DIMENSIONS
OF FAITH

DIMENSIONS OF FAITH

A Mormon Studies Reader

Stephen C. Taysom,
editor

Signature Books | Salt Lake City | 2011

For my mentors, Thomas G. Alexander,
Stephen J. Stein, and Michael S. Taysom

The following articles first appeared as indicated: "God's Chosen People" in *Clio;* "Building Community" in *Communal Societies*; "Buckeye's Laments" in the *Journal of the Illinois State Historical Society;* "Re-placing Memory" in *Religion and American Culture;* and the remaining eleven essays in *Dialogue: A Journal of Mormon Thought* (six) and the *Journal of Mormon History* (five).

Cover design: Ron Stucki

Dimensions of Faith: A Mormon Studies Reader was printed on acid-free paper and was composed, printed, and bound in the United States of America.

16 15 14 13 12 11 6 5 4 3 2 1

Library of Congress Cataloging-in-Publication Data
Dimensions of faith : a Mormon studies reader / Stephen C. Taysom, editor.
pages cm
Includes bibliographical references.
ISBN 1-56085-212-7 (978-1-56085-212-4 : alk. paper) 1. Church of Jesus Christ of Latter-day Saints—History. 2. Church of Jesus Christ of Latter-day Saints—Doctrines. 3. Mormon Church—History. 4. Mormon Church—Doctrines. I. Taysom, Stephen C. editor.
BX8637.D56 2011
289.3—dc22

2011010542

Contents

Editor's Introduction

Origins

I have long had a great admiration for the essay collections produced by Signature Books. As an undergraduate at Brigham Young University, I devoured *The New Mormon History*, *Faithful History*, and *The Prophet Puzzle*, among others. These collections were so valuable because they provided convenient access to some of the finest historical writing on the topic of Mormonism. Several years ago, as a doctoral student at Indiana University, I was in the habit of collecting new articles dealing with Mormonism. It occurred to me that the time was right for the publication of another collection of essays, and you are holding in your hands a book I would love to have had as a graduate student. That way, I could have simply thrust it wordlessly into the hands of those who expressed skepticism about the fitness of Mormonism as an object of serious academic study. Anyone who gives the essays in this book a thorough and fair reading will be left with no reservations on that score.

Happily, the people at Signature Books agreed on the need for a new collection, and I began the painful process of choosing which of the many worthy and cutting-edge articles to include and which to leave out. For every essay that made it into this collection, two or three others had to be sacrificed in the interest of space. Readers should think of this book as an introduction to the kind of fine scholarship that is flowering in the field rather than as anything approaching a comprehensive archive. The collection will be a success if it leads readers to other books and articles in the expanding world of Mormon studies. Moreover, its success will be amplified if it provides writers and researchers with new ideas and approaches to energize their own work.

Mormon Studies

I have been talking about Mormon studies as if it actually exists as a discipline. In fact, there is some debate about the term. Mormon studies, the argument goes, is too exalted and slightly pretentious. In the academic world, when the word *studies* is attached (as in American studies or religious studies), it typically suggests the inclusion of a wide variety of methodological techniques to a subject area. For instance, one would expect such a field to include sociological, anthropological, historical, literary-critical, folkloric, economic, political, and perhaps quantitative/statistical methods under its umbrella. The most common objection to the Mormon studies denomination is that Mormon history is the more accurate term.

It's true that most of what one might consider serious scholarship on Mormonism has traditionally been of a historical bent. This is due in large part to the astonishingly vast manuscript records that document the rise and history of the faith. Out of these records, straight forward narrative histories emerged and continue to form the bulk of scholarly work on Mormonism. However, such narratives have for decades been complemented by more interpretive work that draws on the historical record and applies, tests, works through, and evaluates broader theoretical issues and ideas. Perhaps the first serious effort in this vein was Woodbridge Riley's psychobiography of Joseph Smith. It appeared in 1902. Riley's work was at that time an outlier in its methodological approach, to be sure. But things have changed a little since then.

Now we are at a point where it is no longer necessary, or even helpful, to think of *data* and *interpretation* in tension with one another. They are in tandem. Some researchers are better at mining facts and others are better at offering interpretations of facts. Some gifted few excel at both. In any case, a thriving field of inquiry requires active efforts in both areas. In this anthology, the essays demonstrate with force and clarity that Mormonism is a rich field of inquiry into which theories and methods of a vast array of disciplines are being widely and skillfully integrated.

This book examines Mormonism from a variety of contexts including ritual studies, sexuality, folklore, comparative religion, architecture, collective memory, film studies, literary studies, and Jewish studies. In fact, the essays deal with the entire chronological span of Mormonism from its origins to today: from appearances of Cain/Bigfoot to Wilford Woodruff's vision of the Founding Fathers; from Joseph Smith's founding experiences to Edward Tullidge's reservations about those events; from W. W. Phelps's ghostwritten texts to David O. McKay's natural eloquence; from Mormon women's fiction to Mormon writing on the Holocaust; from anti-Mormon films to healing rituals; from constructions of collective memory to the uses of sacred space in fundamentalist groups. This anthology will provide readers with an example of the entire depth, breadth, complexity, and sophistication of Mormon studies as it is being practiced today.

Voices

The essays are organized under the thematic rubrics of biography, theory, memory, experience, and media/literature. These divisions highlight the developing tendency to engage in a wide variety of theoretical and methodological approaches. I should mention that a number of the contributors are not professional historians. That is, they do not hold a Ph.D. in history and are not professors of history or related disciplines. Mormonism as a field of scholarship has long been open to all who possess the drive and interest necessary to mine the archives and the creativity and vocal power to weave their gleanings into interesting, insightful, and important narratives. In this volume, such voices are complemented by views of professional academics and graduate students in training to become such.

All of this diversity is one of the most attractive elements of the current state of Mormon studies. In this book, there are essays by a medical doctor, a chemist, a university vice president, a college dean, history professors, religious studies professors, a professional editor, independent researchers, and a professor of literature. Graduate students make appearances as well. What binds them together is their commitment to thorough and thoughtful scholarship. In contrast to some other fields of study, there is no Mormon studies elite, cloistered away in one or two academic departments, dictating the tone, tenor, and direction of the field. The voices here are robust and vigorous, not timid or unduly tentative. No one will agree with every conclusion made by every author in this book. As with all good scholarship, there are more debates to come. In that sense, the collection serves as an invitation for others to join the fray if they have the interest. It is an open field, wide enough to accommodate all who put forth the effort and expend the intellectual energy to contribute.

Audiences

As the editor, I naturally feel this book ought to be read by everyone. Tempering my idealistic impulse for the sake of practicality, I hope this collection will serve at least two broad groups of readers. The first are those who have what might be termed a casual interest in Mormon issues. That is, they aren't steeped in the field, they don't spend weekends and vacations doing archival research, and they do not wait with bated breath for the annual conference of the Mormon History Association. Rather, they are, collectively, a thinking, reading, curious bunch. I imagine they might find some of the essays somewhat challenging if they are unaccustomed to academic prose. My hope is that they will be rewarded for struggling through the scholarly jungle and even surprised by the accessibility and ease with which one might come to grips with such essays, provided that they have devoted a little effort to it.

Many of the readers who make up this first audience will be tied to Mormonism in some personal way. Some may be practicing Latterday Saints, others may have left the institutional Church but treasure their cultural heritage. A good number will be somewhere in between. These essays are not intended to be theological treatises, apologetic tracts, or anti-Mormon literature. However, one cannot deny that they will have the potential to change the way readers relate to Mormonism on personal and emotional levels. My hope is that the complexity of Mormonism, and of Mormons, evident in these articles will enrich the reader's relationship with their religion, whatever the nature of that relationship might be.

The second audience consists of those of an academic bent, readers who are familiar with the historiography of Mormonism but who are looking for a digest of some of the most recent scholarship in the field. The breadth and creativity of the essays collected here may provide useful information and perhaps sparks of inspiration for others to apply to their own work. A subset of this group consists of those who teach college students. I have received requests from colleagues for a selection of readings that might be used profitably in courses dealing with Mormonism. The recent emergence of academic departments offering regular courses on the subject has intensified that demand. With these factors in mind, the editorial process that shaped the anthology was informed by the notion that the book might be deployed in undergraduate classrooms. The articles are suitably accessible for undergraduates and particularly useful in courses where the instructor wants to highlight the confluence of data and interpretation in modern scholarship.

How to Read This Book

I spend most of my time teaching undergraduates. Many of them have never read an academic book. My advice to them is not to merely read this book but to step into a boxing ring with it and engage the ideas they encounter there. Take up a pen and analyze the authors' positions. Interrogate them. Express in the margins your agreement and perplexity and contempt and frustration or, on the other hand, your agreement and surprise and joy at what you learn. I would recommend seizing the arguments and ideas and wringing out their implications. To me, reading is not a passive activity. It is a contact sport. I think that religion especially, instead of being treated with solemnity and deference, ought to be thought out and understood so that we're not unduly influenced by proselytizers or lack confidence in our position in the world and so that we understand other people's beliefs.

—Stephen C. Taysom,
Shaker Heights, Ohio
May 31, 2011

The Private versus Public David O. McKay
Profile of a Complex Personality

Newell G. Bringhurst

The public image of David O. McKay, ninth president of the Church of Jesus Christ of Latter-day Saints, is overwhelmingly positive. Impressive in physical appearance, with a large frame, McKay stood six feet one inch, making him the tallest Church president since Joseph Smith. McKay appeared "vigorous and well-preserved" even as an elderly man approaching his eightieth birthday. "His massive, well-groomed mane of white hair tops a handsome face that shines with strong character," an Oregon journalist wrote in the 1960s.[1]

Giving further credence to this positive image are McKay's many accomplishments, first as a member of the Council of the Twelve—a position he was ordained to in April 1906 and held for some forty-five years—and then as Mormon Church president, his tenure lasting from April 1951 until his death in January 1970.[2] McKay's call to the apostleship at the young age of thirty-two came in the wake of an already impressive record of Church service as a missionary to Great Britain from 1897 to 1899, where he served as president of the Scottish Conference, then as a member of the Weber Stake Sunday school superintendence beginning in 1901. In the latter capacity, he inaugurated a number of innovative reforms in teaching and curriculum. He also had been principal of Weber Stake Academy (later Weber State University) from 1902 to 1908, where he presided over the institution's rapidly growing enrollment and expansion of its physical plant.

Early in his apostleship, McKay implemented a successful program of curriculum reform in the Sunday schools, thanks to his position in the general superintendence of the Deseret Sunday School Union commencing in 1906 and service as LDS Church Commissioner of Education beginning in 1919. The following year, McKay was assigned to undertake a one-year tour of Latter-day Saint missions and schools throughout the world. In 1922 he assumed even more responsibilities as president of the European Mission, which meant taking up residence with his family in Liverpool. He remained abroad until 1924. This was critically important in making McKay sensitive to Mormonism's international potential, foreshadowing his later efforts to promote the Church as an international movement.

In 1934 McKay was appointed second counselor in the First Presidency by then-president Heber J. Grant. Following Grant's death in 1945, he was reappointed to this same position by Grant's successor, George Albert Smith. Within the presidency, McKay was actively involved in the day-to-day running of Church administration, especially during the latter years of both Grant's and Smith's administrations as each aging president, in turn, suffered declining health. In 1949 McKay assumed the presidency of the Quorum of the Twelve as senior apostle while concurrently also still serving in the First Presidency.

His own nineteen-year tenure as Church president commencing in 1951 resulted in a number of significant milestones. Total Church membership increased almost threefold from 1,111,000 to 2,931,000. During this period, the number of stakes increased from 184 to 500. In the spirit of McKay's basic creed that "every [Church] member is a missionary," the number of full-time missionaries increased from 2,000 to 13,000. Under his leadership, the Church completed more than 3,700 buildings, including five temples: two in California (Los Angeles and Oakland) and the other three abroad in Switzerland, New Zealand, and London.[3] Completion of the latter three edifices underscored his fundamental commitment to Church growth outside the United States. It also represented a bold departure from Mormonism's longstanding doctrine of "the gathering," whereby all Church members were admonished to gather to Zion, meaning the Intermountain West, in anticipation of the millennium, which was believed to be imminent.[4] McKay described his greatest accomplishment as "making the Church a worldwide organization."[5]

McKay's positive image is further underscored by his lifestyle and statements relative to family and home. Throughout his tenure as president during the 1950s and 1960s, he effectively presented himself as a loving husband to Emma Ray Riggs and devoted father to seven children. His family symbolized an ideal role model for all Latter-day Saints. Reinforcing this idea, President McKay frequently and publicly praised the virtues of his wife, who had been his companion for sixty-nine years. She was, David O. McKay would say, "the sweetest, most helpful wife that ever inspired a man to noble endeavor. She has been an inspiration, my life-long sweetheart, an angel of God come upon the earth."[6] Through poetry written by David and published in various Church periodicals, the Mormon leader's praise of Emma Ray inspired Latter-day Saint readers.[7] The importance that McKay placed on home life is reflected in his oft-quoted statement that "No other success can compensate for failure in the home."[8] On another occasion the Mormon leader characterized "the home [as] the fundamental institution of society."[9] "The dearest possession a man has is his family," he added.[10]

Along with concern for the family, McKay promoted service to others as a responsibility of primary importance that, he said, should take priority over self-interest. "We live our lives most completely," McKay stated, "when we strive to make the world better and happier; [when we] deny self for the good of others."[11] He often quoted the New Testament verse: "He that loseth his life for my sake shall find it" (Matt. 10:39). He interpreted this scripture in the broadest sense, stating that "our lives are wrapped up with the lives of others, and we are happiest as we contribute to their happiness."[12] With effusive praise, his son Llewelyn observed that his father lost himself "entirely" in giving of his energy "to mankind," but that his father was "never less" for having done so, always "greater than he was before."[13]

David O. McKay promoted family and good turns as essential virtues that needed to be embraced by all devout Latter-day Saints. Beyond this, he manifested attitudes and patterns of behavior that were less public and perhaps less idealistic, although without hypocrisy. His concept of family was based on the promotion of self-discipline. "Lack of self-control is the greatest source of unhappiness in the home," he asserted, noting that "children should be taught self-control, self-respect, and respect for others."[14] Accordingly, all problems within McKay's family were handled "quietly and settled ... in strict kindness," recalled Jeanette McKay Morrell, David's younger sister. There were "no company manners in the McKay home," she added. All family members exhibited the "same courtesy and respect for each other" in private as "when the most respected guests were [present] in their home."[15] As David himself explained, "The best lesson that a child can learn is self-control and consideration for the rights and feelings of others."[16]

Discipline within the McKay home was based on "expectations," the oldest son, David Lawrence McKay, recalled. "It was very clear what Mother and Father expected us to do." Both parents set an example by their own "self-disciplined" behavior so that there was never any confusion. "Father never used physical punishment on any of us, but he had a firm rule: 'Never repeat a clear command.'" "Scolding was not a part of [his] repertoire ... Father never talked much. He just looked. And we knew." "The look," as it was termed, generally had the desired effect. Such "gentle loving discipline," moreover, was coupled with high expectations. As David Lawrence recalled, "Father expected the best. No one ever wanted to disappoint him."[17]

Self-discipline was an essential hallmark in David's and Emma Ray's relationship. They never argued openly or in front of their children, preferring to settle all disagreements or controversies in private and away from their children and other outsiders. "I never heard my parents disagree, let alone quarrel," recalled David Lawrence.[18] Such restraint was in keeping with David O.'s strong conviction "that a married couple ought not ever speak in loud tones to each other unless the house is on fire."[19] In fact, he had the advantage in all aspects of his relationship with his wife. Physically, he towered over his petite five-foot-three-inch spouse. More importantly, as the male, his status as head of the family was undisputed, in conformity with principles of Mormon patriarchy that prevailed.[20] In turn, Emma Ray seemingly accepted her subordinate status without question.

Emma Ray, moreover, adjusted to the frequent absence of her ever-busy husband, the family seeing "little" of David, particularly after he became an apostle. His extensive Church responsibilities took him away from home for extended periods of time.[21] As a result, Emma Ray was given wide latitude in running the day-to-day affairs of the household. "Father was gone a great deal too much" for Emma Ray to wait for him to resolve problems, recalled David Lawrence. Thus she made decisions in his absence, but with the essential caveat that what she decided was what "your father would want."[22]

Emma Ray summed up her relationship with David O. in the following revealing manner: "Peace in the home is really a woman's responsibility, and if she wants happiness, she must work for it—yes, and pay for it, too—by being at all times kind, loving, self-sacrificing, ready to help, ready to serve, in fact, loving to do anything the head of the house desires because his desires are also hers."[23] Emma Ray took this concept of submissiveness a step farther, advocating that the "ideal wife" should repress all feelings of anger or frustration in the name of "patience," characterizing it as "the most important ... qualification ... to be a good wife and mother." One must have "patience with children's and husband's tempers, patience with their misunderstandings, with their desires, with their actions." She added the following remarkable statement: "A sure way to bring gloom is to show that your feelings are hurt."[24] Such repressed emotion was reflected in an incident that occurred two weeks after the birth of the McKays' first child:

> The nurse had been discharged, David O. kissed his wife good-bye, and left for a [Sunday school] board meeting. Emma Ray was distressed, and at first she could not believe that her husband would leave her alone with the baby and the dishes. As she started to cry, she remembered her mother's advice: "Don't cry before you're hurt" and "Don't cry over spilt milk." Well, she had asked her mother, "If I can't cry before I'm hurt and I can't cry after I'm hurt, when can I cry?" The obvious answer: "Don't cry at all." Emma Ray told herself not to be foolish, and she quickly vowed that she would never feel bad when David O. had to leave on a Church assignment.[25]

Such strongly held McKay family traits were products of a complex set of factors, some of which transcended and predated the January 1901 marriage of David O. and Emma Ray. A primary factor was the lingering influence of David O.'s parents, David and Jennette Evans McKay. The elder David, a native of Scotland, had immigrated to Utah in 1859 as a fifteen-year-old with his parents, William and Ellen McKay, recent converts to Mormonism. The McKays ultimately settled in Huntsville—a high-mountain community some ten miles east of Ogden. As David O.'s father reached adulthood, he met and married Jennette, the daughter of Thomas and Margaret Powell Evans, natives of Wales who, after converting to Mormonism, migrated to Utah at about the same time as the McKay family. Jennette had grown up in Ogden in fairly comfortable circumstances, thanks to her father's success as a large landowner and landlord.

Following their marriage, David and Jennette also prospered economically, thanks in large measure to timely investments in agricultural land and livestock. Economic success, in turn, made McKay a community leader politically and ecclesiastically—the latter reflected in his appointment as bishop of the Huntsville Ward. It also enabled the couple to build the spacious fourteen-room home David O. was born in and which still stands in the center of Huntsville.[26]

The success of David and Jennette McKay did not come by chance but was the product of two strong-willed, highly motivated individuals seeking to provide adequately for their large family of ten children, eight of whom reached maturity—the oldest being David O., born September 8, 1873. The father has been described as "somewhat of a martinet," reflecting "the very rigidly disciplined Victorian" environment in which he himself was raised. His own family was "very structured … and very motivated," according to a close family member.[27] What David McKay "did, he always did right—second best was never good enough," his grandson Llewelyn R. McKay noted, adding that "it was he who imparted this ideal of perfection" to his son David O.[28] The grandfather clearly embodied the spirit of the family motto emblazoned on the family crest: "manu forti," meaning "with a strong hand."[29] Such influences were profound on the children in the home and particularly evident in the response of David O. to the question, Who is the greatest man you ever met? He replied "without hesitation, 'My father.'"[30]

David O. was also profoundly influenced by his equally strong-willed mother. Described by contemporaries as a woman of exceptional beauty, Jennette had a striking personality to match.[31] "Though high spirited, she was even-tempered and self-possessed. Her dark brown eyes immediately expressed any rising emotion, which, however, she always held under perfect control," recalled grandson Llewelyn.[32] Jennette demonstrated her strong will and initiative in taking over complete management of the family farm when her husband served a Church mission in Scotland for two years from 1881 to 1883. At the time, she had three young children, including David O., then age seven, and was pregnant with a fourth.[33]

A further demonstration of Jennette's strong will was the fact that her husband never practiced polygamy despite being bishop of the Huntsville Ward. Some fourteen families in Huntsville were polygamous, along with an additional five or six in nearby Eden.[34] When asked why he never took a second wife, David reportedly replied, "You don't know my Jennette!" This "handsome, soft-spoken but strong-willed woman" "bore the distinction of being the only Mormon bishop's wife who did not have to share her husband with another woman," wrote granddaughter Fawn McKay Brodie. Jennette's "extraordinary capacity to maintain the Victorian amenities [of monogamy] in so alien an atmosphere was a testament of her ability to get her way."[35]

David catered to Jennette's privileges in other ways. "He refused to let her work in the fields and insisted on obtaining help for her in the house—particularly because he so admired her beautiful hands and lovely, clear complexion."[36] Jennette was also "a very socially proper woman," recalled a McKay relative.[37] She, along with her husband, were "conscious of the immigrant status and the educational deprivations they had suffered as a result" of their displacement from Europe. Jennette was determined that her children "enjoy the advantages" that she and her husband had missed out on. Thus, upon receiving an unexpected gift of $2,500 from her mother, Jennette set aside the money for her children's education, seeing to it that all eight, including David, attended college—a remarkable feat for the time.[38]

Jennette was conscious of the social implications of who her children associated with, according to one family member.[39] She even restricted her children from interacting with the Gunn McKay family who lived in the house immediately north of them. Jeanette's aloofness from her distant relatives was because she was convinced the Gunn McKays were beneath her own family, both socially and economically. Her prejudice was reenforced by the way local residents referred to the "godblessed McKays and the goddamned McKays," one of Gunn McKay's descendants adding that it was "obvious which ones we were."[40]

Jeanette's social concerns notwithstanding, her son chose to reflect on her virtues years later and characterized her as a "saint." "Her influence, and beauty," David noted, "entwined themselves into the lives of her sons and daughters as effectively as a divine presence!" David recalled that his mother "was loved—almost reverenced—by [my father] [,] the best and noblest of husbands and fathers."[41]

Recalling his youth, David confessed to being a "roguish boy."[42] He possessed "the normal vitality of youth" and more, "as evidenced by his aunt's statement while taking care of him as a youngster." She told his mother: "Jennette, if you will just take care of this boy, I'll gladly cook for the threshers!"[43] Years later David referred to his "extremely active, somewhat reckless days of youth."[44] He stated that his mother's influence had given him "the power more than once during fiery youth to keep my name untarnished and my soul from clay."[45] On another occasion he expressed gratitude "for the wise and careful guardianship and training of noble parents" who "kept me from turning to paths that would have ended in an entirely different kind of life!"[46]

More fundamentally, David confessed to being "a doubting youth" relative to his Mormon faith.[47] This despite the fact that he had been ordained to the office of a deacon shortly after his twelfth birthday and then to the higher office of teacher, all in conformity with the recently implemented Churchwide practice of ordaining teenage boys into the Aaronic priesthood.[48] As early as age thirteen, David was bearing his testimony of faith in his quorum meetings.[49] Yet not satisfied with the limits of belief, he said he possessed "an intense desire ... to receive a manifestation of the truth of the Restored Gospel." He prayed "fervently and sincerely ... that God would declare to me the truth of his revelation to Joseph Smith." In this he was disappointed, lamenting that "no spiritual manifestation has come to me. If I am true to myself, I must say I am just the same 'old boy' that I was before I prayed."[50]

McKay's doubts persisted even as he reached adulthood and completed his education, attending first Weber Stake Academy and then the University of Utah where he graduated with a bachelor's degree in 1897. McKay's ambivalence was evident in the response to his mission call to Scotland immediately following graduation. He "was upset with this interruption of his plans" in the wake of having been offered a teaching position in Salt Lake County as soon as he received his degree.[51] David reportedly read the letter from Church headquarters and "flung it across the table with disgust exclaiming: 'Ain't that Hell!'"[52]

Further complicating David's mission call was his lack of preparation. Early in his mission when a woman attacked his theology, he "found out [he] knew nothing about the Bible" and thus could not respond adequately. He immediately sought to remedy this deficiency through an intense course of self-study of the Bible.[53] He was also homesick and depressed. Upon arriving in Scotland, he found it "a gloomy looking place & I ... a gloomy-feeling boy."[54] His insecurities and ambivalence intensified as a result of his appointment as president of the Scottish Conference in June 1898. "I just seemed to be seized with a feeling of gloom and fear [that] ... I would prove incompetent."[55]

He experienced a sudden change in attitude because of two critical events. The first involved his reaction to an inscription emblazoned on a building in the Scottish countryside which read: "Whate'er thou art, act well thy part." "This message struck him forcefully, and he decided to devote himself completely and wholeheartedly to his 'part,' which was the role of missionary."[56] The second event was a particularly moving missionary meeting which he attended with a number of fellow missionaries, a gathering presided over by James L. McMurrin, a councilor in the European mission presidency. As McKay later recalled, McMurrin delivered a discourse in which he directed a number of remarks directly at McKay, stating: "Let me say to you Brother David, Satan hath desired you that he may sift you as wheat, but God is mindful of you." He then added: "If you will keep the faith, you will yet sit in the leading counsels [sic] of the Church." In his diary, McKay noted "that an excellent spirit of love and unity was amongst us. A peaceful Heavenly influence pervaded the room ... It was the best meeting I have ever attended."[57] The experience, he asserted, "was the manifestation for which as a doubting youth" he had prayed for years before.[58] This long and difficult religious odyssey undoubtedly had the cumulative effect of further reinforcing his already strong tendencies toward self-discipline.

David O. McKay was equally affected by his relationship with Emma Ray Riggs and her family's unusual, ambivalent relationship with Mormonism. Both of Emma Ray's parents had initially embraced the Mormon faith. Her father, Obadiah Higbee Riggs, a native of Library, Allegheny County, Pennsylvania, had joined the LDS Church in 1866 at age twenty-two.[59] Emma Ray's mother was Emma Louisa Robbins, a native of San Francisco, whose parents had arrived on the west coast in 1846 as part of Samuel Brannan's *Brooklyn* Mormon contingent.[60] Emma Louisa herself was baptized in 1860 at age nineteen. In May 1867 Emma Louisa and Obadiah were married and sealed in the Endowment House in Salt Lake City.[61]

Obadiah and Emma Louisa were both well-educated and both taught at the University of Utah.[62] Obadiah went on to serve as Utah's territorial superintendent of schools from 1873 to 1877, in which capacity he promoted education reforms intended to increase the quality of teaching throughout the territory.[63] However, his proposals generated controversy and forced him to leave office after his first term.[64]

Obadiah and Emma Louisa had six children. Emma Ray was the fifth child, the only daughter. She was born June 23, 1877.[65] Difficulties developed within the Riggs family when Obadiah took two plural wives, Annie Wilson in 1882 and her younger half-sister, Almina Wilson, in 1884. Eventually both Emma Louisa and Annie Wilson left him, then he was excommunicated and left Utah, abandoning Almina and their small child, Lisle.[66]

He moved to the east coast and changed professions, this time choosing medicine. After graduating from Long Island College Hospital at Brooklyn, Kings County, New York, he moved to Cincinnati and opened a practice there. In 1895 he met and married Hattie Fruhauf, then joined the Reorganized Church of Jesus Christ of Latter Day Saints.[67] In 1900 the family moved to Independence, Missouri. He practiced medicine in Kansas City. Extremely active in the Reorganized Church, Obadiah was a personal acquaintance of its leader, Joseph Smith III.[68]

Meanwhile, his daughter Emma Ray continued to live with her mother in Salt Lake City. She attended the University of Utah, which is where she met David McKay, who along with his younger brother and two sisters was attending the same institution. The four McKays lived in a cottage they rented from Emma Ray's mother.[69] Emma Ray graduated in 1898. She did not immediately become romantically involved with David because he was dating another "beautiful classmate, and Emma Ray was engaged to a fine young man in the business world," according to the recollection of his sister Jeanette.[70]

It was near the time of his graduation in 1897 that David became interested in Emma Ray, which was inconveniently just before his departure for missionary service in Scotland. The young couple corresponded steadily for the first several months that David was gone, from August 1897 to March 1898, followed by a gap of twelve months from March 1898 to the same month the next year when no correspondence was exchanged.[71] It appears they had completely broken off their relationship while Emma Ray dated another young man and experienced other changes in her life. In August 1897 her mother had died suddenly at age forty-seven, after which Emma Ray moved to Cincinnati to join her father there and study piano at the Cincinnati College of Music.[72]

Shortly after the couple renewed their correspondence in early 1899, Emma Ray returned to Utah to teach at Madison Elementary School in Ogden. David returned home from Scotland in August and began to court Emma Ray in earnest even though she now apparently manifested ambivalence about their relationship. A year and a half passed. Finally in early December 1900, David proposed. Emma Ray's response reflects a persistent indecision over the question, "Are you sure I'm the right one?" David answered in the affirmative and just one month later on January 2, 1901, they were married in the Salt Lake temple.[73]

As for the qualities that drew the young couple together, McKay biographer Mary Jane Woodger has suggested several. David and Emma Ray both shared a love of literature, both were well-educated, and both came from prominent families. Emma Ray was drawn by David's charisma and ambition, proclaiming him to be "a young man who is going to amount to something someday." Years later David himself asserted that one should choose a mate "by judgment and inspiration, as well as by physical attraction," adding that "intellect and breeding are vital and important in the human family."[74]

David became the dominant figure not just with his wife and children but also in the extended McKay family, particularly with his three younger brothers and, to a lesser extent, his four sisters and their families as they married and had children of their own. His dominance relative to the McKay clan was evident following the deaths of their parents. First his mother died tragically at the relatively young age of fifty-four in January 1895, then his father passed away at age seventy-three in November 1917. When this happened, young David stepped in to become "the family patriarch," as his niece Fawn Brodie recalled. David "dominated all of the McKay family, to an extraordinary degree, just like an old Chinese patriarch."[75] David influenced his children's choices of spouses, particularly his three oldest children, according to niece Flora McKay Crawford, who said David attempted to influence all members of the extended family with less success.[76] Even so, his brothers and sisters went to him "for advice," Fawn conceded, and "none of his brothers [would] accept a job" without first consulting him.[77]

The positive aspect of their reliance on him was his ability to help them find employment. In 1937 his younger brother Thomas E. McKay lost a political appointment with the Utah State Public Utilities Commission, so David arranged to have Thomas called as president of the Swiss-German mission, a position in which Thomas served from 1938 to 1940 and allowed him to support his family since it was a paying job. Then in 1941 David apparently intervened to have Thomas named as an assistant to the Council of the Twelve, another paid position Thomas served in until his death in 1958.[78]

David's success in helping his brother was offset by a dramatic failure in speculating in land and commodities during the late 1910s and early 1920s. This had adverse economic consequences for all concerned. In making the investments, the McKay brothers chose to borrow needed funds by refinancing the family's Huntsville farm which they had inherited jointly following their parents' deaths. They then invested in Arizona cotton, citrus fruit orchards near Phoenix, Canadian wheat, and cattle and real estate at Birch Creek to the southeast of Ogden. In every case the investments failed,[79] increasing their total mortgage debt to $35,000—a sum considered astronomical at the time. This debt fell mostly on Thomas because he held the mortgage, which was due to the fact that he was the primary resident in the McKay homestead and held the bulk of the surrounding farmland. This financial burden remained "immutable, fixed as the polestar, the absolute around which the [Thomas McKay] family revolved." Thomas, manifesting the McKay family creed of self-control and self-discipline, held in check whatever resentment he might have harbored against his older brother. Instead, Thomas bore his burden over the next thirty years "like Atlas, without hope and without lament," and most importantly without complaint.[80]

David's speculative ventures were an aspect of his attachment to his childhood home and community. He would spend as much time in Huntsville as his extensive Church responsibilities permitted, including weekends and during the summer. In his haste to get to Huntsville, his reputation as a fast and aggressive driver was amply displayed. He would leave Salt Lake City and head north "driving with his foot right to the fire-wall all the way," one family member recalled, adding that it "must have been quite an experience for all of the [Utah state] highway patrolmen."[81] On one memorable occasion in his later years, in receiving a speeding ticket he told the officer: "I'm glad to get this ticket. Some have said I am slowing down [but] this is proof that I'm not."[82] He was always anxious to reach his destination, asserting that "the air is better in Huntsville. That's what keeps me young."[83] He looked upon the high-mountain community as "a cherished haven where he could ... relax from the cares and burdens of his official duties."[84]

He went through the annual ritual of moving to Huntsville for a three-month stay every summer beginning in the 1910s and continuing into the 1950s. With his immediate family, he took up residence in the old homestead, leaving their home in Ogden at first and their Salt Lake City home after 1920. To summer in the mountains, they had to move in with Thomas's family. Even though it would appear to violate the essential privacy of the resident family, Thomas never complained about it, at least not openly. The younger brother had no choice because the homestead was held jointly by eight surviving children through the legal entity known as "the McKay family corporation." In this arrangement the four brothers and four sisters each had an equal voice in making decisions involving the property. In actuality the corporation was dominated by David O. and, to a lesser extent, the four sisters, Jeanette McKay Morrell, Elizabeth McKay Hill, Ann McKay Farr, and Katherine McKay Ricks, who were all assertive, dominant personalities—all clearly taking after their mother. They were "a formidable quartet of big, handsome women who marched through the family's problems in an unbreakable phalanx."[85]

By contrast, the two youngest McKay brothers, William and Morgan, exerted limited influence mainly because lived far away from Huntsville. At the same time, David's third brother, Thomas, may have had the least influence due to his relatively docile personality. He was ill-suited to oppose David and his sisters even on decisions affecting him and his family in a potentially adverse way, which was sometimes the case.[86] "We were the low family of the McKay clan," lamented Thomas's oldest daughter, Flora.[87]

In fact, two of the four sisters, Jeanette and Elizabeth, along with their families, followed the example of their oldest brother, taking up residence in the McKay family homestead every summer to take advantage of the cooler mountain climate and escape the heat of Ogden and Salt Lake City. While this significant influx of relatives invaded the privacy and disrupted the domestic independence of Thomas's family, the fourteen-room house was large enough to accommodate them all even though it lacked the basic amenities of running water and indoor plumbing for many years.[88]

David looked forward to his extended Huntsville stay as more than an escape from the oppressive summer heat of the Wasatch Front. Working on the family farm in Huntsville was one of the few forms of recreation the ever-busy Mormon leader enjoyed.[89] It was an idyllic, temporary escape from the responsibility of being a general authority. Changing his persona to that of a gentleman farmer, working some 400 acres of cultivated land and 2,000 acres of rangeland he shared with his brother, he enjoyed getting out into the fields and asserting a physical robustness going back to his youth. He continued to work his farm acreage alongside his sons and others until well into his eighties.[90]

In particular, he enjoyed being with his horses. His "love for horses [was] proverbial," asserted his sister Jeanette, the horses being "more than farm animals—they were friends and were treated as such."[91] David was not reluctant to "wrestle the horses and ... gave them the whip ... if they didn't mind," a family member said.[92] On occasion David would deliberately "rile up" a team of horses that he was driving, according to the recollection of an old-time Huntsville resident who worked for the Mormon leader. McKay would "tighten up the reins to get [the horses] started up [and] work them up by tightening back on their bits." As a result, "the horses would get ... stampeding a little bit and then [McKay] would start saying, 'Th' go' d' s' bit'!' You could hear him in the back saying, 'Those goddamn sons of bitches.' It would never get fully out, he would only get the first letters of the words." McKay's heavy-handed behavior toward his horses was "to demonstrate how masterful he was" and to prove that he "really knew horses," according to the oberserver.[93]

McKay demonstrated another important skill to residents of Huntsville—his ability as an effective public speaker, an attribute particularly evident during services in the old Huntsville LDS meetinghouse. McKay was dubbed "the silver tongue" and was compared to the three-time Democratic presidential candidate William Jennings Bryan. Like the more famous Bryan, McKay was able to deliver a sermon on virtually any topic with "grand eloquence,"[94] and his sermons, moreover, were "heartening [and] optimistic," avoiding "the complexities of Mormon theology ... 'I bring you a note of encouragement and cheer' [was] a frequent theme ... To thunder over the pulpit and denounce the world for its evil [was] never his technique."[95] McKay "loved to appear before an audience [and] spread himself around," making such oratorical performances a memorable experience for all.[96]

McKay's fondness for Huntsville seemed to validate his well-cultivated public image as a caring, empathic family man.[97] However, family members recall a somewhat different image of him. "He was not a very loving man," asserted a niece, Flora McKay Crawford, who said his interaction with nieces and nephews was minimal.[98] "He never was very loving even to his own children," she added, asserting that he was more loving "to strangers and people that he [thought] he could influence."[99] Such a contrasting negative view was no doubt due in large measure to the fact that Flora was a daughter of Thomas and sister of Fawn Brodie. Fawn's difficulties with David stemmed from her controversial biography of Joseph Smith, *No Man Knows My History,* the firestorm following its 1945 publication bringing to the surface long-standing tensions between members of the Thomas E. and David O. McKay families. Brodie believed, with some justification, that her uncle had played a key role in her excommunication from the LDS Church in May 1946.[100] Reportedly, David was angry about the whole episode, particularly over the extensive publicity it generated. At the same time, he was scrupulously careful not to show his sense of betrayal publicly and avoided discussion of his niece even within the privacy of his own immediate family.[101] Such behavior was in keeping with a longstanding family tradition of avoiding any topic of a controversial nature.[102] It was also in keeping with David's well-honed self-control.

In any case, it seems David was more complex in private than his public image suggested. He was extremely gracious, open, warm, loving, and empathic in public. In the words of historian D. Michael Quinn, "McKay loved intimate association with crowds and individuals, [and] treasured close fellowship" with his fellow Latter-day Saints.[103] However, Francis M. Gibbons, past secretary to the First Presidency, characterized the Church president as "a private person who kept his own counsel and who did not easily admit someone into his inner circle of confidentiality."[104] To some, McKay came across as "arrogant" and "vain," according to one relative. McKay's own son conceded that "if father had any weaknesses, they would be two: He drives too fast; and the other is vanity."[105] "He was a little bit of a showman," a relative admitted.[106] His dress included, on occasion, flowered shirts, but more notably his trademark white, double-breasted suits. He thus broke ranks with his more conservatively dressed colleagues in the Church hierarchy and "intentionally left his snow-white hair slightly longer than the prevailing style to increase its striking effects," noted biographer Gregory A. Prince.[107]

The obvious question is: Why explore the private David O. McKay versus the better-known public side? There is good reason for this because little-known aspects of his background probably influenced his thinking about crucial actions he undertook as Church leader. For example, his own early doubts concerning Mormonism, combined with the unconventional background of his wife's family, likely influenced his tolerance of diversity of various forms. "Sound independent thinking should be encouraged rather than discouraged," he asserted on one occasion, adding that "careful logical analysis, coupled with a sincere desire to find the truth, is praiseworthy." McKay was tolerant of "groups of people interested in doctrine and in Church policies" who met together "independently of Church functions to discuss questions of importance, wherein there appears to be differences of opinion in interpretation."[108] As his son Llewelyn said: "Father's religion is concerned with large, all-embracing spiritual issues which reach out to include rather than to exclude; it unites rather than divides."[109]

Such essential openness and tolerance was evident in McKay's view of different cultures, reinforced by his own early exposure to another culture on his mission and thereafter to other nationalities and races. "When you are in a country other than your own ... [you should] view life from that country's point of view," he admonished his son on one occasion. McKay stressed "the need to learn foreign languages."[110] Such attitudes were in conformity with his desire to extend Mormonism throughout the world and make it a truly international religion. He saw as a major impediment to this goal the Church's policy of excluding men of African descent from ordination to the Mormon priesthood. He sought, unsuccessfully, to change this policy in 1954-56, early in his tenure as Church president.[111]

His ultimate failure to eliminate the ban on black priesthood ordination was, to a significant extent, the product of his own upbringing and background—specifically his tendency to avoid unpleasantness. This had been impressed upon him from his formative years and enforced within his own family. Thus he failed to vigorously promote the repeal of the ban, particularly in the latter years of his administration when he decided he would rather get along with his colleagues and not alienate certain conservative men, notably Harold B. Lee, whose increasing influence by the late 1960s included a firm opposition to loosening the ban on blacks. Consequently, McKay, with deep personal reluctance, continued to deny blacks an entrée to the priesthood—a practice with which he was at least uncomfortable.[112]

McKay's "dislike of confrontations of any kind" affected his relationship with J. Reuben Clark, his longtime associate and counselor in the First Presidency. In varied ways McKay and Clark stood in sharp contrast to one another. In personality, McKay was open, optimistic, feeling that "man's nature was basically good," whereas Clark, in the words of his biographer, "was an unreconstructed pessimist." In administering Church affairs, McKay "favored expansive growth and a more liberal expenditure of funds," whereas Clark "favored slow growth and cautious, even parsimonious, expenditure of funds." In leadership style the two clashed, McKay being willing "to make immediate decisions based on his personal impressions" and Clark demanding "thorough research prior to a decision."[113] Despite such differences, upon becoming Church president in 1951 McKay retained Clark in the First Presidency. This reflected, at least partly, McKay's avoidance of the unpleasant task of letting the conservative, doctrinaire Church leader go. Nevertheless, Clark's retention involved a demotion from first counselor—which Clark had been for seventeen years under previous Church presidents Heber J. Grant and George Albert Smith—to that of second counselor.[114] McKay's longtime friend and associate Stephen L. Richards was made first counselor. Carefully but discreetly, McKay excluded Clark "as much as possible from decision-making." Such exclusion became "nearly total during the last two years of Clark's life."[115]

McKay's avoidance of controversy confirmed his image as an idyllic husband and family man. His family became a role model for all Latter-day Saints who sought peace and harmony in their families. In fact, the McKay family's situation was exaggerated and was, indeed, based largely on myth—a fact that became more and more apparent during the unsettling decade of the 1960s and beyond. It could be further argued that the idyllic, widely publicized images of the McKays—specifically President McKay as a caring but dominant husband acting in perfect harmony with a devoted, deferential wife, Emma Ray—promoted unhealthy expectations of Latter-day Saint women. The reality for Church members was, in any case, much less idyllic, while LDS couples confronted the tensions and marital difficulties experienced by non-Mormon counterparts—problems leading to approximately the same levels of separation and divorce.[116]

Finally, the fact of what might be considered weaknesses of character, specifically McKay's avoidance of controversy, overbearing behavior within his family, and a tendency toward vanity, did not diminish his status as "one of the most important—if not the most important—figure in twentieth century Mormonism" according to biographers Prince and Wright. [117] An awareness of such traits, moreover, make the beloved Church leader more accessible as both a human being and an effective and charismatic leader.

Notes

The author wishes to express his deep appreciation to Gregory A. Prince, Mary Jane Woodger, and Stan Larson, each of whom offered suggestions after reading an earlier draft of this essay, which were useful in correcting errors and providing additional insights into the complex character of David O. McKay.

1. This was later quoted in Terry W. Call's article, "David O. McKay," in the Church News section of the *Deseret News,* Sept. 25, 1993.

2. Four recent book-length studies dealing with various aspects of McKay's life and activities, each providing illuminating insights, albeit from different perspectives, are Gregory A. Prince and William Robert Wright, *David O. McKay and the Rise of Modern Mormonism* (Salt Lake City: University of Utah Press, 2005); Mary Jane Woodger, *David O. McKay: Beloved Prophet* (American Fork, UT: Covenant Communications, 2004); Stan and Patricia Larson, eds., *What E'er Thou Art, Act Well Thy Part: The Missionary Diaries of David O. McKay* (Salt Lake City: Blue Ribbon Books, 1999), and Mary Jan Woodger, ed., *Heart Petals: The Personal Correspondence of David O. McKay to Emma Ray McKay* (Salt Lake City: University of Utah Press, 2005). Also providing an overview of McKay's activities from the perspective of a family member is Jeanette McKay Morrell, *Highlights in the Life of President David O. McKay* (Salt Lake City: Deseret Book, 1966).

3. Richard S. Van Wagoner and Steven C. Walker, "David O. McKay," in *A Book of Mormons* (Salt Lake City: Signature Books, 1982), 87-91.

4. Two book-length discussions of early Mormon millennialism, albeit from somewhat different perspectives, are Grant Underwood, *The Millenarian World of Early Mormonism* (Urbana: University of Illinois Press, 1993), and

Dan Erickson, *As a Thief in the Night: The Mormon Millennialist View* (Salt Lake City: Signature Books, 1998).

5. As quoted in Call, "David O. McKay."

6. Ibid.

7. For various examples of McKay poetry written in tribute to Emma Ray, see Llewelyn R. McKay, *Home Memories of President David O. McKay* (Salt Lake City: Deseret Book), 171-93.

8. David O. McKay, an address delivered before the semi-annual conference of the Church, *Conference Report,* Apr. 1935, p. 116; Apr. 1964, p. 5.

9. McKay, *Home Memories,* 212.

10. Clare Middlemiss, comp., *Cherished Experiences from the Writings of President David O. McKay* (Salt Lake City: Deseret Book, 1955), 19.

11. McKay, *Home Memories,* 235.

12. Middlemiss, *Cherished Experiences,* 176.

13. McKay, *Home Memories,* 272.

14. Ibid., 214.

15. Morrell, *Highlights,* 47.

16. McKay, *Home Memories,* 231.

17. David Lawrence McKay, *My Father David O. McKay* (Salt Lake City: Deseret Book, 1989), 99-191, 219.

18. Ibid., 11.

19. McKay, *Home Memories,* 223.

20. McKay, *My Father,* 12.

21. McKay, *Home Memories,* 39.

22. McKay, *My Father,* 103.

23. Ibid., 12.

24. Ibid., 13.

25. As described by James B. Allen in "David O. McKay," 285, in Leonard J. Arrington, ed., *The Presidents of the Church* (Salt Lake City: Deseret Book, 1986).

26. For a good overview, see Morrell, *Highlights,* 1-39.

27. Hugh Garner, interviewed by Newell G. Bringhurst, Sept. 29, 1988.

28. McKay, *Home Memories,* 23.

29. Morrell, *Highlights,* 2-3.

30. As quoted in Call, "David O. McKay."

31. Morrell, *Highlights,* 10.

32. McKay, *Home Memories,* 3.

33. Morrell, *Highlights,* 23-25.

34. LaVerna Burnett Newey, *Remember My Valley: A History of Ogden Canyon, Huntsville, Liberty, and Eden, Utah, from 1825 to 1976* (Salt Lake City: xxx, 1977), 111-13.

35. Fawn M. Brodie, "The Protracted Life of Mrs. Grundy," n.d., 2, unpublished manuscript in my possession.

36. McKay, *Home Memories,* 26.

37. Quinn McKay, interviewed by Newell G. Bringhurst, Sept. 23, 1988.

38. Francis M. Gibbons, *David O. McKay: Apostle to the World, Prophet of God* (Salt Lake City: Deseret Book, 1986), 26-27.

39. Gunn McKay, interviewed by Newell G. Bringhurst, Sept. 26, 1987.

40. Monroe McKay, interviewed by Newell G. Bringhurst, July 21, 1986.

41. David O. McKay to Lou Jean McKay, May 5, 1921, qtd. in McKay, *My Father,* 131.

42. David O. McKay to Thomas E. McKay, Dec. 12, 1938, qtd. in Morrell, *Highlights,* 29.

43. As quoted in McKay, *Home Memories,* 6.

44. Ibid., 209.

45. As quoted in Leonard J. Arrington and Susan Arrington Madsen, *Mothers of the Prophets* (Salt Lake City: Deseret Book, 1987), 146. Along this same line, McKay further recalled carrying on the following conversation with his mother while a college student: "'Mother, I have found that I am the only one of your children whom you have switched [whipped with a willow shoot].' She said, 'Yes David O., I made such a failure of you I didn't want to use the same method on the other children'" (148).

46. As quoted in McKay, *Home Memories,* 209.

47. As quoted in Morrell, *Highlights,* 38.

48. William G. Hartley, "From Men to Boys: LDS Aaronic Priesthood Offices, 1826-1996," *Journal of Mormon History* 22 (Spring 1996): 89-136.

49. Allen, "David O. McKay," 285.

50. "Prayer Answered in God's Own Due Time," dictated by President McKay, 1938, contained in Middlemiss, *Cherished Experiences,* 16.

51. McKay, *My Father,* 2.

52. According to the recollections of Thomas E. McKay, who was living with his older brother at the time, in Fawn M. Brodie to Dale L. Morgan, 13 June 1963, original in the Dale L. Morgan Papers, Bancroft Library, University of California. While conceding that "a mission was not the top item on

his agenda for the future," Gibbons, in *Apostle to the World*, 35, attributes McKay's reluctance "to a combination of factors," including a family sense of "obligation to start working soon to replenish the McKay family's meager education fund so that his younger brother and sisters could receive university schooling."

53. McKay, *My Father*, 17.

54. As quoted in ibid., 18.

55. Larson & Larson, *Missionary Diaries*, 103.

56. McKay, *My Father*, 24.

57. Ibid., 32.

58. As quoted in "Predictions and Spiritual Manifestations," Oct. 27, 1934, in Middlemiss, *Cherished Experiences*, 13.

59. From information on the Obadiah Higbee Riggs family pedigree chart, original in the LDS Family History Library, Salt Lake City.

60. As noted in Lorin K. Hansen, "Voyage of the *Brooklyn*," *Dialogue: A Journal of Mormon Thought* 21 (Summer 1988): 71.

61. From the Obadiah Riggs family pedigree chart.

62. McKay, *Home Memories*, 171.

63. John Clifton Moffitt, *A Century of Service: A History of the Utah Education Association, 1869-1969* (Salt Lake City: Utah Education Association, 1961), 29-30, 40-42, 282-83, 418-19, 511-13.

64. A more detailed discussion is contained in Newell G. Bringhurst and Frederick S. Buchanan, "The Forgotten Odyssey of Obadiah H. Riggs: Early Pioneer for Education Reform," *Utah Historical Quarterly* 66 (Winter 1998): 48-64.

65. From information on the Obadiah Riggs family pedigree chart.

66. This is according to conversations Lavina Fielding Anderson had with McKay family members, related to the author by telephone, Mar. 7, 1996. See also Bringhurst and Buchanan, "Forgotten Odyssey," 59-69.

67. Susan Easton Black, comp., *Early Members of the Reorganized Church of Jesus Christ of Latter Day Saints*, Vol. 5 (Provo: BYU Religious Studies Center, 1993), 100-19.

68. The extent of Riggs's interaction with Joseph Smith III is evident in the fact that the latter preached at Riggs's funeral in October 1907. See *Saints' Herald*, Oct. 2, 1907, 1899; Oct. 3, 1936.

69. McKay, *My Father*, 1-2.

70. As quoted in Morrell, *Highlights*, 32.

71. McKay, *My Father*, 3-4.

72. As noted by Woodger, *Beloved Prophet,* 40-58; McKay, *Home Memories,* 171-72.

73. McKay, *My Father,* 4-10.

74. Emma Ray quoted in Woodger, *Beloved Prophet,* 32-34; David quoted in McKay, *Home Memories,* 213-14.

75. Fawn M. Brodie, interviewed by Shirley E. Stephenson, Oct. 30, 1975, original in Oral History Collection, Fullerton State University, 3.

76. Flora Crawford, interviewed by Newell G. Bringhurst, Sept. 29, 1988.

77. Fawn M. Brodie to Maurine Whipple, Nov. 12, 1941, in possession of Verda Hale, St. George, Utah.

78. Flora Crawford interview, 1988.

79. Flora Crawford, interviewed by Shirley E. Stephenson, June 5, 1986.

80. Fawn M. Brodie, "Inflation Idyll: A Family Farm in Huntsville," *Utah Historical Quarterly* 49 (1972): 113-15.

81. Hugh Garner interview.

82. Gunn McKay, interviewed by Mary Jane Woodger, July 28, 1995, copy in my possession.

83. As quoted by Van Wagoner and Walker, *A Book of Mormons,* 189.

84. Preston Nibley, *The Presidents of the Church* (Salt Lake City: Deseret Book Co., 1959), 432.

85. Brodie, "Protracted Life," 4.

86. This complicated family arrangement is discussed in detail in ibid.

87. Flora Crawford interview.

88. Brodie, "Protracted Life."

89. McKay, *My Father,* 203.

90. Barrie McKay, interviewed by Newell G. Bringhurst, Sept. 16, 1988.

91. Morrell, *Highlights,* 293-94.

92. Barrie McKay interview.

93. Jarvis Thurston, interviewed by Newell G. Bringhurst, May 16, 1988.

94. Ibid.

95. Fawn M. Brodie to Maurine Whipple, Nov. 12, 1941.

96. Jarvis Thurston interview.

97. As clearly noted and discussed in Morrell, *Highlights;* McKay, *Home Memories;* and McKay, *My Father.*

98. Flora Crawford interview.

99. Flora Crawford interview, 1986.

100. For an extensive discussion of McKay's reaction to Brodie's biography, see Newell G. Bringhurst, *Fawn McKay Brodie: A Biographer's Life* (Norman: University of Oklahoma Press, 1999), 71-115.

101. This according to David's son Edward R. McKay, interviewed by Newell G. Bringhurst, July 23, 1987.

102. This particular McKay family trait is vividly discussed in Brodie, "Protracted Life."

103. D. Michael Quinn, *J. Reuben Clark: The Church Years* (Provo: Brigham Young University Press, 1983), 116.

104. Gibbons, *Apostle to the World*, 32.

105. Gunn McKay's recollection of what David's son told him, noted in his interview by Newell G. Bringhurst, Sept. 23, 1988.

106. Gunn McKay interview, 1995.

107. Prince and Wright, *Rise of Modern Mormonism*, 358-79.

108. McKay, *Home Memories*, 154-55.

109. Ibid., 272.

110. Ibid., 142-43.

111. Armand L. Mauss, *The Angel and the Beehive: The Mormon Struggle with Assimilation* (Urbana: University of Illinois Press, 1994), 117.

112. D. Michael Quinn, *The Mormon Hierarchy: Extensions of Power* (Salt Lake City: Signature Books, 1997), 13-14. See also Newell G. Bringhurst, *Saints, Slaves, and Blacks: The Changing Place of Black People within Mormonism* (Westport, CT: Greenwood Press, 1981), 171-96.

113. Quinn, *J. Reuben Clark*, 116-17.

114. Ibid., 129.

115. Quinn, *Mormon Hierarchy*, 26.

116. In this regard, see Tim B. Heaton, Kristen L. Goodman, and Thomas B. Holman, "In Search of a Peculiar People: Are Mormon Families Really Different?" 87-117, in *Contemporary Mormonism: Social Science Perspectives*, ed. Marie Cornwall, Tim B. Heaton, and Lawrence A. Young (Urbana: University of Illinois Press, 1994).

117. Prince & Wright, *Rise of Modern Mormonism*, xvii.

Sex and Prophetic Power

A Comparison of John Humphrey Noyes, Founder of the Oneida Community, with Joseph Smith Jr., the Mormon Prophet

Lawrence Foster

The close yet often conflicted connection between religious and sexual impulses and their expression has long been noted by scholars.[1] Dynamic new religious movements often experience sharp polarities between efforts to control sexual activity, on the one hand, and to extend sexual expression in new directions, on the other. Such tensions can become intense within a single individual, as Somerset Maugham's short story "Rain" illustrates by describing how a sexually rigid missionary eventually succumbs to the temptations of the flesh.[2] Prophetic religious leaders, in particular, often embody within themselves conflicting tendencies toward extremes of sexual control or license.

The complex relationship between religious and sexual impulses first became a focus of my investigation more than four decades ago when I began studying the Shakers, who introduced strict celibacy into their semi-monastic communities in antebellum America, and the Oneida Perfectionists, who practiced a form of group marriage or "free love," colorfully characterized by Charles Nordhoff as a "combination of polygamy and polyandry with certain religious and social restraints."[3] On the surface, it might seem hard to imagine more diametrically opposed groups. Yet in a host of ways, the two groups were strikingly similar. For example, John Humphrey Noyes, founder of the free-love Oneida Community, developed a theological system that was essentially a mirror image of the one created by the celibate Shakers, and he admired the Shakers as the only group, other than his own, that even approached a correct understanding of the heavenly model of religious and social order.[4]

The curious kinship between these movements which appeared to be such polar opposites is developed more fully elsewhere.[5] This essay, instead, compares the efforts of John Humphrey Noyes to introduce complex marriage during the late 1840s at Oneida, New York, with the efforts of the Mormon prophet-founder Joseph Smith Jr., earlier that same decade, to introduce plural marriage in Nauvoo, Illinois. I shall begin with reflections on the relationship between religious and sexual impulses in new religious movements. Then I shall turn to the religious and sexual dynamics in the Oneida Community, presenting new information about the importance of Oneida's sexual system in maintaining group loyalty. Finally, I shall suggest how understanding the way Oneida's unusual sexual system worked may help us make sense of some of Joseph Smith's most puzzling actions as he introduced polygamous belief and practice in Mormon Nauvoo.

I

As a starting point for these reflections, let us turn to a powerful statement by a Viennese doctor whose work remains influential but controversial, Sigmund Freud. His study, *Civilization and Its Discontents*, begins with this electrifying statement: "The impression forces itself upon one that men measure by false standards, that everyone seeks power, success, riches for himself and admires others who attain them, while undervaluing the truly precious things in life."[6] Freud goes on, in a rare example of willingness to admit his own fallibility, to discuss how his dear friend Romaine Rolland had taken issue with Freud's earlier argument in *The Future of an Illusion* that religion was simply the projection of childish recollections of an all-powerful father figure. Rolland, while admitting that this could well be the primary basis for popular religious belief, argued that a deeper source of religion was an emotion he called "a sensation of 'eternity,' a feeling of something limitless, unbounded, something 'oceanic'"—"a feeling of indissoluble connection, of belonging inseparably to the external world as a whole."[7]

Freud, while admitting that he had never himself experienced such a feeling, speculated that it might well be related to the emotions experienced in sexual union. As he put it: "At its height the state of being in love threatens to obliterate the boundaries between ego and object. Against all the evidence of his senses, the man in love declares that he and his beloved are one, and is prepared to behave as if it were a fact."[8] While one need not accept Freud's speculations about the sources of the sense of oceanic boundlessness, the apparent similarities between the accounts of mystics describing their sense of oneness with God and those of lovers describing their union with each other is nevertheless striking. As one case in point, many of St. Teresa of Avila's ecstatic effusions could easily be read as descriptive of sexual emotions.[9]

Further insight into this relationship is suggested in a brilliant study that may well do for our understanding of the psychology of charismatic religious personalities what William James's *Varieties of Religious Experience* did a century ago for the broader topic of religious experience as a whole. Written by Len Oakes, who for eleven years was a member and historian of a New Zealand commune that could be viewed as a synthesis of the Esalen Institute, a Rajneesh ashram, and the Oneida Community, *Prophetic Charisma: The Psychology of Revolutionary Religious Personalities* presents a brilliant qualitative and quantitative analysis of the development of prophetic leadership in eighteen contemporary New Zealand communal groups.[10]

Most relevant for this analysis is Oakes's chapter on "The Charismatic Moment." It focuses on what Charles Lindholm has described as an "ecstatic transcendent experience opposed to the alienation and isolation of the mundane world."[11] The anthropologist Victor Turner has analyzed this in terms of an emotionally transformative "ritual process" involving an "electrifying blurring of boundaries."[12] In this context, Oakes reflects on the "blurred line between sexuality and mysticism" and the "amoral nature of the charismatic experience," which sometimes provides individuals with "the sense of a truth so great, some ecstasy so powerful, that it takes the group beyond normal morality and into the supra-divine realm."[13] "Such total dissolution of the personality produces an eternal 'moment' wherein but One Thing is needful: to dissolve one's being into the Being of God as mediated by the prophet —the master of the techniques of ecstasy."[14]

But perhaps the most incisive analytical approach to such phenomena is provided by John Humphrey Noyes, who was not only an astute community organizer but also a brilliant, if highly idiosyncratic, social theorist.[15] Noyes summarized the relationship between religious and sexual impulses in antebellum revivalism as follows:

> Revivals are theocratic in their very nature; they introduce God into human affairs. ... In the conservative theory of Revivals, this power is restricted to the conversion of souls; but in actual experience it goes, or tends to go, into all the affairs of life. ... Religious love is a very near neighbor to sexual love, and they always get mixed in the intimacies and social excitements of Revivals.[16]
>
> The course of things may be re-stated thus: Revivals lead to religious love; religious love excites the passions; the converts, finding themselves in theocratic liberty, begin to look about for their mates and their paradise. Here begins divergence. If women have the lead, the feminine idea that ordinary wedded love is carnal and unholy rises and becomes a ruling principle. Mating on the Spiritual plane, with all the heights and depths of sentimental love, becomes the order of the day. Then, if a prudent Mother Ann is at the head of affairs, the sexes are fenced off from each other, and carry on their Platonic intercourse through the grating. ... On the other hand, if the leaders are men, the theocratic impulse takes the opposite direction, and polygamy in some form is the result. Thus Mormonism is the masculine form, as Shakerism is the feminine form, of the more morbid products of Revivals.
>
> Our Oneida Socialism, too, is a masculine product of the great Revival.[17] ...
>
> It is notable that all the socialisms that have sprung from revivals have prospered. They are all utterly opposed to each other; some of them must be false and bad; yet they all make the wilderness blossom around them like the rose. ... [H]owever false and mutually repugnant the religious socialisms may be in their details, they are all based on the theocratic principle—they all recognize the right of religious inspiration to shape society and dictate the form of family life.[18]

II

With the foregoing perspectives in mind, how might the relationship between religious and sexual impulses in the life and prophetic leadership of John Humphrey Noyes and his Oneida Community best be understood? Noyes, despite his fascination with sexuality and the proper forms of sexual expression, always emphasized the primacy of religious over sexual concerns. As he put it in his most important manifesto, his 1848 "Bible Argument Defining the Relations of the Sexes in the Kingdom of Heaven," the first necessity was a restoration of "right relations with God." Only then could "right relations between the sexes" be reestablished.[19] Noyes insisted: "any attempt to revolutionize sexual morality before settlement with God is out of order."[20]

Since John Humphrey Noyes had already securely established the religious foundation for his followers by 1848, his "Bible Argument" primarily addressed how right relations between the sexes could be restored within the holy community he was attempting to found at Oneida. As an extremely shy young adult, Noyes struggled to understand his sexual impulses and determine why many Perfectionists with whom he associated engaged in erratic and often self-destructive experimentation. Noyes concluded that the existing marriage system was unsatisfactory: "The law of marriage worketh wrath."[21] Unrealistic and unnatural restrictions were being placed upon relations between the sexes. In marriage, wives were held in a form of slave-like bondage, while their husbands toiled away in an uncertain and highly competitive external world. Romantic love and the monogamous family merely accentuated the disruptive individualism present in other areas of society.

How were such problems to be overcome? Further individualistic fragmentation—free love outside a community context—was no solution, Noyes argued. Instead of being a disruptive force, why couldn't sexual relations be harnessed to bring people together within a more cohesive community? Noyes wanted believers to share a perfect community of interests, to replace the "I-spirit" with the "we-spirit." If believers were to love each other fully while living in close communal association, they must be allowed to love each other fervently and physically, "not by pairs, as in the world, but en masse." The necessary restrictions of the earthly period, governed by arbitrary human law, would eventually have to give way to the final heavenly free state, governed by the spirit in which "hostile surroundings and powers of bondage cease" and "all restrictions also will cease." A perfect unity in all respects would result. Each should be married to all—heart, mind, and body—in a complex marriage.[22]

This would be achieved by enlarging the home. Selfish loyalty to the nuclear family unit would be replaced by loyalty to the entire community. The way in which this was achieved at Oneida and sustained for more than thirty years has been discussed extensively elsewhere and will be only briefly summarized before I turn to the issues of social and sexual cohesion that the Oneida experiment raised.[23] As the group of some two hundred adults gradually coalesced into a functioning community, individuals came to consider themselves married to the entire group, and they were allowed to exchange heterosexual partners frequently within the group. At the same time, all exclusive romantic attachments were broken up. Such "special love" was seen as an antisocial threat to communal order. All members lived together in one large communal Mansion House, ate together, worked together, had a system of communal childrearing, and shared all but the most basic property in common. Community government was achieved by holding daily religious-and-business meetings that all adults attended; by developing an informal method of group feedback and control known as "mutual criticism"; and by creating an informal status hierarchy known as "ascending and descending fellowship." A difficult system of birth control by "male continence," technically known as "coitus reservatus," was used as the only way of limiting births until the final decade when a "stirpiculture" or eugenics experiment was introduced for some members.

How was Noyes's prophetic leadership and sexual charisma associated with the development of this system? Central to Oneida's success was the acceptance by Noyes's followers of his religious commission and his ultimate authority over all aspects of their lives, including sexual expression. Once that God-like authority was firmly established, Noyes acted as a quintessential patriarchal figure toward both his male and female followers, benevolently allowing them great flexibility in implementing his ideals in practice.[24]

Within this system, a variety of sexual issues was discussed with considerable candor and insight. As one striking example, Noyes included the following reflections at the end of one of his published theological articles:

> Most of the difficulties which have arisen in respects to our social [i.e., sexual] theory, have been based on the idea that woman is a perishable article—that after her first experience in love, she is like an old newspaper, good for nothing. A virgin is considered better than a married woman who has had experience. But the reverse of this should be the case, and when things come to their right hearing, it will be seen that the reverse of the common idea is the truth. It is a scandal to God, and man, and woman, that in the estimation of men, a virgin is better than a married woman. It is true they are so universally preferred, but why? It is because woman has yielded to the worldly idea, and lost her self-respect. She supposes the enigma is solved, and does not carry about with her that fresh consciousness of mystery and worth, that a virgin does. The married settle into the feeling that the enigma is solved, and that makes them less attractive. The principle operates, in the same way, in both sexes.[25]

While many have commented on the role that sex played in the development of the Oneida Community, the key to understanding Noyes's success may be found in the correspondence of Noyes's son Theodore in the 1890s, about a decade after the community broke up. Theodore, who had been unsuccessfully groomed to become his father's successor, wrote a thirteen-page letter in response to some questions about the community's dissolution posed by a perceptive young medical student, Anita Newcomb McGee. She followed up with a four-page letter in which she pressed for more clarity about why the Oneida Community had dissolved.[26] McGee suggested that the community had broken up because of a complex set of factors, including John Humphrey Noyes's advanced age and declining ability to lead; increasing economic prosperity that led to a lessening of communal loyalty; the admission of new and disruptive individuals; and jealousies associated with the "stirpiculture" or eugenics experiment during the final decade of the community's life.[27]

In a response he never sent, Theodore praised Anita McGee's "shrewd summary" but insisted that the causes she identified were secondary to the underlying one. As he put it: "The power to regulate or withdraw sexual privileges, inherent in the community at large and by common consent delegated to father [John Noyes] and his subordinates, constituted by far the most effectual means of government. Father possessed in a remarkable degree the faculty of convincing people that the use of this arbitrary power was exercised for their own good, and for many years there was very little dissatisfaction and no envy of his prerogative. ..."

> But now to come closer, and take the bull fairly by the horns. In a society like the Community, the young and attractive women form the focus toward which all the social [i.e., sexual] rays converge; and the arbiter[,] to be truly one, must possess the confidence and to a certain extent the obedience of this circle of attractions[,] and moreover, he must exercise his power by genuine sexual attraction to a large extent. To quite a late period father filled this situation perfectly. He was a man of quite extraordinary attractiveness to women, and he dominated them by his intellectual power and social "magnetism" superadded to intense religious convictions to which young women are very susceptible. The circle of young women whom he trained when he was between 40 and 50 years of age, were by a large majority his devoted friends throughout the trouble which led to the dissolution.
>
> I must suppose that as he grew older he lost some of his attractiveness, and I know that he delegated the function [of initiating young women into sexual intercourse] to younger men in several cases, but you can see that this matter was of prime importance in the question of successorship and that the lack of a suitable successor obliged him to continue as the social center longer than would have otherwise been the case and so gave more occasion for dissatisfaction.[28]

In short, the Oneida Community can be seen throughout its existence as the lengthened shadow of John Humphrey Noyes, not only in its intellectual and organizational characteristics but also in the way it used mutual sexual attraction to link the community tightly together in pursuit of a comprehensive set of religious and social goals.

III

How may this perspective be relevant to understanding the controversial dynamics of the other great, and ultimately far more influential, "masculine product of the great Revivals," the Mormons? Under their prophet Joseph Smith Jr. during the early 1840s, the Latter-day Saints had begun to introduce plural marriage as an integral part of their larger religious and social preparation for the Millennium. Joseph Smith's first objective was to introduce a new religious worldview and sense of commitment. Yet he also struggled to understand the proper role of human sexuality and how it could be expressed in positive ways.

Like Noyes, who was attempting to "enlarge the family" to overcome the disruptive individualism of his day, Smith was distressed by the social disruption in the "burned-over district" of western New York State. Smith sought, in an acute millenarian effort, "to turn the hearts of the fathers to the children" in the new religious and social order he was developing. Such efforts came to a head, both theologically and practically, during the five years Smith spent in Nauvoo, Illinois, between 1839 and his murder in 1844. Theologically, his concerns were reflected in new sealing ceremonies introduced to link indissolubly the living and the dead, both in this life and throughout eternity. Practically, his concerns were reflected in efforts to achieve closer social ties on earth, most controversially by enlarging conventional monogamous marriage to include a form of patriarchal polygamy based upon Old Testament Hebrew models.[29]

Smith, like Noyes, was a handsome, dynamic, and intellectually attractive figure who clearly saw sexuality in a positive light, even while recognizing that its expression must be carefully controlled. He faced a host of problems as leader of his Church, mayor of his city, and chief business planner for a community that within five years rivaled Chicago in size and appeared to hold the balance of political power in Illinois. With many of his closest and most trusted associates away on lengthy missionary trips, leaving wives and children behind, Smith had to address the complex interpersonal tensions that inevitably resulted. It is within this context—rather than merely as an expression of, or rationalization for, his personal impulses—that Smith's introduction of plural marriage can best be understood.[30]

A vivid expression of Smith's attitudes and concerns can be seen in the remarkable letter he wrote as part of his attempt to convince Nancy Rigdon, daughter of one of his closest associates, to become his plural wife, after she had refused his first proposal. Smith's letter asserts that "happiness is the object and design of our existence," but that this can only be achieved through "virtue, uprightness, faithfulness, holiness and keeping all the commandments of God."

> But we cannot keep all the commandments without first knowing them. That which is wrong under one circumstance, may be, and often is, right under another. A parent may whip a child, and justly too, because he stole an apple; whereas if the child had asked for the apple, and the parent had given it, the child would have eaten it with a better appetite; there would have been no stripes; all the pleasure of the apple would have been secured, all the misery of stealing lost.
>
> This principle will justly apply to all of God's dealings with his children. Everything that God gives us is lawful and right; and it is proper that we should enjoy his gifts and blessings whenever and wherever he is disposed to bestow; but if we should seize upon those same blessings and enjoyments without law, without revelation, without commandment, those blessings and enjoyments would prove cursings in the end. …
>
> Our heavenly Father is more liberal in His views, and boundless in His mercies and blessings, than we are ready to believe or receive … He says, "Ask and ye shall receive, seek and ye shall find;" … no good thing will I withhold from them who walk uprightly before me, and do my will in all things—who will listen to my voice and to the voice of the servant whom I have sent; … for all things shall be made known to them in mine own due time, and in the end they shall have joy.[31]

The letter suggests important perspectives for understanding Joseph Smith's sexual attitudes and his reasons for introducing plural marriage in Nauvoo. It also raises interesting points of comparison with Theodore Noyes's assessment of how his father controlled sexual expression in the Oneida Community. Although many scholars have made head counts of Joseph Smith's probable wives and sought to discover what actually happened in his plural marriages,[32] the *qualitative* questions raised by the introduction of plural marriage—and the larger *social* functions such relationships may have served—have received far less attention.[33]

Smith's proposal to Nancy Rigdon highlights his positive view of sex, as well as his realization that its expression must be controlled.

Marriage and sexual expression were a "gift and a blessing" that could be granted only by proper authority. If proper authority were secured, however, there was "no good thing [God would] … withhold from those who walk uprightly before me, and do my will in all things."[34] During the turbulent final three years of his life, Smith appears to have applied this principle to his core group of about thirty male followers in Nauvoo, where plural marriage was commonly referred to in code as a man's "privileges." For example, in a conversation with his scribe William Clayton authorizing him to marry a young convert to whom he had become attracted in England, Smith added: "It is your privilege to have all the wives you want."[35]

A major reason why Joseph Smith sanctioned such relationships for himself and his closest followers, both male and female, was to bind his followers to him more closely. He believed he was creating a "new Israel," a tribal group indissolubly linked by blood and various forms of "sealing" involving both marriage and adoption. Women whom Smith or his closest associates approached to become plural wives usually were individuals of proven loyalty to the Church. Many of them, especially the daughters of Smith's closest followers, reported that he told them their action would insure their salvation and that of their families, linking them indissolubly to Smith in the hereafter. After such relationships had been established, neither the men nor the women could readily apostatize. Not only were their emotional commitments at stake if they left the Church, so were their reputations.[36]

Perhaps the most puzzling behavior in which Joseph Smith apparently engaged during this period was to ask some of his closest associates to give him their wives. In addition, he may also have sustained sexual relations with some women who were, at the same time, legally married to other men.[37] This phenomenon has been misleadingly characterized as "polyandry" by many Mormon scholars, including Danel Bachman, Richard Van Wagoner, Todd Compton, and George Smith.[38] Compton, for example, in his massive and thoughtful apologetic study, *In Sacred Loneliness: The Plural Wives of Joseph Smith,* asserts that

> fully one-third of his plural wives, eleven of them, were married civilly to other men when he married them. …

> Polyandry might be easier to understand if one viewed these marriages to Smith as a sort of *de facto* divorce with the first husband. However, none of these women divorced their "first husbands" while Smith was alive and all of them continued to live with their civil spouses while married to Smith.[39]

Contrary to almost all other scholars who have looked closely at this phenomenon—with the notable exception of Andrew Ehat and Kathryn Daynes[40]—I believe that the behavior in which Smith apparently engaged could not possibly have been viewed—either by himself or by his loyal followers at the time—as a form of "polyandry." Kathryn Daynes, in her nuanced and arguably definitive study of the development of Mormon polygamy in nineteenth-century Utah, agrees that:

> As Lawrence Foster argues, calling such marriages polyandrous is misleading because polyandry is incompatible with the patriarchal nature of nineteenth-century Mormon marriage. While Mary Ann [Richardson]'s two marriages overlapped, the form of the marriage to each man was different and did not entail the same rights and responsibilities. Marriages for time were perceived as temporary because life on this earth was viewed as ephemeral in the expanse of eternity. Sealings for eternity were thus much more important and took precedence over marriages for time, although they did not necessarily invalidate them.[41]

Although most Mormon scholars who have dealt with this complex issue have unfortunately continued to use the term "polyandry," I believe that Joseph Smith himself could not have considered any of his marital practices to be "polyandrous" because of early Mormon polygamy's intensely patriarchal character. Let me therefore briefly restate here the argument I made in my 1981 study, *Religion and Sexuality,* and then tie it to the comparison of the marital experimentation by Noyes and Smith that I am developing in this essay.[42]

The first two of my three arguments about Joseph Smith's marriages to already-married women have been widely echoed in later scholarship. In the first place, the 1843 revelation on plural and celestial marriage states that civil marriages were not considered valid for eternity. The revelation states: "All covenants, contracts, bonds, obligations, oaths, vows, performances, connections, associations, or expectations, that are not made and entered into, and sealed, by the Holy Spirit of promise, of him who is anointed, both as well for time and for eternity … are of no efficacy, virtue, or force in and after the resurrection from the dead."[43]

Later Mormon theology has assumed that this statement refers only to the afterlife, but in the millenarian context of Nauvoo and early Utah, Mormon leaders were attempting to apply presumptive heavenly standards on earth. Earthly and heavenly standards were viewed as inextricably intertwined; an imminent earthly millennium was to be realized. This meant that existing marriage standards were invalid; only marriages sanctioned under the "new and everlasting covenant" on earth were efficacious. Mormon initiatory ceremonies, from baptism to the more elaborate temple rites, involved a rebirth into a new world that was in the process of realization on earth under Joseph Smith's guidance. Prior to initiation into this new millennial world, however, there was a brief but disruptive interregnum when neither the old nor the new standards were operative and when the basis of social authority was unclear.

A former member of Smith's secret Council of Fifty, which helped to regulate this transition, recalled:

> About the same time [1842][,] the doctrine of "sealing" for an eternal state was introduced, and the Saints were given to understand that their marriage relations with each other were not valid. … That they were married to each other only by their own covenants, and that if their marriage relations had not been productive of blessings and peace, and they felt it oppressive to remain together, they were at liberty to make their own choice, as much as if they had not been married. That it was a sin for people to live together, and raise or beget children, in alienation from each other.[44]

In addition to the supremacy of the revelation on celestial marriage over earthly covenants, there is a second reason why Joseph Smith might have asked for the wives of other men. In a public speech on October 6, 1861, Brigham Young discussed the ways "in which a woman might leave a man lawfully." The primary valid cause for divorce was when "a woman [had become] alienated in her feelings &

affections from her husband." "If the woman Preferred another man higher in authority & he is willing to take her & her husband gives her up—there is no Bill of divorce required."[45] Such a practice of "moving up" in the hierarchy without a formal divorce may well have originated with Joseph Smith.

There is a third, more speculative explanation put forward in *Religion and Sexuality*[46] that might account—within a patriarchal framework—for Smith taking married women as plural wives. According to several nineteenth-century sources, it was possible for what was colloquially called a "proxy husband" to be assigned as a temporary spouse for a woman when her husband was either absent on a long missionary assignment or was otherwise unable to sire children. The children born under such circumstances would be viewed as belonging to the original husband, who was symbolically considered to have become temporarily "dead." Thus, while a man was absent in the service of his Church, his patriarchal "kingdom," which was heavily dependent upon how many children he had, would not suffer loss.[47]

If such extraordinary arrangements were actually sanctioned, they might provide a coherent rationale for Smith's sexual relationships with wives of his close associates. Significantly, a remarkable letter Brigham Young wrote on March 5, 1857, to Mrs. Mary Ann Richardson, a Mormon woman in Manti, Utah, appears to sanction such a "proxy" practice in one unusual circumstance. Responding to a letter from Mrs. Richardson on February 22, Young declared that "if I was imperfect and had a good wife[,] I would call on some good bro[the]r to help me, that we might have increase; that a man of this character will have a place in the Temple, receive his endowments[,] and in eternity will be as tho' nothing had happened to him in time."[48] Although this particular case occurred in Utah, the example and the pragmatic flexibility it illustrates also might reflect a similar pragmatism in some of Joseph Smith's marital alliances in Nauvoo.

An astute early leader of the RLDS movement, Jason Briggs, criticized what he saw as an apparent "proxy" authorization in the revelation on celestial marriage itself. The passage in question states: "And as ye have asked concerning adultery, verily, verily I say unto you, if a man receiveth a wife in the new and everlasting covenant, and if she be with *another* man, *and if I have not appointed [him] unto her by the holy annointing*, she hath committed adultery and shall be destroyed" (emphasis added).[49]

Following the publication of *Religion and Sexuality*, a Mormon in Arizona called me to recount a family memory about such a practice. He said that one of his missionary ancestors, sent out on a missionary trip in 1852 after plural marriage had just been announced, returned home to discover that his wife, without his knowledge, had participated in such a "proxy" relationship in his absence. Although he retained the woman as his wife, he considered her "polluted" and he never subsequently had sexual relations with her.

If such a remarkable Mormon variant on Hebrew levirate marriage was ever practiced by Joseph Smith or his associates, it was only on a limited scale during the emotionally superheated millennial fervor of the transition between the old and new orders in Nauvoo and in early Utah.[50] Such a practice would, however, be of great interest. It might provide a convincing intellectual rationale for some of Smith's most puzzling marital arrangements with wives of his associates, other than the conceptually naive present-day description of them as a form of "polyandry," a term and concept that I have never seen used in nineteenth-century Mormon sources. To suggest that Joseph Smith could have interpreted his relationships with already-married women as "polyandrous" is, in my opinion, tantamount to arguing that Smith was prepared to violate his own fundamental patriarchal marriage principles or that his libido had simply gone wild. I am convinced that the introduction of any form of "proxy" arrangements, even on an extremely limited scale, could only have taken place and been justified under the auspices of the Church-regulated system of patriarchal marriage. If Joseph Smith actually did use a "proxy" justification for his marriages with already-married women, however, that does suggest striking parallels with John Humphrey Noyes's "complex marriage" system at Oneida, through which Noyes became linked sexually and in other ways with wives of his associates.[51]

Even though there may be parallels between what happened in Oneida and in Nauvoo, there are also significant differences, especially arising from the differing size and complexity of the two groups. The

Oneida Community never included more than several hundred adults at its peak, whereas Latter-day Saints numbered in the tens of thousands by the end of the Nauvoo period. Even within the small Oneida group, dissension over complex marriage became so great at first that the practice was temporarily discontinued for a six-month period in 1852 when the group came close to disbanding. In the much larger Mormon community in Nauvoo, conflicts and irregularities proved far more difficult to handle, and they led with almost tragic inevitability to the murder of Joseph Smith and his brother Hyrum on June 27, 1844. Only under Brigham Young's leadership in the relative isolation of the Great Basin region were Latter-day Saints able to implement plural marriage as an integral part of their millennial Zion.

IV

What larger conclusions can we draw from this brief exploratory comparison of the expansion of marital and sexual relationships in the mid-nineteenth-century Oneida and Mormon communities? Although strong sexual impulses undoubtedly do contribute to the sexual hyperactivity displayed by many charismatic leaders, perhaps the most important analytical questions relate to how such practices strengthen or weaken the loyalty of followers to the prophet and his cause.

Two world-significant cases are worthy of brief mention in this regard. The first involves the Muslim prophet Muhammad, founder of the second largest and one of the most rapidly expanding religious movements in the world today. Although hostile stereotypes about Muhammad and Islam are legion in the West, it is worth noting that Muhammad remained monogamous for twenty-five years until the death of his beloved first wife Khadijah, and most of the eleven other women he eventually took as wives during the last twelve years of his life linked him to his closest followers or to the various tribal groups whose support he needed. In addition, except for his first wife, Khadijah, and one later wife, Maria, none of Muhammad's wives bore him any children.[52]

Another instructive case is that of Hong Xiuquan, the millenarian leader of the mid-nineteenth-century Taiping Rebellion in China, the largest civil war in human history, which cost at least 20 million lives between 1850 and 1864. During the flush period of Taiping success when the rebels appeared close to taking control over all of China, Hong acquired an extensive group of consorts and allowed senior associates similar privileges prohibited to the Taiping rank-and-file.[53] While personal pleasure and mental disorder undoubtedly played a part in Hong's actions, attempts to insure the loyalty of his close associates may have been an important factor, as well.

In conclusion, perhaps anthropologist Kenelm Burridge in his fine study, *New Heaven, New Earth*, best summarizes the sexual dynamics of charisma in his cameo essay, "The Prophet." Burridge asks:

> What is the significance of the commonly reported sexual attractions of prophets? Until recently there were few communities in which women were not simply home-makers and child-bearers. Apart from a privileged few, usually elderly and past the flushes of sexual enjoyment, women have played little part in the management of political affairs. They have been in the main uneducated in intellectual matters, untrained in public and managerial techniques. Exchanged or bought in marriage, they have been regarded as chattels who followed their men and did what they were told. Interacting most significantly in the sexual act, the relations between men and women have been largely determined by the overt ordering of different kinds of sexual access. Even if she understood him, of what interest to a Sudanese peasant woman were the Mahdi's dreams of glory, the Caliphate and empire if not, surely, the privileged luxury and influence of being a member of his harem? And much the same may be said of the ladies of New Guinea, whose aspirations are largely realized in being the wife of a rich and important man. On the whole, therefore, the sexual attractiveness of male prophets is to be accounted for less in the amatory skills of the prophet, and more in the conditions of being a woman. Not for nothing did Jupiter come to Danae in a shower of coins. A prophet offers both sexes a wider and more satisfying redemption, and his sexual attractions and virility suggest an awareness of new babies as well as new men: total rebirth, a new community.[54]

Notes

1. Although this relationship has been frequently noted, it has been far less often analyzed. Geoffrey Parrinder, *Sexual Morality in the World's Religions* (Oxford: One World, 1996), provides an overview of sex in the major world

religions. Revealing analyses of such impulses in new and charismatic religious movements include I. M. Lewis, *Ecstatic Religion: An Anthropological Study of Spirit Possession and Shamanism* (Baltimore: Penguin, 1971); William Sargant, *The Mind Possessed: A Physiology of Possession, Mysticism and Faith Healing* (Baltimore: Penguin, 1973); and Susan Jean Palmer, *Moon Sisters, Krishna Mothers, Rajneesh Lovers: Women's Roles in New Religions* (Syracuse: Syracuse University Press, 1994). My first book, *Religion and Sexuality: Three American Communal Experiments of the Nineteenth Century* (New York: Oxford University Press, 1981), which received the Mormon History Association's "best book of the year" award, dealt extensively with such issues and forms the basis for much of the following discussion.

2. W. Somerset Maugham, "Rain," in *The Complete Short Stories of W. Somerset Maugham*, Vol. 1 (London: Heinemann, 1951), 1-38.

3. Charles Nordhoff, *The Communistic Societies of the United States* (New York: Harper, 1875), 271.

4. *Handbook of the Oneida Community* (Wallingford, CT: Office of the Circular, 1867), 60.

5. Foster, *Religion and Sexuality*, 88-90. Also see Stow Persons, "Christian Communitarianism in America," in Donald Drew Egbert and Stow Persons, eds., *Socialism and American Life*, 2 vols. (Princeton: Princeton University Press, 1952), 1:125-51.

6. Sigmund Freud, *Civilization and Its Discontents*, trans. Joan Riviere (1930; Garden City, NY: Doubleday, 1958), 1.

7. Ibid., 2.

8. Ibid., 3-4.

9. For instance, she describes her vision of an angel as follows: "In his hand I saw a great golden spear, and at the iron tip there appeared to be a point of fire. This he plunged into my heart several times so that it penetrated to my entrails. When he pulled it out, I felt that he took them with it, and left me utterly consumed by the great love of God." Quoted in Parrinder, *Sexual Morality*, 218.

10. Len Oakes, *Prophetic Charisma: The Psychology of Revolutionary Religious Personalities* (Syracuse: Syracuse University Press, 1997). Oakes's key argument is that certain childhood experiences may influence prophetic figures to view the world in narcissistic terms, convinced that their own personal experience provides a universally valid paradigm for the world. Oakes's typology of the stages of development of prophetic leadership throughout an individual's life is as suggestive for such figures as Erik Erikson's theory is for normal individuals.

11. Ibid., 144.

12. Ibid.

13. Ibid., 149.

14. Ibid., 150.

15. Excerpts from the letter are printed in William Hepworth Dixon's *Spiritual Wives* (Philadelphia: Lippincott, 1868), 347-53.

16. Ibid., 350.

17. Ibid., 351.

18. Ibid., 352-53. Italics in original removed.

19. For the full text of the "Bible Argument Defining the Relations of the Sexes in the Kingdom of Heaven," see *The First Annual Report of the Oneida Association* (Oneida Reserve, NY: Leonard, 1849), 18-42, rpt. in *Bible Communism: A Compilation of the Annual Reports and Other Publications of the Oneida Association and Its Branches* (Brooklyn: Office of the Circular, 1853), 24-64, and Lawrence Foster, ed., and George Wallingford Noyes, comp., *Free Love in Utopia: John Humphrey Noyes and the Origin of the Oneida Community* (Urbana: University of Illinois Press, 2001), 298-361.

20. "Bible Argument," 28.

21. Ibid., 25.

22. Ibid., 21-22.

23. For major studies that discuss the theory and practice of the Oneida Community, see Robert Allerton Parker, *A Yankee Saint: John Humphrey Noyes and the Oneida Community* (New York: G. P. Putnam's Sons, 1935); Maren Lockwood Carden, *Oneida: Utopian Community to Modern Corporation* (Baltimore: Johns Hopkins University Press, 1969); Spencer Klaw, *Without Sin: The Life and Death of the Oneida Community* (New York: Penguin, 1993). See also Foster, *Religion and Sexuality.*

24. George Wallingford Noyes, *John Humphrey Noyes: The Putney Community* (Oneida, NY: by the author, 1931), 33, writes: "The dogma of Noyes's divine commission became a touchstone in the Putney and Oneida Communities. Those who rejected it were turned away; those who accepted it were bound together in a brotherhood of self-sacrificing quest for the Kingdom of God."

25. *Circular* 1 (30 Nov. 1851): 16.

26. Theodore E. Noyes to Anita Newcomb McGee, Sept. 13, 1891; McGee to Noyes, Nov. 12, 1892, copies in my possession, courtesy Geoffrey Noyes.

27. In Constance Noyes Robertson's documentary compilation, *Oneida Community: The Breakup* (Syracuse: Syracuse University Press, 1972), she develops more fully many of the arguments that Anita McGee broached in her earlier letter.

28. Noyes to McGee, Apr. 15, 1892, copy in my possession, courtesy Geoffrey Noyes.

29. For a more detailed analysis of these developments, see Foster, *Religion and Sexuality*, 123-80. The extreme tensions that such alternative marital and sexual practices generated are described in my "Sex and Conflict in New Religious Movements: A Comparison of the Oneida Community under John Humphrey Noyes and the Early Mormons under Joseph Smith and His Would-Be Successors," *Nova Religio: The Journal of Alternative and Emergent Religions* 13 (Feb. 2010): 34-58.

30. See George D. Smith, "Nauvoo Roots of Mormon Polygamy, 1841-46: A Preliminary Demographic Report," *Dialogue: A Journal of Mormon Thought* 27 (Spring 1994): 1-72.

31. Joseph Smith, Jr., *History of the Church of Jesus Christ of Latter-day Saints: Period 1*, ed. Brigham H. Roberts, 6 vols., 2d ed. rev. (Salt Lake City: Deseret Book, 1948), 5:136.

32. For some of the most important lists of plural wives, see Andrew Jenson, "Plural Marriage," *Historical Record* 6 (May 1887): 219-34; Stanley Snow Ivins's compendium in Jerald and Sandra Tanner, *Joseph Smith and Polygamy* (Salt Lake City: Modern Microfilm, n.d.), 41-47; Vesta P. Crawford Papers, University of Utah Special Collections; Fawn M. Brodie, *No Man Knows My History: The Life of Joseph Smith, the Mormon Prophet*, 2d ed. rev. (New York: Knopf, 1971), 335-36, 457-88; Danel W. Bachman, "A Study of the Mormon Practice of Plural Marriage before the Death of Joseph Smith," MA. thesis, Purdue University, 1975; D. Michael Quinn, "Organizational Development and Social Origins of the Mormon Hierarchy, 1832-1932: A Prosopographical Study," MA. thesis, University of Utah, 1973; Smith, "Nauvoo Roots of Mormon Polygamy"; Todd Compton, "A Trajectory of Plurality: An Overview of Joseph Smith's Thirty-three Plural Wives," *Dialogue: A Journal of Mormon Thought* 29 (Summer 1996): 1-38; Compton, *In Sacred Loneliness: The Plural Wives of Joseph Smith* (Salt Lake City: Signature Books, 1997); and George D. Smith, *Nauvoo Polygamy: "... but we called it celestial marriage"* (Salt Lake City: Signature Books, 2008).

33. Compton's *In Sacred Loneliness* is the first major study to describe in detail the lives of Smith's plural wives as individuals in their own right, although he misleadingly tends to assume that any sexual relationship with a woman constituted a "marriage." For this approach, as applied to Fanny Alger, see Compton's "Fanny Alger Smith Custer: Mormonism's First Plural Wife?" *Journal of Mormon History* 22 (Spring 1996): 174-207; a letter to the editor by Janet Ellington in the *Journal of Mormon History* 23 (Spring 1997): vi-vii; and Compton's response in *Journal of Mormon History* 23 (Fall 1997): xvii-xix. George D. Smith, *Nauvoo Polygamy*, 38-45, carefully assesses the Fanny Alger case and concludes that "the only thing that is well-attested about this relationship is that Joseph and Fanny were seen together in an intimate relationship" (Ibid., 40).

34. Joseph Smith, *History of the Church*, 5:136.

35. Jenson, "Plural Marriage," 225.

36. Especially striking in this respect is the handwritten statement by Helen Mar Kimball Whitney, dated 30 Mar. 1881, in archives, Historical Department, Church of Jesus Christ of Latter-day Saints, Salt Lake City, Utah (hereafter LDS archives), reproduced in Lawrence Foster, *Women, Family, and Utopia: Communal Experiments of the Shakers, the Oneida Community, and the Mormons* (Syracuse: Syracuse University Press, 1991), 137-38.

37. Foster, *Religion and Sexuality*, 159-66.

38. Bachman, "Plural Marriage," 124-36; Richard S. Van Wagoner, "Mormon Polyandry in Nauvoo," *Dialogue: A Journal of Mormon Thought* 18 (Fall 1985): 67-83; and Compton, "Trajectory of Polygamy," 20-31. Brodie, *No Man Knows My History*, 301-04, 335-37, was one of the first to use and develop the concept of polyandry in reference to Joseph Smith's relationships with wives of his associates.

39. Compton, *In Sacred Loneliness*, 15-16.

40. Andrew F. Ehat, "Pseudo-Polyandry: Explaining Mormon Polygyny's Paradoxical Companion," paper presented at the Sunstone Theological Symposium, Aug. 22, 1986, Salt Lake City. More recently, Kathryn Daynes's *More Wives Than One: Transformation of the Mormon Marriage System, 1840-1910* (Urbana: University of Illinois Press, 2001) has become the standard against which all future studies of nineteenth-century Mormon polygamy must be assessed.

41. Daynes, *More Wives Than One*, 81-82. Daynes states, 81, "This form of marriage was not an isolated instance, although it was undoubtedly a rare one."

42. Ehat's argument is that Joseph Smith had "pseudo-polyandrous" connections to women who were already married but that these marriages were for "eternity only" and did not include physical relations on earth ("Pseudo-Polygandry," 15, 19-25). Thus, he saw no need to consider how physical relations between Joseph Smith and his associates' wives might have been justified. It is far from clear, however, that Smith's "pseudo-polyandrous" marriages were unconsummated. Other Mormon historians who have closely analyzed the evidence believe that some of the relationships almost certainly were consummated.

43. *Deseret News Extra*, 14 Sept. 1852, cited in full in Foster, *Religion and Sexuality*, 249-55.

44. John D. Lee, *Mormonism Unveiled; Including the Life and Confessions of the Late Mormon Bishop, John D. Lee* (Hartford: Park, 1881), 146-47.

45. James Beck Notebooks, 1859-65, vol. 1, LDS archives. In the stenographic report of Brigham Young's speech of October 8, 1861, Young states that he and a few others learned this from Joseph Smith himself. For an unau-

thorized transcription of this speech, see Dennis R. Short, *For ~~Wo~~Men Only: The Lord's Law of Obedience* (Salt Lake City: Dennis R. Short, 1977), 85-90.

46. Only two Mormon scholars thus far appear to have been willing to engage my "proxy husband" argument—either positively or negatively. Ehat discounted the argument without actually citing my work, but that was nevertheless a distinct step forward from Richard Van Wagoner's "Mormon Polyandry," which showed no awareness of my detailed argument in *Religion and Sexuality* about how Joseph Smith may have justified his marriages to already-married women. Daynes, *More Wives Than One*, 251, n. 76, took issue with my use of the term "proxy husband," preferring instead "convenience marriage," despite the fact that the latter wording does not appear to have been used during the nineteenth century. Daynes also states: "[T]he term *proxy husband* was used in an entirely different context, and in the early church the term *proxy* was used almost exclusively in relation to the temple." In my opinion, the scattered allegations that have survived about this rare practice do not require that the term *proxy* be used in the same way as when referring to proxy *sealings* in the temple—a point that I believe is supported by the quotations in notes 47 and 50 below. The fact that T. B. H. Stenhouse actually minimizes his reference to the practice, discussing it only briefly in a footnote—rather than highlighting it as another damning example of Mormon "depravity"—suggests that in this instance he was carefully seeking to describe a rare and rather extraordinary phenomenon that he saw more as puzzling than as repulsive. See note 50 below.

47. The fullest source for this argument is John Hyde, who rose to prominence in the LDS Church and then apostatized during the period of the Reformation of 1856-57. The story of his break with the Mormon Church is ably laid out in Daynes, *More Wives Than One*, 82-83, 158. While Hyde may sometimes fail to understand the spirit underlying Mormon actions, his specific factual allegations may well be accurate. He stated:

> As a man's family constitutes his glory, to go on a mission for several years, leaving from two to a dozen wives at home, necessarily causes some loss of family, and consequently, according to Mormon notions, much sacrifice of salvation. This difficulty is however obviated by the appointment of an agent or proxy, who shall stand to themward [sic] in their husband's stead. ... This is one of the secret principles that as yet is only privately talked of in select circles, and darkly hinted at from their pulpits and in their works. They argue that the old Mosaic law of a "brother raising up seed to his dead brother" is now in force; and as death is only a temporary absence, so they contend a temporary absence is equivalent to death; and if in the case of death it is not only no crime, but proper; so also in this case it is equally lawful and extremely advantageous! This practice, commended by such sophistry, and commanded by such a Prophet was adopted as early as Nauvoo.
>
> Much scandal was caused by others than Smith attempting to carry out this doctrine. Several, who thought that what was good for the Prophet should be good for the people, were crushed down by Smith's heavy hand [John C. Bennett, perhaps?]. Several of those have spoken out to the practices of the "Saints." Much discussion occurred at Salt Lake as to the advisability of

> revealing the doctrine of polygamy in 1852, and that has caused Brigham to defer the public enunciation of this "proxy doctrine," as it is familiarly called. Many have expected it repeatedly at the late conferences. Reasoning out their premises to their natural and necessary consequences, this licentious and infamous dogma is their inevitable result (Hyde, *Mormonism: Its Leaders and Designs* [New York: Fetridge, 1857], 87-88).

48. This letter, from the Brigham Young Letterbooks in LDS archives, was kindly called to my attention by Michael Quinn. The letter and its context are further discussed in Foster, *Religion and Sexuality*, 312-14, n. 132. The fullest discussion of the context within which this relationship took place is in Daynes, *More Wives Than One*, 80-81, 251.

49. In the current Utah version of the Doctrine and Covenants, this is verse 41 in section 132.

50. Perhaps the most judicious assessment of this issue was made by the knowledgeable apostate T. B. H. Stenhouse, who stated:

> The Author has no personal knowledge, from the present leaders of the Church, of this teaching; but he has often heard that something yet would be taught which "would test the brethren as much as polygamy had tried the sisters." By many elders it has been believed that there was some foundation for the accusation that Joseph had taught some sisters in Nauvoo that it was their privilege to entertain other brethren as "proxy husbands" during the absence of their liege lords on mission. One lady has informed the Author that Joseph so taught her. All such teaching has never been made public, and it is doubtful if it ever extended very far, if, indeed, at all beyond a momentary combination of passion and fanaticism (Stenhouse, *The Rocky Mountain Saints; A Full and Complete History of the Mormons* [New York: Appleton, 1873], 301).

51. There is another allegation that is worth investigating because it points to a possible parallel between the practices of John Humphrey Noyes at Oneida and those of Joseph Smith in Nauvoo. The allegation is most starkly presented in a bitter tirade by a "Dr. W. Wyl." He asserts that Joseph Smith demanded the total loyalty of his closest followers in *all* things and that as a test of total loyalty he asked some of his closest followers to relinquish their wives to him. According to Wyl: "Joseph Smith finally demanded the wives of *all* the twelve apostles that were at home then in Nauvoo [emphasis in original]." Dr. W. Wyl [Wilhelm Ritter von Wymetal], *Joseph Smith, the Prophet, His Family, and Friends: A Study Based on Facts and Documents* (Salt Lake City: Tribune, 1886), 70. In support of this assertion, Wyl states that Leonora Taylor, first wife of John Taylor, then the president of the LDS Church, "told ladies who still reside in this city, that *all* the wives of the twelve were, in fact, consecrated to the Lord, that is to his servant Joseph [emphasis in original]." Wyl goes on to qualify the statement, however, by saying that Leonora Taylor, Vilate Kimball, and Sarah Pratt "escaped" that fate. Ibid., 71-72.

Corroborating evidence that such demands by the Mormon prophet—if and when they may have been made—did not necessarily lead to liaisons comes from Orson F. Whitney's biography of his grandfather, Heber C.

Kimball. Whitney stated that Joseph asked Heber to give up his wife Vilate to become Joseph's wife, saying that this was a requirement. After enormous inner turmoil, Heber eventually presented Vilate to Joseph. Joseph then wept, embraced Heber, and said that he had only been testing him to find out if his loyalty were absolute! Orson F. Whitney, *Life of Heber C. Kimball* (Salt Lake City: Kimball Family 1888), 333-35.

The reliability of Wyl's allegations can also be investigated by checking one specific quotation he cites from a published sermon by Jedediah M. Grant, one of Brigham Young's closest associates. Wyl said the statement came from volume 1, page 14, of the 26-volume collection of Mormon sermons known as the *Journal of Discourses* (Liverpool, England, 1854-86). According to Wyl, Grant declared: "Do you think that the prophet Joseph wanted the wives of the Twelve that he asked for, merely to gratify himself? No; he did it to try the brethren. But if President Young wants my wives, or any of them, he can have them." Wyl, *Joseph Smith*, 70. Grant's actual published statement, as it appeared in volume 2 [not 1], page 14, of the *Journal of Discourses*, makes substantially the same point, but without mentioning the Twelve or Brigham Young directly: "Did the Prophet Joseph want every man's wife he asked for? He did not, but in that thing was the grand thread of the Priesthood developed. The grand object in view was to try the people of God, to see what was in them. If such a man of God should come to me and say, 'I want your gold and silver, or your wives,' I should say, 'Here they are, I wish I had more to give you, take all I have got.' A man who has got the Spirit of God, and the light of eternity in him, has no trouble about such matters." While Wyl's version does not reproduce the precise wording of the *Journal of Discourses,* he does capture the gist of Grant's statement.

A more substantive inaccuracy can be identified in Wyl's report of an interview of March 30, 1887, that he had with William Law, a long-disaffected former Mormon leader, published on July 31, 1887, in *The Daily Tribune*. This case has been thoroughly investigated by Gordon A. Madsen, "Joseph Smith as Guardian: The Lawrence Estate Case," *Journal of Mormon History*, vol. 6, no. 3 (Summer 2010): 172-211. According to Wyl's report of the interview, William Law criticized Joseph Smith for improperly handling the estate of the Lawrence sisters, who had been placed under his legal guardianship. Based upon a thorough review of the documentary evidence, however, Madsen shows that either Law or Wyl—or both men—made inaccurate statements regarding the matter. I suspect that Wyl may well have accurately reported the substance of an *inaccurate* statement made by Law. Since Law had tried to blot the Mormons out of his mind entirely for nearly half a century after his bitter break from them in the 1840s, it would not be surprising if his memory were less than reliable. The documentable inaccuracy of Law's reported statement nevertheless raises questions about the reliability of other statements that he and/or Wyl made.

52. Rafiq Zakaria, *Muhammad and the Quran* (New York: Penguin, 1991), 43-60.

53. Jonathan D. Spence, *God's Chinese Son: The Taiping Heavenly Kingdom of Hong Xiuquan* (New York: Norton, 1996), 250-51. Two other excellent treatments of the Taiping Rebellion in English are Jen Yu-wen, *The Taiping Revolutionary Movement* (New Haven: Yale University Press, 1973); and Franz Michael, *The Taiping Rebellion: History* (Seattle: University of Washington Press, 1966).

54. Kenelm Burridge, *New Heaven, New Earth: A Study of Millenarian Activities* (New York: Schocken, 1968), 161.

Building Community
The Fundamentalist Mormon Concept of Space

Martha Bradley-Evans

Striking images of the white limestone temple of the Yearning for Zion Ranch in Eldorado, Texas, shown by the media during the 2008 raid on the FLDS community, evoked the LDS temple in Salt Lake City. This kind of visual connection, or "spatial imaginal type," is woven into the social and physical construction of all locations and suggests subtle narratives that are not immediately evident. Although imaginal types exist essentially in the world of the mind, heart, and senses, they are often intentionally or unintentionally represented and approximated in the physical world. Most spaces are complex social, economic, cultural, and physical constructions that carry cultural ideas. They usually are the result of some physical intervention in the landscape. The spaces we create represent the dominant order of things—the values of our society at a given time. Spatial types not only reflect people's relationships, they also influence our activities and beliefs in specific ways and promote particular interests and values.[1] Social order is taught through the environment and reinforced through imagery.

For nineteenth-century Mormons, the pursuit of an earthly paradise, the heavenly Jerusalem, and the millennium were a conceptual framework from which the Church sought to create a utopia. It did so by organizing its people into a divine order on earth rather than waiting for the ideal in the hereafter. The spaces they filled with meetinghouses, temples, and tabernacles anchored a larger environments that was filled with irrigation canals, farm fields, and wide-grid city streets.

This article asserts that the FLDS—the polygamists of Colorado City/Hildale—continue to build community today with patterns from the Mormon world of the 1830s. Mormons brought a conceptual map with them that traveled through Ohio, Missouri, and Illinois to the Great Basin in the second half of the nineteenth century. Historical and sociological attention paid to the fundamentalists has focused on polygamy, communal patterns, and other such distinctive practices. This article considers their spatial world. What does their distinctive sense of space say about their values, beliefs, and history? What does it say about their attitudes and relationships toward each other? What does it say about their relationship with the mother Church?

Sacred Space

Human beings have a built-in desire to find meaning in life. This applies to the quality of our relationships with each other and the physical and visual environments we live in as well as our spiritual and moral inner lives. We seek meaning for a range of reasons—to ground ourselves in the midst of potential chaos or confusion, to mediate conflict or other kinds of potential problems, and to find a sense of spiritual or emotional realities. Much of this proceeds in a spatial arena.

According to art historian Christian Norberg-Schulz, one way that humans grasp for an existential foothold is through the places we inhabit.[2] We not only understand ourselves in relation to these spaces, we partly define ourselves by them. In the same way we maintain gaps between us and other people—in the ways we come together or stay apart, in other words—people orient themselves with, and identify with, "an environment or, in short, when experiencing the environment as meaningful."[3]

Space is not just an ethereal, illusive thing; it has concrete characteristics that are interrelated in complex ways. Substances have shape, texture, and color, and these create the character of the background for our actions and events. The perceptual field allows us to distinguish emotions on a human face as it modulates across a skull—cavities, and protrusions—that enclose or define someone's features. There are boundaries and character to materiality, which in turn form the basis of relationships.

Sacred spaces have an additional purpose as *axis mundi* where we feel centered and elements of the surrounding landscape come together. This is where we have our rituals, embody our myths, and shape certain identities. It is where we speak to our ambitions and what it is that we hold dear. As part of the built environment, sacred space frames our existence in a way that embodies belief. These places introduce an order that extends beyond daily schedules to mediate the differences between the sacred and the profane. Religious leaders often design environments that make a group's abstract spiritual and social concerns concrete.

Trying to better understand spatial relationships, cultural geographers, urban planners, and architectural historians compose "bioregional maps" that show how humans relate to their environment. Rather than representing traditional geography, these maps identify cultural landmarks. In Mormon communities, as historian Richard Bushman writes, it is useful to know how Joseph Smith reshaped the world through his concept of an organized landscape.[4] In the Mormon region, it is helpful to know Smith's concept of a kind of funnel that collected people "from the widest possible periphery and drew them like gravity into a central point." Smith delivered sermons in words and sermons in masonry and city planning.

Plat of the City of Zion

The Plat of the City of Zion was influenced by the U.S. government's Land Ordinance of 1785 in the requirement that any land be surveyed and positioned in a grid before it could be sold. The LDS plat envisioned a town laid out at right angles, altogether about a mile square, with blocks divided into half-acre residential lots. A central area was to accommodate at least twenty-five temples and storehouses for a system of "consecration and stewardship." Residential lots were to contain a brick or stone house set back twenty-five feet from the street and fruit trees and a vegetable garden large enough to sustain a family. The way Mormon homes were clustered together, with communal fields at the periphery of town, it reflected an emphasis on group life. The ideal of a communitarian society was thus promulgated to people and intended to be the blueprint for the population of the earth. "When this square is thus laid off and supplied, lay off another in the same way, and so fill up the world in these last days, and let every man live in the city, for this is the city of Zion," Smith said.[5]

The emphasis on everyone living in a town instead of allowing people to exist on isolated farmsteads beyond the town limits was offset by the pastoral symbolism of Eden imposed on the lots, which were to be graced by gardens and by the urban symbolism of Jerusalem. Beyond these requirements, the plat relied on standard city-building tools—setbacks, zoning, and uniform materials to give the sense of an orderly, homogenous town fabric. Community building became a mixed endeavor of religious and secular activity as public and private enterprise joined together in doing God's will.

The rhetoric of imagery from the Garden of Eden frequently paralleled Smith's concept of kingdom building, placing the Mormon experience in the larger American settlement of the frontier. In 1842 the editor of the *Wasp* wrote, framing the building of Zion with scripture and urban metaphor:

> The wilderness has been made to blossom as the rose; and where hazle brush grew and muskitoes cousined, gardens decorate and the saints rest. ... The country for several miles around is already risen into the great mass of a city, built by the only people of the earth, that while they labor incessantly to make this earth like a garden of the lord, labor also ... to make men fit subjects for his kingdom and coming.[6]

In giving to his people a blueprint for city building, Smith molded space into a sacred backdrop for the effort to build God's kingdom, creating a tension between the sacred and profane. Locating the Mormon experience in a larger stream of history, this was an enterprise that kings and presidents had engaged in throughout time. In the Roman Empire, one found in the architecture and public works the trappings of the empire, of control and domination, religion and commerce symbolized in the grid of the *castrum* that imposed order on the world wherever the empire expanded. For Augustine, the proverbial city of God was distinct from the material city of men, an idea about the Church as a body of ideas and ways of living together in community. The Mormon village, too, would be the embodiment of belief or, as Ben Shann says, the "shape of content."[7]

Smith's concept of Zion was multi-layered. Town and community were rhetorically and figuratively identified as the twin pillars of a literal Kingdom of God. Tilling one's field, preparing wood for fences and barns, digging irrigation canals and diverting springs were all equal to religious ritual—all sacred activity that was dedicated to God. Sacred matter was found in the loam of the earth and the wood of the forests as the hands of the faithful redeemed the land and made the world anew. For Mormons, the physical world had different layers of meaning.

For some, the physical City of Zion resembled towns found throughout New England. It had similarities in its common green and a centralized cluster of public buildings—a tavern, school, church—in a mixture that coalesced and created a sense of identity, meaning, and unity. The tension between dependence and individualism, cooperation and self-reliance, communalism and personal salvation was spatially manifested in both the colonial town and the City of Zion.

According to the revelation, Zion was to consist of agricultural villages even though 30,000 inhabitants, as prescribed in the revelation, was certainly a healthy city and not a village. It was to embody the American values of hard work, mastery of the land, commercial enterprise, and to a point capitalism.[8] These values were at odds with the essence of what the City of Zion represented in its spatial form. The basic *raison d'etre* for these towns was to create a place of refuge, a place of protection, isolation (a place apart from the world), a place to live pure lives dedicated to God rather than as a place of commerce and culture. In fact, in the first version of the plat, there was no allowance made for a commercial zone, although commercial activity would always play out in the Mormon towns. The boundary around the City of Zion was distinct and intended to convey a message to outsiders that this was not another village or town but a city for the faithful—not one that embraced the world and welcomed guests.

As had been true throughout much of the American experience, part of the discussion about what constituted the utopian dream was what constituted the good society. The ideal and the reality on the ground blended together so that it was impossible to distinguish the parts. Zion was what was most hoped for by human beings struggling in a profane world to become perfected men and women.

Bushman points to the significance of Zion as the center place where everything came together. "The city of Zion, moreover, was situated differently in its worldwide geography. New England towns were situated more or less on a level plane, with Boston and a few other commercial centers elevated above the rest. The city of Zion stood at the center of a global vortex; all converts were to turn their faces to Zion. It was a place of refuge. The revelations called Zion the 'center place,' the point where all the saints were to gather. New England towns were dotted more or less evenly across the landscape; Zion was the point toward which all the gathering routes converged."[9]

Unlike in New England towns, Joseph Smith added into the mix a large sacred space for twenty-four temples, the *genius loci* of the Mormon world. These would be more like civic structures than congregational meetinghouses. "The city was the center of gathering, and the temple was the beginning of the city—the center of the center—thus connecting the temple to the whole world.[10] The temple, the city, and the gathering formed a pattern of movement and preparation in a distinctive Mormon geography."[11]

The temple itself, not the twenty-four public buildings called temples, was to demonstrate monumental architecture and the highpoint of the hierarchy of buildings, signaling the pinnacle of Mormon activity. The space within the temple would become increasingly sacred over time, secret and cut off from public view, accessed by only the most faithful. Ordinances and rituals reserved for that sacred space would not take place in other buildings.

In this effort to find a viable form of social and environmental organization, the Mormons were not unlike the Shakers, the Oneida, or other communitarian groups. In important ways their communities were prodigious feats of consistent social and physical design. They reflected their builders' ideas of a common-sense approach to implementing an ethereal vision of earthly paradise and moral superiority.

The Mormon temple was a clear articulation of ideas about hierarchy, priesthood, and gender in a spatial as well as social sense.

As creators of model communities, communards described themselves as "social architects." This metaphor of architecture worked well for activists who wanted to redesign society. They sought to restructure cities and rural spaces in response to the industrial revolution and rapid social change in nineteenth-century America. Their goals incorporated both social and physical change. Most wished to establish self-sufficient settlements based on both industry and agriculture, offering the advantages of city and country to everyone. The city of Zion represented a Mormon version of the same impulse.

As a prophet, Joseph Smith moved people into a spatial vacuum. They created towns that reflected his attitudes. The village grid dominated the land in a way that showed Latter-day Saints to be something like conquerors reclaiming the land for God, taming it for their own use, as the Bible taught. Their homes symbolized their belief in the sanctity of the family, in hearth, with a model of family kingdoms they believed would be theirs in the hereafter.

In choosing an ideal dwelling, the home, as a symbol of social and economic success or religious faith, they resisted the national symbol of an isolated farm house. Mormon villages brought to mind Puritan communities with clusters of homes in close proximity to each other. The model community was a place where conviviality and collective economy prevailed. The ideal hearth was expected to "knit us together mentally and spiritually."[12] In the home, gendered work spaces prevailed. Regular routines of work gave men and women specific roles that were critical to the endeavor.

Brigham Young's Colonization Efforts

After Joseph's death, Mormon space moved west and became part of the country's expansion into the frontier, the colonization of an LDS meaning of existence. Regardless of whether one accepts Frederick Jackson Turner's frontier thesis, unarguably the West represented for most nineteenth-century Americans another chance, a place of refuge and regeneration either as individuals or as groups. Even during the twentieth century, the West was often called the "Last Best Place."

Virtually since the beginning of our country's history, it represented an escape from civilization and the social and economic ills that accompanied it, to the freshness and clean palette the West seemed to promise. For the Mormon people, the West held out this certain promise—a refuge on the western side of the Rocky Mountains that would allow them to build their towns and raise families away from the persecutions they had experienced in the Midwest. Two themes ran through the nineteenth-century story of the Mormon people: the escape from persecution and a chance to build the world anew.

According to Bushman, "The city of Zion rose at the foot of the Wasatch Mountains, and Brigham Young filled up the world with smaller satellite cities. Until the end of the century, the Mormon vortex gathered people with ever-increasing force. And at the center of Salt Lake, the temple anchored the whole system, as it had done in previous Zions."[13]

History of Fundamentalism

As was true of the mainstream Church, fundamentalism had its origins in persecution. Those who continued plural marriage after the official Manifesto of 1890 became increasingly ostracized and were eventually excommunicated from the Mormon Church after 1910. (The 1890 Manifesto began the process of ending Church-sanctioned plurality and was the beginning of a two-decade denouncement of polygamy.) Believing they still had priesthood authority to perform plural marriages and that the mother Church did not, clusters of polygamists grew around the charismatic leadership of men like Joseph W. Musser, John Y. Barlow, and Rulon Allred. Eventually they became more self-conscious in their group identity and their claims to prophetic leadership and separated themselves from society to settle in specific areas. In the mid-1930s the Barlow group moved to Short Creek, a town straddling the Utah/Arizona border.

When the polygamists first started moving into the Arizona Strip in southern Utah/northern Arizona, it was perceived as a place of refuge, only this time Mormons were escaping persecution from their own people who had excommunicated them. In the effort to escape prosecution by law (polygamy was illegal under the Utah Constitution) as well as persecution by the mainstream Church, small groups settled beyond the Wasatch front in a variety of locations. This was an effort to find a place where they could practice their lifestyle in peace, build homes and raise families, and attempt to escape the attention of the Mormon Church in the process.

What shape did their efforts take? What was the form of their new sacred space? It was no longer a "funnel" to attract attention, bringing Saints in from across the world. Short Creek was more of a secret hideout: a dry, dusty, godforsaken place that gave relief to people who were on the lam. Here was land no one else wanted, so the polygamists felt they could stay unmolested. The Vermillion Cliffs to the north created the sense of a redoubt—a fitting metaphor for their new town.

Yet as the fundamentalists built their community, they relied on the Mormon sense of an ordered town, laying out straight streets arranged in a grid, although it deviated at times in Short Creek due to the uneven geography. The town square was reserved for a Church and schoolhouse. They set their homes back from the street in regular patterns so that two decades after settlement, Short Creek looked like a traditional Mormon town in every way. In terms of communal activity, construction was often done cooperatively, fields and herds were managed in shifts by groups of men rather than individuals. Homes, businesses, and other enterprises were community-based, with ties that connected people together rather than separating them through competition.

In some ways the values, beliefs, and practices of capitalism guided the settlement, at least in its businesses' interactions with the outside world, but underlying the whole drama was the idea of a joint effort to provide a space for people to live godly lives away from prying eyes and put into practice doctrines they were told were essential to their salvation. The constructed environment—the buildings, patterns of roads, the ways human beings interact with the terrain—encoded in a tangible way the deeply held and often otherwise unstated cultural, social, and economic values of the residents. It reflected the encouragement of folklorist Henry Glassie to move "away from a concern for the [specific] fabric itself toward the ideas that were the cause of the fabric's existence."[14]

Cultural geographers recommend a paradigm of "cultural diffusion" in examining folk traditions and the way they spread through time and space, and this concept is useful for understanding fundamentalist communities. The architectural traditions traveled west with the pioneers[15] and were adapted to the particularities of the environment. Short Creek finally was settled in the 1930s after a few aborted attempts. The West was already industrialized in some places and exhibited a combination of agricultural, commercial, and industrial exploitation, in common with the East. In Short Creek the difference between the parent community (the core) and its offspring (the periphery) was cultural and barely tangible. To clarify this concept, consider historian Bernard Bailyn's description of the same process or "arc" in British colonization in the seventeenth and eighteenth centuries.

> This arc was nothing so simple as the trade route of an empire ... Nor was it merely an expanding frontier line. It was not a line, an edge, comprehensible in Turnerian terms as such, but a ring of territories, ... separated in important ways from the territories on either side of it. In these linked territories a central culture encountered a variety of different human and physical environments and formed a variety of subcultures, all of which were contained within a single overall system that might be designated "British."[16]

While the core-periphery theory did not originate with Bailyn, his identification of the "orbits of cultural affiliation and derivation" are useful to this discussion. As he saw it, even when developing communities—in this case pockets of polygamist settlers—are located a considerable distance from each other and from their point of origin, they can still be linked to the starting point. The underlying premise of this article is that despite differences on doctrinal issues, the building tradition of the fundamentalist community is connected to the Mormon cultural core.

Housing

As part of the cultural landscape, architecture presents an image that serves as a sort of memory device and creates a reality that is separate from itself. Drawing on the past, it engages the future. Designers draw on images from the past to invent new forms, and this appears to be a basic mechanism of human thinking that happens automatically. Designers manipulate the image through contemplation of a new set of conditions, altering the original meaning and redefining it or thinking about it in a different light. The result is more than an initial remembered image or perception but versions that reach beyond the experiential to the emotional or intellectual realm. Like space itself, the memory continues to order the world and, within its own structure, retains meaningful detail and complexity.

This is certainly true with the evolution of the Mormon house type to conform to the fundamentalist residence. Utah folklorist Austin Fife captured the spirit and character of the nineteenth-century Mormon home in this colorful description:

> In shaping the house exterior, the Utah builders made their meaning clear: gold camps and railroad towns might come and go, but the Mormon communities would stay as permanent fixtures on the land. The West might indeed be wild and woolly, but the civilized world of middle-class America reigned in Utah. The house goes beyond the practicality of shelter in affirming Mormonism as a "correct, wholesome, and successful way of life."[17]

He continues, "Their every [architectural] line bespeaks the will to survive with dignity and the rationale of a well-ordered household in a well-ordered world."

Without a doubt, the interior of the polygamous house, whether shared by multiple wives or inhabited by a single wife and her children, is first of all gendered space devoted to a female sphere. In most situations, polygamous women are ingenious in how they create homes with a version of voluntary simplicity. Frugality, industry, and simplicity are values that play out in the homes and shape the interior space and its use. According to an anthropologist who studies living arrangements among polygamists, "women who built homes and living arrangements [did so] in the face of extremely cramped surroundings and scant materials. The patterns ... show that women access communal goods and rely heavily on the 'sisterhood' for comfortable living."[18]

Each time a polygamous woman welcomes a new wife into her

home, she sacrifices some of her space, her privacy, and her material goods. In the same way, the new wife must change her own expectations about space in the name of the sacred circle she now enters. Each newcomer shares the wealth she brings with her, her time and material goods, with her new husband and with his other wives and children.

There are basically three dominant patterns of living arrangements. These are particularly significant because they impact the ways family members cooperate or function as a family unit in the space they occupy. The first type, a single family dwelling, whether dyadic (the husband comes to visit) or conjugal (the husband and wife live together), provides space for a wife to live separately from her husband's other wives. Her home includes a bedroom, kitchen, bathroom, and some sort of parlor or living room. The plural wife thus lives somewhat independently, though this does not mean she has no interaction on a daily basis with the other wives. Many, for example, share communal yards, driveways, laundry rooms, or other areas. An interesting point is that this was the most typical residential pattern among nineteenth-century pioneer polygamists, just as today, as Jessie Embry found in her oral histories, 55 percent of plural wives live in separate dwellings in the same community and 16 percent live in separate homes in different towns.[19]

In the second type of living arrangement, the dyadic type of unit is doubled up into duplexes or similar complex building structures with two distinct homes sharing a contiguous wall. The third type—and perhaps the most challenging living arrangement to negotiate—is the communal configuration. Here wives maintain separate bedrooms but use all other parts of their home together. This arrangement is more trying in terms of the personal sacrifice required to maintain a harmonious family environment. Because love and respect are highly valued in the fundamentalist culture, extra effort is made in these situations to impose peace and facilitate righteous living. According to Janet Bennion, women in the same house are "forced into both cooperative and competitive activities by virtue of their constant 'elbow rubbing.' In the single or separate dwelling (dyadic), however, there were fewer opportunities for either cooperation or conflict and competition."[20]

In any of the three housing arrangements, the ideal of communal harmony often falls short of the mark. There are financial strains. Bennion speaks of two types of polygamous families, which illustrates the way finances impact lifestyle: a house of necessity, where women live together because they have to, and a house of choice, where each wife has her own home. As the terms suggests, the latter arrangement is preferable. In other words, the issues involving how private space is organized dictate to some degree whether or not individuals are satisfied with their family life. Each family struggles to make its space work as well as possible because there isn't a prophet-sanctioned blueprint, but in any case the solutions are guided by the fundamentalist religio-social philosophy. The end goal is to give each wife a space of her own so she can work, create, and dwell with her own children without interruption. The tension between beliefs in total unity and complete communality on one hand and in privacy and individualism on the other hand is rarely reconciled completely.

One woman in Bennion's study argued "that the concept of unity was not communality per se but of unity in heart and mind and spirit, which occurs only when there exists physical, emotional, and spiritual freedom."[21] She concluded: "Living arrangements are an interplay of ideal and real components, where a husband's perception of his kingdom is the ideal and where co-wives' strategies to meet their economic, sociological, and interpersonal needs are the reality."[22] According to Irwin Altman, when changes in living arrangements occur, it is usually the result of "pragmatic, psychological, and social factors."[23]

But it is in a communal living situation that the Mormon notion of consecration and stewardship finds its fullest range of exploration. In the fundamentalist residences, the interior of the home becomes a drawing board where the shape of the plural family is drawn anew, free of expectations from the monogamous world. New types of family arrangements are drawn with each new attempt to create an ideal family that works well together in every way. Kitchens, dining and living rooms, bathrooms, and other spaces in the home are the common space of all wives, children, and the husband. Women typically organize this space, coordinating and sharing responsibilities for cooking, cleaning, caring for children, or working outside the home. Wives typically have their own bedrooms, although children frequently sleep together in rooms with bunk beds or dorm-like arrangements, the boys and girls separated but children from different mothers sleep together in the same rooms.

The type of living arrangement is determined by the size, shape, and configuration of the home. Typically in the nineteenth century, the Mormon house was a rectangular, two-story, hall-parlor type, meaning there were two rooms on the main floor, one slightly larger than the other, and two rooms on the second level. The common farmer would have attempted to create a symmetrical façade with windows on both sides of a central door. For additional space, the builder extended the house two rooms deep on both levels or added wings to produce "H," "T," or "L" shapes, but the basic idea remained the same. A single centralized block was relatively simple to design and construct, and in fact most farmers had the requisite knowledge to build one. Furthermore, they could be constructed with virtually any material—brick, adobe, timber, or stone. Decoration was moderate, usually Greek Revival, and required no special expertise. There were also vernacular buildings constructed by common folk with little pretension at all to style. Literally hundreds of these homes are still extant in Mormon territory and are a potent reminder of the pioneer heritage of the place.

Function, finances, and a pragmatic attitude toward style also dictated the twentieth-century polygamous home. A new vernacular, the "big house" of Colorado City/Hildale, is determined primarily by the size of the family, the available resources, and the desert climate. The homes are intended to represent in a tangible form the achievement of an earthly paradise. Large, spacious, and solid homes are habitations not unlike those described by Brigham Young as the type "angels may delight to come and visit."[24] In Colorado City the houses are located on spacious lots that allow ample room for orchards, gardens, outbuildings, and other spaces for family activities.

Although the first generation of builders in Short Creek in 1935 sometimes constructed log or timber homes or, in the 1940s, an occasional basement house, more substantial structures were erected as soon as people could afford them. As a group, the houses began as rectangular blocks with moderate if any decoration. As families grew, they added wings or other additions to the central block, often in unimaginative but straightforward ways. Overall aesthetics or styles were not the driving forces behind house design; function was. These were pragmatic workhorses, backdrops to the more important family activity that occurred inside. Often left unfinished, these structures seemed to anticipate growth.

In the same way the houses were meant to be fully utilitarian, landscaping was equally practical, consisting of fruit trees placed along the edges of lots and gardens with tomatoes, corn, and other foods, thereby allowing families a measure of self-sufficiency and independence. Even so, Altman noticed that "transition, change, and experimentation with living arrangements are a hallmark of contemporary Mormon polygynous families." The variables contributing to change include "finances, family size, work requirements, child care, personal desires, interpersonal relationships between wives, and other issues."[25] Furthermore,

> when families described the ideal living arrangements that they would like in the future, they consistently mentioned housing arrangements that include a blend of dyadic and communal features. On the one hand, they want a home for each wife and her children, where they may live independently from day to day, much as in a traditional monogamous family. On the other hand, they also aspire to live near one another and to have a unified, cohesive, and communal family. Thus, they seek a blend of dyadic and communal living arrangements in their hypothetical "dream" home of the future.[26]

So why did the model Mormon town change when fundamentalists established communities? It happened because the relationship between the now secularized Utah community and the fundamentalist town changed in its core/peripheral relationship. Both experienced outside forces: increased competition with other Western communities for markets, growing diversity, and the secularization of society. The ongoing association with the core culture varied over time, but in a potent and essential way this relationship was at the heart of all endeavors.

In the wake of the media attention paid to the 1953 raid and persecution, Short Creek changed its name so that the Utah side took the name Hildale and the Colorado side assumed the name Colorado City. With this decision, a conscious effort was made to start over again despite the disruption from the federal government and to recreate the community institutions that had existed before the raid. There was a heightened sense of isolation and distrust of outsiders—a firm belief that interaction with the outside world threatened the moral fiber of their experiment. Colorado City/Hildale became virtually self-sufficient and increasingly self-conscious as a place apart, distinct, perhaps otherworldly, for here was a community that was totally dedicated to what they considered the work of the Lord.

Despite the change that occurred in the town over the past five decades, it managed to maintain much of its original character and continues to be a distinctly communal community, even though the United Firm has been dismantled by the government. Much of the property is still owned co-jointly. Many new construction projects are United Firm projects. Certainly in this regard, the process of growth constitutes an expansion of sacred space and defense against secularism. Anthropologist Robert Bee recommends paying attention to "the interaction of causal factors" where we can see "a transformation of one condition into another."[27] In the Colorado City/Hildale case, polygamists were mistreated by the government and retrenched, becoming more isolated and suspicious. They were excommunicated by their mother Church and socially persecuted by Mormons in nearby regions. No wonder they retreated from social intercourse with outsiders. Because of this, their community, Colorado City/Hildale has distinct boundaries that are every bit as potent as if they were twenty-foot stone walls.

When you turn off the main highway and drive toward town, you sense you are in a unique place. What you see are straight wide streets lined with a surprising number of very large houses, many unfinished, with insulation board exposed to the front and sides. But the buildings are intact; they provide the requisite shelter for families. You sense the level of industry and see men and women working in fields, in gardens, in orchards. A work ethic seems to prevail and, in fact, seems to be a necessity. The cooperative store, restaurant, various factories, and other enterprises speak to the communal economic endeavor. While it may not be visually explicit, you can sense that this is a group that joins together for activities. The LeRoy Johnson Meetinghouse is the single example of monumental architecture, and that is due to scale more than design—and even though there are several large homes and a few other large structures in town. The meetinghouse is nevertheless an exceptionally large building—an ecclesiastical structure which at first glance resembles a Mormon stake center. It is easily the size of two stake centers, in fact, with a central chamber larger than two basketball courts. Used for general conferences of the Fundamentalist Church and for dances and socials, as well as religious rituals, the chamber is sacred space. The fact that it is not subdivided into smaller units with specific functions speaks to the group orientation of the Church and accentuates the reality of their unity.

Surrounding the central chamber are kitchens, classrooms, offices, and other smaller rooms. Oriented as they are around the periphery, they signal that they are of lesser importance than the central chamber. The finest building materials, craftsmanship, and elaboration of space were lavished on this large, physical monument to their belief in God and community. And they are truly communal. Having property in common with neighbors is almost a technicality, although it demonstrates their high level of commitment to each other. Beyond that, the way the men, women, and children relate to each other is perhaps more important. They share the meetinghouse for key events in their social lives. This building becomes not just a Church or temple, but the sacred backdrop for the activities of the communal organization. It is tangible evidence of their beliefs, the shape of the community's content.

Like Augustine, Plato questions the way men and women live together in community. At one point in *The Republic,* Socrates tells the story of a man who differs from his friends who seek wealth and power over wisdom. Socrates' student asks him if such a life is possible in the real world. Socrates responds that people bear the responsibility to make their environment match the heavenly ideal rather than let their environment dictate their mood: "In heaven there is laid up a pattern of it, methinks, which he who desires may behold, and beholding, may set his own house in order. But whether such an one exists, or ever will exist in fact, is no matter; for he will live after the manner of that city; having nothing to do with any other."[28] In the *Laws,* Plato says that for the world to change, men must first change what they value. There are "three things," he says, "about which every man has an interest; and the interest about money, when rightly regarded, is the third and lowest of them: midway comes the interest of the body; and, first of all, that of the soul; and the state which we are describing will have been rightly constituted if it ordains honours according to this scale."[29] Joseph Smith attempted to provide his people with a vision of how to build a Zion, a "city of God" on the earth. The fundamentalist Mormon community similarly addresses deeper needs than those of the body: the needs of the soul, as spatially manifested in the layout of their towns and design of their houses.

The rural Mormon village, which started out with the Plat of the City of Zion, evolved to become an amalgam of different influences that went through the same kind of metamorphosis that the fundamentalist community continues to experience. Architectural historian Thomas Carter argues that almost as soon as the Mormon pioneers completed their initial stage of settlement, they began building in a modified way. This time, their model was the gentile city, the refined city, based on a concept of the good things of life that spread through European courts to the upper middle classes. The genteel, civil, or urbane life reflected what was called the trappings of polite society in the eighteenth century. A material culture supported the interest in an environment that sustained life but provided beauty and civilization as well. Gentility was interested in beautification, a standard that implied exclusion as well as association and the means for enjoyment that were attainable by refined people. It held out the hope that regardless of the economic realities of one's life, however undignified the scope of one's work, gentility was possible through discipline and the adoption of a few outward forms of higher living. This was an effort to elevate life from what was common to an elite standard of beauty and grace.

In the nineteenth century, just two years after the initial settlement in Nauvoo, the Mormons were busily adorning their city with every imaginable accouterment.

> Our city now presents a lively and beautiful appearance. While it is adorned by the hand of nature in its richest dress, all hands seem engaged in adding to the comforts of the inhabitants. Numbers are

> employed in improving the streets and in removing every nuisance, whilst others are engaged in ploughing, digging, fencing, etc. The female part of the inhabitants are busily engaged in their flower gardens, and all around is health, peace, and happiness; and the songs of Zion are to be heard on every hand, united with those of the feathered tribe in almost every tree.[30]

Brigham Young encouraged his people to be ambitious and to expect much of their cities.

> Let the people build good houses, plant good vineyards and orchards, make good roads, build beautiful cities in which may be found magnificent edifices for the convenience of the public, handsome streets skirted with shade trees, fountains of water, crystal streams, and every tree, shrub and flower that will flourish and grow in this climate, to make our mountain home a paradise ... enjoying it all with thankful hearts, saying constantly, 'Not mine but thy will be done, O Father.'"[31]

Gentility was not only about appearances but had the practical benefit of bestowing social status on its practitioners. "It was a resource for impressing and influencing powerful people and a prerequisite for inspiring trust ... Moreover, it afforded a convenient identity and a definition of position in the confusing fluidity of democratic society ... Refinement held out the hope of elevation from ordinary existence into an exalted society of superior beings. That promise and hope, rooted in the memory of a forbidden old regime, gave gentility its strength."[32]

In Colorado City/Hildale, fundamentalist Mormons are making the same shift from the rural Mormon village to the expectations of a gentile city. That is to say that they are making a conscious effort to create not only a more attractive city (hence more luxurious landscaping) but a refined city that provides a variety of resources, including a university, city park, city zoo, and various new commercial enterprises. These represent a new reaching out to the world and a growing sophistication—a new set of expectations about what represents or creates the good life. The fundamentalists have proven they can survive in the desert of southern Utah. They have learned to successfully eke out a living in the dry arid lands of the Arizona Strip. They have literally made the land "blossom like a rose," a tangible sign of the efficacy of their communal lifestyle and their devotion to God. Now they are refining their efforts.

From their Mormon ancestors, fundamentalists developed the belief that a paradisiacal landscape and fine buildings were signs of inner spirituality, which would be recognized at the Second Coming. Therefore, seeking perfection in even the smallest environmental details helped them to participate in creating an earthly paradise. House types, landscaping, community structures, and networks of roads created and developed an image of a desirable environment and godly lifestyle, which reflects on the earnestness of their faith. Such participation in improving the communal environment and communicating devotion is more important to fundamentalists than creating monumental architecture.

Notes

1. Karen A. Franck and Lynda H. Schneekloth, eds. *Ordering Space: Types in Architecture and Design* (New York: Van Nostrand Reinhold, 1994), 19.

2. Christian Norberg-Schulz, *Genius Loci: Towards a Phenomenology of Architecture* (New York: Rizzoli, 1979), 5.

3. Ibid., 5.

4. Richard Lyman Bushman, "Making Space for the Mormons," Leonard J. Arrington Mormon History Lecture Series, No. 2, Special Collections and Archives, Merrill Library, Utah State University, Logan, Utah.

5. Feramorz Young Fox, "Notes Concerning Joseph Smith's Plat of Zion City," mimeo, LDS Archives, 3. Fox corrects mistaken versions of the plat published elsewhere.

6. *The Wasp*, April 23, 1842.

7. Ben Shann, *The Shape of Content* (Cambridge: Harvard University Press, 1957).

8. See Lowry Nelson, *The Mormon Village: A Pattern of Technique of Land Settlement* (Salt Lake City: University of Utah Press, 1952).

9. Bushman, "Making Space," 10.

10. The importance of building the temple was reiterated by Elder Francis Moon, qtd. in Robert Flanders, *Nauvoo: Kingdom on the Mississippi* (Urbana: University of Illinois Press, 1965), 69.

11. Bushman, "Making Space," 12.

12. John Humphrey Noyes, address on "Dedication of the New Community Mansion," *Oneida Circular*, Feb. 27, 1862, 9.

13. Bushman, "Making Space," 24.

14. Henry Glassie, "Eighteenth-Century Cultural Process in Delaware Valley Folk Building," *Winterthur Portfolio* 7 (1972): 29-57.

15. See Thomas Carter, ed., *Images of an American Land* (Albuquerque: University of New Mexico Press, 1997), 41-62; Fred Kniffen, "Folk Housing: Key to Diffusion," *Annals of the Association of American Geographers* 55 (Dec. 1965): 549-77; Henry Glassie, *Pattern in the Material Folk Culture of the Eastern United States* (Philadelphia: University of Pennsylvania Press, 1968); and Fred Kniffen and Henry Glassie, "Building in Wood in the Eastern United States: A Time-Place Perspective," *Geographical Review* 56 (Jan. 1966): 40-66.

16. Bernard Bailyn, "The Challenge of Modern Historiography," *American Historical Review* 87 (Feb. 1982): 1-24.

17. See Austin E. Fife, "Stone Houses of Northern Utah," *Utah Historical Quarterly* 40 (Winter 1972): 19, qtd. by Thomas R. Carter, "The Tangible Past," *Utah Historical Quarterly* 56 (Fall 1988), 47.

18. Janet Bennion, *Women of Principle: Female Networking in Contemporary Mormon Polygyny* (New York: Oxford University Press, 1998), 114.

19. Jessie Embry, *Mormon Polygamous Families* (Salt Lake City: University of Utah Press, 1987).

20. Bennion, *Women of Principle*, 118-19.

21. Ibid., 121.

22. Ibid.

23. Irwin Altman and Joseph Ginat, *Polygamous Families in Contemporary Society* (Cambridge: Cambridge University Press, 1996), 187.

24. Richard Francaviglia, "The Mormon Landscape: Existence, Creation, and Perception of a Unique Image in the American West," unpublished Ph.D. dissertation, University of Oregon, 1970, 95.

25. Altman and Ginat, *Polygamous Families*, 194.

26. Ibid., 212.

27. Robert I. Bee, *Patterns and Processes: An Introduction to Anthropological Strategies for the Study of Sociocultural Change* (New York: Free Press, 1974), 4.

28. *The Dialogues of Plato*, trans. B. Jowett, 2 vols. (New York: Random House, 1937), 1:851.

29. Ibid., 2:509.

30. *Nauvoo Neighbor*, May 3, 1843.

31. John A. Widtsoe, ed., *Discourses of Brigham Young* (Salt Lake City: Deseret Book, 1925), discourse no. 16.

32. Richard Lyman Bushman, *The Refinement of America* (New York: Vintage Books, 1992), xix.

Mormon Studies in a European Setting

Douglas J. Davies

In 2001, when I was invited to edit a special edition of *Dialogue*, I was particularly grateful for the chance to address readers informally on issues that often remain implicit or are ignored. While these topics are important for what can be called Mormon studies, they also apply to other areas of scholarship. In my introductory paper, repeated here in a slightly modified form, I mentioned my personal involvement in LDS studies, the role of conferences in promoting an exchange of ideas, and finally the contributions by such scholars as those whose articles comprised the special edition of *Dialogue*.

My engagement with LDS material was accidental and stemmed from a postgraduate studentship from the British Social Science Research Council, which I fulfilled at the Institute of Social Anthropology at Oxford. This was in 1969, following my undergraduate studies in anthropology at Durham University. An insightful meeting with the anthropologist Godfrey Lienhardt resulted in the rapid conclusion that I should work more in the sociology of religion rather than become an Africanist. Accordingly, I was taken on by Bryan Wilson, whose research seminar at All Souls College was a creative approach for the study of religious movements. Here I engaged with Mormonism, a religion practically unstudied in the United Kingdom, and of which I had no previous experience or knowledge. Through initial friendly contacts with Latter-day Saint people in Wales, I began a life-long interest, interspersed—as academic life demands—with work on other topics, including Sikhism, Anglicanism, and the themes of death, cremation, and burial.

The mid-1980s provided opportunity for me to revisit much of my earlier research material, particularly the extensive work I had conducted on the Bodleian Library's holding of the *Millennial Star*, a gem of a find for a young postgraduate at a time when academic studies of Mormonism were not particularly extensive. This resulted in the volume Mormon Spirituality: *Latter-day Saints in Wales and Zion.*[1] I helped create a Center for Mormon Studies at Nottingham University, where we were able to develop a small library and host postgraduate students who came to work there on a variety of their own projects. Our numbers were small in terms of graduate students in the U.K., but this was a significant move; our doctorates produced studies on a variety of relevant topics: Craig Marshall on higher education and Mormon student identity, Tyler Moulton from Brigham Young University on the notion of salvation, and Warrick Kearon on music in Mormonism. These students were all active Mormons, mostly employed in the LDS Church Education System (CES), as was Julian Jones, whose M.A. considered members' attitudes about LDS bishops. Barry Fox, who was then head of the Reorganized Church of Jesus Christ of Latter Day Saints in Britain, completed his doctoral work on the history of that movement in the U.K. Much of this research was conducted without the enormous archival reserve available in U.S. centers, and the survey aspects in particular generated their own databases. Even this small focus of LDS study resulted in inquiries from and contacts with interested parties in the media, other Churches, and various LDS members potentially interested in research.

One significant aspect of LDS research in the U.K., which we were able to foster, took the form of two academic conferences, and I will return to a brief description of these after considering the place of academic conferences generally. I must add that I enjoyed general support from LDS Church officials and members in the U.K., including Jeffrey R. Holland before his appointment as one of the Twelve Apostles.

After moving to the University of Durham, I had to leave behind resources that we had garnered at Nottingham and begin afresh. One valuable contribution to our efforts at Durham was made by Armand

Mauss, who spent a short period as a visiting research fellow. His personal and scholarly support were invaluable, especially his advice associated with my book, *The Mormon Culture of Salvation*.[2] Additionally, a variety of visits from American scholars and guest lecturers, including one in December 2001 by Roger Keller, holder of the Richard L. Evans Chair at Brigham Young University, have stimulated undergraduate interest in the LDS religion at Durham. Professor Keller's predecessor in that chair, David Paulsen, also contributed much to my reflection upon LDS spirituality, not least through his friendship.

Such scholarly interaction, stimulus, and support were of particular importance for a subject like Mormonism, taught in a context of minority institutional and cultural status. It is to the credit of both the Nottingham and Durham University Departments of Theology that they hosted this academic venture. Similarly, I gained a great deal from participating in a variety of LDS events in the U.K. and in Utah, including serving as a visiting professor at Brigham Young University. In the final analysis, much scholarly work is initiated and fostered through personal exchange, whether through our original mentors or through subsequent contacts, a point which appropriately brings me to the subject of conferences.

Conferences

Gatherings are, in and of themselves, interesting phenomena. The academic profession would hardly be what it is without academic conferences since they furnish a convenient forum for people to meet and gain a personal sense of each other. Just how we judge scholars is a complex issue that has, as yet, remained beyond much formal scrutiny. Usually we make do with reading what others write, but there is a quality of criticism—or perhaps it would be better to say of appreciation—that comes from listening to someone speak. Better still, our opinions take even greater form when we are able to talk with each other, more truly reflecting the collegial nature of scholarship.

In practice, many conferences have become so large that unless participants have long attended, they can easily be lost or find themselves marginalized amid crowds who all seem to know each other. However, conferences provide a basis for necessary academic politics as people forge or enhance their individual or corporate status, not to mention the role in fostering networking and the whole issue of job-searching. As with academic journals, conferences have both the privilege and responsibility of helping to create and maintain boundaries in disciplines, and here the privilege and responsibility are hopefully framed by an ethical attitude that fosters as much freedom as constraint. Even in the broad world of mainstream academic theology, one sometimes hears colleagues speak negatively of the way in which the academy polices its discipline. Whether acting as a conference organizer, journal editor, or for example as an anonymous referee for major grant-awarding bodies, the issue of personal integrity must be explicit. To what extent are personal prejudices allowed to color our judgment? What degree of freedom do we give to new ideas or interpretations?

Nottingham 1995

These are some of the questions I had in mind as I undertook in 1995 to organize a conference on Mormon studies at the University of Nottingham, based at Derby Hall of which I was then warden. Some thirty individuals attended, many from the U.S. Over several days the delegates heard a great variety of papers, twenty-four of which were subsequently published.[3] This conference was particularly significant in bringing a wide variety of people together who otherwise might not have met.

Durham 1999

Subsequent communication with delegates encouraged me to organize a second conference in April 1999, by which time I had moved to Durham University. Although slightly fewer in number, the delegates said how much they appreciated the collegiality of this event. A major feature of the gathering lay in the fact that three of the most senior of all British scholars in the study of religion agreed to give papers on the topic of Mormonism as a potential world religion. Ninian Smart, whose later death removed a major figure in comparative religion, genially reflected on religious attitudes and spent time talking with many of us there. John Hinnells, a key scholar in Zoroastrian studies and, at the time of the conference, chair of the Association of University Departments of Theology and Religious Studies in the U.K., considered aspects of the definition of religion. Bryan Wilson, Emeritus Fellow of All Souls College at Oxford University and a Fellow of the British Academy, addressed the subject of "Toleration and Religious Pluralism." The other delegates appreciated meeting such colleagues in the informal atmosphere engendered by the conference.

Alongside the challenging themes presented by featured guests, other aspects of Mormonism's international reach were considered by Massimo Introvigne from Italy, with his timely theoretical discussion of "Mormonism and Postmodernity"; Mark Grover on "Coming to Zion Brazilian Style: The Changing Mormon Concept of the Gathering"; and Grant Underwood's typically engaging account of "Mormonism, the Maori, and Cultural Authenticity." It was also particularly good to welcome several younger scholars whose contributions were notable for their scholarly rigor: Henri Gooren's anthropological method was well deployed in his account of Mormon membership in Guatemala, a paper included in the special issue of *Dialogue*. Another equally telling paper was delivered by Staffan Arner on "Mormon-Jewish Relations Yesterday and Today." He brought to the conference a sense of the history of religions for which his University of Uppsala (Sweden) is renowned and did credit to the topic through his deep knowledge of the Mormons in Sweden and practical experience with the LDS presence in Jerusalem. His paper was appreciated and promises future publication.

From the U.S., Eric Eliason gave a polished presentation on "Mapping a New World Religion" from the perspective of the "cultural geography of temples and Pioneer Day celebrations." Notes of a more British kind were sounded by the steady historical craft of Malcolm Thorp on "Popular Millennialism in Britain, 1837-1865" and David Whittaker's enviable competence in covering "Mormon Publishing in the British Empire, 1836-1860."

Returning to the world-religion front, Michael Homer considered the "Historical Foundations of Mormonism as a World Religion," with Malise Ruthven reflecting on "Islam and Mormonism: Common Gnostic Roots" and Roger Keller considering "Non-attachment in Buddhism and Mormonism." I took up the theme of "Death, Transcendence, and World-Religion Status." Other British contributions came from Roy Whitehead, who dwelt on some negative aspects of his Mormon experience in Scotland, while—in directly anthropological terms—Hildi Mitchell analyzed the idea of embodiment in relation to Mormon identity. Shortly afterward she completed her doctoral work in the anthropology of Mormonism in Britain while based at Queens University Belfast. Other significant topics covered by papers included those of gender pursued by Lynn Matthews Anderson, LDS youth delinquency by Bruce Chadwick, and the philosophical aspects of LDS doctrine in its cultural context by David Paulsen.

Not everyone present was expert in LDS topics. For example, among the non-LDS attendees was the Reverend Lionel Atherton, an Anglican priest from Chorley in Lancashire, in whose parish the second British LDS temple had recently opened. Seeking some understanding of Mormonism as part of his ecclesiastical pastoral work, he had been in touch with me and appropriately, I felt, attended the conference. He subsequently did some postgraduate work with me, including a study period in New Zealand where he worked on aspects of LDS life. His appreciation of meeting with academics, many of whom were also LDS, was positively voiced both at the close of the conference and thereafter. This was one example of the importance of maintaining open boundaries in academic ventures on religious topics, allowing for the fact that individuals always possess personal interests and diverse agendas.

One final aspect of the Durham conference needs to be mentioned, which was not in any sense part of the academic program but reflected upon some LDS themes in the musical rather than sentential mode. I had invited the two organists of the College of St. Hild and St. Bede, the venue of the conference—Joseph Ramadan, an undergraduate, and Julian Cooper, a postgraduate—to present a short recital. Cooper's framework of Bach, Boyce, Vierne, and Dupre was augmented by three improvisations by Ramadan on "Come, Come Ye Saints," "The Spirit of God Like a Fire Is Burning," and "How Great the Wisdom and the Love," three hymns which typify, at least to me as a non-Mormon, something essential that suffuses Latter-day Saint spirituality. This was doubtless a first as far as the 1891 Harrison and Harrison organ of Bede Chapel was concerned. The music was, I think, much appreciated by the numerous delegates who sat in the shadowed stillness of that fine building.

Diversity of Interest

If the ability to share music together was a minor aspect of this conference, a major feature lay in its interdisciplinarity, a characteristic also shared by the 1995 gathering. This factor is of importance for any area of study wishing to distinguish itself as a subdiscipline. Mormon studies, for example, cannot depend solely upon historical methodology any more than upon the sociological view of life. The base of Mormon historical and social scientific study groups is well established, while much remains to be gained from interdisciplinary encounters, especially at conferences where numbers are small enough for people of different disciplines to engage with each other. One potential hazard of modern large conferences emerges from the plethora of different topic areas attracting specialists in those areas. Given the small numbers present at both these British conferences, everyone could listen to everything.

In fields related to religious traditions, scholarship is, for a significant number of people, intimately bound with their religious convictions, sometimes with consequences for their status and acceptance within their own Church organization. This can cause problems regarding what people will say or are prepared to hear. Certainly the first of the two conferences I organized witnessed delegates together who were both conservative and liberal. This necessitates a degree of understanding on all sides and raises the issue of judgment over the papers delivered. There is no easy resolution to the difficulties and sensitivities of institutional and personal feelings. Sometimes there are moments of discomfort for some of the delegates. What is important is that a high degree of intellectual integrity is maintained within an overall academic umbrella of responsibility and sense of humanity.

The subject of LDS life provided a key focus for the papers included in the special issue of *Dialogue*, with a degree of historical contextualizing being inevitable. Yet we can see the distinctive influences of literary theory in Givens's "The Book of Mormon and Religious Epistemology," whose wider publications are establishing him as a significant scholar in the literary-cultural aspects of Mormonism's cultural setting. In Seth Kunin's article, "Root and Branch: An Abstract of the Structuralist Analysis of the Allegory of the Olive Tree," we have another form of textual analysis but one derived from structural anthropology, albeit a derivation involving much personal formation by the author. I was committed to including this piece precisely because structuralism has become radically unfashionable. However, having been raised academically when structuralism was in its anthropological prime, and having worked in it a little myself decades ago, I still think it possesses the capacity to provoke thought and engender insight. Scholars who dislike the approach, or general readers who find it overly complex, should take the suggestions it offers and see how they relate to their own preferred ways of interpreting material. Whatever the result, I think it is wise to ponder the thought of someone with expertise both in the literal and cultural interpretation of Hebrew texts and anthropological understanding of what groups do with their sacred writings.

On the level of a more strictly anthropological analysis of social events, Henri Gooren offered results from his extensive fieldwork material from Guatemala in "The Dynamics of LDS Growth in Guatemala, 1948-1998." His wider comparative study of LDS and Pentecostal forms of religious organization have made a significant contribution to the detailed knowledge of social change and religious conversion in South America.

In the issue of *Dialogue*, Warrick Kearon brought to his paper a personal knowledge of LDS congregational and Church organizational life in Britain and a deeply rooted academic background in music. His earlier doctoral studies responded to the need for a scholar in one area to see how his background could be enhanced by the acquisition of new skills, both in social scientific and historical dimensions. His article, "The LDS Sound World and Global Mormonism," shows how significant insights may emerge for historians, sociologists, or musicologists in pursuing Mormon topics in more detailed ways. Armand Mauss is well known as a sociologist of Mormonism, but in "Mormonism's Worldwide Aspirations and Its Changing Conceptions of Race and Lineage," he approached his subject from the perspectives of history and literature.

There are relatively few strict sociologists of religion in Britain, especially among the senior scholars who have taken more than a passing interest in the LDS Church, but Christie Davies is one of them. His support for the two conferences was welcome, especially since he had some prior experience with LDS institutions beyond the U.K. His paper, "Place, Time, and Family in Mormonism," was of a more general and speculative kind rather than a detailed empirical or sociological enterprise but nevertheless reflected the importance of the comparative method. If Mormon studies is to flourish as an identifiable field, then the comparative aspect is vitally important.

My own article on "Gethsemane and Calvary in LDS Soteriology" was the outcome of a particular insight that dawned in a moment but only on the back of several decades of familiarity with Mormon ideas and prompted by the comparative perspective of wider Christian theology and iconography. The academic value given to art and iconography as their own distinctive forms of expression of faith and belief has had an impact upon more established theological disciplines. As a comparative venture, it also shows how one tradition may foster responses in another. For example, I happened to be invited by Rowan Williams, who subsequently became Archbishop of Canterbury, to write the Archbishop of Wales's lent book for 2001 at the time that the fact of Gethsemane, so differently valued by Mormons and other Christians, was on my mind. (Lent books are an Anglican tradition used either individually or by study groups throughout the period leading up to Easter. They offer a means of considering the Christian life in relation to the sufferings and obedience—the passion—in the life of Christ, as told in the New Testament.) My Gethsemane reflections, published as *Private Passions* (Canterbury Press, 2001), were an extended analysis and meditation on what I had come to see as an idiom of betrayal underlying early Christianity. *Private Passions* would never have taken the form it did had I never pondered the LDS commitment to Gethsemane; thus comparative studies can have effects in numerous directions.

All such effects depend, of course, on the prior interests, commitments, and knowledge of individuals. Of the contributors to Dialogue, some were LDS but the majority were not, and as the contributors' list showed, they came from several varied academic backgrounds. These illustrated the possibilities for Mormon studies by scholars of various nationalities and religious backgrounds. One hopes their work beckons others to join us in the same enterprise.

Editor's note: It is unusual to include the introduction (even slightly altered) to one collection of articles as a contribution to a different anthology. I have included Dr. Davies's piece here because it offers such an engaging summary of some of the innovative and daring work being done on Mormon studies topics by European scholars, as well as their interaction with American scholars. This is, in a sense, a sort of bibliographic essay to give readers a sense of the important work being done on Mormonism in places far removed from the Mormon culture region.

Notes

1. Douglas J. Davies, *Mormon Spirituality: Latter-Day Saints in Wales and Zion*, Nottingham Series in Theology (Nottingham: University of Nottingham, 1987).

2. Douglas J. Davies, *The Mormon Culture of Salvation: Force, Grace and Glory* (Aldershot: Ashgate, 2000).

3. Douglas J. Davies, ed., *Mormon Identities in Transition*, a Conference on Mormon Studies, University of Nottingham, 1995 (London: Cassell, 1996).

Wilford Woodruff's Vision of the Signers of the Declaration of Independence

Brian H. Stuy

With the exception of Joseph Smith's visions, few LDS epiphanies are better known than Wilford Woodruff's, especially the ones he said occurred in the St. George temple after its dedication in 1877. According to Woodruff, on two successive August nights, the signers of the Declaration of Independence appeared to him in the spirit and demanded to know why he had not had them baptized in the Endowment House in Salt Lake City or in the newly completed St. George Temple. As Woodruff recounted, they said, "You have had the use of the Endowment House for a number of years, and yet nothing has ever been done for us. We laid the foundation of the government you now enjoy, and we never apostatized from it, but we remained true to it and were faithful to God."

Upon reflecting why the work had not already been performed for these extraordinary individuals, Woodruff recalled: "I thought it very singular, that notwithstanding so much work had been done, and yet nothing had been done for them. The thought never entered my heart, from the fact, I suppose, that heretofore our minds were reaching after our more immediate friends and relatives." Woodruff concluded to take immediate action, and "I straightway went into the baptismal font and called upon brother McCallister [McAllister] to baptize me for the signers of the Declaration of Independence, and fifty other eminent men, making one hundred in all, including John Wesley, Columbus, and others; I then baptized him for every President of the United States, except three; and when their cause is just, somebody will do the work for them."[1]

Church leaders and Sunday school teachers have used this narrative to encourage people to perform proxy work for their deceased relatives. In fact, in just about any Sunday School lesson dealing with temple work, Woodruff's vision is used to bolster and promote diligence in seeking out and performing proxy ordinances for one's ancestors.[2] Its validity as an authentic encounter with the spirit world is never questioned.

Proxy Baptisms in Nauvoo and Salt Lake City

A survey of the Nauvoo temple and Salt Lake City Endowment House baptismal records shows that Woodruff was not the first member of the Church who was concerned about the eternal welfare of some of the prominent figures from history. In fact, saving ordinances were performed for famous personalities as soon as the doctrine of vicarious temple work was revealed.[3] Charlotte Haven, writing home from Nauvoo, reported that she witnessed baptisms for the dead in the Mississippi River in early May 1843:

> We followed the bank toward town, and ... spied quite a crowd of people, and soon perceived there was a baptism. Two elders stood knee-deep in the icy cold water, and immersed one [proxy] after another as fast as [the proxies] could come down the bank. We soon observed that some of them went in and were plunged several times. We were told that they were baptized for the dead who had not had an opportunity of adopting the doctrines of the Latter Day Saints. So these poor mortals in ice-cold water were releasing their ancestors and relatives from purgatory! We drew a little nearer and heard several names repeated by the elders as the victims were douched [bathed], and you can imagine our surprise when the name George Washington was called. So after these fifty years he is out of purgatory and on his way to the "celestial" heaven![4]

In addition to the event Haven witnessed, there were at least three other occasions in Nauvoo when George Washington was baptized.[5] Others for whom this proxy ordinance was performed in Illinois include Benjamin Franklin;[6] Presidents John Adams, William Henry Harrison, Thomas Jefferson, and James Monroe; George Washington's wife, Martha Dandridge Custis Washington; mother Mary Ball Washington; and Thomas Jefferson's wife, Martha Wayles Jefferson.[7] Later in St. George, Woodruff would arrange to have proxy baptisms performed for all of these individuals.

The departure from Nauvoo and exodus to Utah interrupted proxy temple ordinances, but the completion of the Salt Lake Endowment House in 1855 allowed members to once more perform baptisms for the dead. Several took it upon themselves to perform ordinances for prominent individuals, including signers of the Declaration of Independence. One of the first to systematically perform baptisms for the Founding Fathers was Haden Wells Church, who was baptized in 1871 and 1872 for several signers of the Declaration of Independence and for U.S. Presidents Andrew Jackson and James Knox Polk. Haden Church was then confirmed by John D. T. McAllister, who would assist Wilford Woodruff with baptisms in St. George and serve as temple recorder there. Church's wife, Matilda, was proxy-baptized for the signers' wives.[8]

Another individual who had himself baptized for prominent men and women was John M. Bernhisel, Utah's first territorial delegate to the U.S. Congress. Already in Nauvoo he performed baptisms for some distinguished historical figures, then increased his activity for famous "friends" in the Endowment House. His record book indicates that on June 25, 1873 he stood as proxy for American statesman William Henry Seward, journalist Horace Greeley, educator Horace Mann, and Declaration of Independence signer George Clymer.[9] On July 8, 1874, he was baptized for Benjamin Rush, another signer of the Declaration of Independence, and for British political philosopher John Locke and deceased President Millard Fillmore.[10] In August he was baptized for writer Washington Irving and Swiss-American naturalist Louis J. R. Agassiz. The following week Bernhisel's daughter Mary was re-baptized for Mary Ball Washington and Martha Washington, for whom John had already acted as proxy in Nauvoo.[11]

In 1876, most likely in response to the centennial the nation celebrated that year, Bernhisel began systematically arranging for the baptism of all the Founding Fathers and other well-known U.S. leaders. On August 9, he and his daughter Mary went to the Endowment House and were baptized for most of the deceased U.S. presidents and their wives. Bernhisel was also baptized for Revolutionary War hero Patrick Henry.[12]

Two weeks later Bernhisel returned to the Endowment House with a longer list of worthies: the remaining signers of the Declaration of Independence and of the U.S. Constitution, as well as John Tyler, tenth U.S. president, who had been overlooked on August 9.[13] Bernhisel did not perform baptismal work for signers whose proxy baptisms had previously been completed: Charles Carroll, Benjamin Rush, James Wilson, and John Adams.[14]

Woodruff's Proxy Baptisms in the St. George Temple

Upon the completion of the St. George temple in January 1877, proxy ordinances became an important duty for Church members. When Brigham Young addressed the Saints at the temple dedicatory services, he asked members to consider the souls of past generations: "What do you suppose the fathers would say if they could speak from the dead? Would they not say, 'We have lain here thousands of years, here in this prison house, waiting for this dispensation to come? Here we are, bound and fettered, in the association of those who are filthy?'"[15]

Woodruff took these teachings to heart. On Sunday, August 19, he recorded in his journal: "I spent the evening in preparing a list of the noted men of the 17 Century and 18th, including the Signers of the Declaration of Independence and the 16 president[s] of the United States."[16] On August 21 he began standing in for them in the baptismal ceremony in the temple, starting with the signers of the Declaration of Independence except for William Floyd and Thomas Jefferson, whose baptisms he knew had already been performed.[17] He apparently did not know Haden Church and John Bernhisel had previously been baptized for the same people.[18] In fact, *every* signer of the Declaration of Independence had been baptized by proxy before Woodruff performed that ordinance in the St. George temple in 1877.

Woodruff next compiled a list of the U.S. presidents and their wives, omitting Martin Van Buren and James Buchanan because he perceived them as being guilty of crimes against the LDS people.[19] He also eliminated Ulysses S. Grant, who was still alive at that time. Woodruff's presidential listing, however, included only two names for which baptismal work had not already been performed: Zachary Taylor and Abraham Lincoln. Leaving Martin Van Buren off the list was a form of payback, but unknown to him, Bernhisel had performed Van Buren's baptism the previous year.[20] Woodruff had baptisms done for George Washington's parents, grandparents, and great-grandparents and listed forty-five prominent men from two centuries, including such notables as Washington Irving, William Henry Seward, and Daniel Webster, all of whose baptisms had nevertheless been performed in the Endowment House.[21] Also on Woodruff's list were explorers Christopher Columbus,[22] David Livingstone, and Americus Vespucius; theologian John Wesley; and French emperor Charles Louis Napoleon Bonaparte.

Woodruff compiled a list of seventy famous women, many of whom were wives of the men already listed but some of whom were notable in their own right, including English novelists Jane Austen and Charlotte Bronte, English poet and feminist Elizabeth Barrett Browning, and Queen of France Marie Antoinette.[23]

Determining Woodruff's Sources

Biographical information in the St. George Temple Baptismal Records suggests that Woodruff used a reference book to compile his list of prominent men and women. A key to determining the source is the inclusion of birth and death dates and places of birth and death; several records had incomplete information and listed the birthplace, for example, without the date. Others included only the year of an individual's death but not the place or exact day. Thus, Woodruff's baptismal records contained peculiarities that created a kind of fingerprint to compare against other sources.

By analyzing the data, I was able to determine that a two-volume work by Evert A. Duyckinck entitled *Portrait Gallery of Eminent Men and Women of Europe and America*[24] matches the gaps in Woodruff's records, making it almost certain that it was the source Woodruff consulted. Although Duyckinck's volumes contained some individuals not included on Woodruff's list, they contained virtually all the names Woodruff did include and gave the same biographical information. (See Appendix for the list.) Of the forty-five prominent men on Woodruff's list, excluding the presidents and signers, only four do not have biographical essays in Duyckinck's works.[25] Only thirteen of Woodruff's seventy women are not featured in Duyckinck. Nine of the thirteen are related to President George Washington[26] and another two were Euphrosyne Parepa and her mother.[27] The last two were Maria Fackrell and "Mrs Elijah Gibbs."[28]

Comparing the order of Woodruff's names with Duyckinck's also shows Woodruff's dependence on these volumes. The following portion of Woodruff's list demonstrates clearly the strong correlation between Woodruff's order in the baptismal record and Duyckinck's placement of the biographical essay in the second volume of his collection:

Position on Woodruff's List	*page in Duyckinck's volume*
1. Daniel Webster	129
2. Washington Irving	150
3. Michael Faraday	173
4. William Makepeace Thackeray	189
5. John Caldwell Calhoun	203
6. Baron Justin Von Liebig	222
7. Henry Clay	228
8. Edward George Earle Lytton Bulwer	259
9. George Peabody	291
10. Charles Louis Napoleon Bonaparte	304
11. Thomas Chalmers	337
12. William Henry Seward	461
13. Thomas Jonathan Jackson	486
14. David Glasgow Farragut	504
15. Hiram Powers	522
16. Louis John Rodolph Agassiz	528
17. David Livingstone	605

Representative of further matches, showing Woodruff's dependence on Duyckinck, both reported only the year of birth (1801) for the American naval officer and Civil War hero David Farragut and neither gave a death date or year for David Livingston. Duyckinck gave the death of Eva Maria Veigel, wife of David Garrick, as October 1822, identical to Woodruff's entry. A comparison between the two listings shows *not a single instance* in which Woodruff's proxy record contains accurate biographical information not contained in Duyckinck's volumes.[29]

Furthermore, in his journal entries for August 3-5, 1876, Woodruff suggested that he had probably been reading a companion set of Duyckinck's entitled *National Portrait Gallery of Eminent Americans:*

> In my leasure moments of late I have read the life of Daniel Boone the great explorer & pioneer of Kentucky and afterwards Early setler of Louisianna and it is vary Strange that Kentucky should have Cheated him out of his land & home after [his work in] locating the Country & fighting Indians 40 years. Also the Lands in Louisianna that the Spanish Government gave him was taken from him by Congress and he never had any land given him untill he was about 80 years old and a short time before his death.[30]

Woodruff added other details: that Boone lived three months in the wilderness of Kentucky alone without any "bread, sugar, or salt" in an area surrounded by Indians and settled by his family in a fort he built. Duyckinck's biographical essay on Boone included all this information, including "Daniel had been absent two years, during which time he had tasted *neither bread nor salt.*"[31]

Woodruff apparently left Duyckinck's two-volume *National Portrait Gallery of Eminent Americans* in Salt Lake City when he left for St. George on November 1, 1876. This is supported by the evidence that he did not have Daniel Boone, Patrick Henry, or Henry Wadsworth Longfellow baptized even though these were men who were greatly admired and who Woodruff certainly would have considered worthy of proxy attention.[32] It seems, however, that Woodruff continued to read Duyckinck's other two-volume set, and it was from those he drew the majority of his baptismal listing. After settling in St. George, he recorded on December 15, 1876 that he "spent the day in Reading

Livingston's travels in Africa up to the time of his death and to the final resting place of his body in the west Minster Abbey in London. This History was quite interesting."[33]

The Need for Woodruff's Proxy Work

It seems likely that if the signers had literally appeared to Woodruff, he would have used all of the resources at his disposal to compile as complete and comprehensive a list of worthies as he could. His use of Duyckinck's volumes does nothing in and of itself to cause us to question his experience as a literal visitation from the spirit world. But because the baptismal work had been previously performed for every individual who had signed the Declaration of Independence—the very men Woodruff explicitly said appeared to him—we must consider that it would seem unlikely for them to appear to him in 1877 and express unhappiness that it had not been done. Yet this was the main message Woodruff took away from his experience. He said that they told him: "You have had the use of the Endowment House for a number of years, and yet *nothing has ever been done for us*."[34] On at least two other occasions, he spoke of this same experience. In 1892 he described how these individuals "came to me two nights in succession and pleaded with [me] as one man pleads with another to redeem them."[35] Six years later, at the April 1898 general conference, he again said:

> General Washington and all the men that labored for the purpose were inspired of the Lord. Another thing I am going to say here, because I have a right to say it. Every one of those men that signed the Declaration of Independence with General Washington called upon me, as an Apostle of the Lord Jesus Christ, in the Temple at St. George two consecutive nights, and *demanded at my hands that I should go forth and attend to the ordinances of the house of God for them*.[36]

Yet Haden Wells Church and John M. Bernhisel had both done their proxy baptisms in the Endowment House before Woodruff says they appeared to him in St. George. Why would they need to urge Wilford Woodruff to repeat the same ordinances? They could not have been referring to endowments since these were not performed for the dead in the Endowment House.[37]

Previous Visions of Wilford Woodruff

To put Woodruff's encounter with the signers into context, it might be helpful to look at another experience that he often recounted involving visitations from Brigham Young after Young's death. The Salt Lake temple was dedicated in 1893, and reflecting on his accomplishments for that year, Woodruff wrote in his journal: "Two nights in succession before John Taylor[']s Death [in 1887,] President Young [appeared to me and] gave me the Keys of the Temple and told me to go and dedicate it[,] which I did."[38] It seems clear from this that Woodruff believed Young had literally appeared to him from the dead to convey keys that allowed Woodruff to complete and dedicate the temple, which reversed Young's policy of completing the Salt Lake Temple only after a temple in Jackson County, Missouri, had been constructed.[39]

That is the impression of the journal entry in 1893. But at the time of Taylor's death, Woodruff's journal entries conveyed a completely different idea. On March 12, 1887, he said Young had visited him in dreams:

> I dreamed last night that the L D Saints were holding a great Conference at Salt Lake City at the great Temple and thousands of Mechanics were laboring hard to finish the Temple. I was requested to open the Conference as I was [i]n Exile and they might not have me with them long. The Key of the Temple was given me to open it. As I went to the door A large Company were assembled and I overtook Presid[en]t Brigham Young and He asked what the matter was with the great Company at the Door. Some one Answered the Elders did not want to Let the people into the Temple. He said Oh, oh, oh and turned to me & said let all[,] all into the Temple who seek for Salvation. I saw several who were Dead and among the Number my wife Phebe. I Believe there is some meaning to this dream.[40]

He had similar dreams for the next three nights and wrote on March 15: "I dream almost Ev[e]ry night of these great Meetings. I do not understand what those Dreams Mean."[41] It is significant that at the time he had these dreams, Woodruff could not readily interpret them. In their metamorphosis into an actual visitation from Brigham Young, we can see how a dream about the signers of the Declaration of Independence could have evolved into a vision in Woodruff's memory. He attached real importance to his dreams, in any case, and recorded them in his journals.[42] For him, the Lord could reveal principles and truths as easily through a dream as through a vision; some dreams were prophetic. Thus, previous to 1877, he had learned to pay close attention to the meaning of nighttime inspiration and to act on any truth he felt it conveyed.[43]

Significantly, there is no mention in August 1877 in Woodruff's journal of a visit from the country's founders. From his journal alone, the impression is that Woodruff simply decided on his own to perform the work for prominent individuals. In publicly recounting his experiences sixteen years later at the Salt Lake temple dedication, Woodruff's language suggested a dream: "A class of men came to me in the *night visions*, and argued with me to have the work done for them. They were the Signers of the Declaration of Independence."[44]

I suspect that at the time, Woodruff compiled his list of prominent people and went to the St. George temple on August 21, 1877, partly in response to night visions, which is to say because of his interpretation of his dreams. The baptismal records indicate that Woodruff first baptized John D. T. McAllister for George Washington, his family, and the other deceased U.S. presidents—twenty-one individuals in all.[45] McAllister then baptized Woodruff for the signers and other prominent men, resulting in ninety-nine additional baptisms.[46] After completing these, McAllister baptized Lucy Bigelow Young, a plural wife of Brigham Young, for Woodruff's seventy prominent women. Local Saints immediately began serving as endowment proxies for these prominent men and women, completing the work on February 20, 1878.

Seventeen years later, Woodruff had another dream in which he was visited by a distinguished early American from beyond the veil, again motivating him to complete more temple ordinances.

> March 19, 1894—I had a Dream in the night. I met with Benjamin Franklin. I thought He was on the Earth. I spent several hours with him And talked over our Endowments. He wanted some more work done for him than had been done[,] which I promised him He should have. I thought then He died[,] and while waiting for burial I awoke. I thought vary strange of my Dream. I made up my mind to get 2d Anointing for Benjamin Franklin & George Washington.[47]

Conclusion

The 1876 centennial celebrations of the country's independence, coupled with Woodruff's intensive reading of biographies of important leaders and personalities, no doubt prompted his urgency to perform redemptive ordinances for these individuals. For the patriotic Woodruff, the founding fathers of the United States were eminently worthy. Unaware that their proxy baptisms had already been completed, he dreamed they visited him and said that "nothing had been done for them."[48] Acting on these dreams, he compiled a list of worthy individuals from biographical books at his disposal in August 1877. Upon his return to Salt Lake City in September, he told the gathered Saints that he had received a visitation from the Founding Fathers. Each retelling reinforced that idea. Other Church leaders quickly accepted Woodruff's experience, using it as a clarion call to perform temple work. It is apparent from Woodruff's life and teachings that he honestly and sincerely desired the salvation of every son and daughter of God. Woodruff was a man who viewed himself as living in a time when God's hand was moving among the human race, bringing to pass His final work. Woodruff felt that God communicated to His children through dreams, among other means. Thus, it would matter little whether the signers of the Declaration of Independence appeared to him in person or in a dream since, doctrinally and scripturally, he made little distinction between them.[49]

Thus, the issue is not whether Woodruff had a dream or a visitation. The question is what the need was for Woodruff's experience. Since the proxy baptismal work had already been performed for all the individuals on his list, what reason would they have to trouble his mind, by whatever means? Since proxy endowments could not be performed in the Endowment House, that ordinance still remained undone, and this was a lapse that Woodruff corrected, along with the repetition of the baptisms he did not know had already been performed.

A later Church president would be moved by the same desire to insure the salvation of the founding fathers of the United States. Immediately upon becoming president of the Church in November 1985, President Ezra Taft Benson assigned the Family History Library staff to research what proxy work had been completed for the "Founding

Fathers"—signers of the Articles of Association (1774), the Declaration of Independence (1776), the Articles of Confederation (1778), and the members of the Constitutional Convention (1787).[50] Benson's request included research into whether the men's wives and children had been granted the same privileges. Although many ordinances had been done, those omitted were performed by various general authorities before the end of the bicentennial celebration of the Constitutional Convention (1987).[51]

In the days immediately following the Nauvoo revelation on baptism for the dead, Church members felt a similar desire to aid in the salvation of people they felt had been of benefit to them, including family friends, government leaders, and distinguished personages from the past. By performing the proxy work for these individuals, members felt a kinship with them and felt that these "friends" were in some way beholden to them for their salvation. For Latter-day Saints, no group of men represented the greatness of the American society more than the Founding Fathers, especially the signers of the Declaration of Independence. But as this article demonstrates, the desire of many individuals to perform ordinances for these eminent people resulted in duplications and created a cultural legacy that bordered on hero worship. The Church, in a recent issue of the *Ensign* magazine, announced that members should no longer "submit the names of deceased celebrities and historical personalities," stating that "temple work for most of the people in these categories has already been done."[52] In the case of the signers of the Declaration of Independence, that was certainly true.

Appendix:
Proxy Baptisms Performed on August 21, 1877

The names are given in order of baptism, preceded by the St. George Baptismal Record number. A woman's husband's name is given in parentheses as it appeared in the temple record, and the place of residence of the signers of the Declaration of Independence is similarly given in parentheses. After the name, the endowment date and name of the endowment proxy are given. References to Duyckinck's volumes are included if he wrote a biographical sketch about the individual. The italicized names indicate who had previously received a proxy baptism.[53]

John D. T. McAllister officiator, Wilford Woodruff proxy

Signers of the Declaration of Independence[54]

3180. *William Hooper* (NC), Aug. 23, 1877, Charles Smith

3181. *Joseph Hewes* (NC), Aug. 23, 1877, Joseph Harmon

3182. *John Penn* (NC), Aug. 23, 1877, William Richey

3183. *Button Gwinnett* (GA), Aug. 23, 1877, Samuel Bradshaw

3184. *Lyman Hall* (GA), Aug. 23, 1877, Jonathan Platt

3185. *Edward Rutledge* (SC), Aug. 23, 1877, Ute Perkins

3186. *George Walton* (GA), Aug. 23, 1877, John Matthew Mansfield

3187. *Thomas Heyward Jr.* (SC), Aug. 23, 1877, John Peck Chidester

3188. *Thomas Lynch* (SC), Aug. 23, 1877, Peter Edmund Van Orden

3189. *Arthur Middleton* (SC), Aug. 23, 1877, John Foy Chidester

3190. *Samuel Chase* (MD), Aug. 23, 1877, David Moss

3191. *William Paca* (MD), Aug. 23, 1877, Joseph Henry Randall

3192. *Thomas Stone* (MD), Aug. 23, 1877, John Lytle

3193. *Charles Carroll* (MD), Aug. 24, 1877, Thomas Hall

3194. *George Wythe* (VA), Aug. 23, 1877, Joseph Wetherber Carpenter

3195. *Richard Henry Lee* (VA), Aug. 23, 1877, Charles Alphonzo Terry

3196. *Thomas Jefferson* (VA), Aug. 23, 1877, Lorenzo Brown. *Portrait Gallery* 1:279

3197. *Benjamin Harrison* (VA), Aug. 23, 1877, John Lyman Smith

3198. *Thomas Nelson Jr.* (VA), Aug. 23, 1877, Henry William Bigler

3199. *Francis Lightfoot Lee* (VA), Aug. 23, 1877, John Maddison Chidester

3200. *Carter Braxton* (VA), Aug. 23, 1877, Hugh Snape Cousens

3201. *Robert Morris* (PA), Aug. 23, 1877, Hiram Bigelow

3202. *Benjamin Rush* (PA), Aug. 23, 1877, Joseph Orton

3203. *Benjamin Franklin* (PA), Aug. 23, 1877, Moses Martin Sanders. *Portrait Gallery* 1:192

3204. *John Morton* (PA), Aug. 23, 1877, Thomas Cottam

3205. *George Clymer* (PA), Aug. 23, 1877, William Fawcett

3206. *James Smith* (PA), Aug. 23, 1877, John Schmutz

3207. *George Taylor* (PA), Aug. 23, 1877, Mosiah Lyman Hancock

3208. *James Wilson* (PA), Aug. 24, 1877, Heber Christopher Dolbel Riding

3209. *George Ross* (PA), Aug. 24, 1877, George Coombs

3210. *Caeser Rodney* (DE), Aug. 24, 1877, Samuel Walter James

3211. *George Read* (DE), Aug. 24, 1877, William Richey

3212. *Thomas McKean* (DE), Aug. 24, 1877, Isaiah Cox

3213. *Philip Livingston* (NY), Aug. 23, 1877, Addison Everett

3214. *Francis Lewis* (NY), Aug. 24, 1877, Joseph Henry Randall

3215. *Lewis Morris* (NY), Aug. 24, 1877, Harrison Pearce

3216. *Richard Stockton* (NJ), Aug. 24, 1877, Mosiah Lyman Hancock

3217. *John Witherspoon* (NJ), Aug. 24, 1877, Thomas Hall

3218. *Francis Hopkinson* (NJ), Aug. 24, 1877, John Matthew Mansfield

3219. *John Hart* (NJ), Aug. 24, 1877, Josiah Ginle Hardy

3220. *Abraham Clark* (NJ), Aug. 24, 1877, Charles Alphonzo Terry

3221. *Josiah Bartlett* (NH), Aug. 24, 1877, Warren Hardy

3222. *William Whipple* (NH), Aug. 24, 1877, Henry William Bigler

3223. *Samuel Adams* (MA), Aug. 24, 1877, William Grant Perkins

3224. *John Adams* (MA), Aug. 24, 1877, Jacob Gates

3225. *Robert Treat Paine* (MA), Aug. 24, 1877, Hugh Snape Cousens

3226. *Elbridge Gerry* (MA), Aug. 24, 1877, Moses Martin Sanders

3227. *Stephen Hopkins* (RI), Aug. 24, 1877, Ute Perkins

3228. *William Ellery* (RI), Aug. 24, 1877, James Monroe Ide

3229. *Roger Sherman* (CT), Aug. 24, 1877, Oliver John Harmon

3230. *Samuel Huntington* (CT), Aug. 24, 1877, John Lytle

3231. *William Williams* (CT), Aug. 24, 1877, William Burt

3232. *Oliver Wolcott* (CT), Aug. 24, 1877, Samuel William Goold

3233. *Matthew Thornton* (NH), Aug. 24, 1877, Thomas Cottam

Other famous men

3234. Demetrius Parepa, Aug. 24, 1877, Allen Freeman Smithson

3235. *Daniel Webster,* Aug. 23, 1877, William Gant Perkins. *Portrait Gallery* 2:129

3236. *Washington Irving,* Aug. 24, 1877, James Daniel Smithson. *Portrait Gallery* 2:150

3237. Michael Faraday, Aug. 21, 1877, Joseph Henry Randall. *Portrait Gallery* 2:173

3238. William Makepeace Thackeray, Aug. 21, 1877, William Cameron. *Portrait Gallery* 2:189

3239. John Caldwell Calhoun, Aug. 21, 1877, Hugh Snape Cousens. *Portrait Gallery* 2:203

3240. Baron Justin Von Liebig, Sept. 1, 1877, Abner Parker Hardy. *Portrait Gallery* 2:222

3241. *Henry Clay,* Aug. 21, 1877, Moses Martin Sanders. *Portrait Gallery* 2:228

3242. Edward George Earl Lytton Bulwer, Aug. 21, 1877, George Jarvis. *Portrait Gallery* 2:259

3243. George Peabody, Aug. 21, 1877, Charles William Bennett. *Portrait Gallery* 2:291

3244. Charles Louis Napoleon Bonapart[e], Sept. 1, 1877, Thomas H. Chison. *Portrait Gallery* 2:304

3245. Thomas Chalmers, Sept. 1877, George Jarvis. *Portrait Gallery* 2:337

3246. *William Henry Seward,* Aug. 24, 1877, Jesse Wentworth Crosby. *Portrait Gallery* 2:461

3247. Thomas Jonathan Jackson, Aug. 21, 1877, Charles Alphonzo Terry. *Portrait Gallery* 2:486

3248. David Glascoe Farragut, Sept. 1, 1877, Daniel Monroe Thomas. *Portrait Gallery* 2:504

3249. Hiram Powers, Sept. 1, 1877, Samuel Miles. *Portrait Gallery* 2:522

3250. *Louis John Rodolph Agassiz,* Sept. 1, 1877, Charles Alphonzo Terry. *Portrait Gallery* 2:528

3251. David Livingstone, Sept. 1, 1877, Hugh Snape Cousens. *Portrait Gallery* 2:605

3252. Christopher Columbus, Aug. 24, 1877, Adolphus Renie Whitehead

3253. Americus Vespucius, Aug. 21, 1877, Samuel Miles

3254. John Wesley, Aug. 24, 1877, James Godson Bleak

Names absent from the temple record[55]

Lord George Gordon Byron, Nov. 14, 1877, William Parker. *Portrait Gallery* 1:507

Frederic Henry Alexander Von Humboldt, Oct. 24, 1877, Nils Christian Flygare. *Portrait Gallery* 1:466

Count Camillo Benso di Cavour, Oct. 25, 1877, August Henry Frederick Wilcken. *Portrait Gallery* 2:54

Samuel Johnson, Sept. 13, 1877, William Roberts. *Portrait Gallery* 1:5

Thomas Babington Macaulay, Nov. 21, 1877, Andrew Hyrum Whittock. *Portrait Gallery* 2:104

Frederick II of Prussia, Sept. 19, 1877, William Roberts. *Portrait Gallery* 1:60

Edward Gibbon, Sept. 19, 1877, Charles Alfonzo Terry. *Portrait Gallery* 1:75

David Garrick, Sept. 20, 1877, George Frederick Jarvis. *Portrait Gallery* 1:106

Sir Joshua Reynolds, Sept. 20, 1877, Harrison Gray Otis Peck. *Portrait Gallery* 1:169

Robert Burns, Sept. 20, 1877, Silas Gardner Higgins. *Portrait Gallery* 1:204

Johann Wolfgang Goethe, Sept. 20, 1877, Charles Lowell Walker. *Portrait Gallery* 1:226

John Philip Kemble, Sept. 20, 1877, William Roberts. *Portrait Gallery* 1:240

Frederick von Schiller, Sept. 20, 1877, Brigham Jarvis. *Portrait Gallery* 1:310

Henry Grattan, Sept. 20, 1877, Charles Smith. *Portrait Gallery* 1:323

Lord Horatio Nelson, Aug. 22, 1877, James Godson Bleak. *Portrait Gallery* 1:378

John Philpot Curran, Sept. 20, 1877, Charles Alphonzo Terry. *Portrait Gallery* 1:396

George Stephenson, Oct. 24, 1877, Anthony Johnson Stratton. *Portrait Gallery* 1:433

Walter Scott, Oct. 25, 1877, Horatio Harris Merrill. *Portrait Gallery* 1:476

Lord Henry Brougham, Nov. 9, 1877, Thomas Miller. *Portrait Gallery* 1:494

William Wordsworth, Nov. 14, 1877, James Hansen. *Portrait Gallery* 1:544

Daniel O'Connell, Nov. 14, 1877, Severin Nelson Lee. *Portrait Gallery* 2:5

Richard Cobden, Nov. 16, 1877, David Henry Cannon Jr. *Portrait Gallery* 2:71

Oliver Goldsmith, Sept. 19, 1877, Silas Gardner Higgins. *Portrait Gallery* 1:28

Benito Juarez, Nov. 15, 1877, Rudolph Buchman. *Portrait Gallery* 2:124

Wilford Woodruff officiator, John D. T. McAllister proxy[56]

Additional famous men

3159. *George Washington,* Aug. 22, 1877,[57] John Daniel Thompson McAllister

3160. John Washington, Aug. 22, 1877, John Lyde

3161. Sir Henry Washington, Aug. 22, 1877, Ute Perkins

3162. Lawrence Washington, Aug. 22, 1877, Thomas Day

3163. Augustine Washington, Aug. 22, 1877, Hugh Snape Cousens

3164. Lawrence Washington (Augustine's father), Aug. 22, 1877, Charles Alfonso Terry

3165. Lawrence Washington, Aug. 22, 1877, William Richey

3166. Daniel Parke Custis, Aug. 22, 1877, Henry William Bigler

3167. John Parke Custis, Aug. 22, 1877, David Moss

3168. *James Madison,* Aug. 22, 1877, John Lyman Smith

3169. *James Monroe,* Aug. 22, 1877, Henry Eyring

3170. *John Quincy Adams,* Aug. 22, 1877, William Fawcett

3171. *Andrew Jackson,* Aug. 22, 1877, Joseph Harmon

3172. *William Henry Harrison*, Aug. 23, 1877, Moses Franklin Farnsworth

3173. *John Tyler,* Aug. 23, 1877, Matthew Clayton

3174. *James Knox Polk,* Aug. 23, 1877, George Coombs

3175. Zachary Taylor, Aug. 23, 1877, Heber Christopher D. Riding

3176. *Millard Fillmore,* Aug. 23, 1877, John D. T. McAllister

3177. *Franklin Pierce,* Aug. 23, 1877, David Mustard

3178. Abraham Lincoln, Aug. 23, 1877, William White Smith

3179. *Andrew Johnson*, Aug. 23, 1877, Adolphus Rema Whitehead

John D. T. McAllister officiator, Lucy Bigelow Young proxy[58]

Famous women

3255. Elizabeth Christina (Frederick II), Aug. 23, 1877, Anne Eva Knechtel Siegmiller. *Portrait Gallery* 1:61

3256. Eva Maria Veigel, given in temple as "Violet Garrick" (David Garrick), Aug. 23, 1877, Margaret Baird Mathie. *Portrait Gallery* 1:117

3257. Miss Nugent (Edmund Burke), Feb. 20, 1878, Caroline Bleak Hardy. *Portrait Gallery* 1:163

3258. Jean Armour (Robert Burns), Feb. 20, 1878, Elizabeth Thomas Morse. *Portrait Gallery* 1:209

3259. Christiane Vulpius (Goethe), Feb. 20, 1878, Roena Sylvester Jarvis. *Portrait Gallery* 1:237

3260. Mrs. John Philip Kemble, Aug. 23, 1877, Anna Charlotte Eldredge Chidester. *Portrait Gallery* 1:240

3261. Martha Wayles (Thomas Jefferson), Aug. 23, 1877, Anna Laurie Ivins. *Portrait Gallery* 1:282

3262. Charlotte Von Lengefeld (Friedrich Schiller), Aug. 23, 1877, Isabella Hill Romney. *Portrait Gallery* 1:319

3263. Henrietta Fitzgerald (Henry Gratton), Aug. 23, 1877, Mary Ann Heibbet Jeffrie. *Portrait Gallery* 1:327

3264. Miss Herbert (Horatio Nelson), Feb. 20, 1878, Eliza Medlock Campbell. *Portrait Gallery* 1:378

3265. Mrs. Creaugh (John P. Curran), Aug. 23, 1877, Lucy Celestia Bigelow. *Portrait Gallery* 1:401

3266. Fanny Henderson (George Stephenson), Aug. 23, 1877, Mary Elvira Bigelow. *Portrait Gallery* 1:434

3267. Charlotte Margaret Carpenter (Walter Scott), Feb. 20, 1878, Martha Emma Pell. *Portrait Gallery* 1:479

3268. Mary Ann Eden (Henry Lord Brougham), Aug. 23, 1877, Lodemia Elizabeth Chidester Ruby. *Portrait Gallery* 1:506

3269. Miss Milbanke (Lord Byron), Feb. 20, 1878, Sarah Leaver. *Portrait Gallery* 1:516

3270. Mary Hutchinson (William Wordsworth), Aug. 23, 1877, Susan Foy Chidester. *Portrait Gallery* 1:557

3271. Lady Catherine Pakenham (Arthur Duke of Wellington), Aug. 23, 1877, Hannah Gold Perkins. *Portrait Gallery* 1:586

3272. Elizabeth Dykes (Thomas Moore), Feb. 20, 1878, Anna Marinda Colborn Miles. *Portrait Gallery* 1:600

3273. Rachel Donelson (Andrew Jackson), Aug. 23, 1877, Martha Ann Knight Mills. *Portrait Gallery* 1:618

3274. Mary O'Connell (Daniel O'Connell), Aug. 23, 1877, Ann Crosby Thomas. *Portrait Gallery* 2:8

3275. Miss Melbourne (Lord Palmerston), Aug. 23, 1877, Elizabeth Thomas Morse. *Portrait Gallery* 2:41

3276. Princess Charlotte (Benito Juarez), Aug. 23, 1877, Amanda Elizabeth Starr. *Portrait Gallery* 2:125

3277. Abigail Eastman (Ebenezer Webster), Aug. 23, 1877, Laura Ann Amelia Starr. *Portrait Gallery* 2:129

3278. Grace Fletcher (Daniel Webster), Aug. 23, 1877, Hannah Elder Baldwin Crosby. *Portrait Gallery* 2:134

3279. Miss Hoffman (Washington Irving), Aug. 23, 1877, Eliza Ann Lund. *Portrait Gallery* 2:150

3280. Sarah Barnard (Michael Faraday), Aug. 23, 1877, Anna Warren Perkins. *Portrait Gallery* 2:173

3281. Miss Shaw (William Makepeace Thackeray), Aug. 23, 1877, Alice Hulme Thompson Lougee. *Portrait Gallery* 2:189

3282. Martha Caldwell (Patrick Calhoun), Aug. 23, 1877, Johannah Christina Winberg Mansfield. *Portrait Gallery* 2:203

3283. Miss Judkin (Stonewall Jackson), Aug. 23, 1877, Emily Brown Bush Spencer. *Portrait Gallery* 2:189

3284. Mrs. Elijah Gibbs, Feb. 20, 1878, Mary Ann Hibbitt Jeffrey.

3285. Catherine Maria Sedgewick, Aug. 23, 1877, Mary Parker Chidester. *Portrait Gallery* 2:80

3286. Mary Russell Mitford, Aug. 23, 1877, Sarah Anna Arterbury Church. *Portrait Gallery* 2:116

3287. Lady Sidney Morgan, Aug. 23, 1877, Mary Lockwood Kemp. *Portrait Gallery* 2:167

3288. Mary Fairfax Somerville, Aug. 23, 1877, Maria Marks Harman. *Portrait Gallery* 2:219

3289. Letitia Elizabeth Landon, Aug. 23, 1877, Adeliza Alger McArthur. *Portrait Gallery* 2:244

3290. Sarah Margaret Fuller, Aug. 23, 1877, Caroline Smith Coltam. *Portrait Gallery* 2:273

3291. Emily Chubbuch Judson, Aug. 23, 1877, Mary Ann Allen Steers. *Portrait Gallery* 2:321

3292. Elizabeth Barrett Browning, Aug. 23, 1877, Johanna Maria Schultz Nixon. *Portrait Gallery* 2:352

3293. Francis Locke, Aug. 23, 1877, Abigail Finch Kelsey. *Portrait Gallery* 2:411

3294. *Hannah Moore* [More], Feb. 20, 1878, Sarah Kelsey. *Portrait Gallery* 1:43.[59]

3295. Marie Antoinette, Feb. 20, 1878, Alice Hulme Thompson Longel. *Portrait Gallery* 1:87

3296. Maria Theresa, Feb. 20, 1878, Balbina Rohner Wellaner. *Portrait Gallery* 1:87

3297. Frances Burney, Aug. 22, 1877, Anne Thorpe Wells. *Portrait Gallery* 1:139

3298. Mary Ball, Washington's mother, Aug. 22, 1877, Ann Davis McAllister. *Portrait Gallery* 1:123

3299. *Martha Dandridge Washington,* Aug. 22, 1877, Lucy Bigelow Young. *Portrait Gallery* 1:182

3300. *Charlotte Corday,* Feb. 20, 1878, Anna Charlotte Eldredge Chidester. *Portrait Gallery* 1:218

3301. Mrs. John Washington, Aug. 22, 1877, Martha Mecham Bigelow.

3302. Mrs. Henry Washington, Aug. 22, 1877, Abigail Finch Kelsey.

3303. Mrs. Lawrence Washington, Aug. 22, 1877, Johanna Maria Schultz Nixon.

3304. Mrs. Washington (Augustine Washington), Aug. 22, 1877, Sarah Pulsipher Alger

3305. Mrs. Mildred Warner Washington, Augustine's mother, Aug. 23, 1877, Margaret Kay Mustard.

3306. Anne Fairfax (Lawrence Washington), Aug. 23, 1877, Susannah Mahetebel Rogers Keate.

3307. Mary Philipse, Aug. 23, 1877, Jennette Potter Oxborrow. *Portrait Gallery* 1:182

3308. Miss Martha Parke Custis, daughter of Martha Washington, Aug. 24, 1877, Rhoda Mabel Young.[60]

3309. Mrs. John Parke Custis, Aug. 23, 1877, Anna Elmer Smith.

3310. Marie Fackrell, Aug. 23, 1877, Ann Davis McAllister.

3311. Euphrosyne Parepa, Aug. 24, 1877, Lucy Bigelow Young.

3312. Countess Demetrius Parepa, mother of Euphrosyne, Aug. 23, 1877, Minerva White Snow.

3313. Sarah Ford, mother of Samuel Johnson, Aug. 23, 1877, Jane Taylor Smith. *Portrait Gallery* 1:5

3314. *Abigail Smith* (John Adams), Aug. 23, 1877, Catherine Donald Rankin Pimm. *Portrait Gallery* 1:255

3315. Maria Edgeworth, Aug. 23, 1877, Sarah Hallam Worthen. *Portrait Gallery* 1:293

3316. Sarah Van Brugh Livingston, Aug. 23, 1877, Alice Maria Worthen. *Portrait Gallery* 1:334

3317. Jane Austen, Aug. 23, 1877, Sarah Price Smith. *Portrait Gallery* 1:409

3318. Sarah Kemble (John Philip Kemble), Aug. 23, 1877, Marietta Simmons Barney Calkin. *Portrait Gallery* 1:241

3319. Dorothy Payne, Aug. 23, 1877, Elizabeth Reeves Liston. *Portrait Gallery* 1:488

3320. Elizabeth Gurney, Aug. 23, 1877, Orpha Maria Redfield Everett. *Portrait Gallery* 1:529

3321. *Felicia Dorothea Browne* [Hemans].[61] *Portrait Gallery* 1:566

3322. Lydia Huntley, Aug. 23, 1877, Margaret Ried Angier Peck. *Portrait Gallery* 1:605

3323. Anna Murphy, Aug. 23, 1877, Mary Brommelli Eyring. *Portrait Gallery* 2:12

3324. Charlotte Bronte, Aug. 23, 1877, Lucy Bigelow Young. *Portrait Gallery* 2:44

Notes

1. Wilford Woodruff, September 16, 1877, *Journal of Discourses*, 26 vols. (London and Liverpool: LDS Booksellers Depot, 1855-86), 19:229.

2. See, e.g., lesson 39, "The Hearts of the Children Shall Turn to Their Fathers," in the *Doctrine and Covenants and Church History Gospel Doctrine Teacher's Manual* and lesson 15, "Wilford Woodruff–Faithful and True," in the *Presidents of the Church: Priesthood/Relief Society Teacher's Manual* (www.lds.org).

3. Joseph Smith introduced baptism for the dead in Nauvoo in a discourse he delivered at the funeral of Seymour Brunson, a member of the Nauvoo High Council, on August 15, 1840. Smith taught that "people could now act for their friends who had departed this life, and that the plan of salvation was calculated to save all who were willing to obey the requirements of the law of God" (Andrew F. Ehat and Lyndon W. Cook, *The Words of Joseph Smith* [Provo: BYU Religious Studies Center, 1980], 49). Smith based his teaching on a reading of 1 Cor. 15:29, in which a vicarious baptism is cited in support of the resurrection. On January 19, 1841, Smith dictated a revelation formally introducing proxy baptisms, later Doctrine and Covenants 124. Almost immediately the Saints began to perform baptisms for the dead in the Mississippi River. On October 3, Smith instructed people to suspend the ordinance until the baptismal font was installed in the Nauvoo temple. The font was completed on November 8, 1841, and baptisms for the dead recommenced on Sunday, November 21 (ibid., 98).

4. Charlotte Haven to "My dear home friends," May 2, 1843, in *Among the Mormons: Historical Accounts by Contemporary Observers*, eds. William Mulder and A. Russell Mortensen (New York: Alfred A. Knopf, 1958), 123. I was unable to locate a baptismal record for the event Haven describes.

5. The proxies for the three Washington baptisms were Joseph Smith's brother Don Carlos Smith, John Harrington, and Stephen Jones. Nauvoo Baptismal Record Index, microfilm #820155, LDS Family History Library, Salt Lake City (hereafter Nauvoo). The baptismal records from Nauvoo are a collection of notes, often undated, recorded by individuals who participated in the proxy ordinances. The records have been extracted and indexed, with the proxy names listed alphabetically, along with the ordinance dates, who performed the baptisms, and microfilm numbers. I have also drawn from the Endowment House Baptisms for the Dead (hereafter Endowment House) and

St. George Temple Baptisms for the Dead (hereafter St. George), both in the Family History Library. Baptisms were recorded separately from endowments, and each book was microfilmed separately.

6. The proxy work for Benjamin Franklin was performed by John Harrington (Nauvoo, 1841, #820153), Haden Wells Church thirty years later (Endowment House, Aug. 23, 1871, #183384), and John M. Bernhisel (Endowment House, Aug. 23, 1876, #183388). After Woodruff, the Church's International Genealogical Index (IGI) shows that the baptism was repeated again on Mar. 23, 1880, and June 3, 1884, in the St. George temple; on May 20, 1972, in the London Temple; on May 3, 1975, in the Arizona temple; and July 16, 1992, in the Boise temple.

7. In Nauvoo in 1841, these proxies performed baptisms: James Adams (no relation) for John Adams, Stephen Jones for Thomas Jefferson, John Harrington for James Monroe, and both Ebenezar [sic] Robinson and John Harrington for William Henry Harrison (Nauvoo, 1841, 2, 81, 109, 71, 76, #820152-820155). John Adams's baptism was repeated in Utah by Samuel H. B. Smith and by Haden Wells Church (Endowment House, Nov. 15, 1871; April 17, 1872, #183384). Martha Dandridge Custis Washington was baptized three times by John Harrington (Nauvoo, 1841, 174, #820155), John M. Bernhisel (Nauvoo, July 29, 1844, #183379), and Mary Lawrence Bernhisel (John's daughter), Aug. 12, 1874 (John M. Bernhisel, Temple Record Book, Aug. 12, 1874, 188, Family History Library). Mary Ball Washington was baptized in Nauvoo by John Bernhisel and again by Mary Bernhisel in Salt Lake City (Nauvoo, July 29, 1844, #183379; Bernhisel, Temple Record Book, Aug. 12, 1874, 188). Martha Jefferson's baptism was done in Nauvoo by Sarah M. Cleveland (Nauvoo 1841, 87, #820153).

8. Church performed baptisms for twenty-nine of fifty-four signers—just more than half. Why he did not do so for the remaining signers is unknown (Endowment House, Aug. 23, 1871, Apr. 17, 1872, #183384). Oliver Wolcott was baptized by a descendant, Phineas Wolcott Cook (ibid., Sept. 13, 1872, #183384).

9. Bernhisel, Temple Record Book, 176.

10. Ibid., 194.

11. Ibid., 186-188; and Aug. 5, 12, 1874.

12. On this same date, Bernhisel acted as proxy for Presidents John Adams, John Quincy Adams, Millard Fillmore, William Henry Harrison, Thomas Jefferson, Andrew Johnson, James Madison, James Monroe, Franklin Pierce, James K. Polk, and Martin Van Buren (Endowment House, Aug. 9, 1876, #183388). Overlooked were James Buchanan, Andrew Jackson, Abraham Lincoln, Zachary Taylor, John Tyler, and George Washington. Mary was baptized for Abigail Smith Adams, Louisa Catherine Johnson Adams, Anna Tuthill Symnies Harrison, Rachel Donelson Robards Jackson, Martha Wayles Skelton

Jefferson, Dolley Payne Todd Madison, Jane Means Appleton Pierce, and Hannah Hoes Van Buren.

13. Ibid., Aug. 23, 1876, #183388. Bernhisel's listing of the signers of the U.S. Constitution inexplicably omitted Alexander Hamilton, Jared Ingersoll, Daniel Jenifer, and Richard Dobbs Spaight. Bernhisel was previously baptized for Charles Carroll and Benjamin Rush (Bernhisel, Temple Record Book, June 30, 1875, 196; Nauvoo, n.d., #820155).

14. Bernhisel was baptized for Carroll (Bernhisel, Temple Record Book, June 30, 1875, 196), and Benjamin Rush (Nauvoo, n.d., #820154). Mary Sloan was baptized for James Wilson (Nauvoo, June 21, 1843, #820155), but whether Bernhisel was aware of this baptism is unknown.

15. Brigham Young, Jan. 1, 1877, *Journal of Discourses*, 18:30.

16. *Wilford Woodruff's Journal, 1833-1898*, typescript, ed. Scott G. Kenney, 9 vols. (Midvale, Utah: Signature Books, 1983-85), 7:367.

17. Addison Everett had been baptized for William Floyd (St. George, March 13, 1877, #170841). John Hancock's baptism and endowment were performed by his third cousin, Levi Ward Hancock, on successive days (St. George, May 29, 30, 1877, #170843, 170542).

18. Woodruff could have known of Bernhisel's work. On August 9, 1876, the first day Bernhisel performed proxy baptisms, Woodruff was doing live sealings in the Endowment House. However, when Bernhisel returned two weeks later on August 23 to do baptisms for most of the signers of the Declaration of Independence, Woodruff was elsewhere speaking at a funeral. It seems likely that if Woodruff had been aware of any individual names, he would not have performed the ordinances again in St. George, just as he omitted William Floyd and John Hancock. But there are exceptions. Woodruff conducted the sealing of Charlotte Corday to Joseph Smith on September 5, 1870, following her proxy baptism by Josephine Ursenbach (Endowment House, Dec. 29, 1869, #183382). It is difficult to understand Woodruff's perceived need to re-perform Corday's baptism in St. George. (D. Michael Quinn, *The Mormon Hierarchy: Extensions of Power* [Salt Lake City: Signature Books, 1997], 766).

19. *Wilford Woodruff's Journal*, 7:368. Van Buren had refused to assist the Saints during their Missouri troubles in 1838, and Buchanan had sent Johnston's Army to Utah in 1857.

20. Buchanan's proxy baptism was performed on June 4, 1932, in the Salt Lake temple, with endowments following on Oct. 19, 1932, Salt Lake Temple Endowment Records, Book 4T, 924, #184290, Family History Genealogy Library. Van Buren's baptism was repeated May 4, 1938, and he was endowed June 21, 1938, both in the Salt Lake Temple (ibid., Book 6H, 203, #184314).

21. *Wilford Woodruff's Journal*, August 21, 1877, 7:368. On September 6, 1876, John Young Smith was baptized for Daniel Webster, Noah Webster, John

Locke, Horace Greeley, and another name that appeared on Woodruff's list, Henry Clay (Endowment House, Sept. 6, 1876, # 183388). John Bernhisel had been baptized for Washington Irving and Louis J. R. Agassiz on Aug. 5, 1874, and for William Henry Seward on June 25, 1873. See note 10.

22. Although Woodruff appears to be the first to have arranged for Columbus's baptism, he was not the last. The IGI shows repeat baptisms on July 26, 1988, in the Swiss temple; on Jan. 9, 16, 1992, in the Arizona temple; on Mar. 20 and July 10, 1992, in the Provo temple; and Jan. 23, 1993, in the Portland temple. Just as the centennial celebration of America's independence seemed to have prompted Woodruff to seek out the Founding Fathers, so the pentecentennial anniversary of Columbus's discovery apparently generated renewed interest in his salvation.

23. *Wilford Woodruff's Journal,* 7:369.

24. Evert A. Duyckinck, *Portrait Gallery of Eminent Men and Women of Europe and America* (New York: Henry J. Johnson, 1873).

25. The four men are Christopher Columbus, Demetrius Parepa, Americus Vespucius, and John Wesley. Parepa was the father of famed British opera singer Euphrosyne Parepa, whose name and that of her mother also appear in the women's section of Woodruff's listing (see note 27 below).

26. Woodruff did not borrow biographical information from Duyckinck's essay on George Washington and probably consulted Washington Irving's *Life of George Washington.*

27. Euphrosyne Parepa Rosa sang in two opera performances in the Salt Lake Theater in November 1868 (*Deseret News,* "Home Items," Nov. 11, 1868) and must have impressed Woodruff, who held box seats. Woodruff probably obtained her biographical information from her obituary in the *Deseret News* on Jan. 28, 1874. I am indebted to Jennifer Mackley for this information.

28. Maria Fackrell appears to have been a family friend of the McAllisters. Following her baptism here, she was sealed by proxy to John D. T. McAllister as his plural wife, with McAllister's plural wife Ann Davis acting as proxy. Mrs. Elijah Gibbs may have been a family member of Lucy Bigelow Young on her maternal side. Lucy had a great-uncle named Elijah Gibbs. In addition, Lucy's mother, Mary Gibbs Bigelow, was the great-granddaughter of Benjamin Gibbs, who married Dinah Woodruff, a relative of Wilford Woodruff. I am indebted to Jennifer Mackley for this information.

29. In several instances, Woodruff has information not found in Duyckinck's volumes, but the additional information was always inaccurate. For example, Duyckinck's essay listed only the month and year for Baron Justin von Liebig's birth (May 1803), while Woodruff's record listed the birth date as May 18, 1803. Woodruff was nevertheless wrong because von Liebig was born on May 12. (It is possible that he transposed the "18" from the baron's death date, April 18, 1873.) Duyckinck gave the death date for Daniel Webster's wife,

Grace Fletcher Webster, as January 1828. Woodruff made it January 28, but she actually died on January 21. Other inaccuracies include Sarah Margaret Fuller's birth date (listed as 1801, actually 1810); Jane Austin's death date (listed as 1813, Duyckinck has 1819 but it was 1817); Dorothy Payne's death date (listed as 1843, actually 1849), and the addition of the month and year for the birth of Marie Antoinette's mother, Empress Marie Theresa (listed as June 1752, actually May 13, 1717). Since baptismal and endowment records were transcribed from ordinance slips, it is possible that inaccuracies crept in during transcription.

30. *Wilford Woodruff's Journal*, 7:281.

31. Duyckinck, "Daniel Boone," *National Portrait Gallery of Eminent Americans* (New York: Johnson, Fry, & Company, 1862), 1:185; emphasis mine.

32. All of the presidents of the United States for whom Woodruff performed ordinance work had biographical sketches in Duyckinck's *National Portrait Gallery*; however, the biographical data in Woodruff's baptismal records are so different that they preclude reliance on Duyckinck. This fact, and Woodruff's neglect of Daniel Boone, whom Woodruff obviously admired, convince me that Woodruff did not possess this work in St. George. What reference work he did use in compiling his information on the presidents of the United States is not known.

33. *Wilford Woodruff's Journal*, 7:295-96. David Livingstone, for whom Woodruff performed proxy baptism, appears in Duyckinck's *Portrait Gallery*, 2:605, as one of the last sketches in the volume. He is the last person in Duyckinck's essays who also appeared on Woodruff's baptismal list.

34. *Journal of Discourses*, 19:229; emphasis mine.

35. Charles F. Middleton, "Notes from a Priesthood Meeting held in 1892," Historical Department of the Church of Jesus Christ of Latter-day Saints, Salt Lake City (hereafter LDS Church Archives).

36. *Conference Report of the Church of Jesus Christ of Latter-day Saints*, April 10, 1898, 89-90; emphasis mine.

37. Brigham Young specifically forbade proxy endowments in the Endowment House: "Some brethren here are anxious to know whether they can receive endowments for their [deceased] sons or for their [deceased] daughters. No, they cannot until we have a Temple; but they can officiate in the ordinances so far as baptism and sealing are concerned. ... We can attend to these ordinances now before the Temple is built here [in Salt Lake City]; but no one can receive endowments for another, until a Temple is prepared in which to administer them" (Brigham Young, Sept. 4, 1873, *Journal of Discourses*, 16:187). In the Endowment House, there was "baptizing people for the remission of sins, for their health and for their dead friends. ... We also have the privilege of sealing women to men [in monogamous and plural marriages], without a Temple. ... [B]ut when we come to other sealing ordinances, ordi-

nances pertaining to the holy Priesthood, to connect the chain of the Priesthood from father Adam until now, by sealing children to their parents, being sealed for our forefathers, etc., they cannot be done without a Temple. But we can seal women to men [in marriages], but not men to men [in adoption sealings] without a Temple" (ibid., 186).

38. *Wilford Woodruff's Journal,* 9:279, "A Synopsis of Wilford Woodruff Labors in 1893."

39. For more background on Wilford Woodruff's experiences with Brigham Young in relation to building the Salt Lake Temple, see my article, "'Come, Let Us Go Up to the Mountain of the Lord': The Salt Lake Temple Dedication," *Dialogue: A Journal of Mormon Thought* 31 (Fall 1998): 102-05.

40. *Wilford Woodruff's Journal,* 8:429.

41. Ibid.

42. Woodruff dreamed that the ZCMI building burned and that John Taylor solemnized plural marriages in public (*Wilford Woodruff's Journal,* Feb. 17, 1879, 7:456; Dec. 16, 1879, 7:535). He considered some of his dreams to have been prophetic, for instance that his daughter Sarah Emma would die, as she did the next year in 1840 (ibid., Nov. 28, 1839, 1:371; July 17, 1840, 1:485). After recording a dream, he would frequently comment something like "what this dream means, time will soon determine" (ibid., Mar. 26, 1840, 1:429). Thomas G. Alexander documented how Woodruff's dreams changed in response to different concerns and stresses (*Things in Heaven and Earth: The Life and Times of Wilford Woodruff, a Mormon Prophet* [Salt Lake City: Signature Books, 1991], 39-40, 94, 97, 119, 122, 147, 199, 227). In 1890 when governmental pressure was intense, he saw in vision the Church's destruction if he refused to relinquish plural marriage. (See his discourse of Nov. 1, 1891, in Brian H. Stuy, ed., *Collected Discourses of President Wilford Woodruff, His Two Counselors, the Twelve Apostles, and Others* [Burbank: B.H.S. Publishing, 1986-91], 2:287-88.) Given his propensity for viewing dreams as revelation, it is probable that the vision motivating the Manifesto was also a dream.

43. *Wilford Woodruff's Journal,* Oct. 8, 1881, *Journal of Discourses,* 22:331-32.

44. Joseph West Smith journal, Apr. 11, 1893, Special Collections and Manuscripts, Harold B. Lee Library, Brigham Young University, Provo, emphasis mine; also John D. T. McAllister journal, April 7, 1893; *Wilford Woodruff's Journal,* Oct. 8, 1881.

45. McAllister frequently performed proxy ordinances for famous historical personalities. In addition to acting in the confirmation of eleven signers in 1871, he was baptized for the first emperor of Russia and Austria, among others (Endowment House, Aug. 1871, June 12, 1872, #1183384).

46. The baptismal records for the last twenty-four prominent men are missing from the St. George temple records. However, the endowment records

indicate an Aug. 21, 1877, baptismal date, and the list in Woodruff's journal includes them. See appendix.

47. *Wilford Woodruff's Journal,* 9:293.

48. Ibid., Sept. 16, 1877; *Journal of Discourses,* 19:229.

49. See 1 Ne. 1:5-8, 16; 2:2; 3:2; 8:2 ("Behold, I have dreamed a dream; or, in other words, I have seen a vision"); Ether 9:3.

50. President Benson, speaking at the October 1987 general conference, said he had received an earlier assignment from then-president Spencer W. Kimball "to go into the vault of the St. George Temple and check the early records." Benson described locating the original records for the work performed by Woodruff: "I saw with my own eyes the record of the work which was done for the Founding Fathers of this great nation, beginning with George Washington." Benson was ecstatic to learn "the Founding Fathers of this nation, those great men, appeared within those sacred walls and had their vicarious work done for them" (*Conference Report,* Oct. 1987, p. 5).

51. The research on this Founding Fathers project is available in the Family History Library. I wish to thank Lynne Watkins Jorgensen for this information.

52. *Ensign,* July 1999, 65-66. Other historic personalities whose work was performed in the Endowment House in the 1870s include composers Beethoven, Handel, and Haydn (Endowment House, June 21, 1871, #183384), Civil War generals Thomas E. "Stonewall" Jackson and Robert E. Lee (ibid., Apr. 17, 1872), and French King Louis XVI (ibid., July 26, 1871). Endowment House proxy records show that many members used histories in compiling lists of famous people.

53. "I, Wilford Woodruff, went to the Temple of the Lord this morning and was baptized for 100 persons who were dead, including the signers of the Declaration of Independence, all except John Hancock and [William Floyd] (*Wilford Woodruff's Journal,* Aug. 21, 1877, spelling corrected). He then proceeds to list the individuals. Proxy work for William Floyd and John Hancock had been previously performed by relatives: Floyd (Floid) was baptized Mar. 13, 1877, and endowed Aug. 22, 1877, Addison Everett acting as proxy in both ordinances, and John Hancock was baptized May 29, 1877, and endowed the next day, Levi Ward Hancock ("third cousin") proxy.

54. Readers may notice that there are only 99 names on Woodruff's list. He accidentally duplicated Francis Lightfoot Lee, scratched out the duplicate, then forgot to reduce the total.

55. These names are in Woodruff's journal, so there may have been a clerical error whereby a temple recorder neglected to transfer a sheet of records to the permanent record.

56. "When Brother McAllister had baptized me for the 100 names, I baptized him for 21, including General Washington and his forefathers and all of

the Presidents of the United States that were not in my list except Buchanan, Van Buren and Grant. It was a vary interesting day. I felt thankful that we had the privilege and the power to administer for the worthy dead esspecially for the signers of the declaration of Independance, that inasmuch as they had laid the foundation of our Government that we Could do as much for them as they had done for us" (*Wilford Woodruff's Journal*, 7:369).

57. As part of the endowment, men are ordained to a priesthood office, usually that of elder. Woodruff must have held five men in particular esteem because he ordained them to the office of high priest: Christopher Columbus, Benjamin Franklin, Horatio Nelson, George Washington, and John Wesley.

58. "Sister Lucy Bigelow Young went forth into the font and was baptized for Martha Washington and her family and seventy (70) of the eminent women of the world. I Called upon all the Brethren & Sisters who were present to assist in getting Endowments for those that we had been Baptized for to day" (*Wilford Woodruff's Journal*, 7:369).

59. Elizabeth Bernhisel was baptized for More on June 25, 1873, in the Endowment House (Bernhisel, Temple Record Book, 174).

60. Ann Cannon Woodbury did this proxy endowment a second time on Feb. 20, 1878.

61. Apparently Woodruff was unaware that Emily Brown Bush Spencer had performed temple ordinances for Felicia Browne the previous May. The baptism was performed under the name Felicia Dorethea Brown Hemans on May 22, 1877, and the endowment on May 24.

A Mormon Bigfoot

David Patten's Cain and the Conception of Evil in LDS Folklore

Matthew Bowman

In the spring of 1835, while serving a mission in Tennessee and staying with the family of future stake president and Salt Lake City mayor Abraham O. Smoot, LDS apostle David W. Patten claimed to have seen Cain. A 1900 biography of Patten reprinted a letter from Smoot that related, in Patten's words, his claim that while riding his mule back to Smoot's home,

> [I] met with a very remarkable personage who had represented himself as being Cain who had murdered his brother, Abel … I suddenly noticed a very strange personage walking beside me … for about two miles. His head was about even with my shoulders as I sat in my saddle. He wore no clothing but was covered with hair. His skin was very dark … he [said] that he had no home, that he was a wanderer in the earth … He said that he was a very miserable creature, that he had earnestly sought death … but that he could not die, and his mission was to destroy the souls of men … I rebuked him in the name of the Lord Jesus Christ and by virtue of the Holy Priesthood, and commanded him to go hence and he immediately departed out of my sight.[1]

Patten's story has since become mildly famous, an essential piece of Latter-day Saint folklore, and the inspiration for countless campfire tales and at least one full novel.[2] Cain, the first murderer, is a powerful theological symbol of sin in the western religious tradition. For Mormons, he is weighed with a host of roles beyond this; he has been, and sometimes still is, portrayed as a conscious ally of Satan and the father of a cursed race. His changing role in the folklore of Mormonism, then, is worth examining for the insight it provides into the ways in which the Mormon mind has dealt with these issues over the course of its history.

Patten's story has persisted within Mormonism to the present and has been joined by numerous other, similar stories of encounters with Cain, which have been collected in the Fife Folklore Archives at Utah State University. They are often prefaced with statements, such as that offered by a Brigham Young University student in 1972, that "he heard this story from a religion teacher on the B.Y.U. campus. He said the teacher told it as a true story …" Another account, collected from a Deseret Book employee in 1980, begins: "[S]everal people have told me that Cain is still alive. They are actually teaching it in some Seminary classes here [in Salt Lake City]." A BYU anthropology student reported in the 1970s that he had heard the Patten story told as fact by his grandfather. Even Spencer W. Kimball, former president of the Church, recounted Patten's story as fact in his book *The Miracle of Forgiveness*—a book now regarded as a Mormon classic and still widely read more than thirty years after its publication. In his retelling, Kimball noted that Cain's fate—as Cain himself recounted it to Patten—should serve as a warning for those whose sins are heinous enough to prove unforgivable.[3]

Of course, many contemporary Mormons would listen to Patten's story with skepticism. Even the Deseret Book employee mentioned above denied a personal belief in the story her seminary teacher taught her. But that has not stopped the tale from circulating. New variations of similar experiences made their appearance at the Utah State and BYU archives into the 1990s. The story clearly has held a grip upon the Latter-day Saint imagination, and the transformations it has undergone, even in face of increased skepticism, can teach us something about the changing Mormon worldview. Today there is a common point to many of the stories. As told by a BYU student in 1990, his story began, "Did you guys know that Bigfoot is really Cain?" In a 2003 article discussing

Utah folklore, the *Deseret News* (Salt Lake City) noted that "the Bigfoot/Cain idea originated in 1980 following apparent Bigfoot sightings in South Weber" that year.[4]

Indeed, throughout the legendry, Cain is described variously as being "covered in hair," "bigger than anybody [anyone had] ever seen before," "a big, hairy creature," and so forth.[5] The conflation of the two legends shows the transformation of Mormon culture, as reflected in its folklore. In one way, the surrender of Cain's demonic and malevolent origin in favor of an association with the animalistic Bigfoot reflects the gradual decline of supernatural evil in Mormon religious culture. Early Mormons insisted that, contrary to the Enlightenment's "natural religion" which taught that there was nothing in the universe that would offend human rationality, human beings were actually constantly beset by forces divine and demonic and which they might, with the help of a benevolent and interventionist God, learn to master, but which, absent God's help, they had no hope of perceiving. The dichotomy defined their world, and though Mormons continue to insist upon the presence of divine power in their lives, the evolution of Cain stories marks the twists and turns the relationship between this world and the other took.[6]

Further, this dehumanization of Cain reflects the weakening grip of the "curse of Cain" folk doctrine that associated him with the stigmatized African race. Thus, the uncoupling of Cain and the demonic is indicative of a larger process of cultural assimilation and transformation.

The layering of a culturally or religiously specific element such as Mormonism's Cain upon a more widely known folk legend such as Bigfoot is not a unique event. In his study of Three Nephites legends, folklorist Hector Lee noted that new developments in the legend cycle were largely "apocryphal … added by the folk themselves." Rather than emerging from specific Mormon doctrine or culture, they were increasingly homogenous with American culture, reflecting the motifs and, most importantly, lessons of nationally popular urban legends.

Lee asked rhetorically, "How much non-Mormon traditional lore can [the stories] absorb and still remain Nephite stories?" The answer, as the Cain/Bigfoot stories demonstrate, is quite a lot. The unique aspects of Mormon legendry should wither, Lee argued, as the boundary between American and LDS cultures grows increasingly blurry. But folklorist William Wilson has demonstrated that something just the opposite has occurred. In a series of articles, he pointed out that the Three Nephites legends have persisted and adapted even as the insularity of the Mormon community has faded. Indeed, the story has proved strong enough to absorb in its entirety the much better-known legend of the vanishing hitchhiker, a phantom picked up on the side of the road by an unwary driver who disappears from the back seat. When encountered by a Mormon in the tale, the phantom becomes a Nephite and utters some Mormon-specific warning. Thus, though the structure reflects generic American legendry, the content remains Mormon.[7]

I would argue that the assimilation of non-Mormon lore into LDS legend demonstrates the vitality rather than the stagnation of Mormon folklore. As Wilson argued, these stories, even in their modern form, "tell us of a personal God concerned with our individual problems"; they teach of the continuing relevance of the spiritual in everyday life. The persistence of the supernatural figure of Cain through several transformations seems to be consistent with this view, and combined with such stories as the Nephite/hitchhiker legends demonstrates that Mormon folklore is strong enough to maintain a worldview in which the basic supernatural elements of the faith play an essential role. Though the nature of Cain, his role and identity, has changed, placing such a biblical figure in an essentially secular tale such as Bigfoot's is an example of what Jan Brunvand calls "the Bible of the folk," meaning not an interpretation of the Bible but rather story cycles that extend the sacred territory of scripture into seemingly secular topics such as anatomy (a piece of apple in the throat providing a name for the voice box) and botany (a species of trees being cursed because they were used to make Christ's cross).[8] This shift, the preservation of the basic supernaturalism of Patten's tale despite some adaptation, has occurred as earlier meanings of Cain, more overtly demonic and racial in nature, have faded.

The easiest thing to overlook about Patten's story, yet also the most important not to forget, is that he was believed. Smoot's letter citing Patten responded to an inquiry from Joseph F. Smith[9] about, Smoot wrote, "the subject of the visit of Cain to Brother David W. Patten in the state of Tennessee, about which you wrote to me." Smoot filled the story with details, remembering that it was "just twilight" when Patten returned and pronouncing himself quite certain of the date. Clearly, Joseph F. Smith had heard the story and was intrigued enough to investigate, while Smoot's letter made it clear that he also believed it to be fact. After receiving the letter, Smith informed the Quorum of Twelve Apostles about Smoot's description, and Elder Abraham Cannon wrote that this discussion made him reconsider his assumptions; before that day, he wrote, he had "always entertained the idea that Cain was dead." All three men, is appears, took the story seriously.[10]

There is evidence that the story circulated among Mormons throughout the nineteenth century. In 1884, Eliza R. Snow produced a poem discussing the incident, writing about Cain that

> As seen by David Patten, he was dark
> When pointing at his face of glossy jet
> Cain said, "You see the curse is on me yet."
> The first of murderers, now he fills his post
> And reigns as king o'er all the murd'rous host.[11]

Snow presented her poem at a gathering of Church leaders and family celebrating her brother Lorenzo's birthday.[12] Her casual mention of Patten's encounter makes it appear as though the occurrence was known—and accepted—by the audience she wrote for. This was fifty years after the fact.

The Cain of Patten and Eliza Snow, who is condemned by God, reigning in hell, and walking the earth, reflected religious assumptions of nineteenth-century Mormons. Philip Barlow has said that Mormons of this period shared a naive assumption of biblical literalism. In this case, Cain's curse was taken seriously; it was wedded with a more unique belief that Brigham Young termed "spiritual warfare," or a supernatural struggle waged between good and evil over the well-trodden battleground of everyday life. Historian Paul Reeve has noticed the concept of a "spiritual battle between the forces of good and evil manifest in nineteenth-century Mormon theology." Mormon leaders embraced a Pauline conception of sin that identified evil as an external force which, as in the Epistle to the Romans, existed independent of God—a malignant, personified power that threatened to grip humanity. Mormon leaders evoked descriptions of this sort of evil in tangible detail, moving the struggle far from the abstract or merely spiritual realm into the physical reality of everyday life. Supernatural conflict was for these men and women neither a metaphor nor very distant; indeed, leaders took care to bring it home to every Saint. Joseph Smith described the armies of Satan as "wicked men and angels of devils and all the infernal powers of darkness" which sought to destroy the Church and with whom the Saints must be constantly "warring the Christian warfare." Young claimed that "every person who desires and strives to be a Saint is closely watched by fallen spirits ... they are visiting the human family with various manifestations."[13]

Moreover, these struggles were not to be understood as mere temptation to commit sin. Rather, they could be very physical and involve their subjects in hand-to-hand combat. Heber Kimball told of real battles with the forces of Satan—battles as much or more physical than spiritual. He told rapt Utah audiences of the trials visited upon him during his mission in England when "legions of wicked spirits ... as plain as I now see you ... came as near to me as you now are ... they came to me as I was laying hands upon Brother Russell [and] the wicked spirits got him to the door of the room." Kimball said that when he shared these experiences with Joseph Smith, the prophet "told me that he had contests with the devil, face to face. He also told me how he was handled and afflicted by the devil, and said, he had known circumstances where Elder Rigdon was pulled out of bed three times in one night."[14] Jedediah Grant told listeners that Smith was given "revelations showing him the power of Lucifer, the opposite of good, that he might be aware of the strength of his opponent."[15] The physical nature of supernatural evil, a feature largely absent in the present Church, provided Patten's story of Cain with an audience whose worldview was prepared for it.

Indeed, early LDS leaders seemed to revel in spiritual battles that tales such as Patten's described, because as Grant said, "When the kingdom of God is on the earth, you may expect to see a special display or manifestation of the opposite [of] the Gospel ... then the priesthood of the devil may be seen operating."[16] The Saints, perhaps, were pleased with the idea that they had brought Satan from hiding. It meant that the kingdom was rising as it should. Upon offering an oration over the cornerstone of the Salt Lake Temple in 1853, John Young said, "I very well know that, at the commencement of the Temples that have heretofore been built in the name of the Lord, by this people, the devil has always moved his artillery with greater power and activity at that time … I pray that we shall all feel nerved up with power to accomplish the great and glorious work we are called to perform."[17] David Patten's Cain provided the Saints with a clear and definable supernatural antagonist, thus paradoxically underscoring the truth of the work Cain sought to destroy.

Indeed, one of the most famous and well-documented encounters with Cain placed him explicitly in the role that John Young described. The archives of the LDS Church hold a paper marked "from the papers of E. Wesley Smith," president of the Hawaii mission in 1921 when the Laie temple was dedicated. The night before the dedication, he had a strange visitor.

> A man came through the door. He was tall enough to have to stoop to enter. His eyes were very protruding and rather wild looking, his fingernails were thick and long. He presented a rather unkempt appearance and wore no clothing at all … There suddenly appeared in [my] right hand a light which had the size and appearance of a dagger … a voice said "This is your priesthood." [I] commanded the person in the name of the Lord Jesus Christ to depart … [I]mmediately when the light appeared[,] the person stopped[,] and on being commanded to leave, he backed out the door.[18]

A shaken Wesley contacted his brother Joseph Fielding Smith, then an apostle, who identified the apparition as "Cain … whose curse is to roam the earth seeking whom he may destroy." Joseph Fielding echoed John Young's themes almost exactly, describing Cain as a representative of "the spirit of the adversary," of which there was "always unusual evidence … for a period just prior to the dedication of every temple." In a final touch, Joseph directed his brother to "a little book written by Lycurgus A. Wilson on the life of David W. Patten" for further investigation into the matter.[19] Here, then, is perhaps the classic conception of Cain: a physical presence on the earth, an incarnation of supernatural evil sent by Satan, and someone whose primary role was to undo the work of the Church.

Indeed, the motif of Cain trying to disrupt the work of the Saints is echoed throughout the legends. One 1984 tale spoke of a nameless apostle from the 1920s whose car broke down while he was in Mexico. Importantly, the apostle had been "checking up on the mission there." While walking through the desert to find help, he encountered "a very large man about 7 feet tall and very dark and harry [sic] coming towards him ... The Apostle asked him who he was. This man said he was Caine ... [and tried] to over power [the apostle] ... the Apostle cast him out with the authority of the Priesthood."[20]

Another account, collected in 1961, described

> A devout young man who had just recently been called to the office of Bishop. One evening while this man was working late into the night he began to feel as if something was wrong... a monstrous tall dark figure covered with black hair walked in [to his office] ... [T]his figure had the appearance of what one would think Cain to have had ... [T]he Bishop had the feeling that its intent was to destroy him ... [H]e called out "By the authority of the priesthood and the power of God I command you to leave!"[21]

Notice that the protagonists of these stories bear similar characteristics. They are usually dedicated Church servants on Church business when Cain seeks to destroy them. As one might expect, mission officials and missionaries seem to be the most frequent target for the diabolical visitor. Aside from more prominent mission workers like the unnamed apostle, the brother of an apostle, and the apostle David Patten himself, common missionaries have also been plagued by Cain. A story from the 1970s tells of "two boys from the Bear River Valley who had just received their mission calls ... [W]hile they were riding they saw a big hairy creature. It spooked their horses ... They went to their stake president ... he then told them it was Cain." Another story, collected in 1998, describes a giant "Cain-beast which chased two elders to their car."[22]

The ease with which Wesley Smith or the unnamed bishop or apostle dispatched Cain echoes the nineteenth-century themes of spiritual warfare; in these tales, God's power is pitted directly against Satan's in the form of Cain, and of course God triumphs. Similarly, Cain presents little resistance when, for instance, Patten commands him "in the name of Jesus Christ and by the virtue of the Holy priesthood" to leave. Patten said that Cain "immediately departed out of my sight."[23] The unnamed apostle and the bishop of the earlier stories were also able to banish Cain through their priesthood authority. Cain is therefore interpreted through the lens of culture as a player in the battleground of Joseph Smith's restoration, understood through the sacred history that Mormonism wrote for itself. The tales already mentioned engage this motif through overt supernatural conflict between Cain and the power of God. Other tales complicate the neatness of this narrative, for within the borders of Mormon folklore, Cain is not just any demon. It is true that perhaps the single most frequent use of the word *Cain* in the legends and folk doctrine has been in association with the concept of a "curse" of dark skin, a mark of spiritual inferiority, and until 1978 the inability to hold the priesthood. Patten's story, Snow's poem, and other stories used the word "dark," or less frequently "black," to describe Cain's physical appearance. He was also said to be the progenitor of a cursed race, which was another way in which Mormon folklore explained evil to itself.

A case in point is the following tale, retold by William Wilson and Richard Poulson.

> Missionaries tracting … [in] a white section of a town in Georgia were surprised when a huge black Negro came to the door and hurled obscenities at them. His mein was hideous, and the missionaries left, much frightened. Their mission president later told them that the man had been Cain, that the town was very wicked, and that they should no longer labor there.[24]

This story presents a number of problems. First, it is one of the few in which our heroes back down in the face of Cain instead of commanding him to depart. Even the authoritative figure of the mission president in this story avoids a confrontation. In that way, he is reminiscent of the stake president who told two horseback-riding missionaries who their persecutor was and the story ends, although there is a sense that the two young men are able to carry on. Here, by contrast, there seems to be a surrender to Cain. Given the strong racial overtones in this story, with such details as the word *Negro* being used and the specific setting of Georgia, perhaps a racial emphasis was intended. Surrender to Cain might reflect the Church's struggle during a period of its awkward transition in confronting race during the civil rights period.

It is undeniable, of course, that the association of darkness or black skin with evil has ancient roots that are older than Mormonism.[25] However, it is also true that the Mormon belief system, in its way of developing theology or psuedo-theology to explain every practice or speculation, has produced a number of theories that not only associate a dark-skinned Cain with evil but with the African race, widely believed by early Mormons to have been his descendants.[26] John Taylor, third president of the Church, preached that Cain's descendants were preserved through the flood because "it was necessary that the devil should have a representation on Earth as well as God," language that in context implicated Africans and African-Americans. Associations like Taylor's placed Cain's identification as the first black man hand-in-hand with the depiction of Cain as a representative of the adversary; both were thought to represent a challenge to the work of God.

It should be kept in mind that Cain's dark skin was a supernatural brand. Wilson and Poulson noted that "one of the stories current among nineteenth-century Mormons was that when people apostatized from the church, their skin darkened." Conversely, "some tales tell us that when blacks join the Church their skin lightens." This was merely Elder Patten banishing Cain in more generalized language; black skin in the stories was a tangible sign of opposition.[27]

The resurrection of Cain in the folklore of Mormondom, then, has been a complicating factor for a religion often unsure of how to deal with converts of African descent. The presentation of Cain as being not merely a supernatural figure currently present and actively hostile to the ongoing growth of the Church but also as the long-past forefather of a "cursed" race served to emphasize and reinforce sentiments of fear and racism and to strengthen the image of the African race as not only the descendants of the first murderer but as somehow inherently flawed due to that association. The Cain of the stories is often monstrous and occasionally pitiable, particularly in Patten's account, but almost always more demon than man, irredeemably subhuman, and as he told Patten, "a very miserable creature ... [who] could not die" though he sought death—in other words, beyond salvation. It is a profoundly negative image, and one which cannot help but compromise the self-image of African Americans or how other Church members interact with black brothers and sisters.

There is evidence that since the Church's 1978 revocation of its ban on black priesthood holders, there have been social and cultural transitions in the Church that may be the very reason the monstrous image of Cain has been transformed to something else. No longer an archetypical racial slur, Bigfoot is more of a curiosity of nature that lacks the weight of nineteenth-century Mormon demonology. Though the stories seldom do little to rehabilitate Cain's image in that he is still hostile, the emphasis of the legend has shifted. The older stories, from Patten's own experience through the third quarter of the twentieth century, stressed Cain's curse. Cain often spoke of his inability to die and his status as a vagabond. He is presented as an agent of Satan and hell who must be driven off by Saints holding the priesthood power of God. However, newer legends gathered in the 1980s and 1990s de-emphasize the element of supernatural evil and portray a more mundane horror of a bestial Bigfoot. Now Cain rarely speaks. Now his specific mission to destroy the Church has dissolved into the general hostility that one would expect from a wild animal. Perhaps not coincidentally, events in American folklore at the time of the 1978 elimination of the priesthood ban provided the legend cycle's new template.

In October 1967, a man named Roger Patterson filmed thirty seconds of eight-millimeter footage near Bluff Creek, California, showing a large, heavy, hair-covered creature loping away from the camera. At one point the creature turns and stares into the lens before vanishing into the forest. As prominent Bigfoot researcher John Green argues, the film "changed everything." Older stories of Bigfoot, Green notes, spoke of "hairy wild men" and often "don't make a clear division between the 'real' and the 'supernatural.'" Indeed, students of Bigfoot lore regularly trace the beast's ancestry back to such beings as Grendel of Beowulf, the Green Man of medieval legends, and the Wendigo and skin changers who haunted Native Americans. Thus, David Patten's story drew from a traditional genre of supernatural monsters. This sort of legendry has often surrounded the more famous Bigfoot stories of the nineteenth and twentieth centuries. A good example is what future U.S. president Theodore Roosevelt wrote in his 1893 *The Wilderness Hunter.* He said he had heard a "goblin-story" from an old hunter named Bauman and that the story opened a window into the "spectres, and the formless evil beings that haunt the forest depths, and dog and waylay the lonely wanderer"—specifically Bauman and his traveling companion being stalked through a "primeval forest" and ambushed by a huge, fanged, hair-covered, "monstrous assailant" that "buried its teeth in [his companion's] throat. It had not eaten the body, but apparently had romped and gambolled around it in uncouth, ferocious glee, occasionally rolling over and over it; and had then fled back into the soundless depths of the woods." Roosevelt concluded by speculating on the identity of "this half human or half devil, some great goblin-beast."[28]

With the impact of the Patterson film, however, Green and other observers have noticed a parallel understanding of Bigfoot that is scientific rather than supernatural. Bigfoot researcher Loren Coleman thinks another milestone was the publication of Janet and Colin Bord's 1982 *The Bigfoot Casebook* that "put hominology back on track." "Hominology" is Coleman's term for the scientific study of Bigfoot and other bipedal primates such as the yeti, which is now a nearly forty-year school of thought in America. While for many, Bigfoot remains what he always was, a sometimes-supernatural monster that is referred to in the sort of frightful language Roosevelt used, the language of science has begun to seep into the legendry.

Green cites several conclusions about Bigfoot that can be drawn from a consideration of the evidence. Bigfoot is nocturnal, omnivorous, and solitary, and although most sightings report "bluffing or threatening" behavior, "only a very few" describe actual injury, which is similar to encounters with other primates. Most importantly, Green concludes, "they are not some kind of wild humans." Bigfoot is, in short, an animal to be studied as any other species. This is reflected in the growing literature on Bigfoot that bears such titles such as *Big Footprints: A Scientific Inquiry into the Reality of Sasquatch* and *A Field Guide to the Sasquatch*. Even use of the name *Sasquatch* is gaining on the more popular *Bigfoot*, which Green notes with enthusiasm for what it implies about a more serious attitude. Both Coleman and folklorist Linda Milligan have recently seen a decline in stories that associate Bigfoot with UFOs. Milligan perceives that the "published debate" has changed the "thinking of active bearers of the legend" by convincing them of the importance of evidence such as footprints, pieces of hair, a physical description, and the like.[29]

A specific Utah example illustrates how these trends have been realized in a Mormon context. On Sunday afternoon, February 3, 1980, a South Weber high school student named Pauline Markham glanced out of her kitchen window and saw what she identified as "a big, black creature" climbing down a mountain ridge a half-mile away. Markham, a Mormon, reported that she simply put her drinking glass down and "went to church." Early the next morning, her cousin, Ronald Smith, saw a "big dark figure" in his field. He fled into the house, leaving an agitated horse in the pasture. The next morning, odd tracks in the snow had been trampled by hoof prints. The story was pursued by an Ogden *Standard-Examiner* reporter, Jay Barker, who claimed he had also personally encountered Bigfoot three years earlier. At this point in 1980, none of the witnesses—Markham, who is clearly identified as a practicing Mormon, or Barker, who has devoted a great deal of investigation to the events—seem to have associated Bigfoot with Cain. Indeed, all seem to have taken a particularly naturalistic approach to the phenomenon. Smith compared the sound the creature made to that of a cougar, while Barker speculated that sightings faded because Bigfoot "returned to the mountains with its young." He spoke of the "paw prints" it had left. He initially "thought he was looking at an elk"—a mistake that one cannot really imagine David Patten making.

Another man, Sterling Gardner, compared what he believed to be the stench of Bigfoot that agitated his dogs to that of a skunk. However, ten years after the fact, local historian Lee D. Bell noted that South Weber citizens had begun associating these local sightings of Bigfoot with Cain. Twenty-three years later, the *Deseret News* pinpointed this event as the genesis of what it called "the Bigfoot/Cain idea." It is wise to exercise caution when speculating about the turning point in a legend cycle, but whether or not the South Weber sightings drove changes in the folklore, the motifs evident in the encounters illustrate a new path in the legend cycle. Notice that they followed on the heels of the Church's repudiation of the seed of Cain doctrine, at least as implied by the Church's revocation of the priesthood ban, and that naturalism had become the overriding interpretative tool to describe these monsters, now stripped of the supernatural qualities that had defined Cain to Patten and to the storytellers of his tradition.[30]

Accounts gathered in the 1990s for the BYU and Utah State University folklore archives stress features that turn Cain into Bigfoot rather than vice versa. That is, they describe him in terms appropriate for animals, as something with a "big hairy" appearance, and make him less a tormented human. No longer does his appearance imply a contest between the demonic and the divine. Instead, these stories generally end with one party or the other running away. A representative modern story, though more lengthy than most, concerns

> [a] group of Boy Scouts [who were] on a camping trip when they heard strange noises. It was Cain, who chased them through the woods and into a cabin. They locked the door, but Cain tried to climb through the chimney ... The boys prayed, then got the idea to light a fire in the fireplace. The boy who lit the fire saw a big hairy man's face in the fireplace right before it went up in flames. Later they saw Cain running across the field yelping in pain.[31]

This story, collected in 1997, exhibits the main thrusts of newer legends. While the identity of Cain is never questioned, he is depicted—in his seemingly motiveless pursuit, his roof-climbing and "yelping" through the fields—as more of a natural predator than a supernatural emissary of Satan. Though the prayer offered seems to offer a ready made doorway into the sort of mystical confrontation between the priesthood and the powers of Satan that characterized almost every earlier story, the opportunity is not taken. Rather, the Scouts defeat Cain through practical, rational means suitable for a less demon-haunted age. The question of Cain's lineage or skin color is never mentioned at all. He is described solely as "big [and] hairy," *sans* the usual third qualifier—black.

Other stories develop several of these themes. A 1998 tale recounts a giant "Cain-beast," a phrase which emphasizes the brutish nature of this legend's creature, who with no attempt at communication simply "chased two elders to their car." Another collected in the same year told of Cain stalking an old man's farmhouse late at night. It emphasizes Cain's fright potential, telling that "two horses … died in the night from heart attacks because they were so afraid" but then tells us that Cain reacted as any other predatory animal would, fleeing when the farmer awoke. Another story describes a grandfather who looked out his window late at night and "saw a big huge hairy man looking in at him." The grandfather immediately closed the blinds, and upon reopening "saw a huge hairy beast running across his fields. He believed this man to be Bigfoot." Interestingly, the story never explicitly identifies Bigfoot with Cain; however, the teller introduces the story as "grandfather's experience with Bigfoot/Cain." This is a particularly dramatic example of the growing interchangability of the two figures in the legend cycle, a situation reinforced by the content of the legends themselves.

Cain's new activities of stalking barns and running through fields seems far less satanically malicious than Elder Patten's Cain or the gigantic demon that stalked Wesley Smith; they are, indeed, reminiscent of Ronald Smith's horse and the figure in his field.[32] The didacticism of the earlier legends (Snow's poem, Joseph Fielding Smith's instruction to his brother) is downplayed and Cain, rather than a supernatural fiend, is more the stock monster of a campfire tale. He is less a damned soul and more Bigfoot.

Other recent narratives deemphasize or distort earlier theological issues surrounding Cain's origins. A 1998 story rejects the traditional curse entirely, ascribing Bigfoot to an "Indian spirit that turns into a hairy Cain-like creature." Another collected in 1990 mentions the curse but muddles the racial issue, stating that the informant "learned in Seminary that [Cain] was cursed to not die and walk the Earth all Mongoloidy." Notably, neither of these stories associates Cain with Africans; nor do they ascribe to him the demonic motive of overthrowing the Church. One 1997 story illustrates the new trend in Cain's racial identity with noteworthy precision: "A long time ago, maybe Brigham Young's day, [Young] was in a carriage when he saw a big, I mean huge black man. Not like we think of a black man, but his whole countenance was dark and black." This story seeks to preserve the original flavor of the Cain cycle imagery but disassociates Cain from black human beings and from the conceptions underpinning that flavor of story. In addition, none of the stories in the past few paragraphs use racial language to describe Cain. In recent years, it seems that the theological issues of race and damnation have been downplayed in favor of traditional boy scout fare involving Indian spirits, only intended to frighten the listener.[33]

A fascinating retelling of Patten's encounter with Cain, demonstrating in short what the Cain cycle has become, was told in 1997. The teller begins by stating that he learned the tale by reading it in Kimball's *Miracle of Forgiveness,* then he goes on to tell a much different story: "During the early days of the Church in New York state, a brother was riding his horse through a thicket of wood when he came across an extremely tall, frighteningly hairy creature roaming through the trees. This monster-like form stopped the man and told him that he was Cain ... Because of this spotting, many members of the Church believe that Cain is Bigfoot." While this story and Patten's affirm several similar details about Cain—the height, the hairiness—the modern version leaves out Patten's observation of dark skin and replaces it with descriptions such as "frighteningly" and "monster-like." In addition, this story leaves out Cain's diabolic mission and Patten's exorcism of him. In short, racial and religious issues are downplayed; the tale is a horror story whose point is the identification of Cain with the modern monster Bigfoot.

One modern story seems to buck all these trends. It was collected in 1983 from, the collector writes, "my seminary teacher." By implication, though retold here by the student, it was the teacher's experience, related to the students "to teach us not to play with Oui[j]a boards."

> A group of teenaged boys was playing with a ouija board. They were asking simple, fun questions. One of them had the idea to take the board to the graveyard. ... After a while they started asking deeper questions. One boy asked, "Can we see Cane?" The ouija board an-

> swered yes. All of a sudden a huge black man was standing on the hill ... Everyone was scared, so they ran to their car with the black man in hot persuit. The guy driving screeched away, and then drove everybody home ... The next morning he had decided that it never happened, but at breakfast his mom asked why he kept coming and going the night before.[34]

This legend seems to violate the general shift outlined in the last few paragraphs because it identifies Cain as black and conveys supernatural overtones, including the graveyard setting and the use of a Ouija board. It seems as though it would play well with the Latter-day Saints who retold David Patten's story decades earlier. In that sense, it might be important that the teller was a seminary teacher in 1983 and a generation older than the student who recorded it; this may explain the presence of the word *black* rather than *dark* or *hairy* several years after the revocation of the priesthood ban. Additionally, the ban was only five years in the past, making this story's use of *black* a worthwhile contrast to 1990s rhetoric of *Mongoloidy* or *hairy*.

There are, however, features of this tale that reveal an understated shift away from the previous versions of the story. Notice, for instance, that Cain never speaks and that his main concern is with frightening people, whom he simply chases. The story comes from a seminary teacher, but there is no demonstration of priesthood power to deter the pursuer. Further, Cain is neither the focus nor the source of the supernatural element of the story, which is derived from the Ouija board. Indeed, despite the fact that the tale's imagery is a throwback to the nineteenth-century coupling of Cain with demonic evil, it treats the nature of that evil differently than the older legends did. Most apparently, Cain is not presented as a challenger to the growing kingdom of God. Indeed, it is important that the children are not engaged in anything so laudable as missionary work. Rather, Cain enters the story in response to what the storyteller perceives as dangerous, negative behavior. Cain provides punishment for wrong actions and is summoned by human wickedness rather than simply appearing independently. Notice, too, the buildup of the story in the progression from "simple, fun questions" to the fateful question, "Can we see Cane?" What is being dramatized is a slippery slope, which is a classic rhetorical device to warn against engaging in sin. A series of poor decisions on the part of the protagonists leads to their fate, and it is not caused by the aggression of Satan as an antagonist. Evil is now internalized, understood as error on the part of humanity rather than as an external force in its own right. It is not Pauline in the way nineteenth-century Mormon evil was. This story, then, alters the original Cain to fit twentieth-century theology, just as surely as transforming him into the mindless, brutish Bigfoot did.

Historians have noted the diminished role that overt manifestations of the supernatural have played in Mormonism since the nineteenth century. Thomas Alexander's discussion of the "routinization" of "gifts of the Spirit," the discouragement of their exercise outside the lines of Church structure, is a prime example.[35] The transformation of Cain into Bigfoot is illustrative of this trend. The supernatural overtones of the nineteenth-century Cain are not repudiated in that the basic supernatural premises and the associated affirmation of biblical truths are preserved. Even though he has been made over as Bigfoot, Cain is still presumed to be real, as Genesis implies, and therefore confirms the Bible. This is similar to the preservation of gifts of the spirit such as healing—power that any Mormon would strongly defend despite the removal of the Pentecostal-style spontaneity that once accompanied them.

While the supernatural is preserved, its borders have been reframed and reduced so that the new Cain's spiritual malevolence is curtailed, not only through removing the demonic overtones from Cain's story but also through the severance of his link with Africa. Both these developments reflect a new, largely intangible conception of evil. No longer can it be located on a specific continent or in a given skin tone but is something within. Similarly, members are no longer warned, as Brigham Young said, of demons "visiting the human family with various manifestations" even though the basic premise of Cain's existence and the religious assumptions that rest upon it—the validity of the Bible, the literality of Adam and Eve, and the existence of an interventionist God—remain unquestioned. If Cain has been removed as a demonic manifestation, if he no longer represents a material and aggressive, or Pauline, conception of evil, his transformation into Bigfoot still affirms the supernaturalism of his story and confirms the truth claims of Mormonism.

Notes

1. Cited in Lycurgus A. Wilson, *The Life of David W. Patten, the First Apostolic Martyr* (Salt Lake City: Deseret News, 1900) 45-47. Smoot's 1893 letter was to future Church President Joseph F. Smith.

2. Seth Lester, *Clan of Cain* (Bangor, ME: Booklocker, 2001).

3. Folk Collection 8a, Group 7, Box 3, Fife Folklore Archives, Special Collections, Utah State University Libraries, Logan, Utah; Spencer W. Kimball, *The Miracle of Forgiveness* (Salt Lake City: Deseret Book, 1969), 127-28.

4. Lynn Arave, "Living in Utah," *Deseret News*, July 24, 2003, A1.

5. Wilson, *Life of David W. Patten*, 45; Folk Collection 8, Box 73; 8a, Group 2, Box 12; 8a, Group 7: Box 3; Fife Folklore Archives

6. On this distinction, see Catherine Albanese, *Nature Religion in America: From the Algonkian Indians to the New Age* (Chicago: University of Chicago, 1990) 30-34.

7. Hector Lee, *The Three Nephites: The Substance and Significance of the Legend in Folklore* (Albuquerque: University of New Mexico Press, 1949), 56-57; William A. Wilson, "Freeways, Parking Lots, and Ice Cream Stands: The Three Nephites in Contemporary Society." *Dialogue: A Journal of Mormon Thought* 21 (Autumn 1986): 14-25.

8. Jan Brunvand, *The Study of American Folklore* (New York: Norton, 1968), 88; Francis Lee Utley, "The Bible of the Folk," *California Folklore Quarterly* 4 (Jan. 1945): 1-17.

9. Joseph F. Smith was a member of the First Presidency at the time.

10. Qtd. in Wilson, *Life of David W. Patten*, 45; Abraham H. Cannon, "Diary Excerpts of Abraham H. Cannon," Thursday, Nov. 9, 1893, L. Tom Perry Special Collections and Manuscripts, Harold B. Lee Library, Brigham Young University, Provo.

11. Eliza R. Snow Smith, *The Family Record of Lorenzo Snow* (Salt Lake City: Deseret News Company, 1884), 475.

12. Lorenzo Snow was a member of the First Presidency and a future Church president.

13. Philip Barlow, *Mormons and the Bible* (New York: Oxford University Press, 1991), 220-29; Joseph Smith, *History of the Church of Jesus Christ of*

Latter-day Saints, ed. B. H. Roberts (Salt Lake City: Deseret News, 1902-1912), 5:141; Brigham Young, Sept. 1, 1859, in *Journal of Discourses,* 26 vols. (London and Liverpool: LDS Booksellers Depot, 1854-86), 7:237; W. Paul Reeve, "'As Ugly as Evil' and 'As Wicked as Hell': Gadianton Robbers and the Legend Process among the Mormons," *Journal of Mormon History* 27 (Autumn 2001): 132. On Paul's conception of sin as an external force rather than a human action, see Rom. 5:13: "Before the law was given, sin was in the world"; 7:15-17: "I do not understand what I do. For what I want to do I do not do, but [rather] what I hate to do ... it is no longer I myself who do it, but it is sin living in me" (NIV). See also Leon Morris, *The Epistle to the Romans* (Grand Rapids: Eerdmans, 1988) 190-92.

14. Heber C. Kimball, Mar. 2, 1856, *Journal of Discourses,* 3:229-30.

15. Jedediah Grant, Feb. 19, 1854, *Journal of Discourses,* 2:10.

16. Ibid., 2:12.

17. John Young, Apr. 6, 1853, *Journal of Discourses,* 2:40.

18. "Experiences with Cain," n.d., ms. 5273, Church and Family History Archives, Church of Jesus Christ of Latter-day Saints, Salt Lake City.

19. Ibid.

20. Folk Collection 8a, Group 7, Box 3, Fife Folklore Archives.

21. Ibid.

22. Folk Collection 8, Box 73, collected by Lisa Larson, Fife Folklore Archives; "A Night at the Canyon," collected by Whitney Belcher, Wilson Folklore Archives 2204, L. Tom Perry Special Collections and Manuscripts. Interestingly, though the physical manifestations of evil seem to have largely departed from day-to-day Church life, the mission field remains an area in which legends can still be found. See William Wilson's examples of black horsemen and demonic possession in "On Being Human: The Folklore of Mormon Missionaries," *New York Folklore* 8 (Winter 1982): 5-27.

23. Wilson, *Life of David W. Patten,* 47.

24. William Wilson and Richard Poulson. "The Curse of Cain and Other Stories: Blacks in Mormon Folklore," *Sunstone,* Nov./Dec. 1980, 14-26.

25. The American Puritans called the devil that haunted them "Black Man" (Timothy McMillan, "Black Magic: Witches, Race, and Resistance in Colonial New England," *Journal of Black Studies* 25 [Sept. 1994]: 107-08), and Nathaniel Hawthorne used the same term in *The Scarlet Letter* (Boston: Ticknor, 1850), 92. For racial undertones to the Cain folklore in a broader American context, see Stephen Haynes, *Noah's Curse: The Biblical Justification of American Slavery* (New York: Oxford, 2002).

26. Mark Leone, *The Roots of Modern Mormonism* (Cambridge: Harvard University Press, 1979), 168. Leone calls Mormonism a "do-it-yourself theology," saying that "Mormons create their own theology and philosophy in the

literal sense, and in the context of the church[,] they work out for themselves most of the problems faced in life."

27. John Taylor, Aug. 28, 1881, *Journal of Discourses,* 22:304; Wilson and Poulson, "Curse of Cain," 14.

28. John Green, "The Historical Overview and Basic Facts Involved in the Bigfoot or Sasquatch Investigation," *Journal of Scientific Exploration* 18/1 (2004): 37-53. On Bigfoot ancestors, see Robert Michael Pyle, *Where Bigfoot Walks: Crossing the Dark Divide* (New York: Houghton Mifflin, 1995) 3-8; Theodore Roosevelt, *The Wilderness Hunter* (New York: Putnam, 1893), 273-82.

29. Loren Coleman, foreword to Janet and Colin Bord, *The Bigfoot Casebook Updated: Sightings and Encounters from 1818-2004* (Enumclaw, WA: Pinewoods Press, 2005); Green, "Historical Overview," 37-38; Grover Krantz, *Big Footprints: A Scientific Inquiry into the Reality of Sasquatch* (Boulder: Johnson Books, 1992); David Gordon, *A Field Guide to Sasquatch* (Seattle: Sasquatch Books, 1992); Linda Milligan, "The 'Truth' about the Bigfoot Legend," *Western Folklore* 49 (Jan. 1990): 83-98. There is also evidence that Mormon Cain stories have begun to enter the consciousness of mainstream Bigfoot research. See, e.g., Joshua Buhs, *Bigfoot: The Life and Times of a Legend* (Chicago: University of Chicago Press, 2009), 196-97, which contextualizes Patten's encounter with other Christians who used supernatural interpretations of Bigfoot to preserve a spiritual worldview against encroaching science.

30. John Harrington, "Did Bigfoot Visit Small Davis Town? Citizens Buzz," *Ogden Standard-Examiner,* Feb. 12, 1980; Bert Strand, "Eight Hikers Spot Elusive Bigfoot in High Uintahs," *Ogden Standard-Examiner,* Aug. 25, 1977; also Monte Whaley, "Legend of Bigfoot May Be All South Weber Has Left," *Salt Lake Tribune,* Apr. 6, 1996; "Living in Utah," *Deseret News,* July 24, 2003. Lee D. Bell, *South Weber: The Autobiography of One Utah Community* (Salt Lake: K/P Printing, 1990), 513-20, makes many of the same points about the proprietary attitude with which South Weber Mormons approach their Bigfoot.

31. Supernatural Religious Legends, Wilson Folklore Archives, L. Tom Perry Special Collections and Manuscripts.

32. Folk Collection 8, Box 73, collected by Lisa Larson, Fife Folklore Archives; "A Night at the Canyon," collected by Whitney Belcher, Wilson Folklore Archives.

33. "A Night at the Canyon"; Folk Collection 8a, Group 2, Box 12, Fife Folklore Archives; Supernatural Religious Legends, Wilson Folklore Archives.

34. Folk Collection 8a, Group 7, Box 3, Fife Folklore Archives.

35. Thomas G. Alexander, *Mormonism in Transition: A History of the Latter-day Saints, 1890-1930* (Urbana: University of Illinois Press, 1986), 290-98.

The Forms and the Power

The Development of Mormon Ritual Healing to 1847

Jonathan A. Stapley and Kristine Wright

> *Brother Joseph, while in the Spirit, rebuked the Elders who would continue to lay hands on the sick from day to day without the power to heal them. Said he: "It is time that such things ended.* Let the Elders either obtain the power of God to heal the sick, or let them cease to minister the forms without the power."[1] —Parley P. Pratt

Although the miraculous healings that Joseph Smith performed in 1839 on the banks of the Mississippi are well-known to modern Mormons. Parley P. Pratt did not write the first extended account of the events until years after they occurred. Despite the passage of time, his memory nevertheless focused on a theme Smith emphasized throughout his lifetime and that is confirmed through hundreds of contemporary sources. As Mormonism grew, Smith persistently sought to incorporate two elements into the alloy of his people: the power of God to heal and rituals for its implementation. Where mainstream Protestants insisted that the days of miracles were past, Smith was unreserved in combining charisma and ritual into a healing liturgy that challenged these norms. Smith drew on the salvific rituals of his Church and used them to focus the power of God in his people, to overcome death both spiritually and physically, both after this life and during it. This study delineates this developmental process in Mormonism's healing liturgy up to the LDS settlement of the Great Basin.

The Context of Christian Healing

Joseph Smith was born into a world of religious dynamism. In the expanding religious space created by the American Revolution, evangelicalism tempered the strict Calvinism of American religion. Yet this American context was anticipated by the overall history of Christianity, back through the Puritan settlement of New England to the Reformation, the history of the Roman Catholic Church, and to the accounts of Christ's contemporaries. As Mormon ritual development was informed by many aspects of religious history, to understand Mormon healing practices one must comprehend healing in this broader context.

Jesus Christ was known as a healer and great miracle worker, but the King James Bible[2] records that Jesus "ordained twelve ... to preach, and to have power to heal sicknesses, and to cast out devils" (Mark 3:14-15; Luke 9:1-2; Matt. 10:1). The New Testament includes several general statements that people were healed by the apostles, but the precise formula for these healings is not given. Mark 6:13 records that the apostles anointed the sick with oil, but none of the accounts in the New Testament mentions anointing. For example, Peter healed a beggar by commanding him in the name of Jesus to arise and lifting him up by the hand (Acts 3:6-7). Paul healed "a cripple" by simply commanding him to arise, and in another instance he healed a man by first praying and then laying his hands upon him (Acts 14:8-9, 28:7-8). In other healings, people sought to pass under the shadow of Peter for a miraculous cure and Paul sent handkerchiefs and aprons, which he had touched, to the sick and they were healed (Acts 5:15, 19:12). Jesus gave his apostles "power" to heal, which they exercised in a variety of ritualistic fashions.

After Jesus's death and resurrection, the Bible records that he instructed the apostles to go into the world and preach his gospel. He stated that those who believed would be baptized and that the ability to lay hands on the sick to heal was among the "signs that follow" these believers (Mark 16:15-18). Jesus opened the wider Church to participation in healing rituals. Paul classified healing as one of the many spiritual gifts that, like the gifts of tongues and prophecy, were available to the body of Christ (1 Cor. 12). In James 5:14-15, the sick are exhorted to call for the elders to pray for and anoint them to be healed and thereby also have their sins forgiven. This practice was consistent with a world that valued oil for its therapeutic properties and viewed physical and spiritual health as being intricately entwined.[3]

Early Christians inhabited a magical world in which the sacraments of the Church secured and restored life,[4] and the earliest records indicate that both lay men and women participated in anointing the sick.[5] As Christianity expanded, the Church competed with indigenous magic for the healing of their people, and in the sixth century, Bishop Caesarius of Arles, in what is now France, relying on James, championed the clerical distribution of oil.[6] He also encouraged Church members to seek healing through the Christian sacraments instead of from folk magics which persisted in spite of clerical antipathy into the milieu of Joseph Smith.[7] By the end of the Carolingian Renaissance, the rites of anointing the sick for health had merged with the rites of penance and death into a unified sacrament for the dying.[8] Anointing the sick was practiced as well as this preparation for death, or "extreme unction"; and both frequently involved anointing various parts of the body including the five sense organs. After the eleventh century, anointing the sick fell out of use and extreme unction was the only anointing, besides those of baptism, confirmation, and ordination, generally performed in the Roman Church.

Reformation Churches rejected extreme unction as a serious departure from biblical Christianity and viewed the anointing of the sick with disapprobation.[9] John Calvin was perhaps the most ardent critic of these rituals, claiming that they are "merely playacting" and that "unction has no divine authorization or promise." He claimed that healing, like the rest of the New Testament miracles, was a witness of the gospel's validity but that, after the biblical era, no such powers were available from God.[10] By the end of the sixteenth century, the extreme Protestant view that "divine grace could not be conjured or coerced by any human formula" was normative among Reformation Churches.[11] And while the seventeenth- and early eighteenth-century "lived religion" of Protestant England did not completely exclude miraculous healing,[12] the Puritan establishment which settled New England held to a worldview that maintained the cessationist tradition.

Reformed theology rejected as both absurd and blasphemous the idea that people could wield the power of God. The Puritan interaction with God was obsessed with this Calvinist separation between people and His power. In the ritual vacuum created by selective Puritan anti-sacramentalism, folk magic flourished. Magic persisted throughout the history of Europe and, as the Reformers observed, mingled with Christianity. Early Americans engaged in divination, treasure seeking, and healing, although their clergy decried such practices.[13] This persistence highlights the deep human yearning to access power to change one's immediate situation as well as a willingness to circumvent authoritarian customs in the process. Furthermore, many early Mormons, including Joseph Smith himself, descended from a culture that particularly bucked clerical constraints on supernatural folk religion.[14]

By the time of the First Great Awakening, self-declared Calvinist evangelists like George Whitefield preached a gospel that allowed for concepts that had traditionally lain outside the bounds of their formal association. After the Revolution, popular evangelicalism further expanded Arminian beliefs and pushed strict Calvinism to the sidelines of American religion.[15] Participants in the revivals of the Second Great Awakening often experienced enthusiastic visions, jerking, fainting, and other ecstatic manifestations.[16] Some religious groups sought to find a rejuvenation of scriptural charisma exhibited by glossolalia and even healing. However, this healing was generally limited to the prayer of faith. Methodists frequently prayed over their sick, seeking miraculous cures.[17] It is important to note that such healings were viewed as manifestations of God's grace and not miracles elicited by the power of faith, a ritual invocation of God's power, or charisma *per se*.[18] Nonetheless, groups outside American orthodoxy like the Shakers were founded on the great miracles of their early participants, and healings resulted from members laying hands on the afflicted.[19]

A few isolated religious communities anointed the sick in antebellum America. In the early eighteenth century, the Welsh Baptists of the Delaware Valley administered to the sick by anointing with oil;[20]

however, such rituals appear to have been quite rare.[21] Later that century, a community within the Separate Baptist movement also engaged in anointing the sick. This influential but short-lived group was a collaborative union of Arminian and Calvinist Baptists in the South. However, Baptist historians note that the Separates eventually abandoned the practice of anointing and adopted the Philadelphia Confession of Faith in 1787.[22] By the late eighteenth century, the "Tunkers" apparently developed a healing ritual from a deathbed practice similar to extreme unction in which they anointed the sick three times on the head or on the afflicted area of the body.[23] However, despite the occasional manifestation of an anointing, healing rituals were otherwise absent from American Christianity. The conservative Briton Charles Buck succinctly summed up the normative evangelical view of such activities in his popular *Theological Dictionary:* "The passage ... from St. James respecting the anointing with oil, has been a source of difficulty to some pious minds; but in order to understand it, it is necessary to observe that anointing with oil was an ordinance for the miraculous cure of sick persons (Mark 4:13). But since those extraordinary gifts are ceased, as being no longer necessary for the confirmation of the Gospel, of course there is no warrant now for using the ceremony."[24] Not only were rituals for healing invalid, but the gift of healing had become anachronistic.

Joseph Smith and Early Mormonism

Sickness and early mortality were omnipresent in the world of Joseph Smith. Coinciding with Joseph's annual visits to the Hill Cumorah was the death of his oldest brother, Alvin, while the death of his and Emma's first child occurred in the first stages of his translation of the Book of Mormon. These losses poignantly illustrate Smith's familiarity with mortal suffering. The Smith family believed in medical science, employing physicians as needed—successfully in the case of Joseph's leg; but in the case of his brother, their mother ultimately blamed practitioner incompetence and the misuse of calomel for the death.[25] Lucy herself was known in the community as something of a folk healer[26] and much of the Smith family's life revolved around folkways, notably demonstrated by their involvement in the folk divination characteristic of the period.[27] However, the Smiths were also heavily invested in the Christian death culture that permeated American society.[28] As one Palmyra neighbor later recalled, they "were the best family in the neighborhood in case of sickness. One was at my house nearly all the time when my father died."[29]

The Smith family was deeply religious even if some members were unChurched.[30] Palmyra had its cohort of Christian groups—Presbyterians, Methodists, Calvinist Baptists, Episcopalians, and Quakers. Lucy and three of the children formally affiliated.[31] The family's grief at Alvin's death, however, was intensified when one minister intimated that he was destined for hell because he was not baptized.[32] Years earlier, Joseph Smith witnessed firsthand the enthusiasm of frontier revivalism and subsequently sought the comfort of God's grace.[33] The resulting theophany, now known as the First Vision, likely steeled him against the criticism of creedal Christians; but one detail of this communication, as recorded in his 1838 account, seems to have strongly informed Smith's later religion-making: God's condemnation of those Churches which profess "a form of Godliness but ... deny the power thereof."[34] Having already defied standard religious practice by engaging in folk magic, once the power of God was within the reach of Joseph Smith, he vigorously employed it to assuage the mortal suffering he knew so well.

A critical step in that developing theology was Smith's translation and publication of the Book of Mormon. This new scripture was an iconoclasm against the ritual proscriptions that still governed American religion, powerfully informing his restoration theology which aimed at re-living the biblical world. The book claimed that "the work of miracles and of healing did cease, not because God's power was withdrawn, but because of the iniquity of the people" and that if the faith sufficient for miracles is not present then the people have insufficient faith for salvation (Morm. 1:13, 9:7-9; Moro. 7:37-38). The Book of Mormon prescribes no form for healing, but the specific accounts of Abish and Zeezrom emphasize charismatic power and touch (Alma 19:28-30, 15:4-10).

In the first year after the Church of Christ (LDS) was organized, Smith engaged in its rapidly expanding revelation and organization, the culmination of which was the proto-endowment of June 1831.[35]

Three months after the first meeting of the Church, Joseph Smith received a revelation limiting miracles but also emphasizing healing and exorcism.[36] While traveling west from New York in the fall of 1830, Mormon missionaries met Sidney Rigdon in Ohio. Rigdon, a minister who had split from Alexander Campbell over the necessity of spiritual gifts, almost immediately traveled to New York to meet the prophet. During Rigdon's stay, Smith received a revelation directed toward him and fellow convert Edward Partridge. As part of these instructions, the voice of the Lord declared that "whoso shall ask it in my name, in faith, they shall cast out Devils; they shall heal the sick; they shall cause the blind to receive their sight, & the deaf {~~the~~\to} hear, & the dumb to speak, & the lame to walk."[37] These words reinforced the resurrected Jesus's teachings to the Twelve, which opened up charismatic gifts to the entire Church.

On January 2, 1831, the faithful gathered for the third conference of the Church. At this meeting, Smith dictated a revelation that required Church members to move to "the Ohio" and indicated that they would there be "endowed with power from on high."[38] In February, Smith again revealed that the elders of the church were to be "endowed with power."[39] During this time, Smith's continued amplification of the Bible narrative showed that Melchizedek had been a high priest, an office lacking in the nascent Mormon Church. The revelation stated "that every one being ordained after this order and calling should have power by faith" to work great miracles.[40]

The Mormons gathered at their conference in Kirtland, as "there was a revelation received, requiring the Prophet to call the elders together, that they might receive an endowment … The Melchizedek priesthood was introduced for the first time and conferred on several of the elders. In this chiefly consisted the endowment."[41] The preceedings of the conference were somewhat controversial.[42] Still, Church members understood this endowment to include great healing powers as illustrated by Jared Carter's account of his wife's healing. She had fallen from a wagon and was gravely injured: "I conversed with her and told her that she need not have any more pain[.] I also spoke of my Brother [S]imeon & told her that he was one that was endowed with power from on high and that she might be healed if she had faith. After this

Brother Simeon conversed with her & … took her by the hand and said I command you in the name of Jesus Christ to rise up & to walk[,] and she arose & walked from room to room." Near the same time and in the same account, Carter told of his child being healed by Joseph Smith. He wrote that Smith "came to my house and I told him that I had faith that the babe might be healed. He then spoke in the name of the Lord that it should be according to my faith. The child was healed immediately."[43] These healing accounts are a recapitulation of the apostolic healing forms explicitly exemplified in the New Testament.

While the proto-endowment was limited to a select few men who were ordained at the June conference, the effect on the community was a documented increase in healing performance.[44] During these early years of the Church, Mormon healing typically involved an individual praying to God for the afflicted person and then laying hands on him or her, which was according to the pattern that Jesus declared would follow true believers. For example, before the proto-endowment, Newel Knight traveled to Ohio with the other New York Church members. His aunt broke her shoulder. Newel "went to see my aunt, and immediately on my entering the room she said, '…if you will lay your hands upon me, I shall be well and able to go on the journey with you.' I stepped up to the bed, and, in the name of the Lord Jesus Christ, rebuked the pain with which she was suffering, and commanded her to be made whole; and it was done."[45]

These early Mormons did not use consecrated oil, nor did they invoke priesthood authority in healing.[46] Frequently those administering to the sick laid their hands on the afflicted area. For example, on October 26, 1831, Joseph Smith healed William McLellin's sprained ankle by placing his hands on it.[47] This method was endorsed by the only two instances in modern Mormon scripture that describe forms for administering to the sick, both of which were delivered in 1831. Smith received a revelation declaring that the elders of the Church "shall pray for, & lay their hands upon" the sick in the name of the Lord.[48] Smith also delivered a revelation to William McLellin that exhorted him to "lay your hands upon the sick and they shall recover."[49] McLellin followed this instruction; and his journal, a valuable resource for understanding early Mormon healing praxis, recounts many such healings.[50]

Orson Pratt also recorded similar healings in his missionary diary. On June 15, 1833, Pratt visited the Harvey home and found their daughter terribly ill: "She had been sick about 12 weeks and vomited much blood; and it was supposed by many that she could not live many days. She was desirous that I should pray for her that she might be healed, at the same time covenanting before God to obey the Gospel. Therefore I prayed for and laid my hands upon her in the name of Jesus Christ and she was immediately healed."[51] This account is illustrative of the tendency for missionaries to administer ritual healings contingent upon commitment to the Church or baptism.[52] The rituals of the Church were seen as a conduit to God's power, and converts were frequently healed upon their baptism or confirmation.[53]

Extensive ritual application is the embodiment of Mormonism's early commitment to the signs that Jesus, the Book of Mormon, and Joseph Smith all revealed would "follow them that believe."[54] The idea that all believers could have access to healing power is illustrated by an area of practice often misunderstood by modern observers—ritual healing by women.[55] Though female healing was not formalized until the later Kirtland period, forms of the practice were exhibited earlier. Despite Smith's early revelation that the elders be called to lay hands on the sick, when Joseph Smith Sr. first gave patriarchal blessings publicly in 1835, he sometimes bestowed the "gift of healing" or the "power to heal" on women.[56] One of the most extraordinary accounts of healing during this period in Kirtland was later recorded by Sarah Studevant Leavitt decades after the fact. While her daughter lay critically ill, Leavitt prayed fervently. In response, an angel appeared and instructed her "to call Louisa up and lay my hands upon her in the name of Jesus Christ and administer to her and she should recover."[57] This ritual formulation is precisely that contemporarily described by William McLellin and Orson Pratt.

Anointed and Sealed

After the first Kirtland conference, the concept of the "endowment of power" expanded with Joseph Smith's revelations that the Lord required a temple for people to receive it. Smith's concern that his people be filled with God's power, however, did not change. Several months before the rituals now frequently called the "Kirtland Endowment" were delivered, Smith stood before the Twelve Apostles and preached: "You need an endowment brethren in order that you may be prepared and able to overcome all things, and those that reject your testimony will be damned[,] the sick will be healed[,] the lame made to walk[,] the deaf to hear[,] and the blind to see through your instrumentality."[58] The Church at large shared Smith's perspective, which was reported in the local media.[59]

The Kirtland Temple rituals included an anointing. In January 1836, Joseph Smith Sr. was the first to receive this rite. The administrators anointed his head with consecrated oil and then sealed blessings upon him.[60] Several were healed by the laying on of hands at the later dedication of the temple;[61] and after the pentecostal endowment during the subsequent Solemn Assembly,[62] the elders went from door to door administering the sacrament of the Lord's supper, healing the sick, and casting out devils.[63] Eliza R. Snow remembered that from that point forward, "the sick and the lame came [to the temple] to be healed, and would throw away their crutches and go home whole."[64] Starting with its dedication, the Mormon temple became a sacred space not only to receive the power of God but also to exercise it.[65]

Before Joseph Sr.'s anointing, there are few extant accounts of anointing the sick, all of which involve Joseph Smith. All but one of these anointings was executed in the months immediately preceding this ceremony.[66] By 1834, Smith was familiar with Buck's *Theological Dictionary,* whose injunction against the ritual use of oil, declaring that the "extraordinary gifts are ceased," practically defied Smith to engage in the practice.[67] Though the dictionary was used for the *Lectures on Faith* and Smith later used it in explicating the doctrine of baptism for the dead, he does not quote from the anointing entry so it is not certain whether Smith was aware of the specific entry on anointing.[68] Still, the ritual use of oil was consistent with Smith's Restorationist innovation. There is also no doubt that the Saints were aware of Smith's pre-temple ritual anointing of the sick; in one case the anointing was performed at an elders conference and in another Smith was asked to perform the ritual by community members.[69]

Immediately after the temple anointing was revealed, it was

adapted to healing. While Joseph Smith had anointed the sick previous to the Kirtland temple rituals, only after these ceremonies did Church members administer the new healing unction. Furthermore, the pattern set out in the temple anointing—use of consecrated oil and subsequent sealing of blessings—was not previously employed for the sick and became the standard form for anointing in the Church. Several priesthood leaders later recalled that Smith, through the Kirtland rituals, "had taught them the ... anointing of their head and sealing their blessings on each other with the laying on of hands."[70] The Kirtland temple rituals were patterned after the biblical consecration of priests and symbolized a conferral of power as well as the purification and sacralization of the participants (Ex. 29:1-9; Lev. 8:1-13). The precise reasons for adapting the temple anointing form to healing are not extant; however, with the biblical exhortation that the sick should seek ritual anointings to be healed, the adaptation was likely a natural evolution for early Mormons. As with the earlier ritual of laying hands on the sick, the area of affliction was frequently anointed. One month after the general participation in the Kirtland temple dedication, William McLellin again recorded in his journal an example at a sacrament meeting: "Being called upon[,] we anointed, prayed for[,] and laid our hands upon A. Culbertson's sore leg."[71] Wilford Woodruff participated in the temple rituals the following year on April 3, 1837, and kept the surplus oil from his anointing. Later when his wife was gravely ill, pronounced dead in a reminiscence, he used the oil to heal her.[72]

As with the proto-endowment of June 1831, the temple "endowment of power" of 1836 appears to have elevated Mormon energy and focus on ritual healing. After the temple dedication in March, women participated in "blessing meetings," where Church members gathered for communal outpourings of the Spirit and blessed each other in the name of the Lord.[73] Joseph Smith Sr. continued to publicly bestow on women "power" to heal their family members, with the blessings becoming more and more explicit.[74] In 1837 he specifically authorized one sister to "lay thy hands on thy children" when the elders were unavailable.[75] In these early years, there is no question that Church leaders viewed with primacy the ritual administration of the elders of the Church, but female participation in ritual healing also became normative during this time.[76] After the Smith family fled from Kirtland in 1838 for its brief stay in Far West, Missouri, Lucy Mack Smith participated in the healing of a Mormon girl: "[She] was taken very ill, and her life despaired of, in fact it seemed impossible for her to get better. The mother of the Prophet, Mrs. Lucy Smith, came and blessed the child, and said she should live. This was something new in that age, for a woman to administer to the sick."[77] That same year while on a mission in Maine, Phoebe Woodruff administered to her apostle husband, Wilford, when he fell ill.[78] The apostolic missions appear to have spread the practice of female ritual healing as British women were also anointing the sick by 1838.[79]

While anointing became more and more common after the Kirtland Temple rituals, there still remained a diversity among Mormon healing rituals. Individuals continued to lay their hands on the sick without anointing.[80] Baptism and confirmation remained a frequent source of physical healing for converts and instances of simply commanding the sick to rise still occurred. There was also additional innovation in healing praxis. Perhaps, in a mixture of folk medical healing and Church ritual, the sick drank consecrated oil.[81] Following the biblical precedent of the Apostle Paul (Acts 19:12), members of the Quorum of the Twelve sometimes touched or sent handkerchiefs to people in order to heal them.[82] Joseph Smith Sr. issued the first extant instruction on such healing as part of Lorenzo Snow's December 1836 patriarchal blessing where he declared that Lorenzo would have faith "like that of Peter [and] thy shadow shall restore the sick—the diseased shall send to thee their handkerchiefs and aprons and by thy touch their owners shall be healed."[83] Such activities were rare compared to other means of healing; however, they illustrate the degree to which the early Mormons sought to embody the power of the biblical apostles and modeled their healing practices on New Testament precedents.

In the development of their various healing practices, the most important concept to these Mormons was the idea that people had access to the power of God and the implicit authority to wield it. They do not appear to have been concerned with the theological constructions of grace, magic, and sacrament in relation to their healing activities. This desire for charisma is most simply viewed in the vocal rebukes of disease and the laying on of hands. Further, Joseph Smith envisioned the endowment as the conferral of this power upon the Saints. Just as individuals received power through rituals, oil for anointing was consecrated by ritual. It appears that Mormons viewed consecrated oil as having power, manifested by the consumption of oil as well as its application to the afflicted area of the body. While the use of handkerchiefs could be viewed as a form of magic descending from the use of Catholic relics, gifts associated with the "king's touch" and royal cramp rings,[84] Mormons at the time appear to have viewed their use as a logical extension of biblical precedent and as a conduit to the healing power given by God to the individual.[85] Joseph Smith's early involvement with folk divination did, however, leave him open to ritual possibilities that the Protestant establishment viewed as anathema.[86]

Not surprisingly, Mormonism's hallmark practice of healing practice was criticized by antagonists of the Church. The Mormon claims of working "miracles and super-natural cures" were among the litany of accusations presented by the citizens of Missouri against the Saints in 1833.[87] Anti-Mormons were never hesitant to castigate healings, especially those that failed,[88] and there is no question that such attacks struck a sensitive area. Caroline Crosby remembered a crippled brother, Joel Dury, at whose home in Kirtland meetings were frequently held. She wrote, "He had been afflicted for years, and although he always seemed strong in the faith, yet he was not healed, which proved a great stumbling block to many unbelievers."[89]

Ineffectual healing rituals also produced tension among believers. The remarkable healings of infants and even animals formed a puzzling contrast with individuals of great faith who remained afflicted. Wilford Woodruff remembered laboring as a missionary with David Patten, who when their mule fell incapacitated, laid his hands on and blessed it. The mule arose. At first Woodruff felt that such a blessing was sacrilegious, but grew to see it as a gift from God.[90] The ritual healings of animals were not regular events, sporadically occurring on the trek west and into the Utah period;[91] however, they highlighted the power of the administrant over nature and the devil. Conversely, when Joseph Smith preached to the Twelve preparatory to the 1836 Kirtland endowment and informed them that they would be endowed with power to heal all manner of disease, he also cautioned them, "Let me tell you that you will not have power after the endowment to heal those who have not faith, nor to benifit them."[92] Smith placed the burden of faith on all parties participating in healings.[93]

Even while linking successful healing to the faith of participants, Joseph Smith still grappled with the failed outcomes of ritual administrations. Soon after moving to Kirtland in 1831, he dictated a revelation: "He that hath faith in me to be healed, & is not appointed unto death, shall be healed." This caveat left open the possibility that God, in his wisdom, might have good reason to not allow an individual to be healed. The subsequent sentences further affirmed that healing was to be sought and that "the lame who hath faith to leap shall leap"; still, those who lack faith "have power to become my sons," an allusion to conversion and salvation.[94] The idea that the Lord would allow death for His own reasons likely informed Smith's theodicy regarding infant mortality[95] and was not far from the Protestant beliefs in providence.[96] However, this Mormon providence began and ended at the deathbed. Instead of submitting to the "afflictive providence" of their Protestant peers,[97] Mormons approached healing by God's power with an ethic similar to that of early nineteenth-century physicians where "the Lord might give and the Lord take away—but until he did, the physician dared not remain passive in the face of those dismaying signs of sickness which caused his patient anxiety and pain."[98]

As they sought to use God's power to heal with an ethic similar to that of physicians, as a matter of faith, early Mormons also wrestled with the degree to which they should engage medical science. Much later, and in language reminiscent of the Protestant divine healing movement of the era, Helen Mar Kimball Whitney lamented, "What a pity we cannot always have faith like a little child, and instead of calling upon doctors who have no faith in the ordinances, call on the Great Physician, who giveth freely to all and upbraideth not. When we can do this, there will be less suffering and fewer graves to weep over."[99] Some early Mormons controversially espoused beliefs that all medicine was satanic, but Joseph Smith clarified that while Mormons were free to believe as they wished, all sickness was not from the devil and that God had "ordained for the use of man" many herbs and plants for medicine.[100] The 1833 revelation known as the "Word of Wisdom" had outlined the benefit of Thomsonian or botanic medicine which Mormons embraced over the more traditional heroic allopathic remedies.[101] As a consequence, Mormons frequently employed a mixture of ritual and botanic healing[102] as outlined in the even earlier revelation that "whosoever among you that are sick, & have not faith to be healed, but believeth, shall be nourished with all tenderness with Herbs & mild food, and that not of the World."[103]

Nauvoo: Ritual Expansion

After the Mormons were expelled from Missouri, Joseph Smith rebuilt his city in Illinois. In Nauvoo, Smith expanded the endowment of power, first offered to a small group of high priests and then to the body of the priesthood in Kirtland, to the entire Church—both men and women. Furthermore, through progressive levels of ritualization, Smith equipped Church members with the ritual forms to channel this power to heal.

Building upon the Kirtland experience, Smith envisioned the Nauvoo temple as a distinctive site for healing.[104] He expanded the traditional salvific ordinance of baptism to include the dead and also modified it to benefit the health of the living.[105] Both of these rituals were performed by male priesthood holders, and Smith considered them to be uniquely temple rites.[106] In 1841 the Twelve published an epistle to the Saints in the *Times and Seasons* that the temple was to be a place for the Lord's servants to be "endued from on high" and that the font would be "a place, over which the heavenly messengers may watch and trouble the waters as in days of old, so that when the sick are put therein they shall be made whole."[107] Church leaders led out in employing the ritual,[108] and "baptism for health" was practiced commonly from that period forward as an explicit rite of the Church. Still, Smith envisioned focusing God's power in the Saints through the ritual endowment. For Smith, receiving this power was of paramount importance.

The founding of the Female Relief Society, coupled with anticipation of the Nauvoo temple endowment, ushered in a further amplification of ritual healing. Women sometimes administered to the sick in more formal settings in conjunction with their regular meetings. Minutes of the Female Relief Society of Nauvoo reveal how women felt empowered by greater access to healing rituals. On April 19, 1842, "Mrs. Durfee bore testimony to the great blessing she received when administered to after the close of the last meeting by Prest. E[mma] Smith & Councillors Cleveland and Whitney. She said she never realized more benefit thro' any administration, that she was healed, and thought the sisters had more faith than the brethren."[109] Female ritual healing apparently caused some controversy, however. Joseph Smith rebuked the detractors on April 28, 1842, "according to revelation" which he newly preached that day. In the context of Paul's teachings to the Corinthians on spiritual gifts, he reiterated Christ's teaching that the signs that follow true believers, "whether male or female," included the healing of the sick.[110] He stated that it was proper for women to administer to the sick by the laying on of hands and further asserted that when the temple was complete, the "keys of the kingdom" would be given to them "as well as to the Elders."[111]

Anticipating this communal increase in knowledge and power, Smith preached about these "keys of the kingdom" a few days later.[112] An onlooker quoted Smith as saying: "The Prophets spoke of being endowed With power from on High[.] They spoke of power that was of God[.] They spoke of ~~power~~ works by it performed[,] [t]o heal the sick by the prayer of faith[,] [t]o cast out Deavils [and] raise the Dead[.] And will declare the Council of God[.] This in connection with all the gifts [c]omposed the Endowment of those sent to preach."[113] Three days later, on May 4, Smith revealed the expanded endowment rituals to several close associates. When one of the men who had received these rituals died, Smith stated that he had "anointed him … to receive knowledge, and power."[114] Similarly, just one week after receiving temple rituals with his wife, Mary Fielding, in 1843, Patriarch Hyrum Smith blessed one woman that she would "be endowed with power."[115] Joseph Smith intended all the Saints, both men and women, to be endowed with power, including the power to heal.

As with the Kirtland temple anointing, the rituals of the Nauvoo temple were adapted to healing and other purposes from the earliest moments. These rituals, unlike those of the Kirtland temple, are generally regarded by Latter-day Saints as too sacred to publicly detail; however, much has been published with the consent of the Church. The Nauvoo temple rituals are the foundation for modern Mormon temple liturgy, which includes a washing and anointing where, as the initiates "are washed, they will be spiritually cleansed. As they are anointed, they will be renewed and regenerated in soul and spirit."[116] In the dramatic presentation now commonly referred to as the endowment, the Saints in Nauvoo were instructed in the "true order of prayer,"[117] often called the "prayer circle."[118] The advent of the Nauvoo endowment ceremonies introduced a greater complexity to healing, for as with Kirtland temple anointing and baptism, these salvific rituals were adapted to healing.

The prayer circle was viewed as an especially effective means of supplicating for the sick[119] and was also used to consecrate oil.[120] In conjunction with the laying on of hands, the temple prayer ritual was used to heal the sick.[121] Children were washed and anointed before being sealed to their parents[122] and the sick were washed and anointed for their health.[123] Washing and anointing the sick became a regular healing practice, being administered by both men and women.[124] While the first extant account of washing and anointing the sick occurred after the death of Joseph Smith, the practice reflects his ritual dynamism in adapting salvific rituals to healing and was executed by his successors: "President Young and H. C. Kimball, assisted by their wives and Sister Whitney, washed and anointed for their health their three little children."[125] Empowered by their rituals, early Mormons continued their quest to experience the biblical precedent of curative miracles.

The Nauvoo temple was the locus for Joseph Smith's ultimate theology aimed at bridging mortality and immortality. In a revolutionary move, he opened the temple doors to the sick and the dying. In ancient Israel such people experienced severe restrictions in relation to the temple as they were considered unclean, yet Smith administered rituals for their healing and sanctification. In the temple, he bound the living and the dead in eternal relationships and prepared men and women to reign in eternity as royal heirs of God. Healing has not been considered to be a significant part of Smith's sacral development; however, the adaptation of salvific rituals to heal the sick, the formalization of the temple as a sacred space for healing, and his consistent teaching that the endowment entails a bestowal of healing power illustrates how Smith used the same tools to bind his people into a celestial society that was not only spiritually but physically whole. Several scholars have noted Joseph Smith's revelatory and liturgical passion to conquer death.[126] With the development of the Mormon healing liturgy, this war on death was not only spiritual but tactile, ever-present, and continually waged for mortal life.

Joseph Smith's administrations to the sick highlight the complexity of Mormon ritual healing during this time. He occasionally commanded the sick to rise[127] and healed others by passing along his handkerchief.[128] On one occasion he anointed a woman's broken finger[129] and on another a little girl's throat.[130] When those close to him were critically ill, such as his wife or a young girl in his charge, Smith baptized them for their health.[131]

With Smith's revelation on female ritual healing, Mormon women engaged in Nauvoo's healing activities. Church leaders specifically set apart women to administer to the sick[132] and spoke favorably of women healing in general conference.[133] Emmeline Wells remembered Relief Society women meeting sick immigrants and ministering to them with healing rituals.[134] Church authorities facilitated healing rituals performed by women;[135] after the martyrdom, Patriarch John Smith continued the practice of blessing women to heal the sick.[136] Highlighting this focused ritual energy, Bathsheba Smith wrote to her missionary husband in 1842 about their sick infant: "I took him to the fount and had him baptised and sinse then he has not had any feavor. He is about well now. Looks a little pail. I anointed him with oil a good many times."[137]

Joseph Smith's claim to restore God's power to heal and the extensive ritualization surrounding the gift of healing exposed Mormons to the argument that their practices were magical.[138] They deflected this criticism by insisting on a biblical witness of history that affirmed their ritual forms.[139] Baptism for health was practiced "in Soloman's temple, and all temples that God commands to be built."[140] This position had rhetorical potency, and even some non-Mormon critics of American orthodoxy pointed to Mormon healing as an "external evidence" of Mormonism's biblical veracity.[141] Additionally, Latter-day Saints sought to purge what they considered actual dark magic from among them. Brigham Young remembered that some were practicing evil "necromancy" in Nauvoo[142] and the Nauvoo High Council acted against a practitioner of explicitly magical healing.[143]

The Trail West: A Union of Faith

After the death of Joseph Smith, the Saints fled from Nauvoo, carrying their healing rituals with them. These sacred rites provided for a meaningful expression of faith as well as the deepening of communal ties. Furthermore, the healing practice on the western trail functioned to train Mormons in the use of the new and expanded healing liturgy, thus serving as a pattern for the rest of the nineteenth century. Curative anointings, washing and anointings, and baptisms were all performed along the western trail, in Winter Quarters then beyond the borders of the United States, wherever the Saints were located. The vanguard pioneer company of 1847 exemplifies poineer healing practice. When company member Norton Jacobs suffered joint pain and fever, Charles Harper anointed his head and back, then baptized him for his health.[144] When Brigham Young became critically ill a few days later, the leaders held a prayer circle in the mountains, then subsequently "washed and anointed [him] all over."[145] He recovered and the company arrived in the Salt Lake Valley later that month. Upon their arrival, they dammed City Creek and conducted rebaptisms and baptisms for health in the resulting pond.[146] Pioneer healings were frequently communal in nature and employed a variety of rituals.[147]

Female participation in healing and blessing during this time was normative.[148] With the accessibility of the endowment of power, women administered to each other with greater frequency. Over 10 percent of the inhabitants at Winter Quarters were sick in December 1846.[149] Louisa Barnes Pratt wrote of her experience during this time, "The shaking ague fastened deathless fangs upon me, from which there was no escape. ... The sisters were moved with sympathy. They assembled at my tent, prayed, annointed me with oil, and laid their hands upon me."[150] The following spring, several sisters administered to a child in a manner that highlights continued Mormon willingness to combine healing rituals with frontier medicine. In Utah, a writer for the *Woman's Exponent*, probably editor Emmeline B. Wells, remembered the healing of a sick child: "The little one had not seen or spoken for two days, its eyeballs were dried over, [and] the sisters were called in to administer[:] Sister Elizabeth Ann Whitney, Sister Vilate, Sister Laura Pitkin and Presendia Kimball and one or two others. They administered, anointing the child with oil, and bathing its eyes with milk and water, and it was restored to life and health miraculously, but the sisters gave God the glory."[151]

The post-Nauvoo period was characterized by a heightened fluidity in ritual healing. Participation in temple ceremonies increased communal feelings between men and women by prescribing their mutual ritual participation. An ethos of unity,[152] which informed these activities, served to subvert the prevalent notion of "separate spheres" within the realm of healing administrations and contributed to a social order of non-hierarchical blessings and healings.[153] George A. Smith reflected on the power of this union when preaching at the temple: "We are now different from what we were before we entered into this [temple] quorum. ... When a man and his wife are united in feeling, and act in union, I believe they can hold their children by prayer and faith and will not be obliged to give them up to death until they are fourscore years old."[154] Illustrative of this faith union, men and women administered to the sick together.[155] For example, on March 17, 1847, Patty Sessions noted: "[Mary Pierce] was buried. I went to the funeral. Brigham preached. I then visited the sick. Mr. Sessions and I went and laid hands on the widow Holmons ^step^ daughter. [S]he was healed."[156]

Healing ritual performance during the migration to the Great Basin guided Latter-day Saint practice for the remainder of the century. While anointing the sick was the most common form of ritual healing, men continued to wash and anoint the sick during the Utah period.[157] Similarly, baptism for health was the most commonly performed temple ritual for the living for many years.[158] Men and women also continued to administer to the sick collaboratively. For example, Andrew and

Elizabeth Ferguson in Scotland sought to unitedly heal their three-year-old son. Ferguson recorded: "Satterday little William is very ill. had to wait upon him all night … I anointed him with consecrated oil, & his mother & I laid hands upon him & Praid over him."[159]

Women also remained potent healers. Louisa Barnes Pratt, who was anointed by women at Winter Quarters during her illness, later served as a missionary wife in the Pacific Islands and contributed to the spread of female administration throughout the world. Her husband, Addison, recorded many ritual healings and baptized the native sick for their health,[160] while Louisa carried out a similar ministry among the women and children:

> The natives … have great faith in the ordinances of the Gospel such as baptism and the laying of hands of recovering the sick to health. I brought with me a bottle of consecreated [sic] oil which was blessed by brother Brigham Young and other of the authorities, previous to my leaving Salt Lake. The females had great faith in the oil, when I told them from whence I had brought it, and by whom it had been blessed. They would frequently bring their young children to me when they were sick to have me annoint them, give them oil inwardly, and lay my hands upon them in the name of the Lord.[161]

Like the healing handkerchiefs earlier, consecrated oil was sometimes the conduit to the power of those who had blessed it. However, it also illustrates the faith of the participants and how the community of Saints expanded with the application of healing rituals.

Although the post-Nauvoo period can be seen as a period of adapting healing rituals to a variety of circumstances, it can also be described as one of institutionalization in which ritual performance acted as the pattern for future Mormon practices. The typical LDS response to illness was to seek out the forms of healing that Joseph Smith had introduced to the Saints in Kirtland and then Nauvoo. Continuing Smith's vision of spiritual power and healing played a significant role in the settlement of Utah. The later establishment of temples as curative edifices through anointings, washings and anointings, baptisms, and the consecration of oil held a central position in the lives of Mormon pioneers.[162]

Conclusion

In antebellum America, Mormonism stands out in its vigorous development of ritual healing. However, the most striking aspect of the Mormon healing liturgy is the adaptation of salvific rites to healing. The first Mormon ritual employed for healing was laying hands on the afflicted area of the sick. Over time this practice evolved to follow the pattern set when the heavenly messengers laid hands on Joseph Smith's head for the conferral of priestly authority. Smith took oil from the temple, which for millennia had been used to consecrate priests and kings to make them holy, and poured it on the sick. The imagery of priests being anointed in preparation for entering the presence of God, and the Mormon parallel of having such anointings "sealed" in its temples, a term connoting the binding of heaven and earth, heightens the potency of the symbolism when applied to the afflicted. Later and more explicitly in Nauvoo, Church leaders adapted baptism and the new temple rites as healing rituals.

Smith's passion to conquer death is strikingly manifest in the development of Mormon healing rituals where this battle was aimed, not only at the post-mortal sphere but also at the omnipresent mortality of this life. This impetus to circumvent death appeared in the language of many early patriarchal blessings such as John Smith's blessing bestowed on Lydia Leavitt Snow in 1845: "Tis thy privilege to heal the sick in thine house to preserve thy children from the grasp of the destroyer in the absence of thy companion and if thy Faith does not fail thee thou shalt never be called to mourn the loss of a child for thy children shall grow up around thee like healthful plants."[163]

While Joseph Smith is most often remembered as a religious innovator, a compelling leader of a religious community, and a prophet of God by those who believe his message, he is rarely portrayed as a healer. However, a central feature of Smith's ministry was his legacy of healing rites, emphasizing the connection between these ritual forms and the endowment of spiritual power, which early Mormons received through their temple ceremonies. Many authors have noted the flurry of temple activity that occurred in Nauvoo immediately preceding the Mormon exodus and have attributed it to a desire to be sealed as families. However, under the tutelage of Joseph Smith, early Saints also understood the temple rituals as a bridge between the forms and the power—the rites that would bequeath the gifts of the Spirit, heal those who were ill, and bind a community of believers together both in sickness and in health, in life and death.

Notes

For those interested in more complete endnotes, please consult the original publication in the *Journal of Mormon History*.

1. Parley P. Pratt, *Autobiography of Parley Parker Pratt* edited by his son, Parley P. Pratt (New York: Russell Brothers, 1874), 325. See accounts in *Wilford Woodruff's Journal, 1833-1898*, typescript, ed. Scott G. Kenney, 9 vols. (Midvale, UT: Signature Books, 1983-85), 1:347, 6:377; Wilford Woodruff, *Leaves from My Journal*, Bk. 3, Faith-Promoting Series (Salt Lake City: Juvenile Instructor Office, 1881), 75-79; "History of Brigham Young," *Deseret News*, Feb. 24, 1858, 401 (an account compiled by Church historians but absent from Young's diary); "History of Wilford Woodruff," *Deseret News*, July 28, 1858, 93; Orson F. Whitney, *Life of Heber C. Kimball, an Apostle: The Father and Founder of the British Mission* (Salt Lake City: Kimball Family, 1888), 262-63, with an extended narrative attributed to Kimball; J[oseph] B. Noble, "Early Scenes in Church History," *Juvenile Instructor*, May 1880, 112. See also Jedediah M. Grant, Dec. 17, 1854, and Heber C. Kimball, Dec. 17, 1854, *Journal of Discourses*, 26 vols. (London and Liverpool: LDS Booksellers Depot, 1854-86), 2:232-34; *Wilford Woodruff's Journal*, 5:23; Heber Kimball to Joseph Fielding, et al., July 25, 1839, Commerce, IL, photocopy, MSS 670, L. Tom Perry Special Collections and Manuscripts, Harold B. Lee Library, Brigham Young University, Provo (hereafter Perry Special Collections); George A. Smith, loose diary pages, July 22, 24, 1839, MS 1322, Box 1, fd. 5, LDS Church History Library, Salt Lake City, also on *Selected Collections from the Archives of the Church of Jesus Christ of Latter-day Saints*, 2 vols., DVD (Provo: Brigham Young University Press, [Dec. 2002], 1:32); Lavina Fielding Anderson, ed., *Lucy's Book: A Critical Edition of Lucy Mack Smith's Family Memoir* (Salt Lake City: Signature Books, 2001), 765-76.

2. Mormons were assiduously biblical, mustering commonsensical if not idiosyncratic interpretations of the King James Version to support their beliefs and practices. See Philip L. Barlow, *Mormons and the Bible: The Place of Latter-day Saints in American Religion* (London: Oxford University Press, 1991), 43-46, 62-73.

3. Jeffrey John, "Anointing in the New Testament," in Martin Dudley and Geoffrey Rowell, eds., *The Oil of Gladness: Anointing in the Christian Tradition* (Collegeville, MN: Liturgical Press, 1993), 50-51.

4. Amanda Porterfield, *Healing in the History of Christianity* (New York: Oxford University Press, 2005), 60-62; John Halliburton, "Anointing in the Early Church" in Dudley and Rowell, *The Oil of Gladness,* 82-83.

5. The landmark study of early Christian unction is Antoine Chavasse, *Étude sur l'onction des Infirmes dans l'Église latine du IIIe au XIe Siècle,* vol. 1 (Lyon: Librairie du Sacré-Cœur, 1942). Chavasse's second volume, never published, was summarized in *L'Église en Prières: Introduction à la Liturgie,* ed. A. G. Martimort (Paris: Desclée & Cie, 1961), 580-94, and in Placid Murray, "The Liturgical History of Extreme Unction," *Studies in Pastoral Liturgy,* Vol. 2, ed. Vincent Ryan (Dublin: Gill & Son for the Furrow Trust, 1963): 18-38. More accessible are Frederick S. Paxton, *Christianizing Death: The Creation of a Ritual Process in Early Medieval Europe* (Ithaca, NY: Cornell University Press, 1990), 27-32; and Lizette Larson-Miller, "Women and Anointing the Sick," *Coptic Church Review* 12 (Summer 1991): 37-48.

6. Paxton, *Christianizing Death,* 48-51, 55-59, 78-79.

7. In one excellent example, Caesarius encouraged mothers to come to the Church to receive oil with which to anoint their families and to be physically healed through the Eucharist. Germain Morin, *Sancti Caesarii Arelatensis Sermones,* 2 vols., *Corpus Christianorum: Series Latina,* Vols. 103-04 (Turnholti, Belgium: Brepols, 1953), 2:751. Eligius (590-660) provides an informative list of magic practices over which the Church hoped to hold primacy: the use of amulets, passing an individual through forked trees, house calls by magicians (*Spicilegium,* ed. Luc d'Achéry, vol. 2 (1723; rpt., Farnborough, England: Gregg Press, 1967-68), 97.

8. We recommend Paxton's entire volume, *Christianizing Death,* to the interested reader.

9. Geoffry Rowell, "The Sacramental Use of Oil in Anglicanism and the Churches of the Reformation," in Dudley and Rowell, *The Oil of Gladness,* 137-41. Note that Rowell describes seventeenth-century British Baptists who controversially anointed the sick. See also Jane Shaw, *Miracles in Enlightenment England* (New Haven, Conn.: Yale University Press, 2006), 33-50.

10. Ford Lewis Battles, trans., and John T. McNeil, ed., *Calvin: Institutes of the Christian Religion,* 2 vols. (Philadelphia: Westminster Press, 1960), 2:1,466-68; Robert Bruce Mullin, *Miracles and the Modern Religious Imagination* (New Haven: Yale University Press, 1996), 12-25.

11. Keith Thomas, *Religion and the Decline of Magic: Studies in Popular Beliefs in Sixteenth- and Seventeenth-Century England* (Hammondsworth, England: Penguin Books, 1971), 65. Richard Godbeer, *The Devil's Dominion: Magic and Religion in Early New England* (New York: Cambridge University Press, 1992), 16, critiques Thomas's sweeping generalization and asserts a more nuanced relationship between magic and religion among Protestants. Still, Godbeer affirms the general antipathy of established clergy to magic.

12. Shaw, *Miracles in Enlightenment England,* 21-33. Shaw's entire volume is insightful. Note particularly, miraculous healings associated with the Baptists, Quakers, Charles II, and others, pp. 33-97.

13. The complexity of New England religion and its interaction with magic are treated and contextualized by Godbeer, *The Devil's Dominion;* David Hall, *Worlds of Wonder, Days of Judgment: Popular Religious Beliefs in Early New England* (New York: Alfred A. Knopf, 1989); and Jon Butler, *Awash in a Sea of Faith: Christianizing the American People* (Cambridge, MA: Harvard University Press, 1990). For an introduction to folk healing, see Wayland D. Hand, "The Folk Healer: Calling and Endowment," *Journal of the History of Medicine and Allied Sciences* 26 (July 1971): 263-75. Mark Ashurst-McGee, "A Pathway to Prophethood: Joseph Smith Junior as Rodsman, Village Seer, and Judeo-Christian Prophet," M.A. thesis, Utah State University, 2000, is an excellent treatment of folk magic and its influence on early Mormonism; also D. Michael Quinn, *Early Mormonism and the Magic World View,* 2d ed. rev. (Salt Lake City: Signature Books, 1998); John L. Brooke, *The Refiner's Fire: The Making of Mormon Cosmology, 1644-1844* (Cambridge, MA: Cambridge University Press, 1994).

14. Steven Fleming, "The Religious Heritage of the British Northwest and the Rise of Mormonism," *Church History* 77 (March 2008): 73-104.

15. Nathan O. Hatch, *The Democratization of American Christianity* (New Haven, CT: Yale University Press, 1989), 59-62, 170-79; Roger Finke and Rodney Stark, "How the Upstart Sects Won America: 1776-1850," *Journal for the Scientific Study of Religion* 28 (Mar. 1989): 27-44. Arminianism, instigated by Dutch Reformed theologian Jacobus Arminius (1560-1609), includes resistible grace, conditional election, and a general atonement, rejecting Calvinist determinism.

16. Leigh Eric Schmidt, *Holy Fairs: Scotland and the Making of American Revivalism,* 2d ed. (Grand Rapids: William B. Eerdmans Publishing, 2001), xiv-xxviii.

17. John H. Wigger, *Taking Heaven by Storm: Methodism and the Rise of Popular Christianity in America* (Urbana: University of Illinois Press, 2001), 104-24. On the controversy of early Methodist healing, see Henry D. Rack, "Doctors, Demons, and Early Methodist Healing," in W. J. Shiels, ed., *The Church and Healing: Papers Read at the ... Ecclesiastical History Society* (Cambridge, England: Crampton & Sons, on behalf of Basil Blackell, Oxford, 1982), 137-52.

18. E. Brooks Holifield, *Health and Medicine in the Methodist Tradition* (New York: Crossroad, 1986), 36, states that Wesley "had not expected the cure and did not look for such cures, because he believed that God did not intervene in accord with 'the will' of men and women." However, he encouraged followers to pray for the sick and noted miraculous outcomes (36-38). The small Reformed Methodists, from which Brigham Young and Heber Kimball converted, criticized the fact that in mainstream Methodism "blessings given

in answer to prayer are suspended upon the condition of faith" (Wesley Bailey, "History of the Reformed Methodist Church," in Israel Daniel Rupp and John Winebrenner, eds., *History of All the Religious Denominations in the United States*, 2d ed. (Harrisburg, PA.: John Winebrenner, V.D.M., 1849), 384.

19. See, e.g., Benjamin Seth Young, *The Testimony of Christ's Second Appearing: Containing a General Statement of All Things Pertaining to the Faith and Practice of the Church of God in this Latter-Day*, 2d ed. rev. (Albany, NY: E. and E. Hosford, 1810), 479, 487. Susan Juster, *Doomsayers: Anglo-American Prophecy in the Age of Revolution* (Philadelphia: University of Pennsylvania Press, 2003), 72-73, notes a few other eighteenth-century examples of healing by touch.

20. Morgan Edwards, *Customs of Primitive Churches* (Philadelphia: N.p., 1768), 94-5; Edwards, *Materials towards a History of the Baptists in Pennsylvania* (Philadelphia: Joseph Crunkshank and Isaac Collins, 1770), 28, 57; Edwards, *Materials towards a History of the Baptists in Jersey* (Philadelphia: Thomas Dobson, 1792), 17-20. See also Shaw, *Miracles in Enlightenment England,* 35, 46-7.

21. For example, Owen Thomas (1692-1760), who was reverend of the influential and prominent Welsh Tract Church in the 1740s, indicated that he had administered the rite only three times (Edwards, *Materials towards a History of the Baptists in Pennsylvania,* 22-3).

22. C. Dirck Keyser, "The Virginia Separate Baptists and Arminianism, 1760-1787," *Virginia Baptist Register,* 1984, 1,110-38; A. H. Newman, *A History of the Baptist Churches in the United States* (New York: Christian Literature Co., 1894), 302.

23. Donald F. Durnbaugh, *Fruit of the Vine: A History of the Brethren, 1708-1995* (Elgin, IL: Brethren Press, 1997), 120; *Minutes of the Annual Meetings of the Church of the Brethren: Containing All Available Minutes from 1778 to 1909* (Elgin, IL: Brethren Publishing House, 1909), 19, 30, 50. The Tunkers were also called the Dunkers and are now typically known as the Old German Baptist Brethren. That they anointed the area of affliction is attested by Edwards, *Customs of Primitive Churches,* 94.

24. Charles Buck, "Unction," in *A Theological Dictionary,* 4th American ed. (Philadelphia: A. Griggs & Dickinson, 1815), 512. Matthew Bowman and Samuel Brown, "The Reverend Buck's Theological Dictionary and the Struggle to Define American Evangelicalism, 1802-1851," *Journal of the Early Republic* (Fall 2009): 441-73, highlights the central role that Buck's dictionary played in defining evangelical consensus in antebellum America.

25. Anderson, *Lucy's Book,* 493. On Joseph's leg surgery, see LeRoy S. Wirthlin, "Nathan Smith (1762-1828), Surgical Consultant to Joseph Smith," *BYU Studies* 17 (Spring 1977): 319-37.

26. Orrin Porter Rockwell's sister recalled that Lucy "doctored many persons in Palmyra" (Mrs. M. C[aroline] R[ockwell] Smith, Statement, Mar. 25,

1885, in Arthur B. Deming, ed., *Naked Truths about Mormonism*, Apr. 1888, 1). Another Palmyra resident said Lucy "knew the virtues of remedial roots and herbs, and was ever ready to administer and assist when her lowly neighbors were sick or dying" (Mrs. Dr. Horace [Anne R. Webster] Eaton, *The Origin of Mormonism* [New York: Woman's Executive Committee of Home Missions, 1881], 3).

27. See Ashurst-McGee, "Pathway to Prophethood," 99-117; cf. Hand, "The Folk Healer."

28. Samuel Brown, "The 'Beautiful Death' in the Smith Family," *BYU Studies* 45/4 (2006): 121-50. Christians of the early republic observed a stylized deathbed ritual, the "good" or "beautiful" death, which focused upon calm acceptance of death and attendance by family and friends who were allowed a window into immortality.

29. Orlando Saunders, interviewed by William H. Kelley and Edmund L. Kelley, Palmyra, New York, Mar. 6, 1881, in Dan Vogel, ed., *Early Mormon Documents*, 5 vols. (Salt Lake City: Signature Books, 1996-2003), 2:85.

30. Richard Lyman Bushman, *Joseph Smith: Rough Stone Rolling* (New York: Alfred A. Knopf, 2005), 30-56.

31. Milton V. Backman, *Joseph Smith's First Vision: Confirming Evidences and Contemporary Accounts*, 2d ed. (Salt Lake City: Bookcraft, 1980), 61-75. For the Smith family's congregational participation, see Bushman, *Rough Stone Rolling*, 36-38.

32. William Smith, interviewed by E. C. Briggs, 1893, in Vogel, *Early Mormon Documents*, 1:512-13.

33. D. Michael Quinn, "Joseph Smith's Experience of a Methodist 'Camp-Meeting' in 1820," posted online for a time at www.dialoguejournal.com, copy in authors' possession.

34. Dean C. Jessee, ed., *The Papers of Joseph Smith*, 2 vols. (Salt Lake City: Deseret Book, 1989-92), 1:273. This excerpt is from Joseph Smith's 1839 history, later canonized in the Pearl of Great Price as JS-H 1:19.

35. The meaning of "endowment" has evolved. Today Mormons employ it to refer to the dramatic ritual performed in temples, but originally it described the conveyance of charismatic power in association with an ordination. Gregory A. Prince, *Power from on High: The Development of Mormon Priesthood* (Salt Lake City: Signature Books, 1994), 15-21, discusses the chronology leading up to the June 1831 conference.

36. Revelation, July 1830, in Robin Scott Jensen, Robert J. Woodford, and Steven C. Harper, eds., *Revelations and Translations: Manuscript Revelation Books*, Joseph Smith Papers series, eds. Dean C. Jessee et al. (Salt Lake City: Church Historian's Press, 2009), 37; D&C 24:13.

37. Revelation, Dec. 7, 1830, in ibid., 65; D&C 35:9.

38. Revelation, Jan. 2, 1831, in ibid., 75; D&C 38:32, 38; Donald Q. Cannon and Lyndon W. Cook, eds., *Far West Record: Minutes of the Church of Jesus Christ of Latter-day Saints, 1830-1844* (Salt Lake City: Deseret Book, 1983), 5.

39. Revelation, Feb. 1831, in Jensen et al., *Manuscript Revelation Books,* 109; D&C 43:16.

40. "Old Testament Manuscript 1" in Scott H. Faulring, Kent P. Jackson, and Robert J. Mathews, *Joseph Smith's New Translation of the Bible: Original Manuscripts* (Provo: BYU Religious Studies Center, 2004), 127; JST Gen. 14:30-31. Sidney Rigdon was the scribe for this portion of the manuscript.

41. John Corrill, *A Brief History of the Church of Christ of Latter Day Saints* (St. Louis: By the author, 1839), 18. Corrill was an active participant in early Mormonism as an official historian but later left the Church and published this volume.

42. Cf. Bruce N. Westergen, ed., *From Historian to Dissident: The Book of John Whitmer* (Salt Lake City: Signature Books, 1995), 69-71; Ezra Booth to editor, Oct. 31, 1831, *Ohio Star,* Nov. 3, 1831, online at "Misc. Ohio Newspapers," *Uncle Dale's Readings in Early Mormon History,* www.sidneyrigdon.com.

43. Jared Carter journal, unpaginated, near June 6, 1831, microfilm of holograph, LDS Church History Library. Ezra Booth, who published an antagonistic commentary on the events of the conference, described the first ordination of the meeting: "[Lyman Wight] was ordained to the gift of tongues, healing the sick, casting out Devils, and discerning spirits; and in like manner he ordained several others"; Booth to editor.

44. In the months leading up to the conference, Joseph Smith purged the Church of what he viewed as false manifestations of the Holy Spirit (fainting, jerking, barking) but simultaneously encouraged what he viewed to be genuine charismatic power like healing (Robert J. Woodford, "The Historical Development of the Doctrine and Covenants," Ph.D. diss., Brigham Young University, 1974, 2:643-47; revelation, Mar. 8, 1831, in Jensen et al., *Manuscript Revelation Books,* 125-9; D&C 46).

45. Newel Knight autobiography, in Vogel, *Early Mormon Documents,* 4:65.

46. We found only two instances of the ritual use of oil, neither of which is reliable: a story from the Erastus Snow family in Andrew Karl Larson, *Erastus Snow: The Life of a Missionary and Pioneer for the Early Mormon Church* (Salt Lake City: University of Utah Press, 1971), 16, repudiated by the account of Milando Pratt in Elden Jay Watson, ed., *The Orson Pratt Journals* (Salt Lake City: By the author, 1975), 502; and a retrospective anonymous account in *Jefferson County Genealogy,* Apr. 11, 2002, 8-10, purporting to be a reprint of "Anointing Bowl Found," *Watertown Daily Times,* Dec. 10, 1898, although the article is not in the newspaper cited. In any case, the article in the latter publication purports to be about a piece of pottery unearthed from the Hill Cumo-

rah and allegedly used to store olive oil for healing blessings, specifically to raise someone from the dead.

47. Jan Shipps and John W. Welch, eds., *The Journals of William E. McLellin, 1831-1836* (Provo and Urbana: BYU Studies and University of Illinois Press, 1994), 45.

48. Revelation, Feb. 9, 1831, Jensen et al., *Manuscript Revelation Books,* 101; D&C 42:44.

49. Revelation, Oct. 29, 1831, in Shipps and Welch, *Journals of William E. McLellin,* 46; D&C 66:9. Note that the headnote to D&C 66 claims that the revelation was delivered on October 25, 1831, at a Church conference. However, McLellin's diary is clear that he transcribed the revelation from Joseph Smith's dictation on October 29, 1831.

50. Shipps and Welch, *Journals of William E. McLellin,* 40, 43, 66, 67, 71, 72, 96, 136, 138.

51. Watson, *Orson Pratt Journals,* 17, 18, 22.

52. See, e.g., Stanley B. Kimball, *Heber C. Kimball: Mormon Patriarch and Pioneer* (Urbana: University of Illinois Press, 1986), 48; Whitney, *Life of Heber C. Kimball,* 178-79; Lycurgus A. Wilson, *Life of David W. Patten, the First Apostolic Martyr* (Salt Lake City: Deseret News, 1900), 8-9.

53. Jonathan A. Stapley and Kristine Wright, "'They Shall Be Made Whole': A History of Baptism for Health," *Journal of Mormon History* 34 (Fall 2008): 69-112.

54. Mark 16:17; Morm. 9:24; revelation, Sept. 22-23, 1832, 1835 D&C 4:11; 1981 D&C 84:65-72; cf. Jensen et al., *Manuscript Revelation Books,* 283.

55. Jonathan A. Stapley and Kristine Wright, "Female Ritual Healing in Mormonism," *Journal of Mormon History* 37 (Winter 2011): 1-85.

56. H. Michael Marquardt, *Early Patriarchal Blessings of the Church of Jesus Christ of Latter-day Saints* (Salt Lake City: Smith-Pettit Foundation, 2007), 36, 47, 56. In all these early blessings, the power to heal was associated with the health of their children.

57. Juanita Leavitt Pulsipher, ed., "History of Sarah Studevant Leavitt (1875)," 9, Ms 62, Special Collections, Marriott Library, University of Utah, Salt Lake City.

58. Dean C. Jessee, Mark Ashurst-McGee, and Richard L. Jensen, eds., *Journals, Vol. 1: 1832-1839,* in the Joseph Smith Papers series, general editors Dean C. Jessee et al. (Salt Lake City: Church Historian's Press, 2008), 98, 68; cf. Feb. 14, 15, 1835, ordinations of the Twelve (Fred C. Collier and William S. Harwell, eds., *Kirtland Council Minute Book* [Hannah, UT: Collier's Publishing, 2002), 72-76). Butler, *Awash in a Sea of Faith,* 245, mistakenly states that Smith adopted an intolerance for healing rituals during this time due to Butler's misreading of Smith's Nov. 17, 1835, diary entry.

59. Consider the quotation of an anonymous letter to the *Ohio Atlas*, Mar. 18, 1836, in "Mormonism," *Painesville Telegraph*, May 20, 1836, 768, and response in [Oliver Cowdery?], "The 'Atlas' Article," *Messenger and Advocate*, Apr. 1836, 303.

60. Jessee et al., *Journals*, 1:167. Joseph F. Darowski, "An Endowment from on High: 1831-1842," paper presented at the Mormon History Association annual meeting, May 2007, Salt Lake City, audio recording in our possession.

61. Benjamin Brown letter, Mar. 27, 1835, in John W. Welch and Erick B. Carlson, eds., *Opening the Heavens: Accounts of Divine Manifestations, 1820-1844* (Provo and Salt Lake City: Brigham Young University Press and Deseret Book, 2005), 336.

62. Scholars frequently refer to the combined Kirtland temple rituals as the "Kirtland endowment" even though the endowment, at the time, was thought to be what came after the rituals, not the rituals themselves. Smith wrote of the meetings: "The brethren continued exhorting, prophesying and speaking in tongues until 5 o clock in the morning—the Saviour made his appearance to some, while angels minestered unto others, and it was a penticost and enduement indeed, long to be remembered" (Jessee et al., *Journals*, 1:207, 215-16).

63. Erastus Snow autobiography, 29-30, in *Selected Collections*, 1:31; also Edward Leo Lyman, Susan Ward Payne, and S. George Ellsworth, eds., *No Place to Call Home: The 1807-1857 Life Writings of Caroline Barnes Crosby, Chronicler of Outlying Mormon Communities* (Logan: Utah State University Press, 2005), 43-44.

64. Anonymous, "Quarterly Conference of the Primary Associations of Weber Stake of Zion, opened at 10 a.m., June 11," *Ogden Daily Herald*, June 11, 1881, 2.

65. The Kirtland temple was frequently the location for patriarchal blessings, Church meetings, and activities where visions, prophecy, and glossolalia were common.

66. Collier and Harwell, *Kirtland Council Minute Book*, 58-59 [Sept. 8, 1834]; Jessee et al., *Journals*, 1:112, 122 [Nov. 28, Dec. 14, 1835].

67. Buck, "Unction," in *A Theological Dictionary*, 512. Mormons used the idea that the heavens were sealed as a foil in responding to critics.

68. Samuel Brown and Matthew Bowman, "Joseph Smith and Charles Buck: Enthusiasm, Common Sense, and the Living Witness of History," paper presented at the Mormon History Association annual meeting, May 24, 2008, Sacramento, California, photocopy in our possession.

69. Collier and Harwell, *Kirtland Council Minute Book*, 58-59; Jessee et al., *Journals*, 1:122.

70. Franklin D. Richards, Feb. 12, 1893, in *Collected Discourses*, ed. Brian

H. Stuy, 5 vols. (Sandy, UT: B.H.S. Publishing, 1987), 3:227-28; also Merle H. Graffon, ed., *Salt Lake School of the Prophets: Minute Book, 1883* (Palm Desert, CA: ULC Press, 1981), 20-21; George A. Smith, Mar. 18, 1855, *Journal of Discourses,* 2:215. Note, however, that the sealing by the laying on of hands was not usually employed. At meetings organized for the purpose, individuals were anointed and the rituals were sealed *en masse* by a presiding authority's prayer, with uplifted hands and shouts of hosanna (e.g., Lyndon W. Cook and Milton V. Backman Jr., eds., *Kirtland Elders' Quorum Record, 1836-1841* [Provo: Grandin Book, 1985], 9, 11, 12, 27, 29).

71. Shipps and Welch, *Journals of William E. McLellin,* 217.

72. *Wilford Woodruff's Journal,* 1:128, 306; Woodruff, *Leaves from My Journal,* 66-67. This is the first mention of anointing the sick in Woodruff's voluminous diaries.

73. Lyman et al., *No Place to Call Home,* 43-44.

74. Marquardt, *Early Patriarchal Blessings,* 73, 104, 147.

75. Ibid., 166. See also Joseph Smith Sr.'s patriarchal blessing to Eda Rogers in 1837, excerpted in Carol Lynn Pearson, *Daughters of Light* (Salt Lake City: Bookcraft, 1973), 65.

76. In her important essay, Linda Newell, "Gifts of the Spirit: Women's Share," 112, makes an unsubstantiated claim that during this period "women were as likely to heal or be healed as were men." Joseph Smith's July 30, 1840, sermon indicates an important shift in that direction: "Furthermore if the Saints are sick or have sickness in their families, and the Elders do not prevail[,] every family should get power by fasting & prayer & anointing with oil & [if they] continue so to do their sick shall be healed[;] this also is the voice of the Spirit" (Andrew F. Ehat and Lyndon Cook, eds., *Words of Joseph Smith: The Contemporary Accounts of the Nauvoo Discourses of the Prophet Joseph* (Provo: BYU Religious Studies Center, 1980), 37. On the elders' institutional mandate to administer healing rituals, see Cook and Backman, *Kirtland Elders' Quorum Record,* 22-23.

77. Anonymous, "A Representative Woman: Mary Isabella Horne," *Woman's Exponent,* June 15, 1882, 9. The author was likely Emmeline B. Wells, who was not in Missouri and hence would have been passing on another woman's memory. See also Augusta Joyce Crocheron, *Representative Women of Deseret: A Book of Biographical Sketches to Accompany the Picture Bearing the Same Title* (Salt Lake City: J. C. Graham & Co., 1884).

78. *Wilford Woodruff's Journal,* 1:235.

79. Joseph Fielding diary, Dec. 16, 1838, microfilm of holograph, LDS Church History Library. Addison Pratt also instructed native women to anoint the sick during his first mission to the Society Islands in 1846 (S. George Ellsworth, ed., *The Journals of Addison Pratt* [Salt Lake City: University of Utah Press, 1990], 292-93).

80. For example, the missionary diary of Orson Pratt, which ends in late 1837, and the Kirtland Elders' Quorum Record include several healings by the laying on of hands only after the institution of the Kirtland temple rituals (Watson, *Journals of Orson Pratt,* 79, 80, 84, 85, 87; Cook and Backman, *Kirtland Elders' Quorum Record,* 20, 22, 41, 43).

81. George D. Smith, ed., *An Intimate Chronicle: The Journals of William Clayton* (Salt Lake City: Signature Books, 1995), 6. This practice endured into the twentieth century.

82. Whitney, *Life of Heber C. Kimball,* 165; Smith, *An Intimate Chronicle,* 31; *Wilford Woodruff's Journal,* 1:409. Kimball appears to have healed by passing along other articles of clothing as well. Mary Ellen Kimball diary, undated entry preceding July 5, 1857, microfilm of holograph, LDS Church History Library.

83. Joseph Smith Sr., patriarchal blessing for Lorenzo Snow, Dec. 15, 1836, MS 1330 1, in *Selected Collections,* 1:31. That Lorenzo healed via handkerchief is attested to in Eliza R. Snow Smith, *Biography and Family Record of Lorenzo Snow* (Salt Lake City: Deseret News Company, 1884), 264-65.

84. Shaw, *Miracles in Enlightenment England,* 64-75; Thomas, *Religion and the Decline of Magic,* 227-35. The use of healing by coffin canes and the cherished handkerchiefs kept by Mormons from the Nauvoo era took on a character similar to Catholic relics. See Heber C. Kimball, Mar. 15, 1857, *Journal of Discourses,* 4:294; Steven G. Barnett, "Canes of the Martyrdom," in James B. Allen, ed., "The Historian's Corner," *BYU Studies* 21, no. 2 (1981): 205-11. We found another individual who was healed by using a cane, described in John Albiston's letter to the editor, Apr. 30, 1848, in the *Millennial Star,* May 15, 1848, 158. For a healing cane carved from a tree used in the Nauvoo temple, see Charles Kelly, ed., *The Journal of John D. Lee, 1846-47 and 1859* (Salt Lake City: University of Utah Press, 1984), 67-8.

85. From the late nineteenth-century Divine Healing movement through Pentacostalism to the present, handkerchiefs have been used to heal the sick. See Michael S. Stephens, *Who Healeth All Thy Diseases: Health, Healing, and Holiness in the Church of God Reformation Movement* (Lanham, MD: Scarecrow Press, 2008), 70n23; Amy Sitar, "Praying for Power: Dispositions and Discipline in the Azusa Street Revival's Apostolic Faith," *Poetics* 36 (2008): 458; R. Marie Griffith, "Material Devotion: Pentecostal Prayer Cloths," *Material History of American Religion Project Newsletter,* Spring 1997, 1-3; Douglas H. Pessoni, *With Healing in His Wings: A Complete and Concise Presentation of God's Healing Gospel,* 3rd ed. (Vancouver, BC: CCB Publishing, 2008), 111.

86. Ashurst-McGee, "Pathway to Prophethood," similarly argues that Smith's involvement in folk magic prepared him for his role as prophet.

87. Minutes and resolutions, July 20, 1833, reported in *Missouri Intelligencer and Boon's Lick Advertiser,* Aug. 10, 1833, qtd. in William Mulder and A. Russell Mortensen, eds., *Among the Mormons: Historic Accounts by Contempo-*

rary Observers (New York: Alfred A. Knopf, 1958), 79. Several Church leaders projected their use of oil for anointing the sick onto the Missourians' critique: George A. Smith, June 20, 1869, Aug. 13, 1871, *Journal of Discourses,* 13:79, 14:212; John Henry Smith, Jan. 16, 1881, reported in the *Deseret News,* Apr. 20, 1881, 178. One missionary wrote in his 1833 diary, "We, at the close of the meeting laid hands on his little children, which appeared to excite some opposition" (John Sims Carter diary, Apr. 13, 1833, microfilm of holograph, LDS Church History Library).

88. J. Spencer Fluhman, "Anti-Mormonism and the Making of Religion in Antebellum America," Ph.D. diss., University of Wisconsin-Madison, 2006, 97-101.

89. Lyman et al., *No Place to Call Home,* 33-34.

90. Abraham H. Cannon diary, Nov. 9, 1893, photocopy of holograph, Perry Special Collections. Cannon summarizes Woodruff's account as part of a conversation with the First Presidency and Twelve.

91. Ibid.; Donna Toland Smart, ed., *Mormon Midwife: The 1846-1888 Diaries of Patty Bartlett Sessions* (Logan: Utah State University Press, 1997), 36; John Doyle Lee journal, Feb. 1846-Aug. 1846, Mar. 14, 1846, microfilm of holograph, LDS Church History Library; Horace K. Whitney journal, Apr. 24, 1846, microfilm of holograph, LDS Church History Library; cf. Helen Mar Whitney, "Our Travels beyond the Mississippi," *Woman's Exponent,* Feb. 1, 1884, 135; Lavina Fielding Anderson, "Mary Fielding Smith: Her Ox Goes Marching On," *Dialogue: A Journal of Mormon Thought* 14 (Winter 1981): 99-100; Luisa Steele Jensen, "The Story of My Grandmother Nancy Bailey Steele," microfilm of typescript, LDS Church History Library; Donald G. Godfrey and Rebecca S. Martineau-McCarty, eds., *An Uncommon Common Pioneer: The Journals of James Henry Martineau, 1828-1918* (Provo: BYU Religious Studies Center, 2008), 130. Walter Murray Gibson wrote to Brigham Young in 1862 about the native Hawaiians' propensity for charismata. In doing so, he noted, "It has been common for native elders to lay hands upon a tired and worn out horse to give him fresh vigor" (Letter, Jan. 16, 1862, Brigham Young Office Files, Box 28, fd. 21, LDS Church History Library, a reference provided by Ardis E. Parshall).

92. Jessee et al., *Journals,* 1:98.

93. This perspective is illustrated by a later sermon by Orson Pratt, Nov. 2, 1873, *Journal of Discourses,* 16:290. On several occasions, Joseph Smith blamed failed healings on lack of faith. See Jessee et al., *Journals,* 1:122, 348; Corrill, *Brief History of the Church of Christ of Latter Day Saints,* 46; Ehat and Cook, *Words of Joseph Smith,* 191-92; Editor, "Physician Heal Thyself," *Times and Seasons,* Sept. 15, 1843, 325-26.

94. Revelation, Feb. 9, 1831, in Jensen et al., *Manuscript Revelation Books,* 65; D&C 42:48-52. On Sept. 29, 1839, Joseph Smith said that "many of the

righteous shall fall a prey to disease to pestilence &c ... by reason of the weakness of the flesh and yet be saved in the kingdom of God[,] [s]o that it is an unhallowed principle to say that such and such have transgressed because they have been preyed upon by disease or death" (Jessee et al., *Journals,* 1:352-53).

95. *Wilford Woodruff's Journal,* 2:153. In 1835 Mormon evangelist Amasa Lyman wrote of a child's funeral invoking providence (Amasa Lyman diary, Sept. 9, 1835, in *Selected Collections,* 1:37).

96. For an overview of antebellum views of divine providence, see Lewis O. Saum, *The Popular Mood of Pre-Civil War America* (Westport, CT: Greenwood Press, 1980), 3-26. See Jonathan R. Baer, "Perfectly Empowered Bodies: Divine Healing in Modernizing America," Ph.D. diss., Yale University, 2002, 49-50, for a treatment of Evangelical theodicean interactions with healing. In relation to infant mortality, see Paula Bernat Bennett, "God's Will, Not Mine: Child Death as a Theodicean Problem in Poetry by Nineteenth-Century American Women," in *Representations of Death in Nineteenth-Century U.S. Writing and Culture,* ed. Lucy E. Frank (Ashgate, England: Ashgate Publishing, 2007), 125-40.

97. Heather D. Curtis, *Faith in the Great Physician: Suffering and Divine Healing in American Culture, 1860-1900* (Baltimore: Johns Hopkins University Press, 2007), 27-34, 40. Even Arminians viewed resignation to suffering as a mark of piety by the 1830s (Holifield, *Health and Medicine in the Methodist Tradition,* 72).

98. Charles E. Rosenberg, "The Therapeutic Revolution: Medicine, Meaning, and Social Change in Nineteenth-Century America," in Morris J. Vogel and Charles E. Rosenberg, eds., *The Therapeutic Revolution: Essays in the Social History of American Medicine* (Philadelphia: University of Pennsylvania Press, 1979), 11.

99. Helen Mar Kimball Whitney, "Life Incidents," *Woman's Exponent,* July 1, 1880, 18. Note that Whitney herself suffered from serious and chronic illness, which forms a constant theme in her journal (Charles M. Hatch and Todd M. Compton, eds., *A Widow's Tale: The 1884-1896 Diary of Helen Mar Kimball Whitney* [Logan: Utah State University, 2003]).

100. Cannon and Cook, *Far West Record,* 96-97.

101. Thomson's botanic medicine was viewed as "sectarian medicine" and championed by the great figures of the Second Awakening. This shift was part of a wider revolt against institutional elites. See Hatch, *The Democratization of American Christianity,* 28-30, 129. Rosenberg, "The Therapeutic Revolution," 3-25, introduces and contextualizes the practices of American physicians during the nineteenth century. Robert T. Divett, "Medicine and the Mormons: A Historical Perspective," *Dialogue: A Journal of Mormon Thought* 12 (Fall 1979): 16-25, outlines Mormonism's interaction with these medical trends.

102. See, e.g., Oliver Cowdery to Dr. S. Avord [Samson Avard], Dec. 15,

1835, Oliver Cowdery Letter Book, Henry E. Huntington Library, San Marino, CA:

> I made inquiry on the subject of your coming to this place to establish yourself as a Botanic Physician. We are a people who design living near the Lord, that our bodies may be healed when we are sick, for a general rule, though our faith is yet weak, being young, weak and surrounded by a wicked enticing world—When, however, we have need of an earthly physician, and in many instances we have, we call upon our highly esteemed friend and brother Dr. F. G. Williams, universally known through this country as an eminent and skilful man. I may say in short, he is also a Botanic Physician—which course of practice is generally approved by us.

103. Revelation, Feb. 9, 1831, in Jensen et al., *Manuscript Revelation Books*, 101; cf., D&C 42:48-52. An excellent example is Joseph Smith's unsuccessful administration because the sick individual's "faith was not sufficient to effect, a cure," after which Emma administered a botanic cure (Jessee et al., *Journals*, 1:122. For a more in-depth treatment, see Lester E. Bush Jr., *Health and Medicine among the Latter-day Saints: Science, Sense, and Scripture* (New York: Crossroad, 1993), 89-93; N. Lee Smith, "Herbal Remedies: God's Medicine?" *Dialogue: A Journal of Mormon Thought* 12 (Fall 1979): 37-60.

104. For example, Thomas Gregg, *History of Hancock County* (Chicago: Chas. C. Chapman & Co., 1880), 374-75, printed an account of "I. R. Tull, Esq., of Pontoosuc" who related:

> In the fall of 1843 I went to Nauvoo to buy calves, and called on a blind man who had one to sell. I bought his calf, and being curious to learn his history, went in and saw his wife, with two little twin infants in a cradle, and great destitution. He told me that he had a nice home in Massachusetts, which gave them a good support. But one of the Mormon elders preaching in that country called on him and told him if he would sell out and go to Nauvoo, the prophet would open his eyes and restore his sight. And he sold out, and had come to the city, and had spent all his means, and was now in great need. I asked why the prophet did not open his eyes. He replied that Joseph had informed him that he could not open his eyes until the temple was finished, and then when the temple was finished he would open them, and he should see better than before! And he believed, and was waiting patiently for the last stroke to be made on the temple.

Joseph Smith took Emma to the temple for her health, and people were generally known to seek healing there (Jessee, *The Papers of Joseph Smith*, 2: 490; Gregory R. Knight, ed., "Journal of Thomas Bullock [1816-1885]: 31 August 1845 to 5 July 1846," *BYU Studies* 31 [Winter 1991]: 70). For a period, Brigham Young administered to the sick at the temple daily (Brigham Young Office Journal, July 12, 1845, photocopy of manuscript, Brigham Young Papers, MS 0566, Marriot Library).

105. For a complete history of baptism for health, see Stapley and Wright, "'They Shall Be Made Whole.'"

106. Joseph Smith, conference minutes, *Times and Seasons,* Apr. 15, 1842, 763. Note that soon after this sermon, Joseph started baptizing for health outside the temple, a practice that soon became normative.

107. "An Epistle of the Twelve, Nauvoo, October 12, 1841," *Times and Seasons,* Oct. 15, 1841, 569. For the allusion to troubling the waters, see John 5:4.

108. See, e.g., *Wilford Woodruff's Journal,* 2:138, 175, 177; Willard Richards journal, Apr. 15, 16, 27, 28, 1843, in *Selected Collections,* 1:31.

109. Nauvoo Relief Society minutes, Apr. 19, 1842, in *Selected Collections,* 1:19. After that same meeting, "Mrs. [Abigail] Leonard was administered to for the restoration of health by Councillors Cleveland & Whitney."

110. Beyond Jesus's explicit teaching that the signs following true believers included their laying hands on the sick to heal, Joseph Smith also gave a lengthy sermon on "signs," a code word for rituals, just a month earlier. He noted that the "sign of the healing of the sick" was the laying on of hands (*Wilford Woodruff's Journal,* 2:161-62). A splendid example of this phenomenon is the 1843 healing of a child by Jane Manning James, an African American convert (Jane Manning James autobiography, 2-3, microfilm of typescript, LDS Church History Library).

111. Nauvoo Relief Society minutes, Apr. 28, 1842; Ehat and Cook, *The Words of Joseph Smith,* 114-19. See also Jessee, *Papers of Joseph Smith,* 2:378-79, an entry from the Book of the Law of the Lord. As Mormons now base their healing liturgy on priesthood authority, it is hard to understand a time when it was not (see *Wilford Woodruff's Journal,* 2:162, 267). However, even in Smith's day some questioned the propriety of female ritual healing and whether the Relief Society was infringing on the role of a bishop in ministering to the poor (Jill Mulvay Derr, Maureen Ursenbach Beecher, and Janath Russell Cannon, *Women of Covenant: The Story of Relief Society* [Salt Lake City: Deseret Book, 1992], 32).

112. Jessee, *Papers of Joseph Smith,* May 1, 1842, 2:379. This entry is also from the Book of the Law of the Lord and summarizes Smith's sermon about the "keys of the kingdom" or "certain signs" being necessary "to be endued with power."

113. Joseph Smith's discourse, May 1, 1842, recorded by Oliver Olney, in Ehat and Cook, *The Words of Joseph Smith,* 1996.

114. "Minutes of a Special Conference," *Times and Seasons,* Sept. 15, 1843, 331-32.

115. Marquardt, *Early Patriarchal Blessings,* 222.

116. James E. Faust, *To Reach Even unto You* (Salt Lake City: Deseret Book, 1980), 82. Note that in modern Mormon parlance, *soul* refers to one's physical existence. For scholarly treatments of the Mormon temple liturgy, see Andrew F. Ehat, "Joseph Smith's Introduction of Temple Ordinances and the 1844

Mormon Succession Question," M.A. thesis, Brigham Young University, 1982; David John Buerger, *The Mysteries of Godliness: A History of Mormon Temple Worship* (San Francisco: Smith Research Associates, 1994).

117. Boyd K. Packer, *The Holy Temple* (Salt Lake City: Bookcraft, 1980), 4.

118. D. Michael Quinn, "Latter-day Saint Prayer Circles," *BYU Studies* 19 (Fall 1978): 79-105.

119. As an antecedent, when the elders of the Church in Kirtland received their temple anointings, leaders organized them for supplication and on February 1, 1836, "petitions were presented for prayers in behalf of those who were sick" (Cook and Backman, *Kirtland Elders' Quorum Record,* 5, 6, 8).

120. Stanley B. Kimball, ed., *On the Potter's Wheel: The Diaries of Heber C. Kimball* (Salt Lake City: Signature Books, 1987), 125, 218; Smith, *An Intimate Chronicle,* 218. Consecrating oil at prayer circles continued well into the Utah period. See, e.g., *Wilford Woodruff's Journal,* 5:229; John Pulsipher, *A Short Sketch of John Pulsipher* (N.p.: N.p., 1970), 34; Donald G. Godfrey and Brigham Y. Card, eds., *The Diaries of Charles Ora Card: The Canadian Years, 1886-1903* (Salt Lake City: University of Utah Press, 1993), 426. William B. Smart, *Mormonism's Last Colonizer: The Journals of William H. Smart, April 11, 1898-October 24, 1937,* CD-ROM (Logan: Utah State University Press, 2008), Jan. 27, Feb. 23, 1901, included with the book, *Mormonism's Last Colonizer: The Life and Times of William H. Smart.*

121. Kimball, *On the Potter's Wheel,* 123, 125, 129. Adaptations of this practice are seen in the Utah period. See, e.g., Lucy Meserve Smith to George A. Smith, Apr. 19, 1851, in *Selected Collections,* 1:33; Oliver B. Huntington diary, Jan. 27, 1887, 159-61, holograph, Perry Special Collections.

122. Heber C. Kimball, Dec. 27, 1857, in *Journal of Discourses,* 6:191; Andrew Ehat, ed., "'They Might Have Known That He Was Not a Fallen Prophet': The Nauvoo Journal of Joseph Fielding," *BYU Studies* 19 (Winter 1979): 160; Joseph F. Smith, comp., "Sealings and Adoption, 1846-1857," 561-62, microfilm 183374, Special Collections, LDS Family History Library.

123. Lyman et al., *No Place to Call Home,* 64-65.

124. The precise formulations for these healing rituals are not extant; however, texts written over sixty years later are similar to the temple ritual. Relief Society women later claimed that Joseph Smith taught them to wash and anoint the sick (Stapley and Wright, "Female Ritual Healing in Mormonism"). Whether or not these are homologous, men and women were washed for their health both inside and outside of Utah temples (Stapley and Wright, "'They Shall Be Made Whole,'" 88-95).

125. Helen Mar Kimball, "Scenes from Nauvoo, and Incidents from H. C. Kimball's Journal," *Woman's Exponent,* Aug. 15, 1883, 42. Note that this serialized episode is an excerpt from the Heber C. Kimball diary, Dec. 28, 1845,

kept by William Clayton (see also Devery S. Anderson and Gary James Bergera, eds., *The Nauvoo Endowment Companies, 1845-1846: A Documentary History* [Salt Lake City: Signature Books, 2005], 210). Two days later, one of the children, Brigham Willard C. Kimball, was included in the temple prayer for his sickness (233). We cannot find earlier accounts of a washing and anointing for health. Men and women administered together as part of the Quorum of the Anointed (Willard Richards diary, June 26, July 9, 1845, holograph, in *Selected Collections,* 1:31; Kimball, *On the Potter's Wheel,* 105).

126. See, e.g., Douglass James Davies, *The Mormon Culture of Salvation: Force, Grace and Glory* (Aldershot, England: Ashgate Publishing, 2000), 84-112; M. Guy Bishop, "To Overcome the 'Last Enemy': Early Mormon Perceptions of Death," *BYU Studies* 26 (Summer 1986): 63-79; Samuel Brown, "Joseph Smith's Death Conquest: Sacerdotal Genealogy and the Great Chain of Being," paper presented at the American Academy of Religion meeting, Nov. 18, 2006, Washington, D.C.

127. See, e.g., Pratt, *Autobiography of Parley Parker Pratt,* 325.

128. Newel Knight, Autobiography and Journal, 1846, unnumbered pages, 96-97, microfilm of holograph, LDS Church History Library; "History of Wilford Woodruff," 93; Woodruff, *Leaves from My Journal,* 78-79; *Wilford Woodruff's Journal,* 5:53; Levi James Taylor, Pleasant Green Taylor Family Record, 1917, 5-6, microfilm of typescript, LDS Church History Library; William G. Hartley, *My Best for the Kingdom: History and Autobiography of John Lowe Butler, a Mormon Frontiersman* (Salt Lake City: Aspen Books, 1993), 114, 452n49.

129. Scott H. Faulring, ed., *An American Prophet's Record: The Diaries and Journals of Joseph Smith,* 2d ed. (Salt Lake City: Signature Books, 1989), July 27, 1843, 400.

130. Margaret McIntire Burgess, "Mothers in Israel," *Relief Society Magazine,* Jan. 1918, 14.

131. Jessee, *The Papers of Joseph Smith,* Oct. 5, 1842, 2:486; Lucy Walker Kimball autobiography, n.d., 7, microfilm of typescript, LDS Church History Library.

132. Elizabeth [Ann Smith] Whitney, "A Leaf from an Autobiography," *Woman's Exponent,* Nov. 15, 1878, 91; Anonymous, "In Memoriam," *Woman's Exponent,* June 1, 1879, 251.

133. Brigham Young sermon, Apr. 9, 1844, Thomas Bullock account, in *Selected Collections,* 1:18. The speech was edited for Joseph Smith et al., *History of the Church of Jesus Christ of Latter-day Saints,* ed. B. H. Roberts, 7 vols., 2d ed. rev. (Salt Lake City: Deseret Book, 1948), 6:322.

134. Emmeline B. Wells, "Relief Society Memories," *Relief Society Bulletin,* May 1914, 4-5.

135. Kimball, *On the Potter's Wheel,* 122.

136. See, e.g., John Smith's patriarchal blessing for Lydia Snow, in William Snow autobiography, 35, digital copy of holograph, Perry Special Collections; John Smith patriarchal blessing for Loenza A. Kingsbury, in Joseph C. Kingsbury diaries, Feb. 19, 1847, 34-36, digital copy of holograph, Perry Special Collections; John Smith patriarchal blessing for Cathrine Campbell Steele, in Irene M. Bates and E. Gary Smith, *Lost Legacy: The Mormon Office of Presiding Patriarch* (Urbana: University of Illinois Press, 1996), 117.

137. Bathsheba B. Smith to George A. Smith, Oct. 12, 1842, qtd. in Kenneth W. Godfrey, Audrey M. Godfrey, and Jill Mulvay Derr, eds., *Women's Voices: An Untold History of the Latter-day Saints, 1830-1900* (Salt Lake City: Deseret Book, 1982), 122.

138. See, e.g., J. B. Turner, *Mormonism in All Ages: Or the Rise, Progress, and Causes of Mormonism* (New York: Platt and Peters, 1842), 290-97.

139. On the Mormon use of the "witness of history," see Brown and Bowman, "Joseph Smith and Charles Buck." For an example of the deflection of criticisms regarding miraculous healings in 1846 Wales, see Ronald D. Dennis, ed. and trans., *Prophet of the Jubilee* (Provo: BYU Religious Studies Center, 1997), 24-28, 70-78, 107-19, 128-31, 156-60.

140. W. W. Phelps to William Smith, Dec. 25, 1844, *Times and Seasons*, Jan. 1, 1844, 759. See also Brigham Young sermon, Apr. 6, 1845, *Selected Collections*, 1:18. While some might point to holy wells in Europe as an antecedent to baptism for health, Latter-day Saints clearly drew from salvific baptism and contextualized it biblically. Smith may have nevertheless blessed one well for healing. See Harriet A. Preston, "A Moment of Peace," *Relief Society Magazine*, Jan. 1920, 19; Alexandra Walsham, "Reforming the Waters: Holy Wells and Healing Springs in Protestant England," in *Life and Thought in the Northern Church, ca.1100-ca.1700*, ed. Diana Wood (Woodbridge, England: Ecclesiastical History Society/Boydell Press, 1999), 237-55; Judith F. Champ, "Bishop Millner, Hollywell, and the Cure Tradition," in *The Church and Healing*, 135-64.

141. Ann Taves, *Fits, Trances, and Visions: Experiencing Religion and Explaining Experience from Wesley to James* (Princeton, NJ: Princeton University Press, 1999), 183, with the rhetoric of spiritualist A. J. Davis to this effect.

142. Fred C. Collier, ed., *The Office Journal of President Brigham Young, 1858-1863, Book D* (Hannah, UT: Collier's Publishing, 2006), 83.

143. Fred C. Collier, ed., *The Nauvoo High Council Minute Book* (Hannah, UT: Collier's Publishing, 2005), Mar. 11, 1843, 103.

144. Ronald O. Barney, ed., *The Mormon Vanguard Brigade of 1847: Norton Jacob's Record* (Logan: Utah State University Press, 2005), 193-94.

145. George A. Smith, "Memoirs of George A. Smith," 348, July 18, 1846, MS 1322, Box 1, fd 2, in *Selected Collections*, 1:32; Barney, *Mormon Vanguard Brigade of 1847*, 211-12.

146. Journal History, Aug. 7, 1847, 1, in *Selected Collections,* 2:1; George A. Smith, "Memoirs of George A. Smith," 361, Aug. 6-7, 1846; Barney, *Mormon Vanguard Brigade of 1847,* 238.

147. For other examples of men administering washing and anointings for the sick on the trail, see Kelly, *Journals of John D. Lee,* 95; Job Smith, Diary and Autobiography, 1849-77, 23-5, digital copy of holograph, Perry Special Collections. For examples of baptism for health on the trail, see Stapley and Wright, "'They Shall Be Made Whole,'" 83-86. For examples of healing prayer circles, see Juanita Brooks, ed., *On the Mormon Frontier: The Diaries of Hosea Stout,* 2 vols. (Salt Lake City: University of Utah Press, 1964), 1:170; Samuel W. Richards diary, Sept. 12, 1846, microfilm of holograph, Perry Special Collections. Richards was in New York, having gone east on a mission while the body of the Church moved west.

148. Besides the examples of female ritual administrations contained in this section, see Maureen Ursenbach Beecher, ed., *The Personal Writings of Eliza Roxcy Snow* (1995; rpt., Logan: Utah State University Press, 2000), 151, 176, 181, 190, 208, 209; Smart, *Mormon Midwife,* 81, 83, 84, 93, 100, 102, 103; Sarah De Armon Pea Rich, *Journal* (Provo: Brigham Young University, 1960), 53-54; Helen Mar Whitney, "Scenes and Incidents at Winter Quarters," *Woman's Exponent,* Dec. 1, 15, 1885, 98, 106.

149. The bishop's census indicated that of the 3,483 inhabitants at Winter Quarters, 386 were sick. See Brooks, *On the Mormon Frontier,* 1:219. Richard Bennett, *Mormons at the Missouri: Winter Quarters, 1846-1852* (Norman: University of Oklahoma Press, 1987), 131-47, contextualizes the degree of sickness, mortality, and suffering in Winter Quarters.

150. S. George Ellsworth, *The History of Louisa Barnes Pratt: Mormon Missionary Widow and Pioneer* (Logan: Utah State University Press, 1998), 87.

151. Anonymous, "A Venerable Woman: Presendia Lathrop Kimball," *Woman's Exponent,* June 1, 1883, 2.

152. See comments on the union of faith through healing in Lucy Meserve Smith to George A. Smith, Apr. 19, 1851, qtd. in Jill Mulvay Derr, "'Strength in Our Union': The Making of Mormon Sisterhood," in *Sisters in Spirit: Mormon Women in Historical and Cultural Perspective*, eds. Maureen Ursenbach Beecher and Lavina Fielding Anderson (Urbana: University of Illinois Press, 1992), 167. See also Helen Whitney's description of an 1855 "union of faith" as she and men healed together (Hatch and Compton, *A Widow's Tale,* 71).

153. The diversity of spiritual administrations was not limited to adults. Sarah G. Richards wrote that in Winter Quarters,

> There were about a dozen or 15 [children] sitting there, and two or three grown persons ... Soon however I saw one of the little boys (there were none over 14 years old ...) rose from his seat and went to another ... put his hands on his head and began to say something to him ... then he turned off and

spoke in tongues a few minutes then went to his seat ... One of the little boys went over and put his hands on the head of Brother Joseph Young, Senr and he was so much moved with the action even before the interpretation was given that tears coursed each other down his cheeks bedewing his venerable beard" (Sarah G. Richards to Zina D. H. Young, July-Dec. 1889, qtd. in Martha Sonntag Bradley and Mary Brown Firmage Woodward, *Four Zinas: A Story of Mothers and Daughters on the Mormon Frontier* [Salt Lake City: Signature Books, 2000], 162-63).

154. George D. Smith, *An Intimate Chronicle,* 221. Note that Smith's reference to a quorum refers to the Quorum of the Anointed, the organization he set up to administer temple rituals to men and women.

155. For instance, midwife Patty Sessions anointed and laid hands on the sick and suffering with her husband, David (Smart, *Mormon Midwife,* 75, 78, 180, 208). When Sessions wrote that "we" laid hands on the sick, she may have meant women or men and women together (79, 81, 93; see also Beecher, *The Personal Writings of Eliza Roxcy Snow,* 180).

156. Smart, *Mormon Midwife,* 75.

157. See, e.g., John Lyman Smith diary, June 10, 1855, digital copy of holograph, Perry Special Collections; Robert Glass Cleland and Juanita Brooks, eds., *A Mormon Chronicle: The Diaries of John D. Lee, 1848-1876,* 2 vols. (San Marino, Calif.: Huntington Library, 2003), 1:221; Godfrey and Martineau-McCarty, *An Uncommon Common Pioneer,* 44; Thomas Searles Terry diary, July 14, 1857, LDS Church History Library; Donald G. Godfrey and Kenneth W. Godfrey, eds., *The Diaries of Charles Ora Card: The Utah Years, 1871-1886* (Provo: BYU Religious Studies Center, 2006), 135; Donald G. Godfrey and Brigham Y. Card, eds., *The Diaries of Charles Ora Card: The Canadian Years, 1886-1903* (Salt Lake City: University of Utah Press, 1993), 194, 196; L. W. Macfarlane, *Yours Sincerely, John M. Macfarlane* (Salt Lake City: L. W. Macfarlane, 1980): 277; Kym Ney, ed., Allen Russell Autobiography and Journal, typescript, July 1, 1894; June 10, 15, 17, 27, 1896; Apr. 2, 1905; Mar. 22, 1907, holograph in possession of Brandon Gull; [Joseph F. Smith], "Editors' Table," a sermon at the funeral of Joseph H. Grant, *Improvement Era,* Feb. 1918, 354.

158. Stapley and Wright, "They Shall Be Made Whole," Figure 2, 96.

159. Andrew Ferguson diaries, Nov. 11, 1854, digital copy of holograph, Perry Special Collections.

160. See, e.g., Ellsworth, *Journals of Addison Pratt,* 215-16, 278-79, 292-93, 478.

161. Ellsworth, *History of Louisa Barnes Pratt,* 128.

162. While physical healing is no longer performed in temples, it was an important function of temples through the past two centuries (Stapley and Wright, "They Shall Be Made Whole").

163. John Smith patriarchal blessing for Lydia Snow, in William Snow autobiography, 35. Cf., John Smith patriarchal blessing for Jennetta Richards, Jan. 22, 1845, Knecht family records, cited in Irene M. Bates, "Patriarchal Blessings and the Routinization of Charisma," *Dialogue: A Journal of Mormon Thought* 26 (Fall 1993): 19-20.

A Uniform and Common Recollection
Joseph Smith's Legacy, Polygamy, and Public Memory, 1852-2002

Stephen C. Taysom

An Introduction to Historical Consciousness

Historians have long doubted that it is possible to recount the past by just telling it "as it really was."[1] The process of researching, selecting, and emplotting historical evidence within a narrative structure is idiosyncratic and may be employed to further a host of goals. Within communities, history represents a way of appropriating the past in order to serve the needs of the present. Maurice Halbwachs's[2] work emphasized the role history plays as the "collective memory" of a community. Halbwachs argued that "no memory is possible outside frameworks used by the people living in society to determine and retrieve their recollections."[3] This process involves the retention of useful historical emplotment points coupled with the suppression of evidence which threatens to undermine a community's structures.

Halbwachs views collective memory as a social process that "express[es] the general attitude of the group; [it] not only reproduce[s] [the group's] history but also define[s] its nature and its qualities and weaknesses."[4] As will be argued below, this process is much more complicated than simply reproducing the past. Indeed, the process of creating a historical consciousness, or public memory, derives from a variety of impulses designed to serve the immediate needs of the community;

the need to capture the past for its own sake is not important to the functional creation of historical consciousness.

Religious communities in particular tend to be quite rigid regarding their official interpretations of the past. Halbwachs noted:

> [W]hat is peculiar to the memory of religious groups is that, while the memories of other groups permeate each other mutually and tend to correspond, the memory of religious groups claims to be fixed once and for all. It either obliges others to adapt themselves to its dominant representations, or it systematically ignores them; contrasting its own permanence with the instability of others, it relegates them to an inferior rank.[5]

As this paper will show, this process becomes even more complicated when the memories of religious groups present a challenge to the same groups' current situations. Then they too must find a way to reinterpret the past.

While Halbwachs's approach is useful, it does have limitations, including the idea that a collective memory can be forgotten. The research presented here indicates that communities often construct a historical consciousness, or public memory,[6] in which a certain emplotment scheme is agreed upon or enforced by a group of elites but which exists in tension with competing public and private memory systems.

The idea of emplotment is borrowed from Hayden White. He argues that "historical discourse should not be regarded as a mirror image of the set of events that it claims simply to describe." Rather, it should be viewed as "a given set of events, arranged more or less chronologically but encoded so as to appear as phases of a process with a discernible beginning, middle, and end, [which] may be emplotted as a Romance, Comedy, Tragedy, Epic, or what have you, depending upon the valences assigned to different events in the series as elements of recognizable archetypal story-forms."[7] While no attempt will be made to classify the public memories in this article as specific story forms, my idea of historical consciousness depends upon the theory, articulated by White, that events are selected, arranged, and emplotted rather than "discovered and recovered." Historian James Deetz made a similar observation when he wrote, "[W]hat we do is construct [rather than reconstruct] the past, and in so doing, decide what is important and what is not. ... [S]uch constructions invariably reflect the values and biases [I would add goals] of the time they were written."[8] The most important point here is that history and the past are not the same thing. The literal past is completely inaccessible; it is fixed and unchangeable. History is fluid, malleable, infinitely changeable, and open to a myriad of potentially conflicting interpretations.

The theory of historical consciousness developed here consists of six basic elements. First, as is the case with collective memory, a discourse develops from which certain historical elements are dropped and others emphasized. Second—and this is where my thinking diverges from Halbwachs's—the community does not literally forget its own past. Rather, it agrees upon an official narrative in tension with the public memories of other communities and private memories of individuals. Third, when the historical narrative is brought from above, institutional sanctions are often imposed upon those who openly criticize or seek to undermine the discourse, while at the same time rewards are parceled out to those who reinforce the approved consciousness. Fourth, historical consciousness is both functional and heavily presentist. In other words, the narrative is designed to serve the needs of the community at the time as defined by the controlling parties. Thus, the emplotment points of the narrative shift as the needs of the community change. This approach often puts the creators of the history at odds with liberal or intellectual forces which profess to find the value of history in studying the past "for its own sake" rather than seeking to further the goals of community elites. Fifth, historical consciousness is defined in many ways by what is left out of the narrative; these remnants are frequently emplotted in counter-narratives which function as public histories for competing communities. Finally, people may inhabit multiple communities simultaneously and in the process partake of multiple, discrete, and sometimes competing narratives. Attempts by such individuals to harmonize the varying public memories are often met by resistance from elites who seek to punish such behavior.

This paper is, more particularly, a study of how one community, the Church of Jesus Christ of Latter-day Saints, has constructed and reconstructed a historical consciousness of its past. The object is to apply the principles described above to the creation of memory within various Mormon communities on the issue of plural marriage. While polygamy is the general issue around which this article revolves, the historical narratives that emerge from this context touch on a wide range of issues, not all of which may be dealt with here. Among these are the ownership of history, the need to appropriate and carefully sculpt the image of the founder, the role of women, the part played by popular culture, and the importance of public history (especially historic sites) in the construction of historical consciousness.

We will begin by recounting the so-called facts relative to the Mormon doctrine of plural marriage and its demise, followed by an exploration of the creation of related narratives and how public memories have changed from 1852 to the present.

Emplotment Points: 1820-1890

According to Joseph Smith, it was in the spring of 1820 when he first saw God. Confused by the "war of words and tumult of opinions" raging among various revival groups in and around his home in western New York state, he retired to a stand of trees near his family's farm to ask God which Church was right. What happened next has been narrated in a number of different ways but the story is consistent on several points. Depending on the account, either God the Father or Jesus Christ—or in the official account, both—appeared to Smith, indicated that his sins were forgiven, and told him not to join any Church because "all religious denominations were believing incorrect doctrines, and none of them was acknowledged of God as his church and kingdom."[9]

This experience had little noticeable impact on Smith's life at first, as he continued the pursuits of a teenager in a poor farm family for the next three years. In 1823 he again recorded an experience with the divine in which this time an angel told him of a book buried in a hill near his home. The book, he said, contained the text of what is known as the Book of Mormon, which he translated "by the gift and power of God" between 1827 and 1830. On April 6, 1830, he and six followers organized the Church of Christ (later renamed the Church of Jesus Christ of Latter-day Saints) in Fayette, New York.

Over the course of the next fourteen years, his Church grew to include tens of thousands of members, many immigrating thousands of miles over land and sea to gather with the Church. During this period, the sect's headquarters moved from New York to Ohio to Missouri and—following its violent expulsion from Missouri—to a small town on the Mississippi River in west-central Illinois. Smith dubbed this city Nauvoo, and from his arrival there in 1839 until his murder in nearby Carthage in 1844, he introduced new doctrines which inspired and enraged the religious and non-religious alike. Among these was the doctrine of "plurality of wives."

A central tenet of the Mormon faith, under which other doctrines can be categorized, is the premise of a restoration of ancient forms. Smith believed that God had called him to restore ancient religion, including the practices of the Old Testament patriarchs. Among the practices this belief imposed on adherents was a commitment to polygamy. Early in his prophetic career, Smith demonstrated an intense interest in the Bible, undertaking what he called an inspired revision of King James's text in the summer of 1830. As he worked on rewriting the Bible, Smith was confused by the contradiction between the Bible's injunction against adultery and the practice of polygamy among some Old Testament figures. Following his usual course, Smith asked God for clarification on the matter. The answer, referred to as the "revelation on plural marriage," was committed to paper in July 1843, although Smith apparently had been practicing this style of marital relationship from the early or mid-1830s.[10]

The document Smith produced announced that Abraham and other ancient patriarchs were under no condemnation for having taken "many wives and concubines" because "the Lord commanded it."[11] As part of the restoration, Smith was then commanded to enter into this practice, something he later claimed he was reluctant to do. He kept the practice private until the early 1840s when he introduced it to several key advisors. He used their reactions to his secret to gauge their loyalty. Some resisted, including his first wife, Emma, for whom the actual text of the document cited above was written out in a losing attempt to convince Emma the doctrine was of God.

Joseph's clerk wrote that when Emma was presented with the

revelation, "she did not believe a word of it and appeared very rebellious," a turn of events that "much troubled" Joseph.[12] She vacillated throughout the early 1840s, variously refusing to countenance even the thought of plural marriage and at other times participating in her husband's marriage ceremonies. One thing is clear: she knew that her husband taught and practiced polygamy during his lifetime, a fact that would later carry great importance.

In the 1840s, Smith introduced a new mix of doctrines closely related to plural marriage and centered on what came to be known as the temple endowment. This ceremony represented (and continues to represent) a process of initiation in which faithful Mormons are instructed in what they believe are the most sacred rituals connecting God and man. The ultimate goal of these rituals is to guide the participants along the path to godhood.[13] The 1840s marked a major shift in Mormon cosmology. Previous teachings through the 1830s, including those found in the Book of Mormon, were similar to those of other Protestant sects of the time, the major difference being not the message but the delivery: Mormons believed God continued to communicate with people on the earth and that the canon was not closed; but beyond that, they preached a straightforward brand of Protestant Christianity.

The introduction of the endowment rites and plural marriage at Nauvoo changed everything. At first, Smith kept these teachings close to the vest and said the public fiction—the rumors of polygamy—amounted to "false epithets and charges." As late as 1844, people stood trial in Nauvoo for "falsely" charging Smith with this practice.[14] Before the Mormon prophet could fully explore and develop all the theological implications of these new teachings, he and his brother Hyrum were murdered while in jail at Carthage, Illinois. Following some confusion, the Church eventually came under the control of the Quorum of the Twelve Apostles, headed by Brigham Young, who had come to fully embrace the doctrine of plural marriage.

Brigham Young and Smith's widow, Emma Smith, had never cared for one another. In the months following Smith's murder, the tension between the two became palpable. Emma regarded her husband's successor as a profane, loutish brute, while he accused her of being a greedy, conniving thorn in the side of the Church. While the situation in Nauvoo grew bleaker, Emma and Brigham quarreled at every opportunity, wrestling over Joseph's estate, for instance, and engendering even deeper feelings of bitterness. In late 1845 when Nauvoo faced invasion by armed groups laying siege to the city, Young decided to lead his followers to the uncharted west and abandon the city. In February 1846 the first company struggled across the frozen Mississippi River toward Iowa and from there to the Great Basin where Young intended to rebuild the Mormon promised land, this time in the American West. Noticeably absent from the pioneering party were Emma Smith and her children, who remained in Nauvoo.

By 1852, Young had made considerable progress in taming the wilds of what became Utah Territory. In August that year, safely ensconced behind the Wasatch Mountains, Young directed apostle Orson Pratt to announce at general conference that plural marriage had become an important element of LDS doctrine. The chief design of this principle, Pratt said in this public discourse, was for a "numerous and faithful posterity to be raised up and taught in the principles of righteousness and truth."[15] Throughout the remainder of the nineteenth century, polygamy grew in importance until it came to be regarded as the centerpiece of Mormon theology. By the 1870s, the U.S. government had had enough of what it considered to be the "immoral" conduct of the Mormons and exerted legal pressure for them to abandon it. The Edmunds Act (1882) and the Edmunds-Tucker Act (1887) disenfranchised Mormon women, disincorporated the Church, and confiscated Church property valued at more than $50,000.[16]

In 1890, after nearly a decade of living "on the underground" to hide from U.S. marshals, Mormon President Wilford Woodruff, prompted by prophetic visions, came to the conclusion that Utah statehood and the future ability of the Church to own and operate temples depended upon the abolition of plural marriage. In September of that year, he issued a declaration known as the Manifesto.

That is the skeleton story. Now let's consider how these events have been emplotted to construct public memories.

Public Memory Phase 1, 1852-1890: The RLDS Challenge

In 1860, Joseph Smith's oldest son, Joseph Smith III, then twenty-eight years old, agreed to assume leadership over a group of former Mormons who had rejected human divinization and plural marriage. This group, officially the Reorganized Church of Jesus Christ of Latter-Day Saints, maintained that the elder Joseph Smith had not had anything to do with temple rites or plural marriage. They charged that Brigham Young had invented these blasphemies after Smith's death. Emma was still bitter about her late husband's polygamous relationships and Young's appropriation of her late husband's role as president of the Church. She told her children that their father was innocent of the charges by the apostolic upstart, a position she maintained until the end of her life. For instance, in 1876 a Mormon from Utah traveled east to pay Emma a visit, and during their conversation he asked if Joseph had "any more wives than you" and if she believed "he received the revelation of plural marriage." To both queries, she responded, "not to my knowledge."[17]

As president of the RLDS Church, Joseph Smith III actively preached against Brigham Young and the Utah Church, charging Young with soiling the good name of the Church founder by associating him with these odd doctrines. In the RLDS newspaper and in public speeches, the younger Smith and his associates continually strove to separate his father from the Brighamite heresies being practiced with abandon in Utah. In the process, they created a public memory in which Joseph Smith Jr. had had nothing to do with the doctrinal innovations of the 1840s. The RLDS public memory effectively froze Mormon history in 1839 before the troublesome doctrines of the Nauvoo period appeared. As early as 1855, Joseph Smith III asserted that "the Mormons of Salt Lake City are not the Mormons of my father's faith. They teach doctrines which are bound to carry those believing [in them] and practicing them to eventual destruction, but my father never taught or believed them."[18]

The combined charges of lying and defiling the memory of the founder enraged Brigham Young. When the Smith boy came of age and assumed leadership of the RLDS Church, Young set out to counter his assertions. When plural marriage was officially announced in August 1852, Young mentioned that after Smith received the revelation and had it transcribed, "sister Emma burnt the original."[19] Over the next twenty-five years, Young repeatedly mocked Emma Smith's flaws and rebelliousness. In October 1866, Young told the assembled Mormons that "Emma has made her children inher[i]t lies. … [T]o my certain knowledge Emma Smith is one of the damnedest liars I know of on earth. … [Joseph himself] told me that she was a child of hell, and literally the most wicked woman on this earth."[20]

Six years later, more than a decade after the organization of the RLDS Church, Young again took on Emma and her sons:

> As for the doctrine that is promulgated by the sons of Joseph, it is nothing more than any other false religion. We would be very glad to have the privilege of saying that the children of Joseph Smith, Junior, the Prophet of God, were firm in the faith of the Gospel, and following in the footsteps of their father. But what are they doing? Trying to blot out every vestige of the work their father performed on the earth. Their mission is to endeavor to obliterate every particle of his doctrine, his faith and doings. These boys are not following Joseph Smith, but Emma Bideman. Every person who hearkens to what they say, hearkens to the will and wishes of Emma Bideman. The boys, themselves, have no will, no mind, no judgment independent of their mother. I do not want to talk about them. I am sorry for them.[21]

Young's assertion notwithstanding, he continued to speak about the Smiths frequently until his 1877 death. As strong as his rhetoric was, his effort to discredit Emma and her sons represented only one prong in the creation of a particular brand of historical consciousness by the second LDS president. He spoke often to remind his followers and the RLDS Church that Joseph Smith had been involved in plural marriage. Many of Joseph's plural wives lived in Utah, where their connection with him was made common knowledge by the Church. His most famous wife, a poet and one of the few prominent female leaders, Eliza Roxcy Snow, was identified as Eliza R. Snow Smith in official publications.[22] Never missing an opportunity to respond to the RLDS, Young gave a short address in Provo in 1855 and reminded the audience no fewer than five times that it was the "Prophet Joseph [who had] revealed this holy law and order to the Latter-day Saints."[23] In response to the counter narrative being offered by the Smith sons and widow and the RLDS Church, Young made every effort to link Joseph Smith to polygamy.

The third prong of the nineteenth-century historical tactic was the increasingly important role played by plural marriage in Mormon theology. During Joseph Smith's lifetime, the question of whether or not plural marriage was required for exaltation was ambiguous, perhaps stemming from Smith's attempts to keep the practice secret from the general public and from rank-and-file Mormons. His own references, as recorded by those closest to him, were always veiled and often parabolic. A fine example of this is found in a letter he wrote to Nancy Rigdon. Apparently he had approached her about becoming one of his plural wives, but she rejected the notion out of hand. In his letter to her, Joseph Smith never mentioned polygamy or even marriage. Instead, he explained, "[T]hat which is wrong under one circumstance, may be and often is, right under another." In a curious parable, he added that "a parent may whip a child, and justly too, because he stole an apple; whereas, if the child had asked for the apple, and the parent had given it, would have eaten it with a better appetite, there would have been no stripes—all the pleasures of the apple would have been received, all the misery of the stealing lost."[24] Smith wrote in this type of obscure style and told recipients to burn his letters once they had read them.

Another example of this ambiguity was recorded by William Clayton, an English convert to Mormonism who served as Smith's secretary and close friend from 1842 until Smith's death in 1844.[25] On May 16, 1843, Smith and Clayton stayed at the home of another Mormon, the brother of one of Smith's plural wives, Benjamin F. Johnson. In the evening the men engaged in a discussion of the afterlife, and Smith gave "some instructions on the priesthood." During the course of this conversation, he "put his hand on [Clayton's] knee and said … nothing but the unpardonable sin[26] can prevent him from inheriting eternal glory[,] for he is sealed up by the power of the priesthood unto eternal life having taken the step which is necessary for that purpose."

Clayton had yet to receive the temple endowment and gain admittance into Smith's elite Quorum of the Anointed (he would on Feb. 3, 1844), but he had just taken his first plural wife on April 26, 1844. It seems logical that the step Smith referred to was Clayton's entrance into polygamy. The matter is complicated, however, because Smith then told the small group at Johnson's home that "except a man and his wife enter into an everlasting covenant and be married for eternity by the power and authority of the Holy Priesthood they will cease to increase when they die."[27] He did not make a direct reference to plural marriage, mentioning only authorized sealings of men and women as a requirement for exaltation, but Clayton's account is nonetheless valuable in that it provides one of the few contemporary records of Smith's teachings on the subject. As demonstrated below, later reminiscences became more specific and would place a heavier emphasis on polygamy than did this earlier contemporary account.

Although Smith may have never made the point specifically, Young and others interpreted the revelation on plural marriage to mean that, at least theoretically, the practice was required for full salvation.[28] Especially after 1852, Young drew a hard line, asserting that "the only men who become Gods, even the Sons of God, are those who enter into polygamy."[29] On another occasion, after reminding the audience that "Joseph received a revelation on *celestial marriage,*" Young told those who were "determined not to enter into a plural marriage" that they could look forward to an eternal life lived "single and alone, for ever and ever, and be made servants, while others receive the highest order of intelligence and are bringing worlds into existence."[30] The emphasis on the phrase *celestial marriage* is mine and is important. As the context of this passage clearly illustrates, Mormon doctrine after 1852 equated celestial marriage with plural marriage. When the practice was officially acknowledged in the fall of 1852, Young had the revelation that had introduced plural marriage and served as the theological basis for Mormon temple sealing (now D&C 132) published.[31] Although the revelation never had an official title during Smith's lifetime, it was published in the *Deseret News* as "The Principle and Doctrine of Having Many Wives and Concubines, A Revelation to Joseph Smith, Jr., 12 July 1843."[32]

From this point forward, Young made a concerted effort to associate salvation in the highest heavenly kingdom with polygamy, based on this text. In a later address, he related an incident which typified his public discourse during the period, saying that according to Smith, those who did not enter into polygamy would have no spouses in the hereafter, that only polygamous marriages would be eternal. Again, there are no accounts from Smith's lifetime documenting that he stated this; such accounts enter the historical record after 1852.

Heavily influenced by Young's interpretation of Section 132, later accounts by Smith's former associates have no trace of the ambiguity that characterized their earlier, contemporary notes. For example, in 1874, William Clayton wrote, "[F]rom him [Smith] I learned that the doctrine of plural and celestial marriage is the most important doctrine ever revealed to man on earth and that without obedience to that principle no man can ever attain to the fullness of exaltation in the celestial glory."[33] Nowhere in Clayton's earlier writings can we find such a stern statement from Joseph Smith. Some of the founder's disciples may have reached such a conclusion, but there is scant evidence that he himself made the point explicit.

More evidence for this ambiguity may be found in another statement recorded by Clayton one night in March 1843, again at Benjamin Johnson's home. Clayton recorded Smith as having said, "In the celestial glory there was three heavens or degrees, and in order to obtain the highest a man must enter this order of the priesthood and if he don't he can't obtain it." Just before recording this statement, Clayton wrote, "I feel desirous to be united in an everlasting covenant to my wife and I pray that it may soon be."[34] Apparently, Clayton viewed plural marriage as possible without an eternal sealing since he was already a polygamist though not yet sealed to anyone for eternity.

In 1856, Apostle Wilford Woodruff wrote of a meeting he attended with Brigham Young in which they read again "the revelation on patriarchal marriage [section 132]." During the course of the discussion, they pondered, "[W]hat does the saying mean that sayes all shall be damned that does not keep this law unto whom it is revealed? Does it mean that they shall take more wives than one or be damned?"[35] Woodruff recorded that the group decided that the reference was to "the whole law with its covenants," not just to plural marriage.[36]

But Young and others, still puzzled by the ambiguity of the revelation and one preceding it dealing with the three degrees of glory, took action to provide a more concrete interpretation, adding a few words to Section 131 five months later, defining "this order of priesthood," a requirement for exaltation, as "the new and everlasting covenant of marriage."[37] It seems strange that Young and Woodruff felt the revelations needed clarification, given the tone of Apostle Orson Pratt's address in August 1852 forcefully arguing that plural marriage was required for Mormons to "inherit the blessings and promises made to Abraham, Isaac and Jacob." (The promise of these blessings remains a central part of the sealing ceremony in LDS temples today.) Significantly, Pratt believed the only possible way to receive those blessings was to engage in plural marriage. According to the revelation on marriage, godhood consisted chiefly of the "continuation of the seeds forever and ever."[38] The gods, it says, "shall be from everlasting to everlasting, because they continue; then shall they be above all."[39] Pratt interpreted this to mean that gods would need multiple wives in order to fulfill such a requirement. With this interpretation of the link between polygamy and the promised fecundity of those covered by the Abrahamic covenant, the use of the word *everlasting* in this context logically referred to polygamy. At least, from 1852 on, this was the accepted interpretation of what it meant to live a life as god—the kind of life promised in the revelation to all who "entered into the new and everlasting covenant."

Further evidence linking the "new and everlasting covenant"[40] with polygamy in 1852 and afterward is found in Pratt's warning that "there will be foolish among the wise who will not receive the new and everlasting covenant in its fullness; and they will never attain their exaltation; they will never be counted worthy to hold the scepter of power over a numerous progeny that shall multiply themselves without end, like the sand upon the seashore."[41] Pratt believed that exaltation would only be granted to those who obeyed the "new and everlasting covenant in its fullness."

One of the first major attempts to make the case for the exalting nature of plural marriage came in 1853 when Brigham Young sent Orson Pratt to Washington, D.C., to publish a periodical called *The Seer.* In the paper's prospectus, Pratt promised to "fully publish" the "views of the Saints in regard to the ancient patriarchal order of matrimony, or plurality of wives, as developed in a Revelation, given through Joseph, the Seer."[42] Young chose the nation's capital for this publication as a lobbying device. Perhaps, Young thought, if a strong enough case could be made for the morality of plural marriage, the government would leave Mormons to enjoy their desert solitude unmolested.

While this did not happen, *The Seer* nevertheless shed light on the central role polygamy was beginning to play in LDS theology. Pratt republished Smith's revelation on marriage under the title: "Celestial Marriage: A Revelation on the Patriarchal Order of Matrimony, or Plurality of Wives."[43] He devoted hundreds of pages to demonstrating that polygamy was not inconsistent with Christian principles, again placing heavy emphasis on Abraham and the promises of "eternal increase" which Mormons associated with the Abrahamic covenant. In a series of rhetorical questions, Pratt asked his readers, "[I]f plurality is offensive in the sight of God, why was Abraham, who practiced it, called a Friend of God? Why require all the families of the earth, to be adopted into the family of a polygamist in order to be saved? Why choose a polygamist to be the Father of all saved families?"[44] *The Seer* clarified that plural marriage was part of the "restoration of all things" and that those who lived the "law of the gospel" in its entirety were by default polygamists. He cited the forty-fifth Psalm as evidence that "the great Messiah who was the founder of the Christian religion, was a polygamist, as well as the patriarch Jacob and the prophet David from whom He descended according to the flesh." More dramatic still was Pratt's claim that "God the Father had a plurality of wives."[45] The implication of these and similar passages was that full integration into the hereafter involved polygamous marital relationships.

In an 1856 journal entry, Wilford Woodruff referred to the necessity of keeping "the whole law." Apparently the membership had begun to think that a monogamous temple marriage constituted partial fulfillment of the law. Woodruff wanted people to know that the highest degree of glory would only be achieved by those who obeyed the whole law, meaning polygamy. Further evidence for this interpretation may be found in a sermon delivered by then-Apostle Joseph F. Smith: "The marriage of one woman to a man for time and eternity by the sealing power is a fulfillment of the celestial law in part—and is good as far as it goes." Then Smith reminded his listeners that monogamous marriage in the temple represented "only the beginning of the law, not the whole of it," and "whoever has imagined that he could obtain the fullness of blessings pertaining to this celestial law, by complying with only a portion of its conditions has deceived himself; he cannot do it."[46] Orson Pratt similarly remarked in 1880 that "if a man has no divine right to marry two wives or more in this world, then marriage for eternity is not true, and your faith is all vain, worthless, good for nothing; for as sure as one is true the other must be true."[47]

This evidence points to the fact that Young and his fellow leaders were engaged in altering the historical consciousness of the Mormon people by linking the theology of exaltation and the temple endowment with plural marriage. By the mid-1850s, Brigham Young believed the new covenant of marriage and celestial marriage to be one and the same, which were, in turn, coterminous with plural marriage. Based on statements and publications of LDS leaders during the mid-to-late nineteenth century, they believed Section 132 referred to plural relationships only and that polygamy was mandatory. And in fact, Young's attempt to strengthen the connection between plural and celestial marriage was successful. In 1881, Artemesia Beman Snow wrote, "I have lived in the order of Celestial marriage thirty-five years; I have no wise—I have no desire—to have it changed or abolished." Thirty-five years earlier, Snow's husband "first asked my consent to take other wives [and] I freely gave it, believing such an order of marriage to be a pure and holy principle."[48] Likewise, Zina D. H. Young, one of Brigham Young's plural wives, reminisced in 1874 about the early days when she and her "sister wives" had "bravely commenced to live in the newly-revealed order of celestial marriage."[49] Only in her 1874 account, not in any earlier narrative, does she refer to this kind of marriage as "celestial." In 1859, John D. Lee, an adopted son of Brigham Young, recorded in his diary that "Mary Ann Lee ... was the 16th Woman that was seal[e]d to me in the New & Everlasting covenant."[50]

In 1879, Woodruff provided evidence in a speech at the St. George temple that Young's vision of the meaning of Section 132 and the link between polygamy, the Abrahamic covenant, and godhood had firmly taken root. Joseph Smith, said Woodruff, had received a revelation from God in which He commanded the Saints to

> [h]ave our wives and children sealed to us for time and eternity that we may have them with us in our family organization in the resurrection to dwell with us forever in the eternal worlds[,] that we may have an increase of posterity forever in connection with Abraham, Isaac and Jacob and all the ancient patriarchs. God our heavenly father, knowing that this was the only law ordained by the Gods of eternity that would exalt immortal beings … commanded Joseph Smith the Prophet and the Latter-day Saints to obey this law or you shall be damned.[51]

Although some may argue that Woodruff could have had in mind either monogamous or plural marriages, later that year when he spoke of the divine law given to the ancient patriarchs, he wrote that "God says we shall be damned if we do not obey this law, Congress says we shall be damned if you do obey it."[52] Congress never opposed monogamous Mormon marriages, so there was no question he meant plural marriage.

From the 1850s on, the individuals cited (Lee, Snow, Woodruff, and Zina Young), reflecting Brigham Young's view, had come to see both celestial marriage and the new and everlasting covenant of marriage as polygamy. Such a thorough indoctrination would soon prove to be a difficulty which twentieth-century LDS leaders would have to negotiate. After Young's death in the late summer of 1877, his successor, John Taylor, continued to maintain the public memory Young had fashioned. As noted earlier, from the 1870s on, the Church faced increasing pressure from the federal government to abandon polygamy. The Edmunds Act, passed in 1882, landed more than 1,300 Mormon men in prison for "unlawful cohabitation." Failing to break the back of the Mormon practice with the Edmunds Act, the government tried again and in 1887 passed the Edmunds-Tucker Act, which declared the children of polygamous unions to be illegitimate, among other draconian provisions. The Mormons responded by sending leaders "underground" while simultaneously challenging the legitimacy of the laws. This forced the association of polygamy with Joseph Smith more firmly into Mormon thought. During this period, John Taylor spoke at length of the necessity of practicing polygamy at all hazards because "if they would not enter into this covenant, then the kingdom of God could not go one step further." Taylor emphasized, as Young had done many times, that "it was the Prophet of God [Smith] who revealed [plural marriage] to us in Nauvoo, and I bear witness of this solemn fact before God, that He did reveal this sacred principle to me and others of the Twelve, and in this revelation it is stated that it is the will and law of God that 'all those who have this law revealed unto them must obey the same.'"[53]

When Taylor died in hiding in July 1887, Wilford Woodruff assumed leadership of the Church. Another Mormon of long standing and friend of Joseph Smith from the 1830s, Woodruff was an ardent polygamist who faced a grave dilemma. The U.S. Supreme Court had finally ruled on the Edmunds-Tucker Act and had directed law enforcement officials to seize more than $3 million worth of Church property, including the temples. They also emphasized that if Woodruff wanted statehood for Utah, and he clearly did, he would have to abandon polygamy. To the shock and horror of many Mormons, Woodruff declared in his Manifesto of 1890 that "we are not teaching polygamy or plural marriage, nor permitting any person to enter into its practice."[54] As disingenuous as this claim may have appeared, it soon became clear that Woodruff was serious, at least about slowing down the number of authorized plural marriages.

For the next decade, the Church struggled with its identity. Despite the Manifesto, half the members of the Quorum of the Twelve took additional wives within one year.[55] In 1904, Joseph F. Smith (the founder's nephew and fifth Church president) was called before a Senate committee investigating the continued practice of polygamy in connection with the seating of a Mormon senator, Reed Smoot. Humiliated by the experience, Smith issued a so-called second manifesto decrying plural marriage and announcing that "all such marriages are prohibited, and if any officer or member of the Church shall assume to solemnize (perform) or enter into any such marriage he will be deemed in transgression against the Church ... and excommunicated therefrom."[56] The most prominent casualty of this new policy was John Taylor's son, apostle John W. Taylor, who refused to abide by the new law and was excommunicated in 1911. As the Mormon polygamous chapter slowly and painfully came to a close, Mormon public memory had to be re-fashioned.

Public Memory Phase 2(A), 1904-1933
The Rise of Mormon Fundamentalism

While the Church undertook to find and excommunicate people practicing and sanctioning polygamy during the early decades of the twentieth century, it was left to deal with a public memory that held polygamy as an essential doctrine, necessary to the success of the Church and to the exaltation of individual members. If the task of recasting that public memory were not difficult enough at this point, another counter-narrative arose from an unexpected source. The RLDS Church grew more slowly than its Utah-based cousin, and by the turn of the century it became clear to some RLDS members that their hope that Joseph Smith Jr. had not been involved with plural marriage was misguided. In any case, the LDS Church did not feel it needed to compete with the RLDS counter-narrative anymore, and after 1904 it was a moot point anyway. What did emerge was the so-called Mormon fundamentalist movement. During the second decade of the twentieth century, as the Church began to track down and punish polygamists, a group introduced a secret revelation it said had been received in 1886 by then-Church President John Taylor. The first mention of this revelation came in February 1911 when Church leaders convened to consider the fate of John W. Taylor, son of John Taylor, who told the assembled leaders that "my father received a revelation which however was never presented to the Church."[57] The text, which John W. Taylor claimed he had discovered in the Church's vault, consisted of God saying:

> My son John, you have asked me concerning the New and Everlasting Covenant, how far it is binding upon my people. Thus saith the Lord, All commandments that I give must be obeyed by those calling themselves by my name unless they are revoked by me or by my authority. And how can I revoke an everlasting covenant; for I the Lord am everlasting and my everlasting covenants cannot be abrogated nor done away with; but they stand forever.

Following this statement, the revelation reiterated the necessity of obeying the principle of plural marriage: "As I have heretofore said by my servant Joseph, All those who would enter into my glory must and shall obey my law."[58] Interestingly, here was God, like Brigham Young before, dropping Joseph Smith's name in connection with the new and everlasting covenant of marriage, which now was clearly intended to mean plural marriage. It brought to mind the earlier fashioning of public memory on this topic.

According to the fundamentalist narrative, after this 1886 revelation, President Taylor ordained a number of men to carry on the practice of plural marriage in the future when the Church would do away with it, a development foretold to Taylor. These men and their plural wives started their own Church and began their own version of history, one that posed a unique challenge to mainstream Mormons. After all, the fundamentalists used a narrative consistent with nineteenth-century mainstream Mormon ideals. For example, they continued to identify the "works and blessings of Abraham" and the promise of "eternal increase" with polygamy as the mainstream Church had done after 1852. After quoting the LDS temple marriage ceremony in which participants were promised "the blessings of Abraham, Isaac and Jacob," one leading fundamentalist asked, "[I]f it is not expected that the contracting parties shall live the law by which Abraham received his promise of countless and eternal increase, why promise them the blessings of Abraham?"[59]

To counter this narrative, Church leaders, exercising their prerogatives as prophets, seers, and revelators, set out to redefine the connection between plural marriage and celestial marriage and the relationship between the Abrahamic covenant, eternal increase, and polygamy. As late as 1898, Church leaders were still saying that Mormons "believed in and practiced plurality of wives—more properly celestial marriage."[60] But just one year later, the first hint of a change in definition came when Dr. James Talmage, a leading Mormon intellectual and future apostle, published a "series of lectures on the principle doctrines" of the LDS Church. Collectively entitled *The Articles of Faith,* this book became a profoundly influential expression of LDS belief. In it, Talmage defined celestial marriage as "the system of holy matrimony, involving covenants as to time and eternity," in "the order of marriage that exists in the celestial worlds," skillfully avoiding mention of plural marriage and instead emphasizing the eternity of the marriage covenant.[61] In October 1901, Talmage further revised LDS ideas about celestial marriage in an official publication asserting that in celestial marriage, "plurality of wives was an incident[al] [doctrine]—never an essential."[62] Talmage—the first Mormon to earn a Ph.D.—was one of the first leaders to remain a monogamist.[63] Faced with the scriptural statement that in order to enter the "celestial glory" one must enter into "the new and everlasting covenant of marriage," and coming of age when polygamy was forbidden, Talmage could not make sense of the old phrase.[64] His new definition caught on, so that six years after his revisionist essay, another author who was briefly sketching Joseph Smith's prophetic career could explain that "in connection with the ordinances performed in the temple is another very important principle—the eternity of the marriage covenant—commonly referred to as 'celestial marriage.'"[65]

That this concept was new and needed reinforcing is evident by the fact that any mention of celestial marriage in LDS publications between 1901 and the early 1950s included the new definition. For example, Charles W. Penrose of the Church's First Presidency wrote in 1920 of "the heavenly order of celestial marriage; that is, matrimony for time and all eternity."[66] Similarly, J. M. Sjodahl wrote in 1927 that the "revelation of celestial marriage" dealt solely with the "eternal duration of the marriage relation."[67]

With this new definition in wide use, leaders decided to make an official statement to concretize it. In 1933, President Heber J. Grant declared, "Celestial marriage—that is, marriage for time and eternity—and polygamous marriage are not synonymous terms. … Monogamous marriages solemnized in our temples are celestial marriages."[68] Unlike nineteenth-century sermons on the plurality of wives, Joseph Smith's name was not invoked. From the time the First Presidency expressed a change of interpretation, it became a central pillar of Mormon historical consciousness. A book of quotes from LDS leaders on a variety of topics in 1948 included Grant's explanation under the heading, "The Nature of a Celestial Marriage."[69]

After the 1950s, no explanatory notes accompanied the term *celestial marriage* in LDS publications; it simply had come to be understood as the eternal union between a man and a woman when solemnized in an LDS temple.[70] This redefinition required a change in Mormon exegesis for the revelation on plural marriage. In an official book of commentary on the Doctrine and Covenants published in the 1920s, a new interpretation emerged for the first time. In the nineteenth-century context, Section 132 had been known as the "revelation on plural marriage."[71] Now the new commentary divided up the revelation to reveal that the first half of the text "deals with celestial marriage—marriage for eternity. ... [I]n the sections following, plural marriage is the subject."[72] Notice that at this early stage in the creation of a new public memory, each mention of celestial marriage was accompanied by a new definition such as marriage for eternity or temple marriage, indicating that the writers were keenly aware of the lingering vestiges of an old public memory. The commentary offered no explanation for the context of the revelation, which would obviously tie the historical moment to Joseph Smith to plural marriage.

At about the same time, Church Historian (and later Church president) Joseph Fielding Smith, son of Joseph F. Smith, published a textbook on LDS history for use in Church schools. *Essentials in Church History* would remain in print for fifty years and exert tremendous influence on countless Mormon readers. As in the exegetical work already noted, Smith dealt with the revelation in sections. The point of the revelation, according to Smith, was to teach that marriage between a man and a woman can be eternal and that people may become like God in every way. In a separate section, Smith added that "this revelation also contains the doctrine of plural wives."[73] He made very little mention of Joseph Smith's involvement with plural wives and no mention of Emma Smith.

In 1930, B. H. Roberts, a Church leader and historian, published the six-volume *Comprehensive History of the Church of Jesus Christ of Latter-day Saints*.[74] This massive work added further support to the new public memory. Roberts himself had initially expressed tremendous shock and confusion over the Manifesto but had come to accept it and worked to help other Mormons do the same. He took pains in his history to point out that what nineteenth-century leaders had referred to as the revelation on plural marriage had as its "primary principle ... *the eternity of the marriage covenant*." This, he said, had been "obscured by the discussion of and the popular clamor concerning the plurality feature of the new marriage system" (emphasis in original).[75] Roberts argued that plural marriage was a conditional, temporary, and relatively minor aspect of "celestial marriage," which he defined—in step with a statement to be issued three years later—as "the marriage system that obtains in the celestial worlds."[76] He held that plural marriages may fit under the rubric the celestial pattern but that they are secondary to monogamous marriages performed by proper authority in LDS temples.

During this second phase of public memory, many Mormons were still alive whose parents had been polygamists and who firmly believed the older views. However, as time passed, fewer Mormons came to identify personally with polygamy. By the 1950s, they had become so thoroughly Americanized that they tended to display a split opinion about the topic. Although proud of the sacrifices their pioneer ancestors had made, as modern Americans and models of family values, they were uncomfortable with their heritage of socio-sexual experimentation. Raised on *Essentials in Church History* and similar volumes, and never having heard of Joseph Smith's own plural relationships in sermons or official publications, the new public memory began to take root.

Public Memory Phase 2(B), 1933-Present

Joseph as Monogamist and the Redemption of Emma

Although fundamentalist groups continued to thrive on a small scale, their ability to convert mainstream Mormons to their cause eventually diminished, and the Church's emphasis on debunking the 1886 revelation likewise stopped. With the fundamentalist threat minimized, mainstream Church leaders now competed with the public memory their predecessors had created in an earlier period. Historians became the new target of Church suspicions and the public memory from Brigham Young's time became a forbidden field, particularly the close link publicized by earlier Mormons between Joseph Smith and polygamy or Young's vilification of Emma. As the first part of this second phase took hold—and with it a new interpretation of Section 132 and the nature of celestial marriage—the emplotment of the new Mormon public memory took another turn.

Interpretations of Section 132 tended to repeat the exegesis laid out by Smith and Sjodahl in the 1920s. A 1981 commentary on the Doctrine and Covenants quoted Smith and Sjodahl verbatim regarding the division of the revelatory text, adding that the main portion dealt with "the everlasting covenant of marriage," while a small aside covered "plural marriage within the new and everlasting covenant."[77] The new and everlasting covenant had clearly become something different from plural marriage, and because polygamy was identified as a smaller part of a larger system, monogamous eternal marriages had become theologically normative. A BYU professor of LDS history reiterated this view in a recent volume of commentary: "The plurality of wives is an appendage to the greater principle of eternal marriage."[78] This represents a clear departure from Young's interpretation that directly equated the two.

The context was also revised. In a teacher's manual on the Doctrine and Covenants published in 1984, it was suggested that Joseph Smith had questions when he read in the Bible about "the life of Abraham, not only regarding Abraham's having more than one wife, but also on the very nature of the marriage relationship."[79] Little evidence exists to suggest that Smith had anything on his mind except the plurality issue, but if Section 132 is read in a way to emphasize monogamy, it may be reasonable, or perhaps even necessary, to conclude that marriage in general was his concern. In histories written during this time, attempts were made to minimize the importance of polygamy to nineteenth-century Mormons. One example should suffice. In 1950 a widely distributed book appeared in which apostle LeGrand Richards claimed that "only a few of the members of the Church ever lived the principle of plural marriage—never over three percent."[80] Although subsequent research showed this to be a gross underestimation, the book remained continuously in print for more than fifty years and is still read by many LDS missionaries.

In addition to the issues related to Section 132, a newly refurbished portrait of Emma Smith began to emerge. Over the course of a half century to the 1970s, Emma's name had all but disappeared from Mormon history. Although she was no longer the villain of the early public memory, she had also ceased to play any other role. The Smiths' family life was rarely mentioned. This began to change in the 1970s when the Church staged a massive campaign to defeat the Equal Rights Amendment. Part of the intent was to make sure that liberal forces at work in the movement did not unduly influence Mormon women.[81]

Soon official Church publications carried stories about Emma's life, emphasizing her loyalty to Joseph. She was no longer the "most wicked woman on earth" but was instead referred to as the "elect lady." In the late twentieth century, references to her almost always used this title in both official and popular LDS literature. The phrase originally appeared in a revelation in the summer of 1830 in which Emma was told that her "sins are forgiven thee and thou art an elect lady."[82] This occurred more than a decade before the troubles at Nauvoo over polygamy, yet it is the image the architects of the new Mormon public memory gravitate to. They overlook a later and much harsher treatment that is found, not surprisingly, in Section 132. In a seldom-quoted reference, Emma is told to "receive all those that have been given unto my servant Joseph ... to abide and cleave unto my servant Joseph and to none else." This instruction came with the ominous warning that "if she abide not this commandment she shall be destroyed, saith the Lord. ... I will destroy her if she abide not in my law." The definition of "my law" is evident in the passages about plural marriage and command to "receive ye therefore my law."[83] Brigham Young liked to draw from this threat when publicly measuring Emma's character. Although she did not obey the law of plural marriage, no mention of this was made in recent, official Church commentaries on the revelation.

Thus, Emma once again became part of the Mormon public memory, but mainly as a character witness for her husband and model for proper womanly behavior. No recent mention was made of Emma's refusal to accept polygamy or the tension it caused between her and Joseph. In a 1979 article in the Church's *Ensign* magazine, only this cryptic evaluation of the conflict was offered: "[T]he tumultuous events of the last few months before Joseph's death put additional strains on Emma and Joseph," followed immediately by the ameliorating assurance that, as ever, "love and consideration are evident."[84]

In 1976 the Church's historical division published a one-volume history of the Church to replace *Essentials in Church History*. The new volume, *The Story of the Latter-day Saints,* makes no mention of Emma's reaction to polygamy, and the only post-1839 references to her include her position as head of the women's auxiliary, her attempt to hide the body of her dead husband after his death in order to discourage relic seekers, and her decision to stay in Nauvoo rather than head west with Young.[85] None of these accounts mention her throwing pregnant plural wives down the stairs or attempting to poison her husband in retaliation for his marriages to other women—stock stories from the nineteenth-century public memory. Instead, a story of loyalty despite hardship has emerged. In a recent address to Mormon women, the leader of the female auxiliary said, "[I]n a very literal way, Emma Smith's influence [for good] continues to ripple through generations."[86] In order to fully redeem Emma, her story usually ends around 1839, much like the RLDS public memory, when she was still the "elect lady," before God had threatened to destroy her.

With Emma back at his side, Joseph was able to take on a new role in the public view as well, and this is probably the main reason for Emma's reappearance in history. Joseph is now portrayed not only as an exemplification of Mormon virtues but as someone living with his one wife and devoting his life to her. This involves a further diminution of the importance of polygamy in interpreting Section 132 and of Smith's connection with the practice. In 1994 a chronology appeared in the Church's official magazine listing "key events in the life and ministry of the Prophet Joseph Smith."[87] Included on the timeline were "the revelation on celestial marriage" and Joseph's "sealing to Emma Smith for time and eternity." Section 132 was referred to, naturally, by its twentieth-century nomenclature as celestial marriage. Plural marriage was never mentioned, nor were Joseph's other marriages listed in the chronology or otherwise, although his sealing to Emma was featured prominently.

More in-depth pieces have revealed the same altered public memory. In 1989, the Church published an article celebrating the most important doctrinal contributions made by Joseph Smith. Included were "priesthood, the word of God, and temples." The discussion of temples in the article centered on "the eternal sealing of families," including the sealing of husband and *wife.* The authors pointed out that "Joseph and Emma Smith were sealed for time and eternity on 28 May 1843," without mentioning Smith's other eternal sealings or polygamy in general.[88] Two years later another article appeared in the *Ensign* stating that "the Prophet had seen in vision that marriage should be for eternity. It is no wonder that he so vigorously taught the Saints to love their spouses fully, to be tender and faithful. His own love for Emma and the children illustrated his firm conviction that families can be forever." Adding that Smith often exhorted his followers to treat their families with kindness, the author wrote, "Joseph certainly practiced what he preached. He knew the importance of a loving marriage that would endure eternity. His concern for Emma was revealed in the vigils he kept over his wife when she was sick, attending to her needs and praying for her health."[89] It is significant that Emma is painted in both accounts as a sympathetic character to illustrate Joseph's devotion and concern for her. Like the first article, the second piece made no mention of plural marriage. It would have been unthinkable for an architect of nineteenth-century Mormon history to ignore plural marriage and celebrate Joseph's marriage to Emma, yet such is the very core of the new public memory.

In an interesting twist, the Church decided in the late 1990s to publish a volume of teachings from Church presidents to be used in church classes. Inexplicably, they skipped Joseph Smith and went directly to Brigham Young. In the chronology of Young's life, the manual listed his first marriage, but no others. Several of his quotations were altered from "wives" to "wife" in an effort to remove references to polygamy. The manual for the following year on the teachings of Joseph F. Smith displayed marks of the same editorial techniques. One could read either of these books in their entirety and never know the men were polygamists. Similarly, there has been little mention of Joseph Smith's plural marriages in official Church publications since at least the 1950s.

This new public memory also appears in Mormon popular culture. In the 1990s a Mormon artist, Liz Lemon Swindle, became famous for paintings of figures from Church history. One of her favorite subjects has been Emma Smith. In a number of paintings, she portrays Emma and Joseph together enjoying an obviously close and loving relationship. There is no evidence of other wives or of tensions between

Joseph and "the wickedest woman that ever lived," as Brigham Young dubbed her. Using Swindle's art on the cover, a number of books have emerged furthering this picture of wedded bliss in a traditional household. Written by Gracia N. Jones, the books are titled *Joseph and Emma: Their Divine Mission* and *Priceless Gifts: Celebrating the Holidays with Joseph and Emma*. Of Emma, the author writes, "[T]here is no doubt that Emma put her whole soul into the effort of helping to lay the foundation of the kingdom of God. Her faith in the truthfulness of (Joseph's) mission caused Emma to turn her back on parents, social position, security and all things a girl holds dear, to share a beggar's life with her prophet husband, whose entire energy was directed toward fulfilling God's commandment to take the message of the Restoration to the whole world."[90] Along with these paintings and books, a number of statues, medallions, and decorative plates depicting Emma Smith are extremely popular among Mormons.

In 1990, Mormon seminary teacher Gerald Lund began publishing what would become the most popular fiction series in LDS publishing history, *The Work and the Glory*. The author follows the fictional Steed family from their conversion in the early 1830s through immigration to the Salt Lake Valley under Brigham Young. Throughout the books, the Steeds rub shoulders with Joseph Smith and other Church leaders and witness the most dramatic events in Church history. The narrator provides helpful interpretive explanations for "difficult" areas of Church history, which usually means explaining away areas that do not comport with the current public memory. Polygamy is mentioned, and it is tied to Joseph Smith, but in the broader context of monogamous marriage and the importance of temple rites. Joseph's relationship with Emma is likewise portrayed sympathetically, even sentimentally, especially in the volume covering the period in Nauvoo. Emma's conflicts with other plural wives are never discussed. In fact, the author takes liberties with the historical record and occasionally disregards facts altogether. For example, he describes a scene in which Joseph organizes the female Mormon auxiliary, the Relief Society. Emma Smith is placed at the head of the organization and her assistants are announced. One of them is Eliza R. Snow. Lund, in the voice of one of the main characters, notes that "Eliza … was not married. …

[T]his would tell the sisters that this was an organization of sisters, not just of wives."[91] Within three months, Eliza would marry Joseph Smith, a fact Lund never mentions.

The *Work and the Glory* has reached a tremendous number of Mormons, and the books are frequently mentioned in LDS meetings. Typical responses to the books indicate that the reader's faith has been strengthened and they have gained new insights into LDS history. For example, readers responding at *Amazon.com* noted, "Brother Lund has made church history come alive for me. I've read many different church history books. These I can relate to. It's like I'm there living it as it happens" and "My Sunday school teacher read us part of this one. It included the martyrdom [of Joseph Smith]. It was extremely sad. If you want a kid to really understand the concept of hatred and how truly evil the mob was, this is the book to read. It hit me over the head like a club just what the Saints went through."[92] Many similar responses are recorded, all of which support the notion that these books work effectively to support the intended memory regarding plural marriage. The entire series of nine volumes has been reprinted in paperback, a rare occurrence in Mormon fiction.

Conclusion

At the outset of this paper, I listed six basic elements in the theory of public memory. The first element holds that a discourse develops in which certain emplotment points are dropped and others emphasized. This has been the case with Mormon perspectives on plural marriage. The second element of the theory is that members of the community do not literally forget their collective past, they simply agree upon an official version. Most Mormons know that polygamy played a central role in the lives of their predecessors in the Church. They certainly know that Joseph Smith, Brigham Young, and other leaders had multiple wives, yet the Church still publishes material which blots out these facts, and the membership largely accepts this public memory without comment.

The third point of my theory of public memory holds that institutional sanctions prevent individuals from undermining the intended public view while rewarding those who help build it. In September

1993, six scholars were excommunicated for publishing material the Church deemed "faith destroying." Among these was historian D. Michael Quinn, whose work on LDS leaders and post-manifesto polygamy presented an open challenge to the new Mormon public memory. On the other hand, Gerald Lund, author of The *Work and the Glory* series, was sustained as a General Authority of the Church at the April 2002 LDS general conference. In his first speech in this position, he referred specifically to his research on the life of Joseph Smith for his books, commenting that "it was my privilege to spend about 10 years in an intensive and extensive study of his life, of his writings, of his teachings, and of those who knew and loved him, and I came to know that here is a prophet of prophets."[93] Clearly he viewed his task as helping to build the public memory of Joseph Smith rather than exploring his life in an academic fashion—and the Church rewarded his efforts.

The fourth element of the theory holds that public memory is functional and presentist. The key elements of the public memory are chosen based upon the Church's needs at the time the narrative is constructed. This was true in the case of Brigham Young's response to the RLDS challenge, in Joseph F. Smith's effort to recast the public memory after the Manifesto, and in the Church's current attempts to emphasize the family-values platform in the life of Joseph Smith.

Fifth, the emplotment points left out of public memory narratives often turn up in counter-narratives produced by competing communities. This has been most clearly illustrated in the case of the fundamentalist counter-narrative that emerged in the second decade of the twentieth century and in the academic counter-narrative currently emerging. In both cases, elements of the story which tend to disrupt the mainstream LDS public memory are discarded, or sometimes hidden, but these bits play central roles in the counter-narratives.

The final element of public memory, as I defined it, holds that individuals may be members of many discourse communities and, as such, take part in varying, even competing public memories. Any attempt to harmonize these systems can elicit institutional punishment. In early 1981 a faculty member at Church-owned Brigham Young University attempted to explain why some statements from Church leaders in the nineteenth century conflicted with statements made by current leaders.

In a pointed response, apostle Bruce R. McConkie, leading Mormon theologian and son-in-law and protégé of Joseph Fielding Smith, warned the professor that "there is no need to attempt to harmonize conflicting views," suggesting instead that the professor "echo what I say or remain silent." As Elder McConkie asserted further: "I hold over you the scepter of judgment," hinting at consequences for further shedding light on a discarded official history.[94] In the same year, apostle Boyd K. Packer delivered an address to Mormon educators and castigated historians for telling the whole truth about their past, noting that "some things that are true are not very useful."[95] This philosophy is evident in the various phases of Mormon public memory. Packer made the case that historians should write "faithful history," which essentially consists of emplotting only the events from the historical record that mesh with the current memory version. Packer's speech was in direct response to Mormon scholars who sought to harmonize their academic research and the public memory of their religious community.

Historical consciousness has clearly been an important element in the history of the LDS Church. It remains to be seen just where the next constructed historical consciousness will take the Church, but several things are clear. The historical consciousness of the Church will change as the institution's interests and needs shift. The architects of the history will continue to re-emplot historical events and reinterpret historical texts according to current imperatives. Jan Shipps, a prominent non-Mormon scholar of LDS history, has argued that the stories I call historical consciousness narratives represent denominational, confessional, or apologetic histories and the authors of these narratives, according to Shipps, have considerable latitude to emplot events as long as they use "what amounts to a canonized body of evidence composed of the testimony believers have left behind."[96] She suggests that as long as the evidence comes from faithful Mormons, it will fit comfortably into devotional narratives. I have attempted to demonstrate in this essay that some of the evidence most potentially damaging to the historical consciousness comes from faithful Mormon sources. Material clearly coming from an anti-Mormon source is much more easily explained away than are dissonant statements from the likes of Brigham Young.

On June 27, 2002, the anniversary of the murder of Joseph Smith, the LDS Church dedicated a temple in Nauvoo, Illinois, and some 300,000 Mormons and interested non-Mormons toured the building over the period of two months before the dedication. The services were broadcast live via satellite to meeting houses all over the world. The original temple in Nauvoo was burned by a mob in 1846. The new temple is a replica of the old one, and the Church and its members celebrated their return to Joseph Smith's "city beautiful." It was not only a celebration of the repossession of the land but also a celebration of the triumph of historical consciousness; in all of the festivities, no one mentioned plural marriage or the close relationship nineteenth-century Mormons saw between polygamy and temple rituals. Clearly, history may be emplotted and told in such a way that it eclipses the so-called real past. A more useful partial history constructed with a message in mind is usually more apparent. For groups anchoring their present authority to an epic past, such constructions are not only useful but necessary.

Notes

1. This concept of what might be called the idealized view of history was famously espoused by Leopold von Ranke, *Fürsten und Völker von Südeuropa im sechzehnten und siebzehnten Jahrhundert,* ed. W. Andreas (Wiesbaden, Germany: 1957), 4.

2. Maurice Halbwachs, *On Collective Memory,* trans. Lewis A. Coser (Chicago: University of Chicago Press, 1992). Halbwachs (1877-1945) was among the most influential students of sociologist Emile Durkheim. A Frenchman of German extraction, Halbwachs attended the prestigious Ecole Normale Superieure and later occupied a professorial chair at the Sorbonne.

3. Ibid., 43.

4. Ibid., 59.

5. Ibid., 92.

6. Throughout this article, I use "public memory" and "historical consciousness" interchangeably to convey a full meaning of the concept better than I think either term alone would do.

7. Hayden White, *Tropics of Discourse: Essays in Cultural Criticism* (Baltimore: Johns Hopkins University Press, 1978), 106.

8. James Deetz and Patricia Scott Deetz, *The Times of Their Lives: Life, Love, and Death in Plymouth Colony* (New York: Anchor Books, 2000), 11.

9. Joseph Smith, "Church History," *Times and Seasons*, Mar. 1, 1842, 707.

10. It is not clear exactly when Smith began taking additional wives or how many women he married during his lifetime. The most recent estimate places the date of the first marriage in 1833 and the number of wives in the low 30s. See Todd Compton, *In Sacred Loneliness: The Plural Wives of Joseph Smith* (Salt Lake City: Signature Books, 1997).

11. D&C 132:35.

12. William Clayton's Nauvoo Journal Two, July 12, 1843, LDS Archives, Salt Lake City, also in George D. Smith, ed., *An Intimate Chronicle: The Journals of William Clayton* (Salt Lake City: Signature Books, 1995), 110.

13. David John Buerger, *The Mysteries of Godliness: A History of Mormon Temple Worship* (San Francisco: Smith Research Associates, 1994). The doctrine of human divinization is spelled out in D&C 132.

14. For example, a Dr. Foster stood trial in 1844 for accusing Smith and others of plural marriage, among other things. See entry for April 27, 1844, in Scott Faurling, ed., *An American Prophet's Record: The Journals and Diaries of Joseph Smith* (Salt Lake: Signature Books, 1989), 474.

15. *Deseret News Extra*, Sept. 14, 1852.

16. Several academic histories of plural marriage have been published over the last twenty years, including B. Carmon Hardy, *Solemn Covenant: The Mormon Polygamous Passage* (Urbana: University of Illinois Press, 1992), Richard S. Van Wagner, *Mormon Polygamy: A History* (Salt Lake: Signature Books, 1989), and Sarah Barringer Gordon, *The Mormon Question: Polygamy and Constitutional Conflict in Nineteenth-Century America* (Chapel Hill: University of North Carolina Press, 2002).

17. Statement of Nels Madsen, LDS Archives, reproduced in Linda King Newell and Valeen Tippetts Avery, *Mormon Enigma: Emma Hale Smith* (New York: Doubleday, 1984), 298.

18. Joseph Smith III to Emma Knight, May 24, 1855, Utah State Historical Society Library and Archives, Salt Lake City.

19. *Journal of Discourses*, comp. George D. Watt, et al., 26 vols. (Liverpool: Latter-day Saints Book Depot, 1854-1886), 6:281.

20. Brigham Young address, Oct. 1, 1866, LDS Archives, Brigham Young Collection.

21. *Journal of Discourses*, 15:126. Emma married Lewis Bidamon in late December 1847. In the above account, the scribe misspelled her new surname.

22. See Augusta Joyce Crocheron, *Representative Women of Deseret: A Book of Biographical Sketches* (Salt Lake City: J. C. Graham & Co., 1884), 1-9, for an example of Eliza Snow being addressed as Eliza Snow Smith. The author writes that after Smith's murder in 1844, "Eliza, widowed, turned again to the work Joseph had established" (3).

23. *Journal of Discourses,* 3:266.

24. Joseph Smith to Nancy Rigdon, no date, in Dean C. Jessee, ed., *Personal Writings of Joseph Smith,* 2d ed. (Salt Lake: Deseret Book, 2002), 538-39. This letter first surfaced in the *Sangamo Journal* in Illinois on August 19, 1842, and was probably written in 1841. The newspaper received the letter from the former Smith confidante and member of the First Presidency John C. Bennett. Research and witness testimony have demonstrated that the letter, despite being published by Bennett, was in fact written by Joseph Smith.

25. For an excellent biography of this important witness to the behind-the-scenes events in Nauvoo, see James B. Allen, *No Toil Nor Labor Fear: The Story of William Clayton* (Provo: Brigham Young University Press, 2002.)

26. According to Mormon theology, "if ye deny the Holy Ghost when it once has had place in you, and ye know that ye deny it, behold, this is a sin which is unpardonable" (Alma 39:6). Joseph Smith gave further meaning to this term in a revelation from 1832 which stated that the unpardonable sin consists of "having denied the Holy Spirit after having received it, and having denied the Only Begotten Son of the Father, having crucified him unto themselves and put him to an open shame" (D&C 76:35).

27. Smith, *Intimate Chronicle,* 102.

28. In Mormon theology, salvation is offered unconditionally to nearly everyone regardless of their behavior during their lifetime. However, there are different degrees to heaven, and the term *exaltation* is used to refer to "life with God as God." It is reserved for those who strictly adhere to Mormon teachings and covenants.

29. Brigham Young address, Aug. 19, 1866, in *Journal of Discourses,* 11:272. In this address, as in many others during this period, Young used language drawn directly from Smith's revelation on marriage which also promised that men could become "gods, even the sons of gods."

30. Discourse by Brigham Young, Aug. 17, 1873, LDS Archives.

31. Unless explicitly stated, all references in this paper to the Doctrine and Covenants refer to the 1981 edition.

32. *Deseret News Extra,* Sept. 14, 1852.

33. Statement by William Clayton made on Feb. 16, 1874, reprinted as "William Clayton's Testimony," *Historical Record,* May 6, 1887, 225-26.

34. Smith, *Intimate Chronicle,* 102, emphasis added.

35. The text of the revelation paraphrased by Woodruff reads: "[P]repare thy heart to receive and obey the instructions which I am about to give unto you; for all those who have this law revealed unto them must obey the same. For behold, I reveal to you a new and an everlasting covenant; and if ye abide not that covenant ye are damned."

36. *Wilford Woodruff's Journal, 1833-1898,* ed. Scott G. Kenney, 9 vols. (Midvale, UT: Signature Books, 1983-1985), 4:411.

37. Beginning with the 1876 edition and continuing to the present, this text was known as section 131 of the Doctrine and Covenants; cf. *Deseret News,* Sept. 24, 1856.

38. D&C 132:19.

39. D&C 132:20-21.

40. Since 1843, the term "new and everlasting covenant" was associated with marriage and LDS temple theology. However, it was not a new term for Mormons. The first recorded instance of its use was in a revelation received by Smith in April 1830 indicating that the entirety of the doctrines and ordinances of the new church would constitute this new covenant. Frequently in the 1830s, Mormon leaders ended correspondence with the phrase, "yours in the new and everlasting covenant." This stopped after the term took on a new meaning in the 1840s. For a more in-depth treatment, see Thomas G. Alexander, "'A New and Everlasting Covenant': An Approach to the Theology of Joseph Smith," in Davis Bitton and Maureen Ursenbach Beecher, eds., *New Views of Mormon History: Essays in Honor of Leonard J. Arrington* (Salt Lake: University of Utah Press, 1987), 43-62.

41. Orson Pratt, "Celestial Marriage," delivered Aug. 29, 1852, in *Journal of Discourses,* 1:58-62.

42. *The Seer: Prominent Works in Mormon History,* photo reprint edition (Salt Lake City: Eborn Books, 2000), 1 (Jan. 1853).

43. Ibid., 7.

44. Ibid., 187 (Dec. 1853).

45. Ibid., 172 (Nov. 1853).

46. *Journal of Discourses,* 20:24.

47. Ibid., 21:296.

48. "Artemesia Beman Snow on Polygamous Marriage," reproduced in Andrew Karl Larson, *Erastus Snow: The Life of a Missionary and Pioneer for the Early Mormon Church* (Salt Lake: University of Utah Press, 1971), 747.

49. Zina D. H. Young, as quoted in Edward Tullidge, *Women of Mormondom* (New York: Tullidge & Crandall, 1877), 327.

50. Robert Glass Cleland and Juanita Brooks, eds., *A Mormon Chronicle:*

The Diaries of John D. Lee, 1848-1876 (San Marino, CA: Huntington Library, 1955), 1:191.

51. *Wilford Woodruff's Journal*, Feb. 22, 1879, 7:456.

52. Ibid., 7:457.

53. *Journal of Discourses*, 24:229.

54. D&C, Official Declaration 1.

55. D. Michael Quinn, "LDS Church Authority and New Plural Marriages, 1890-1904," *Dialogue: A Journal of Mormon Thought* 18 (Summer 1985): 9-105.

56. *Conference Report*, Apr. 6, 1904, 75.

57. Minutes of Council of Twelve Meeting concerning Fellowship of John W. Taylor, Feb. 22, 1911, LDS Archives.

58. "Revelation given to John Taylor, September 27, 1886, copied from the original manuscript by Joseph F. Smith, Jr., August 3,1909," John Taylor Papers, LDS Archives, copy in author's possession.

59. B. Harvey Allred, *A Leaf in Review* (Caldwell, IN: Caxton Publishers, 1933), 187.

60. B. H. Roberts, "Comment on Dr. Reiser's Letter," *Improvement Era*, May 1898, 7.

61. James E. Talmage, *The Articles of Faith* (Salt Lake City: Deseret News Press, 1899), 458. This book has remained in print and relatively unchanged for more than one hundred years and is not likely to go out of print soon. It is one of a handful of books, along with Talmage's *Jesus the Christ*, which LDS missionaries are permitted to read while on their missions.

62. James E. Talmage, "The Story of Mormonism," *Improvement Era*, Oct. 1901, 12.

63. Talmage received a Ph.D. from Illinois Wesleyan University in 1896; he married eight years earlier. In 1926, another apostle, John Widtsoe, edited a volume of the *Discourses of Brigham Young* which contained no references to plural marriage. Widtsoe and Talmage were used by the Church to shape and implement the new public memory partly because both were intelligent spokesmen and first-generation European converts who had no personal or sentimental ties to plural marriage. This background made them unusual in LDS leadership circles at this time and unusually well qualified to dismantle the historical consciousness of an earlier age. Unfortunately, these two men and their contributions to LDS history have gone largely unstudied.

64. D&C 131:2.

65. William Halls, "The Mission of Joseph Smith," *Improvement Era*, Dec. 1907, 2.

66. Charles W. Penrose, "The Edict of a Century," *Improvement Era,* Apr. 1920, 6.

67. J. M. Sjodahl, "Temple Marriage an Antidote Against Divorce," *Improvement Era,* Oct. 1927, 12.

68. "Official Statement from the First Presidency of the Church of Jesus Christ of Latter-day Saints," rpt. in *Deseret News,* Church section, June 17, 1933.

69. Daniel H. Ludlow, *Latter-day Prophets Speak* (Salt Lake City: Bookcraft, 1948), 301.

70. For examples of the new definition of celestial marriage, see the following: Ernest Anderson, "What a Chance You Take," *Improvement Era,* July 1950, 7; A. C. Lambert, "The Book of Doctrine and Covenants," *Improvement Era,* Oct. 1951, 10; Hugh B. Brown, "The LDS Concept of Marriage," *Ensign,* Jan. 1972, 60; Spencer W. Kimball, "The Importance of Celestial Marriage," *Ensign,* Oct. 1979, 3; N. Eldon Tanner, "Celestial Marriages and Eternal Families," *Ensign,* May 1980, 15; Dean L. Larsen, "Marriage and the Patriarchal Order," *Ensign,* Sept. 1982, 6; Robert L. Millet, "The Ancient Covenant Restored," *Ensign,* Mar. 1998, 36.

71. For evidence of this association between Section 132 and polygamy, see *Journal of Discourses* 6:362, 13:194, 16:166, 17:360-61, 21:10-11, 22:127, 25:309, 26:122, 26:340.

72. Hyrum M. Smith and Janne M. Sjodahl, *The Doctrine and Covenants with Historical and Exegetical Notes* (Salt Lake: Deseret Book, 1921; rpt. 1978), 831.

73. Joseph Fielding Smith, *Essentials in Church History* (Salt Lake: Church of Jesus Christ of Latter-day Saints, 1921), 341.

74. B. H. Roberts, *A Comprehensive History of the Church of Jesus Christ of Latter-day Saints,* 6 vols. (Salt Lake City: Church of Jesus Christ of Latter-day Saints, 1930).

75. Ibid., 2:95.

76. Ibid., 93.

77. *The Doctrine and Covenants: Student Manual* (Salt Lake City: Church of Jesus Christ of Latter-day Saints, 1981), 327.

78. Joseph Fielding McConkie, *Revelations of the Restoration: A Commentary on the Doctrine and Covenants and Other Modern Revelations* (Salt Lake City: Deseret Book, 2000), 1,058.

79. *The Doctrine and Covenants and Church History: Gospel Doctrine Teacher's Supplement* (Salt Lake City: Church of Jesus Christ of Latter-day Saints, 1984), 159.

80. LeGrand Richards, *A Marvelous Work and a Wonder* (Salt Lake City: Deseret Book, 1950), 401.

81. For an account of Church opposition to the ERA, see D. Michael Quinn, *The Mormon Hierarchy: Extensions of Power* (Salt Lake: Signature Books, 1997), 373-406, passim.

82. D&C 25:3.

83. D&C 132:24, 52-54.

84. Valeen Tippetts Avery and Linda King Newell, "The Elect Lady: Emma Hale Smith," *Ensign*, Sept. 1979, 65.

85. James Allen and Glen Leonard, *The Story of the Latter-day Saints* (Salt Lake City: Deseret Book, 1975; 2nd rev. ed., 1992).

86. Virginia U. Jensen, "Ripples," *Ensign*, Nov. 2000, 78.

87. "Highlights in the Life of the Prophet," *Ensign*, June 1994, 24.

88. Donald Q. Cannon, Larry Dahl, and John Welch, "The Restoration of Major Doctrines through Joseph Smith: Priesthood, the Word of God, and the Temple," *Ensign*, Feb. 1989, 7.

89. Brent L. Top, "'I Was with My Family': Joseph Smith—Devoted Husband, Father, Son, and Brother," *Ensign*, Aug. 1991, 22.

90. Gracia N. Jones, *Joseph and Emma: Their Divine Mission* (Alpine, UT: Covenant Communications, 1999).

91. Gerald N. Lund, *The Work and the Glory*, 9 vols. (Salt Lake: Bookcraft, 2001), 6:289-90.

92. These responses are far from definitive but represent what I have also personally heard in LDS meetings on many occasions.

93. Gerald Lund, "The Opportunity to Serve," *LDS General Conference Report*, Apr. 2, 2002.

94. Bruce R. McConkie to Eugene England, Feb. 19, 1981, copy in author's possession.

95. Boyd K. Packer, "The Mantle is Far, Far Greater than the Intellect," *BYU Studies* 21 (Summer 1981): 259-78.

96. Jan Shipps "Remembering, Recovering, and Inventing What Being a People of God Means: Reflections of Method in the Scholarly Writing of Religious History," in *Sojourner in the Promised Land: Forty Years among the Mormons* (Urbana: University of Illinois Press, 2000), 184.

Re-placing Memory

Latter-day Saint Use of Historical Monuments and Narrative in the Early Twentieth Century

Kathleen Flake

In the winter of 1905, leaders of the Church of Jesus Christ of Latter-day Saints[1] departed from Utah on two seemingly disparate missions to the east coast. One contingent went to defend their Church at Senate hearings in Washington, D.C.; the other to Vermont to dedicate a monument to Church founder Joseph Smith. These forays into national politics and religious memory refashioned LDS identity and public perception of Mormonism for the remainder of the twentieth century. They also illuminate one of the quotidian mysteries of religion: how it adapts to the demands of time yet maintains its sense of mediating the eternal.

It is axiomatic that religious communities are not exempt from the human condition; they must adapt to their temporal circumstances or die. What is not as often recognized is that Churches bring a particular burden to this task because they offer their believers the hope of transcending time. Indeed, it is doubtful that religious identity can survive the awareness of certain kinds of change. This is more true of some religious communities than others, especially those characterized as sectarian or set apart from their culture. Formed in response to a sense of an immediate divine call, which aggrandizes the expectation of imperviousness to time, and yet originating in a literate era which inevitably documented their changes over time, the Latter-day Saints are among those communities most susceptible to feeling the conflict between time and eternity, history and faith. And at no time had the Latter-day Saints felt the conflict more keenly than the winter of 1905.

After many years of resistance, the Church was about to cease practicing their doctrine of plural marriage, or polygamy, as their antagonists called it, and as a consequence, subordinate their divine law to the anti-polygamist law of the land. This was a change of enormous magnitude for Mormons, and the particular mission of Church leaders traveling east in the winter of 1905 was to negotiate the change without destroying the very Church they were trying to save by abandoning plural marriage. Thus, one of the two sets of travelers was charged with convincing the state that the Church had changed enough and the other was to convince the faithful that it had not changed at all.

The Washington-bound group of travelers was led by Reed Smoot, LDS apostle and new U.S. Senator for the State of Utah.[2] His election the previous year had catalyzed a nationwide protest and prompted U.S. Senate hearings on charges that the Saints were still practicing polygamy, notwithstanding promises to the contrary which had enabled Utah's statehood ten years earlier. Polygamy, like Smoot himself, however, represented a deeper problem to the protestors. Through plural marriage, the nineteenth-century Church had earned a reputation for theocratic despotism and civil anarchy. It was widely believed that Mormons obeyed priestly leadership at the expense of the nation and its elected lawmakers. A trial on these charges had been fifty years in the making, and this may explain the length and intensity of the Senate investigation that began in 1903 and was not resolved until 1907. What is left in the national archives of petitions against Smoot fills eleven feet of shelf space, the largest such collection in the archives. During the hearing, spectators lined the halls of the U.S. Capitol waiting for limited seats in the committee room and filled the galleries to observe floor debates. For those who could not see for themselves, journalists and cartoonists depicted each day's admission and outrage. Ultimately the four-year Senate investigation created a 3,500-page record of testimony by one hundred witnesses on every peculiarity of Mormonism: its polygamous family structure, ritual worship practices, "secret oaths," open canon, economic communalism, and theocratic politics.[3]

Smoot's journey, however, and his trial before the Senate provide only the context for this essay, not its subject.

In the middle of the public uproar and Senatorial demands that the LDS Church change its ways, a second group of Utahns embarked on a pilgrimage that would include the dedication of a monument to the Church founder, who was the revelator of its doctrine of plural marriage. At the head of the delegation to Vermont was the founder's nephew and namesake, contemporary Church president Joseph F. Smith. Only three days earlier, President Smith had given Smoot permission to inform his Senatorial colleagues that two of the Church's apostles would be dismissed for their practice of plural marriage.

This was the first disciplinary measure ever taken by the Church in obedience to federal anti-polygamy law and signaled the end of more than a half century of open hostility between the Church and its host nation.[4] However stabilizing this action was for the Church's external relations, it had the potential to be exceedingly destabilizing internally. The faithful believed that plural marriage was a divine commandment given through the martyred prophet, Joseph Smith; members themselves had sacrificed much to live the principle. Thus, solving the Church's problem with the government required Smith to undermine adherence to plural marriage without lessening people's confidence in other revelations or the revelators, namely Joseph Smith and Joseph F. Smith himself as successor. How he managed to do that is the subject of this essay.[5]

In sum, I argue that the dedication trip to Vermont was both a means and a symbol of President Joseph F. Smith's creation of a new future out of a Mormon past. The first section of this article lays the groundwork for my argument by showing how plural marriage had become central to the LDS belief system, including the understanding of Joseph Smith as a prophet. Section two describes the Vermont dedication ceremony and the meaning given to Smith's birth marker as it memorialized Mormonism claims to have (1) restored the ancient Church order, (2) received divine authority, and (3) continued to receive revelation. Section three argues that these three claims, inscribed on the Vermont monument, were given particular force by the way LDS Progressive-Era leaders used the Church founder's autobiographical narrative. Specifically, the story of Joseph Smith's original theophany, or First Vision, as it is denominated within the Church, achieved during this period the primacy once accorded plural marriage. This allowed the Latter-day Saints to forget, as a practical matter, the once-definitive marriage practice.[6] The fourth section of this essay uses theories of narrative and myths of origin to show how the First Vision narrative allowed the Latter-day Saints to jettison plural marriage without destroying their identity, much less their confidence in Joseph Smith as Church founder.

Jan Shipps argues that the Church's transition to modernity required an increased emphasis on individual boundary maintenance. Nothing in this essay contradicts her conclusion; rather, I offer a definition of the "somehow" in her observation that "somehow the responsibility for boundary maintenance had to be shifted from the corporate body to the individuals in that body, and that shift had to be legitimized in such a way that it would gain general acceptance."[7] In addition, this essay attempts to show how, despite the apparent shift to stronger individual boundaries, the Latter-day Saints maintained an unusually strong corporate identity throughout the twentieth century. Thus, the fifth and final section returns to Joseph F. Smith and his colleagues to show that their return trip to Utah effected and symbolized changes the LDS Church had to make to negotiate its corporate survival within the host culture. The dedication party's decisions about where to go and not go, what to say and not say, on their way home reveals subtleties about what was to be remembered or forgotten about nineteenth-century Mormonism. More obvious to the Church's project of collective memory was its reconstruction of historical sites and schedule of historical commemorations. These, too, are discussed, but it is important that the details of what follows not obfuscate the general explanatory power of the story itself. Ultimately, this essay argues that the LDS Progressive-Era efforts to change and remain the same illuminate a task common to all communities that seek the divine in real time and who successfully hold to that pursuit over time. Nevertheless, before this particular story can be used to illuminate general principles of resourcefulness, the Latter-day Saints' particular crisis of faith must be defined.

The Mormon Problem

From their earliest beginnings, Mormons tested America's Constitutional commitment to free exercise of religion. The governor of Missouri considered Latter-day Saints to be such a problem that he issued an extermination order against them in 1838 and drove them from the state with a militia. State officials in Illinois took actions that precipitated the murder of the Church founder in 1844 and expulsion of his followers by local mobs. In 1857 the federal government dispatched its army to the Rocky Mountains to subdue the Mormons. The so-called Utah War caused trauma and expense but little change. Brigham Young was deposed as governor, but the Mormons continued to build their kingdom of God in the West while North and South fought a real war. Between 1862 and 1896, the nation turned to the instrumentalities of law to change the Mormons by jailing polygamists, revoking franchise, denying citizenship, disinheriting children, confiscating property, and disincorporating their Church. In 1890 the Church's promise to abandon polygamy made possible the territory's admission to the union of states in 1896. But a few years later, to the nation's chagrin, the Smoot hearing demonstrated that Church economic, political, and familial orders, including polygamy, remained in place. Thus by December 1905, when Senator Smoot and President Smith left Salt Lake City on their respective missions, the nation was once again trying to solve that complex of differences that had become known simply as "the Mormon problem."[8]

Proposed remedies included not only removing Smoot from office but also amending the Constitution to deny public office to those who espoused polygamy. Convinced that the draconian laws of the late nineteenth century were about to be called into service again, Church leaders had to convince the nation that this time the Latter-day Saints really would change. Words would not suffice. Therefore, the contingent heading for Washington, D.C., carried with it news about the dismissal of apostles John W. Taylor and Matthais Cowley, two of the Church's most powerful and popular leaders. Disciplining these two was the first punitive action taken by the Church against its members for polygamy, notwithstanding fifty years of federal anti-polygamy law.[9]

By striking down two of their own, the Church satisfied the Senate. More immediately, however, this dramatic action made clear to the rank-and-file Saints that the Church was serious about abandoning plural marriage. Immediate attention was required to shore up the faith of members who had staked so much on the principle. While Joseph F. Smith's ultimate goal in sending Smoot to the Senate was to "make us [the Church] assume our real position and standing in the midst of the earth,"[10] he first had to ensure that the hearing did not knock the Church off its feet.

Mormonism's capacity to adapt to its social environment has been credited to its doctrine of continuing revelation. Jan Shipps noted that at several junctures in LDS history, "disappointment was overcome as revelation ... strengthen[ed] the ritual and institutional dimension of this developing religious tradition."[11] Continuing revelation is not of itself sufficient to legitimize change, if only because of the conflict inherent in undoing a past revelation, even with a present one. Undermining a part of someone's religious conviction can endanger the whole of it. This is especially true where the part in question is integrated into the whole as plural marriage was. The enduring willingness of the Saints to sacrifice respect, property, liberty, and life in order to maintain the practice between 1841 and 1905 is a measure of the doctrine's significance. Less noble, but equally telling, is the longer history of lying about the practice by an otherwise sternly ethical people. No doubt, persecution made the Saints hold to the principle less critically than they might have done. But again, more than the psychology of persecution is required to explain the Saints' persistent practice of a uniquely antisocial form of family life.[12]

Several forces contributed to the LDS Church's conflation of religious faith and marital practice. Each of these forces had to be dealt with if Joseph F. Smith was to change the marriage practice without destroying the faith. The first of these two can be characterized as historical. Joseph Smith spent the last three years of his life implementing an ecclesiology of temple worship that made plural marriage, or "celestial marriage" as it was also called by the faithful, the highest sacrament of the Church. As Joseph Smith's final prophetic effort, plural marriage was given added significance by those who had entered into the practice under his tutelage. Thrust into leadership by Joseph Smith's murder, these early initiates organized the Utah Church according to their understanding that celestial marriage constituted the fulfillment of Joseph Smith's mission to restore the fullness of the gospel of Jesus Christ.

Smith himself called celestial marriage "a new and an everlasting covenant" instituted for the fullness of "[God's] glory," and Brigham Young agreed.[13] In 1852, shortly after the grant of territorial status to Utah and arrival of the last refugees from Illinois, the decision to make plural marriage a Church-wide practice was justified on the grounds that it was a revelation "given [by God] to our Prophet, Seer, and Revelator" about eleven months before he was "martyred for the testimony of Jesus."[14] Later, when the Reorganized Church of Jesus Christ of Latter Day Saints (RLDS), led by Smith's son, identified itself in opposition to polygamy and denied that the founder had ever practiced it, the Utah Church's identity became further defined in terms of plural marriage. Not only for the nation, but for the Saints as well, the test of a true believer was acceptance of plural marriage in both theory and practice. Any successful attempt to stop the practice had to find within Smith's life and thought an equally powerful assertion of Mormon doctrinal identity.

A second force that sustained plural marriage came from the Church's long contest with the federal government. Though not all Latter-day Saints practiced polygamy, all were subject to and affected by government sanctions against the Church. Raided by federal marshals, its members accused of barbarism and immorality by Protestant ministers and dime novelists, the entire Church population lived for decades in an atmosphere of fear, antagonism, and shame. After the failure of the U.S. Army to effect sufficient change in mid-century, the forms and forums of American law were increasingly employed to impose the nation's moral sensibilities upon the Saints. Naturally then, as federal law became the instrumentality for imposing Protestant morality on them, the Saints' resistance to the law was framed increasingly in legal terms. For example, in 1870 in response to more aggressive federal efforts to enforce anti-polygamy statutes in the Utah Territory, the following statement was endorsed by the Saints:

> The doctrine of Celestial Marriage or plurality of wives was revealed to the prophet Joseph Smith and by him established in the Church of Jesus Christ of Latter-day Saints as a revealed law of God, therefore be it Resolved that we the members of said Church, in general mass meeting assembled do now most earnestly and solemnly declare before Almighty God that we hold that said order of marriage is a cardinal principle of our religious faith affecting us not only for time, but for all eternity and as sacred and binding as any other principle of the Holy Gospel of the Son of God.[15]

Beyond any theological significance it may have had, this resolution was an explicit First Amendment claim to protection of LDS marriage practices. The way the Latter-day Saints saw it, "free exercise of [LDS] religion" could only be preserved if the country ceased to criminalize Church-sanctioned marriages. Six years later, as they felt the Poland Act's efforts to make anti-polygamy laws effective, the Saints strengthened their legal argument by canonizing Smith's revelation on celestial marriage. For the first time in 1876, the Book of Doctrine and Covenants added Smith's revelation, which was written in 1843. Thus, the doctrine was canonized thirty-three years after its formalization by Smith and twenty-four years after its publication by Young. The choice to formalize it in scripture strengthened their "free exercise" claim in federal courts. It also complicated the succeeding generation's task of disposing of the practice: proscription of plural marriage would have to be established with the same legitimacy and formality as had its prescription.

Finally, in addition to the history of polygamy and the effects of litigation surrounding it, the Saints' marital practices were integrated with their doctrines of salvation and Church administration. During Joseph Smith's lifetime, plural marriage was practiced secretly among the elite leadership. Consequently, at the time of his death in 1844, the doctrine was not well developed by sermon or other public exposition. This omission had been thoroughly corrected by the turn of the century. Indeed, thirty years prior to inheriting the burden of doing away with the practice, then-apostle Joseph F. Smith had said in a sermon, "I understand the law of celestial marriage to mean that every man in this Church, who has the ability to obey and practice it in righteousness and will not, shall be damned. I say I understand it to mean this and nothing less, and I testify in the name of Jesus that it does mean that."[16] For the Latter-day Saints, damnation was to cease to progress in the hereafter. Though not equivalent to traditional Christian notions of hell, it did mean that one would not go to heaven. For the Saints, monogamy constituted a rejection of Joseph Smith's teaching that "there are three heavens ... and in order to obtain the highest a man must enter into this order of the priesthood [meaning the new and everlasting covenant of marriage]; and if he does not, he cannot obtain it."[17] The bracketed definition was inserted into the published scripture to make explicit the relation of "this order of priesthood" and the revelation that followed in the text, namely, plural marriage. This equation of celestial marriage and exalted priestly authority led naturally to the belief that such marriages were a legitimating requirement for high Church office.

Because plural marriage constituted for the Saints an "order of the priesthood," to not practice it was to lack a form of priesthood authority prerequisite to leading the congregation of the Church. This meant that plural marriage was a necessary condition of LDS leadership position and priestly power. When Senator Hoar observed to Joseph F. Smith, during Smith's 1904 testimony in the Smoot hearing, that the New Testament "apostle says that a bishop must be sober and must be the husband of one wife," Smith responded, "At least."[18] Hoar was amused, but Smith could not have been. His task was formidable. To ensure the temporal survival of the Church, he had to amend the Saints' belief while defending polygamy's divine origin. Dedicatory services held throughout the Church involved not simply remembering but also forgetting.

Retracing Their Steps

On December 18, 1905, President Joseph F. Smith and the remaining members of his administration boarded a specially designated train car that would carry them from Salt Lake City to Sharon, Vermont.[19] Before returning to their headquarters behind the Rocky Mountains, this aging, second generation of leaders and their mature children would travel 5,500 miles and visit the formative sites of their faith, preaching the Mormon past and future in the East and Midwest. The trip to Vermont, with its choices of where and where not to go and what meanings to assign to Joseph Smith's life while commemorating his birth both symbolized and affected twentieth-century Mormonism. Ultimately when Joseph F. Smith dedicated the monument, the nephew not only remembered the uncle, he initiated a collective forgetting of the founder's last revelation: plural marriage. In its place, he gave renewed significance to Joseph Smith's first revelation, which permitted the expression of LDS difference in terms of religious belief, not practice; namely, a non-Trinitarian theology and claims to unique revelatory authority. In short, Joseph F. Smith created a new and more socially tolerable source of otherness for his Church where existing differences with the rest of the country were threatening it with extinction.

No one was better suited to the task of melding past and present into a new future than "Joseph F.," as he was called by the faithful. Notwithstanding the familiarity of this reference, both his pedigree and his personality made him a formidable figure in Church circles. He was a curious combination of frontier toughness, political sophistication, and religious certainty. He had been present at every stage of the Latter-day Saint colonization of the vast intermountain territory of the American West and had traveled widely throughout the United States, the Pacific Islands, and Europe. For a self-educated frontiersman, he had a surprising breadth of knowledge and facility with argument, as the Senate hearing committee would discover. While he was his people's undisputed leader in spiritual matters, having served in the highest counsels of Church government since 1867, he was also captain of the Church's many industrial, commercial, and political enterprises. Politically, he had served both his Church and state as colonist, city councilman, legislator, Washington lobbyist, and drafter of Utah's constitution. It was Joseph F. who engineered the Church's alignment with the Republican Party, and who defended Smoot against those within the Church who called for his resignation rather than have the Church endure the scrutiny of a Senate investigation.

The source of his people's confidence in Joseph F. was, however, probably not a function of his skilled leadership but his identity with all the trials they had endured to date.[20] His character and personality were shaped in an environment of extraordinary personal sacrifice and by experiences of abject loss and extreme terror. Born in 1838, he was immediately caught in the Saints' brutal flight to Illinois, catalyzed by Missouri's extermination order. Over the next few years, he saw the Mormon utopia, Nauvoo, Illinois, created out of a swamp on the Mississippi River and then evacuated by force of mob violence. On his thirty-sixth birthday, Smith wrote in his journal, "my soul has never thoroughly dispelled the darkening shadows cast upon it by the lowering gloom of that eventful period."[21] The Church's second exodus in six years was precipitated by the murder of Joseph F.'s father and uncle. He was five and a half at the time. The memories of the escape from Illinois were sufficiently traumatic that he did not visit the site of his father's violent death until 1906 despite having been in the vicinity several times. He matured in Utah Territory under circumstances that continued to school him in the destructive antagonism between his Church and the United States. His mother died from the hardships of building a homestead in the barren Salt Lake Basin, making him an orphan at thirteen. His temper earned him an early mission call at the age of fifteen to the Sandwich Islands. When he returned five years later, he found "all Utah" aflame with the war spirit and "preparing to resist the impending invasion of Salt Lake Valley."

President James Buchanan had sent the U.S. Army to subdue the Mormon kingdom, and Smith's first night home from the mission field was spent "molding rifle bullets from a pig of lead." "I then proceeded to the front," he said.[22] For the next forty years, he was on the front line in every battle his Church fought with the nation, including of course the furor over plural marriage. Smith had five plural wives and forty-two children by the time he was subpoenaed to testify in the Smoot hearing. The following year at age sixty-seven, when he boarded the train to Joseph Smith's Vermont birthplace, Joseph F. embodied his Church no less than the man he sought to memorialize.

Arriving on December 22, the party from Salt Lake City, joined by Mormons from New York and Boston, must have nearly overwhelmed the little hamlet of South Royalton. The town rose to the occasion, however, and greeted the Latter-day Saints with a resolution "recognizing the right of said [LDS] persons to worship God according to the dictates of their own conscience." In a "broad spirit of toleration," they offered the Utah delegation use of the town hall. Their hospitality was no doubt warmed by the financing incident to hauling to such a remote place "the largest polished shaft we know of in America, and perhaps the world." The spectacle of its installation included planking roads, shoring up bridges, shearing off groves of trees when granite went awry, and hitching as many as twenty-two horses to a special wagon and, behind them, another four horses with a battering ram "for the last push."[23] Why all the effort? President Smith had stated the goal at the Church's general conference the previous October. The Saints must, he said, proclaim "that 'Mormonism' is a living, moving entity; that it is not dead nor sleeping, but that it is alive and awake, growing and advancing in the land; and let the world know it."[24] The celebration of Joseph Smith's legacy was meant to signal that the movement he founded had both the intention and the resources necessary to continue on a grand scale.

Of course, this message was intended for critics who declared that "the Smoot case will abolish Mormonism without war."[25] But the outside world was not Smith's only audience. The monument sent a strong message to believing but demoralized Latter-day Saints. Testimony solicited from Church leaders during the Smoot hearing had at times challenged LDS beliefs. Especially difficult had been Joseph F. Smith's testimony that the "guidance" he received from God was "the same as any other member of the church."[26] Thus, it was serendipitous that the centennial of Joseph Smith's birth came at a time when the faithful needed something to celebrate and needed particularly to celebrate him as the first in a succession of modern prophets. Significantly, for its first public celebration of Joseph Smith in the twentieth century, the Church chose an occasion unrestrained by any theological or ecclesiastical associations except those that the dedication party brought with them. Memorialization of a birth is the blankest of slates upon which to write a retrospective memory. Thus, the monument in Vermont was susceptible to embodying not only the nature and the permanence of LDS claims about their founding prophet but also their claims about the nature and permanence of their Church.

The dedication ceremony celebrated not only the Latter-day

Saint difference from but also similarity to their fellow citizens. For example, Joseph F. responded to Royalton's welcome by hosting a patriotic meeting and inviting everyone to the festivities. Going east as they did in the midst of the crisis posed by the Smoot hearing, the Mormon party was not unaware of the renewed attacks on their patriotism and never failed to remark on their identification with America's origins. Calling the first members of the Church the "pilgrim fathers No. 2," one LDS speaker reminded his listeners that the Mormons were "descended of stock from New England—from Massachusetts, New Hampshire, Rhode Island and Vermont and from everywhere else."[27] In Boston, apostle and future Church president George A. Smith noted that "'Mormon people have been the builders of a great commonwealth in the … Western country. And now for the first time they have turned their faces back, as it were, to begin to build in New England."[28] Like the decision to send Smoot to Washington in the first place, the monument erected to Joseph Smith's memory signaled the Church's intent to come out from behind the mountains and claim a place in America at large. Whereas Smoot's election constituted a claim to participate in America's future, the monument staked a claim to America's past. For the Saints, the dedicatory ceremonies marked an attempt at homecoming and healing: "And now we come back. The west and the east meet here. … [W]e want your friendship; and you have ours."[29] Joseph F. Smith's party had come to celebrate their Church's New England origins with New Englanders and to express their shared history and citizenship with all Americans at every stop along the way.

There was, however, also an exclusivity to their dedicatory celebration when they reflected upon the historical significance of reversing their pioneering trek and remembered the losses which characterized their youth. Indeed, all the Latter-day Saints assembled in memorial services throughout the Church were "reckoning the time from the birth of their prophet, leader and organizer."[30] According to that reckoning, their history not only "repeated the labors and successes of the Pilgrim Fathers" but also was "the fufillment of the dreams of the ancient prophets. … Jerusalem, Shechem, and Capernaum rise again from the great American Desert, and the Lord has remembered His promise to Jacob."[31] Rehearsals of Church history during the dedication were preludes to claims of survival and even triumphant growth in numbers and status. Such reckoning typifies the work inherent in commemoration, especially in times of crisis.

Maurice Halbwachs inaugurated the concept and many have built upon his studies of collective remembering.[32] Central to his thesis is the insight that commemoration is inevitably a function of selective memory and entail the equally important task of forgetting. As David Thelan put it: "People develop a shared identity by identifying, exploring, and agreeing on memories. ... In the course of taking a picture or creating an album they decide *what* they want to remember and *how* they want to remember it."[33] In 1905 the Latter-day Saints were about to turn the American landscape into their scrapbook. During Joseph F. Smith's administration, the Church began to recover and reconstruct the sites of its early history in New York, Ohio, Missouri, Illinois, and Iowa. Consistent with Pierre Nora's observation generally, the Latter-day Saints felt the need for "places of memory" at the very time when they felt at risk of a breach with their past.[34] The Utahns' claim to a piece of Vermont was a collective act of remembering which helped them forget a past they could not carry with them into the future. They would be so successful that eventually they would hardly be aware that they were agreeing to forget and, if made aware, would tend to think they were forgetting only Joseph Smith's immediate successors, who practiced plural marriage. In fact, however, the Progressive Era Saints were in the process of forgetting Joseph Smith's legacy.

Leaving overt historicizing to others, Joseph F. Smith's participation in the dedication was limited to blessing the monument. His prayer stipulated the elements of Joseph Smith's mission that would be carried forward into the twentieth century. Thanking God for "the great Prophet and Seer of the nineteenth century," Joseph F. made an offering of each element of the monument in terms of its religious significance. The huge cement foundation symbolized the primitive Church or "the foundation Thou has laid, of Apostles and Prophets, with Jesus Christ, Thy son, as the chief corner stone." Upon this foundation was laid a four-foot-thick, thirty-ton granite base "typifying the rock of revelation."

Lastly, erected on the base and measuring a foot for each year of his life, a thirty-eight-and-a-half-foot shaft of granite represented Joseph Smith. The shaft was polished to symbolize Smith's "reflecting the light of heaven" and crowned to illustrate successful completion of his earthly mission and the possibility for all to be similarly glorified.[35] These three elements—a foundational restoration of Christ's Church from apostasy, a base of continuing revelation from heaven, and an assertion of Joseph Smith's revelatory power and divine authority bestowed to those who follow—are arguably the core elements of LDS doctrine. They summarize the Church's message and frame its identity within American denominationalism. In place of a nineteenth-century emphasis on theocratic and familial kingdom-building, the Latter-day Saints were turning now to less grandiose but still large claims regarding the restoration of the primitive Church, divine sponsorship, and living prophets. These claims were carved in stone literally on the surface of the Joseph Smith monument. Figuratively, they would be as indelibly inscribed on twentieth-century Latter-day Saint identity through the reorientation of the Church's doctrinal priorities.

Carved on the monument's northerly side was a reference to Joseph Smith's initial theophany in 1820 when he was instructed not to join any existing Church. Other surfaces were devoted to Smith's subsequent experiences of angelic restoration of knowledge and authority to organize "the Church of Jesus Christ in its fullness and perfection."[36] Arguably, these assertions of restored truth, authority, and Church order constitute the creative material out of which the LDS Church adapts itself over time. Moreover, because these claims comprise both the boundaries and content of Latter-day Saint identity—the sense of separateness from non-Mormons and of internal coherence as Mormons—they mark the outside limit of what may be changed without disturbing the sense of continuity with their past. Virtually every other aspect of LDS belief is relatively fungible, making the Church extraordinarily adaptable and identifiable at the same time. This can be seen by the deployment of these claims both to compensate for the loss of celestial marriage and to defend against the threat this loss posed to the prophet's legacy, especially as it authorized the prophets who succeeded him.

Putting First Things First

Joseph Smith claimed to have received many revelations, all of which were, to varying degrees, indices of his prophetic stature and were mined for their theological significance by successive generations of believers. This is especially true of what is called the First Vision. According to Smith's own account, it occurred in 1820 when concerns about competitive revivalism motivated the fourteen-year-old Smith to try to determine which evangelical Church to join.

Relying on biblical injunction to pray for wisdom, he retired to the woods to ask "which of all the sects was right (for at this time it had never entered into my heart that all were wrong)—and which I should join."[37] The canonized account of the vision states that two divine personages appeared to Smith and identified themselves as God and Jesus Christ. As foreshadowed in his restatement of his question, they "answered that I must join none of [the Churches], for they were all wrong."[38] Hence, two key teachings of Mormonism make their first appearance in this First Vision.

Of greatest import in the nineteenth century was the instruction not to join any of the existing Churches. This private message to Joseph Smith about a widespread apostasy was publicly taught ten years later in the publication of the Book of Mormon. The other doctrine was implicit in Smith's description of God and the Son as "personages" and marked an immediate and radical break with traditional creeds. However, if noted at all by Mormonism's early critics, Latter-day Saints' belief in a godhead of three separate personages was considered only one among many unpleasantly distinctive elements of Mormonism and secondary in concern to the faith's new scripture, priesthood hierarchy, economic communalism, temple building, modern revelation, and of course plural marriage.[39]

Many factors contributed to the relative lack of interest in the First Vision by nineteenth-century believers and nonbelievers. Most have been identified by Latter-day Saint scholars in a variety of articles attempting to validate the historicity of the event or its relationship to developments in LDS doctrine.[40] Though these studies disagree on the First Vision's theological implications, what matters for our purposes is that all agree, in the words of James B. Allen, author of the most extensive study, that "the weight of evidence would suggest that it [the First Vision] was not a matter of common knowledge, even among Church members, in the earliest years of Mormon history."[41] As Allen's research makes apparent, though the First Vision was used in a sermon as early as 1883, the turning point in the First Vision's status occurred during the administration of Joseph F. Smith and, significantly for the purposes of this essay, contemporaneous with the Smoot hearing and its immediate aftermath. The story was first used in LDS Sunday School texts in 1905, in priesthood instructional manuals in 1909, as a separate missionary tract in 1910, and in histories of the Church in 1912. Moreover, in 1907 the Smith family farm in Palmyra, New York, was purchased and passed into Church ownership in 1916 and a grove of trees on the site, where Joseph Smith was assumed to have had the First Vision, became an increasingly popular pilgrimage site, culminating in centennial celebrations in 1920. By mid-century, Joseph Smith's account of his theophany was denominated the "Joseph Smith Story." Eventually this story would be granted the status of "the beginning point, the fountainhead, of the restoration of the gospel in this dispensation."[42] In the First Vision, Progressive-Era president Joseph F. Smith, whose tenure lasted until his death in 1918, had found a marker of LDS identity whose pedigree was as great as, and would be made greater than, that of plural marriage for the twentieth-century Saints.

The First Vision contained all the elements necessary to fill the historical, scriptural, and theological void created by the abandonment of plural marriage. Where plural marriage was revered as Joseph Smith's last revelation, the First Vision, as its referent indicates, was equally appealing. It also, like polygamy, was an idea that could be characterized as having attracted persecution. Already, by claiming to be the only true Church in a religiously plural society, nineteenth-century Saints had not endeared themselves to their neighbors. Moreover, though it was not of as much note as the Book of Mormon or other doctrines, the Saints' rejection of Trinitarianism appears to have been a source of some antagonism. Joseph Smith's mother recounted, "The different denominations are very much opposed to us. ... The Methodists also come, and they rage, for they worship a God without body or parts, and they know that our faith comes in contact with this principle."[43]

Whether the Methodists knew this from accounts of Joseph Smith's theophany did not matter to the twentieth-century Latter-day Saints: they believed it to be so.[44] From here it was a small step to finding in the First Vision a source of the Latter-day Saints' continuing identity with their forebears. In 1909, still feeling the aftershocks of the Smoot hearing through negative press reports, Joseph F. Smith told the Church: "From the day that the Prophet Joseph Smith first declared his vision until now … the enemy to direct revelation from God and to the inspirations that come from the heavens to man has been arrayed against this work."[45] New emphasis on the First Vision maintained a sense of religious difference from neighbors and, as such, provided the equally necessary sense of internal cohesiveness and historical continuity in terms of persecution.

Significantly, however, the First Vision changed the arena of confrontation over differences from social action to theological belief, a necessity created not only by the experience of persecution but also by Supreme Court law. In *Reynolds v. U.S.*, the Court made clear that America would tolerate only differences in religious thought, not religiously motivated actions that competed with social mores.[46] New emphasis on the First Vision reframed the Latter-day Saints' necessary sense of otherness to fit safely within the politics of American religion. Unlike his teachings on plural marriage, Joseph Smith's First Vision placed his followers at odds with Churches, not the state, and shifted the battle from issues of public morality to theological tenets.

Like plural marriage, however, the First Vision was capable of being formalized as doctrine fundamental to the faith. An account of it had been added to the Church's scriptural canon in 1880 on motion of Joseph F. Smith, then a counselor in the LDS presidency. Thus, this first revelation to Joseph Smith was susceptible to obtaining the same formal authority becoming formalized and assuming as central a role as his last. Moreover, in 1902 under the direction of Joseph F. Smith, the text of the founder's autobiography was divided into chapters and verses and integrated by reference to the rest of LDS scripture. This served to give the First Vision status equal to the visions of biblical and Book of Mormon prophets.

The successful formalization of the First Vision and its placement at the core of LDS identity is neatly summarized by an apostle called to his position during the Smoot hearings: "One outstandingly distinguishing feature of this Church is divine authority by direct revelation. The appearing of the Father and the Son to Joseph Smith is the foundation of this Church. Therein lies the secret of its strength and vitality. ... What God is, is answered. His relation to his children is clear. His interest in humanity through authority delegated to man is apparent. The future of the work is assured."[47]

The "assurance" provided by the First Vision was in no small part due to its synthesis of ideas so necessary to LDS faith: an immanent God, modern revelation, and divine imprimatur for ecclesiastical authority. Despite such extravagant endorsement of the First Vision's theological substance, however, its significance cannot be fully appreciated if seen merely as a container for LDS theology. The twentieth-century role of the First Vision, especially as contextualized within Joseph Smith's autobiography, can only be appreciated when viewed as a narrative, even a story of origins or a myth with the capacity to order the reader's experience of time. The Latter-day Saints had a particular need for order during Joseph F. Smith's administration; so it is that during these years the First Vision emerges not only as a source of doctrine but also as the modern Church's master narrative.

Mormonism's Master Narrative

Joseph Smith's autobiography covers only his early years and is commonly referred to within the Church as the "Joseph Smith Story." As indicated by the broad attribution in its title, the narrative is deemed to communicate the essence of Smith's life and work; notwithstanding the fact that it covers only a few events during a nine-year period that, significantly, preceded the organization of the Church in 1830. The events around which the narrative is constructed are: (1) Smith's First Vision in 1820 of the Father and the Son; (2) several appearances between 1823 and 1827 of an angel named Moroni who instructed Smith and directed him to the hiding place of the record he would publish as the Book of Mormon; and (3) an appearance in 1829 of the resurrected John the Baptist who ordained Smith and another colleague to priestly authority.

While other versions of Smith's autobiography include additional events, and the contemporaneously kept record of Smith's life is voluminous, only these early events were legitimized by canonization and employed as Smith's "story."[48] Why they were considered sufficient to constitute the essences if not the whole of Smith's biographical significance and deemed worthy of canonization can be deduced in part from the earlier discussion of the dedication of the Joseph Smith monument. Namely, these three events in Joseph Smith's life correspond directly to the three principles memorialized in the 1905 dedication ceremonies and lie at Mormonism's core: a foundational restoration of Christ's Church from apostasy, a base of continuing revelation from heaven, and an assertion of Joseph Smith's revelatory power and divine authority bestowed to those who follow.

As a narrative, however, the autobiography places these principles in a plot that, by definition, is an ordering of events in time and allows readers to experiment with the world offered by the plot. In theory, by sympathetic participation with a narrative and by interpreting the writer's offered order of events, readers construct meaning for themselves. "It is," Ricoeur argues, "the very heart of reading that explanation and interpretation are indefinitely opposed and reconciled."[49] Reconciliation of contemporary oppositions by its readers is anticipated by the other names given to the Joseph Smith story, namely, the "Joseph Smith Testimony" and, in the most recent version of LDS scripture, "Joseph Smith—History." In appealing to these types of discourse—story, testimony, history—the autobiography signals its narrative uses that do more than merely state a theological principle.

Naturally the "reconciled" meaning the reader derives from any story will depend upon the immediate questions he or she brings to it. Thus, one way to understand the appeal or explanatory power of a given narrative in a given time is to consider its community of readers and their circumstances. For the Joseph Smith story, which achieved its popularity in the LDS Church between 1905 and 1920, this means seeing it through the eyes of a Church readership struggling in the midst of external attack and on the verge of internal schism over the abandonment of prior commitments and wanting to know whether their Church was still "the only true and living Church on the face of the whole earth."[50] From its very first sentence, there can be no doubt that Joseph Smith's 1838 canonized autobiography is an explanatory defense of Church origins:

> Owing to the many reports which have been put in circulation by evil-disposed and designing persons, in relation to the rise and progress of the Church of Jesus Christ of Latter-day Saints, all of which have been designed by the authors thereof to militate against its character as a Church and its progress in the world—I have been induced to write this history, to disabuse the public mind, and put all inquirers after truth into possession of the facts, as they have transpired, in relation both to myself and the Church.[51]

After a brief introduction, the narrative begins immediately by describing the tension in Smith's search for religious certainty amid competing truth claims, and it ends ten printed pages later with the hero's receipt of heavenly endowment of power to organize a Church.

In the different accounts of his experience, Joseph Smith emphasized different motivations for his 1820 prayer. As indicated above, in the canonized version of the story, Smith's First Vision was prompted by his concern to know which of the contending denominations was God's Church.[52] Dictated in 1838, just months after Smith was forced from Kirtland, Ohio, by mob action, this version reflects its contemporaneous circumstances: an organized and hunted Church in combat with its neighbors. The account is, therefore, not surprisingly preoccupied with persecution, using the word seventeen times in its ten pages. On one level, then, the story's appeal to the early twentieth-century Church, embattled in another anti-polygamy campaign and fearing constitutional disfranchisement, is obvious. By his own account, Joseph Smith's sense of persecution was aroused by accusations regarding his family's poverty and local treasure-hunting activities, as well as other aspersions on his own integrity.

For twentieth-century readers of the account, however, what mattered most were those portions of the story related to allegations of heresy by Protestant critics, as indicated above by Joseph F. Smith's conclusion that persecution resulted primarily from his uncle's doctrine of God. In addition, Progressive-Era Saints, so small in numbers and capital relative to the larger population, must have been drawn to the story's portrait of endurance and certainty of purpose:

> It caused me serious reflection then, and often has since, how very strange it was that an obscure boy, of a little over fourteen years of age, and one, too, who was doomed to the necessity of obtaining a scanty maintenance by his daily labor, should be thought a character of sufficient importance to attract the attention of the great ones of the most popular sects of the day, and in a manner to create in them a spirit of the most bitter persecution and reviling. But strange or not, so it was, and it was often the cause of great sorrow to myself.
>
> However, it was nevertheless a fact that I had beheld a vision. I have thought since, that I felt much like Paul, when he made his defense before King Agrippa, and related the account of the vision he had when he saw a light, and heard a voice; but still there were but few who believed him; some said he was dishonest, others said he was mad; and he was ridiculed and reviled. But all this did not destroy the reality of his vision. He had seen a vision, he knew he had, and all the persecution under heaven could not make it otherwise; and though they should persecute him unto death, yet he knew, and would know to his latest breath, that he had both seen a light and heard a voice speaking unto him, and all the world could not make him think or believe otherwise.
>
> So it was with me. I had actually seen a light, and in the midst of that light I saw two Personages, and they did in reality speak to me; and though I was hated and persecuted for saying that I had seen a vision, yet it was true; and while they were persecuting me, reviling me, and speaking all manner of evil against me for so saying, I was led to say in my heart: Why persecute me for telling the truth? I have actually seen a vision; and who am I that I can withstand God, or why does the world think to make me deny what I have actually seen? For I had seen a vision; I knew it, and I knew that God knew it, and I could not deny it, neither dared I do it; ... I had found the testimony of James to be true—that a man who lacked wisdom might ask of God, and obtain, and not be upbraided.[53]

This was the Latter-day Saints' "perfect man," whom they memorialized in polished granite: the seeker who became a prophet by means of theophany and unwavering public witness.[54] It was a model of perfection under pressure that they themselves aspired to when they built a monument to him in 1905 and began reading his story with renewed interest.

The second pivotal event in the narrative is the appearance of an angel who, according to the account, repeatedly instructed Joseph Smith about the meaning of biblical scripture and directed him to a new scripture, the Book of Mormon. This is the second of the three themes celebrated by the Joseph Smith monument: restored truth through divine communication with a prophet. For twentieth-century LDS leaders, the numerous biblical references made in Joseph Smith's account of the angel's instruction provided an additional basis for demonstrating the holy pedigree of several LDS doctrines. As one Church leader explained:

> At the second vision that the Prophet Joseph received, ... [a]mong the things that were revealed to him was the principle of vicarious work for the dead, and the principle of the gathering of the people, principles of our Church that are unique to it. These were given by the angel Moroni. He also read from the book of Malachi about the hearts of children being turned to their fathers, and the fathers' hearts to the children. He read to him the eleventh chapter of Isaiah, which refers to the gathering; and other principles he explained to the young man. Today we have heard read how much has been given for temples and for temple buildings, and this shows that the Latter-day Saints believe in the principle revealed to the Prophet Joseph as early as 1823.[55]

Here the practice of performing ordinances vicariously for the dead, a particularly twentieth-century initiative of the Church, is validated by the Joseph Smith story.[56] Though Smith had introduced baptism for the dead as early as 1840, the primary focus of his Nauvoo discourses had been the role of the temple in relation to doctrines of deification and celestial marriage or its sanctifying import for the living. As discussed below, the definition of celestial marriage would be adapted and a new priority assigned to vicarious work for the dead during the twentieth century. Though not the sole source by any means, the Joseph Smith story became an important authorizing agent for twentieth-century theologizing on LDS temples and priesthood.

Most fundamentally, however, the narrative account of Moroni's appearance to and education of Joseph Smith conveys the necessity of revelation and its triumph over worldly opposition. The narrative makes the latter point when it relates a failed attempt to validate the Book of Mormon's historical claims by showing its purportedly ancient script to Columbia University professor Charles Anthon. According to the account, once Anthon realized the source of the characters, he withdrew his endorsement, "saying, that there was no such thing now as ministering of angels."[57] In Professor Anthon's reaction, later readers of the Joseph Smith story would see, as did Smith himself in his 1832 account, the fulfillment of the learned-man prophecy of Isaiah 29 and be reminded that they should not expect, neither would they need, worldly assistance. When, in 1905, the dedication party included in its itinerary a prayer meeting on the hill where Joseph Smith said he retrieved the Book of Mormon record, they came away with a renewed conviction of "the truth of the latter-day work and the for[e]telling its ultimate triumph over opposing powers."[58] Thus, the second of Smith's visions also was a useful source of interpretation of present events and source of continuity with their past.[59]

The final event in the canonized version of Joseph Smith's story occurs in 1829 and illustrates the same principles as the previous events: ongoing revelation in an atmosphere of opposition but with promises of triumph. Motivated by questions during his work on the Book of Mormon, Smith prayed again for guidance. Implicit in the result of the prayer is concern for authority. An account of baptism in the Book of Mormon left Smith and his scribe, Oliver Cowdery, wondering how to receive a remission of sin if, as they believed, no existing Church were an acceptable agent of God. The short of the story is that a resurrected John the Baptist appeared to Smith and Cowdery, ordained them with authority not only to baptize but also to organize a Church, and promised that further authority would be bestowed in the future. The words Smith ascribed to the angelic visitor provide the pre-Church beginnings of Churchly authority to receive continuing revelation: "Upon you my fellow servants, in the name of Messiah I confer the Priesthood of Aaron, which holds the keys of the ministering of angels, and of the Gospel of repentance, and of baptism by immersion for the remission of sins; and this shall never be taken again from the earth, until the sons of Levi do offer again an offering unto the Lord in righteousness."[60]

The endowment of authority and promise of permanence, like the experiential knowledge of God modeled in the First Vision, and the idea of a continuing knowledge from God illustrated in the second, provided the foundation upon which the Latter-day Saints could tolerate a changing Church. Thus, Smith's story is also denominated his "testimony" or witness of the divine origins of the Church, its authority, and its future possibilities. No less than other cannonized narratives, the official account of Joseph Smith's early years begins "a history directed by a 'promise' and moving to a 'fulfillment.'"[61] When, in the first decades of this century, the Latter-day Saints broke finally with their immediate past, they found present stability—not merely theology—in Joseph Smith's testimony of promises made prior to the organization of their Church. Herein lay the greatest strength of the Church's new twentieth-century uses of the Joseph Smith story as a myth of Mormon origins.

To the extent that Joseph Smith's canonized story is concerned exclusively with events that occurred prior to the organization of the Church, the narrative's concerns are primordial and function like other myths of origination. "In recounting how these things began and how they will end," said Ricoeur, "the myth places the experience of [the reader or listener] in a whole that receives orientation and meaning from the narration. Thus, an understanding of human reality as a whole operates through the myth by means of a reminiscence and an expectation."[62] The Joseph Smith story was able to capture the attention of Church members in the Progressive-Era because it oriented them, giving authority and order to their contemporary experience of crisis and providing hope for the future in its promise that their bond with the sacred would not be broken.[63] Throughout the Joseph Smith autobiographical account of Mormon origins, the reader's *expectation,* to use Ricoeur's term, is shaped by promises of a divine relationship, revelation, and authority, all of which eased the Church's entry into the twentieth century.

Probably the most extravagant and comforting promise was the last, namely, that the authority by which the Church could be organized (and, implicitly, susceptible to reorganization) "shall never be taken again from the earth." The believing reader of the Joseph Smith story was thereby assured that Smith's restoration would be permanent. With this promise, Smith's canonized story *cum* testimony *qua* history of Church origins climaxed in an affirmation of unchangeable ecclesiastical authority that mediates divine knowledge and power.

Richard L. Bushman concluded his biography of Joseph Smith's early years with the observation, "What distinguished Mormonism [in the nineteenth century] was not so much the Gospel Mormons taught ... but what they believed had happened—to Joseph Smith, to Book of Mormon characters, and to Moses and Enoch. ... Mormonism was history, not philosophy."[64] As implied by reference to Moses and Enoch and by placing Smith in such company, it is obvious to anyone familiar with the LDS reworking of the traditional Jewish and Christian canon that the Mormon sense of history is a cosmological one.[65] Thus, it is also possible to elaborate on Bushman's observation to conclude that what distinguished Mormons was the conviction that the cosmological order was expressed immediately in the mundane.

Note, for example, that Smith's canonized autobiography was placed in LDS scripture immediately following the LDS version of Moses's and Abraham's theophanies and is of a type with them: a type bearing promise of fulfillment in a new aeon in God's relation to his people. A sermon by one who participated in the revival of Joseph Smith's story illustrates his relation to this biblical type: "There has been some reference here today to the First Vision of the Prophet Joseph, which we look upon as the dawn of this last dispensation, the dispensation of the fullness of times."[66] This sense of new time, a "fullness" of time, given by Joseph Smith's narrative of primordial Church events contributed significantly to the third-generation Latter-day Saints' capacity to embrace change in Church doctrines and programs without a loss of identity or loss of continuity with their past.

For the Latter-day Saints, Progressive Era changes were ordered within a cosmology of promise and fulfillment, which lent stability to efforts to revoke the theocracy, economic communalism, and plural marriage of the previous generation. The Latter-day Saints' confidence in their cosmology may have been shaken by the defensive and prevaricating testimony of Church witnesses at the Smoot hearing, by the confusion and disarray in Church policy, and by the removal of Taylor and Cowley, but the history of their pre-Church judgment and bond with the sacred, as explained in Joseph Smith's story, was a means of restoring origins of their confidence through the constructive capacity of both nineteenth-century writer and his twentieth-century readers. The Latter-day Saints managed the dislocating experience of passage into the twentieth century by inscribing their present experience onto Joseph Smith's, which promised changeless duration, even the "fullness of times." In placing confidence in the promises of divine presence, revelation, and authority that, as the angel promised, "shall never be taken again from the earth," not in particular practices or doctrines, the believing reader of Joseph Smith's testimony could appropriate a future in which failure was impossible.

The Joseph Smith Story was no less effective in providing a new basis for individual LDS identity. In the process of inscribing their own experiences onto his, believing readers made Joseph Smith the model of modern Latter-day Sainthood. A Church authority and major interpreter of doctrine during this period wrote, "The whole latter-day work was initiated by Joseph Smith's search for truth. ... Thus came the first great vision of Joseph Smith; and as a consequence of his search for truth came the other revelations, and the enduring light-giving structure of the Church. ... It is understood that every worthy member of the Church must likewise seek and find truth for himself."[67] The *sine qua non* of Latter-day Saint religious experience was to seek and find the true Church through revelation. Thus, also as a pattern for individual spirituality, the Church's new emphasis on the Joseph Smith Story effectively strengthened Joseph Smith's status as a prophet.

Ultimately, however, Mormonism's transition had to be made collectively. To remain the same to itself and others, it had to enter the twentieth century as a people, not merely as believing individuals. Acts of collective memorial; new emphasis on restored order, authority, and revelation; and a shared mythos of origination provided a non-discursive redefinition of Latter-day Saint identity. Discursive redefinition was also necessary, however. Certain subjects could not be discussed and new names had to be found for others, just as certain places were remembered and others were not. The return itinerary of the dedication party both effected and symbolized this final way of changing and remaining the same.

Accentuating the Positive, Eliminating the Negative

Leaving Vermont the day after the dedication, Joseph F. Smith and his party traveled to Massachusetts and held public services in Boston in the afternoon and evening of December 24, 1905. Christmas Day was occupied by a visit to the Massachusetts homestead of the progenitors of Joseph Smith. From there the party traveled to Palmyra, New York, paying homage at the Smith family farm and its sacred grove, site of the First Vision. They held a prayer meeting at the Hill Cumorah, reputed discovery site of the Book of Mormon. From New York, the party traveled to Kirtland, a small town in northern Ohio where Smith had gathered his followers on the new frontier in 1831, eight months after organizing the Church in New York. This was the final site of the commemorative activities related to Joseph Smith's role in the Church. The travelers made only one more stop on their way home. On a two-day visit to Chicago, they spent the majority of time observing local industries, such as the Swift Stockyards and the Jeffries Automobile Factory, and paying respects to various businessmen.

Thus, the travelers retraced the Church's steps as far as Kirtland, Ohio, and the final years of Smith's ministry went unremarked upon. In geographic terms, this meant the party did not visit Independence, near Kansas City, Missouri, and site of Joseph Smith's first attempt to build an American Zion. Neither did they stop in Nauvoo, the town from which the Latter-day Saints fled to the Rocky Mountains. Nauvoo lies on the western border of Illinois midway between Chicago and Omaha and, like Independence, has powerful associations with developments in LDS doctrine. For example, plural marriage was first practiced in Nauvoo, as were the nascent forms of theocratic government that would find full expression in Utah. Similarly, the anti-capitalist principles that had characterized Utah's economy were first practiced in Missouri. Finally, though Kirtland was the site of the first LDS temple, the ceremonies and oaths of such concern to the Smoot hearing panel were performed only later in Nauvoo. In sum, the practices that placed the Church in conflict with American institutions were largely a product of LDS history in Missouri and Illinois, and to these sites the dedication party did not go.

While stopping at either Independence or Nauvoo would have been a detour for the travelers, it would have been no more so than Kirtland, to which they backtracked from Cleveland "going at a slow pace, because of the condition of the road and of the hills and hollows, at the old-fashioned ox-team speed."[68] Moreover, in an itinerary that took them by train from Chicago to Omaha, Nauvoo was directly in their path. If they had not spent two days in Chicago, one might explain the omission in terms of time constraints; but whatever the reason, the result was that their itinerary emphasized the less controversial stages of Joseph Smith's life, and their sermons, to Church member and nonmember alike, similarly emphasized his less controversial ideas.[69] In this respect, too, the dedication party illustrated a means by which Mormonism transformed itself during the period.

Avoidance of certain topics was to be expected from the travelers. Since the 1880s the Church had abandoned all efforts to defend plural marriage to outsiders and had become careful even among members to not say much publicly. Only at local conferences of the Saints where nonmembers were unlikely to overhear had the subject been taught. It was no surprise, then, that the few allusions to polygamy during the Vermont trip were indirect and defensive. In Chicago, for example, Joseph F. Smith assured visitors: "We are not seeking for women; we have women of our own and they are as good and pure as ever women were on the earth."[70] On other subjects, too, the Church became increasingly careful, and its public discourse changed on such subjects as theocracy, millennialism, and deification. For example, the phrase "fullness of the gospel" was sometimes employed to represent primitive Christianity, not, as had been the case, all ordinances and truths ever revealed in the Bible and then some. Past emphasis on deification shifted to appeals for ethical perfection: "'Mormonism' is to benefit mankind. Obedience to it makes good men better, and bad men good. No man dare continue in wrongdoing and still claim membership in the Church of Jesus Christ of Latter-day Saints. That is one of the distinctive features of our people, and of this work." So said President Smith to the Vermonters, and his companions repeated the message throughout their trip: "If the Gospel will not make us better, by obedience to its precepts, then it is no better than any other religion. ... The religion that will make men the best of all in the world is the best religion and that religion has been embraced by the members of this Church, for it is the religion of Jesus Christ."[71]

Significantly, the message to member and nonmember became indistinguishable during this period. Instead of being admonished to do the works and receive the blessings of Abraham, the Saints were encouraged to manifest Yankee virtues and Progressive-Era values. Exhortations to missionary work overtook the other elements of nineteenth-century millennialism: growth, not gathering to Zion, was the rallying cry. During Joseph F. Smith's tenure, immigration to Utah was officially ended, and the Church began to build centers of membership abroad. Finally, celestial marriage was redefined in terms of the eternity, not the multiplicity, of the marriage covenant. It became understood exclusively as temple marriage for time and eternity.

The version of Mormonism lived publicly in the twentieth century was that taught in the first years of Joseph Smith's life and preached in New York and Ohio. The more exotic doctrines from the Missouri and Illinois periods remained in temples and were thus privately practiced. As Jan Shipps noted in her analysis of a conference address given by Joseph F. Smith ten years later:

> By concentrating on what the Mormons regard as essential principles of the gospel—the nature of God, Christ's role as Savior, the restoration of the Church and its place, and the place of the priesthood in humanity's quest for salvation and eternal life—Joseph F. Smith conveyed to the Saints his confidence that the changes which had occurred during his tenure were not changes which had in any way diminished the strength of the relationship between God and his chosen people.[72]

Whatever gap may have been created by redefining *inter alia* plural marriage as temple marriage, gathering as growth, and deification as moral perfection was bridged by the classic restorationist claims enumerated in the dedication of the monument to Smith. Studies show that the incidence of sermons at LDS General Conference on the theme of an apostasy by the primitive Church nearly quadrupled in the decades at the turn of the century. The assertion that the LDS Church was the "only true Church" tripled. Mention of fellowship with other faiths was lower than at any other time except between 1830 and 1859.[73] This development is even more pronounced given that, during this period, other restorationist Churches were minimizing their claims to primitive Christianity and choosing between evangelical or fundamentalist forms.[74]

In addition to these interpretive strategies that minimized Joseph Smith's revelation on plural marriage, the Church had to act more formally to reposition his revelations within Church dogma, both because the Senate demanded it and because the Saints needed it. Specifically in response to the Senate's demand, the Church canonized its abandonment of plural marriage by adding the 1890 Manifesto against polygamy to the *Book of Doctrine and Covenants* as an "official declaration."[75] The Church-owned *Deseret News* announced without fanfare: "A new edition of the Doctrine and Covenants has just been prepared and is for sale at the Deseret News Book Store. ... [In addition to a concordance] the edition also contains the official declaration generally known as the Manifesto of President [Wilford] Woodruff. We call special attention to this edition of one of the four standard works of the Church."[76]

The inclusion of the Manifesto in scripture was not introduced or later explained by the Church leadership. Silence on the new publication was profound, although it was a matter of considerable concern among Church leadership and many alternatives were considered.[77] Publicly, however, it was treated simply as an editorial determination like the addition of a concordance. Having so legitimated the Manifesto, it was necessary to account for the Church's nearly fifteen years of disobedience to it. The official explanation was that post-Manifesto marriages were few in number, initiated by individuals, and caused by understandable differences of interpretation:

> Since that time [1890] the Church has not performed any plural marriages or authorized any violation of the law thus forbidden. But there were some persons who construed the language of that Manifesto to signify plural marriages within the boundaries of the United States, that being 'the land' wherein the laws spoken of extended. They, therefore, went or removed to Mexico and thus acted on that which they

> believed to be right without violating the Manifesto. They looked on plural marriage within the United States as *malum prohibitum* and not *malum in se*.[78]

Published in 1911 in Church periodicals and pamphlets, this legalistic interpretation of the recent past and disclaimer of Church involvement attempted to satisfy insiders and outsiders that the institution was not responsible for polygamy's continuation into the twentieth century. Such had been the official position throughout the Smoot hearings, and the Church reiterated it whenever asked. Eventually outsiders lost interest and insiders accepted the interpretation at face value. Those members who needed particular reassurance received it privately. One very upset, post-Manifesto polygamous wife sent her brother to Joseph F. Smith to ask whether her marriage was legitimate. She turned to Smith not because he was president of the Church but because he had performed the ceremony. In an interview years later, the brother said Smith told him "to tell his sister that her marriage was o.k., but he had had to say what he did in Washington to protect the Church."[79] Those members, however, who could not accept the change and who contracted plural marriages after an injunction by Smith in 1904 were subjected to Church disciplinary courts beginning in 1911.[80]

For those who were willing to change, the effect of abandoning polygamy was cushioned doctrinally by three strategies. First and most obvious, the Church did not repeal Joseph Smith's revelation as canonized in the Doctrine and Covenants as Section 132. Indeed, the Manifesto was subordinated by placing it at the back of the book and labeling it a "declaration," not a revelation, thus making it of unequal weight to the other material within the main text. As stated by its own terms, the Manifesto's addition to the Doctrine and Covenants was understood to memorialize only a suspension of Church law out of respect for "laws enacted by Congress ... pronounced constitutional by the court of last resort."[81] True to the *Reynolds* decision, the Latter-day Saints would believe but would not act—except in the afterlife, that is. Second, then, change in marital practice was palliated by continuing commitment to the doctrine. The Church continued the practice to the extent that males whose previous wives were deceased were permitted to have subsequent marriages sanctioned by temple ordinance, believed to ensure marital status after death. Finally, through sermon and other doctrinal exposition, celestial marriage was equated exclusively with eternal marriage rather than plural marriage. Though this had been a defensive strategy in legal arguments since 1880, it now was universally applied within the Church as well.[82]

By avoiding Independence, Missouri, and Nauvoo, Illinois, the 1905 dedication party avoided even more than problematic theology, however. These were also the sites of martyrdom and persecution, the memory of which fueled the Saints' desire for political independence. Missouri was legendary among the Latter-day Saints for "mobocracy" or state-sanctioned efforts to exterminate Mormonism. In Illinois, Joseph Smith and his brother Hyrum were murdered while in the governor's protective custody. Although these places would not be forgotten and, in the next few years, would be developed as sites of pilgrimage, the 1905 centennial celebration's emphasis was not on justice and struggle but on forgiveness and progress.

Joseph F. Smith's progressiveness was also demonstrated in more subtle initiatives as he reframed the Church's sense of its past, shaping its history onto the American terrain and directing his people's attention beyond the Rocky Mountains to where he believed their future lay. Besides the Vermont birthplace, Joseph F. oversaw the purchase of the Smith family farm in New York; various plots of land in Missouri associated with the Church's continued expectation of Christ's second coming; the jail in Carthage, Illinois, where Joseph and Hyrum Smith were murdered by anti-Mormon mobs; and a cemetery near Omaha at Winter Quarters, Iowa, dedicated to those who did not survive the forced exodus from Illinois. Each of these places was a rich mine of Mormon history and, as such, was a uniquely powerful resource for the constructive maintenance of Mormon identity under stress. These sites constitute the focus of Mormon monument building and pilgrimage to this day.

Finally, Joseph F. Smith's constructive use of the Church's more distant and less morally complicated past was facilitated by the variety of centennials that occurred in the early twentieth century, beginning as we have seen with Joseph Smith's birth date. Where centennial anniversaries did not provide the occasion, Joseph F. developed his own. For example, paramount among identity markers for the Latter-day Saints was, of course, the heroic arrival of the pioneers to the Salt Lake Valley on July 24, 1847. Individual communities sometimes had held celebrations on this date to honor their aging settlers, and Joseph F. Smith's predecessor was known for planning the Pioneer Jubilee in 1897. Smith was the first, however, to incorporate a ritual celebration of the event into the Church calendar. Not waiting for a centennial occasion, he announced in 1905 that July 24 would be celebrated by the Church's Sunday schools. Characteristically, he did so with an eye to the future, not the past; on resourcefulness and triumph, not privations and travail; on rights, not wrongs.

He personally instructed his people:

> The leading purpose of the celebration is to provide an object lesson to our young people and create within their hearts feelings of patriotism and loyalty [to] those who pioneered the way to our western homes ... The object lesson should be given by a procession representing the condition of the Saints when they crossed the plains between the Missouri River and the Rocky Mountains. ... It is not the intention to make every Twenty-fourth of July an occasion for so elaborate a celebration, but it is hoped that it may be sufficiently frequent to keep alive in the hearts and the memories of our youth the instructive lessons of our pioneer life.[83]

As demonstrated by their annual "Pioneer Days" and reconstruction of LDS historical sites across the United States, the Latter-day Saints prove Connerton's hypothesis that "images of the past ... are conveyed and sustained by (more or less ritual) performances," not merely by texts.[84] The Saints demonstrate, also, however, that the combination of text and ritual is an especially powerful means of shaping the past to ensure a future.

Conclusion

It is of limited, if any, use for us to construe the LDS Church's actions during the Smoot hearings as "an intentional response to particular and variable social and political contexts."[85] We can only observe that central to the dynamism of LDS history during the Progressive Era was "inertia," or persistency, as Connerton would call it, or inherent "grammar" and tradition, to use Ricoeur's terms, of narratives and rituals employed by Joseph F. Smith to maintain both his peoples' religious faith and their American citizenship. The point of this analysis is not that Smith consciously invented or planned his way into the solutions that hindsight has shown to be so effective. Like most historical actors, he was subject to his share of ironic results and unintended consequences. Certainly he did not intend a four-year Senate investigation when he sent Smoot to the Senate in 1903 or the five grueling days he spent on the witness stand at "the seat of war" in Washington.[86] Nevertheless, and notwithstanding the variety of intentions and opportunities that competed for causal power in the years during which Mormonism changed, the actions taken by Joseph F. Smith beginning in 1905 remain key to understanding the present shape and success of the LDS Church.

Notes

This essay has benefited greatly from the comments of Richard Bushman, Jan Shipps, and Jed Woodworth. I also thank those members of the North American Religion Section of the American Academy of Religion and the BYU Smith Institute for the Study of Latter-day Saint History who, in 1999 and 2002 respectively, heard and offered suggestions on significant portions of this essay. Of course, I remain solely responsible for its content.

1. The term "Mormon" is heavily freighted with both historical and theological baggage. It originated in the nineteenth century as a pejorative reference for members of the LDS Church, for whom the Book of Mormon is scripture. To a biblically based American culture, the term communicated succinctly the extreme otherness of the Church. During the period discussed here, "Mormon" retained its highly negative connotation. Understandably, the Church objected to its use as a denominator and preferred to be referred to as Latter-day Saints, which expressed the believer's sense of continuity with primitive Christianity.

2. The nearest analogy to a Latter-day Saint apostle is probably found in the office of Catholic cardinal, though the comparison can fail to express the extent of the apostle's plenary authority over LDS Church affairs at all levels of administration. Technically, an apostle is a lifetime-appointment priesthood

office held by fifteen men, three of whom comprise the First Presidency and the remainder of the Quorum of the Twelve Apostles. Upon the death of the Church's president, his successor is chosen from among the apostolic quorum, another source of concern to the protestors.

3. The secondary literature on each of these topics is voluminous. The most complete guide to it is available in James B. Allen, Ronald W. Walker, and David J. Whittaker, eds., *Studies in Mormon History, 1830-1997: An Indexed Bibliography* (Urbana: University of Illinois Press, 2000). For aid in finding primary materials, see David J. Whittaker, ed., *Mormon Americana: A Guide to Sources and Collections in the United States* (Provo: BYU Studies, 1995). A particularly helpful source for primary documents related to the Church's history of conflict with the American government is Susan L. Fales and Chad J. Flake, comps., *Mormons and Mormonism in U.S. Government Documents: A Bibliography* (Salt Lake City: University of Utah Press, 1989). Both primary and secondary materials are available on CD-ROM from several sources, the most scholarly of which is *New Mormon Studies CD-ROM: A Comprehensive Resource Library* (Salt Lake City: Smith Research Associates, 1998). The LDS Church's canon, as well as other documentation of its beliefs and practices, are available at the Church's official web site, http://www.lds.org.

4. See, generally, Sarah Barringer Gordon, *The Mormon Question: Polygamy and Constitutional Conflict in Nineteenth-Century America* (Chapel Hill: University of North Carolina Press, 2002); Leo Lyman, *Political Deliverance: The Mormon Quest for Utah Statehood* (Urbana: University of Illinois Press, 1986); and Edwin Firmage and Richard Mangrum, *Zion in the Courts: A Legal History of the Church of Jesus Christ of Latter-day Saints* (Urbana: University of Illinois Press, 1988).

5. For a comprehensive account of the changes to Mormonism during this period, see Thomas G. Alexander, *Mormonism in Transition: A History of the Latter-day Saints, 1890-1930* (Urbana: University of Illinois Press, 1986).

6. Of course, public curiosity periodically requires the Church to dispose of the subject or comment on their present relationship to plural marriage such as in the September 8, 1998, CNN interview of Church president Gordon B. Hinckley. "When our people came West, they permitted it on a restricted scale," he explained, but "that's 118 years ago. It's behind us" (from a transcript previously available at CNN and lds.org but no longer available; copy in author's possession).

7. Jan Shipps, *Mormonism: The Story of a New Religious Tradition* (Urbana: University of Illinois Press, 1985), 116.

8. See, e.g., C. P. Lyford, *The Mormon Problem: An Appeal to the People* (New York: Phillips and Hunt, 1886); Dyer Daniel Lum, *Utah and Its People: Facts and Statistics Bearing on the "Mormon Problem." By a Gentile* (New York: R. O. Ferrier, 1882).

9. On the Taylor-Cowley incident, see Victor W. Jorgensen and B. Car-

mon Hardy, "The Taylor-Cowley Affair and the Watershed of Mormon History," *Utah Historical Quarterly* 48 (Winter 1980): 4-36.

10. Joseph F. Smith sermon, *Seventy-fourth Semi-annual Conference of the Church of Jesus Christ of Latter-day Saints,* Nov. 1901, 70; hereafter cited as *Conference Reports.*

11. Shipps, *Mormonism,* 148. The evolution of the theology of revelation is analyzed in William R. Persons, "An Analysis of Changes in the Interpretation and Utilization of Revelation in the Church of Jesus Christ of Latter Day Saints, 1830-1918," Ph. D. diss., Iliff School of Theology, Denver, 1964.

12. A number of dates could be chosen to mark the beginning and end of LDS polygamous practices. The emphasis here is not on Joseph Smith's own conviction but on the larger Church's adherence to polygamy, so I have chosen a limited period. These dates represent the years between Joseph Smith's extension of the practice to others within the Church and Joseph F. Smith's first disciplining of members for the practice, discussed below. The broadest definition would circumscribe events between 1833 and 1911. Joseph Smith himself appears to have practiced polygamy as early as 1833 (Todd Compton, *In Sacred Loneliness: The Plural Wives of Joseph Smith* [Salt Lake City: Signature Books, 1997]). Church discipline was not applied to the Church at large until 1911 when the first excommunications occurred. For a comprehensive treatment of LDS marital customs, using data on individuals who practiced plural marriage and the effects of the anti-polygamy campaign on those customs, see Kathryn M. Daynes, *More Wives Than One: Transformation of the Mormon Marriage System, 1840-1910* (Urbana: University of Illinois Press, 2001) and Jessie L. Embry, *Mormon Polygamist Families: Life in the Principle,* Publications in Mormon Studies, vol. 1 (Salt Lake City: University of Utah Press, 1987). For a discussion of the public misrepresentation of plural marriage, see B. Carmon Hardy, *Solemn Covenant: The Mormon Polygamous Passage* (Urbana: University of Illinois Press, 1992), 363-80.

13. The Doctrine and Covenants of the Church of Jesus Christ of Latter-day Saints (Salt Lake City: LDS Church, 1981), 131:11-12; 132:4, 6; hereafter D&C. Those who did not agree formed their own Churches emphasizing other principles. Most notably, the Reorganized Church of Jesus Christ of Latter Day Saints (RLDS) ordered themselves on the contrary principle that Smith had never practiced polygamy and that his sons, who stayed in Illinois with their widowed and anti-polygamous mother, had sole authority to lead the Church their father had founded. For the history of the RLDS (now Community of Christ), see Inez Smith Davis, *The Story of the Church* (Independence, MO: Herald House, 1977). For a description of the many groups organized out of Smith's Nauvoo Church after his death in 1844, see Steven L. Shields, *Divergent Paths to the Restoration: A History of the Latter Day Saint Movement* (Bountiful, UT: Restoration Research, 1975).

14. Orson Pratt, "Celestial Marriage," in *Journal of Discourses,* 26 vols.

(Liverpool, Eng.: F. D. Richards, 1855-86), 1:53-66. This sermon was delivered in the Salt Lake Tabernacle on August 29, 1852. Technically Joseph Smith's revelation regarding plural marriage was not his last. As indicated, he practiced the principle as early as 1833 but did not reduce it to writing until 1843. Hence, the 1852 sermon in Utah Territory is incorrect that the doctrine was received by Joseph Smith in the last year of his life. The sermon is correct, however, to the extent that Church members did not learn of this principle, if at all, until the last months of Smith's life. Thus the Latter-day Saints experienced plural marriage as Joseph Smith's last revelation.

15. Minute Book of the School of the Prophets, Mar. [30], 1870, Scott G. Kenney Papers, Special Collections and Manuscripts, J. Willard Marriot Library, University of Utah, box 12, fd. 9.

16. Joseph F. Smith, "Law of Celestial Marriage," in *Journal of Discourses,* 21:9-13. This sermon was delivered at the funeral services of pioneer settler William Clayton, Salt Lake City, Dec. 7, 1879.

17. D&C 131:11-12.

18. U.S. Senate, 59th Cong., 1st sess., Committee on Privileges and Elections, *Proceedings before the Committee on Privileges and Elections of the United States Senate in the Matter of the Protests against the Right Hon. Reed Smoot, a Senator from the State of Utah, to Hold his Seat,* S. Rept. 486 (Washington, D.C.: Govt. Print. Off., 1904-1906), 4 vols., serial set 2932-2935, 1:210, emphasis added; hereafter cited as *Proceedings.*

19. Apostles Heber J. Grant and George Teasdale were sent to England and Mexico, respectively, beyond the reach of Senate subpoena. A third known advocate of polygamy in the apostolic quorum, Marriner W. Merrill, was too ill to travel and would die within two months. Taylor and Cowley were still in flight from Senate subpoenas and Smoot was preparing for trial in Washington, D.C.

20. There is no scholarly biography available on the life of Joseph F. Smith. The LDS Church has published the following book-length treatments: F. M. Gibbons, *Joseph F. Smith: Patriarch and Preacher, Prophet of God* (Salt Lake City: Deseret Book, 1984); Joseph Fielding Smith Jr., *Life of Joseph F. Smith, Sixth President of The Church of Jesus Christ of Latter-day Saints* (Salt Lake City: Deseret Book, 1938; rpt., 1999). See also Scott Kenny, "Joseph F. Smith," in *The Presidents of the Church: Biographical Essays,* ed. Leonard J. Arrington (Salt Lake City: Deseret Book, 1986), 178-209.

21. Qtd. in Preston Nibley, *Presidents of the Church* (Salt Lake City: Deseret Book, 1971), 147.

22. Joseph F. Smith, "My Missions," *Deseret Evening News* (Salt Lake City), Dec. 21, 1901. Notwithstanding such preparations on both sides, the battle between the LDS Church and U.S. Army was a bloodless one. The conflict is chronicled in Norman F. Furniss, *The Mormon Conflict, 1850-1859*

(New Haven: Yale University Press, 1960; rpt., Westport, CT: Greenwood Press, 1977).

23. *Proceedings at the Dedication of the Joseph Smith Memorial Monument* (Salt Lake City: privately published, 1906), 1-14; hereafter cited as *Dedication.*

24. Joseph F. Smith sermon, in *Conference Reports,* Oct. 1905, 96.

25. Murat Halstead, introduction to J. H. Beadle, *Polygamy: Or the Mysteries and Crimes of Mormonism,* rev. ed. (Philadelphia: World Bible House, 1904), xvi.

26. *Proceedings,* 1:96. Joseph F. Smith's statement responded to the idea that a belief in prophetic leadership subverted obedience to civil law.

27. *Dedication,* 17.

28. Ibid., 54.

29. Ibid., 17.

30. Ibid., 29.

31. Ibid., 30-31.

32. For Maurice Halbwachs's foundational studies, see Halbwachs, *Les Cadres Sociaux de la Mémoire* (Paris: Presses Universitaires de France, 1925); Halbwachs, *La Mémoire Collective* (Paris: Presses Universitaires de France, 1950). More recent studies include: E. Hobsbawm and Terence Ranger, eds., *The Invention of Tradition* (Cambridge: Cambridge University Press, 1983); David Lowenthal, *The Past Is a Foreign Country* (Cambridge: Cambridge University Press, 1985); and Paul Connerton, *How Societies Remember* (Cambridge: Cambridge University Press, 1989). For the critical adaption of collective memory to the American context, see James McConkey, ed., *The Anatomy of Memory: An Anthology* (New York: Oxford University Press, 1996); John Bodnar, *Remaking America: Public Memory, Commemoration, and Patriotism in the Twentieth Century* (Princeton: Princeton University Press, 1992); Michael Kammen, *Mystic Chords of Memory: The Transformation of Tradition in American Culture* (New York: Alfred A. Knopf, 1991); Edward T. Linenthal, *Sacred Ground: Americans and Their Battlefields* (Urbana: University of Illinois Press, 1991).

33. David Thelan, "Memory and American History," *Journal of American History* 75 (Mar. 1989): 1,123, emphasis added.

34. Pierre Nora, "Between Memory and History: Les Lieux de Mémoire," *Representations* 26 (Spring 1989): 7-25.

35. *Dedication,* 22.

36. Ibid., 26.

37. All relevant references that follow are to the canonized account published as "Joseph Smith—History: Extracts from the History of Joseph Smith,

the Prophet," in The Pearl of Great Price (Salt Lake City: The Church of Jesus Christ of Latter-day Saints, 1981), 47-59; hereafter cited as JS-H. For an analysis of other versions, see Dean C. Jessee, "The Early Accounts of Joseph Smith's First Vision," *BYU Studies* 9 (Spring 1969): 275-96.

38. JS-H, 1:19.

39. Anti-Mormon literature is prolific. A contemporary indictment of Mormonism that catalogues the traditional bases for complaint and their relative weight is Frank Cannon and Harvey J. O'Higgins, *Under the Prophet in Utah: The National Menace of Political Priestcraft* (Boston: C. M. Clark, 1911), earlier published as an eight-issue serial in *Everybody's Magazine*. An interpretation of the literature, taking for its title a phrase used in *Cosmopolitan* magazine in 1911, is Terryl L. Givens, *The Viper on the Hearth: Mormons, Myths, and the Construction of Heresy* (New York: Oxford University Press, 1997).

40. Thomas G. Alexander, "The Reconstruction of Mormon Doctrine: From Joseph Smith to Progressive Theology," *Sunstone*, July/Aug. 1980, 24-33; James B. Allen, "The Significance of Joseph Smith's 'First Vision' in Mormon Thought," *Dialogue: A Journal of Mormon Thought* 1 (Autumn 1966): 29-45; James B. Allen, "Emergence of a Fundamental: The Expanding Role of Joseph Smith's First Vision in Mormon Religious Thought," *Journal of Mormon History* 7 (1980): 43-61; Richard Lloyd Anderson, "Circumstantial Confirmation of the First Vision through Reminiscences," *BYU Studies* 9 (Spring 1969): 373-404; David L. Paulsen, "The Doctrine of Divine Embodiment: Restoration, Judeo-Christian, and Philosophical Perspectives," *BYU Studies* 35 (1995-96): 7-94; and Dan Vogel, "The Earliest Mormon Concept of God," in *Line Upon Line: Essays on Mormon Doctrine*, ed. Gary James Bergera (Salt Lake City: Signature Books, 1989), 17-33.

41. Allen, "Emergence of a Fundamental," 53.

42. Milton V. Backman Jr., "First Vision," in *Encyclopedia of Mormonism*, ed. Daniel H. Ludlow, 4 vols. (New York: Macmillan, 1992), 2:515-16.

43. Lucy Smith, *Biographical Sketches of Joseph Smith, the Prophet, and His Progenitors for Many Generations* (Liverpool, Eng.: S. W. Richards, 1853), 146.

44. See, e.g., Joseph F. Smith's statement that "the greatest crime that Joseph Smith was guilty of was the crime of confessing ... that he saw those Heavenly Beings. ... That is the worst crime he committed, and the world has held it against him. ... He suffered persecution all the days of his life on earth because he declared it was true" (qtd. in *Two Sermons by President Joseph F. Smith*, Sermon Tract, no. 1 (Chattanooga, TN: Southern States Mission, 1906).

45. Joseph F. Smith sermon, in *Conference Reports*, Apr. 1909, 4.

46. *Reynolds v. U.S.*, 98 US 145, at 166 (1879): "Laws are made for the government of actions, and while they cannot interfere with mere religious belief and opinions, they may with practices."

47. David O. McKay, *Gospel Ideals: Selections from the Discourses of David O. McKay, Ninth President of the Church of Jesus Christ of Latter-day Saints* (Salt Lake City: Improvement Era, 1953), 85.

48. At least eight accounts of the First Vision were produced during Joseph Smith's life. The one chosen by the LDS Church as the official version was dictated to a scribe in 1838 and published originally in a Latter-day Saint newspaper in 1842. The texts of all eight accounts are found in Dean C. Jessee, ed., *The Papers of Joseph Smith*, 2 vols. (Salt Lake City: Deseret Book, 1989-92), 1:3-7, 127-28, 267-75, 389-91, 405-09, 429-30, 444, 448-49, 461.

49. Paul Ricoeur, *From Text to Action, Essays in Hermeneutics*, vol. 2, trans. Kathleen Blamey and John B. Thompson (Evanston, IL: Northwestern University Press, 1991), 124.

50. D&C 1:30.

51. JS-H, 1:1.

52. In an earlier account, Joseph Smith characterized the primary motivation for his prayer in classic revivalist and primitivist terms: "My mind become exceedingly distressed for I become convicted of my sins and by searching the scriptures I found that mankind did not come unto the Lord but that they had apostatised from the true and liveing faith and there was no society or denomination that built upon the gospel of Jesus Christ as recorded in the new testament and I felt to mourn for my own sins and for the sins of the world" (Jessee, *Papers of Joseph Smith*, 1:5-6). In this, his 1832 account, his question was more personal: how was he to be saved if none of the Churches acted consistently with the Bible? The answer was similarly personal yet included a rejection of false religion and promise of judgment: "Joseph, my son, thy sins are forgiven thee. go thy way. walk in my statutes and keep my commandments behold I am the Lord of glory. ... behold the world lieth in sin at this time and none doeth good, no not one they have turned asside from the gospel and keep not my commandments they draw near to me with their lips while their hearts are far from me" (Jessee, *Papers of Joseph Smith*, 1:6-7. By 1838, Smith's object in writing and his circumstances had shifted to defending his Church. Hence, his representation of the First Vision likewise changed to meet this institutional purpose. As discussed above, this later purpose was much more responsive to the conditions of the twentieth-century Church as well.

53. JS-H, 1:23-26.

54. *Dedication*, 10.

55. Anthon H. Lund sermon, in *Conference Reports*, Apr. 1920, 19, 21.

56. James B. Allen, Jesse L. Embry, and Kahlile B. Mehr, *Hearts Turned to the Fathers: A History of the Genealogical Society of Utah*, 1894-1994 (Provo, Utah: BYU Studies, Brigham Young University, 1995), 59-90.

57. JS-H, 1:65.

58. *Dedication,* 67. Smith's identification of Anthon with the learned man in Isaiah 29 is discussed in Richard L. Bushman, *Joseph Smith and the Beginnings of Mormonism* (Urbana: University of Illinois Press, 1988), 86-89.

59. The search for true knowledge and unhelpfulness of temporal means and unbelieving people was a favorite theme in LDS sermons. See, e.g., Frank Y. Taylor sermon, in *Conference Reports,* Apr. 1905, 30; also sermons by Joseph F. Smith and Hyrum M. Smith *Conference Reports,* Apr. 1903, 2; Apr. 1910, 68.

60. D&C 13, emphasis added.

61. Paul Ricoeur, *The Symbolism of Evil,* trans. Emerson Buchanan (Boston: Beacon, 1967), 262.

62. Ibid., 6.

63. The entire history of the LDS Church can be written as a crisis of authority. See, e.g., Marvin S. Hill, *Quest for Refuge: The Mormon Flight from American Pluralism* (Salt Lake City: Signature Books, 1989). The crisis that came to a head during the Smoot hearing may have had its origin in the disappointed expectations of a Second Coming after the Civil War and the increasing dominance of the LDS kingdom by the federal government during the 1870s and 1880s. Certainly by the early twentieth century, however, when the Smoot hearing precipitated the dismissal of Taylor and Cowley, the Saints needed reassurance that their Church was truly capable of fulfilling its millennial mission or it was, for that matter, simply true.

64. Bushman, *Beginnings of Mormonism,* 188-89.

65. Shipps, *Mormonism,* 109-29; Kathleen Flake, "'Not to Be Riten': The Nature and Effects of the Mormon Temple Rite as Oral Canon," *Journal of Ritual Studies* 9 (Summer 1995): 1-21.

66. Lund, *Conference Reports,* 19.

67. John A. Widtsoe, *Evidences and Reconciliations,* ed. G. Homer Durham (Salt Lake City: Bookcraft, 1960), 46.

68. *Dedication,* 68.

69. A historical study of Joseph Smith's theology during this period is found in Ronald K. Esplin, "The Significance of Nauvoo for Latter-day Saints," *Journal of Mormon History* 16 (1990): 71-86; T. Edgar Lyon, "Doctrinal Development of the Church during the Nauvoo Sojourn, 1839-1846," *BYU Studies* 15 (Summer 1975): 435-46. See also Shipps, *Mormonism,* 67-86, for an analysis of the increasingly esoteric nature of Joseph Smith's teachings.

70. *Dedication,* 86.

71. Ibid., 42, 57-58.

72. Shipps, *Mormonism,* 145.

73. Gordon Shepherd and Gary Shepherd, *A Kingdom Transformed: Themes*

in the Development of Mormonism (Salt Lake City: University of Utah Press, 1984), 229-59.

74. Richard T. Hughes, "Why Restorationists Don't Fit the Evangelical Mold, Why Churches of Christ Increasingly Do," in *Re-Forming the Center: American Protestants, 1900 to the Present,* ed. Douglas Jacobsen Jr., and William Vance Trollinger (Grand Rapids: Eerdmans, 1998), 194-213.

75. The 1890 Manifesto was entitled "Official Declaration 1" and placed at the back of the Doctrine and Covenants. It reads as follows:

> To Whom It May Concern:
>
> Press dispatches having been sent for political purposes, from Salt Lake City, which have been widely published, to the effect that the Utah Commission, in their recent report to the Secretary of the Interior, allege that plural marriages are still being solemnized and that forty or more such marriages have been contracted in Utah since last June or during the past year, also that in public discourses the leaders of the Church have taught, encouraged and urged the continuance of the practice of polygamy—
>
> I, therefore, as President of the Church of Jesus Christ of Latter-day Saints, do hereby, in the most solemn manner, declare that these charges are false. ... Inasmuch as laws have been enacted by Congress forbidding plural marriages, which laws have been pronounced constitutional by the court of last resort, I hereby declare my intention to submit to those laws, and to use my influence with the members of the Church over which I preside to have them do likewise.
>
> There is nothing in my teachings to the Church or in those of my associates, during the time specified, which can be reasonably construed to inculcate or encourage polygamy; and when any Elder of the Church has used language which appeared to convey any such teaching, he has been promptly reproved. And I now publicly declare that my advice to the Latter-day Saints is to refrain from contracting any marriage forbidden by the law of the land.
> —Wilford Woodruff, President of the Church of Jesus Christ of Latter-day Saints

76. *Deseret Evening News,* Dec. 18, 1908, 4. The other three referenced "standard (canonized) works" are the Bible, the Book of Mormon, and the Pearl of Great Price which contains the Joseph Smith History, the Articles of Faith, and other items.

77. Charles W. Penrose (Liverpool) to Joseph F. Smith (Salt Lake City), Mar. 31, 1908, Kenney Collection, box 11, fd. 15.

78. James R. Clark, ed., *Messages of the First Presidency of The Church of Jesus Christ of Latter-day Saints, 1833-1964,* 6 vols. (Salt Lake City: Bookcraft, 1965-1975), 1:224.

79. Stanley S. Ivins diary, Nov. 29, 1944, Kenney Collection, box 11, fd. 14B. In his 1904 appearance at the Smoot hearing, Joseph F. Smith testified that "there never has been a plural marriage by the consent or sanction or knowledge or approval of the Church since the manifesto" (*Proceedings,* 1:130).

80. On October 5, 1910, all stake presidencies (diocesan level of Church administration) were notified by letter from the First Presidency that they were to excommunicate or disfellowship any member in violation of the 1904 prohibition of plural marriage. See Clark, *Messages of the First Presidency,* 4:216. Marriages between 1890 and 1904 were not actionable unless they were a source of public embarrassment. See, e.g., Anthony W. Ivins diary, Jan. 7, [1911], Anthony W. Ivins Collection, Utah State Historical Society, Salt Lake City. The seminal articles evaluating the evidence of post-Manifesto polygamy are D. Michael Quinn, "LDS Church Authority and New Plural Marriages, 1890-1904," *Dialogue: A Journal of Mormon Thought* 18 (Spring 1995): 9-104; and Kenneth L. Cannon II, "After the Manifesto: Mormon Polygamy, 1890-1906," *Sunstone,* Jan.-Apr. 1983, 27-35.

81. Excommunication of polygamists is based on a contest of authority rather than plural marriage per se. Mormon fundamentalists dispute the legitimacy of authority claimed by Church leaders to suspend the practice of plural marriage. As with most internecine arguments, the literature on this subject is voluminous and excited. See, e.g., Dennis R. Short, *Questions on Plural Marriage with a Selected Bibliography and 1600 References* (Salt Lake City: privately published, 1975). A more accessible and scholarly discussion of the "monogamous triumph" in Utah is Hardy's *Solemn Covenant,* 336-62.

82. See Hardy, *Solemn Covenant,* 297-99; Alexander, *Mormonism in Transition,* 60.

83. Joseph F. Smith, "Celebration of the Twenty-fourth of July by the Sunday Schools," *Juvenile Instructor,* Mar. 1905, 178-79.

84. Connerton, *How Societies Remember,* 4.

85. Ibid., 103-04.

86. George A. Smith (Salt Lake City) to Reed Smoot (Washington, D.C.), Feb. 27, 1904, Reed Smoot Collection, box 51, fd. 10, L. Tom Perry Special Collections, Harold B. Lee Library, Brigham Young University, Provo.

The Translator and the Ghostwriter
Joseph Smith and William W. Phelps

Samuel M. Brown

In 1845, almost a year after the murder of Joseph Smith, John Taylor published a pamphlet titled *The Voice of Truth, Containing the Public Writings, Portrait, and Last Sermon of President Joseph Smith*. This pamphlet compiled political material published in the last years of Smith's life, including official correspondence with James Arlington Bennett, John C. Calhoun, Henry Clay, the *Washington Daily Globe,* an *Appeal to Vermont's "Green Mountain Boys,"* the "Pacific Innuendo," "A Friendly Hint to Missouri," and Smith's presidential platform: *Views of the Powers and Policy of the Government of the U.S.* The sixty-four-page booklet concluded with an appendix, "Joseph Smith's Last Sermon, Delivered at the April Conference, 1844." The appendix, Smith's most famous public sermon (now called the King Follett Discourse), stands apart from the body of the pamphlet. This mystical and colloquial account differs from the formal polemics of the eight political texts, which are prone to pedantic, multilingual asides.[1]

The difference in style in this case resulted from a difference in authorship. William Wines Phelps ghostwrote the political material.[2]

The story of the ghostwritten pieces and their displays of linguistic prowess provide an important window into Smith's desire to be seen as a skilled translator and sacred linguist, a hunger Phelps shared. Though the multilingual displays came to embarrass Mormons even as they attributed the writings to Smith, these writings had once expressed the prophet's desire for recognition as a master of language. The reason for writing the material and the intended benefit of their publication provide a vital window into early Mormonism, illuminating Smith's and Phelps's self-conceptions, the nature of textual attribution and collaborative authorship in early Mormonism, and the religious valences of translation in early Mormonism.

Understanding the purpose of the ghostwritten material requires situating these projects from 1843-44 within the histories of Smith and Phelps from the 1830s on. From the beginning, command of ancient languages figured prominently in Smith's religious activity. In the 1820s he reported that an angel bestowed on him gold plates inscribed in "Reformed Egyptian" (a shorthand Hebrew-Egyptian hybrid) that he undertook to translate using stones he called "interpreters." In the early 1830s, Smith revised portions of the King James Version of the Bible, in this case augmenting and correcting the English text, again by supernatural means. In the same period, he sent his followers to found a Hebrew-named city, Zion, and revealed various words from what he termed the Adamic language, including a new name for God (Ahman) and one or more place names (Adam-ondi-Ahman and perhaps Zomas).[3]

By 1835 Smith added direct translation from Egyptian to his repertoire when he analyzed and then translated into what became the Book of Abraham a collection of funerary papyri purchased that summer at Kirtland, Ohio. During his sustained encounter with the papyri, Smith organized a Hebrew School in Kirtland, an amplification of his School of the Prophets that was run by Joshua Seixas, a freelance Hebraist visiting Oberlin College but with connections to the conservative Andover Seminary in central Massachusetts.[4] Upon the place to which the Saints fled after the Missouri Mormon War of 1838, Smith also bestowed a Hebrew name, Nauvoo. He would continue to study Hebrew, often with the help of Jewish convert Alex Neibaur, until the end of his life. As evidence of his familiarity with Greek, he puzzled through the etymology of the word *paradise* in an 1843 sermon exploring life after death.[5] In his last two public sermons (the King Follett Discourse and the Sermon in the Grove), he undertook a radical retranslation of the first sentence of the Hebrew Bible to explain his vision of God's nature.[6] In the same sermons he gave his listeners to understand that he could decipher German, Greek, Hebrew, and Latin.[7]

Throughout his life, he denied aspirations to book learning, and he and his followers mocked as the heirs of Babylon the "priestcraft" of Protestant clergy who "spiritualized" the Bible and wrapped themselves in creedal apostasy from the original faith. Still, however unlearned, he considered himself a preeminent translator. Indeed, translation figured prominently in the title he assumed at the founding of the Church in April 1830—he was "a seer, a translator, a prophet, an apostle of Jesus Christ" (D&C 21:1). Throughout his career, he struggled with the fact that the educated mainline Protestant clergy defamed him as a semi-literate rural "plough boy" or "illiterate vagrant hanging on the skirts of society," while the newer Methodist and Baptist clergies (themselves only slowly embracing seminaries) sided with the traditionalists in rejecting Smith's claims to respectability.[8] Generally only established clergy knew Greek, Hebrew, and Latin; before the dramatic expansion of the Second Great Awakening, mainline clergy in fact were expected to master these languages—early colleges could refuse to graduate the monolingual aspiring minister. Orators, clergymen, and some writers were known to sprinkle their sermons, essays, and stories with foreign terms and phrases as marks of their erudition. Beyond learned circles, scattered foreign phrases or names figured in certain popular metaphysical traditions; in general, commoners enjoyed little direct access to ancient languages.[9]

Despite his considerable exertions, Smith never commanded much respect for his language scholarship outside his Church. The man who sold him Egyptian papyri in 1835 seems merely to have sought a buyer for his tattered wares, and other men who complimented his translation skills were simple hoaxers. In 1843, a group of Illinoisans claimed to have unearthed bell-shaped plates from an Indian burial mound near Kinderhook and brought them to Smith for translation. He died before he could fall fully victim to the hoax, though his followers remained convinced of the plates' validity for many decades.[10]

In general, Christian critics were not sympathetic to Smith's quest or appreciative of his achievements. They saw his claim to translate the

Book of Mormon as charlatanism and, after Howe proposed the Spaulding theory in 1834, plagiarism. They mocked him for a meager command of the King's English, citing the Book of Mormon as one of many proofs. Representing his peers, Mormon critic Thomas Sharp (ghostwriting for former Mormon William Harris) complained that Smith and his colleagues "could scarcely write their own language."[11] Palmyra critic Abner Cole jeered at Smith as a "*spindle shanked* ignoramus," possibly mocking both his well-known limp (the sequel of a childhood bone infection) and his lack of education.[12] When Smith attempted to gain traditional knowledge of ancient languages in the 1830s, critics mocked him further, wryly stating that inspiration failed him because he had taken to studying Hebrew. One observer commented acerbically: "Whether the stones had become rusty, or whether the gift of the Spirit had withdrawn ... is not fully revealed."[13]

Even his followers criticized his language at times. During the meeting in the fall of 1831 when it was decided to publish Smith's revelations as the *Book of Commandments*, some present criticized the poor language in the collection. In response, Smith promulgated a revelation aimed at the critics, saying "his language you have known; and his imperfections you have known; and you have sought in your hearts knowledge, that you might express beyond his language." The revelation challenged "the most wise" of the critics to improve upon "the least" revelation from the *Book of Commandments*.[14] The noted itinerant William McLellin accepted the challenge. When they reprinted the exchange in 1844, Smith's editors commented that McLellin, who had by then defected from the Church, had "more learning than sense," and his revelation was a "vain attempt of a man to imitate the language of Jesus Christ."[15]

The insults of critics seem to have bothered Smith, not least because he appreciated his own inadequacies in language. He wrote in a personal letter in 1832, "Oh Lord God; deliver us in thine own due time from the little narrow prison, almost as it were, total darkness of paper, pen and ink; and a crooked, broken, scattered and imperfect language."[16] Three years later, he noted in his diary, "O may God give me learning even Language and [e]ndo[w] me with qualifications to magnify his name."[17] The Book of Mormon anticipated these feelings of inadequacy, as several prophetic authors warned that their language too was imperfect, and the reader who could not overlook these flaws risked damnation (1 Ne. 19:6; 2 Ne. 33:4, 11; Ether 12:23-25). The theme persisted into Smith's own revelations, most explicitly an 1831 revelation canonized as LDS Doctrine and Covenants 67 (see esp. vv. 5–7).

Phelps's Linguistic Aspirations

By contrast, the flamboyant William W. Phelps, recipient of the 1832 letter pleading for power over language, may have represented the salve for Smith's wounds. Having edited anti-Masonic papers in the 1820s and pondered a run for lieutenant governor of New York, Phelps came to Mormonism early. An unaffiliated Christian seeker, he could not resist the story of an angel descending from heaven. He accepted baptism in June 1831,[18] after which Smith put him to work almost immediately. Within a year, the first Mormon newspaper, *The Evening and the Morning Star*, began publication in Independence, Missouri, with Phelps as editor. Having long considered himself a great legal and journalistic talent and something of a linguist, he made what disaffected Mormon Ezra Booth characterized in 1831 as "no little display as an editor of a parti[s]an newspaper" in New York and "made the dupes believe he was master of fourteen different languages, of which [he] frequently boasted."[19] Phelps's claims to linguistic knowledge likely compensated for a lack of a prestigious education. Inaugurating a public correspondence in the Church paper with editor Oliver Cowdery, Phelps explained in 1834, "My source of learning, and my manner of life, from my youth up, will exclude me from the fashionable pleasure of staining my communications, with the fancy colors of a freshman of Dartmouth, a sophomore of Harvard, or even a graduate of Yale."[20]

Though outsiders and perhaps modern observers would likely dismiss such a disclaimer as false modesty, Phelps positioned himself as a self-made man, thus protecting himself from criticism. Regardless of the source of his learning or extent of his modesty, he did treasure the meaning of the written word, as indicated by an 1832 editorial in the *Star*: "The art of writing is one of the greatest blessings we enjoy. To cultivate it is our duty, and to use it is our privilege. By these means the thoughts of the heart can act without the body: and the mind can speak without the head, while thousands of miles apart, and for ages after the flesh has mouldered back to its mother dust. ... It is one of the best gifts of God to man, and it is the privilege of man to enjoy it."[21] After Smith revealed a sample of pure Adamic language in 1832, Phelps proudly sketched out a preliminary grammar for those terms.[22]

Phelps would be allowed the pleasure of editing the Church periodical for only a brief period. While he was printing the *Book of Commandments* in 1833, vigilantes destroyed the printing press, bullied him, and ransacked his home. The *Star* moved to Kirtland and a new press, while Phelps remained behind in Missouri. After fighting for Mormons' rights for two more years, he returned to Kirtland in May 1835 and began working on the Doctrine and Covenants and transcribing patriarchal blessings, among other duties, all of which he performed as a boarder in the Smiths' home.[23] He likely enjoyed his return to *de facto* Church headquarters and advertised the significance of the blessings he transcribed, but he also may have been awaiting the opportunity for greater creativity. Smith, by then, had his hands full with political, military, and administrative problems, not to mention Church governance, and had scant time left over for public writing projects.

In June a visitor arrived in Kirtland who brought hope to both Smith and Phelps regarding the mastery of ancient languages. Michael Chandler, visiting Cleveland with a collection of Theban mummies and funeral papyri, stopped by with an offer for the Mormon prophet, who purchased the collection and promptly reported that they contained the writings of biblical Joseph and Abraham. He shared the find with Phelps, Oliver Cowdery, and soon Warren Parrish. Other assistants played minor roles in Smith's interactions with the Egyptian relics.

These initial encounters with the papyri yielded a number of unpublished documents known collectively as the Kirtland Egyptian Papers (KEP). Primary among these documents is a notebook entitled "Egyptian Alphabet" or "Grammar and A[l]phabet of the Egyptian Language" (hereafter GAEL). Beyond controversial manuscripts of the Book of Abraham with hieroglyphs beside paragraphs of English text, this alphabet, primarily in Phelps's hand, is the main document in the KEP collection. Since their publication in 1966, the KEP have occasioned considerable debate because they are not Egyptian and yet are clearly related to the Book of Abraham that Smith published in 1842.[24] In the interest of distancing Smith and the Book of Abraham from the GAEL, Mormon scholar Hugh Nibley suggested that Phelps may have competed adversarially with Smith over the papyri and produced the alphabet, with input from Warren Parrish, but without significant oversight from the prophet.[25] Critics have suggested that this assertion lacks reliable documentary support and merely reflects Nibley's quest to limit "dissonance."[26] In fact, both sides appear to have overstated their respective cases, deflecting attention from the meaning of the Egyptian project and the nature of the relationship between Phelps and Smith.

They began work immediately after acquiring the Abraham papyri, according to an entry in the *History of the Church* that claims Smith spent the latter half of July working on the alphabet.[27] The prophet's diaries do not cover that period, but the source of the *History of the Church* entry is Willard Richards, who had easy access to both Phelps and Smith at the time (1843).[28] In addition, a letter from Phelps to his wife, Sally, likely penned on July 19-20, 1835, confirms his involvement with the papyri at that time: "God has so ordered it that these writings and mummies have been brought into the Church," he wrote, saying that he had "just locked up" the "sacred writings" "when your letter came, so I had two consolations of good things in one day."[29] Phelps thus confirmed his access to the papyri, which were generally kept under lock and key, and that he and Smith made active use of them. An apparent addendum to the July 20 letter by Smith himself confirms Phelps's involvement in the interpretation of the papyri. Smith told Sally that her husband would "return [home to Missouri] and teach ... hid[d]en things of old times ... the tre[as]ures hid in the sand."[30] Later in the same letter, Phelps proudly anticipated that "these records of old times when we translate and print them in a book will make a good witness for the Book of Mormon."[31] His enthusiasm was mixed with the prophet's to the extent that he employed the first-person plural to describe the translators.

Like his peers, Phelps believed in the mystical nature of hieroglyphs, writing in 1834 that the "Egyptians could astonish the universe … concealing their arts in mystical characters or hieroglyphics."[32] In this respect, he and his prophet joined a chorus of other voices concerned with the deep meaning of hieroglyphs and primal language.[33]

The burst of activity on the documents did not last long, much to Phelps's frustration. Two impatient months later, he complained to his wife that "nothing has been doing in the translation of the Egyptian Record for a long time, and probably will not for some time to come."[34] Attention had turned to preparations for harvest, other publication projects, and the reopening of the School of the Elders. Phelps did, however, receive a personal revelation from Smith on September 22. In the revelation, he discovered that he would "have the desires of his heart in the gift that pertaineth to writing the law of God and in being an instrument in writing to lift up an ensign to the Nation[s]." The blessing further reassured him that he would be "a lawyer in Israel," would be "renowned among men," who "shall acknowledge his superior wisdom," and that he would acquire "understanding in all science and languages." Though the blessing tempered this praise with warnings that God would "chasten him because he taketh honor to himself," Smith promised his scribe notoriety and power,[35] and a note to Sally Phelps confirmed Smith's appreciation for Phelps's skill. William, Smith wrote, was a man of "merits and experiance and acquirements," with whom "but few can compete" and on whom "[G]od in his wisdom hath bestowed gifts."[36]

A little more than a week after this reassuring revelation of October 1, 1835, Smith's diary, written in Oliver Cowdery's handwriting, noted that the prophet had "labored on the Egyptian alphabet in company with Brs O Cowdery and W W. Phelps."[37] Four weeks later Smith added a third scribe, Warren Parrish, who shortly received a personalized revelation promising that "he shall see much of my ancient records and shall know of hid[d]en things and shall be endowed with a knowledge of hid[d]en languages."[38] Three days later Smith displayed "the Alphabet of the ancient records" in company with "the Mumies."[39] As part of their language and translation projects, Smith dispatched Cowdery to New York to purchase language texts, and the scribe returned on November 20 with Hebrew grammars and lexica, Greek primers, and

"Webster's English Lexicon."[40] On December 26, Smith "commenced stud[y]ing the Hebrew Language in company with Bros Parrish and Williams."[41] Several days later, Phelps complained to his wife that he was not among those first language scholars: "I want to study Hebrew, and I have not as yet been able to begin."[42] He enrolled in Seixas's class the next month, and Seixas placed him in the same advanced class as the prophet, which evidenced either Phelps's aptitude or his centrality to the effort. Both Smith and Phelps were proud of this recognition from Seixas.[43]

After a dramatic spring, finally marked by the epochal dedication of the Kirtland temple in March, Phelps returned to Missouri in April 1836 at Smith's instruction. In the aftermath of the Kirtland banking disaster, Parrish turned against Smith in 1837, briefly leading a seceding Church of Christ before giving up on Mormonism entirely. Smith dispatched Cowdery to Missouri in October, then in light of the mass apostasy in Kirtland fled the city with Sidney Rigdon in January 1838. Though Smith initially intended to continue his translation in Missouri and maintain relations with Cowdery and Phelps, the Far West High Council excommunicated Cowdery in April 1838 and Phelps gradually lost his place in the Church that year, starting with his excommunication in March because of alleged financial misconduct and ending with full estrangement by October. Bereft of his scribes, Smith appears to have abandoned the Egyptian grammar project by late 1837.[44]

Phelps remained outside of Mormonism for almost two years. Financially devastated and eager to regain access to Smith, whom he continued to esteem a prophet and seer, Phelps pleaded for forgiveness in June 1840. Smith accepted the prodigal scribe's repentance, and Phelps's apology was triumphantly printed in the *Times and Seasons*, accompanied by an expression of gratitude to once again be "wielding his pen in the cause of truth." Editor Don Carlos Smith, younger brother of the prophet, continued, "We hope Elder Phelps will continue to contribute his favors and they shall have a place in our little sheet."[45]

After a brief stay in Kirtland, Phelps made his way to Nauvoo, arriving in August 1841 eager to prove his worth to his magnanimous leader.[46] He began offering material to the Church paper even before he arrived, starting with an essay on prayer that displayed familiarity with Johann von Mosheim's *Ecclesiastical History,* which was a standard reference for educated Christians.[47] Smith responded to these overtures by naming Phelps Church historian in December 1842, later assistant to Willard Richards, and assigning him to work on the revisions to the Doctrine and Covenants, among other projects. With Smith as mayor starting in 1842, Phelps became city clerk and fire warden in February 1843.[48]

Challenges to Smith as Translator

Nauvoo represented a busy and increasingly public period for Smith and his Church. He requested that the federal government make reparations for the loss of LDS life and land in Missouri, he planned to build a hotel to house visiting heads of state, and he established ties with national newspapermen like James Arlington Bennett of the New York *Sun* and James Gordon Bennett of the New York *Herald*. All these efforts marked an ambitious scope for Mormonism of the 1840s.

With greater fame came greater criticism. The writings of a wandering British expatriate, the Anglican divine Henry Caswall, demonstrates the cost of notoriety. Caswall, then in Madison, Indiana, had noted the "Mormonites" in his 1839 history of American religions as "one of the grossest impostures ever palmed on the credulity of man." Among other outrageous idiosyncrasies, he noted that the Mormons "consider the study of the Hebrew language to be a religious duty."[49] Situated at Kemper College outside St. Louis in 1842, Caswall decided to investigate Mormonism personally. This decision ultimately resulted in two more books. Beyond Anglican concerns about the crudeness of the American frontier and the Mormon religion, Caswall's ultimate indictment focused on Smith's proclaimed translation ability. By Caswall's 1842 account, he entered Nauvoo with a six-hundred-year-old Greek psalter, reportedly a family heirloom, and according to his vitriolic reminiscence the simple-minded Mormons thought the psalter was a lost book of the Bible which their prophet could translate. When Caswall met Smith, he found "a coarse, plebeian person in aspect, [whose] countenance exhibits a curious mixture of the knave and the clown [and whose] dress was of coarse country manufacture." The visiting scholar reportedly displayed the psalter to Smith, feigning ignorance of its origin, and heard in reply, "It ain't Greek at all; except, perhaps, a few words. What ain't Greek, is Egyptian; and what ain't Egyptian is Greek. This book is very valuable. *It is a dictionary of Egyptian Hieroglyphics.*" By Caswall's account, Smith pointed at the "capital letters at the commencement of each verse" and said, "Them figures is Egyptian hieroglyphics; and them which follows, is the interpretation of the hieroglyphics, written in the reformed Egyptian." By Caswall's now-triumphant account, the disgraced charlatan fled in embarrassment, leaving the visiting divine to announce to his Mormon audience that he had caught their famed translator in a fraud.[50] But such an accusation against Smith, who owned a Greek lexicon and had some limited understanding of Greek, was a derisive exaggeration—one that Smith's critics were nevertheless eager to gleefully summarize in 1843.[51] When Mormons recounted the visit and the minister's "old manuscript," they portrayed Caswall as something like an Anglican spy.[52]

Caswall was not the only one to criticize Smith's linguistic credentials in 1842. A Yale-trained classicist and sometime Congregational minister, Professor Jonathan Baldwin Turner of Illinois College (later a noted abolitionist and Christian proto-socialist), commented on the "valorous translator" of Mormonism that Smith rendered the Book of Mormon "into what HE CALLS the English language."[53] Earlier, Alexander Campbell had complained of the Book of Mormon that "it has not one good sentence in it" beyond those plagiarized from the Bible.[54] An 1840 editorial in a Baptist journal complained that the language "frequently violates every principle and rule of grammar."[55] More generally, Illinois historian Henry Brown said after meeting Smith that "he is, upon the whole, an ordinary man; and considering his pretensions, a very ordinary man."[56]

As Smith aspired to be a statesman and prophetic figure, he confronted accusations of a shabby intellect and hucksterism from many sides. Simultaneously his people knew and advertised that he could unlock the secrets of ancient scripture as a translator. These threats to the credibility of Smith's seeric/prophetic status caused considerable distraction. This was the context in which Phelps began sustained public ghostwriting for Smith.

Phelps as Smith's Ghostwriter

Phelps's first obvious ghostwriting effort in Nauvoo began with a Latin-titled poem, "Vade Mecum," or "Go with Me," published in the *Times and Seasons*.[57] In this poem, Phelps invited Smith to join him on a voyage into the next life, implicitly committing himself forever to the prophet he had once betrayed. Phelps's poem was followed by Smith's poetic rejoinder, "A Vision," an expanded paraphrase of the 1832 "Vision" of Smith and Rigdon. (By tradition, Smith's revelation is called "The Vision," while the poem is called "A Vision.") The experience of Smith and Rigdon was rapidly canonized and is now Doctrine and Covenants Section 76. It included a glimpse of heaven ("celestial kingdom"), hell ("outer darkness" or "perdition"), and the gradations between them.[58] After a wordy preamble, the poem dramatically amplified the depiction of hell to move beyond the 1832 revelation and emphasize outer darkness as the fate of all apostates. Phelps, who had made public in 1835 his belief that perdition contained "millions of the children of this world," may have been making a convoluted apology to Smith for his prior disloyalty.[59] The prophet—whose forays into poetry were limited to two pieces of memorial doggerel in his 1842 Book of the Law of the Lord (a section of his official diary devoted to memorials to the faithful) and a few scrawled lines in Barbara Neff's autograph book—appears to have found these conversing poems sufficiently compelling to have his own name attached to the response that was also written by Phelps, as Michael Hicks has carefully demonstrated. Importantly, this poem intentionally and explicitly refuted suggestions from a local politician that Smith was different than the ancient prophets in that he only prophesied in prose. Phelps's poem, "A Vision," proved that Smith, too, possessed the literary skill of an Isaiah.[60]

Shortly thereafter, Smith enlisted Phelps to respond to the long-standing claim (first made by E. D. Howe in his influential 1834 *Mormonism Unvailed*) that the Mormons derived their name from the Greek term *mormo,* a root meaning "frighten" and sometimes associated with dark supernatural forces. The word confronted any reader of Webster's 1828 dictionary as well as standard Greek lexicons, and Methodist critic Daniel Kidder resurrected the claim in his 1842 diatribe.[61] This claim served, much as Caswall's psalter, to demonstrate

Smith's over-reach as a translator, so clumsy he inadvertently let the truth out, allowing himself to be indicted by the language of the New Testament. The rebuttal etymology, attributed to Smith (who never claimed knowledge of Danish, Anglo-Saxon, or Gothic) and penned by Phelps, begins by explaining that "there was no Greek or Latin upon the plates" and reiterating the distinctive nature of "*Reformed Egyptian.*" In closing this explanation, Phelps offers unrelated translations for the word "good" in a string of languages. "We say from the Saxon, *good;* the Dane, *god;* the Goth, *goda;* the German, *gut;* the Dutch, *goed;* the Latin, *bonus;* the Greek, *kalos;* the Hebrew, *tob;* and the Egyptian, *mon.* Hence, with the addition of more, or the contraction, mor, we have the word MORMON; which means, literally, more good."[62] This fanciful etymology brought the problem back to Phelps's and Smith's perceived strength, the Egyptian language, while it was meant to demonstrate their familiarity with many languages, including the Greek that Howe, Kidder, and Caswall claimed had betrayed them.[63]

There is some suggestion that Smith may have considered, then rejected, Phelps as an editor in the spring of 1843. That was when the *Wasp* became the *Neighbor* under John Taylor's editorship and Taylor continued to edit the *Times and Seasons,* a post he had assumed in November 1842. Smith's cousin George A. Smith reported in a diary entry for May 15, 1843, that the prophet had inquired about Phelps's suitability as an editor. George A. replied: "[When] it came to the cool discretion necessarily [e]ntrusted to an editor in the control of public opinion, the soothing of enmity, he was deficient, and would always make more enemies than friends. But for my part I would be willing, if I were able to pay Phelps for editing a paper, providing nobody else should have the privilege of reading it but myself." To this, "Joseph laughed heartily and said I had the thing just right."[64] With this ambivalent appreciation of his skills, Phelps did not take over the *Times and Seasons* or the *Nauvoo Neighbor.* Instead he continued to ghostwrite for his prophet.

That fall, Phelps felt emboldened to request support for his wife in the form of a city lot, phrasing his request as a melodramatic poem on November 7, 1843.[65] Two days after the poetic request, Smith "called at the office with a letter from Jas A Bennett and gave instruction to have it answered." Four days later, Smith "heard Judge Phelps read [the] letter to Jas A. Bennet and made some corrections," then took Phelps to the Mansion house and had Phelps "read [the] letter which I [Smith] had dictated to Gen James Arlington Bennet[t] which pleased me much." That evening Phelps again read the letter to Dr. John Bernhisel and William Clayton, and the next day Smith had it read to Edward Southwick, a friendly attorney from Dixon, Illinois.[66] In this official response, Phelps took his prior flourishes to a whole new level, engaging the haughty Bennett in a contest of great apparent erudition;[67] "Were I an Egyptian, I would exclaim, Jah-oh-eh, Enish-goon-dosh, Flo-ees-Flos-is-is; [O the earth! the power of attraction, and the moon passing between her and the sun.][68] A Hebrew; Haueloheem yerau;[69] a Greek, O Theos phos esi;[70] a Roman, Dominus regit me;[71] a German, *Gott gebe uns das licht;*[72] a Portugee, Senhor Jesu Christo e libordade;[73] a Frenchman, Dieu defend le droit."[74]

The Bennett correspondence proved so popular that the *Neighbor* exhausted its run and had to reprint the document in the following number.[75] On November 17, Smith deeded the lot to Sally Phelps, likely indicating his satisfaction with his clerk's work.[76] The ghostwriting assignments continued to proliferate. On November 21, Smith "gave W W. Phelps instructions to write an appeal to the citizens of Vermont," a project that would ultimately be published and distributed as *General Joseph Smith's Appeal to the Green Mountain Boys*.[77] Phelps completed the statement by December 3 when he read it to assembled Church leaders who "dedicate[d] [it] by prayer."[78] A repeat performance the next day attracted an overflow audience and a report in the *Nauvoo Neighbor*.[79] Phelps was apparently the sole individual to read the *Appeal* in public, possibly because only he could pronounce the polyglot perorations he included:

> Were I a Chaldean I would exclaim: Keed'nauh ta-meroon le-hoam elauhayauh dey-shemayauh veh aur'kau lau gnaubadoo, yabadoo ma-ar'gnau oomeen tehoat shemayauh allah. (Thus shall ye say unto them: The gods that have not made the heavens and the earth, they shall perish from the earth, and from under these heavens.)[80] An Egyptian, Su-e-eh-ni; (What other persons are those?)[81] A Grecian, Diabolos bassileuei;

(The Devil reigns.)[82] A Frenchman, Messieurs sans Dieu; (Gentlemen without God.)[83] A Turk, Ain shems; (The fountain of light.)[84] A German, sie sind unferstandig; (What consummate ignorance!)[85] A Syrian, Zaubok; (Sacrifice!)[86] A Spaniard, Il sabio muda conscio, il nescio no. (A wise man reflects, a fool does not.)[87] A Samaritan: Saunau! (O stranger!)[88] An Italian: Oh tempa! oh diffidanza! (O the times! O the difference!)[89] A Hebrew: Ahtauh ail rauey. (Thou God seest me.)[90] A Dane: Hvad tidende! (What tidings!)[91] A Saxon. Hwæt riht; (What right!)[92] A Swede: Hvad skilia: (What skill!)[93] A Polander: Nav-yen-shoo bah pon na Jesu Christus; (Blessed be the name of Jesus Christ.)[94] A western Indian: She-mo-kah she-mo-keh teh ough-ne-gah. (The white man, O the white man, he very uncertain.)[95] A Roman: Procul, O procul este profani! (Be off, be off ye profane!)[96] But as I am[,] I will only add; when the wicked rule the people mourn.[97]

This appeal to the militia of Smith's natal state was intended to shame frontier enemies by emphasizing his New England roots, perhaps also advertising the Nauvoo Legion, the city militia, as an important military body in U.S. geopolitics. Always battling against the popular stereotype that depicted him as an unlearned manual laborer with a tenuous command of language, Smith allowed Phelps free rein as a demonstration of Mormon erudition. Even so, Vermonters were unimpressed; several Green Mountain Boys wrote an insulting response which they forwarded to anti-Mormon editor Thomas Sharp in February 1844, mocking the "lofty strains" of the *Appeal*.[98]

Regardless of actual results, Smith continued to use Phelps as his ghostwriter in 1844. On January 26, he "instructed Bro Phelps to write a piece on the situation of the nation—referring to the President's Messages &c."[99] Three days later, the official diary notes that Smith "gave some instructions concerning an address to the paper for Bro Phelps to write—views on the powers and policy of the Government of United States &c."[100] On February 5, three days after Phelps received his second anointing, Smith "heard read my views of the Gen Government."[101] John Bernhisel proposed possible changes to the platform at the time, demonstrating the occasional input of other advisers to collaboratively authored material, much as he had done in the Bennett correspondence of 1843.[102] The *Times and Seasons* reported on a public reading of the statement on February 9:

> On Friday evening last ... a public address, of General Joseph Smith's to the citizens of the United States was read by Judge Phelps. The address is certainly an able document, big with meaning and interest, clearly pointing out the way for the temporal salvation of this union, shewing what would be our best policy, pointing out the rocks and quicksand where our political bark is in danger of being wrecked, and the way to escape it and evincing a knowledge and foresight of our political economy, worthy of the writer.[103]

This political platform again displayed Phelps's fascination with foreign, particularly biblical, languages. He invoked the Bible, "As a Chaldean might exclaim, *Beram etia elauh beshmayauh gauhah rauzeen:* (Certainly there is a God in heaven to reveal secrets;),"[104] and interposed a German phrase: "(A Dutchman might exclaim: *Ein erlicher name ist besser als Reichthum* (a good name is better than riches),"[105] then inserted a Hebrew proverb, "Sedaukauh teromain goy, veh ka-sade le-u-meem khahmaut," which he translated as "Righteousness exalteth a nation, but sin is a reproach to any people,"[106] along with various untranslated Greek and Latin phrases.[107] These snippets from foreign languages must have seemed to Phelps and Smith to be fitting evidence of a great statesman and scholar.

Later that month, Phelps penned the "Pacific Innuendo" at Smith's request.[108] Though it lacks the polyglot flourishes typical of other Phelps creations, the rhetorical style is otherwise consistent with his documented authorship.[109] Another composition, "A Friendly Hint to Missouri," was published over Smith's name in March 1844 and contained a single obscure Latinism (*felo de se,* an archaic legal reference to suicide), while recommending in Phelps's overweening style that Missouri repent.[110] Smith had specifically "instructed [Phelps] to write" the essay.[111] Church historians writing in the 1850s changed the critical word "instructed" to "dictated" to ascribe authorship of the statement directly to Smith.[112] The same historians engaged in similar revisions for the Vermont *Appeal*[113] and the presidential platform, converting the ghostwriter into a passive scribe in both instances.[114]

At the end of February, Smith asked Phelps to create a statement to be presented to meetings of the Relief Society.[115] The statement, "The Voice of Innocence," rebutted claims of polygamy arising out of *City of Nauvoo vs. Orsimus Bostwick*. Bostwick had accused Hyrum Smith of polygamy, thereby impugning the virtue of Nauvoo women, and was being tried for slander.[116] After Phelps's editorial was "unanimously" acclaimed by the Relief Society and subjected to Emma Smith's final edits, the statement was published March 20, 1843, in the *Nauvoo Neighbor* over Emma's signature. In it Phelps continued to demonstrate his knowledge of Latin as he recommended that good citizens encountering dissolute men should "write with indelible ink, upon every such villain: *Vitare perditoris*! Beware of the wretch!"[117]

An angry retort to Francis Blair's *Daily Globe*, which had mocked Smith's presidential platform and gave satisfaction to the critics in Warsaw,[118] was published over Smith's name but featured Phelps's florid rhetoric and an obscure Latinism ("*Unitas, libertas, caritas esto perpetua*!"), the latter inspired by the English-language masthead of the *Nauvoo Neighbor*.[119] Finally, an irate rebuke of Henry Clay for his reluctance to commit to the Mormons partakes of the same style with another Latinism (*vox reprobi, vox diaboli*), echoing a prior swat at Martin van Buren in the *Appeal to the Green Mountain Boys*.[120] Phelps had written the letter for Smith, who did not hear it read until Phelps completed it.[121]

John Taylor assembled the ghostwritten political pieces and published them as *The Voice of Truth* in 1845. Though they are clearly attributed to Joseph Smith throughout the pamphlet, Phelps's name stands out on the inside leaf as the person who registered the copyright, and his poem, "The Cap Stone," appears on the back cover without attribution.[122] The material is coherent, thematically and rhetorically, and it is possible that Taylor and others judged the quality of the material in deciding to highlight Phelps's writing throughout. Phelps may have played a role, as well, as suggested by his copyright, though the evidence is uncertain. Taylor cannot have failed to know that Phelps ghostwrote the chosen pieces but seems to have believed that Smith was best honored by ascribing the political writings to him.

The King Follett Discourse, included in *The Voice of Truth* almost as an afterthought, demonstrates a dramatically different style. There Smith warned, "I do not calculate to please your ears with superfluity of words or oratory, or with much learning." The amateur Hebraist then criticized the use of "James" for the Greek "Jakobos" in the

Authorized Version of the New Testament and retranslated the Hebrew of the opening line of Genesis.[123] His invocation of linguistic knowledge, though milder than Phelps's, still demonstrated his conviction that ancient languages could reveal important secrets, as well as his desire to reveal those secrets.

Despite evidence to the contrary, the attribution of the entire pamphlet to Smith stuck. For a prophet who had hoped, however incorrectly, to establish intellectual credibility through public statements, the period after his martyrdom was no time to reveal the man behind the curtain. Those aware of Phelps's role likely saw Smith's supervision of his scribe's efforts as the most important factor in deciding authorship. Wilford Woodruff ignored Phelps's contributions when he revisited the pamphlet in 1848: "Those letters & writings are of much interest & show the spirit of the times & the mighty rebuke of wicked men by that great, good, & wise Prophet Joseph. I was much edified in reading it."[124] Many authors afterward have attributed these writings to Joseph Smith, even using them occasionally as evidence of Smith's knowledge of ancient languages.[125] Louis Zucker followed the attribution to Smith, citing "Ahtau ail rauey" as evidence of Smith's use of Hebrew outside Mormon scripture proper.[126] William Hamblin, in a somewhat confusing argument with Lance Owens over Smith's capacity to read the Kabbalistic *Zohar,* implied that Smith was the source of these Latin and Aramaic quotations, while simultaneously hoping to distance Smith from the claim that he had mastered such languages.[127] Less charitably, Thomas Gregg, a contemporary chronicler of Mormonism, mocked Smith as the author of Phelps's polyglot displays.[128]

However, other contemporaries openly recognized Phelps's authorship. "Mr. Skiniway," a pseudonym for a disaffected Mormon, spoke to the heart of the matter in a letter to the *Warsaw Signal* dated April 13, 1844. Appreciating the significance of the political correspondence, Skiniway noted that "the readers of the 'Nauvoo Neighbor' would suppose, from the articles which appear in that paper, that Joe was one of the greatest statesmen and scholars of the age." He continued insultingly, "In relation to Joe's Scholarship, we have only to say that he is one of the greatest *ignoramuses* of the age; and has not even had the advantages of a common country schooling." To prove his low view of

Smith's intelligence, Skiniway, implicitly recognizing that the polyglot displays demonstrated erudition, noted that "all the *articles*, to which Joe[']s name has appeared of late, as well as his *Statesman*-like 'Views of the Powers and Policy of the Government of the United States,' were written by the immaculate William W. Phelps, Esq., the City Attorney for the *Holy City* and Private Secretary to his holiness *Joe*."[129] The writer impugned Phelps's integrity by recalling his sworn testimony against Smith in 1838. Phelps promptly published a response denying his 1838 allegations, claiming they had been made under duress and threat of violence and were a mere "hoax." He did not, however, deny that he was the ghostwriter of the published political material.[130]

In the late nineteenth century, B. H. Roberts, without explicitly citing contemporary evidence, came to a similar conclusion regarding the authorship of at least the Mormon etymology, the Bennett correspondence, the presidential platform, and the appeal to Vermont. Roberts, unimpressed with the polyglot Judge Phelps, recalled that Phelps "had some smattering knowledge of languages, which he was ever fond of displaying." Roberts justified deleting from the published *History of the Church* what he saw as Phelps material on the grounds that it represented mere "displays of pedantry" and left Smith "open to ridicule."[131] In this regard, he followed Oliver Huntington, who in 1847 complained of Phelps that "he knew seemingly everything for a man, and all the learning was his."[132] However, Roberts could not separate himself entirely from presenting the prophet as language scholar, retaining the Hebrew proverb and Aramaic phrase in the presidential platform when he republished it in 1900.[133] Van Orden, in his review of Phelps as political scribe, added two items, "Pacific Innuendo" and "Friendly Hint to Missouri," to Roberts's list of ghostwritten documents.[134] Neither Roberts nor Van Orden described the extent of Phelps's ghostwriting or analyzed what Smith and Phelps hoped to accomplish from their multilingual flourishes.

Phelps and Viator

Phelps did not limit himself to ghostwriting for Smith. In mid-1843, he assumed the persona of Viator (the Christian "wanderer," a not uncommon pseudonym in antebellum journalism) in collaboration with

Willard Richards, whom Smith had commissioned to write as if he were a non-Mormon addressing the Eastern press that spring.[135] In July 1843, Viator wrote to the Boston *Daily Bee*. In this first letter, he made explicit reference to the *mormon* etymology ("The meaning of Mormon, the prophet Joe says, is 'More Good,' and no matter where it is, the Mormons will have it") and made pro-Mormon statements while claiming to be unconverted. He closed with a melodramatic Latin cry, "O Gladius! O Crumena!"[136] The rhetorical style is typical Phelps, and he read the letter to Smith at the same time he read the letter he had composed for Smith's signature addressed to James Arlington Bennett.[137]

Viator offered a political commentary the next month, with an introduction in the *Neighbor* from Taylor that described him as "a man of sound sense and discernment, and of no ordinary legal talents." In defending the Nauvoo City Charter, which Viator called a "Magna Charta," he argued as a legal expert for the charter's broad scope.[138] In October, Viator took on Warsaw anti-Mormons by arguing that he was "under the suspicion or jealousy of that firm of filth [anti-Mormons]," responding dismissively with reference to a cross-linguistic pun and signing the letter Philo Viator, a malformed Greek-Latin abbreviation intended to mean a friend of Viator.[139]

Shortly thereafter, publication of the James Arlington Bennett correspondence in the *Times and Seasons* was introduced in words difficult to attribute to anyone but Phelps: "Mr. Editor, I occasionally drop into the Prophet's office, and take a sly peep at matters and things; and in one of these moments of observation I spied a letter from Gen. Bennet, to Lieut.-Gen. Joseph Smith, and also the reply, both of which I thought a little TOO GOOD to be lost among the rubbish, so I take the liberty to forward you a copy for publication. VIATOR."[140]

Understanding Phelps's involvement with Viator helps to illuminate his desire to engage ancient languages. Specifically, Viator, "one of the Literati, not the Prophet," published a new translation of Isaiah 18 "from the ms of Michaelis" in September 1843.[141] The editors acclaimed the translator as "a man of great tact and genius, and of no mean literary attainments. … It is evident that a great deal of obscurity is removed from this hitherto mysterious chapter, by the translation of our friend; and we would respectfully invite him to proceed with his researches, whether his interpretations are orthodox or not."[142] Phelps had made similar attempts, including translations of Isaiah 2, 60, and 62, in the back pages of his 1835 diary.[143] These attempts likely evolved from his involvement in the Seixas Hebrew class. Further suggestions of Phelps's interest in Bible translation comes from his 1843 interpretation of 1 Corinthians 15 "from an old translation," his unpublished versions of the Lord's Prayer, and his 1841 essay, "Despise Not Prophesyings."[144] He relished not just evidence of his linguistic acumen but actual involvement in translating sacred texts.

He may have employed still another pseudonym, that of "Gad the Seer," in reference to a popular figure in the Old Testament apocrypha.[145] The modern Gad wrote a response when Joseph Smith was arrested in Dixon, Illinois, on June 23, 1843, addressed to James Gordon Bennett of the *New York Herald* and published in the *Neighbor.* The letter sarcastically denounced the Missourians. An important clue to the authorship is in an associated letter to the *Neighbor* which requested, "I hope you will publish my communications just as I send them. As I am half lawyer half priest, and the rest of the requisites being made up of nobility, not within the scrutiny of Babylonish curiosity, it will consist of *truth.*"[146] Phelps was, at the time, Nauvoo city attorney but had been called "Judge" at least since his appointment as Caldwell County justice in 1837; he had long understood himself to be a self-taught legal authority even when he wasn't actually practicing law.[147] In addition, a May 1843 poem, "The Mobbers of Missouri," is signed "A Lawyer in Israel"—a title he claimed by revelation and emphasized during his receipt of the second anointing.[148] Further, his signed advertisement for the office of city clerk is headed "*Suum cuique tribuito,*" a famous reference to a principle of Roman law ("allot to each his own") which he presents as an obscure pun (offenders "sued quickly for tribute").[149]

Post-martyrdom Activities

After Smith's death, Phelps continued to demonstrate his interest in languages and translation. He assisted John Taylor in preparing the Hebrew references in the King Follett Discourse for publication in the *Times and Seasons,* the version used for the *Voice of Truth.*[150] His fascinating 1845 short fiction, "Paracletes," incorporated special Hebrew names for the epochal angels of creation.[151] In Winter Quarters, Phelps taught Greek lessons, one auditor recording his translation of 2 Peter 1:17 in a way that suggested God had a Father.[152] In the 1860s, Phelps would offer translations for a variety of the code names used in the 1835 Doctrine and Covenants. These late translations are inconsistent, indicated by his varying definitions of "Shalemanasseh" and his failure to recognize "Shinehah" and "Olehah" from Smith's scriptures. They are imaginative, though, particularly "a tried broken Pillar" and "everlasting helpmeet."[153] Interestingly, Phelps may have learned a partial lesson after the exodus to Utah. In an 1857 statement, rather than employ variations on the Latin *vox populi, vox diaboli*, he merely used the English, "the voice of the people, the voice of the devil!"[154]

His ongoing interest in languages is manifest in his work on the Deseret Alphabet, an attempt to liberate American English from the vagaries of historical orthography.[155] He flaunted his knowledge of "Hebrew and other linguistic studies" to Richard Burton when the explorer passed through Salt Lake City in 1860.[156] During the Howard Egan trial of 1851, Phelps quoted Homer and Virgil in his client's defense. (Egan was acquitted for murdering his wife's non-Mormon lover.)[157] Phelps's interest in Egyptian would continue through his discussions of astrology in comments for the *Deseret News* in 1851.[158] In 1858 he created another whimsical etymology in the spirit of *mormon*, presenting it in a short essay on comets. "The word *Comet*, allowing all deference to the witty Greek theme *Kome*, (hair) and the sedate opinion of Dr. Webster, from the Latin, *Cometa*, 'an opaque, spherical, solid body,' &c. was anciently doubtless understood, from old Hebrew, *Komaz etah*, to mean a 'brilliant, passing globe.'"[159]

Phelps again tried his hand at deciphering "hieroglyphics or characters and Hebrew coin letters" when someone found an inscribed copper coin "on the Colorado river" in 1860. He informed the questioners that the coin was "a Nephite Senine or farthing" issued by a King Hagagadonihah in AD 95 and suggested that Hebrew-Egyptian hieroglyphics employed Arabic numerals, just as he had implicitly claimed in one of the Kirtland Egyptian Papers documents.[160] The same year he made a similar claim about a relic from Ohio and provided an idiosyncratic translation of purported Hebrew.[161]

Phelps and the Kirtland Egyptian Papers

Phelps's desire to master ancient languages appears to account for the final reference in Smith's writings to the Kirtland Egyptian Papers. In November 1843, after calling twice in a day to recite the James Arlington Bennett correspondence, Phelps returned a third time that evening "enquir[ing] for the Egyptian grammer."[162] Two days later, Smith's diary noted the "idea of preparing a grammar of the Egyptian Language."[163] The presence of Egyptian phrases in the political correspondence suggests that Phelps used the KEP as a reference when he displayed his linguistic prowess, while at the same time suggesting that the project was never actually finished. The Egyptian project irrupted more generally into the letter when Phelps advertised Smith's great power by proclaiming, "Ecce veritas! Ecce cadaveros! Behold the truth! Behold the mummies!"[164] Phelps's use of the KEP showed his great interest in the documents and also his probable important contributions to their authorship. However, neither he nor Smith appears to have returned to the project before Smith's death in June 1844. For those brief months, though, the ghostwriting projects brought the Egyptian documents back to Smith's attention.

Chronologically the first use of Egyptian in Phelps's political writings demonstrates the incompleteness of the KEP. *Mon* from the *mormon* etymology is absent from the extant manuscripts.[165] It is tempting to see the etymology merely as Phelps's sarcastic response to Mormon critics, but there are several reasons why this may not be the case. Phelps used Egyptian phrases from the Kirtland Egyptian Papers in other documents and later proposed a similar etymology for "comet" in apparently full seriousness, and he approvingly cited the etymology in defense of the Church.

In the popular 1843 letter to James Arlington Bennett, Phelps presented a string of words taken in strict order from the GAEL. There *Jah-oh-eh* means "the earth under the government of another," while *Enish-go-on-dosh* represents a fixed star, specifically as it relates to *Jah-oh-eh*—"the power of attraction it has with the earth." *Flo-ees* refers to the moon, specifically in its ability to eclipse the sun, while *Flos-is-is* refers to "the sun in its affinity with Earth and moon."[166] Each is a relational astronomical term that describes the interactions of three heavenly bodies. The translation offered in the Bennett letter is a paraphrase of the original definitions: "O earth! the power of attraction, and the moon passing between her and the sun." Notably, this use of *Enish-go-on-dosh* (without *Oliblish* or *Kae-e-vanrash*) violates its use in both the GAEL and the published description of Facsimile 2 in the *Times and Seasons* as one of a triumvirate of "governing creation[s]"; this discordance may suggest Phelps's relative lack of involvement with the facsimile legend.[167]

In the *Appeal to the Green Mountain Boys*, the translation of *Su-e-ehni* does not closely match the definition employed in the GAEL ("who, whence, &c an interrogative pronoun through its degrees"), but quotes nearly directly from documents comprising the smaller "Egyptian alphabet," one of them in Smith's handwriting ("what other person is that or who").[168] Phelps almost certainly had the Egyptian papers in front of him when he drafted the political correspondence, but he appears to have preferred the prophet's definition to his own, though it is possible that Smith recommended the modification. In short, though Smith may have overseen the effort, Phelps appears to have made autonomous use of the KEP in 1843, and this effort may have brought the documents back to Smith's attention after a long hiatus. Despite publication of extracts from the Book of Abraham in 1842, Smith does not seem to have been concerned again with the Egyptian grammar documents until Phelps came calling with his letter to James Arlington Bennett in hand.

Conclusion

Careful review of the scribal activity of W. W. Phelps in the last year or so of Joseph Smith's life points to and illuminates several important aspects of the Church founder's creative work. First, it demonstrates his reliance on a ghostwriter for the bulk of his published political statements and correspondence, though his doctrinal statements do not demonstrate the same evidence of ghostwriting. The well-documented drafting of the Bennett correspondence during the time when several similar political statements were written provides a reasonable overview of the process by which Smith authored several of the late documents attributed to him. He assigned topics, provided some guidance on the content required, then reviewed the work of his lieutenants before final approval.

Second, that Smith allowed Phelps to continue to include what are now embarrassing multilingual asides in his official correspondence provides a glimpse of both men's desires. Language was a sign of erudition or access to biblical mysteries and mattered a great deal to both of them. Not to be left behind by seminary-trained ministers or scholars, they hoped to demonstrate their familiarity with ancient-language texts. Many writers of the era adorned their phrases with snippets from foreign languages, but few could compete with Phelps's excesses. That the ghostwritten documents failed to impress critics suggests misjudgment on Smith's part rather than his failure as a translator. That most of Phelps's translations are reasonably correct would probably have validated Phelps's self-perception and, by extension, his prophet's. In work that was certainly his own, such as the exegesis of Genesis 1:1, Smith demonstrated a hunger for learning, though his philological reach was more focused than that of his creative amanuensis.[169] When early Latter-day Saints attributed Phelps's work to Smith, they would not have offended their prophet, who continued to study German and Hebrew until shortly before his death.[170]

Third, and perhaps most controversially, Phelps's ghostwriting provides additional evidence regarding the provenance of the Kirtland Egyptian Papers. Specifically, the documents are incomplete; they do not appear to have been accessed directly during the publication of the Book of Abraham in 1842; and Phelps, ceaselessly seeking new linguistic knowledge, appears to have been a major force in the creation of at least the GAEL.[171] While Smith appears to have been involved in supervising the project, it seems unlikely, though not impossible, that the grammar was actively used in producing the Book of Abraham. Smith's use of collaborators in his writing and linguistic projects began before the Egyptian project and continued throughout his career.[172] This evidence supports Nibley's initial impression of Phelps's important creative role, though without Nibley's reliance on allegations of conflict between the men: Smith needed Phelps, and Phelps needed Smith.

In this instance, peeling back the layers of tradition proves useful in finding Joseph Smith's actual voice, which, while narrower in scope than previously thought, is less susceptible to criticism. At the same time, Smith's great drive to assemble the apparatus required to comprehend human language—a vision shared by his assistant and amanuensis, W. W. Phelps—shows through clearly.

Notes

I am grateful to the following colleagues for their linguistic input: Kevin Barney (Aramaic and Hebrew), Andrew Brown (Spanish), Hugh Brown (Italian), Kristine Haglund (German), and Susan Hamilton (Latin). I am also grateful to the anonymous reviewers of the *Journal of Mormon History,* whose comments significantly improved this essay. This version of the essay has been revised from the original publication.

---

1. *The Voice of Truth, Containing General Joseph Smith's Correspondence with Gen. James Arlington Bennett; Appeal to the Green Mountain Boys; Correspondence with John C. Calhoun, Esq.; Views of the Powers and Policy of the Government of the United States; Pacific Innuendo, and Governor Ford's Letter; a Friendly Hint to Missouri, and a Few Words of Consolation for the "Globe;" Also, Correspondence with the Hon. Henry Clay* (Nauvoo, IL: John Taylor, 1844). The pamphlet reprints the Bullock version of the Follett Discourse, published in the Conference Minutes of the *Times and Seasons,* Aug. 15, 1844, 612–17. King Follett was a fifty-five-year-old elder who had recently died when building a well; a bucketful of rocks had fallen on him (Donald Q. Cannon, "The King Follett Discourse: Joseph Smith's Greatest Sermon in Historical Perspective," *BYU Studies* 18 [Winter 1978]: 179-92).

2. Since publication of the original essay, I have become more comfortable with designating some of Smith's published works as resulting from "collaborative authorship" rather than simply ghostwriting, though the difference is not particularly substantive.

3. On "Ahman" and "Adam-ondi-Ahman," see Robert J. Matthews, "Adam-ondi-Ahman," *BYU Studies* 13 (Autumn 1972): 27-35. On "Zomas," see Ezra Booth in E. D. Howe, *Mormonism Unvailed* (Painesville, OH: Howe, 1834), 199. The use of "Zomar" in the Kirtland Egyptian Papers may reflect the same term. See "Grammar and Alphabet of the Egyptian Language," 23, photographically reproduced by Jerald and Sandra Tanner, *Joseph Smith's Egyptian Alphabet & Grammar* (Salt Lake City: Modern Microfilm Company, 1966); for discovery of this source by Sidney B. Sperry, see note 24. For more on the Adamic language in early Mormonism, see Samuel Brown, "Joseph (Smith) in Egypt: Babel, Hieroglyphs, and the Pure Language of Eden," *Church History* 78:1 (Mar. 2009): 26-65.

4. Shalom Goldman, "Joshua/James Seixas (1802-74): Jewish Apostasy and Christian Hebraism in Early Nineteenth-century America," *Jewish History* 7 (Mar. 1993): 65-88; Louis Zucker, "Joseph Smith as a Student of Hebrew," *Dialogue: A Journal of Mormon Thought* 3 (Summer 1968): 41-55. I treat these issues at length in chapter 5 of my book, *In Heaven as It Is on Earth: Joseph Smith and the Early Mormon Conquest of Death* (New York: Oxford University Press, 2012).

5. Scott H. Faulring, *An American Prophet's Record: The Diaries and Journals of Joseph Smith, Jr.* (Salt Lake City: Signature Books, 1989), June 11, 1843, 384.

6. Kevin Barney, "Joseph Smith's Emendation of Genesis 1:1," *Dialogue: A Journal of Mormon Thought* 30 (Winter 1997): 103-35.

7. Stan Larson, "The King Follett Discourse: A Newly Amalgamated Text," *BYU Studies* 18 (Winter 1978): 193-208; Andrew Ehat and Lyndon Cook, eds., *Words of Joseph Smith: The Contemporary Accounts of the Nauvoo Discourses of the Prophet Joseph Smith* (Provo: Grandin Book, 1991), 379-411.

8. Nancy Towle, *Vicissitudes Illustrated in the Experience of Nancy Towle, in Europe and America,* 2d ed. (Portsmouth, NH: John Caldwell, 1833), 157; John A. Clark, *Gleanings by the Way* (Philadelphia: W. J. & J. K. Simon, 1842), 345.

9. Paul K. Conkin, *The Uneasy Center: Reformed Christianity in Antebellum America* (Chapel Hill: University of North Carolina Press, 1995), 270, discusses the relevance of mastering biblical languages to protect the Bible from higher criticism.

10. Stanley B. Kimball, "Kinderhook Plates Brought to Joseph Smith Appear to Be a Nineteenth-century Hoax," *Ensign,* Aug. 1981, 66-74.

11. William Harris, *Mormonism Portrayed* (Warsaw, IL: Sharp & Gamble, 1841), 9. Clark, *Gleanings by the Way,* 292, similarly mocked the language of Smith's Book of Mormon in 1842.

12. Abner Cole, Palmyra *Reflector,* June 30, 1830, qtd. in Spencer Fluhman, "Anti-Mormonism and the Making of Religion in Antebellum America," Ph.D. diss., University of Wisconsin, 2006, 33.

13. J. B. Turner, *Mormonism in All Ages: Or the Rise, Progress, and Causes of Mormonism* (New York: Platt & Peters, 1842), 40.

14. Robin Scott Jensen, Robert J. Woodford, and Steven C. Harper, eds., *Revelations and Translations: Manuscript Revelation Books*, vol. 1, Revelations and Translations series, *The Joseph Smith Papers*, eds Dean C. Jessee, Ronald K. Esplin, and Richard Lyman Bushman (Salt Lake City: Church Historian's Press, 2009), 203.

15. *Times and Seasons,* Apr. 15, 1844, 496.

16. Dean Jessee, comp. and ed., *Personal Writings of Joseph Smith,* rev. ed.

(Salt Lake City: Deseret Book, 2002), Nov. 27, 1832, 287; also in the *Times and Seasons,* Oct. 15, 1844, 673.

17. Faulring, *American Prophet's Record,* Dec. 22, 1835, 90-91. His scribe was "unwell."

18. William Phelps, "Letter No. 7," *Messenger and Advocate,* May 1835, 115.

19. Booth in Howe, *Mormonism Unvailed,* 274.

20. William Phelps, "Letter No. 1," *Messenger and Advocate,* Nov. 1834, 22.

21. W. W. Phelps, "Writing Letters," *The Evening and the Morning Star,* Sept. 1832, 49-50.

22. This is available in Jensen, Woodford, and Harper, eds., *Revelations and Translations,* 1:265. Phelps's grammar is appended to a May 26, 1835, letter to his wife (VMSS 810, Harold B. Lee Library, Brigham Young University).

23. Walter D. Bowen, "The Versatile W. W. Phelps: Mormon Writer, Educator, and Pioneer," M.A. thesis, Brigham Young University, 1958, 62-63; Howard Searle, "Early Mormon Historiography," Ph.D. thesis, University of California, Los Angeles, 1977, 150, 158. In his published correspondence with Cowdery, Phelps advertised the significance of patriarchal blessings (W. W. Phelps, "Letter No. 9," *Messenger and Advocate,* July 1835, 146-47).

24. Mormon scholar Sidney B. Sperry rediscovered the Kirtland Egyptian Papers in LDS Church Archives in 1935 but little came of the discovery until 1966 when former Mormons published a purloined microfilm (Tanner and Tanner, *Joseph Smith's Egyptian Alphabet & Grammar*) rpt. as a bound photostat by H. Michael Marquardt, comp. and ed., *The Joseph Smith Egyptian Papers* (Cullman, AL: Printing Service, 1981).

25. Hugh Nibley, *The Message of the Joseph Smith Papyri: An Egyptian Endowment* (Salt Lake City: Deseret Book, 1975), 2; Hugh Nibley, "The Meaning of the Kirtland Egyptian Papers," *BYU Studies* 11:4 (Summer 1971): 359-62, 391-93.

26. Edward Ashment, "Reducing Dissonance: The Book of Abraham as a Case Study," in *The Word of God: Essays on Mormon Scripture,* ed. Dan Vogel (Salt Lake City: Signature Books, 1990), 225-28.

27. Joseph Smith Jr. et al., *History of the Church of Jesus Christ of Latter-day Saints,* ed. B. H. Roberts, 2d ed. rev. (Salt Lake City: Deseret Book, 1902-1912), 2:235-36, on *New Mormon Studies: A Comprehensive Resources Library* CD-ROM (Salt Lake City: Smith Research Associates, 1998).

28. Searle, "Early Mormon Historiography," 222; William V. Smith, *A Joseph Smith Commentary on the Book of Abraham,* 2d ed. (Provo: Brigham Young University/Book of Abraham Project, 2002), 226; PDF files available through "Search," *The Book of Abraham Project,* www.boap.org.

29. W. W. Phelps to Sally Phelps, in Bruce A. Van Orden, ed. "Writing to

Zion: The William W. Phelps Kirtland Letters (1835-1836)," *BYU Studies* 33:3 (1993): 554-56.

30. Jessee, *Personal Writings*, 360. I agree with Nibley, "Kirtland Egyptian Papers," 358, that this is a reference to the Book of Abraham.

31. W. W. Phelps to Sally Phelps, July 19-20, 1835, in Van Orden, "Writing to Zion," 554-56.

32. W. W. Phelps, "Reflections for the Fourth of July, 1834," *The Evening and the Morning Star*, July 1834, 173. This cultural commonplace even made it into Noah Webster's 1828 *American Dictionary of the English Language*, s.v. hieroglyphic.

33. Brown, "Joseph (Smith) in Egypt," esp. 36-40, 48-50.

34. W. W. Phelps to Sally Phelps, Sept. 11, 1835, in Van Orden, "Writing to Zion," 563.

35. William Phelps, "Diary 1835, January-June," 30-33, MS 3450, Church History Library, Church of Jesus Christ of Latter-day Saints, Salt Lake City (hereafter Church History Library). Oliver Cowdery transcribed the blessing into Church records Oct. 3, 1835. Another 1831 warning to Phelps appears in D&C 58:40-41.

36. Leah Y. Phelps, "Letters of Faith from Kirtland," *Improvement Era*, Aug. 1942, 529, qtd. in Ashment, "Reducing Dissonance," 227.

37. Faulring, *American Prophet's Record*, 35.

38. Ibid., Nov. 14, 1835, 59.

39. Ibid., Nov. 16-17, 1835, 65-66.

40. Ibid., Nov. 17, 1835, 66. By "Lexicon," Smith probably means Webster's *American Dictionary*. Webster's *Improved Grammar of the English Language* (1831) is less likely, *lexicon* being a term common at the time to mean a vocabulary list.

41. Faulring, *American Prophet's Record*, 91.

42. W. W. Phelps to Sally Phelps, Jan. 5, 1836, Church History Library.

43. Faulring, *American Prophet's Record*, Feb. 19, 1836, 134. The *History of the Church* 2:397, reports the same material.

44. Donald Q. Cannon and Lyndon W. Cook, eds., *Far West Record: Minutes of the Church of Jesus Christ of Latter-day Saints, 1830-1844* (Salt Lake City: Deseret Book, 1983), 145-50; Brigham Young, "Extracts of the Minutes of Conferences," *Times and Seasons*, Nov. 1839, 15. Former Mormon William Swartzell noted on July 26, 1838, that a house was being built in Adam-ondi-Ahman for Smith to engage in "translating the heiroglyphics [sic] of the Egyptian mummies" (William Swartzell, *Mormonism Exposed, Being a Journal of a Residence in Missouri from the 28th of May to the 20th of August, 1838* [Pekin, OH: By the author, 1840], 25).

45. Don Carlos Smith, "We Are Favored," *Times and Seasons,* Feb. 1, 1841, 304.

46. Bowen, "Versatile W. W. Phelps," 95-101.

47. W. W. Phelps, "Pray without Ceasing," *Times and Seasons,* June 15, 1841, 451. Mosheim's *Ecclesiastical History, Ancient and Modern,* was widely published in English translation in the United States in the late eighteenth and early nineteenth centuries.

48. *History of the Church,* 5:273; Searle, "Early Mormon Historiography," 214-17; *History of the Church,* Feb. 11, 1843, 5:270.

49. Henry Caswall, *America and the American Church* (London: J. G. & F. Rivington, 1839), 322-23.

50. Henry Caswall, *The City of the Mormons; or, Three Days at Nauvoo, in 1842* (London: J. G. & F. Rivington, 1842), 5, 19-21, 24, 28-29, 34-27, 43; emphasis his.

51. "The Mormon Prophet and the Greek Psalter," *Warsaw Message,* Nov. 15, 1843, Dale Broadhurst's transcription at "Newspapers of Illinois," *Uncle Dale's Readings in Early Mormon History,* www.sidneyrigdon.com/dbroadhu/IL/sign1843.htm, unpaginated.

52. [John Taylor], "Reward of Merit," *Times and Seasons*, Oct. 15, 1843, 364-65.

53. Turner, *Mormonism in All Ages,* 17; emphasis his.

54. Alexander Campbell, "Delusions," *Millennial Harbinger,* Feb. 7, 1831, 95.

55. *The Religious Herald,* Apr. 9, 1840, qtd. in Terryl L. Givens, *The Viper on the Hearth: Mormons, Myths, and the Construction of Heresy* (New York: Oxford University Press, 1997), 86.

56. Henry Brown, *The History of Illinois, from Its First Discovery and Settlement to the Present Time* (New York: Winchester, 1844), 403, qtd. in Givens, *Viper on the Hearth,* 84.

57. W. W. Phelps, "From W. W. Phelps to Joseph Smith: The Prophet," *Times and Seasons,* Feb. 1, 1843, 82. A version of this poem became the LDS hymn "Come to Me, Will Ye Come." The title is actually an intelligible Latin pun, playing on the meaning of *vade mecum* and its etymology. The poem was a reworking of his prior hymn "Indian Hunter" (Michael Hicks, "Joseph Smith, W. W. Phelps, and the Poetic Paraphrase of 'The Vision,'" *Journal of Mormon History* 20 [Fall 1994]: 70).

58. Joseph Smith, "The Answer to W. W. Phelps, Esq. A Vision," *Times and Seasons,* Feb. 1, 1843, 82-85.

59. W. W. Phelps, "Letter No. V," *Messenger and Advocate,* Mar. 1835, 82.

60. Hicks, "Poetic Paraphrase," 63-84, esp. 72. Notably, the British editor of the *Millennial Star*, perhaps unaware of the exchange over Smith's prophetic

credentials that "A Vision" hoped to answer, admitted the relatively low quality of this poem but defended Smith's prophetic credentials ([Thomas Ward], "Editorial," *Millennial Star,* Aug. 1843, 62-3).

61. Howe, *Mormonism Unvailed,* 21; Daniel P. Kidder, *Mormonism and the Mormons: A Historical View of the Rise and Progress of the Sect Self-styled Latter-day Saints* (New York: Methodist Episcopal Church, 1842), 81-82.

62. Joseph Smith to the Editor, *Times and Seasons,* May 15, 1843, 194. The etymology was reprinted in *Millennial Star,* Dec. 1843, 125. B. H. Roberts deleted the additional translations from the etymology in editing *History of the Church,* 5:399-400. Phelps's translations of "good" are essentially all correct, although the Gothic word appears to be misspelled.

63. According to Terryl L. Givens, *By the Hand of Mormon: The American Scripture that Launched a New World Religion* (New York: Oxford University Press, 2002), 81, the etymology represents an instance of Bakhtin's "authoritative discourse"; this suggestion misses the broader social and intellectual context of this exercise by Phelps and Smith. Stuart Gallacher, "Mormon: An Example of Folk Etymology," *Western Folklore* 8 (Jan. 1949): 22-24, proposes a folkloric analysis that is interpretively limited.

64. George A. Smith diary, qtd. in *History of the Church,* 5:390.

65. Bowen, "Versatile W. W. Phelps," 107-8.

66. Faulring, *American Prophet's Record,* Nov. 14, 1843, 426-27.

67. The correspondence is printed in the *Times and Seasons,* Nov. 1, 1843, 371-75. Some of the fury of the letter may be a response to Bennett's veiled and somewhat hostile reference to his recent baptism at the hand of Brigham Young, which he labeled little more than a "frolic."

68. This is a composite summary from entries in the GAEL, as discussed below. Brackets in original.

69. This is an incomplete rendering of "fear God" (Eccles. 12:13).

70. This is an almost correct rendition of 1 John 1:5: "God is light."

71. This is correct Latin and means "the Lord rules me."

72. This is correct, archaic German and means "God give us light."

73. This is an almost correct rendition of "Lord Jesus Christ is liberty."

74. The French is essentially correct and means "God defends the right," though not in the sense of "the righteous."

75. "For the Neighbor," *Nauvoo Neighbor,* Dec. 6, 1843, 3; and "In consequence of the numerous calls," Dec. 13, 2-3.

76. Faulring, *American Prophet's Record,* 427.

77. *General Joseph Smith's Appeal to the Green Mountain Boys* (Nauvoo, IL: Woodruff and Taylor, 1843).

78. Faulring, *American Prophet's Record,* 430.

79. [John Taylor], "A Public Meeting Was Called," *Nauvoo Neighbor,* Dec. 6, 1843, 2.

80. Aramaic, the Semitic language in which portions of the Masoretic text of the Old Testament are written, was termed Chaldean in the nineteenth century. Joshua Seixas, who taught Hebrew to Smith and his colleagues in 1836, had written a brief Aramaic primer that may have been used in the Hebrew school. His transliteration scheme is apparent in this excerpt. This phrase is drawn directly from KJV Jeremiah 10:11, an Aramaic verse, and differs only by omitting the italicized "even."

81. This is drawn from the KEP, Document 4, as noted below.

82. Aside from a missing definite article, this is correct.

83. This is correct.

84. This appears to be a reference to the *ayini cem* (or *ayin-i cem*), an Alevi religious festival of union, meaning essentially "a gathering of ritual music." The Alevi have long been grouped with other so-called Dervish groups of Sufi mystics and ascetics, though the Alevi are distinct. In any case, this is not Turkish for "fountain" and "light."

85. This is a melodramatic translation of "They are uncomprehending." Phelps makes the phonetic substitution of *f* for *v* and fails to capitalize *Sie* but is otherwise essentially correct.

86. I have been unable to determine what Phelps intended here.

87. This is malformed Spanish. *El sabio medita, el nescio no* would be a more correct phrasing. Phelps may have been trying to use *muda* ("changes") with *conscio* as a malformed version of *conciencia* ("consciousness") in the sense of "changes his mind."

88. Phelps isn't far off. There is a word in Samaritan Aramaic from the root for "hatred" ("one who hates") that could be transliterated, using Seixas's scheme, as *saunau*. I conjecture that Phelps was relying on his memory for this mildly garbled translation.

89. This appears to be an attempt at *O i tempi, o la differenza,* which would correspond with the English translation. *Diffidenza,* on the other hand, means "diffidence."

90. This is Hagar's statement to the angel (Gen. 16:13). Bearing the Seixas transliteration scheme in mind, this is basically correct. The English is the verbatim KJV translation.

91. Phelps appears to be essentially if not idiomatically correct. *Hvad* does mean "what," and *tidende* is the word for "tidings" or "times." It appears in the name of several Danish newspapers.

92. The two words are both Anglo-Saxon and mean something like what Phelps describes, though the word combination may not have the same meaning. Hwæt is an adverb or interjection meaning "why," "lo," or possibly "what." *Riht* means "right," "correct," or "erect."

93. Phelps appears to have employed false cross-linguistic homophony. The Swedish word for "skill" is *skicklighet.* The word *skilja* means "to distinguish or separate."

94. The transliteration is nonstandard and difficult to guess at. It does not correlate well at all with actual Polish, though perhaps Phelps meant to invoke *nazwa*, "name." "Blessedness" in Polish is based on *Błogosław-*.

95. According to correspondence of November 28, 1857, from the famous Belgian Jesuit Pierre de Smet, this phrase is Lenape-Delaware for, "White man, you have been very unjust with us" (*Précis Historiques,* Oct. 15, 1859, online at http://users.skynet.be/pater.de.smet/pj-b-f/pagina177.htm). The first Mormon missionaries to a native group were to the Delaware who were being relocated to an area near Fort Leavenworth (Lori Elaine Taylor, "Telling Stories about Mormons and Indians," Ph.D. diss., State University of New York at Buffalo, 2000).

96. Phelps is quite close here. The Latin phrase is probably best translated "Be far from me, O profane things."

97. *The Voice of Truth,* 16-17.

98. Dan Vogel, *Early Mormon Documents,* 5 vols. (Salt Lake City: Signature Books, 1996-2004), 1:595-98.

99. Faulring, *American Prophet's Record,* 442.

100. Ibid., Jan. 29, 1844, 444; Richard D. Poll, "Joseph Smith and the Presidency, 1844," *Dialogue: A Journal of Mormon Thought* 3 (Autumn 1968): 19, suggests Phelps as co-author of the presidential platform.

101. Scott Kenney, ed., *Wilford Woodruff's Journal,* typescript, 9 vols. (Midvale, UT: Signature Books, 1983-85), 2:346, 348; Faulring, *American Prophet's Record,* 445. Phelps read the platform to a public audience three days later. Though Woodruff writes the tantalizing phrase, "views were written & were read by Wm. W Phelps," he may have been specifying merely that Phelps made a copy and read from it.

102. Faulring, *American Prophet's Record,* Feb. 19, 1844, 446.

103. [John Taylor], "Public Meeting," *Times and Seasons,* Feb. 15, 1844, 441.

104. The statement was initially published in the *Times and Seasons,* May 15, 1844, 528-33. The Aramaic is from Daniel 2:28, and both the transliteration and the translation are almost correct. A mocking response from Francis Blair's *Globe* of Washington, D.C., was printed in the *Times and Seasons,* Apr. 15, 1844, 511. See also *The Voice of Truth,* 33.

105. *The Voice of Truth,* 35. This is correct except for minor typographical errors.

106. *The Voice of Truth,* 31. This is Proverbs 14:34. The Hebrew has several minor transliteration errors but is basically correct.

107. For example, *Amor vincit omnia* (love conquers all).

108. Faulring, *American Prophet's Record,* Feb. 16, 21, 1844, 446-47.

109. [W. W. Phelps,] "Pacific Innuendo," *Times and Seasons,* Feb. 15, 1844, 442-43.

110. Joseph Smith [W. W. Phelps], "A Friendly Hint to Missouri," *Times and Seasons,* Mar. 15, 1844, 473-74.

111. Faulring, *American Prophet's Record,* Mar. 18, 1844, 457.

112. Searle, "Early Mormon Historiography," 228, dates the writing of this section of the official history to 1854-57. Cf. *History of the Church,* 6:245 ("dictated") and Faulring, *American Prophet's Record,* Mar. 8, 1844, 428 (Smith "had instructed [Phelps] to write" the document).

113. Compare *History of the Church,* 6:80 ("dictated") with Faulring, *American Prophet's Record,* Nov. 21, 1843, 428 ("Gave WW Phelps instructions").

114. Compare *History of the Church,* 6:189 ("dictated the heads of my pamphlet") with Faulring, *American Prophet's Record,* Jan. 29, 1844, 444 ("gave some instructions concerning an address to the paper for Bro Phelps to write").

115. Faulring, *American Prophet's Record,* Feb. 28, 1844, 449: "Phelps writing on O. F. Bostwick for women."

116. Ibid., Feb. 26, 1844, 448.

117. Emma Smith [W. W. Phelps], "The Voice of Innocence from Nauvoo," *Nauvoo Neighbor,* Mar. 20, 1844. This is a malformed Latin warning to "avoid the destroyer."

118. Thomas Sharp, *Warsaw Signal,* Apr. 17, 1844.

119. [W. W. Phelps], "The Globe," *Times and Seasons,* Apr. 15, 1844, 507-10. The *Neighbor* masthead was "Our Motto—The Saints' Singularity—is Unity Liberty Charity." The Latin is recognizable but grammatically flawed. See also *History of the Church,* 5:304-05.

120. Joseph Smith [W. W. Phelps], "Gen. Smith's Rejoinder," *Times and Seasons,* June 1, 1844, 544-48. There he used *vox Matty, vox diaboli* in reference to van Buren as the voice of the devil.

121. Faulring, *American Prophet's Record,* May 15, 19, 1844, 479-80.

122. The authorship of the poem is made clear in W. W. Phelps, "The Cap Stone," *Times and Seasons,* Aug. 1, 1845, 991. Smith had died by the time of

publication, so he could not have secured copyright, but Phelps's copyright (as opposed to that of a more senior ecclesiastical authority) is nevertheless important.

123. *The Voice of Truth,* 59-64.

124. Kenney, *Wilford Woodruff's Journal,* Feb. 7, 1848, 3:316.

125. David Brion Davis, "The New England Origins of Mormonism," *New England Quarterly* 26 (June 1953): 157, incidentally but correctly invokes the Mormon etymology as evidence of Smith's desire to be seen as an erudite divine.

126. Zucker, "Joseph Smith as a Student of Hebrew," 48.

127. William J. Hamblin, "'Everything Is Everything': Was Joseph Smith Influenced by Kabbalah?" review of "Joseph Smith and Kabbalah" by Lance Owens, *FARMS Review of Books* 8:2 (1996): 251-325.

128. Thomas Gregg, *The Prophet of Palmyra* (New York: J. B. Alden, 1890), 490-94. The section is entitled "The Prophet as a Linguist."

129. Mr. Skiniway (pseud.), "Mr. Editor, April 13, 1844," *Warsaw Signal,* Apr. 24, 1844.

130. His affidavit of May 20, 1844, is published in the *Nauvoo Neighbor,* June 12, 1844, 255.

131. *History of the Church,* 6:75, 90. See discussion in Searle, "Early Mormon Historiography," 321.

132. Oliver Huntington diary, 1:163, qtd. in Bowen, "Versatile W. Phelps," 135.

133. B. H. Roberts, *The Rise and Fall of Nauvoo* (Salt Lake City: Deseret News, 1900), 396-97.

134. Bruce A. Van Orden, "William W. Phelps's Service as Joseph Smith's Political Clerk," *BYU Studies* 32 (Winter-Spring 1991): 88-89.

135. On Willard Richards and the Viator correspondence, see Jeffery Johnson, "Joseph Smith, Willard Richards and the *Boston Bee,*" presentation at the Mormon History Association 2008 conference, Sacramento, CA. I thank Johnson for sharing his Viator materials with me for the revised version of this essay.

136. "O the sword! O the purse!" *Times and Seasons,* Sept. 1, 1843, 305-06. A litany of countries visited by Mormon elders echoes Phelps's usual collection of foreign phrases.

137. Faulring, *American Prophet's Record,* Mar. 17, 1843, 334. Jeffery Johnson and colleagues determined after publication of the original version of this essay that the Viator letters I identified are in fact in Phelps's handwriting, providing independent confirmation of my stylistic analysis.

138. Viator (pseud.), "Vested Rights of Nauvoo," *Nauvoo Neighbor,* Aug. 30, 1843, 2-3.

139. Philo Viator (pseud.), "To the Editor," *Nauvoo Neighbor,* Oct. 11, 1843, 3. "Philo" is a Greek prefix meaning essentially "lover of."

140. Viator (pseud.), "For the Times and Seasons," *Times and Seasons,* Nov. 1, 1843, 371.

141. This suggests Phelps may have had access to a copy of the Hebrew Bible edition of Johann Heinrich Michaelis (1668-1738).

142. Viator (pseud.), "From the *Boston Bee,*" and [John Taylor], "There Is Something So Very Novel," *Times and Seasons,* Sept. 1, 1843, 306-07.

143. Phelps, "Diary 1835." Phelps decoded the names Jesus ("first born"), Christ ("anointed"), Enoch ("consecrated"), and Joseph ("to spread out[,] to enlarge"). The translations are not paginated. Phelps re-used his Isaiah 60 translation for his 1854 *Deseret Almanac* (Salt Lake City: W. Richards, 1854), 10.

144. Faulring, *American Prophet's Record,* Apr. 8, 1844, 468; W. W. Phelps, "Despise Not Prophesyings," *Times and Seasons,* Feb. 1, 1841, 297-99. The translation of the Lord's Prayer (Matt. 6:9-13) is in the 1835 diary, along with a more polished but undated "literal translation" and attempt to translate Luke 2:3-4. See "Translation," MS 16929, Church History Library.

145. Gad the Seer popularly referred to an apocryphal book mentioned in the Old Testament (1 Chr. 29:29). The lost book was mentioned by various Latter-day Saints (J. Goodson, "Dear Sir," *Messenger and Advocate,* Oct. 1836, 398; E. Snow and B. Winchester, "An Address to the Citizens of Salem (Mass.) and Vicinity," *Messenger and Advocate,* Oct. 1836, 398; *Times and Seasons,* Nov. 1, 1841, 581).

146. Gad the Seer (pseud.), "To the Editor of the Neighbor," *Nauvoo Neighbor,* July 26, 1843.

147. Bowen, "Versatile W. W. Phelps," 154-55. In February 1844, he would speak "concerning his appointment as a Lawyer in Israel" (Kenney, *Wilford Woodruff's Journal,* 2:346).

148. "A Lawyer in Israel" (pseud.), "The Mobbers of Missouri," *Nauvoo Neighbor,* May 31, 1843. The poem focuses on the 1833 destruction of Phelps's printing press and is characteristically somewhat more polished than the standard Mormon poem of the period. "A Lawyer in Israel" was the title Smith gave Phelps in the revelation of September 1835.

149. Mayor's Clerk [W. W. Phelps] to the Editor, *Nauvoo Neighbor,* May 10, 1843. The advertisement may indicate a misunderstanding of the Latin, though fanciful word play is also a possibility. Phelps writes "offenders *sued quickly* for *tribute* are dealt with according to law," matching through italics the English to Latin words. If this is a pun rather than a mistranslation, it is unlikely to have made any sense to its intended audience.

150. Barney, "Joseph Smith's Emendation," 116-18.

151. Samuel Brown, "William Phelps's 'Paracletes': An Early Witness to Joseph Smith's Divine Anthropology," *International Journal of Mormon Studies* 2 (Spring 2009): 62-81.

152. Maurine Carr Ward, ed., *Winter Quarters: The 1846-1848 Life Writings of Mary Haskin Parker Richards* (Logan: Utah State University Press, 1996), Feb. 21, 1847, 191: "Had them (L & S) cite their lessons in Greek to Br Phelps[,] who trancelated these words[,] and he received from God the Father honer [and] Glory[,] which afterwards read[,] and he recived in presence of *God's Father* honer and Glory," emphasis added.

153. David J. Whittaker, "Substituted Names in the Published Revelations of Joseph Smith," *BYU Studies* 23 (Winter 1983): 111.

154. "Celebration of the Twenty-Fourth of July," *Millennial Star,* Oct. 15, 1857, 307. John C. Bennett, *The History of the Saints; or, An Exposé of Joe Smith and Mormonism* (Boston: Leland and Whiting, 1842), 281, had invoked *vox populi, vox Dei* in his indictment of the Saints.

155. Bowen, "Versatile W. W. Phelps," 154-55. On the broader effort, see Ronald G. Watt. *The Mormon Passage of George D. Watt: First British Convert, Scribe for Zion* (Logan: Utah State University Press, 2009), 141-59.

156. Richard Burton, *The City of the Saints,* ed. Fawn Brodie (New York: Alfred A. Knopf, 1963), 279. Burton also discovered a Hebrew insignia on Phelps's weathervane and ultimately decided that he was "a little *tête-montée* on certain subjects," a pejorative French idiom signifying addle-brained self-importance.

157. Bowen, "Versatile W. W. Phelps," 160. Phelps served as co-counsel with George A. Smith.

158. Ibid., 161.

159. W. W. Phelps, "The Comet," *Deseret News,* Sept. 22, 1858, 127. The transliteration and verbal declension are slightly off, but *kumaz* does mean a small orb, such as used in jewelry, and *'atah* as a verbal root refers to "passing by." Of note, this meaning of *kumaz* is obscured by the KJV (Ex. 35:22; Num. 31:50) which uses "tablets." Phelps's Latin and Greek are correct, and his quotation from Webster is correct, at least in the 1828 edition. Scholars side with Webster in seeing a reference to the comet's tail as its "hair."

160. "An Old Nephite Coin," *Deseret News,* Dec. 12, 1860, 321. KEP, Document 2, is titled, "Egyptian counting."

161. Journal History, Oct. 9, 1860, qtd. in Bowen, "Versatile W. W. Phelps," 170.

162. Faulring, *American Prophet's Record,* Nov. 13, 1843, 427.

163. Ibid., Nov. 15, 1843, 427.

164. W. W. Phelps, "For the Times and Seasons," *Times and Seasons*, Nov. 1, 1843, 374.

165. The Egyptian papers do contain one possible candidate for "good." *Beth* is represented to mean "good to the taste, pleasing to the eye," though this may not have been preferred, given its obvious Hebrew meaning (house) that could have opened Smith and Phelps to ridicule. In the KEP, goodness is a subset of the broader meaning of *beth*, which does signify a residence (GAEL, 13).

166. GAEL, 24, 27, 30, 33.

167. "A Fac-simile from the Book of Abraham, No. 2," *Times and Seasons*, Mar. 15, 1842, 720a.

168. These documents are EA3, EA4, and EA5. I am grateful to William Schryver for correcting an error on this point in the original essay.

169. Bowen, "Versatile W. W. Phelps," 112-13 has misapprehended the situation by labeling Phelps merely a "spokesman."

170. Faulring, *American Prophet's Record*, Mar. 20, 1844, 460; May 23, 1844, 481.

171. Christopher Smith, "The Dependence of Abraham 1:1-3 on the Egyptian Alphabet and Grammar," *John Whitmer Historical Association Journal* 29 (2009): 38-54 has taken issue with my original essay, suggesting that Phelps had only a minor role in the KEP and that at least the first three distinctive verses of the Book of Abraham derive directly from the GAEL. As I have shown, Phelps was an active participant in Joseph's linguistic activities in the Kirtland period, and Phelps's excitement and sense of ownership of the papyri argues for his involvement in the hieroglyphic quest (see my "Joseph (Smith) in Egypt" for this quest generally and Phelps's early involvement). Our disagreement dances around the old polemic surrounding Joseph Smith's seeric-prophetic credentials. I am more interested in understanding how Smith and Phelps sought to establish and protect their credentials and what role the use of ancient languages played socially and religiously. The problem of textual dependence or derivation in Smith's Egyptian project depends on intractable documentary evidence, in my view.

172. The argument of Smith, "Dependence of Abraham 1," that Phelps's creative involvement in KEP must have been minimal because his political ghostwriting took place in the 1840s does not do justice to the clear evidence of Phelps's involvement, his personality and early interest in such projects, and Smith's general *modus operandi* of collaborative authorship from the earliest phases of his religious career.

"Scandalous Films"

The Campaign to Suppress Anti-Mormon Motion Pictures, 1911-1912

Brian Q. Cannon and Jacob W. Olmstead

In 1911, LDS leaders confronted a new form of opposition: hostile depictions of the Church, its history, and its missionaries on the silver screen. During this time, the influence of the motion picture industry was rising rapidly. As a result of competition within the industry, the quality of films was improving, substantial multi-reel feature films were being imported from Europe, and theaters were beginning to attract large numbers of middle-class viewers. The film industry in the early 1910s was rapidly acquiring recognition as a powerful force for education as well as entertainment.[1] Under these circumstances it seemed that the Church was compelled to take this new medium and its portrayals of Mormonism seriously.

Missionaries were the first to raise an alarm about anti-Mormon silent films they encountered in Europe, and they attempted, somewhat unsuccessfully, to combat the negative images of Mormonism they purveyed there. In Salt Lake City, Church leaders were not immediately touched directly by this development, but within a matter of months the release of several films in the United States drew not only local Mormons and missionaries but also the First Presidency into the fray. In their quest to stem the tide, Church leaders worked with civic organizations such as the Salt Lake Commercial Club and state and local officials. The Church's efforts reflected an increased sensitivity to public opinion during this era.[2] While the effort to influence the film industry yielded few victories with regard to film censorship, it did engender significant cooperation between Mormons and non-Mormons in Utah as both groups endeavored to promote positive perceptions of Utah, her history, her residents, and Mormonism itself. Moreover, this historical episode was important because it forced authorities to consider the Church's relationship to film, the potential role of film in enhancing or diminishing the Church's reputation, and the best ways for the Church to respond to cinematic portrayals of its history and culture. Shortly after its brush with anti-Mormon cinema in 1911-1912, the Church began working with friendly film makers, hoping that favorable films would improve the Church's image.[3]

Anti-Mormon Films and Plays in England, Late 1911

Spanning the years 1910-1914, a vigorous campaign swept through Great Britain, led by individuals who were bent on exposing Mormonism's "vile" practice of polygamy. Religious leaders, lecturers, books, and newspapers blamed Mormons and their missionaries for an erosion of conservative Victorian values. "The Mormon Problem"—polygamy and the possibility that missionaries might be luring young women to Utah for harems—concerned government officials in many lands including Sweden, the Netherlands, and Great Britain. The European trend grew out of a similar movement in the United States; in 1910 and 1911 muckraking journalists were publishing what they called new evidence of corruption and fresh marriages in the Church, and the reports rapidly made their way to Europe. At the same time, lecturers such as Hans Peter Freece hired by opponents of the Church in the United States traveled abroad to launch an anti-Mormon campaign.[4]

Given that the anti-Mormons' campaign coincided with the film industry's rapid development and film producers' quest for marketable tales, it is not surprising that at the height of this crusade against the LDS Church, Nordisk Films released an hour-long feature film on October 2, 1911, in Copenhagen entitled *Mormonens Offer* (*A Victim of the Mormons*). At the time, Denmark was a world leader in silent movies and Nordisk Films was a distinguished production studio. The founder, Ole Olsen, was the first European film maker to eye the dollar value of the so-called Mormon Problem as a sensational topic for films.[5] His approach to all films was to emphasize sensational issues to "rouse people's emotions." Publicity for the film suggests that Olsen and others at Nordisk believed Mormon themes would produce handsome profits and at the same time win support for the film industry by attacking a perceived social ill. The plot of *A Victim of the Mormons* was typical of anti-Mormon books, plays, and lectures of the era. A program designed to advertise the film in Danish warned, "He who sees this film and reads this text booklet is warned against the deception of Mormonism." The film traces the travails of a young woman named Florence who is lured to Utah by an unscrupulous Mormon missionary named Larson. When Florence comes to her senses, it is too late and the pair are aboard a ship to America. The story turns into a cat-and-mouse chase between the Mormon elder and Florence's brother, George, and suitor, Leslie. In the end, Larson is accidentally killed and Florence is set free.[6] Of particular interest is a temple scene with an amalgamation of the Salt Lake temple's baptistry, complete with oxen, and a set of organ pipes patterned after those in the Salt Lake Tabernacle.[7]

On October 10, not long after it premiered in Denmark, *A Victim of the Mormons* was released in England.[8] An ad in the English film trade paper *Bioscope* promised theater owners large returns under the headline, "This Great Winner Creates a Record Booking."[9] Only days after *A Victim of the Mormons* was released, ads in *Bioscope* touted the film's "enormous demand" and the fact that the studio would soon be "reissuing a 2nd run copy," also that "the song of the shrewd successful showman" would be "the Mormons are coming, Hur-rah! Hur-rah!"[10] Theater programs similar to those produced in Denmark informed London audiences of the film's release date, length, and plot, while editorializing about the "pernicious doctrines" of Mormonism. Here was a "drama which ... should do more to counteract the growth of Mormonism in this country than all the preaching against it, even by the most noted clerics," the program read. The film would "open the eyes of those foolish members of the gentler sex who are unluckily too easily gulled by the oily tongue of the deceiver"—by those "vampires" who "sow the seeds of the hated cult of Mormonism."[11]

The arrival of the film in England coincided with production of a popular play entitled *Through Death Valley, or The Mormon Peril.*[12] After Rudger Clawson, president of the European Mission, became aware of the film, he sent the First Presidency in Salt Lake City an optimistic letter reporting, "Our enemies are trying to stir up trouble for us with moving picture shows and theatrical performances, but usually the offering is so rank and abominable, that the mark is over-reached and the shaft falls harmless at our feet." He continued, "Just enough interest has been aroused in the subject to create a good demand for our literature and doubtless good results will follow." To illustrate his point, he wrote of a theater in which *A Victim of the Mormons* was being shown. After being denied permission by the manager to distribute tracts at the exits, the elders stood in the street instead and experienced much success in dispensing the literature. The tract they most likely circulated was headlined *£200 Reward* and offered cash to anyone who had knowledge of an instance wherein a woman had been captured and taken to Utah by Mormon elders. This publication by the British Mission, which reprinted a letter to the *Liverpool Express* written by Volney S. Peet, a non-Mormon newspaper editor in Salt Lake City who had campaigned vigorously against anti-Mormon sentiment, was available for distribution since August 10. The tract's effectiveness was great enough to warrant an order of 173,000 in February 1912.[13]

Despite Clawson's original optimism, by mid-December his confidence had turned to misgivings. "The moving picture show agitation is still on," he wrote to the First Presidency. "The 'Mormon' play is a prominent feature, and with other things, attracts large crowds. It is undoubtedly retarding the work more or less in the mission, as it serves to emphasize the prejudice already in the minds of the people against us. A living picture is, after all, quite a live thing, and often times makes a lasting impression on the mind. *A Victim of the Mormons* and *Through Death Valley, or The Mormon Peril* are plays that are in every sense lurid and sensational." In despair, elders in the mission wrote to Clawson asking what they could do to stop the presentation of such films and plays. Due to his lack of success in obtaining a fair hearing in the British newspapers, Clawson responded, "I presume it would be about as easy to inaugurate some method that would prevent the newspapers lying about us, as it would be to prevent these picture shows doing the same thing!"[14]

As mission leaders scrambled to develop a method for combating the bad publicity generated by the films, the *Liverpool Daily Post and Mercury* reported more bad news:

> In view of the crusade going on throughout the country against Mormonism, the extraordinary cinematography film entitled, *A Victim of the Mormons* which is being shown at the Garston Picturedrome this week, is particularly interesting, and there was a crowded audience at that popular house last night.
>
> The picture had just begun after the interval when something of a sensation occurred in the body of the hall. A man rose and exclaimed, "I protest against this picture being shown in this hall to-night." Immediately there was an uproar, the lights were promptly turned up, and the interrupter was speedily ejected through a door at the rear of the hall.[15]

The owner of the theater claimed he had received a letter from the "Mormon Brotherhood" threatening trouble if the film continued to be shown. It is unknown if the disturbance was a gimmick to create controversy about the film or if it was caused by a Church member who had had enough. In any case, the *Millennial Star* attempted to discredit the incident by noting that similar disruptions took place at other locations "almost simultaneously." Clawson, undoubtedly concerned by the attraction this report would bring to the film, said he felt insulted by the suggestion that the Church was involved. He wrote in the *Millennial Star* that because the show itself would be "insufficient, apparently, to keep up the interest to fever heat, a clumsy dodge is resorted to." In an effort to counter the report, Clawson wrote to the *Liverpool Daily* denying that the Mormon leadership had threatened the theater owner or had played any part in the disturbance. The newspaper, however, declined to print Clawson's letter.[16]

By December, the standard response in Britain was for elders to distribute tracts and pamphlets to exiting audiences outside the theaters. The primary tract until December 21 was *£200 Reward*, at which time Clawson published *The Anti-Mormon Moving Pictures and Play*.[17] The tract directly rebutted the film and was tailored to the mission's strategy of handing out literature the evening of a performance. It educated people regarding the crusade against Mormonism, mentioning specifically *A Victim of the Mormons* and the play, *Through Death Valley, or The Mormon Peril,* as the most recent examples of the smear campaign. A copy of the *Liverpool Daily Post and Mercury*'s exposé on the Garston Picturedrome incident and Rudger Clawson's response to the paper were also included.[18]

In the last three months of 1911, Clawson was desperately seeking an appropriate method to counter the films; however, in February and March 1912, his letters to the First Presidency switched from frustration to confidence. Returning to his original impressions, he said he was elated by the dividends the mission's efforts were reaping. Many of the conferences in the mission—Hull, Norwich, and York—had reported favorable responses to the tracts. Clawson quoted an elder, "We distributed tracts at each performance to those in attendance and as a result we have had quite a number of strangers at our meetings. Some of them remarked that they could readily see the absurdity of the pictures and were led by curiosity to our gatherings. Many of them seemed quite favorably impressed."[19]

While *A Victim of the Mormons* made its debut in England at the apex of persecution and intolerance toward the Latter-day Saints, Clawson detected a difference between these films and other media such as lectures and newspaper reports. Prophetically, he wrote, "It is easy to be seen that the managers of these picture shows are largely influenced by mercenary motives in their attack upon the Mormons! I imagine these disreputable shows will go as long as the almighty dollar goes with them, but when the dollar fails to show up the pictures will sink unto oblivion." The *Millennial Star* printed a story to illustrate Clawson's point. After the elders in the Norwich Conference had distributed literature at a theater presenting *Through Death Valley, or The Mormon Peril,* "the receipts at the theatre for the week were surprisingly low. The manager of the company was very angry over the results. He has stated that he had not made enough to pay the actors, and he blamed it to our tracts." While this story deals with a play rather than a film, it nevertheless illustrates Clawson's general point. The suspicion that the films were motivated by a desire to exploit a controversy for money rather than out of malice, combined with the missionaries' success in curbing the impact of the films, gave Clawson and the Latter-day Saints residing in England some hope for the future.[20]

Combating Anti-Mormon Films in the United States

As Clawson, missionaries, and members in Great Britain felt they were finally coming to grips with anti-Mormon films like *A Victim of the Mormons,* the Church across the Atlantic to the west was only beginning to confront this problem. Late in 1911 the trade journal *Moving Picture World* announced that *A Victim of the Mormons* was slated for release by Nordisk Film's American subsidiary, the Great Northern Film Company, during the first week of February. The full-page image that appeared in the magazine was an inaccurate and indelicate depiction of inside of the Mormon temple; the photo showed several white-robed women crowded on a platform above a temple baptismal font, awaiting baptism by a man in the water below. This was highly offensive to Church members.[21]

The First Presidency learned from Lester Park, a Mormon in the theater business, that this was not a film to be ignored. In an era of short, one-reel films, this three-reel film had a fully developed plot and was likely to dazzle audiences, Park advised the Church sometime before January 6. Park had been in the film industry for years and thought this was only "the seventh three-reel" film to ever appear. Writing to the editor of *Moving Picture World,* Park identified himself as a Church member, as well as a "film exchange representative" and "moving picture exhibitor," and then "vigorously" protested the film's release.[22]

Close on the heels of Park's ominous news came word of another cinematic attack upon the Mormons: a film called *The Mountain Meadows Massacre,* distributed by a French firm, Pathé Frères, the largest film company in the world at the time. The film had been released on the West Coast and was seen by Utahns vacationing there. The Church contacted the Salt Lake Commercial Club, which was the state's foremost booster organization and a model of Mormon and Gentile cooperation, to warn them of how the film slandered Utah.[23]

While Church leaders fretted about *A Victim of the Mormons,* news of *The Mountain Meadows Massacre* initially attracted more attention from Utah's business community, igniting a firestorm of protest.[24] The Salt Lake Commercial Club and Utah Development League sent telegrams to the New Jersey headquarters of Pathé to complain that the film was "a libel on the state of Utah," and "respectfully demand" that Pathé remove the film from circulation. The Commercial Club also petitioned its sister organization, the Los Angeles Chamber of Commerce, to ask it to lobby Pathé's Los Angeles subsidiary. The Utahns wanted the film "withdrawn at once." If Pathé spurned their request, the Utah businessmen would contact their Congressional delegation and the National Board of Censorship, they said. The National Board was a private organization that had close ties to the motion picture industry.[25]

Theater owners and Utah's governor echoed the complaints about the *Mountain Meadows Massacre* film. The mayor of Ogden promised to do "all in [his] power" to keep all Pathé films out of Utah if the company refused to meet their demands. Likewise the Alhambra Theatrical Company, which operated theaters in Utah, Idaho, and Wyoming, warned that it too would "refuse to show" any Pathé pictures unless *The Mountain Meadows Massacre* were withdrawn.[26]

Behind the scenes, LDS leaders instructed Eastern States Mission President Ben E. Rich to contact the National Board to have the film "condemn[ed]." What they didn't know was that the board had already approved the film two months earlier. The *Deseret News* heard about the controversy and called the film "a fake" even though the Church's overall strategy was to work quietly behind the scenes and downplay its connection to the effort to have the film censored. The massacre itself had never been a "concern [of] the Church," the *Deseret News* emphasized, since its leaders had played no role in the event. It was "a crime for which no one was responsible but those who committed it," the paper opined. The Church opposed the film because of how it dredged up a demoralizing historical event in a way that was injurious to "the fair name of Utah." "Uncritical" viewers might "transfer the odium of long ago to the present" and associate Utah with murder and mayhem. It made Utah appear to be a place of "murders and cutthroats" at an inauspicious time, three years before the San Francisco World's Fair, and would prejudice "hundreds of thousands" who were going to pass through the state on their way to California.[27]

Three days after receiving the Commercial Club's telegram, Pathé Frères pointed out that if they withdrew the film at the behest of Utah, this of itself would generate "adverse newspaper comment against Utah." The company nevertheless offered to remove the film from circulation provided that the Commercial Club would reimburse them for their expenses—a fair proposition in the sense that it offered something to both the company and the club. However, the club saw this as blackmail and thought that to participate in such an arrangement would open them to the possibility of future blackmail by other film producers. Several weeks later when Rich visited Pathé Frères, its officers, most of whom were French, feigned ignorance of American and Mormon history, claiming they could not see why anyone would take umbrage at it when it was a film set in the past and, even at that, laid no claim to historical accuracy. Rich reported that the Pathé representative with whom he spoke said his company's officials were "hot over the pre-emptory telegrams" they had received and felt that if the club had really been concerned about the issue, it would have purchased the film.[28]

Meanwhile the Los Angeles Chamber of Commerce condemned both films but informed the Salt Lake businessmen that only the General Film Company, the official distribution agency for major motion picture producers, could suppress them, and as a creation of the studios the distributor would probably not do so. The chamber apparently did not appeal to them.[29]

While the LDS Church maintained a relatively low profile in the largely unsuccessful campaign against *The Mountain Meadows Massacre,* it far more vigorously and successfully worked on several fronts to suppress *A Victim of the Mormons.* In addition to contacting Apostle and Senator Reed Smoot about the film, the First Presidency instructed President Rich to petition the National Board of Censorship to condemn it before its scheduled release. While they apparently assumed the board wielded "dictatorial" power and could prevent a film's release, the board in reality could merely recommend changes to films they reviewed.[30]

The board had been established by the People's Institute, along with motion picture producers and exhibitors, to review films prior to their release and identify offensive scenes or subtitles that needed to be eliminated before a film could receive the board's stamp of approval. Such notables as Andrew Carnegie, Anthony Comstock, Samuel Gompers, and Shailer Matthews sat on the board's first executive committee. Its stated policies were to "insist that there be no sensationalism and no representation of crime except with the object of conveying a moral lesson" and that "certain socially forbidden themes" and "anything of a sacrilegious nature" would be proscribed. While film makers were not legally bound to obtain the board's authorization, doing so helped them market their products, so on that basis the board exerted substantial leverage. Thus, the First Presidency's decision to lobby the National Board was shrewd and sensible even though it overestimated the board's coercive powers.[31]

The First Presidency approached William H. Swanson, president of the Rex Motion Picture Company, and asked him to present their case against the hated *Victim of the Mormons* to the Great Northern Film Company. Swanson was a good choice because, as a New York businessman and owner of the Salt Lake City Film Exchange, he had one foot in both worlds. He also served on the board of the Motion Picture Distributing and Sales Company (MPDSC), which was the distributor of Great Northern films. On yet another front, the First Presidency consulted with Utah Governor William Spry, who pledged to write to the National Board of Censorship on behalf of the state, protesting the film's release "on the grounds of injury which will come to the state of Utah" as a result of the film's "malicious misrepresentation against the Mormon people."[32]

On January 9 the governor sent his protest to Swanson, who was to deliver it to the National Board. Spry requested that the film be suppressed, along with another, *The Mormon*, which he learned was slated for release later that month. *The Mormon* was shorter than *A Victim of the Mormons* and was the work of the American Film Manufacturing Company, an independent producer. Its depiction of an attack by Mormons on a nineteenth-century wagon train "to secure new wives" compounded Utah's indignation. Governor Spry wrote "on behalf of the people of Utah" to object to both films on grounds they would "tend to revive and kindle prejudice against this state" and thereby "retard" the state's economic development. He maintained that "there is so much of inspiration in the present day labors of the people of Utah" that "resort need not be had to ... false stories, such as those in question, whose rehearsal slanders a state and a people." Instead of resorting to fiction, he suggested, why not ask the state of Utah to "suggest themes for picuture [sic] drams [sic] regarding Utah that will be truthful and elevating."[33]

Before communicating with the National Board, Swanson contacted John R. Freuler, an officer of the American Film Company, which had produced *The Mormon*. Inasmuch as this film was a regular release slated for distribution through the MPDSC, Swanson, as a member of the board, was able to wield substantial influence. He persuaded other members of the board to "use what influence we can to persuade them not to release" the film. The company's representative pledged "in every way possible [to] rectify any objections to the issuance of the film," suggesting that merely removing all mention of Mormonism from the title would "perhaps eliminate criticism." Swanson claimed victory in this incident, and perhaps the film received a more narrow distribution than otherwise, but it was nevertheless released under the original title on January 25 in New York City.[34]

While Church leaders had concerns about *The Mormon*, they were still more interested in preventing circulation of *A Victim of the Mormons* because it was longer and more sophisticated and focused on contemporary missionaries rather than historical issues. In an effort to explain the Church's position, Swanson communicated with the National Board of Censorship and Ingvall Oes, the producer's agent in New York City. Although the MPDSC purchased and distributed all the one-reel films from the Danish producer, *A Victim of the Mormons* was being marketed independently as a "special release," so Swanson had to rely largely on his persuasive powers with Oes. Multiple-reel feature films like *A Victim of the Mormons* were financially risky, Oes reminded him. The Great Northern, like most producers of feature films, had decided to manage that risk by selling exclusive rights for *A Victim of the Mormons* on a state-by-state basis to local theater owners or exchanges. Under these conditions, Oes advised Swanson, the only way to prevent the film from being shown in the United States would be for Utah to purchase screening rights to the 45,000 feet of film that had already been imported for $6,750.[35]

Swanson apparently agreed with Oes's solution and passed the recommendation on to Governor Spry, who became furious. He rejected the filmmaker's offer to sell the film to the state, accused Oes of blackmail, and in early February publicly threatened to "use every influence at my command" to "prohibit the exploitation of motion pictures in the state of Utah." This oblique threat left people wondering if he would attempt to ban all films or only the ones he considered to be offensive.[36]

Gearing up for what might be a perilous battle against the entire movie industry, Spry, an honorary member of the Salt Lake Commercial Club, sought the club's assistance. The Commercial Club had been asked to oppose the film on January 11, but the club, which included non-Mormon businessmen, had declined to do so because the film "deal[t] with a religious subject wholly" and the club had a policy of avoiding religious questions. In light of recent developments, though, non-Mormons decided to set that policy aside and cooperate with the governor to prevent the Church's defamation. On January 22, prominent non-Mormon businessmen and members of the Salt Lake Commercial Club including Simon Bamberger, John Dern, Daniel Jackling, William McCornick, George T. Odell, and Samuel Park lodged a protest with the National Board of Censorship objecting to anti-Mormon films on the grounds that they would be "prejudicial to progress here." Smoot and some of his western colleagues in the Senate, at his request, likewise protested against unfavorable films about Mormonism.[37]

Continuing his campaign on behalf of Utah and the Church, Swanson wrote for the trade paper, *Moving Picture World,* about the "grave complaints and protests" of theater owner Lester Park and the Salt Lake Commercial Club. "It is impossible to resist the conclusion," maintained Swanson, "that the Mormons are [being] attacked as a religious sect and made the objects of hatred, ridicule and contempt," which he found "decidedly inexcusable." Although *Moving Picture World* published Swanson's essay, it continued to advertise the films.[38]

Swanson was actually a highly effective emissary. Isaac Russell, a Mormon journalist in New York City whose uncle was President

Rich, was even more effective with the National Board of Censorship, although his role was largely hidden from public view. A Stanford graduate with important social and political connections, he had previously lobbied for the Church in New York City on matters relating to the media and public relations. He met with his friend John Collier, who was the educational secretary at the Board of Censorship, regarding *A Victim of the Mormons*. In their candid conversation, Russell learned that the National Board consisted of a board of directors or executive committee, a general committee, and a censoring committee on which dozens of prominent citizens sat. Usually between one and three representatives from the censoring committee were assigned to review a film before it was shown in theaters. Two members of that committee, a Mrs. Whaley and a Mr. Sonnichsen, had already viewed and approved *A Victim of the Mormons,* contingent upon minor deletions, well before anyone in Salt Lake City had even heard of the film. On the strength of this approval, the producer's agent in New York had ordered copies of the film from Denmark and advertised screening rights. This placed the National Board in a sticky situation with regard to the producer and the censors who had approved the picture. Collier warned that the board had a longstanding policy of disregarding "sectional protests"; for instance, they had recently turned a deaf ear toward protests from Catholics over a film's "historically true" depiction of "a corrupt and licentious Pope." He admitted, however, that when a film proved to have "a propagandist purpose—while it is used for a crusade on some question before the Courts"—the board would work to suppress the film. Russell seized upon this point to argue that *A Victim of the Mormons,* with its charge that missionaries were kidnapping women and dragooning them into plural marriage, "ha[d] been used as a propaganda against the Mormons." Such anti-Mormon films "hurt [the] missionaries, and injure[d] their good name." Russell believed this argument "impressed [Collier] more than anything else." Collier agreed to bring the matter before the board's executive committee, presenting any arguments and evidence which the Church might prepare in favor of the film's suppression. Collier asked Russell to draft a letter for him, and Russell recommended to Rich that the Church officially register "a vigorous religious protest."[39]

Rich cabled Salt Lake City the information and prepared his own protest letter for the board. He also asked other mission presidents to send "their protests in behalf of safety of elders." At least one president, James E. Robinson, replied with a wire detailing problems caused in California by the presentation of an anti-Mormon film.[40] Robinson said that in San Francisco, a film had been shown entitled *An Episode of Early Mormon Days,* depicting the Mountain Meadows Massacre and portraying Joseph Smith and Brigham Young as conspirators in the massacre. The film, which Robinson called "fake and foreign to the truth," had nearly caused a riot. The *Salt Lake Tribune* reported that at one showing "several Mormons were among the audience, and took such exception to the production that for a time, a fight seemed imminent."[41]

In his letter to the National Board, Russell placed the recent outpouring of anti-Mormon sentiment within the context of Utah and Mormon history so the board would understand the Church's strenuous opposition to depictions of missionaries as recruiters for polygamous harems. Admitting that many older Mormons, including President Joseph F. Smith, continued to live with plural wives, Russell said the ascendant generation was committed to monogamy and was "striving by every possible means to work away from the old issue" that had been so divisive in Utah. Russell attributed recent adverse publicity regarding polygamy to Thomas Kearns and Frank Cannon who had become embittered in the wake of their political defeats, coupled with the Cannon family's fall from prominence in the Church after George Q. Cannon's death. Russell averred that Kearns's and Cannon's bitterness provided the "basis" for four anti-Mormon articles which had appeared in national magazines in 1910. At the same time, the Interdenominational Council of Women had hired Hans P. Freece to lecture against Mormon missionaries.

Freece arrived in Europe "about the same time" as the magazine articles and was the inspiration for Danish filmmakers portraying Mormons as kidnappers of young women, Russell speculated. He denied that Mormons had ever imported girls for polygamy. The film would be interpreted by Westerners as "a libel" not only because it impugned the honor of Mormons but because it threatened Utah's reputation and commercial interests. The Commercial Club, comprised of Mormons and "Gentiles," wanted to "boost the region" and "welcome the tourist, to make him at home, to get him over certain old ideas about the west." The club possessed strong ties to similar clubs in thirteen states in the West and to businesses in the East. It would be unwise, Russell warned, to "keenly anger" such a large and influential group. Knowing that the Board of Censorship was itself struggling to counter critics who charged that it was merely a pawn of the film industry, Russell urged the board to avoid the wrath of Western businessmen by taking "a broad stand against films which are morally libels upon large classes of citizens" and which inspired "hatred."[42]

The protests from Russell, Rich, Smoot, the Commercial Club, and especially Governor Spry were persuasive. Walter Story, secretary for the National Board, told reporters that protests from Utah were "pouring in ... by the sackful" and that "the Salt Lake commercial bodies were making a howl." After receiving Spry's protest letter, the chair of the general committee, Thomas R. Slicer, viewed the film and then invited three other members of the executive committee, including Collier, to see it. On January 24 the executive committee noted that the situation "appeared quite serious to all"; two members agreed to contact the producer's agent, Ingvald Oes, and inform him that in order to retain the board's approval, the producer would have to "eliminate" the "objectionable character" of the film by removing all references to Mormonism. The prescribed changes were so extensive that they would "mutilat[e]" the film, the *New York Morning Telegraph* averred.[43]

The following week, on January 31, eleven members of the general committee met at the request of the executive committee to discuss Oes's reaction to the board's ultimatum. They learned that Oes had refused to make changes. The crucial issue for the board in their deliberations was not the reputation of Utah or of the Church; rather it was the board's standing and the fear that in the West "the seeing of this picture with the approval of the Board would greatly damage the confidence which it has endeavored to obtain throughout the country at large." Fearing, as Russell had shrewdly pointed out to Collier, that the board's "reputation and usefulness" would be compromised unless it rescinded its earlier approval, the board voted to revoke its approval of the film. Three representatives were appointed to inform Oes that "this action ... was understood to prohibit the use by the importer" of any suggestion "that the film had been passed by the National Board of Censorship." Thus, the film and its advertisements, which had previously carried the National Board's stamp of approval, would have to be altered slightly, potentially impairing the film's marketability.[44]

Word of the board's favorable decision reached Utah by the end of the week. On February 3, Spry received a *New York Morning Telegraph* article on the topic. Jubilant, Spry tried to claim credit for the victory by providing reporters with copies of his telegrams to the board. Perhaps misunderstanding the National Board's powers, the *Salt Lake Telegram* reported that as a result of the decision, the film would not be released unless it was "changed and the name or title ... eliminated." Similarly, the *Tribune* informed readers that the Board had "ban[ned]" the film, while the *Deseret News* hailed Spry for having "done the State splendid service in securing the repression" of the film, also recognizing the Commercial Club, which "so ably seconded his efforts on behalf of the good name of the State."[45]

Meanwhile, Oes and the Great Northern Film Company denounced the "Mormon racket" that had induced the National Board to rescind its approval and indicated that they would "go right ahead" and distribute the film. The *Morning Telegraph*, the New York daily that covered the film industry more fully than any other paper in the city, applauded Oes's stand and derided the board, observing correctly that the National Board "cannot suppress anything. It is a subsidized body without official standing." The paper's editor asked, "How much longer will the producers of picture plays permit the interference of this discredited body?" The paper printed a letter from Alexander E. Mackie, a non-Mormon who claimed to have lived in Utah for forty years. Brazenly arguing that the film depicted Mormonism accurately, Mackie contended that "it would have been the proper thing for our brainy censors to have replied to the Governor of Utah in words to the effect that when Utah cleared her skirts of traitors, lecherous scoundrels, polluters of the home, enticers of young girls, and robbers of ignorant foreigners, it might be time enough to suppress [the] films."[46]

Others interpreted the incident as evidence of the Church's considerable political clout. For instance, Governor Spry received a copy of an editorial from the *Memphis Appeal* decrying "the political influences" wielded by "the Mormon Church, backed by the Mormon Governor." Although the editor admitted that tales of unsavory proselyting tactics might be "colored to some extent," he held that "the Mormon Church is an evil that should be suppressed. ... Consequently if the suppressed picture show would have helped to strengthen public opinion against the teachings of Brigham Young it would have been well for the people at large."[47]

In retrospect, it seems strange that no one raised the issue of free speech in defense of the film. The National Board lacked legal authority to abridge anyone's Constitutional rights, but there had been government censorship of films as early as 1909 and filmmakers did not challenge it in the courts on First Amendment grounds until 1915, and even then the challenge was rejected by the U.S. Supreme Court.[48]

As the press weighed the merits of the board's decision, William Swanson traveled to Salt Lake City and was hailed as a hero for helping "suppress several sets of libelous moving picture films which are uncomplimentary to the state and the people of Utah." Swanson met with Governor Spry and with the First Presidency, who lavished praise and "recognition" upon him. He admitted that his role in suppressing the films had been "little" but pledged to work further with the Commercial Club to persuade the National Board, now that it had withdrawn its approval of *A Victim of the Mormons,* to outright "condemn" it and to condemn *Mountain Meadows Massacre* as well. Meanwhile, Isaac Russell received no public recognition for his efforts.[49]

The celebration over the National Board's ruling was short-lived. One week after Swanson's February 10 arrival, Joseph F. Smith learned of yet another anti-Mormon film, *Marriage or Death,* which the National Board was supposedly reviewing. Swanson agreed to try to prevent the film's release. After Swanson obtained the names of the production company's officers, President Smith cabled President Rich to ask him to contact the company. It turned out to be none other than Pathé, the distributor that had been willing to withdraw *Mountain Meadows Massacre* if the state of Utah would buy every copy of it.[50]

Initially Rich was hopeful. The secretary of the National Board informed him that the board had not yet reviewed the picture and there was still time for the Church to lobby against it. But when Rich visited Pathé's headquarters, he was told that the National Board had actually approved the film three months earlier; the board's secretary had somehow overlooked this in the board's records. Moreover, Rich learned that the film was already playing in New York theaters, having been released two days earlier. Owners of the company claimed they had "no desire to fight the Church" but could not see why the Church would be concerned: "their contention," reported Rich, "is that the scenes displayed are of events that are supposed to have happened long ago, and that no one pretends to believe the moving picture story any more than he would a story in a yellow backed novel." To prove they were not singling out Mormons for persecution, an official told the mission president the company was also filming *The Hunchback of Notre Dame* with its unfavorable portrayal of the Catholic clergy. They expected the Catholics to "make a rumpus when it comes out." Pathé had invested thousands of dollars in each film, and they could not justify withdrawing expensive films from circulation "simply because someone's feelings are hurt."[51]

Rich also learned that on February 8, just a few days after the board's general committee had withdrawn their approval of *A Victim of the Mormons*, another anti-Mormon film, *The Danite*, which was a two-reel production by Selig Studios in Chicago, had been approved by representatives of the board's censoring committee.[52] Although the term "Mormon" never appeared in the film, its connection to the Church was apparent to anyone familiar with Mormon history. The film was advertised in *Motion Picture World* on February 17 and opened two days later in New York—at least the first reel with the first half of the film was shown two days later; the next evening, the reel with the concluding half was shown.[53]

Rich was discouraged and disillusioned. Anti-Mormon films were consistently previewed by the board's censoring committee well before he or any other Church official had even heard of them. By the time they learned about a film, it was too late to act. After members of the Board of Censorship approved a film, it was practically "suicid[al]" for the board to reverse itself, Rich had been told. The general committee had made an exception in the case of *A Victim of the Mormons,* but the decision had driven a wedge between members of the censoring committee and the general committee. The board had been heavily criticized in influential papers. Particularly, allegations that the board had bowed to the wishes of the Church had damaged its credibility. Rich learned, probably from Russell who had visited with the board's executive secretary, that "the strongest weapon that could be used against [the board] would be to say that at the behest of the Mormon Church it withdrew approval it had formerly given." In other ways, too, the board's reversal of its stand on *A Victim of the Mormons* had proved to by a pyrrhic victory. The Great Northern Film Company released the film anyway and capitalized on the Church's intervention to advertise the film. Although the evidence today is unclear, Rich claimed he had it on "good authority" that the board had "'crawfished' on its [pro-Mormon] decision" in the face of "hostile criticism" from the press. The film was released without modification in the six states where showing rights had been sold prior to the board's decision. According to rumors which reached Rich, the company had modified the film somewhat before selling it in other states. However, the title, with its reference to Mormonism, remained unchanged everywhere.[54]

Rich wrote to Senator Smoot, enclosing Rich's letter to the First Presidency about his dissatisfaction with how things had proceeded. The National Board, he explained, was "a creature of the film companies, who use it merely for the advertising it brings them." The Church's protests had "accomplish[ed] little except to advertise the films and thus increase their circulation." He recommended that Congress create a truly official "national" board with power to review films, bar the mailing of advertisements of offensive films, and prohibit "ship[ping] such pictures from one state to another."[55]

While Rich believed that the entire episode demonstrated that vigorous federal regulation of the cinema was necessary, he and others who sought to suppress anti-Mormon films also felt the episode was a reminder of the silver screen's power for good or ill. As Rich noted, the film industry was "growing to an immense size." Indeed, this realization was probably the most important legacy of these unfavorable films. Governor Spry came to see the potential for shaping opinions and reaching mass audiences. "I believe it is today furnishing amusement and education to a greater number of people than any other one agency," he said. Ben Rich saw little redeeming merit in the film industry's products, which seemed to "plant the spirit of murder and robbery in the minds of young Americans," but he was convinced that a properly regulated film industry might "be used for an immense amount of good." Driving home the same point that films could help as well as hurt the Church, Rex Swanson thought the Church could commission its own favorable film about Mormonism. Later that year, with the memory of their brush with anti-Mormon films fresh in their minds, Church authorities entered into a cooperative agreement with the Ellaye Motion Picture Company regarding the production of a ninety-minute feature film, *One Hundred Years of Mormonism.*[56]

Although exposure to anti-Mormon films in 1911-1912 convinced some Church and civic leaders that films possessed potentially immense manipulative or educational power, others believed the same incidents demonstrated that the influence of films upon public opinion was evanescent. The *Deseret News* recalled in mid-March that just a few weeks earlier "some of our correspondents" had been "very much concerned" about anti-Mormon films. In retrospect, it appeared to the editor that there had been "hardly any ground for alarm." In the nineteenth century, the Church had been assaulted by slanderous novels, but these were now "forgotten." Likewise, "falsehoods presented in the film" under discussion "will have the same fate." Why was anyone concerned? Had not God promised, "No weapon that is formed against thee shall prosper"?[57]

One perceptive Utah resident, George A. Hicks of Spanish Fork, believed Mormons should draw a different lesson from their encounter with spiteful films. Writing to the *Salt Lake Tribune* on February 21, Hicks castigated filmmakers who sought to make money by sensationalizing Mormon history and depicting demoralizing incidents like the Mountain Meadows Massacre, then pointed out that Mormons were guilty of the same offense. In February someone had delivered two lectures in LDS chapels in central Utah on the massacre of Mormons at Hauns Mill in Missouri and the murder of Joseph and Hyrum Smith in

Illinois. The lectures were accompanied by illustrations. "If it is wrong to represent acts of violence committed by a few of the Mormon people against Gentiles, so it is also wrong to blame the whole of the people of Missouri and Illinois for what only a few of them were guilty of," Hicks reasoned. He argued that Mormons should scrutinize their own versions of history for misrepresentation as sensitively and closely as they scrutinized films about the Church produced by outsiders.[58]

Conclusion

In both the United States and Great Britain, the flood tide of anti-Mormon films soon subsided. Never again in the silent film era would such a barrage of anti-Mormon portrayals be produced within the space of only a few months. Nearly ninety years after the release of *A Victim of the Mormons* and other anti-Mormon films in 1911-1912, the brouhaha has nearly been forgotten, and except for an archival copy of *A Victim of the Mormons*, none of the feared films has survived.

However, the controversy deserves to be remembered for several reasons. The release of anti-Mormon films had an impact upon the Church's missionary efforts. In Britain baptisms declined from 2.98 per missionary in 1910 to 1.6 in 1911. In the Eastern States Mission where Ben E. Rich and Isaac Russell worked to turn the tide of anti-Mormon propaganda, baptisms fell from 1,920 in 1911 to 1,433 in 1912, a decline of over 25 percent. Although other factors certainly contributed to the trend, anti-Mormon films were probably partly to blame.[59]

The controversy was equally important for fostering interreligious cooperation. The LDS Church gained little by petitioning the National Board, but its success in uniting with secular organizations like the Salt Lake Commercial Club was remarkable. At a time when religious tensions remained strong in Utah society, Utah business leaders came together out of a concern for the image of the state and its residents and, remarkably, to contradict invidious stereotypes. The precedent established in 1912 was repeated nine years later when another unfavorable film, *Riders of the Purple Sage*, appeared.[60]

The Church managed to establish indirect influence over at least some of the members of the National Board, with lasting effects. Four members of the review committee examined *A Mormon Maid*, in 1917.

Passing it on to the general committee, the reviewers said it "involve[d] a question of controversy with the Mormon Church" that might "cause a great deal of opposition on the part of that organization." When the general committee reviewed the film, Miriam S. Price recalled the previous "trouble in Utah" over *A Victim of the Mormons*. When a fellow committee member aired the opinion that the board should not concern itself with "the difficulties which this picture might encounter in Utah," Price disagreed and urged the board to "not pass a picture offensive to a religious sect." Ultimately a majority of the committee rejected Price's viewpoint and approved the film, but it did adopt her recommendation to the producer to add a warning that the film did not depict contemporary conditions in Mormon country. This was a small concession but one that at least acknowledged that polygamy was no longer sanctioned by the LDS Church.[61]

The most enduring legacy of this brush with anti-Mormon films in 1911-1912 was the Church's awareness of the potential films had for reaching, educating, and influencing vast audiences. In the April 1912 general conference, David O. McKay referred to *A Victim of the Mormons* and acknowledged its "stronger means of disseminating knowledge, even than the press." The apostle explained, "When you read a book, you depend upon the printed page for your mental pictures. If those characters are readily interpreted, the reader will probably get the idea or the picture which the author intended to express; but when you may sit and see it acted, see it portrayed as naturally as though it were being enacted in the every-day life, then the mental pictures are given as definitely and as rapidly as the motions of the actors can portray them." In line with this new appreciation of the power of motion pictures, Church leaders cooperated with a friendly producer, hoping to see favorable films improve the Church's image. Long after the plots of films like *A Victim of the Mormons* had been forgotten, fascination with the silver screen remained. As the twentieth century progressed, films became a key element in the Church's proselyting and public relations efforts. The events of 1911-1912 helped set the stage for those developments.[62]

Notes

1. Garth Jowett, *Film: The Democratic Art* (Boston: Little, Brown and Company, 1976), 51.

2. Thomas G. Alexander, *Mormonism in Transition: A History of the Latter-day Saints, 1890-1930* (Urbana: University of Illinois Press, 1986), 239-57, examines some of the Church's key attempts during this era to foster favorable views of the Church and its membership.

3. The fullest discussion of anti-Mormon silent films is Richard Nelson, "A History of Latter-day Saint Screen Portrayals in the Anti-Mormon Film Era, 1905-1936," M.A. thesis, Brigham Young University, 1975. Nelson's unpublished study draws upon Danish sources regarding the film, *A Victim of the Mormons,* and Mormon pamphlets printed in England that attacked the film. It also effectively draws upon film trade publications including *Moving Picture News* and *Moving Picture World,* as well as Utah newspapers and the *New York Morning Telegraph.* A much briefer study covering a broader time period is Richard Alan Nelson, "From Antagonism to Acceptance: Mormons and the Silver Screen," *Dialogue: A Journal of Mormon Thought* 10 (Spring 1977): 59-69. William J. Roper and Leonard J. Arrington, in *William Spry: Man of Firmness, Governor of Utah* (Salt Lake City: Utah State Historical Society, 1971), devote roughly one page to a discussion of Spry's protest of *A Victim of the Mormons* and erroneously conclude that Spry's protest "had the desired effect"(p. 95). Alexander, *Mormonism in Transition,* 242, mentions the existence of films "which focused on accounts of the Mountain Meadows Massacre, plural marriage, and atrocities of the Danites."

Building upon previous scholarly work, this paper utilizes new sources, including the correspondence of Eastern States Mission President Ben E. Rich, European Mission President Rudger Clawson, the First Presidency, and Utah Governor William Spry, as well as the files of the National Board of Censorship in investigating the efforts by religious, governmental, and commercial leaders to suppress anti-Mormon films.

4. Nelson, "History of Latter-day Saint Screen Portrayals," 25. A Utah native who studied law at Columbia College, Freece went to Europe in 1910 as a representative for the Interdenominational Council of Women to lecture on Mormonism. His "eye witness" accounts of life in Utah played a significant role in rallying anti-Mormon sentiment in Europe. For a more detailed description of Freece and the anti-Mormon crusade in Great Britain, see Malcolm R. Thorp, "'The Mormon Peril': The Crusade against the Saints in Britain, 1910-1914," *Journal of Mormon History* 2 (1975): 73-75.

5. The film, *A Victim of the Mormons,* boasted top Danish actors. Vlademar Psilander was the most popular early twentieth-century Danish actor, and he played the Mormon elder. August Blom, the director, was respected in the industry. See Nelson, "History of Latter-day Saint Screen Portrayals," 29, and

The Cinema in Denmark (Copenhagen: Danish Film Foundation, 1970), 3-4, qtd. in Nelson, 25.

6. A partial copy of the film is available for viewing in the Historical Department Library, Church of Jesus Christ of Latter-day Saints, Salt Lake City. A copy is also located at the Danish Film Museum in Copenhagen. See Nelson, "History of Latter-day Saint Screen Portrayals," 24-28.

7. Given the semi-accurate depiction of the temple baptistry, the set was possibly based upon exposés describing temple rituals such as *Baptism for the Dead: The Font Resembling Somewhat the "Molten Sea" of Solomon's Temple* (London: n.p., 1911). Edwin D. Hatch, "Moving Picture Misrepresentations," *Millennial Star,* Nov. 9, 1911, 710, illustrates the agitation that such depiction of sacred rituals engendered in Latter-day Saints.

8. Nordisk Films Company's marketing pamphlet, *A Victim of the Mormons,* in Nordisk Release Heralds, folder 132, vertical files, Margaret Herrick Library Special Collections, Academy of Motion Picture Arts and Sciences and Academy Foundation, Beverly Hills.

9. "A Victim of the Mormons," *Bioscope,* Oct. 5, 1911, 8.

10. "Jury's Imperial Pictures, Ltd.," *Bioscope,* Oct. 12, 1911, 66.

11. *A Victim of the Mormons* marketing pamphlet.

12. The authorship of this play is unclear. A search of the collections of the British Library, the Library of Congress, and libraries in Utah revealed no works with this title.

13. *£200 Reward* (Liverpool: Millennial Star, 1911); Rudger Clawson, "The Anti-'Mormon' Moving Pictures and Play," *Millennial Star,* Dec. 21, 1911, 808; Rudger Clawson to the First Presidency, Nov. 7, 1911, Letters to the First Presidency, box 9, MS 481, Rudger Clawson Papers, Manuscripts Division, J. Willard Marriott Library, University of Utah, Salt Lake City; Rudger Clawson to the First Presidency, Feb. 21, 1912, Clawson Papers.

14. Rudger Clawson to the First Presidency, Dec. 15, 1911, Mar. 5, 1912, Box 9, Clawson Papers.

15. The article in the *Liverpool Daily Post and Mercury,* Dec. 12, 1911, was reproduced in Rudger Clawson, "Anti-'Mormon' Moving Pictures," 809.

16. Ibid., 808-11.

17. The tract, *Anti-Mormon Motion Pictures and Play,* cost "one shilling and three pence per pound" and was sold to investigators (Nelson, "History of Latter-day Saint Portrayals," 31).

18. Rudger Clawson to Frances M. Lyman, Dec. 19, 1911, in Rudger Clawson, "European Mission Report Made by Elder Rudger Clawson of the Council of the Twelve," p. 91, box 8, Clawson Papers; Clawson to the First Presidency, Feb. 21, 1912; Clawson, *Anti-Mormon Moving Pictures.*

19. Rudger Clawson to the First Presidency, Mar. 12, 1912, Letters to the First Presidency, box 9, Clawson Papers.

20. "European Mission Report," 91, Clawson Papers; "The Anti-'Mormon' Drama," *Millennial Star*, Feb. 22, 1912, 124-25. Clawson's optimism was premature in the face of continued attacks in the British press and physical violence and threats to missionaries. In 1913, Clawson noted that by almost every measure, missionaries had been less successful in 1912 than in 1911. Baptisms, visits to families, and the number of gospel conversations had declined. Clawson reported that "the spirit of prejudice took hold of the minds of the people to the extent that it was indeed difficult to get a gospel conversation" ("European Mission Report," 144).

21. "A Victim of the Mormons," *Moving Picture World*, Dec. 30, 1911, 1,085. The film had already been screened in Australia and South Africa, as well as in Europe. See "European Mission Report," 91. A small advertisement for a film entitled *An Episode of Early Mormon Days* appeared in the December 9 issue of *Moving Picture World*. However, the Church paid no attention to this film ("List of the Best Films Released during the Week of Dec. 11th, 1911," *Moving Picture World*, Dec. 9, 1911, 787).

22. *Salt Lake City Directory, 1911* (Salt Lake City: R. L. Polk & Co., 1911), 776; Nelson, "History of Latter-day Saint Screen Portrayals," 44-45, 174; *Motion Picture World*, Jan. 27, 1912, copy in Scrapbook no. 1, 1909-1916, box 1, William Spry Papers, L. Tom Perry Special Collections Library, Harold B Lee Library, Brigham Young University, Provo; First Presidency to Ben E. Rich, Jan. 6, 1912, folder B-13, box 2, Scott G. Kenney Collection, L. Tom Perry Special Collections Library, Harold B. Lee Library, Brigham Young University, Provo. Feature films were pioneered by European producers like Nordisk. Prior to 1912, all three-reel feature films shown in America had been produced abroad. For information on the European role in their manufacture, see Tino Balio, ed., *The American Film Industry*, rev. ed. (Madison: University of Wisconsin Press, 1985), 109-13; Robert Sklar, *Movie-Made America: A Cultural History of American Movies* (New York: Vintage Books, 1975), 37.

23. "Moving Pictures Libel, Utah Travelers Report," *Salt Lake Herald Republican*, Jan. 10, 1912, 2; "Business Men See Libel in Utah Film," *Salt Lake Tribune*, Jan. 11, 1912, 16. For information on Pathé Frères, see Anthony Slide, *The American Film Industry: A Historical Dictionary* (New York: Greenwood Press, 1986), 259; Gene Fernett, *American Film Studios: An Historical Encyclopedia* (Jefferson, NC: McFarland, 1988), 162-64. The Salt Lake Commercial Club, originally known as the Chamber of Commerce, was established in April 1887. Organized to promote the economic growth of Salt Lake City and Utah and, for the sake of economic development, to minimize religious and political divisions, the club promoted home industry and attracted population and capital to Salt Lake City. Membership in the club was diverse and included individuals from the Mormon, gentile, and apostate communities who agreed to set political and religious divisions aside. By 1912 the club had 1,200 mem-

bers statewide including the most prominent Utah business leaders ("Officers and Board of Governors of the Commercial Club," *Deseret News*, Jan. 20, 1912, 3:11; Thomas G. Alexander and James B. Allen, *Mormons & Gentiles: A History of Salt Lake City* (Boulder: Pruett Publishing, 1984], 104-05).

24. The heated reaction of the Salt Lake City Commercial Club and similar organizations such as the Utah Development League was to be expected; they had invested time and cash in attracting out-of-state business and promoting stability and wealth. One of the Commercial Club's many projects was the printing in January 1912 of 40,000 promotional booklets ("Big Advertising Deal," *Deseret News*, Jan. 25, 1912, 14). In that same month, at a combined conference of the Utah Development League (including many of the Commercial Club), the Utah Press Association, and Native Sons of Utah, promoters decided to spend upward of $50,000 over the next few years to advertise Utah to the East ("Citizens Are Uniting for Greater Utah," *Salt Lake Tribune*, Jan. 24, 1912, 1). Businessmen felt the previous year's advertising campaign in Europe and the United States had been successful and anticipated that 1912 would surpass 1911 in economic growth ("Salt Lake Looms on Map of World," *Salt Lake Tribune*, Jan. 6, 1912, 10; "Business and Trade," *Salt Lake Tribune*, Jan. 7, 1912, 6).

25. "Business Men See Libel in Utah Film," *Salt Lake Tribune*, Jan. 11, 1912, 16; Charles Dwight Willard, *A History of the Chamber of Commerce of Los Angeles, California* (Los Angeles: Kingsley-Barnes & Neuner, 1899), 58-70. Although the Salt Lake and Los Angeles organizations were not formally affiliated, some of Salt Lake's foremost entrepreneurs were frequently in Los Angeles on business and the film was being produced and screened in Los Angeles. In 1911, Californians had filed on over one-third of the out-of-state homesteads in Utah. Utah had held one "land show" in Los Angeles and was planning to hold another ("Los Angeles May Help Suppress Films," *Salt Lake Herald Republican*, Jan. 13, 1912, 3; "Great Result in Advertising Utah," *Deseret News*, Jan. 11, 1912, 5).

26. First Presidency to Ben E. Rich, Jan. 10, 1912, folder B-13, box 2, Kenney Collection; "Protesting against Moving Picture Film," *Deseret News*, Jan. 13, 1912, 3; "Moving Picture Co. Takes Definite Steps," Jan. 16, 1912, 3; "A Vigorous Protest Made," *Ogden Evening Standard*, Jan. 15, 1912, 8.

27. First Presidency to Ben E. Rich, Jan. 10, 1912; Ben E. Rich to First Presidency, Feb. 23, 1912, folder 2, box 35, Reed Smoot Collection, L. Tom Perry Special Collections Library, Harold B. Lee Library, Brigham Young University, Provo; "A Timely Protest," *Deseret News*, Jan. 11, 1912, 4; "Should Be Suppressed," *Deseret News*, Jan. 22, 1912, 4.

28. Pathé Frères to Joseph E. Caine, Jan. 12, 1912, qtd. in "Company Demands Payment to Quit," *Salt Lake Tribune*, Jan. 13, 1912, 9; Rich to First Presidency, Feb. 23, 1912. Offering to sell film rights to a group that was interested in suppressing a film was a strategy the National Board of Censorship

occasionally promoted. See, e.g., the letter drafted by W. D. McGuire, executive secretary for the National Board, for possible use by distributors Hiller and Wilkes, [1917], box 105, Records of the National Board of Review, New York Public Library, New York City.

29. "Mountain Meadows Films Obnoxious," *Deseret News*, Jan. 20, 1912, 1. For information on the General Film Company, see Balio, *American Film Industry*, 103-06, 145-49.

30. First Presidency to Ben E. Rich, Jan. 6, 1912; First Presidency to Reed Smoot, Jan. 6, 1912, folder B-13, box 2, Kenney Collection; "Business Men See Libel in Utah Film," *Salt Lake Tribune*, Jan. 11, 1912, 16.

31. The National Board claimed in 1911 that filmmakers "believe[d] it to be to their commercial advantage" to produce films that met the board's standards. As historian Shelley Stamp has observed, the board's bulletin of approved films enjoyed wide circulation among municipalities and civic organizations. Consequently the approval of a film could enlarge its prospective audience. "The influence of reformers [on the board] was real," historian Lary May found. While their stamp of approval was beneficial to filmmakers, it was not essential. At least 15 percent of the films produced in the early 1910s were not even submitted for review. "Censors Destroyed Evil Picture Films," *New York Times*, May 14, 1911, p. 5; Minutes of the Meeting of the General Committee, Jan. 19, 1917, box 121, Records of the National Board of Review; Shelley Stamp, "Moral Coercion: Or the National Board of Censorship Ponders the Vice Films," in Matthew Bernstein, *Controlling Hollywood: Censorship and Regulation in the Studio Era* (New Brunswick: Rutgers University Press, 1999), 42; Lary May to the Editor, *American Historical Review* 87 (June 1982), 913. See also Lary May, *Screening out the Past: The Birth of Mass Culture and the Motion Picture Industry* (New York: Oxford University Press, 1980), 54-59; Robert Fisher, "Film Censorship and Progressive Reform: The National Board of Censorship of Motion Pictures, 1909-1922," *Journal of Popular Film* 4:2 (1975): 143-56.

32. First Presidency to Ben E. Rich, Jan. 6, 1912; First Presidency to Reed Smoot, Jan. 6, 1912; Nelson, "History of Latter-day Saint Screen Portrayals," 35.

33. William Spry to National Board of Censorship, Jan. 9, 1912, box 3, Spry Papers; "Governor Spry Stops Slander," undated newsclipping, Scrapbook, 1909-1916, 1:112, box 1, Spry Papers; "The Mormon: A Western Drama to be Released by the American Film Co.," undated clipping, Scrapbook, 1909-1916, 1:114, box 1, Spry Papers. *The Mormon* is referred to in some sources as *The Mormons*.

34. William H. Swanson to William Spry, Jan. 29, 1912, box 3, Spry Papers; Swanson to Spry, Jan. 11, 1912, box 3, Spry Papers; "Helped Suppress Libelous Films," *Deseret News*, Feb. 10, 1912, 2; Nelson, "A History of Latter-day Saint Screen Portrayals," 41, 52-53; "Heeds Request for Suppression of Film,"

Salt Lake Tribune, Feb. 4, 1912, 28. For information on the MPDSC, see Slide, *American Film Industry,* 221-22.

35. William H. Swanson to William Spry, Jan. 11, 29, 1912, box 3, Spry Papers; Balio, *American Film Industry,* 111.

36. William Spry to William H. Swanson, Jan. 19, 1912, box 3, Spry Papers; "'Victim of Mormons' Prohibited," *Salt Lake Telegram,* Feb. 3, 1912, 8; "Heeds Request for Suppression of Film." One New York newspaper interpreted Spry's statement to mean that he would "banish all pictures from Utah" ("Mormon Governor Threatens to Bar Films in Utah," *New York Morning Telegraph,* Jan. 28, 1912, section 4, part 2, p. 1.

37. "Business Men See Libel in Utah Film," *Salt Lake Tribune,* Jan. 11, 1912, 16; "Victim of Mormons, Title of New Film," *Salt Lake Tribune,* Jan. 12, 1912, 14; First Presidency to Ben E. Rich, Jan. 6, 1912; McCornick et al. to National Board of Censorship, Jan. 22, 1912, box 2, folder B-13, Kenney Collection; Ben E. Rich to Reed Smoot, Jan. 23, 1912, box 35, folder 2, Smoot Papers; Smoot to Rich, Jan. 25, 1912, box 35, folder 2, Smoot Papers. One of the films mentioned in the telegram, *A Mormon Victim,* was clearly *A Victim of the Mormons.* But the identity of the other, entitled *Lured by the Mormons,* is unclear.

38. "The Sectarian Film Once More," *Moving Picture World,* Jan. 27, 1912, 282; William H. Swanson to William Spry, Jan. 29, 1912, box 3, Spry Papers.

39. Walgren, "Inside the Salt Lake Temple," 6-9; Isaac Russell to Ben E. Rich, Jan. 22, 1912, box 4, folder 16, Kenney Collection; "Minutes of the Special Meeting of the General Committee Held at the National Board of Censorship Offices, January 31, 1912," Minutes of Special Review Meetings, box 121, Records of the National Board of Review, New York Public Library. Documentation of Russell's previous public relations work for the Church is found in Isaac Russell to Theodore Roosevelt, Feb. 2, 1911; Theodore Roosevelt to Isaac Russell, Feb. 4, 1911; Isaac Russell to Brother [B. H.] Roberts, Feb. 8, 1911; Russell to Roberts, May 6, 1911; Russell to Roberts, May 13, 1911, box 4, Kenney Collection. Collier's position on the board is identified in "Censor Board Bows to Mormon Mandate," undated news clipping, Scrapbook 1, 1909-1916, p. 115, Spry Papers. *A Victim of the Mormons* was reviewed by representatives of the National Board on December 5 in New York City. The two reviewers approved the film, contingent upon "complete elimination" of two scenes in which "attack and struggle between [a] Mormon and [a] girl" were portrayed or suggested. "Voting Record of Films Viewed, November and December 1911," Special Reports, box 163.

40. Ben E. Rich to First Presidency, Jan. 22, 1912, box 4, folder 16, Kenney Collection.

41. "Moving Pictures Stir Up Feeling," *Deseret News,* Jan. 25, 1912, 5. Robinson's telegram is quoted in "Massacre Picture Nearly Causes Riot," *Salt Lake Tribune,* Jan. 25, 1912, 5.

42. Isaac K. Russell to National Board of Censorship, Jan. 24?, 1912, box 4, folder 16, Kenney Collection.

43. "Mormon Film Has 'Em Wobbly," *New York Morning Telegraph,* Jan. 30, 1912, p. 2; "Minutes of the Special Meeting of the General Committee"; "Heeds Request for Suppression of Film"; "Mormon Governor Threatens to Bar Films in Utah," *New York Morning Telegraph,* Jan. 28, 1912, sect. 4, pt. 2, p. 1.

44. "Minutes of the Special Meeting of the General Committee"; "Heeds Request for Suppression of Film"; "Mormon Governor Threatens to Bar Films."

45. "'Victim of Mormons' Prohibited," *Salt Lake Telegram,* Feb. 3, 1912, 8; "Heeds Request for Suppression of Film"; "Bad Films Repressed," *Deseret News,* Feb. 5, 1912, 4.

46. "Mormon Governor Threatens to Bar Films in Utah"; "'Mormon' Film to Be Censored by National Board," *New York Morning Telegraph,* Jan. 31, 1912, p.1; "Film 'Censors' Right on the Job," *New York Morning Telegraph,* Feb. 1, 1912, p. 12; "A Victim of the Mormons, the National Board of Censorship, and the Falsehoods Spread by the Utah Press," *New York Morning Telegraph,* Feb. 18, 1912, sect. 4, pt. 2, p. 1; "Mormonism Jolted by Utah Man," *New York Morning Telegraph,* Feb. 11, 1912, sect. 4, pt. 2, p. 1. Alexander Mackie does not appear in Salt Lake City directories for 1911-1912, nor in Utah census indexes for 1880, 1900, or 1910. It is possible that the author of the letter was a Utah resident but writing under a pseudonym. Although it was not the city's largest paper, the *New York Morning Telegraph,* which printed Mackie's letter, was an important player in the city's journalism community. It was edited and managed by an experienced newspaperman, William E. Lewis, who had previously worked for the *Kansas City News,* the *Chicago Times,* the *New York Journal,* and the *Philadelphia North American.* Nelson served as editor and general manager of the *Morning Telegraph* for over two decades (Albert Nelson Marquis, ed., *Who's Who in America: A Biographical Dictionary of Notable Living Men and Women in the United States* [Chicago: A. N. Marquis and Co., 1924], 1978).

47. The *Memphis Appeal* was quoted in "Action of Mormon Governor of Utah Teaches a Lesson," undated clipping, Scrapbook 1, 1909-1916, p. 111, Spry Papers.

48. In *Mutual Film Corporation v. Ohio* (1915), the Supreme Court ruled that Constitutional guarantees of freedom of speech and freedom of the press did not extend to the movie industry, which was "a business, pure and simple, originated and conducted for profit, like other spectacles" (Jowett, *Democratic Art,* 120; Richard S. Randall, *Censorship of the Movies: The Social and Political Control of a Mass Medium* [Madison: University of Wisconsin Press, 1968], 12, 18-21).

49. "Helped Suppress Libelous Films," 2; "Will Aid Effort to Suppress Films," *Salt Lake Tribune,* Feb. 11, 1912, 16.

50. First Presidency to Ben E. Rich, Feb. 17, 20, 1912, box 2, folder B-13,

Kenney Collection. *Marriage or Death* was advertised in *Motion Picture World,* Feb. 17, 1912, 614. A review in the *Morning Telegraph* described it as "another Mormon story picturing the horrors of the religious fanaticism of a few years ago. A young girl is about to be forced into wedlock with a Mormon when she is rescued by cowboys, her family having been previously forced out of the country because of their refusal to comply with the Mormon demand. The scenes are supposedly laid in Utah, the action taking place in the time of the Mormon settlement of that then-wilderness country" ("Marriage or Death," *New York Morning Telegraph,* Feb. 25, 1912, sect. 4, pt. 2, p. 3).

51. Ben E. Rich to First Presidency, Feb. 23, 1912.

52. This film, written by Mckee Rankin, was loosely based upon his popular five-act Broadway production, *The Danites,* produced by the American Play Company for a hit run in New York, as well as in Europe (Nelson, "History of Latter-day Saint Film Portrayals," 66-68). A copy of the Broadway script is in folder 201, William Selig Collection, Special Collections, Margaret Herrick Library, Academy of Motion Picture Arts and Sciences and Academy Foundation.

53. "Selig," *Moving Picture World,* Feb. 17, 1912, 614; "Pictures Are Released," *Deseret News,* Feb. 24, 1912, 2; "The Danites," *New York Morning Telegraph,* Feb. 25, 1912, sect. 2, pt. 4, p. 3; Nelson, "History of Latter-day Saint Screen Portrayals," 68. Installments of longer, multi-reel films were sometimes released on succeeding days, as was the case with this film.

54. Ben E. Rich to First Presidency, Feb. 23, 1912; Ben E. Rich to Reed Smoot, Feb. 29, 1912, box 35, folder 2, Smoot Collection; "Mormon Governor Threatens to Bar Films in Utah," *New York Morning Telegraph,* Jan. 28, 1912, sect. 4, pt. 2, p. 1. The board's general committee asked on January 29 that all references to Mormonism be removed from the film, but Rich assumed the board had retreated to a position taken by two members of the censoring committee in November, which was that any "suggestion of force on the part of the Mormon" or of "struggle on the part of the girl" be excised. The minutes do not indicate that the board retreated or restored approval of the film. Nor did the producer imply in its advertisements that it had the board's endorsement. The board had been opposed by the Great Northern Film Company and the *New York Morning Telegraph,* and the censoring committee took umbrage that it was not being further consulted. Irene Langford, the "only member of the theatrical profession" on the censoring committee, resigned in protest, complaining, "The attitude taken by the board in regard to the protest of the Mormons ... is only another proof of [an] uncertain policy ... It simply shows that the pictures are passed upon utterly without regard to their merit[s] as plays" ("Miss Irene Langford Resigns from the 'Censorship' Board," *New York Morning Telegraph,* Feb. 25, 1912, sect. 4, pt. 2, p. 1; see also "Mormon Meddlers Being Ignored by Film Manufacturers," *New York Morning Telegraph,* Mar. 1912, sect. 4, pt. 2, p. 1). Evidence of internal opposition is also found in the April 18, 1912, addition to Minutes of the Special Committee of the General Committee,

Jan. 31, 1912, box 121, National Board of Review Records, noting the censoring committee's request to be present and vote whenever the general committee considered overriding them.

55. Ben E. Rich to Reed Smoot, Feb. 29, 1912; Ben E. Rich to First Presidency, Feb. 23, 1912. Rich, who emerged from his encounter with the National Board of Censorship convinced that federal police power was the only effective means of regulating films, followed the path Progressive reformers had trod, who preferred working with voluntary organizations but soon turned to the state to enforce standards. Smoot failed to follow up on Rich's recommendation, and although others in Congress had suggested film censorship bills, none of the bills came before the Senate for a vote. Perhaps Smoot did not agree fully with Rich's assessment of the board's inefficacy.

In April 1912, David O. McKay quoted a missionary letter in the April 1912 LDS general conference: "It is a shame that the men and women composing the national board of censorship for moving pictures cannot see the untruthfulness of the picture [*A Victim of the Mormons*] and reject it." In 1917, Joseph F. Smith asked the National Board to suppress *A Mormon Maid*. In correspondence with the board in 1921 at Heber J. Grant's behest, Senator Smoot threatened to support a federal board of censorship if the existing board did not suppress the British film, *Riders of the Purple Sage*. See *Report of the Eighty-Second Annual Conference of the Church of Jesus Christ of Latter-day Saints* (Salt Lake City: LDS Church, 1912), 53-54; Joseph F. Smith to Cransten Brenton, Chairman of the Executive Committee of the National Board of Review, Mar. 23, 1917, box 105, Records of the National Board of Review; Heber J. Grant to Reed Smoot, Aug. 24, 1921, qtd. in Nelson, "History of Latter-day Saint Screen Portrayals, 131; Reed Smoot to National Board of Review, July 2, 1921, box 78, Records of the National Board of Review. For further information on Smoot's campaign against *Riders of the Purple Sage,* consult Nelson, "History of Latter-day Saint Screen Portrayals," 128-39.

56. Ben E. Rich to Reed Smoot, Feb. 29, 1912; William H. Swanson to William Spry, Jan. 29, 1912, box 3, Spry Papers; William Spry to National Board of Censorship, Jan. 9, 1912, box 3, Spry Papers. According to Levi Edgar Young, the Ellaye Motion Picture Company "entered into a contract with the Church authorities to produce the history of 'Mormonism.' The agreement stipulated that the Church was merely to sanction the production of the historical scenes, which the company had chosen to enact" (Levi Edgar Young, "'Mormonism' in Picture," *Young Woman's Journal,* Feb. 24, 1913, 77). According to Richard Nelson, the company "agreed to relinquish control over the final release version to the Church in return for LDS sanction" (Nelson, "History of Latter-day Saint Portrayals," 73-77). It is unclear whether or not the Church helped finance the film. Several days prior to its Feb. 1, 1913, premiere, the First Presidency communicated its "approval" of the film but on Feb. 5 withdrew it on the advice of William T. Nuttall, the film's manager, having been informed that "outside of Utah and its vicinity the exhibition will be benefited rather than injured by the

absence of our endorsement" (First Presidency to Utah Moving Picture Company, Jan. 24, 1913; First Presidency to P. A. Thompson, Feb. 5, 1913, box 2, folder 14, Kenney Collection).

57. "As to Those Films," *Deseret News*, Mar. 13, 1912, 4. The quoted scripture appears in 3 Ne. 22:17 and Isa. 54:17, with slight variation in D&C 71:9, 109:25.

58. "Why Not Reciprocate," *Salt Lake Tribune*, Feb. 25, 1912; "Mormon Hypocrisy and Motion Pictures," undated clipping, *New York Morning Telegraph*, Scrapbook 1, 1909-1916, p. 113, box 1, Spry Papers.

59. Statistical Reports of the British Mission for the Years Ending 31 December 1910 and 31 December 1911, British Mission Manuscript History, 16 April 1908-5 April 1913, LDS Historical Department Archives; Eastern States Mission Reports, Presiding Bishopric, "Financial, Statistical and Historical Reports of Wards, Stakes and Missions, 1884-1955," as extracted by the LDS Historical Department Archives staff.

60. "Miss Irene Langford Resigns from that 'Censorship' Board," *New York Morning Telegraph*, Feb. 25, 1912, sect. 4, pt. 2, p. 1; Nelson, "History of Latter-day Saint Screen Portrayals," 130-35.

61. Minutes of the Meeting of the General Committee, Jan. 19, 1917, "General Committee Minutes of Special Review Meetings, 1917-1934," box 121, National Board of Review Records.

62. *Report of the Eighty-Second Annual Conference*, 53.

Buckeye's Laments

Two Early Insider Exposés of Mormon Polygamy

Gary James Bergera

On Wednesday, February 7, 1844, the Whig-oriented *Warsaw Message* published, on its front page, a satirical poem about Joseph Smith. Titled "Buckeye's Lamentation for Want of More Wives," it demonstrated an insider's awareness of Nauvoo's most secret goings-on. Because Warsaw, Illinois, was situated about twelve miles south of the bustling headquarters of Smith's Latter-day Saint Church, the newspaper liked to tweak the noses of the LDS faithful. As Thomas Gregg, the paper's thirty-five-year-old editor, explained, "The poem ... comes to us post marked 'Nauvoo.' It is not perfect in versification, but contains some hits at the Prophet, his Apostles, and their practices, which most readers will understand."[1] Smith learned of the 104-line poem that afternoon and, according to his later official history, quickly dismissed it as "a piece of doggerel ... evidently the production of Wilson Law [an LDS dissident], and breathing a very foul and malicious spirit."[2]

The feisty Gregg represented the older residents of Illinois who had become leery of the Mormons' growing political power, but he urged peace even while stirring the pot of contention.[3] Less than five months earlier, in late September 1843, Gregg had editorialized that while he despised "the whole system of Mormonism," he nonetheless urged nonviolence: "Let it suffice for the present to say that *our* remedy must be a peaceable one … We can advocate no measure of redress that does not carry along with it the doctrine of Obedience to the Laws, from the beginning to the end."[4]

Two months after its initial appearance, "Buckeye's Lamentation," together with a longer but equally cheeky companion poem entitled "The Buckey's First Epistle to Jo," ran again, this time in the *Message*'s successor, the *Warsaw Signal,* which had been re-acquired by twenty-five-year-old Thomas C. Sharp. The *Signal* was actually the *Message*'s forerunner, but Sharp had sold the paper to Gregg, who had renamed it and operated it for several years, then sold it back to Sharp. Much like Gregg, Sharp opposed Smith's Church; but unlike Gregg, who was a Quaker, Sharp advocated its violent overthrow. "War and extermination is inevitable!" he thundered against the Mormons before year's end. "CITIZENS ARISE, ONE and ALL!!! – Can you *stand* by, and suffer such INFERNAL DEVILS! to ROB men of their property RIGHTS, without avenging them. We have no time for comment, every man will make his own. LET IT BE MADE WITH POWDER AND BALL."[5]

"Buckey's First Epistle," running twenty-two stanzas of six lines each, totaled 132 lines. "Buckeye's Lamentation," which was thirteen stanzas long, was reprinted with only minor alterations, mostly converting italics to small capital letters, though four words were changed. Two days after the two poems' publication on April 25, Joseph Smith mentioned in his diary that he had seen the "Warsaw Signal about Mormonism." The later historians who expanded Smith's diary into an official Church history said he "read in the *Warsaw Signal* a vile article against the Saints,"[6] apparently treating the two poems as one. The next issue of the weekly *Signal* did not appear until May 1.

The value of Buckeye's poetry lies not in its creative expression but in its accurate, albeit sensationalized, parallels to historical facts.[7] By 1844, Smith's doctrine of plural marriage had become one of Illinois's better-known secrets. Despite his and others' denials, Smith himself had married (or been "sealed" to) thirty-plus women, while many of his closest disciples had taken an equal, or greater, number of plural wives.[8] This circle of confidants does not include other potential authors of the poems such as parents, siblings, children, friends, and colleagues.

Buckeye's verses evinced an understanding not only of Mormon polygamy's practice but, just as importantly, of its theology. The author seems clearly to have been a knowledgeable insider-turned-dissident who wanted to expose Smith's scandalous secrets—particularly those involving a young woman named Nancy—while also dropping enough hints to enable readers to venture a tentative identification.

The first of the two poems, "Buckeye's Lamentation," is preceded by an author's note, reading in part: "It is time that all should know that there are hundreds and thousands in Nauvoo who will neither worship the image nor bear the yoke of the tyrant." The poem begins by noting Buckeye's feigned fear that he will not be saved in heaven because he only has "one lone wife" (ln. 5), and not "half a score" (8), since "beardless Joe" Smith (12) teaches that salvation depends on the number of wives a man has.[9] Monogamy was the practice anciently, the poem asserts, but Heaven's gate has become narrower. Smith received permission "to open the broad way" (16) "of greater glories far" (26) by sanctioning multiple wives. In fact, "the prize" (33) is no longer "some lone twinkling star" (28), or even two wives (29), but ten, since "with it you will shine as bright / as the bright shining sun" (35-36). In heaven, such husbands will "reign like mighty Gods, / creating worlds so fair; / at least a world for every wife / that you take with you there" (37-40). Men who do not embrace a plurality of wives "will find a bitter fate" (44), for as in Jesus's parable of the talents (Matt. 25:14-30), those few wives will be given to a more deserving husband.

Through the end of the sixth stanza, overlooking the sarcasm, Buckeye presents a plausible explanation for plural marriage.[10] In fact, it is possible to draw a rationale for Mormon polygamy from sympathetic sources that is similar to what Buckeye proposes. Theoretically, a plurality of wives facilitates the passage into mortality of a larger number of spirits than results from normal birth and conversion rates. "For if I will raise up seed unto me," God says in Smith's Book of Mormon, "I will command my people" (Jacob 2:30).[11] In fact, Smith's revelation on plural marriage, recorded in mid-1843, stipulated that plural wives "are given unto [the husband] to multiply and replenish the earth, according to my commandment, … that they may bear the souls of men; for herein is the work of my Father continued, that he may be glorified"

(D&C 132:63). "When Lorenzo Snow was twenty-nine years old," the biographer of one of Snow's plural wives explained, "the Prophet, Joseph Smith, had a talk with him and Lorenzo was told it was urgent that he marry right away and do his part in replenishing the earth."[12]

Likewise, after the resurrection of the righteous, polygamy will aid in peopling other worlds, according to Apostle George A. Smith, who said the practice will "exalt mankind to celestial glory and increase."[13] "[T]he Prophet taught us," an early Mormon elaborated, "that Dominion & powr in the great Future would be Comensurate with the n[umber] of 'Wives Childin & Friends' that we inheret here," "that our great mission to earth was to Organize a Neculi of Heaven to take with us. To the increace of which there would be no end."[14] "I understand," another of Smith's followers reported, "that a Man's Dominion will be as God's is, over his own Creatures[,] and the more numerous[,] the greater his Dominion."[15] Sarah Rich, the first wife of Apostle Charles C. Rich, consented to polygamy because she believed that "those holding the Priesthood of Heaven might, by obeying this Order attain to a higher glory in the eternal world."[16] When Joseph Smith invited seventeen-year-old Lucy Walker to become his wife, he told her "this principle ... would prove an everlasting blessing to my father's house and form a chain that could never [be] broken, worlds without end."[17] For worthy men, plural marriage was thus "a privilege with blessings."[18] "It is your privilege," Joseph Smith told his male secretary, "to have all the wives you want."[19] "The Lord had given him the keys of this sealing ordinance," Smith's cousin remembered, and "he felt as liberal to others as he did to himself ... and said to me 'You should not be behind your privileges'."[20]

In the remaining seven stanzas, Buckeye reports that Smith sometimes sanctioned a friend or a faithful priesthood bearer to take another man's wife or daughter: "Some priest or king, may claim your wife / because that you are poor" (51-52). Those who reject Smith's counsel risk damnation; those who obey are forever blessed: "He'll seal you up, be damned you can't, / no matter what you do[;] / if that you only stick to him, / he swears he'll take you through" (62-64). This "secret doctrine" (73), Buckeye continues, is taught and practiced by Smith and the "red rams," referring to red-headed apostles Brigham Young and

Orson Hyde (74), "though they deny it publicly" (75), and even by Smith's older brother and Church Patriarch, Hyrum (83). In fact, Buckeye implies that Hyrum has already taken a widow as a plural wife: "For sure, 'twould be quite impolite, / if not a great disgrace, / to have a widow sister fair / spit in a Prophet's face!" (85-88) Still, Buckeye asserts, Joseph Smith, "at snaring[,] beats them all, / and at the rest does laugh; / for widows poor, and orphan girls, / he sets his snares around for all, / and very seldom fails / to catch some thoughtless Partridges, / Snow-birds or Knight-ingales!" (89-96) Some women are not so easily "drag[g]ed to hell" (99), Buckeye says, especially those "whose sires have bled in days gone by, / for their dear country's cause; / and who will still maintains its rights, / its Liberty and Laws!" (101-04)

Again using sources friendly to Joseph Smith, Buckeye's allegations find support. To that man who is given ten talents "shall be given more," Smith taught, "and from him that had but one should be taken … and given to him who had ten. This, so far as I could understand," explained one of Smith's followers, "might relate to families."[21] Rejecting these teachings imperiled one's soul: "All those who have this law revealed unto them," God said to Smith in the revelation on plural marriage, "must obey the same. For behold, I reveal unto you a new and an everlasting covenant; and if ye abide not that covenant, then are ye damned; for no one can reject this covenant and be permitted to enter into my glory" (D&C 132:3-4). One faithful father who agreed to "consecrate" his teenage daughter to Smith was promised: "[T]he thing that my servant Joseph Smith has made known unto you and your Family … shall be rewarded upon your heads with honor and immortality and eternal life to all your house both old & young."[22] "If you will take this step," one of Smith's plural brides reported him saying, "it will insure your eternal salvation & exaltation and that of your father's household & all of your kindred."[23] In fact, only those who accepted the doctrine of plural wives[24] were worthy to receive the Church's highest blessing: the "promises that worthy men could become kings and priests and that women could become queens and priestesses in the eternal worlds," this guaranteeing their exaltation in the Celestial Kingdom.[25]

By the time of "Buckeye's Lamentation," in early February 1844, Mormonism's "red rams," apostles Young and Hyde, had already been sealed, as Buckeye says, to three and two plural wives, respectively.[26] Of the remaining ten members of the Quorum of Twelve Apostles, Heber C. Kimball had taken a plural wife in 1842, Parley P. Pratt in July 1843, Willard Richards in January 1843, and John Taylor in December 1843 and again in February 1844. Apostle Ezra Taft Benson would marry polygamously in April 1844, as would Lyman Wight, probably in May 1844, John E. Page sometime in 1844, Orson Pratt later that fall, George A. Smith in November 1844, and Wilford Woodruff in April 1846. In addition, Smith's brother Hyrum had, in August 1843, married as his first plural wife Mercy Rachel Fielding Thompson, sister of his legal wife, Mary Fielding Smith, and relict of Robert B. Thompson, who had died in August 1841.

Joseph Smith himself had married some thirty-plus women by this time, in addition to his first wife.[27] Of these, four were widows and four, though not orphans *per se,* had lived with Smith as their *de facto* guardian. The widows—Agnes Coolbrith Smith (m. January 1842), Martha McBride Knight (m. August 1842), Fanny Young Murray (m. November 1843), and Delcena Johnson Sherman (m. before July 1842)—ranged in age from thirty-three to fifty-seven; Smith's charges—Sarah and Maria Lawrence (both m. May 1843) and Emily Maria and Eliza Dow Partridge (both m. March 1843)—were from seventeen to twenty-two years old.[28] Notice that Buckeye also correctly identifies by surname four of Smith's plural wives: the Partridge sisters, Eliza Roxcy Snow (m. June 1842), and Martha Knight: the "thoughtless Partridges, / Snow-birds or Knight-ingales!"

Not all plural wives greeted the practice enthusiastically, as Buckeye writes;[29] and not all would-be wives, despite threats of damnation, submitted to Smith's solicitations.[30] One of Smith's intended wives said she would "sooner go to hell as a virtuous woman than to heaven as a whore."[31] "Teach it to someone else," replied another woman.[32] In referring to those whose fathers had "bled in days gone by, / for their dear country's cause," Buckeye may have meant Cordelia Calista Morley, daughter of Isaac Morley, a veteran of the War of 1812. With Smith's blessing, Isaac took his first plural wife in January 1844, about the same time, according to Cordelia's autobiography, that "plural marriage was introduced to me by my pearents from Joseph Smith asking their consent … [for] me to be his wife. Imagine if you can my feelings to be a plural wife. Something I never thought I ever could be[,] I [k]new nothing of such religion and could not [ac]cept it. Neither did I."[33] Following Smith's death, however, Cordelia changed her mind and was sealed to him posthumously in January 1846.[34] Finally, some writers[35] have interpreted Buckeye's closing reference to "Libery and Laws!" as a nod to his identity as one or both of the renegade Mormon brothers Wilson and William Law. On the other hand, Buckeye may have simply been saluting other prominent dissidents like himself.

The second of Buckeye's two poems focuses on Smith's slanderous charges against the poet. In the first five stanzas, Buckeye trumpets his earlier broadside and calls himself a "certain chief" who had "learned to sing" and "turn'd out a poet great, / or some such thing" (3-6). "Like some great herald," he proclaims Smith's "wicked ways, / your tyran[n]y, your sin and shame, / in these last days" (10-12). People should know "there is still one child who dare / and will be free" (lns. 17-18). Buckeye reveals that he "lives in Nauvoo," where he once was a true friend "to you, / in days that's past," until Smith slandered him, throwing "fair fame to blast" (21-24). Only then did the poet see that "you were not what you had been," displaying instead iniquity "in every way; / And from fair virtue's paths did lean[,] / vile plans to lay" (26-30).

The next eleven stanzas address Smith's courtship of a young woman for whom Buckeye has strong romantic feelings. "Have you forgot," he asks Smith, "the snare you laid / for Nancy, (lovely Buckeye maid?) / … assisted by that wretched bawd / who kept the house" (31-32, 35-36). Nancy would not yield to Smith's doctrines, "although the scriptures you did wield / in your relief" (41-42). Faced with rejection and the threat of exposure, Smith "chang'd your lovers sighs, / and vengeful hate flash'd in your eyes" (49-50). "Circulating lies" (53), Smith hoped to "destroy her fame, / and give to her a ruin'd name, / so that if she should ever proclaim / what you had tried; / your friends might turn on her the shame / and say she lied" (55-60). Instead of cowering, Nancy "met you face to face / … and like a counterfeit she nail'd / you tightly down" (63-66). "Although you tried," Buckeye gloats, "to make this gentle creature … eat her words, / … strong in truth, she in that hour / told you you lied" (67-72). Humiliated, Buckeye says,

Smith went to Nancy's father and admitted that "what she had said, was true," but explained that he had simply been testing her virtue to "keep herself all pure and free / from base seducers like to me, and Joab vile," both of whom, Smith had been told by God, would attempt to "beguile" her (75-84). Though pained by Smith's "slanderous tongue" (85), Buckeye would have said nothing of Smith's infamy, provided Smith repent (89). Instead, Smith continued to voice his "slanders vile" (91), which Buckeye—"this child" (92)—now refuses to bear any longer: "Although by nature he is mild, / and well disposed; / thy sins from continent to isle / shall be exposed" (93-96).

While giving vent to his anger, Buckeye discloses his own shaken faith in Smith and promises to expose "Missouri's deeds ... / though perpetrated in the night, / by hirelings who thought it right / to do thy will / by cabin conflagration bright[,] / to scalp and kill" (98-102). Buckeye pleads for Smith to repent and "think, how mighty and sublime / thy calling first [is,] / and in black sackcloth bow thee down / low in the dust / ... and I'll forgive" (103-14). Otherwise, "your dark deeds in Nauvoo, / as well as in Missouri too[,] / like Hamlet's ghost shall rise to view" (115-17). Buckeye may be a "child" (125), but he can trace his lineage back to William Wallace and Robert the Bruce, champions of Scottish freedom, who "for Liberty did raise / the sword, and broke / (as I intend in these last days) / a tyrant's yoke" (129-32).

From a variety of sources, it is clear that "Nancy," the "lovely Buckeye maid," is Nancy Rigdon, daughter of Sidney Rigdon, one of Smith's two counselors in the three-man First Presidency.[36] According to Rigdon biographer Richard S. Van Wagoner,[37] thirty-one-year-old Marinda Nancy Johnson Hyde, though civilly married to Orson Hyde, was sealed to Smith about this time and was probably the "wretched bawd / who kept the house." Marinda asked Nancy in April 1842 to accompany her to talk with Smith. Smith was unable to meet the two women, and Nancy later mentioned the episode to twenty-three-year-old Francis ("Frank") M. Higbee, who at the time was courting Nancy.[38] John C. Bennett, one of Smith's boosters-turned-traitors, cautioned Higbee that Smith was interested in nineteen-year-old Nancy. Higbee allegedly told Nancy of Smith's interest, and when she subsequently met Smith, she spurned his advances. Within the next few days, Smith sent Nancy a pleading letter to change her mind. The letter read, in part: "That which is wrong under one circumstance, may be and often is, right under another. … Everything that God gives us is lawful and right; and it is proper that we should enjoy His gifts and blessings … Our Heavenly Father is more liberal in his views, and boundless in his mercies and blessings, than we are ready to believe or receive." Nancy told her family of the encounter and gave the letter to Higbee, who handed it to Bennett, who soon published it. Relations between the Rigdons and Smith soured, and some of Smith's followers publicly branded Nancy a prostitute.[39]

Smith succeeded in accounting for his actions in such a way to satisfy everyone involved except Higbee. Meeting privately with him on June 29, 1842, Smith explained that his criticisms of Higbee had been spoken "in self defense." Smith later told a small group of followers that he would attack the credibility of anyone who violated his trust, that those who did so were covenant-breakers and liars, especially if they threatened his or his people's safety, and it did not matter if his criticisms of them were true or not. According to Smith's secretary, Higbee seemed "humble, and promised to reform."[40] Higbee, however, remembered the encounter differently and never forgot Smith's rationalization. In recounting this same episode, Buckeye reported Smith's contention that he had merely been preparing Nancy to resist the amorous overtures of young men such as Buckeye and lechers like Joab (one of John Bennett's well-known *noms de plume*).[41] By 1844, Bennett's own extramarital escapades circa 1841-42 had become common knowledge. For Buckeye, Smith's assertion that he had been protecting Nancy was a *coup de grâce* which "burning tears from me have wrung" (86). Still, Buckeye forbore, and only after subsequent slanders did he, like the Scottish patriots, dare to break the "tyrant's yoke."

In this second poem, Buckeye shows his hand most clearly to be Nancy Rigdon's suitor, Francis Higbee.[42] In addition to calling himself Buckeye, signaling his status as Ohio-born, he scatters throughout his verses the following hints regarding his identity:

- He is a "child" living in Nauvoo, who was both a friend and follower of Smith until Smith slandered him;

- He is familiar with Smith's teachings on plural marriage and knows some of those who took other wives, including Hyrum Smith, Brigham Young, Orson Hyde, and others of the Quorum of Twelve Apostles; he also knows that Joseph Smith married widows and orphans and the identities of four wives; he knows that some women rejected Smith's proposals, including women whose fathers were veterans;
- He is well acquainted with Nancy Rigdon. He knows that Smith proposed to her and what arguments Smith used to persuade her; he knows that Nancy rejected the prophet, that Smith and others attempted to discredit her, and that Smith admitted his guilt but explained he had been preparing her for seduction by others;
- He knows about being saved in mortality as a king and priest or queen and priestess.

Of these clues, Francis Higbee seems to satisfy the greatest number.[43] Born in 1820 in Tate, Ohio, to Elias Higbee and Sarah Elizabeth Ward (m. 1818), Francis's family joined the Mormon Church in Ohio in early 1832. Like other new Latter-day Saints, the Higbees moved to Jackson County, Missouri, the following year but left in 1835 to settle in Kirtland, Ohio, another Mormon stronghold. In 1836 they relocated to Missouri, left again, and by early 1839 had migrated to Illinois and helped establish Nauvoo. Like others, it may have taken the Higbees years to recover from the horrors associated with their experiences in Missouri. Francis's father, Elias, was a county judge in Missouri, a leading officer in the Church's Missouri quasi-militia sometimes called the Danites, and accompanied Joseph Smith to Washington, D.C., to plead the Mormons' case for redress in 1839-40. Elias was Church recorder from 1838 until June 1843 when he died from cholera. His passing devastated his forty-two-year-old wife and seven or so children, ranging in age from four to twenty-three. Smith had scolded Elias the previous year for not being "as diligent as you ought to have been, … [to] make your children industrious,"[44] but now at his funeral said that in the resurrection Elias would "come forth and strike hands with the faithful, and share the glory of the kingdom of God for ever and ever."[45]

In 1841, twenty-one-year-old Francis was elected a colonel ("a certain chief") in the Nauvoo Legion, a county-wide militia, with Smith and John Bennett as his superior officers. About this time, Francis became serious about Nancy Rigdon, whom he had met in Missouri. He apparently began seeing her in early 1842. Nancy had been born in Pennsylvania, but Francis seems to have thought she was from Ohio, probably because her parents had married there in 1820 and Ohio was where several of her siblings were born.

At about the same time as Joseph Smith's proposal to Nancy in April 1842, allegations erupted that Bennett and others had defiled several young women and said that Smith had sanctioned such behavior.[46] By this time, Smith had been sealed to at least eight women, and for nearly ten months, from September 1840 to July 1841, Bennett had lodged with him and was evidently privy to Smith's first plural marriage on April 5, 1841. Bennett seems to have felt authorized to initiate others into his version of plural marriage. Smith worried that Bennett was exposing the Church to criticism and decided by mid-May 1842 to rid himself of his counselor. Bennett apparently confessed his guilt prior to resigning the mayorship of Nauvoo and membership in the Church, then left town in June and was succeeded as mayor by Smith. Prior to his departure, Bennett announced under pressure that he had never known Smith "to countenance any improper conduct whatever either in public or private; and that [Smith] never did teach to me in private that an illegal, illicit intercourse with females, was under any circumstance justifiable, and that I never knew him to so teach others."[47] When Smith became connected to women, it was through a marriage sealing ceremony performed by an authorized priesthood holder, whereas Bennett believed that a marriage ceremony was unnecessary.[48]

Francis Higbee's brother Chauncey was among the city's young men who fell under Bennett's spell. Despite swearing to an affidavit virtually identical to Bennett's, Chauncey, as a lesson to all, was formally expelled from the Church on May 24, 1842, "for unchaste and unvirtuous conduct towards certain females, and for teaching it was right, if kept secret, &c."[49] To counter any suspicion of complicity after Chauncey invoked Joseph Smith's name in his defense, Chauncey was sued for "slander[ing] and defam[ing] the character of the said Joseph

Smith, and also the character of Emma Smith, his wife."[50] Chauncey felt his situation differed little from that of Bennett, who at this point had not been disciplined, or from Smith's own younger brother William, who was never punished for his sexual liaisons.

The Higbees were furious at what they perceived to be Joseph Smith's hypocrisy. In fact, Smith became worried they might attempt to convince the brother of a woman Smith intended to court to disrupt his plans, and Smith therefore called the brother away on a mission to get him out of town.[51] For a brief time, Francis collaborated with John Bennett, who denied any wrongdoing and on July 8, 1842, began publishing a series of letters to expose Smith.[52] Francis gave Bennett the letter Smith had sent to Nancy, which had the unintended effect of ending Francis's relationship with her. Chauncey initiated a civil action against Smith so he could call women as witnesses who could be forced to admit to immorality with Smith.[53]

After some three months, Smith dropped his own suit and went into hiding, trying to avoid extradition to Missouri. Authorities there wanted to charge him with an attempted assassination of a former governor. In addition, the Higbees had retreated from their earlier threats of reprisal.[54] Smith no doubt sensed that a trial might expose his marriage teachings. "I want [all] to understand," a chastened-sounding Francis wrote in late November 1842 to the editor of a Nauvoo newspaper, "that I have no feelings against Joseph." He had "fully satisfied myself that [Smith] has been called of God, to do a great, and mighty, work in the earth, and let it suffice to say I am fully satisfied with him.—All our former difficulties (if such they might be called), were forever effectually settled before I left."[55] "My object," Chauncey later added, "is not to vindicate or anathamatise either party"; but "free from the shackles of party litigation," he "desire[d] peacefully to pursue the duties of my daily avocation; while—thankful for the boon—I hope long to remain a citizen of our flourishing city."[56]

"If … I have done anything to injure my character," Smith himself confessed four months later, "I am sorry for it; and if you will forgive me, I will endeavor to do so no more. I do not know that I have done anything of the kind. But if I have, … I want you to come boldly and frankly, and tell of it; and if not, [for]ever after hold your peace."[57]

When the Higbees' father passed away in June, the *Times and Seasons* editorialized: "He has raised a large family—all to respectability—all to ultimate usefulness."[58] But Smith offered a mild rebuke to Francis and Chauncey when, during the funeral sermon, he advised "the mourners" to "do as the husband and the father would instruct you, and you shall be reunited."[59]

Francis soon relocated to Cincinnati until mid-summer 1843 when he returned to Nauvoo and found his name linked to ongoing efforts to extradite Smith to Missouri. He had not, in fact, forgiven Smith for his overtures to Nancy Rigdon. Maybe he had shared his feelings on the topic with others. "My father's death has been enough," he wrote to Smith on September 8, 1843, anxious to clear his name,

> when taken in connection with other things of less moment, to engage my whole attention without seeking to draw down upon my own head, the heads of my mother's family, another scourge, such as we suffered in Missouri. Who suffered more and hazarded life oftener than did I—God forbid that ever I should be instrumental in bringing destruction not only upon my friends, but upon myself and relatives—Then, Sir, please read this, or announce to the public that the charge with which I stand charged is <u>false, false, false,</u> and greatly oblige.[60]

Within weeks Francis participated in a special "pleasure party and dinner" hosted by Smith,[61] who subsequently "expressed himself satisfied that Col. Frances M. Higbee was free, even of reproach or suspicion, in that matter."[62] But rumors of Higbee's disloyalty would not die. In late December, Smith expanded Nauvoo's police force, which doubled as a personal security force, in response to Missouri's efforts to capture him.[63] During his charge to the forty new recruits, Smith declared:

> My life is more in danger from some little dough-head of a fool in this city than from all my numerous and inveterate enemies abroad. I am exposed to far greater danger from traitors among ourselves than from enemies without ... and if I can escape from the ungrateful treachery of assassins, I can live as Caesar might have lived, were it not for a right-hand Brutus. ... Judas was one of the Twelve Apostles, even their treasurer, and dipt with their Master in the dish, and through his

> treachery, the crucifixion was brought about; and *we have a Judas in our midst.*[64]

Almost immediately, William Law, who was one of Smith's counselors in the First Presidency, and William Marks, who was president of the Nauvoo Stake, were told that Smith had reference to them.[65] Both had rejected Smith's teachings on plural marriage, and Law in particular was an increasingly vocal critic.[66] Smith tried to reassure the two that he had not meant them,[67] but in the course of his comments he linked the unnamed traitors with a rejection of polygamy: "Mayor [Joseph Smith] spoke on Spiritual Wife system, and explained, The man who promises to keep a secret and does not keep it[,] he is a liar, and not to be trusted. ... When a man becomes a traitor to his friend or country who is innocent, treacherous to innocent blood[,] [I] do consider it right to cut off his influence so that he could not injure the innocent, but [it is] not right to meddle with that man without testimony, law & trial."[68]

The Nauvoo City Council asked Francis on January 5, 1844, what he knew about Law and Marks. "Have received the impression from rumor that Mr. Law, Mr. Marks and probably one or two others could not subscribe to all things in the Church, and there were some private matters that might make trouble," he replied.[69] Annoyed at Higbee's mention of "private matters," Smith said before the close of the meeting that he "thought Francis Higbee had better stay at home and hold his tongue, lest rumor turn upon him and disclose some private matters which he would prefer kept hid. Did not believe there was any rumor of the kind afloat [regarding Smith's private matters], or [Higbee] could have told some of the names of his informants. Thought the young men of the city had better withdraw from [Higbee's] society, and let him stand on his own merits. I by no means consider [Higbee] the standard of the city."[70]

William Law's account of Smith's remarks suggest that the official minutes may not do full justice to Smith's warning:

> Joseph made another speech, and in it said that F. M. Higbee had better be careful or a train of facts would be disclosed concerning him that he would not like; gave us to understand that [Higbee] was conniving with Missouri &c., and that [Higbee] only disgraced anyone who

> associated with him, and that [Smith] had denied him the privilege of [entering] his house (or words like that) and would not allow him to associate with his females &c; that he had been called on to lay hands on him when he stank from a cause that he did not like to name (or such a saying).[71] I did not believe the story at all, and cannot see why he should tell it.[72]

During the next few days, Higbee fumed over Smith's accusations and before the end of the week sent what Smith called "a long equivocating letter charging me with having slandered his character and demanding a public trial before the Church. It contains no denial of the charges which he accuses me of having spoken against him, but is full of bombast."[73] Barely able to contain his anger, Higbee replied:

> The inconsiderate, the unwarented, and unheard of attack you made upon my character on the 6th inst before the City Council impels me to demand an investigation of you, and that without delay[,] before the eclesiastical powers. For if I am guilty of either of those charges, omitting the guilt of the whole, I most unquestionably am not worthy a name among a people making as great proffesions as do the people called mormons. It is said I seek the hours of the midnight assassin to seize my victim, when no one is near to bear witness of the crime or attest the unhallowed deed, that I sympathized with the afflicted and oppressed, that I may devour their vitals, that I seek the mantle of religion to envelop my scorpion body, that I may better practeice my nefarious designs. Then sir, if I am acting in this sphere, am I not acting in the sphere of a hypocrite, and am I not a dark body suffered a place on the fair escutcheon of our religion? In deciding this question, let us not sever the moorings of Christianity, [for if we do, do we not] plunge into the mad sea of revenge? persuade the mariner to sell his compass? or Washington his sword? persuade an intelegent man to pluck out his eyes, to enjoy the unmitigated horrors of blindness? Truth is our compass in the stormy sea of life; before which wealth, power, authority, talent and genious tremble, as did Felix on his thrown; when Heaven and Earth shall pass away[,] [t]ruth shall arise like the angel on Manoah's sacrifice, upon the flame of Natures funeral pyre, and ascend to her source, her heaven and her horne, the bosem of the Holy, and eternal God.[74] ...
>
> Sir, you have struck a blow at evry thing which renders existance sweet; you have sought to blast evry proud hope, and evry fond expectations by throwing into free circulation reports, the truth of which,

God is some day to judge. The cause of your course towards me has astonished many, from the fact that they can not divine the reason, and as for myself I am as ignorant of the cause, as a child unborn. As for the opinion which I always, and still entertain, with regard to the propriety of one mans having more than one woman, or this spiritual business, I am not ashamed to avow, in your presence or in the face and eyes of the world; I have repeatedly said and am still of the same opinion "fixed and determined as the polar star" that any revelation commanding or in any wise suffering sexual intercourse under any other form than that prescribed by the laws of our country, and which has been ratified by special revelation through you, is of HELL; and I bid defiance to any or all such. As far as my character and influence extends, I am willing, not only willing but determined, to oppose it, under evry form it can present itself. Whether [or not] my name shall be sounded, my opposition to such a hellish fabrication shall be known, at the peril of my life, my fortune and my sacred honor. "Though the people should riot and pro[t]e[s]t in insurrection[,] though tyrants should rage and threaten distruction, though the hurricane should lay upon the bed of the sea; though the earthquake should tear the globe in peices; though the stars should fall from their sphere, and the frame of nature be dissolved I know virtue will protect her votaries while the good men will remain tranquil amidst the ruins of the world.["]

That man who pursues a course different from that which I have persued and am still determined to persue, may reach the regions of pleasure when the happy companions [of] contentement, friendship, Knowledge, wealth, dignity, and fame shall greet him, but alas! how soon must he according to the inevitable decree of Heaven, be consigned to sorrow, remorse and dispair. Then sir[,] with me it is virtue or vice. I am a devoted friend to virtue, and Sir a court or council of the church must declare no[thing] otherwise immediately; or I shall think you unjust [i]n the extreme; then Sir I cla[i]m the right of investigation, I claim the right to a fair and impartial and public trial; and that without delay. From your mere ipse dixit [unfounded assertion] I shall extricate myself, for bear it I will not; I am quite determined not to remain quiet under the foul imputations cast upon me.[75]

Smith ignored Higbee's demand for a public investigation, and word soon surfaced that Francis intended to publicly sue Smith for slander.[76] Smith responded by arranging to have Higbee tried before

Nauvoo's municipal court "for absenting himself from City Council without leave, when summoned as a witness, and for slanderous and abusive language towards one of the members of the Council [i.e., Smith]."[77] Instead of a trial, however, Smith and Higbee cobbled a tentative reconciliation. According to the official minutes:

> Mayor [Smith] announced that all difficulties between him & Francis M. Higby [were eternally buried] and he was to be his friend forever & F. M. Higby said I will be his friend forever and his right hand man. And A[lderman] Hiram Smith stated that all aspersions which may have been supposed to have been cast upon Higby are ~~false~~ a mistake[,] tis not so. Mayor explained at length [illegible] what, in substance, he had said at previous councils on the same subject. ... F. M. Higby spoke stating his distraction of mind the past week, glad the difficulties are settled shall be his friend as said before. The observations by the mayor before the council on the 5th inst. concerning F. M. Higby were ordered to be stricken from the minutes.[78]

Unfortunately, the *détente* proved short-lived, and three weeks later "Buckeye's Lamentation for Want of More Wives" appeared in the *Warsaw Message*.

Before the end of the month, on February 26, 1844, Higbee again crossed paths with Smith. By now a practicing attorney, as was his brother Chauncey, Francis represented Orsimus F. Bostwick, whom Hyrum Smith had charged with slandering him in connection with "certain females of Nauvoo."[79] The mayor's court found Bostwick guilty, and Francis informed the tribunal that he would appeal the decision to the circuit court, which he felt would be less biased, knowing the influence Joseph Smith wielded over the city's legal system.[80] Smith countered: "I told Higbee what I thought of him for trying to carry such a suit to Carthage [the county seat]—it was to stir up the mob and bring them upon us."[81] Ten days later, Smith addressed a general gathering of Nauvoo's citizens and placed Francis Higbee on notice:

> [W]e have a gang of simple fellows here who do not know where their elbows or heads are. ... [I]f there is any case tried by the authorities of Nauvoo, they want it appealed to Carthage to the circuit court. ...
>
> From this time I design to bring such characters who act against

> the interests of the city before a committee of the whole; and I will have the voice of the people, which is republican, and is likely to be the voice of God; and as long as I have a tongue to speak, I will expose the iniquity of the lawyers and wicked men.[82]

"I despise the man who will betray you with a kiss," Smith added; "and I am determined to use up[83] these men, if they will not stop their operation. … I will disgrace every man by publishing him on the house top, and who will not be still and mind his own business."[84] "Wo to the man or lawyer," the women of Nauvoo joined in, "that filthies himself by advocating such rotten hearted raven's rights," meaning the right to defend oneself in court on the charge of insulting the Church.[85]

Before the end of March 1844, people were becoming increasingly aware that dissidents were organizing themselves into a knowledgeable cabal as Smith, in particular, lashed out at Chauncey Higbee, for instance. "The lies that C. L. Higbee has hatched up as a foundation to work upon" Smith said, included the claim that Smith had "had men's heads cut off in Missouri" and that he had "wanted to kill and put out of the way" the dissidents. "I won't swear out a warrant against them," Smith postured, "for I don't fear any of them: they would not scare off an old setting hen. I intend to publish all the iniquity that I know of them. … I am willing to do anything for the good of the people."[86] Smith's critics had, in fact, met to discuss how best to expose Smith's iniquities, and tensions escalated. On April 1, the Higbees were arrested for "assaulting the police" but were acquitted. Chauncey was then arrested for "using abusive language to and insulting the city marshal while in the discharge of his official duty."[87] Chauncey reciprocated by having the complaining policemen arrested for "false imprisonment." Nauvoo's municipal court intervened, released the three policeman, and ruled that Higbee was a "very disorderly person," noting that the suit was "malicious" and ordering "that said Higbee pay the costs."[88]

Smith's opponents demanded that their complaints be aired fully during an upcoming Churchwide general conference. Unwilling to give his enemies a forum, Smith decided differently. "It had been expected by some that the little petty difficulties which have existed would be brought up and investigated before this conference," he announced, "but it will not be the case; these things are of too trivial a nature to occupy the attention of so large a body."[89] Ironically, Hyrum Smith tried to defuse the situation during the same conference by saying the Laws had "done a great deal of good … I do not believe that the Messrs. Laws would do anything against me."[90] Joseph Smigh was not pleased with this olive leaf.[91] On April 17, he confronted Chauncey with evidence that Chauncey had threatened him. The next day, Smith had William and Wilson Law formally expelled from the Church for "unchristianlike conduct."[92] This was the catalyst for the Higbees, Laws, and other dissenters meeting on April 21 to form a new Church. A few days later, on April 26, a skirmish broke out between three of the dissenters, including Chauncey, and Nauvoo policemen when the latter asked for help in bringing a prisoner to the mayor's office. They were arrested for "resisting the authorities of the city."[93] The previous day, "Buckey's First Epistle" had appeared in the *Warsaw Signal,* together with the reprint of "Buckeye's Lamentation."

Eight days later, Francis formally charged Joseph Smith with slander and had him arrested by the circuit court in Carthage, hoping to forego a hearing in Nauvoo. It is unclear what immediately prompted the suit; perhaps others of Higbee's immediate circle had talked about Smith's earlier accusations against him. Smith petitioned Nauvoo's municipal court the same day to allow him to respond to Higbee's charges and to force Higbee to justify why Smith should remain under arrest.[94] During the May 8 proceeding, which Higbee did not attend, Smith proved good on his threat to try to expose Higbee.[95] According to the published minutes:

> Joseph Smith sworn … Francis M. Higbee said he was grieved at me, and I was grieved at him. I was willing on my part to settle all difficulties, and he promised if I would go before the City Council and tell them he would drop every thing against me forever. I have never mentioned the name of Francis M. Higbee disrespectfully from that time to this; but have been entirely silent about him; if any one has said that I have spoken disrespectfully since then, they have lied: and he cannot have any cause whatever. I want to testify to this court of what occurred a long time before John C. Bennet left [t]his city. I was called on to visit Francis M. Higbee; I went and found him on a bed on the floor.

[Here follows testimony which is too indelicate for the public eye or ear; and we would here remark, that so revolting, corrupt, and disgusting has been the conduct of most of this clique, that we feel to dread having any thing to do with the publication of their trials; we will not however offend the public eye or ear with a repetition of the foulness of their crimes any more.][96]

Bennet said Higbee[97] pointed out the spot where he had seduced a girl, and that he had seduced another. I did not believe it, I felt hurt, and labored with Higbee about it; he swore with uplifted hands, that he had lied about the matter. I went and told the girl's parents, when Higbee and Bennet made affidavits and both perjured themselves, they swore false about me so as to blind the family. I brought Francis M. Higbee before Brigham Young, Hyrum Smith and others; Bennet was present, when they both acknowledged that they had done these things, and asked us to forgive them. I got vexed, my feelings had been hurt; Higbee has been guilty of adulterous communication, perjury, &c.; which I am able to prove by men who heard them confess it. I also preferred charges against Bennett, the same charges which I am now telling: and he got up and told them it was the truth, when he pleaded for his life, and begged to be forgiven; this was [Bennett's] own statement before sixty or seventy men; he said the charges were true against him and Higbee. I have been endeavoring to throw out shafts to defend myself, because they were corrupt, and I knew they were determined to ruin me: [Higbee] has told the public that he was determined to prosecute me, because I slandered him, although I tell nothing but the truth. Since the settlement of our difficulties, I have not mentioned his name disrespectfully; he wants to bind up my hands in the circuit court, and make me pay heavy damages for telling the truth. In relation to the conspiracy, I have not heard Francis M. Higbee say he would take away my life; but Chauncey Higbee [and two others] … said they would shoot me, and the only offence against me is telling the truth.

Although Hyrum Smith had earlier insisted that such accusations were "a mistake," he and others now joined their testimony to Joseph Smith's regarding Francis's reported depravity:

Brigham Young, sworn, With regard to Francis M. Higbee, at the time that is spoken of, I stopped opposite Mr. Laws' store, we had been conversing with Dr. Bennet when I came into the room, Francis Higbee rather recoiled and wished to withdraw; he went out and sat upon a pile of wood. He said it is all true, I am sorry for it, I wish it had never happened. I understood Bennet who related some of the circumstances, he cried and begged of us to forgive him, and said if he could be permitted to stay in the city as a private individual he should be happy; that was about what he said; it is true, I am sorry for it I wish it had never been so; as we came up, Dr. Bennet, Mr. Higbee, and Mr. Smith, had been talking about it, I have not mentioned it before, I knew of the whole affair, it was on the 4th of July, or a few days after[;] it was shortly after I came from England. I was in the City Council when Mr. Higbee said all was settled. ...

Hyrum Smith swore,—I recollect a settlement of difficulties between Francis M. Higbee and my brother Joseph, about which some of the court may recollect. I recollect Dr. Bennett asking forgiveness of the [Masonic] Lodge when there was about sixty present—Francis M. Higbee acknowledged that it was the truth, that he was sorry, and had been a thousand times: he acknowledged his connection with the woman on the hill; I did think he was with Dr. Bennet at the time, the statement of Bennet was, that he was guilty, he was sorry and asked forgiveness, he said he had seduced six or seven, he acknowledged it, and said if he was forgiven, he would not be guilty any more. Francis said he knew it was true, he was sorry and had been a hundred times; the very things that we had challenged him with, he acknowledged. I told Francis that it had better be settled[.] [H]e said, Joseph had accused him—if his character was gone all was gone, he said he would settle it and they went into the room, he did not deny any charge, he said he was sorry, that he wanted it buried, and it was agreed to do so. Francis did not say any thing about his sickness, but Dr. Bennet ... doctored him in the time of his sickness. ...

Heber C. Kimball, sworn—I think it is near two years: I had some conversation with Francis Higbee, he expressed himself indignant at some things; he expressed himself that he was sorry, he would live a new life, he never would say a word against President Joseph Smith; he had an inclination to write that what he published was false. ... The last time I conversed with him, he said, "if I had taken your council, I should now have been a man looked on with respect; he said he was not connected with the people that opposed President Smith and never would"—he much regretted the course he had taken.[98]

At the end of the hearing, the court discharged Joseph Smith and ruled that "Francis M. Higbee's character having been so fully shown, as infamous, the court is convinced that this suit was instituted through malice, private pique and corruption; and ought not to be countenanced; and it is ordained by the court that said Francis M. Higbee pay the costs."[99] To underscore his commitment to expose Higbee, Smith had the court record, including his own testimony, published in the *Nauvoo Neighbor* the next week.

Before the end of the month, Higbee issued his own public statement to the *Warsaw Signal:*

> The nature of the above case was as follows:—On the 1st day of May, 1844, I sued out a *capias,* from the Clerk of the Circuit Court, of the Fifth Judicial District of Illinois, against Joseph Smith, who, immediately on being arrested obtained a writ of *habeas corpus,* from the Municipal Court at Nauvoo, that he might under that garb or semblance of justice, extricate himself from the just demands of violated law, as has always been the case before when men have attempted to bring him to justice. On the return of said writ before the Municipal Court, Joseph Smith in justification of his own wickedness, corruption and infamy, swore first, as follows: "That I was grieved at him, and he was grieved at me," but he does not tell the cause of my "grief," neither does he give the world to understand the cause of his. He, as well as I, recollects well, the cause which first induced me to question his pretentions to sincerity, and which gave rise as he says, to my 'grief:' which was the base attack he (Joseph Smith) made upon the virtue of Miss Nancy Rigdon, in 1842, to whom I was at that time paying my addresses. The attack was of so base, so loathesome, and of so detestable a character, that I could not conceal my feelings from the base seducer, and I assailed Joseph Smith about the matter; in (as I think quite likely,) rather a rough manner, for I felt much excited indeed; when he (Smith) assured me I must keep perfectly dark, and be quiet, or he would serve a *quietus* upon me—But I could not feel reconciled towards Joseph, and I made another assault upon him, in front of Mr. James Ivin's store, (or where he at that time kept,) and he upon that occasion told me he would blow my character to the four winds, if I did not be still, for God would deal with him, if I would be still and mind my own business, and that I was only exciting and agitating the attack, he made upon Nancy for the sake of insuring to myself an imperishable name, (or some words to that effect.)
>
> The excitement upon my part was still on the increase, for as I reflected upon the matter, the more and more I became astonished; to

think that Joseph Smith, a man professing to be a Messiah, sent by the God of Heaven to revolutionize and christianize this depraved and fallen generation, would have the presumption to attack the virtue of any female, with whom I was corresponding, and that too under the cloak of Christianity, was more than I could or ever will bear from him or any other man made in the image of his God;—I care not what his pretentions of Christianity may be, or how many revelations he may call to his aid—he is a dark fiend from the Tartarian regions,[100] and hell stands wide to swallow him up; and I would here recommend that Joseph Smith should look well to the west, for the figure of the Lord hath written it upon the wall "Mene, Tekel, Upharsin."[101]

Smith discovered my feelings and commenced raging against me, by assailing my character in every corner of the street and in any private circle, and he soon commenced his outrageous attacks upon my character from the public stand. I met Smith in the public street before Hiram Smith's office, about that time (in '42,) when he presented his hand for my acceptance, I carried mine behind me, and refused to accept his, when he stated that he was sorry the things had assumed such an aspect, for he always loved me and did still, and I was a good boy, and every body knew it, and if every body did not know it, they were not as smart as he was. At that time he eulogized my moral worth to the skies, but could not come [to] it, for I still persisted, and utterly refused to extend my hand to any one so base, so lost to every sense of honor and virtue.

The above is a brief statement of some things that passed between Joseph and myself, about the time he made the attack upon the virtue of Miss Nancy, sufficient, however, to acquaint the public with the reasons for my feeling towards him, as he stated I did. As for himself he could not succeed in his unhallowed attempts, and that is what made him feel so bad, but all the *man* had to do, I suppose in mitigation of the crime, was to offer up the entrails of a lamb, if John T. Barnett would sell another, as he did when Mr. Samuel Pratt repeated his attempts.[102]

Joseph Smith continues his statement before the Municipal Court, at great length with regard to myself, during which statement he (Joseph) tells but one falsehood, and that includes all the man said from the time he rose to swear, until he closed his testimony—which was a lie of the basest kind, and constitutes him a *perjured villain*, and so he stands on the docket of that Court, and what is still more painful and desperate, is to know as I do verily know, that he stands before the Bar of Heaven and own[s] [i.e., admits] that he has lied, and that too, for the sole purpose of destroying him who has never harmed the hair of any man's head, or injured any female under Heaven.[103]

Smith continued to go toe-to-toe with his critics. The day after his testimony against Higbee, he saw to it that Wilson Law was cashiered from Nauvoo's militia for "ungentlemanly and unofficer-like conduct."[104] The next day, the Laws, the Higbees, and others began distributing the prospectus for a new independent publication, the *Nauvoo Expositor*, promising "to give a full, candid and succinct statement of FACTS AS THEY REALLY EXIST IN THE CITY OF NAUVOO[,] *fearless of whose particular case the facts may apply.*"[105] "It shall be the organ through which we will herald the Mormon ribaldry," Francis explained. "It shall also contain a full and complete exposé of his *Mormon Seraglio or Nauvoo Harem*—; and [the prophet's] unparelleled and unheard of attempts at seduction. As it regards Joe I am as well satisfied that he excells Solomon, Tiberius, or even the black prince of Dahomeny himself, among the women as I am that he is the bigest villain that goes unhung."[106]

On the 12th, Smith seethed:

> All the lies that are now hatched up against me are of the devil, and the influence of the devil and his servants will be used against the kingdom of God. … I never told you I was perfect; but there is no error in the revelations which I have taught. … I testify that no man has power to reveal it but myself—things in heaven, in earth and hell; and all shut your mouths for the future.[107]

Within the week, Chauncey returned briefly to Nauvoo's municipal court to represent a complainant in a civil case.[108] Two days later, Francis and three others were officially excommunicated "for apostasy."[109]

On May 23 word circulated that William Law intended to charge Joseph Smith with adultery.[110] Two days later, on the strength of Law's affidavit about Smith living in "an open state of adultery," two indictments were issued against Smith.[111] Francis Higbee's testimony was rejected, according to Smith's history.[112] Smith gave a feisty public response: "The Lord has constituted me so curiously that I glory in persecution. I am not nearly so humble as if I were not persecuted. If oppression will make a wise man mad, much more a fool. If they want a beardless[113] boy to whip all the world, I will get on the top of the mountain and crow like a rooster: I shall always beat them."[114] He decided he would not avoid the trial and traveled the next day to Carthage, Illinois, where he hoped to "have the indictments against me investigated." However, since one of the witnesses was absent, the case was postponed until October and Smith returned home.[115]

On May 29 the *Nauvoo Neighbor* published affidavits from three women who had, two years earlier, testified that Chauncey Higbee had seduced them. Smith's history noted that this was done "to show the character of the men who are now seeking to destroy my life and usefulness, and overthrow the work of the Lord which He has commenced through my instrumentality."[116] The editor of the *Neighbor* explained:

> After all that this Chauncey L. Higbee has done in wickedly and maliciously using the name of Joseph Smith to persuade innocent females to submit to gratify his hellish lusts, and then blast the character of the most chaste, pure, virtuous and philanthropic man on earth, he, to screen himself from the law of the land and the just indignation of an insulted people, and save himself from the penitentiary, or whatever punishment his unparalleled crimes merit, has entered into a conspiracy with the Laws and others against the lives of those who are knowing to his abandoned conduct, thus hoping to save himself from the disgrace which much follow an exposure, and wreck his vengeance and gratify his revenge for his awful disappointment.[117]

Not everyone was convinced. The *Warsaw Signal* editorialized: "No Joe, these affidavits are but evidence against yourself. They show conclusively, that the females of your city, are taught by you, to hold virtue, chastity, decency and propriety, eh! every thing that gives adornment to the character of the sex, as subservient to your will and desire. … Shame where is thy blush?"[118]

Two days later, on June 4, Smith wondered about his prospects if he were to sue the Laws and others for "perjury, slander, etc.," perhaps on behalf of one of the women implicated in his alleged adultery.[119] Before the end of the week, the first (and only) issue of the *Nauvoo Expositor* appeared, publishing three affidavits attesting to Smith's revelation on plural marriage. "Infinite are the gradations which mark this man's attempts for power," wrote Francis Higbee of Smith.

> Is it not a shame and a disgrace, to think we have a man in our midst, who will defy the laws of our country; the *laws* which shed so gentle

> and nourishing an influence upon our fathers, which fostered and protected them in their old age from insult and aggression; shall we their sons, lie still and suffer *Joseph Smith* to light up the lamp of tyranny and oppression in our midst? God forbid, let the departed spirits of *our fathers*, cry from the ground against us. Let us arise in the majesty of our strength and sweep the influence of tyrants and miscreants from the face of the land, as with the breath of heaven.[120]

Smith was outraged and feared more exposures; he convened the city council on June 8 and 10 and orchestrated passage of a new ordinance and resolution declaring the *Expositor* a public nuisance and ordering its destruction.[121] During these meetings, Hyrum Smith insisted that his brother's revelation on "a multiplicity of wives" was "in answer to a question concerning things which transpired in former days, and had no reference to the present time."[122] He said William Law had confessed to adultery and that Francis Higbee "had the P** [pox, meaning syphilis]."[123] Joseph Smith admitted to preaching plural marriage "on the stand from the bible, shewing the order in ancient days, having nothing to do with the present times," after which Hyrum again stressed that the revelation "was in reference to *former* days, and not the present times."[124]

Following destruction of the *Expositor*,[125] most dissenters left Nauvoo, hoping to avoid arrest and fearing for their lives.[126] On June 12, Smith was arrested for causing "a riot" and appeared before Nauvoo's court, which freed him. Five days later he was again arrested and discharged. Informed that angry citizens were gathering in Warsaw to storm Nauvoo,[127] Smith mobilized the Nauvoo Legion and declared martial law. He then decided to escape to the west, believing that the Saints would be safer without him; but when told that troops were being sent to occupy the city and that he would be protected, he returned to Nauvoo to stand trial. While imprisoned in nearby Carthage Jail, Joseph and Hyrum were killed on June 27, 1844. The Higbees and Laws were not directly involved in the assassination, but their rhetoric helped to ignite the volatile situation. If dissenters hoped their actions would cause the demise of polygamy, they underestimated the power of Smith's revelation.

The Higbees continued for a time to practice law in and around Nauvoo. Chauncey married Julia May White in 1854 in Quincy, then resettled to Pittsfield. That same year, he was admitted to the bar and elected to the Illinois general assembly. Four years later he joined the state senate. In 1861, he was elected as a circuit judge. He was appointed a member of the appellate court in 1877 and served as president of First National Bank, of which he was a charter member. He supported construction of the Pittsfield East School and a new Methodist Episcopal church. He remained in Pittsfield and died in 1884.[128]

Francis is more difficult to track. A Mormon source claims he was arrested in mid-1846 for anti-Mormon activities,[129] but he was still residing in Hancock County four years later when census takers identified him as a merchant and his younger brother Jackson as a clerk.[130] He reportedly died in New York.[131] Whether or not he married and had descendants is unknown. While he may have had help in composing the two Buckeye poems,[132] they reflect aspects of his life, personality, and temperament that seem to mark him as their principal creator. The poems are significant as evidence of the controversial environment in which Joseph Smith was assassinated, particularly with regard to the beginnings of plural marriage, as well as being artifacts of the author's own stormy encounter with Mormonism.

Appendix

BUCKEYE'S LAMENTATION FOR WANT OF MORE WIVES.
(*Warsaw Message*, Feb. 7, 1844, 1; *Warsaw Signal*, Apr. 25, 1844, 3)

1.
I once thought I had knowledge great,
But now I find 'tis small;
I once thought I'd Religion, too,
But I find I've none at all.
For I have got but *one lone wife*,
And can obtain no more;
And the doctrine is, I can't be saved,
Unless I've *half a score!*

2.

The *narrow gate* that Peter kept,
In ages long ago,
Is locked and barred since he gave up
The keys to *beardless* JOE.
And Joe proclaims it is too small,
And causes great delay,
And that he has permission got
To open the *broad way.*

3.

The narrow gate did well enough
When Peter, James, and John,
Did lead the saints on Zion-ward,
In *single file* along:
When *bachelors,* like good old *Paul,*
Could win the glorious prize,
And *maids,* without a *marriage rite,*
Reach "mansions in the skies."

4.

But we have other teaching now,
Of greater glories far;
How a *single glory's* nothing more
Than some lone twinkling star.
A *two-fold* glory's like the moon,
That shines so sweet at night,
Reflecting from her gracious lord
Whatever he thinks right.

5.

A *tenfold* glory—that's the prize!
Without it you're undone!
But with it you will shine as bright
As the bright shining sun.
There you may reign[133] like mighty Gods,
Creating worlds so fair;—
At least a *world* for every *wife*
That you take with you there.

6.

The man that has got ten fair wives,
Ten worlds he may create;
And he that has got less than this,
Will find a bitter fate.
The one or two that he may have,
He'd be deprived of then;
And they'll be given as *talents* were
To him who has got *ten*.

7.

And 'tis so here, in this sad life–
Such ills you must endure–
Some *priest* or *king*, may claim your wife
Because that you are poor.
A *revelation* he may get—
Refuse it if you dare!
And you'll be damned *perpetually*
By our good *Lord* the *Mayor!*[134]

8.

But if that you yield willingly,
Your daughters and your wives,
In spiritual marriage to our Pope,
He'll bless you all your lives;
He'll *seal you up,* be damned you can't,
No matter what you do—
If that you only *stick* to him,
He swears he'll *take* you *through*.

9.

He'll lead you on to[135] the broad gate,
Which he has opened wide—
In *solid column* you shall march,
And enter side by side.
And no delay you'll meet with there,
But "*forward march*" you shall:—
For he's not only our *Lord* Mayor
But *Lord* Lieutenant-ral.[136]

10.

This is the secret doctrine taught
By Joe and the *red rams**—
Although in public they deny—
But then 'tis all a sham.
They fear the indignation just,
Of those who have come here,
With hands thats clean and honest hearts,
To serve the Lord in fear.

11.

Thus, all the *twelve* do slyly teach,
And slyly practice, too;
And even the *sage Patriarch,*
Wont have *untied his shoe:*
For sure, 'twould be quite impolite,
If not a great disgrace,
To have a *widow* sister fair
Spit in a Prophet's face!

12

But Joe at snaring beats them all,
And at the rest does laugh;
For *widows* poor, and *orphan girls,*
He can ensnare with <u>chaff,</u>
He sets his snares around for all,—
And very seldom fails
To catch some thoughtless *Partridges,*[137]
Snow-birds[138] or *Knight*-ingales![139]

12. [sic]

But there are hundred[140] other birds
He never can make sing;
Who wont be driven nor *draged* to hell,[141]
By *prophet, priest* nor *king:*
Whose sires have bled in days gone by,
For their dear country's cause;
And who will still maintains its rights,
Its *Liberty* and *Laws!*

*B. Y. & O. H.[142]

The Buckey's First Epistle to Jo.
(*Warsaw Signal*, Apr. 25, 1844, 1)

1
Friend Jo, I have been told of late,
That you had got it in your pate
A certain chief, to vent his hate,
Had learned to sing;
And had turn'd out a poet great,
Or some such thing.

2
Because the "Warsaw Message" came
With tidings from that *state* of fame,
Like some great herald to proclaim
Your wicked ways,
Your *tyrany*, your *sin* and *shame*,
In these last days.

3
With Buckey's trumpet sounding clear,
That Democrat and Whig might hear,
And *Priest-rid* Mormons, who in fear,
Bow down to thee;
That there is still one child who dare
And will be free.

4
That Buckeye child lives in Nauvoo,
And some there are, who know how true
A friend, he ever was to you,
In days that's past,
Till *slanders base* around you threw
Fair fame to blast.

5
Till for himself he's fairly seen
That you were not what you had been,
But that iniquity you'd screen
In every way;
And from fair virtue's paths did lean
Vile plans to lay.

6

Have you forgot the snare you laid
For Nancy, (lovely Buckeye maid?)
With all your priestly arts array'd
Her to seduce;
Assisted by that wretched bawd
Who kept the house.

7

But she, in virtues armour steel'd,
Was proof against what you *reveal'd,*
And to *your doctrines* would not yield
The least belief;
Although the scriptures you did wield
In your relief.

8

And when you saw, she would detest
Such doctrines, in her noble breast,
And did d[e]pise the man, 'tho priest;
Who taught them too
A sallow, yellow, lustful beast,
Poor Joe, like you.

9

'Twas then you chang'd your *lovers sighs,*
And vengeful hate flash'd in your eyes
When you found out she did despise
You as a man;
So took to circulating lies,
Your usual plan.

10

Just that you might destroy her fame,
And give to her a ruin'd name,
So that if she should ever proclaim
What you had tried;
Your friends might turn on her the shame
And say she lied.

11

But Joe, in this you fairly tail'd,
Though you her father's house assail'd
She met you face to face; *you* quail'd
Before her frown,
And like a counterfeit she nail'd
You tightly down—

12

Although you tried, by priestly power
To make this gentle creature cower
And eat her words, that you might tower
In priestly pride;
But strong in truth, she in that hour
Told you you lied.

13

And when you found it would not do,
Then like a coward paltroon,[143] you
Acknowledg'd what she had said, was true
Unto her sire;
But then you'd nothing more in view
Than just to try her—

14

And put her on her guard, that she
Might keep herself all pure and free
From base seducers like to me,
And *Joab*[144] vile—
For that it was *reveal'd* to thee
We would beguile.

15

O Jo! O Jo!! thy slanderous tongue
Some burning tears from me have wrung,
And I had thought t' have held my tongue
And nothing said—
If thou had'st but repentance shown
And shut thy head.

16

But thy repeated slanders vile
Shall not be long borne by this child;
Although by nature he is mild,
And well disposed;
Thy sins from continent to isle
Shall be exposed.

17

Missouri's deeds shall come to light
Though perpetrated in the night,
By hirelings who thought it right
To do thy will—
By cabin conflagration bright
To *scalp* and kill.

18

Repent, repent, there still is time—
And add no more dark crime to crime,
But think, how mighty and sublime
Thy calling first—
And in black sackcloth bow thee down
Low in the dust—

19

And put away far from thy heart,
Each wicked, *sensual,* sinful art;
And from the truth no more depart
Long as you live—
But stop and make another start,
And I'll forgive.

20

If not, your dark deeds in Nauvoo,
As well as in Missouri too—
Like *Hamlet's* ghost shall rise to view
With *old white hat*[145]—
Then tremble tyrant, for but few
Will sanction that.

21

But I must stop this long epistle,
"My pen is worn down to the gristle,"
And 'tis the poet's only missill
In truth's relief—
For, be it known to all, this child
Aint yet a chief—

22

'Tho he his lineage can trace
Back to the *Bruce*[146] and *Wallace*[147] days,
When they for Liberty did raise
The sword, and broke
(As I intend in these last days)
A tyrant's yoke.

Notes

1. *Warsaw Message,* Feb. 7, 1844, 3. Ironically, Joseph Smith had just disciplined a follower for preaching the very thing Buckeye accused him of: "polygamy, and other false and corrupt doctrines" (see "Notice," *Times and Seasons,* Feb. 1, 1844, 423).

2. Joseph Smith et al., *History of the Church of Jesus Christ of Latter-day Saints. Period I* (Salt Lake City: Deseret Book Co., 1973), 6:210. I cite the published history when it does not differ materially from the manuscript version. In his diary, Smith does not mention having seen the poem, and his reaction is probably a later interpolation by LDS historians. See Scott H. Faulring, ed., *An American Prophet's Record: The Diaries and Journals of Joseph Smith* (Salt Lake City: Signature Books/Smith Research Associates, 1989), 445. The Church's historians may have assumed that Law was the author since three weeks earlier the Church had published one of Law's poems. See "Farewell, Illinois," in Ebenezer Robinson to John Taylor, Nov. 20, 1843, *Times and Seasons,* Jan. 15, 1844, 412-13; see also "Love of God" by "W. L." in *Times and Seasons,* Jan. 1, 1841, 270.

3. By the fall of 1840, Nauvoo counted more than 2,400 residents. Eighteen months later, its population had grown to 4,000. By 1845, there were more than 11,000 residents, nearly half the population of the county and only

1,000 shy of Chicago's. James E. Smith, "Frontier Nauvoo: Building a Picture from Statistics," *Ensign*, Sept. 1979, 17-19, found that "cities the size of Nauvoo were rare in the American West" and that "the Mormons almost singlehandedly caused Hancock County to be the most populated county in Illinois by the time of the 1845 Illinois State census" (17-18). It was second only to "Chicago and St. Louis in the region," according to Glen M. Leonard, *Nauvoo: A Place of Peace, a People of Promise* (Salt Lake City and Provo: Deseret Book and BYU Press, 2002), 179.

4. In John E. Hallwas, *Thomas Gregg: Early Illinois Journalist and Author* (Macomb: Western Illinois University, 1983), 47. Gregg was a self-taught newspaper man who once wrote a feature story under the name "a Buckeye." He was an abolitionist and teetotaler. He founded a total of eight newspapers and four magazines during his lifetime.

Other examples of "Buckeye" used as a pen name include a newspaper series by Samuel Sullivan Cox, written from Europe in the 1840s under the *nom de plume*, "A Buckeye Abroad." See Henry Howe, *Historical Collections of Ohio: An Encyclopedia of the State,* 2 vols. (Cincinnati: State of Ohio, 1902), 1:204; also "Buckeye," "The Grand Union Barbecue," *Harper's Weekly,* Oct. 12, 1861, 647. In 1841, U.S. President William Henry Harrison was known as "the Buckeye president."

5. *Warsaw Signal,* June 12, 1844, 2. See also the editorials reprinted in John E. Hallwas and Roger D. Launius, eds., *Cultures in Conflict: A Documentary History of the Mormon War in Illinois* (Logan: Utah State University Press, 1995), 79-81, 247-51.

6. Faulring, *American Prophet's Record,* 474; Smith, *History of the Church,* 6:345. Again, the account in the *History of the Church* is probably a later addition.

7. Buckeye was not the first to publicize Joseph Smith's doctrine of marriage. Almost two years earlier, John C. Bennett had published a series of letters in the nearby *Sangamo Journal* detailing what he had seen or learned, which he expanded in *The History of the Saints* (Boston: Leland & Whiting, 1842). For more on Bennett's activities, see Andrew F. Smith, *The Saintly Scoundrel: The Life and Times of Dr. John Cook Bennett* (Urbana: University of Illinois Press, 1997). Another early insider exposé was Oliver Olney's *The Absurdities of Mormonism Portrayed* (Hancock County, IL: the author, 1843).

8. See the data in George D. Smith, "Nauvoo Roots of Mormon Polygamy, 1841-46: A Preliminary Demographic Report," *Dialogue: A Journal of Mormon Thought* 27 (Spring 1994): 1-72. The fact of Joseph Smith's polygamy is generally accepted by historians today, but not entirely. For a contrary opinion based on Smith's own denials, see Richard and Pamela Price, *Joseph Smith Fought Polygamy* (Independence, MO: Price Publishing, 2000).

9. In citing the poetry, I have put line numbers in parenthesis and inserted a solidus at each line break. In addition, I have removed the capital-

ization at the beginning of each line, the emphasis (italics, small capitals), and superfluous dashes. For the full punctuation, see the appendix.

10. Another possible early explication was Udney Hay Jacob's *The Peacemaker,* excerpts from which were published in 1842 in Nauvoo by "J[oseph] Smith, Printer." See Lawrence Foster, "A Little-known Defense of Polygamy from the Mormon Press in 1842," *Dialogue: A Journal of Mormon Thought* 9 (Winter 1974): 21-34.

11. "[W]hat if," asks twentieth-century LDS educator Danel W. Bachman, "God was interested in raising up a certain lineage or a group of children through a special core of spiritual elite, who had been initiated into the mysteries of God and were thereby qualified to instruct others? How better might this be expeditiously accomplished than through multiple wives? These women might perpetually bear children of the men of modern Israel—'holy men' whom God had 'reserved' and chosen" (Bachman, "A Study of the Mormon Practice of Plural Marriage before the Death of Joseph Smith," M.A. thesis, Purdue University, 1975, 96).

12. Mildred H. Bray, "Elenor Houtz Snow (Fifth Wife of Pres. L. Snow)," typescript, 2-3, Archives, Church of Jesus Christ of Latter-day Saints, Salt Lake City, hereafter LDS Archives. LDS historian Kathryn M. Daynes observes: "Joseph Smith's counseling [another of his followers] to marry a fecund woman is consonant with a second reason for plural marriage: 'to multiply and replenish the earth, according to my commandment'" (*More Wives Than One: Transformation of the Mormon Marriage System, 1840-1910* [Urbana: University of Illinois Press, 2001], 29).

13. George A. Smith to Joseph Smith III, Oct. 9, 1869, in the Journal History, LDS Archives, for that date.

14. In Dean R. Zimmerman, ed., *I Knew the Prophets: An Analysis of the Letter of Benjamin F. Johnson to George F. Gibbs, Reporting Doctrinal Views of Joseph Smith and Brigham Young* (Salt Lake City: Horizon Publishers, 1976), 47.

15. In Andrew F. Ehat, "'They Might Have Known That He Was Not a Fallen Prophet': The Nauvoo Journal of Joseph Fielding," *BYU Studies* 19 (Winter 1979): 154.

16. "Autobiography of Sarah DeArmon Pea Rich," typescript, 36-37, LDS Archives.

17. "Statement of L[ucy] W[alker] [Smith] Kimball," n.d., typescript, LDS Archives.

18. Sarah M. Kimball, in Augusta J. Crocheron, *Representative Women of Deseret, A Book of Biographical Sketches to Accompany the Pictures of the Same Title* (Salt Lake City: J. C. Graham & Co., 1884), 26.

19. In "William Clayton's Testimony," Feb. 16, 1874, rpt. in George D. Smith, ed., *An Intimate Chronicle: The Journals of William Clayton* (Salt Lake City: Signature Books / Smith Research Associates, 1995), 557.

20. George A. Smith to Joseph Smith III, 1869.

21. Benjamin F. Johnson, *My Life's Review: Autobiography of Benjamin F. Johnson* (Orem, UT: Grandin Book, 1997), 84.

22. In "A Revelation to N[ewel] K. Whitney," July 27, 1842, rpt. in *The Essential Joseph Smith* (Salt Lake City: Signature Books, 1995), 165.

23. Helen Mar Kimball, in Richard S. Van Wagoner, *Sidney Rigdon: A Portrait of Religious Excess* (Salt Lake City: Signature Books, 1994), 293. "The promise was so great," Kimball admitted, "that I willingly gave myself to purchase so glorious a reward." See also Donna Hill, *Joseph Smith: The First Mormon* (Garden City, NY: Doubleday, 1977), 355.

24. "[T]hese [sealing] ordinances," LDS scholar Andrew F. Ehat writes, "were being administered to those who were at least willing to believe in the divinity of plural marriage. ... Acceptance of plural marriage was a demonstration that they would obey the actual laws that God taught were absolutely prerequisite to such blessings" (Ehat, "Joseph Smith's Introduction of Temple Ordinances and the 1844 Mormon Succession Question," M.A. thesis, Brigham Young University, 1982, 74-75).

25. Leonard, *Nauvoo,* 260-61.

26. Young had married Lucy Ann Decker in mid-June 1842 and Augusta Adams and Harriet Elizabeth Cook on November 2, 1843. Hyde had married Martha Rebecca Browett in February-March 1843 and Mary Ann Price on July 20, 1843. Young would marry a fourth wife, Clarissa Decker, in May 1844. These and other dates come from Smith, "Nauvoo Roots of Mormon Polygamy," and from subsequent correspondence with the author (copies in my possession).

27. This is according to Todd M. Compton, *In Sacred Loneliness: The Plural Wives of Joseph Smith* (Salt Lake City: Signature Books, 1997), 4-7.

28. The Partridge sisters lived with Joseph and Emma Smith for three years following the death of their father on May 27, 1840. Their mother remarried on September 27, 1840. Smith was appointed guardian of the Lawrence sisters in 1841 following the death of their father. Their mother remarried in late 1841. Smith's critics would later point to his relationship with the Lawrence sisters, whom he had married, as evidence of adultery.

29. See Smith, "Nauvoo Roots of Mormon Polygamy," 22-24.

30. Ibid., 24-26.

31. In Ronald W. Walker, "Rachel R. Grant: The Continuing Legacy of the Feminine Ideal," *Dialogue: A Journal of Mormon Thought* 15 (Autumn 1982): 109.

32. Sarah M. Kimball, in Crocheron, *Representative Women,* 26.

33. Cordelia Calista Morley Cox, "Autobiography," ca. Mar. 17, 1909, L.

Tom Perry Special Collections, Harold B. Lee Library, Brigham Young University, Provo.

34. Compton, *Sacred Loneliness*, 8.

35. See, e.g., Bachman, "Mormon Practice of Plural Marriage," 264-65; and Ehat, "Joseph Smith's Introduction of Temple Ordinances," 276n377.

36. See Bachman, "Mormon Practice of Plural Marriage," 265.

37. The following account is from Van Wagoner, *Sidney Rigdon*, 294-302.

38. Francis M. Higbee to the editor, *Warsaw Signal*, May 29, 1844, 2.

39. But see the editor's notice in *The Wasp*, Sept. 3, 1842.

40. Smith, *History of the Church*, 5:49.

41. See William Smith's "Bennettiana; The Microscope with Double Diamond Lenses," *The Wasp Extra*, July 27, 1842. William was Joseph Smith's younger brother.

42. For one writer's approach to Higbee and other dissidents, see Ted Gibbons, *Like a Lamb to the Slaughter: The Nauvoo Expositor, Traitors, and Treachery* (Orem, UT: Keepsake Paperbacks, 1990).

43. Wilson Law was born in Northern Ireland in 1807. In 1818 his family immigrated to Pennsylvania and later to Canada. He was baptized and ordained an elder in Nauvoo. In 1841 he was elected to the city council and promoted to brigadier general in the Nauvoo Legion. On July 22, 1842, he presented a public resolution attesting to Smith's good character; two weeks later was elected major general of the legion, replacing John Bennett. In mid-August, Smith said Law was of "noble stature, of noble hands, and of noble deeds" (Smith, *History of the Church*, 5:109). On December 25, 1842, he married Elizabeth Sikes, who died fifteen months later. By 1844 the thirty-seven-year-old joined his younger brother William, a counselor in the LDS First Presidency, in opposing plural marriage. He and his brother were excommunicated on April 18 and discharged from the legion on May 9, 1844. He helped to found the *Nauvoo Expositor*. By 1850, he was living in Pennsylvania and died ca. 1877. While he was aware of Mormonism's secret doctrines, he was not connected to Ohio or to Nancy Rigdon and had not been repeatedly "slandered" by Smith.

44. Smith, *History of the Church*, 4:503.

45. Ibid., 5:421.

46. Again, see Van Wagoner's treatment in *Sidney Rigdon*.

47. Affidavit dated May 17, 1842, in Smith, *History of the Church*, 5:11.

48. See the affidavits, first published by the LDS Church in the *Nauvoo Neighbor*, May 29, 1844, rpt. in Price and Price, *Joseph Smith Fought Polygamy*, 135-42.

49. Smith, *History of the Church,* 5:18.

50. See the documents reprinted in Price and Price, *Joseph Smith Fought Polygamy,* 146-55.

51. See Compton, *Sacred Loneliness,* 349.

52. Francis also neglected his duties in the Nauvoo Legion. In early June 1842, he was tried for negligence after failing to hold a court of assessment on May 14 and court of appeals on May 28, "thereby depriving the Legion of the use of the Funds which would have been assessed, & has suffered delinquents to escape Justice." Higbee "admitted his guilt" and was allowed to continue to serve. See "Capt. John H. Tippets versus Francis M. Higbee, Col.," June 3, 1842, Nauvoo Legion Papers, LDS Archives.

53. See Price and Price, *Joseph Smith Fought Polygamy,* 154-55.

54. See, e.g., the public certificate from Elias and Francis denying one of Bennett's allegations in the *Times and Seasons,* Aug. 1, 1842, 874.

55. Francis M. Higbee to Elias Higbee, Nov. 28, 1842, in the *Times and Seasons,* Dec. 15, 1842, 47.

56. Chauncey L. Higbee to the editor, *The Wasp,* Dec. 3, 1842.

57. Smith, *History of the Church,* 5:328.

58. "Death of Elias Higbee," *Times and Seasons,* June 15, 1843, 233.

59. Smith, *History of the Church,* 5:530.

60. Francis M. Higbee to Joseph Smith, Sept. 8, 1843, in the Journal History; underlining in original.

61. Smith, *History of the Church,* 6:42-43.

62. See *Times and Seasons,* Sept. 15, 1843, 331, reporting remarks delivered Oct. 9, 1843.

63. For more on Nauvoo's police force, see John Lee Allaman, "Policing in Mormon Nauvoo," *Illinois Historical Journal* 89 (Summer 1996): 85-98.

64. Smith, *History of the Church,* 6:152.

65. Ibid., 162-70.

66. Law's objections are detailed in Lyndon W. Cook, *William Law* (Orem, UT: Grandin Book, 1994), 11-34.

67. Nonetheless, Smith's official *History of the Church* (6:170) reported him thinking: "What can be the matter with these men [e.g., William Law, William Marks, et al.]? Is it that the wicked flee when no man pursueth, that hit pigeons always flutter, that drowning men catch at straws, or that Presidents Law and Marks are absolutely traitors to the Church, that my remarks should produce such an excitement in their minds. Can it be possible that the traitor … is one of my quorum [i.e., First Presidency]?" Though these thoughts

are not recorded in his diary, they are probably representative of Smith's suspicions.

68. Nauvoo City Council Minutes, Jan. 3, 1844, LDS Archives. Smith's comments do not appear in the published version in the *History of the Church,* 6:162-65.

69. Smith, *History of the Church,* 6:168.

70. Ibid., 169.

71. Smith implies that Higbee had contracted a venereal disease. This is the first, but not the last, mention of it.

72. William Law diary, Jan. 7, 1844, in Cook, *William Law,* 45-46.

73. Smith, *History of the Church,* 6:174.

74. The references are to Antonius Felix, the former slave who became governor of Judea and trembled when the apostle Paul spoke to him (Acts 24:24-27), and to Manoah, the Danite father of Samson, who is said to have seen an angel ascend to heaven in the flame of his sacrifice (Judges 13:19-20).

75. Francis M. Higbee to Joseph Smith, Jan. 10, 1844, Joseph Smith Papers, LDS Archives; underlining in original.

76. Smith, *History of the Church,* 6:176.

77. Ibid., 178.

78. Nauvoo City Council Minutes, Jan. 16, 1844. These are summarized in Smith, *History of the Church,* 6:178. Where the references to Higbee were "ordered to be crossed out," they were subsequently published verbatim in Smith's *History* (6:169).

79. Smith, *History of the Church,* 6:225. Bostwick's allegations, although not specified in the official history, had to do with Hyrum's and others' polygamy. Bostwick allegedly bragged that he could "take a half bushel of meal, obtain his vile purpose, and get what accommodation he wanted with almost any woman in the city" (in "Virtue Will Triumph," *Nauvoo Neighbor,* Mar. 20, 1844, 2).

80. Unlike other municipal courts in Illinois, Nauvoo's mayor automatically served as chief justice and the city's aldermen as associate justices. "Thus," write legal historians Edwin Brown Firmage and Richard Collin Mangrum, "the lawmaker was also the law interpreter, creating a concentration of power that was absent" elsewhere (*Zion in the Courts: A Legal History of the Church of Jesus Christ of Latter-day Saints, 1830-1900* [Urbana: University of Illinois Press, 1988], 86-87; 92-105).

81. Smith, *History of the Church,* 6:225. Francis appealed the court's decision (326).

82. Ibid., 237-38.

83. Smith's use of the phrase "use up" must have been disconcerting to his audience. Consider, e.g., Brigham Young's later use of the term in reference to the Utah War. As U.S. troops approached, he boasted that "we could go out and use them up, ... [but] we do not want to kill men (*Journal of Discourses*, comp. George D. Watt, 26 vols. [Liverpool: Latter-day Saints Book Depot, 1854-86], 5:234; cf. 1:171, 10:110; *History of the Church*, 2:181; 6:559).

84. Smith, *History of the Church*, 6:238, 239.

85. "Virtue Will Triumph," *Nauvoo Neighbor*, Mar. 20, 1844, 2.

86. Smith, *History of the Church*, 6:272.

87. Ibid., 285. According to the *History of the Church*, Higbee had threatened to shoot a policeman two days earlier. What prompted such a threat is not explained.

88. Ibid., 285-86.

89. Ibid., 287-88.

90. Qtd. in Cook, *William Law*, 50n26.

91. "My brother Hyrum called in the evening," Joseph Smith later reported, "and cautioned me against speaking so freely about my enemies, &c., in such a manner to make it actionable. I told him that six months would not roll over his head before they would swear twelve as palpable lies about him as they had about me" (Smith, *History of the Church*, 6:403).

92. Ibid., 6:341.

93. Ibid., 344; see also 348-49. The *Nauvoo Expositor* said they committed the "*very enormous* offence of refusing to assist the *notorious* O[rrin] P[orter] Rockwell, and his '*dignity*' John P. Green, in arresting a respectable and peaceable citizen, without the regular process of papers" (June 7, 1844, 3). The three men appealed the verdict to the municipal court but did not appear when that court convened on June 3. The court sent the case back to the mayor's court for dismissal or a rehearing (*History of the Church*, 6:426; *Nauvoo Expositor*, June 7, 1844, 3).

94. Smith, *History of the Church*, 6:356.

95. See Joseph Smith's testimony in "Municipal Court," *Nauvoo Neighbor*, May 15, 1844, rpt. in *Times and Seasons*, May 15, 1844, 538-39. While the testimony of Smith and others was later reprinted in the official history (*Deseret News*, Aug. 12, 1857, 1-2), it was deleted from the twentieth-century revision.

96. This bracketed paragraph appears in the published minutes. Most historians have tended to accept Smith's charges without question. Some have speculated that the deleted testimony concerned possible homosexual activity (D. Michael Quinn, *Same-Sex Dynamics among Nineteenth-Century Ameri-*

cans: A Mormon Example [Urbana: University of Illinois Press, 1996], 268, 362n121), but I suspect not.

97. This may actually refer to Chauncey Higbee.

98. See the testimony in "Municipal Court," *Nauvoo Neighbor,* May 15, 1844, rpt. in the *Times and Seasons,* May 15, 1844, 539-41.

99. This amounted to a little over thirty-two dollars (see Smith, *History of the Church,* 6:427). Higbee appealed the decision to the circuit court in McDonough County ("Circuit Court," *Nauvoo Expositor,* June 7, 1844, 3).

100. Higbee has in mind the Russian Mongols who had converted to Islam and ate raw meat—in other words, the most exotic people he could think of.

101. Dan. 5:25-28: "Thou art weighed in the balance, and art found wanting."

102. Higbee refers to an incident recorded in Bennett's *History of the Saints,* 231, when Smith allegedly sacrificed a lamb to atone for trying to coerce an unwilling participant.

103. Higbee to the *Warsaw Signal,* May 29, 1844, 2.

104. Smith, *History of the Church,* 6:362. Among the witnesses against Law, Cyrus H. Wheelock testified: "I heard Mr. Law say ... he knew Mr. Smith was the greatest villain, and guilty of the darkest deeds of any man on the earth—he said Mr. Smith was a whoremaster—all his religion was to carry out his points—He did not know but that he was guilty of every thing but murder." John Scott added: "I was at Mr. Laws a few days before they were cut off ... he said he did not believe that ever there was a more cursed scoundrel than Joseph Smith ever hung between the heavens and the earth, he said it voluntarily" ("Evidence taken at a Court Martial held on Major General Wilson Law," May 9, 1844, Nauvoo Legion Papers).

105. Smith, *History of the Church,* 6:363, 444.

106. Francis M. Higbee to Thomas Gregg, May 1844, Chicago Historical Society, Chicago. By "dark prince," Higbee may have meant the Brazilian slave trader Francisco Felix de Sousa, who allegedly had 1,000 women in a harem and worked from the Kingdom of Dahomey in west Africa, now the Republic of Benin, whose king had thousands of wives and an army of female soldiers (*Wikipedia*).

107. Smith, *History of the Church,* 6:366-67.

108. Ibid., 379.

109. Ibid., 398.

110. Ibid., 403.

111. Ibid., 405.

112. Ibid.

113. This may refer to "Buckeye's Lamentation," line 12, "beardless Joe."

114. Smith, *History of the Church,* 6:408.

115. Ibid., 413; "Circuit Court," *Nauvoo Expositor,* June 7, 1844, 3.

116. Smith, *History of the Church,* 6:407.

117. Ibid.

118. "Last Resort of Joe," *Warsaw Signal,* June 5, 1844, 2.

119. Smith, *History of the Church,* 6:427.

120. Francis M. Higbee, "Citizens of Hancock County," *Nauvoo Expositor,* June 7, 1844, 3. The last two lines echo the closing stanzas of "Buckeye's Lamentation": "Whose sires have bled in days gone by, / for their dear country's cause; / and who will[,] still maintains its rights, / its *Liberty* and *Laws!*"; and "Buckey's First Epistle": "When they for Liberty did raise / the sword, and broke / (as I intend in these last days) / a tyrant's yoke."

121. Smith, *History of the Church,* 6:432.

122. "City Council, Regular Session, June 8th [and 10th], 1844," *Nauvoo Neighbor,* June 19, 1844, 2 (the last eight words of Hyrum's remarks were omitted from the *History of the Church,* 6:435).

123. Ibid.

124. Ibid., 3. Again, the last eight words of Joseph's comments, as well as all of Hyrum's testimony quoted here, do not appear in *History of the Church,* 6:441. Both men's assertions were intended to disprove the affidavit, published in the *Nauvoo Expositor,* of a man whose twenty-nine-year-old daughter had been sealed to Smith a year earlier on June 1, 1843 (see Compton, *Sacred Loneliness,* 543-57).

125. Francis reportedly threatened that any who "lay their hand upon it [the press] or break it, they may date their downfall from that very hour, and in ten days there will not be a Mormon left in Nauvoo" (in Smith, *History of the Church,* 6:451; cf. Orrin Porter Rockwell's testimony of Higbee's threats, 457).

126. Ibid., 450.

127. See the special issue of the *Warsaw Signal,* June 14, 1844. Francis told the angry Illinoisans of "his personal knowledge of the Mormons, from their earliest history, through their hellish career in Missouri and this State—which has been characterized by the darkest and most diabolical deeds which has ever disgraced humanity."

128. See *The Official Magazine of the Isaac Higbee and Sophia Somers Family Organization,* July 1957, 1:18-22.

129. Leonard, *Nauvoo,* 602.

130. *The 1850 Census of Illinois, Hancock County* (Richland, WA: Locust Grove Press, 1977), 136.

131. Andrew Jenson, *Autobiography of Andrew Jenson* (Salt Lake City: Deseret News Press, 1938), 178.

132. In September 1903, ninety-one-year-old Joseph A. Kelting, while swearing to his knowledge of Joseph Smith's marriages, recited virtually verbatim a handful of verses from "Buckeye's Lamentation," which he placed in the mouth of William Law. It is not clear if Kelting, or his aide, was suggesting Law wrote the poem or was merely using the poem to give voice to Law's criticisms (Kelting Affidavit, Sept. 11, 1903, LDS Archives).

133. The *Warsaw Signal* has "shine."

134. Smith was appointed mayor of Nauvoo following the resignation of John Bennett on May 19, 1842.

135. The *Warsaw Signal* has "through."

136. Smith was named lieutenant general of the Nauvoo Legion by Illinois's governor on March 10, 1841. The last general commander to hold such a rank was George Washington. Buckeye's addition of "-ral" seems simply to have aided the poem's rhyming scheme.

137. Emily Dow Partridge and her sister Eliza Maria Partridge.

138. Eliza Roxcy Snow.

139. Martha McBride Knight.

140. The *Warsaw Signal* has "a hundred."

141. The *Warsaw Signal* has "Who wont be dragged to hell."

142. Brigham Young and Orson Hyde.

143. Variant of "poltroon," a "spiritless coward, a mean-spirited wretch" (*Webster's Third New International Dictionary*).

144. John C. Bennett.

145. Bennett claimed that Smith signed a love letter to one woman as "Old White Hat" (*History of the Saints*, 235).

146. Robert the Bruce.

147. William Wallace.

God's Chosen People

Mormon Representations of the Jewish Other in Holocaust Literature

Reinhold R. Hill

Mormonism has struggled to form a unified doctrine regarding Judaism and Jewish identity since its founding in the early nineteenth century. On Sunday morning, October 24, 1840, ten years after the founding of the Church of Jesus Christ of Latter-day Saints, Mormon apostle Orson Hyde ascended the Mount of Olives and dedicated Israel for the return of the Jews. Noticeably absent from Hyde's dedicatory prayer is any mention of proselyting or missionary efforts: the land was dedicated for the return of the Jews and not for Mormon missionary efforts.[1] Nonetheless, Hyde's words also indicate Mormon christocentrism and a conception of the Jewish need for repentance and humility when he asks "in the name of thy well-beloved Son, Jesus Christ," to have the land restored to its prior glory and to soften the hearts of the rightful inhabitants of the land.[2] Hyde's assumption that the Jews are the rightful inhabitants of Israel illustrates an early theological ambiguity about the relationship of Jew to Gentile and Mormon to Jew that continues to influence contemporary theological, historical, and literary representations of Jews and Judaism in Mormon works. In this paper I explore the representation of one marginalized group (Jews, Judaism, and the Jewish Holocaust) by another (Mormons) and argue that Mormon representations of Jewish life and experience, especially the experience of the Holocaust, will necessarily be flawed if Mormon authors do not recognize the competing worldviews of the groups. Through the examination of Margaret Young's *House without Walls* (1991), and Eugene England's "Summer Solstice" (1995), my paper explores the preferability of a poetics of impasse over a poetics of representation.

Mormons view themselves as God's chosen people, but unlike most other Christian faiths, they do not regard themselves as the successors to God's covenant with Israel. In Mormon theology, the Abrahamic covenant is alive, and Mormons hold divine birthright through their ritual adoption into the covenant. Certainly, Mormonism views itself as "a new and everlasting covenant," but it is not one that replaces God's original covenant with his chosen people. Joseph Smith, founder of the Church of Jesus Christ of Latter-day Saints and "translator" of the Book of Mormon, taught that the Jews were God's chosen people and that contemporary attitudes about Jews and Judaism were antithetical to God's teachings. "O ye Gentiles," the Book of Mormon reads, "have ye remembered the Jews, mine ancient covenant people? Nay; but ye have cursed them, and have hated them, and have not sought to recover them. But behold, I will return all things upon your own heads; for I the Lord have not forgotten my people."[3]

According to Steven Epperson, the Book of Mormon "is for all its christocentrism peculiarly pitched toward the realization of God's covenant with Israel. Israel's covenant dominates the text the way a 'main theme' presides through the exposition, development, and recapitulation of a sonata."[4] Epperson argues that Smith was unique among religious leaders of the nineteenth century because he did not actively seek to proselyte or convert Jews (37). Indeed, Smith was critical of such efforts among the Christian denominations as attested by the passage from the Book of Mormon above (Epperson, 37, 52). The theme of separate and distinct covenant communities is further developed through Smith's revelation of the books of Moses. According to Smith's interpretations, two separate covenant communities develop through Judah and Joseph, with Mormons receiving their birthright primarily through Joseph (Epperson, 50-54). In the Doctrine and Covenants, Mormon scripture containing modern revelation, Smith clearly envisions two distinct communities when he writes, "Let them, therefore, who are among the Gentiles flee unto Zion. And let them who be of Judah flee unto Jerusalem, unto the mountains of the Lord's house."[5] Nonetheless, Smith did not seek to align his new faith with either Christianity or Judaism but to set up a new faith community borrowing liberally from both traditions but independent of them (Epperson, 59).

Smith's feelings about Jews and Judaism, however, were not without their contradictions. In order to more fully understand the Bible and other ancient scripture, Smith sought to learn Hebrew and other ancient languages. Joshua Seixas, son of Rabbi Gershom Medes Seixas, a prominent Jewish leader, was hired to teach Hebrew in Kirtland, Ohio (Epperson, 80-82). Epperson cites Moshe Davis to suggest that this period of interaction between Smith and Seixas was of crucial importance to the development of early Mormon theologies (85). Nonetheless, the friendly encounter between Smith and Seixas aroused in Smith "an inclusive, conversionist impulse" (Epperson, 88). Seixas did not embrace Smith's "restored" gospel and their interactions brought Smith to write that he had interacted with one of the "peculiar people" who practiced "true piety [and,] real religion" (in Epperson, 89). Epperson concludes, "For a man who claimed that he was told by divine revelation that 'all the sects ... were an abomination' in the sight of the Lord, such adjectives as 'true' and 'real' for another religious community were hardly trivial" (89).

Nonetheless, Smith's views of the Jews and Judaism were not shared by all early Mormon leaders. Many of the early leaders continued to hold the views they brought with them from their previous Christian affiliations, and Epperson divides the early leadership into two distinct camps with Smith, Hyde, and Brigham Young, the second leader of the church, in one camp and Sidney Rigdon, a Campbellite minister before his conversion to Mormonism; Oliver Cowdery, a teacher and editor of Mormon publications; and Orson Pratt in the other. Rigdon, Cowdery, and Pratt held traditional views of the Jews and Judaism, believing that the Jews followed an apostate religious tradition and were responsible for the crucifixion of Jesus Christ (Epperson, 105-205).

Interest in the gathering of the Jews to Jerusalem has not waned in LDS theology. Ezra Taft Benson, a secretary of agriculture in the Eisenhower administration and Mormon apostle, was the first to cite the Second World War as a tool for the gathering. After denigrating the world's treatment of the Jews, Benson indicated that a gathering of monumental importance was about to take place:

> While in Europe, traveling through the war-torn countries, I was deeply impressed with the fact that the Lord had used, as a means of prodding the Jews and bringing about a fulfillment of his purposes, legalized persecution under the great and terrible Nazi program. The Jews were persecuted and driven, I presume, like no other people under heaven. … One hardly ever hears reference to the prophecies regarding Judah's return. Yet, the promises are clear that it would be one of the great events of the last days.[6]

Benson appears to imply that the Holocaust perpetrated by the Nazis served a higher purpose—to spur the Jews to return to their homeland. To be fair to Benson, he discusses the Holocaust in detail in his address:

> I remember standing on the ruins of what was the largest Jewish ghetto in Europe, in the Jewish section of Warsaw, Poland, in August 1946. … Here 250,000 descendants of Judah had lived prior to the war. Under the Nazi rule … some 150,000 Jews from other parts of Europe were brought into that area. Then finally the entire section was destroyed, wiped out by bombing after the people had been robbed and ravaged. … We visited some of the concentration camps and the crematoriums where it is estimated, six million of the sons and daughters of Judah lost their lives, reducing their world population from seventeen to eleven million. (72-79)

Benson's view of the Holocaust is hardly unique among religious thinkers.[7] While early Mormon authorities taught that God would yet honor his covenant with Judah, the means by which the covenant would be fulfilled remained unclear. In the same speech in which he credits the Holocaust with encouraging the Jews to return home, Benson cites Doctrine and Covenants 45:51-53:

> Then, no doubt, will be realized the fulfillment of the glorious statement made by the Lord in the Doctrine and Covenants through the Prophet Joseph [Smith] with reference to Judah, which I read in conclusion: And then shall the Jews look upon me and say: What are these wounds in thine hands and in thy feet? Then shall they know that I am

> the Lord; for I will say unto them: These wounds are the wounds with which I was wounded in the house of my friends. I am he who was lifted up. I am Jesus that was crucified. I am the Son of God. And then shall they weep because of their iniquities; then shall they lament because they persecuted their king. (79)

Benson's address indicates that the Jews will see Christ at his second coming, accept him as their promised Messiah, and repent of their "iniquities." Nonetheless, the role that Mormons would play in this "conversion" of the Jews is not clear.

Benson goes to great lengths to relate Mormonism to Judaism:

> There is a great affinity for the Jews by the Mormons. The Jews have endured great persecution and suffering. This we understand, for our people have also undergone severe persecutions and extermination.[8] Indeed, the man we revere as a modern prophet, Joseph Smith, was martyred for his testimony in 1844. In 1846 our people had to leave the United States in exodus because of the threat of annihilation. ... But our affinity toward modern Judah is not prompted out of mutual suffering; it is prompted out of a knowledge of our peculiar heritage. Jeremiah has prophesied that in the latter times, "the house of Judah shall walk with the house of Israel, and they shall come together" (Jer. 3:18).[9]

Benson seeks to verify his understanding when he cites a meeting with David Ben-Gurian, "We need to know more about the Jews, and the Jews ought to know more about the Mormons. When we understand one another, perhaps we will understand why David Ben-Gurian said to me on one of my visits to Tel Aviv, 'There are no people in the world who understand the Jews like the Mormons'" (Benson, 97). Benson is not entirely clear as to why the Jews ought to know more about the Mormons, but implicit in the connection is that the Mormons hold a truth that the Jews do not have. This implicit assumption has caused much misunderstanding in interactions between Mormons and Jews.

The impossibility of reconciling Other and self is not unique to Mormon popular literature or criticism. Trinh Minh-ha has written that the conversation about the Other is essentially a conversation about silence: "'Them' [the Other] always stands on the other side of the hill, naked and speechless ... 'them' is only admitted among 'us,' the discussing subjects, when accompanied or introduced by an 'us.'"[10] That is, the Other is rarely given voice in any cultural setting unless it is to exoticize (and thereby colonize) the difference represented by the category of other. The impossibility of rendering the Other is manifest in the way the Other is admitted into society, in the presence of "us," accompanied by one of "us." We are not interested in the Other unless we can see ourselves, or a benefit to ourselves, in the examination.

Nonetheless, the question of otherness is difficult to address in terms of Mormon perceptions of the Jewish Other. Mormons often perceive Jews and Judaism in a more favorable light than they do other Christian denominations. The general acceptance by Mormons of Jews as one of God's covenant people contrasts sharply with the Mormon view of other Christian denominations as apostate religious traditions. Nonetheless, the question remains whether or not such views and their subsequent representations are based in the reality of the specific worldviews and beliefs of Mormons and Jews or are based in Mormon perceptions of similarity.

Margaret Young's *House without Walls* is a text that is difficult to categorize: it is part romance, part Holocaust fiction, part religious didacticism. The novel opens with the protagonist, Sarah Sinahson, returning home to Hamburg from the Bergen-Belsen concentration camp. Sarah, a 1930s Jewish convert to Mormonism, is stunned that her house is still standing, and her memory is taken back to the blessing left on the house by the two Mormon missionaries years earlier. Everyone in Sarah's family is dead, but upon seeing her house, she remembers a different time and place. She remembers her conversion to Mormonism. Young is honest about the motivations of many young converts when she describes Sarah's crush on the handsome Mormon boy Hans, but the novel describes much more than an attachment to Mormonism because of romantic fancy. Sarah is possibly saved by her Mormon connections when her father insists that she go to a local Mormon family for shelter. Sarah is housed for a time in a forest cottage, but when her benefactors are killed in a bomb raid, she is forced to fend for herself, is captured by the Nazis, and is sent to the concentration camp.[11]

Sarah does not return to Mormonism after her experience in the camps. Instead, she marries Abraham, a rabbi from her pre-war community in Hamburg, so that she can emigrate to the United States with him. Once in the United States, Sarah begins a new, Jewish life with Abraham. Together they have a son, Isaac. The final two-thirds of the novel revolve around Isaac's relationship with the daughter of Sarah's pre-war Mormon boyfriend. Isaac is drawn to Mormonism, converts, and returns to Germany as a Mormon missionary. Young attempts to further complicate the plot by having Sarah and Abraham visit Isaac in Germany during the Munich Olympics.

For all of the novel's emphasis on Mormon christocentric values of salvation, it portrays a surprisingly vibrant picture of Jewish culture. When Young explores Abraham's life before the Holocaust, the reader is given a clear sense of Jewish tradition:

> Abraham Cohen was the fourth in a family line of rabbis. It was the Jewish custom that every firstborn male child should belong to God. The father paid a token sum for his son's release to his care.
>
> Abraham was the firstborn of his father's family. Though the elder Rabbi Cohen, Samuel, had fulfilled the requirements of the Law in buying his boy back, Abraham understood throughout his life that he was expected to become a servant of God, a scholar of Judaism, a rabbi. He fulfilled the expectations magnificently. He not only learned the writings of past scholars and prophets—the *nauvey*—but loved them.[12]

Young respects Jewish tradition and life, and she attempts to instill in her reader an appreciation of this tradition.

Young describes Jewish ritual, tradition, and ceremony with obvious reverence. Her descriptions of Jewish life appear honest and sincere. The pictures are convincingly drawn through minute description that incorporates a liberal smattering of Hebrew words and phrases to lend an authentic feel to her text:

> Simon and an acquaintance of Rabbi Silverstein assisted with the child's circumcision. The wine was slipped into the eight-day-old infant's mouth, and the rite of Brith Milah was performed: the child was put under the covenant of his fathers and circumcised as a token of his identity. For had not God said, "My covenant shall be in your flesh for an everlasting covenant"?

> The child, whom Abraham symbolically named Isaac, cried vigorously as the ritual was performed. Abraham took him in his arms and whispered, "*Shah, shah,*" and the cries quieted to whispers. "Oh this will be a good boy," Abraham prophesied to all present—and to the world. (100)

The covenant of God with Judaism is emphasized throughout Young's discussion of Jewish life and tradition. We are shown Abraham teaching his son the significance of Hanukkah, the meaning of the festival, and its application to modern life. The description Young gives the Passover is particularly infused with emotion in light of the description she has given the Holocaust:

> Sarah cleaned the house for a week in preparation for Passover. ... [When the Passover ritual began] Isaac squirmed in his chair, eyes glowing. Abraham nodded to him.
>
> "What makes this night different from all other nights?" the child asked, and Isaac and Abraham spoke the ritual conversation. The family recited the plagues of God on the Egyptians and remembered the passing over of the Angel of Death. (114)

On a personal, visceral level, Young's descriptions draw in the reader. A Mormon audience will be drawn to the story because it appeals to the faithful: it describes a similar religious culture that has a rich religious tradition, and which Mormon theology embraces as a chosen, covenant community. But this is the problem with the story and with the novel as a whole. The picture drawn by Young is a Mormon picture of a Jewish experience. Thus, the novel is trapped in a peculiar Mormon worldview that cannot reasonably represent the experience of the Holocaust in any terms except those that relate to Mormon ideals of redemption. That is, the novel presents a picture of the Holocaust and life after the Holocaust that demonstrates Mormon christocentric values. In the world of the novel, if Sarah will not return to Mormonism (though clearly her heart is drawn in this direction), then God will take Isaac. Isaac's loss occurs when he is married to his Mormon girlfriend, Elsa, in a Mormon temple ceremony. While Abraham was not comfortable with Isaac's decisions to serve a Mormon mission and marry this Mormon girl in a ceremony in which he cannot participate, at the novel's conclusion Abraham sounds a tone of reconciliation that conforms to a Mormon worldview when he compares the temple destroyed in Jerusalem to the Mormon temple in Salt Lake City:

> My son, if this were a Jewish wedding, you would crush a glass in remembrance of the destruction of our temple. For you, perhaps you don't remember the destruction of your temple, since this one is—since it has been restored to you. I think maybe there is good in this. Maybe it is good to remember that in his own time, in his own way, God restores whatever man destroys. Therein is your hope. And mine. (222)

In some forms of conservative Judaism, especially the Judaism portrayed by Young, one would expect the father to be distraught because he is losing a son who is marrying outside God's covenant, while for the Mormon reader, it is clear that Abraham cannot attend his son's wedding because he is not Mormon, because only worthy, practicing Mormons may enter Mormon temples. Young has done a good job of establishing Abraham's identity as a conservative Jew, but the Jewish view is lost in Young's telling because she seems unaware of the differing perspectives of Mormonism and Judaism, which causes her portrayal to break down. Perhaps more importantly for this discussion, Abraham speaks of God's redemption as an action by God rather than a result of human action. The gulf between the views of redemption, in this case redemption brought about by God's intervention, and seeing redemption as a result of human endeavor, results in an incommensurable separation between the competing worldviews. The implications of Young's ending are clear: Mormonism, particularly the restoration tendencies of Mormonism, provides hope for redemption through God's literal redemption. In Young's conception, much of the lesson of the Holocaust must be glossed over because the Holocaust does not yield such a redemption.

Nonetheless, the portrait she paints is as accurate as any can be that attempts to address and reconcile the difference between the belief systems of Mormons and Jews. Young's novel is further problematized by her husband's preface to the book. In his introduction, Bruce Young discusses the Mormon doctrine of posthumous temple work that allows those who did not receive Mormon ordinances in this life to receive them in the next. According to Young, "the names of some of those killed in the Holocaust, the Nazi destruction of the Jews, have been placed in files at the Provo Temple" (xiv), and he and his spouse have done Mormon temple work in their behalf:

> There was something terribly anonymous in their persecution and murder. They were treated not as individuals but as nameless members of a despised race. Temple work, we have felt, somehow reverses that process. Those who were destroyed en masse are redeemed one by one. Those deprived of names and voices are given names and voices again. We think of them as individuals, one at a time. (xiv)

Jewish reaction to the practice of posthumous baptism for victims of the Holocaust was understandably negative. Ernest Michel, chairman of the World Gathering of Holocaust Survivors, led the protest against the Mormon practice after learning that his parents, victims of Auschwitz, were posthumously baptized into a Christian faith.[13] According to the newswire, the Mormons who had themselves baptized for Holocaust victims did so because they were motivated by "love and compassion" after visiting Holocaust memorials. They did not realize that what they did might be offensive. There is clearly an incommensurability between the language used by the Mormons motivated by compassion and the language of the relatives of the Holocaust victims. Church leaders have agreed to remove from the Church's genealogical index the names of Holocaust victims who do not have Mormon relatives, which will effectively halt temple baptisms of the victims. Nonetheless, in Mormonism, there is no exaltation (God's highest reward for the faithful) for the non-Mormon. All the righteous, if they are to receive this reward, must undergo conversion to Mormonism and receive all Mormon ordinances.

Louis Zucker, the first Jewish professor at the University of Utah, writes, "Mormons, I think, are in the habit of magnifying similarities between Judaism and Mormonism and etherealizing the differences into shadow. We should have a clearer and truer knowledge of each other."[14] Any meaningful dialogue between Mormons and Jews is restricted by the inability of resolving the difference between Mormon and Jewish worldviews. Zucker expresses part of the distance in his discussion of Mormon interpretations of the Old Testament in relation to Jewish understanding:

> There simply is no meeting ground between the Mormon line of argument and the Pharisaic or Rabbinic development of Scripture in the Talmud. The one speaks of Salvation in the next world; the other speaks of Halachah, the way, ethical conduct in human relations. The knowledgeable Jew is also aware of over 2000 years of Jewish experience and thought, of challenge and response, after the Old Testament. (Zucker, 43)

The otherworldliness of Mormon interpretation contrasts with the this-worldly emphasis of Jewish interpretation, to say nothing of messianic thought versus christocentric thought. The regimens provided by the different focus in worldviews challenge assumptions of salvation and redemption that cause difficulties for Mormon writers attempting to incorporate the Jewish Other into their texts.

Eugene England's personal essay "Summer Solstice" draws a picture that is strikingly different from Young's. England's essay is set in Idaho on his ninth birthday. He realized, after seeing Claude Lanzmann's account of the Holocaust, *Shoah*, that in his childhood, his ninth birthday coincided with the beginning of the Nazi liquidation of the Warsaw ghetto. Drawing from several sources, including Lucy Dawidowicz's *The War Against the Jews*, England creates parallel worlds, the world of a nine-year-old Mormon boy in Idaho and the world of a nine-year-old Jewish boy in the Warsaw ghetto. Instead of focusing on aspects of religion or culture, England focuses on experience. He remembers helping his father on the farm that day, playing with his friends, and rushing to the movies. He describes his despair when he learns that the price of seeing a movie has increased, and he does not have enough to go to the movie, and then he contrasts these experiences with those of the children in the Jewish orphanage on the day of the liquidation of the ghetto:

> By four o'clock in the afternoon, about when I, eight time zones away, had run the morning's first load of wheat out of the pit and turned off the elevator, six thousand people were being loaded into forty cattle cars, packed so tight they could only stand. After a journey of fifteen

> hours, without water or toilets, they were put onto a siding with other trains at the small town of Treblinka. Twenty cars at a time were disconnected and pushed to a small locomotive for the four miles to the camp. Suddenly the car doors were opened and a variety of guards, Ukranian, Latvian, German, began pushing them out of the cars, beating them with whips and clubs, and screaming, "Get out, get out. Hurry. Leave the baggage. Get undressed! You're to be disinfected."[15]

Eugene England repeatedly contrasts his experience as a nine-year-old boy in Idaho with the experiences of the Jews in the Warsaw ghetto. Instead of minimizing differences, England magnifies them. He seems to force the reader to an impasse that must be reconciled. The differences in the experience elicit the desire to grasp and to comprehend, even if such comprehension is elusive. As England evokes historical figures and personal experience, the reader seeks to reconcile his or her experiences with the experiences of the Other, but England does not allow such reconciliation to occur.

He describes, as does the historian Dawidowicz, how the orphanage's leader insures that the children have clean clothing and fresh water for their journey. Korczak, the leader of the orphanage, takes one of the children, England's imagined Julek, by the hand and escorts the children to the train station. Korczak is given the opportunity to leave the children, but he does not. Again at Auschwitz he is encouraged to leave the children but refuses. England takes the reader inside the gas chamber and describes the horrific annihilation of the ghetto:

> At this point the record ends. ... I feel I must try to speak for them, to imagine a voice for at least one, and so have chosen nine-year old Julek to take us all the way into that chamber ...
>
> *Then the door opened and they pushed us inside one big room. Some fell down but the doctor still held my hand. He tried to keep us standing against the wall, but when they closed the doors everyone began crying and pushing back to get out the door. Then I heard a loud engine start up at the back. ... The doctor yelled at us to stand still and breathe quietly and soon it would end. ...We fought each other to climb up and get air. ... I could feel the doctor under me, and he pushed me up and held me until there was no breath to breathe.* (55-57, italics in the original)

England feels compelled to write this story for those who cannot. The desire to give voice to and represent the Other is natural, but it, in fact, undermines England's essay by minimizing the gap between his experience and the experience of the imagined Julek. He presumes to speak for the Other when he cannot know fully what it was like.

England, however, does not end his essay in the gas chamber. Instead, he returns the reader to Idaho and the normalcy of life:

> As I awoke in the dark on August 7, 1942, about the time Julek Jacobowicz died, I realized my father was standing by the bed, his hand on my shoulder. "We need to get going," he said quietly. "Your grandpa wants to go with us today, so let's help with his chores." We ate and got down to Grandpa's by 5, in time for Dad to milk the last big black and white Holstein. ... (57)

The contrast at this point of the essay could not be more striking: England's return to the juxtaposition of his experience with what has just occurred to Julek evokes the gap between the individual experiences. England implies rightly that his experience as a nine-year-old, indeed the experiences of all who have not experienced the disaster, make it impossible to grasp the events that are the Holocaust.

Instead of taking the traditional Mormon approach to understanding Judaism and the Jewish experience by focusing on perceived religious similarities, England maximized the difference of the experiences, thus allowing the reader to glimpse the gap between what it meant to be a young Jewish victim of the Holocaust and a young Mormon boy in rural Idaho. It is through this unfilled gap that the force of the Holocaust is brought to the reader—it is the gap that evokes the disaster, that promotes the grappling with the unspeakable and the unknowable.

Margaret Young's book is trapped in a Mormon conception of Jewish life. Where Young attempts to explore what it means to be Jewish only insofar as the Jewishness is related to Mormonness, England draws a stark contrast between the lived experiences of the Mormon and Jewish youths that allows for the potential of conceiving the Other. England's focus is on his life, action, and experience, and his interest is in trying to understand the separation between his lived experience and the experience of Julek. It is clear that Julek's experience is not his. The experience of the Other is clearly differentiated from the experience of the self, and the readers are driven to attempt to reconcile the difference between their own lived experiences and the experiences of Julek and Eugene, a redemptive act that brings the reader out of his or her own realm of knowledge and experience toward that of the Other. England's poetic of impasse drives his essay beyond representation and provides an opportunity to gain a glimpse of the horror of the war through the examination of his experience and the experience of the Other.

The selection of genre is important to the success of England's essay. By contrast, Young's *House without Walls*, which is trapped in a universalizing view of literature, seeks out a lesson to be learned. The lesson, in the end, is that redemptive hope might rise from the ashes of the Holocaust. England offers no such universalizing experience or lesson. He does not seem interested in teaching a lesson but rather in exploring the difference between his understanding and the understanding of someone else. The focus of his essay establishes a common ground of experience (his) in contrast to another experience (the Holocaust), which forces the reader to attempt to reconcile the impasse. No such gap exists in Young's novel because the experience of one is universalized into the experience of the reader. Because of this approach, and the intended audience of the novel, the difference of the reality of the experience cannot be reconciled. Instead of providing testimony, as England's essay does, Young creates a fiction that unwrites itself because of the gulf that exists between Jewish and Mormon worldviews. In the end, it is the uniqueness of the experiences that England focuses on that establishes a common ground for examining the event, a common ground that does not elide the Other, but that maximizes the Other to force a reconciliation and thereby allow a glimpse of the disaster.

Notes

1. Orson Hyde, *A Voice from Jerusalem, or a Sketch of the Travels and Ministry of Elder Orson Hyde* (Boston: Albert Morgan, 1842), 28-35.

2. Hyde, 30.

3. 2 Ne. 29: 5, 1-10.

4. Steven Epperson, *Mormons and Jews: Early Mormon Theologies of Israel* (Salt Lake City: Signature Books, 1992), 34.

5. D&C 133:12, 13; Epperson, *Mormons and Jews*, 64.

6. Ezra Taft Benson, *Conference Reports of the Church of Jesus Christ of Latter-day Saints*, Apr. 1950, on the *LDS Collectors Library 1997 CD-ROM* (Salt Lake City: Infobases, 1996], 77-79.

7. See, e.g., Richard L. Rubenstein, *After Auschwitz: History, Theology, and Contemporary Judaism*, 2d ed. (Baltimore: Johns Hopkins University Press, 1992), 157-200, for a thorough summary of diverse theological assumptions about the Holocaust.

8. Benson is referring to early persecution of the Latter-day Saints in New York, Ohio, Missouri, and Illinois. For a Mormon account of the events leading to Missouri Governor Lilburn Boggs's "extermination" order, see Leonard J. Arrington and Davis Bitton, *The Mormon Experience*, 2d ed. (Chicago: University of Illinois Press, 1992). A more balanced approach, perhaps, is found in Stephen C. LeSueur, *The 1838 Mormon War in Missouri* (Columbia: University of Missouri Press, 1990).

9. Ezra Taft Benson, *The Teachings of Ezra Taft Benson* (Salt Lake City: Bookcraft, 1988), 95.

10. Trinh T. Minh-Ha, *Woman, Native, Other: Writing Postcoloniality and Feminism* (Bloomington: Indiana University Press, 1989), 65, 67.

11. Douglas Tobler, "The Jews, the Mormons, and the Holocaust," *Journal of Mormon History* 18 (Spring 1992): 59-92, reports incidents of Mormons helping Jewish friends, which no doubt influenced Young's novel.

12. Margaret Young, *House without Walls* (Salt Lake City: Deseret Book, 1991), 11.

13. Associated Press, "Mormons, Jews Sign Agreement on Baptized Holocaust Victims," May 5, 1995, online at "The Issue of the Mormon Baptisms of Jewish Holocaust Victims," *JewishGen* (www.jewishgen.org/infofiles/ldsagree.html).

14. Louis C. Zucker, "A Jew in Zion," *Sunstone*, Sept.-Oct. 1981, 35-44.

15. Eugene England, "Summer Solstice," *The Sewanee Review* 103:1 (1995), 51.

Preaching the Gospel of Church and Sex

Mormon Women's Fiction in the *Young Woman's Journal*, 1889-1910

Rebecca de Schweinitz

In 1889, Utah newspapers and periodicals informed readers about the start of a new monthly magazine, the *Young Woman's Journal* (*YWJ*). Initiated and first edited by Susa Young Gates, a daughter of Brigham Young, and directed to girls and young, unmarried women in the Latter-day Saint Church (LDS), the journal was meant to contain "the most elevating ideas of the Daughters of Zion."[1] The *YWJ* published poems, stories, and articles written overwhelmingly by women. It analyzed "great" books like *Anna Karenina* and discussed topics such as women's health, education, clothing, suffrage, and marriage. The *YWJ* reveals similarities and differences in the experiences and attitudes of Mormon women and women nationally and shows LDS women's efforts to promote their Church and sex.

The *YWJ* was not the first periodical directed to a female Mormon audience, the *Woman's Exponent* having been in existence since 1872. Scholars have long acknowledged the *Exponent*'s role as a feminist forum but have given less attention to the *YWJ*.[2] Both journals demonstrated a commitment to the LDS Church and to the woman's movement.[3] The *YWJ*, however, is unique in at least two respects. First, it was directed to a younger female audience. Second, it employed fiction to communicate ideas. As an 1890 article in the *YWJ* explained:

"The aim and object of this publication has been set forth many times. … The present generation demand amusement, and … lessons … are more vividly taught, more deeply impressed through the medium of books … than through homilies and sermons."[4] Like non-fiction articles in both the *Woman's Exponent* and the *YWJ*, fictional stories in the *YWJ* advanced the lessons of women's rights. The content of those stories outlines a shift in Mormon experiences and anxieties before and after Utah achieved statehood as through the pages of the *YWJ* experienced LDS women expressed their beliefs about religion and gender to their younger counterparts.

"Seek Ye Out of the Best Books"

Fiction was not a medium initially available to Mormon women. For forty years the LDS church taught its members to read only "solid, truthful and useful" material and warned against the dangers of fiction. Mormon officials, like many other nineteenth-century evangelical religious leaders, believed that reading fiction wasted time that could be spent reading scripture or otherwise building Zion and that it undermined the appeal of truth, which appeared tame and uninteresting in comparison to the romance and exaggeration of personality and circumstance in popular literature. In the early 1880s, Mormon anti-fictionists stepped up their attack. The completion of the transcontinental railroad and escalating migrations to Oregon and California brought the Saints increasingly into contact with "gentiles," including their earthy ideas and the shoddy dime novels and sensational tabloids of the Eastern states. In addition, the Godbeite and Christian Science movements generated concern among Church leaders.[5] George Q. Cannon, Mormon apostle, territorial legislator, and owner and editor of the *Juvenile Instructor,* a quasi-official periodical for youth, lead the assault, equating novel reading with drinking alcohol. "It is a species of dissipation," he insisted. "The mind, under the influence of such a habit, is stimulated and the imagination unduly fed, until such people are almost unfitted for the every-day work of life. … They are only happy when they can take refuge, as a dram drinker would to liquor," in their "stories of fiction."[6]

During this same period, other LDS leaders came to realize that despite the Church's position, Mormon youth liked to read fiction. Unlike Cannon's concern for imaginative narratives, these officials believed that fiction could be "good, pure, elevating," and an "effective and pleasing method of teaching doctrine [and] illustrating principle."[7] By 1890 the Church modified its stance; instead of condemning fiction outright, leaders differentiated between good and bad stories and advocated Mormon "home literature." Through fiction written by Church members, the older generation could reach out to and guard the youth of Zion, harness the power of the press, encourage creativity, and promote self-reliance.[8]

Producing a distinctive literature became a special mission for women in the LDS community. Having long been involved in Utah's non-fiction literary endeavors, and with a decided interest in securing sound influences for their children, women enthusiastically embraced the crusade to construct an original body of fictional writing.[9] Like other Americans at the time, Mormons believed that women possessed a unique spirit and temper and that their distinct moral virtues could be used "to the fullest extent for the establishment of righteousness on earth," including the development of home literature.[10]

Despite, or partly because of, nineteenth-century women's high level of literary productivity, historians and literary theorists have usually treated early women's fiction with disdain. Deemed inartistic, imitative, and void of "the singular qualities of the concerns with which they were trying to deal," scholars have traditionally dismissed it as sentimental and didactic.[11] Feminist scholars, however, have re-evaluated early women's literature and found a constant political enterprise even in the most sentimental writing. Written by women, for women, and about women, fiction writing gave the presumed weaker and silent sex a way to participate in the debate over women's access to power and to contribute to the development of a positive gender consciousness. Scholars suggest that while on the surface, women's fiction appeared to simply reflect entrenched cultural values, a closer look reveals that it frequently questioned some traditional social prescriptions even as it reinforced others.[12] And indeed, although many stories ended with women giving up autonomy and worldly aspirations, female characters often acquiesced to traditional gender ideals only after exploring other possibilities, showing a desire for achievement, challenging the idea of female subordination, and identifying conflicting definitions of womanhood.[13] Underneath the contrived plot lines, lofty language, and conspicuous moralizing, Mormon women's fictional stories suggest how their authors understood the world and their place in it. Although stylistically immature, *YWJ* fiction provided women with a valuable outlet for investigating their particular values and concerns.

"Eve's Curse"

The *YWJ* emerged not only at the same time Mormon leaders embraced fiction as a suitable means for teaching but also during a time when the LDS Church faced attacks on its unique beliefs and place in American society, specifically about polygamy. In 1870, when Utah Territory extended suffrage rights to women, the federal government and national women's leaders expected LDS women to vote themselves out of the purportedly degrading practice of plural marriage.[14] When they did not, reformers and politicians decided to rid the country of this reputed evil themselves. In the early 1880s, Congress passed anti-polygamy legislation, culminating in 1887 with the Edmunds Tucker Act which made polygamy a crime, disincorporated the Mormon Church, and disfranchised the women of Utah. Many LDS women, as believers in their Church and active suffragists, fought the negative stereotypes and used their Church organization, the Relief Society, to show the benefits of their unconventional way of life. They organized mass meetings, signed petitions, and held conferences. Many women, including a number of *YWJ* fiction writers, pleaded with Congress, the U.S. president, and national women's rights leaders to help them retain their right to vote and practice their religion, including its more peculiar parts.[15]

Understandably, national suffrage leaders found it difficult to reconcile Utah women's dual commitments to female rights and a seemingly perverse and patriarchal religion.[16] LDS women often countered that their religion actually provided the basis for feminist beliefs. They explained that "the real elevation of woman" was one of the "prime objects" of those who received the "Gospel light." The establishment of the Relief Society in 1842, they said, represented the "dawning of a new age" for women, which would eventually restore the "natural" equality of the sexes.[17] Susa Young Gates claimed that the founding of the LDS women's organization represented "the earthly beginning of woman's emancipation," and others saw the 1848 Seneca Falls convention as the "temporal" manifestation of the "spiritual" equality their female Relief Society signified.[18] Although nineteenth-century Mormonism retained its patriarchal characteristics, guided by a male hierarchy, women exercised a remarkable degree of authority within the formal women's auxiliary and in the culture at large.

The Relief Society was intended to be a charitable organization, but its members practiced spiritual gifts such as healing the sick through the exercise of priesthood power.[19] Eliza R. Snow, who was a founding member and second president of the organization (a position she, like the male head of the Church, held until her death), claimed that all worthy sisters "not only have the right, but should feel it a duty ... to administer to our sisters in these [priesthood] ordinances, which God has graciously committed to His daughters as well as to His sons."[20] Snow and other women were referred to as "priestesses." Some male leaders called Susa Young Gates the thirteenth apostle, suggesting that her relative status and influence made her comparable to the twelve male apostles who stood, with the president of the Church, at the top of the organization's hierarchy.[21] Although the Church's women's organizations lost much of their autonomy and claim to limited priesthood authority in the twentieth century, early Mormon women defended their religion as liberating and used its principles to form their own distinct brand of feminism.[22]

When LDS women became involved with the national suffrage movement during the 1870s, they readily accepted its expansive ideology for their own woman's rights movement in Utah. Local Relief Societies served as the nucleus of community suffrage associations, and many female Church leaders participated in national and international conferences, became officers in the National American Woman Suffrage Association, and established close friendships with women such as Susan B. Anthony and Anna Howard Shaw.[23]

While Utahns eagerly championed the causes of feminism, their continued defense of polygamy distinguished and estranged them from the national leaders. Many Mormon women linked their feminism directly to plural marriage, saying it provided them with female networks and helped them achieve a degree of independence; it freed some of them from household and child-care obligations, compelled others to become financially independent, and provided a means for limiting family size (plural wives presumably engaged in sex less frequently).[24] But polygamist women often encountered difficulties in trying to articulate, in acceptable nineteenth-century terms, the independence they felt plural marriage gave them. Polygamy rejected Victorian ideals of monogamy, romantic love, and nuclear families—ideals that some *modern* feminists reject but that most nineteenth-century feminists faithfully supported. [25]

Passage of the Edmunds Tucker Act incensed Mormon women. It disrupted families, took away Utah women's right to vote and act as full citizens, and effectively ended a social experiment that some LDS women had come to regard, or at least to defend, as liberating. Although not all Mormons personally accepted the doctrine of plural marriage, and most did not practice polygamy, Church members rallied together to defend their right to this "holy principle" until 1890 when the Church's Manifesto unexpectedly rescinded the practice.[26] The Manifesto surprised and confused some members, and a number of Mormons continued to "live in plurality," but the Church generally struggled to put plural marriage behind it and convince the country that Mormons shared America's basic moral, religious, and political values.

Utah's Scribbling Women

The *YWJ*'s emergence in the late 1880s, with Susa Young Gates as its creator and editor, is not surprising. Gates was among the most outspoken promoters of home literature and was a prolific writer herself. She also defended polygamy and zealously supported women's rights.[27] As the daughter of Mormonism's most famous polygamist, she often had to defend Mormonism to non-Mormon associates. But for Gates and other LDS women, explaining their positions on Church and sex to outsiders was less important than teaching these things to their younger "sisters" in the gospel.

Writing fiction proved to be an attractive way for women to express their thoughts on religion and gender to a new generation. Between 1906 and 1908, for example, twenty different women contributed fiction annually to the *YWJ*.[28] Like Gates, some of them were well-connected to the Church's hierarchy or held Church leadership positions; many were active in the woman's rights movement. The writers, however, did not all fit the same mold; some of them raised large families while others had no children, and the group included university professors and women with little formal education, legislators and homemakers, immigrants and native Utahns, rural women and those who spent time in far-away urban centers like New York City. Some were plural wives, while others were in conventional marriages or unmarried. Despite their varied backgrounds, their shared culture, as well as the time in which they lived, shaped their lives and views. The fiction in the *YWJ* is most striking for what it reveals about its authors' commitments to Mormonism and independent womanhood and for its messages to LDS girls growing up in a time that brought changes to both Mormons and women.

"What Can We Do with Our Girls?"

The *YWJ* emerged at the same time the Church abandoned plural marriage. It was also the time during which women lost the right to vote in Utah, the number of non-Mormons passing through or settling in the territory considerably increased, and Utahns began an earnest campaign for statehood that included a push for woman's suffrage. These issues inform *YWJ* fiction between 1889 and 1896 when Utah became a state.

The fiction during these years explored three main topics: women's equality, polygamy, and LDS doctrines. First, older women wanted to instill in their daughters and younger sisters in the gospel a sense of independence—an understanding of themselves as individuals with the same rights men enjoyed. Second, the writers challenged popular images, especially of polygamous wives, that portrayed Mormon women as degraded slaves. They tried to explain why plural marriage went wrong and to establish it as an honorable legacy both for the Church and for women. Third, they advocated Church doctrines, especially those of special significance to women. Faced with the rising prominence of "the woman question" on the national stage and an influx of non-believers, the *YWJ* affirmed the compatibility of Mormon beliefs with the idea of independent womanhood. Three serialized stories demonstrate how LDS women authors explored these themes.[29]

One *YWJ* story, "The Western Boom" by Ellen Jakeman, centered on a young woman, Mrs. Lawson, who married outside the faith and left Utah.[30] Soon she realized there was a stark contrast between her husband's "standard of the world" and her own.[31] He dressed her elegantly, knowing "that a well dressed and handsome wife was a good advertisement for a business man," but at the same time he refused to help the poor. Mrs. Lawson reminisced about her father, a devoted believer who "had always ... acted as if he were but the steward of his wealth," saying that whatever his family did not need "belonged to the poor."[32] The young woman learned her lesson well (albeit the hard way) that "no girl properly taught in the principles of the Church of Jesus Christ of Latter-day Saints, can ever accept the counterfeits [non-Mormon men] of the world and be satisfied."[33]

LDS women were deeply concerned about teaching young women to value "gospel truths" and recognize the differences between Saints and Gentiles. Increased contact with the outside world undermined Mormon notions of self-sufficiency and retrenchment. More importantly, LDS women feared that the end of polygamy reduced women's chances to wed within the faith, making non-believers more attractive marriage partners. One editorial asked readers to "notice the great preponderance of girls over boys ... then subtract ... the young men who are not as respectable as they might be." The author encouraged girls to choose "honorable" spinsterhood over the "hollow farce" of an ungodly marriage, noting: "Today single women are spoken of respectfully, and marriage is at a discount."[34] Her editorial concluded with, "What an emancipation!"[35]

Articles and stories in the *YWJ* repeatedly counseled young women to reject marriage rather than wed outside the faith and presented singleness in positive terms. The fiction also articulated feminist reassessments of women's choices, roles, and capacities. Jakeman explained that initially Mrs. Lawson hid her unhappiness and sought to make amends when her husband was displeased. The author narrated:

> She was learning to crush back sorrow into her soul, to feed upon the vitality of her youth, that he might not see [her sorrow] and be annoyed, and he congratulated himself, that because he could not see it, that it did not exist; and to deceive her (for her own good) to decide what was good for her, and to take away her womanhood and treat her like a child.[36]

Jakeman's message to young women in this passage was clear: they should not simply sacrifice themselves and try to please their husbands. Moreover, treating a woman as anything less than an autonomous individual defied the very essence of womanhood; to do so, in fact, was to treat them as something altogether different—a child.

Furthering his deceit, and reflecting Jakeman's view of independent womanhood, Mr. Lawson was said to have concealed a letter from his wife's "folks in Utah." When Mrs. Lawson discovered this, she protested that he would not want her to take "the same liberty" with his mail, to which Mr. Lawson responded: "A husband may do many things with perfect propriety that would be very unbecoming a wife."[37] Mrs. Lawson reflected with "trepidation" that he seemed to consider her "absolutely his."[38] Her uneasiness deepened when, for the first time, he called her "Mrs. Lawson."[39] She responded by throwing back her head and giving "way to an irresistible impulse to laugh, and long, loud and ringing came the unnatural sound from the white agonized lips, and Mrs. Lawson fell full length on the floor like one dead."[40] This episode led the maid to declare: "Men are cowards, brutes, hypocrites, deceivers, goats!" and Jakeman to proclaim:

> Oh! the love that men have for women is … often deadly in its selfishness … Men … demand that a woman yield her name and person to the marriage vow … her habits of life, taste in dress and society, principles, religion, and the very teachings that she received at her mother's knee. Before marriage he is a humble slave, afterward, too often a heartless and unconscious tyrant.[41]

Mrs. Lawson again asserted her independence, this time by giving money to a vagrant. After her "simple act of justice," Mrs. Lawson walked "proudly out of the room … without waiting to hear what Mr.

Lawson would say."[42] Although angry, he could not help but "admire what he had been unable to crush out—her truth."[43]

Jakeman and other writers promoted sexual equality, as did a *YWJ* editorial stating that women have "the same rights as man to liberty and equality."[44] An 1890 article suggested that: "In times past, women have ... done many improper things; and one of them is they often preferred men's opinions to their own and even yielded points of conscience. ... A course of self-reliance and self-assertion will restore our credit."[45] In reporting to readers on National Women's Council activities, the *YWJ* maintained, "There is no difference between the intelligent woman and the intelligent man."[46] In an address before the National Woman's Suffrage Convention, reprinted in the *YWJ*, Emily S. Richards declared: "Equal civil and political rights is largely the natural and normal outcome of Utah settlement. ... There has been a constant tendency toward independence, self-culture and self-reliance among women."[47] Mormon fiction urged young women to demand this independence and equality. It also, however, defended plural marriage, a practice that non-Mormons saw as contrary to emergent feminist principles.

The letter that Mr. Lawson withheld from his wife carried news about the "crusade against polygamy" and its author lamented the suffering of families and hypocrisy of those involved in the "inquisition," saying, "If they were morally clean themselves; if they really cared for morality I could believe them sincere."[48] Mrs. Lawson was shocked to find her husband unsympathetic to the situation. She reflected:

> Knowing the cause of [her uncle's] imprisonment, the honor and nobility of his character, the esteem in which he was held by the community ... it had never occurred to her that her husband would look upon him in any other light than a political prisoner, as indeed, most of the honorable men outside of the Mormon Church, and acquainted with surrounding conditions did.[49]

Jakeman suggests that while ignorant outsiders viewed polygamy as "a sort of barbarous slavery," the true source of depravity in the world lay in its double moral standard. "A man's virtue," she asserted, "must be preserved as sacredly inviolate as that of the purest woman."[50] Most

Mormon women did not seem to understand that polygamy in some ways actually sanctified a different sexual standard for men. Instead, like Jakeman, they upheld it as a solution to men's licentiousness, criticized the federal government for enacting legislation that separated family members, and sometimes even justified the actions of those who defied anti-polygamy laws and the Church's rescinding order.[51]

With the Woodruff Manifesto, some LDS women felt they had to defend polygamy both to those outside the Church as well as to young women in the Church who had seen it destroyed—who saw families torn apart and a way of life ridiculed and condemned. One plural wife's child explained:

> After the Manifesto came the hardest time. Up until then people practiced polygamy because of their religion ... they had the consolation that they were doing right. ... The persecution did not matter—but when the Church renounced polygamy all the heroism was gone.[52]

Women like Jakeman worried that the new generation might become disillusioned. Perhaps they were disillusioned themselves by the reversal on plural marriage and needed to legitimize their lives. They asserted that it was not a shameful heritage and that Mormon women still had "advantages over the women of the outside world, given us through the gospel."[53] Fiction writers stressed that, rather than enslave women, polygamy had represented a righteous, liberating principal that non-members and some Mormons misunderstood. Their stories explained that God had revoked the practice because of misapprehension and misapplication, not because of political expediency or theological wavering.

Jakeman and other women took the opportunity to affirm basic Mormon tenets in their fiction. Although women sometimes accompanied their husbands on proselytizing missions, the Church did not specifically invite them to serve as missionaries, or "certify" them as such, prior to 1898.[54] Women were assigned to other types of "mission work." For instance, Brigham Young appointed Louisa Greene Richards to her "calling" as editor of the *Woman's Exponent* as if it were a mission call, and Eliza R. Snow sent Bathsheba W. Smith "on a mission to preach retrenchment all through the South [of Utah] … [and] woman's rights … if she wished."[55] Gates was "set apart" to perform her editorial duties. A later *YWJ* editor felt "as much called of God as any missionary" to do her work.[56] While individual fiction writers did not receive formal callings to write for the *YWJ*, many considered their literary efforts commensurate with missionary work.[57] They were told that as they assisted with "home industries," they were "doing just as much as an Elder who went forth to preach the Gospel."[58] Writing fiction helped build Zion and offered women an opportunity to interpret and teach religious principles.

Throughout "The Western Boom," Jakeman discusses such basic Christian concepts as faith, repentance, and baptism. She also explores more distinctive religious beliefs about social justice. Individuals are portrayed as stewards of worldly assets intended for the common good rather than for individual enrichment, which reflected Mormon ideas about individuals being inseparable from larger kinship networks and the Relief Society's focus on charity. One thinks of paying tithes and fast offerings for the benefit of the poor or about the underlying Law of Consecration, a code that involved sharing community resources according to need—something members considered a "higher law." Jakeman's stories affirm the significance of temples and the LDS belief that righteous families would be reunited after death and live together eternally because of ordinances performed in a temple. In one scene, an old man miraculously saves Mrs. Lawson's child from a fire because the child had "a great work to do for its dead ancestors," and in another place a repentant apostate reveals that in committing adultery he has sinned both against his wife and against God, "inasmuch as I had entered into holy covenants with Him [in the temple]."[59]

Another serialized story with similar themes was Louisa Greene Richards's "Lights and Shades," which contrasted two women, Gwen and Chloe. [60] Gwen, "dear clever girl that she was," began her "married life right" by insisting that her fiancée, Jacob, kneel with her to pray for guidance and meet with the local bishop before taking such an important step.[61] Chloe, on the other hand, hastily wed Edward, a young stranger. When the Church requested both husbands leave home for a few months to help a company of emigrants, Chloe "moaned" and "cried," while Gwen stood firm and told her to "be a woman—be brave."[62]

Gwen embodied Richards's ideal of Mormon womanhood. Prudent, independent, God-centered, and courageous, Gwen also, not incidentally, wanted to know about polygamy. On her own initiative, she approached the bishop's two wives to "inquire ... the secret of the success they were making in a life which she knew ... was difficult to live." The women acknowledged having to learn "one, two, or three little lessons" but claimed they "never had any just cause for jealousy," that with the Lord's Spirit "there can be no difficulty in living in plurality, any more than there is out of it."[63] The first wife further explained: "Some of our people enter into that sacred order without due reflection or preparation and before the Lord has actually revealed it to them; and so they make failures of it."[64] Richards presented polygamy as an ideal that only "worthy" men and women who had prepared themselves, and who were "called" to, could successfully practice. She explicitly linked feminism to polygamy. It was because Gwen was an independent woman that she was drawn to polygamy. She initiated the discussion of the topic and "joyously breathed the covenant" which soon made her "one with them," meaning her husband and his first wife, "forever."[65]

Richards suggested that polygamy created strong female relationships, not immoral men. In her story, the bishop's wives are drawn toward each other and Gwen herself is attracted to polygamous women. The husbands and their feelings have seemingly little to do with the relationships Richards describes. Polygamy empowers rather than enslaves women. Moreover, according to "Lights and Shades," the Manifesto was issued, not because of pressure from outside Utah, but at least partly because some Mormons did not understand and live the practice correctly.

Plural marriage is not the only religious principle Richards discusses. Her stories refer to prayer, faith, obedience, and other more complex Mormon beliefs. One scene depicts Gwen receiving personal revelation. With "her spirit eyes," she saw mothers happily reunited with their children who had died in "baby innocence."[66] Her own son dies a few months later, but Gwen receives comfort as she reflects on this vision.[67] Richards emphasized doctrines which taught that individual women, not just male leaders, received revelations. The idea that women would be reunited in the next life with children who died appealed to women in a period of improving but still high infant and child mortality rates. And while ideas about "family reconstitution" in the afterlife were not unique to nineteenth-century Mormons, LDS Church members believed they possessed exclusive rituals that qualified them to live eternally with their family members.[68]

Susa Young Gates's serial, "Seven Times," also defended polygamy, discussed Mormon beliefs, and upheld visions of female independence. In her story, a "professor" approaches Clara with a marriage offer. He explains that his first wife is "quite willing that I should take this step."[69] Clara "felt a sort of longing to be near his wife … she simply wanted to be near the Professor's wife, almost more than she cared to be near him."[70] Clara, however, went against her own better judgment, listened to her father, who advised her to "put him off," unwisely married a handsome yet irresponsible young man, and consequently found her married life a "disappointment."[71] In this story Gates both affirmed polygamy and suggested that marriage was not always fulfilling, a lesson she knew from personal experience since her own first marriage, which she described as "a most unfortunate one," had ended in divorce.[72]

Gates used the father, Marcus Jones, as an example of those who abused polygamy. He taught his family "that a proposition from a good man who was married, and had proved his virtue and integrity was worthy of a girl's most sincere consideration." He did this, however, with "the personal application in mind"—supporting plural marriage as long as he was the one to get another wife.[73] Clara's weak and corrupt father is countered by the virtuous and strong personality of an old maid, Aunt Ellen, who condemns Jones and admonishes Clara to stand firm in her values.

Another forceful female character in Gates's narrative was Margery, a non-member from Scotland who had moved to Utah to be near her uncle even though she refused to accept the LDS faith. She also refused overtures from Don, an honorable young Mormon, insisting she could not "be had for any man's asking."[74] Don loved Margery, but after wise Aunt Ellen counseled that "the love of a man to woman and woman to man, is not the pivot around which all eternity turns," he determined "not to sell his birthright" by marrying a non-Mormon.[75] When Margery overheard Don's attitude, she plotted revenge by feigning interest in the Church. Convinced of her sincerity, Don asked her to be with him "forever and ever," to which she "proudly and coldly" replied: "Ye'd best seek to your own poor, crazy Mormons for a wife. For I'm never sic' a fool as to sell my womanhood for a mess o' pottage like that."[76] Margery eventually converted, but only after her nephew almost died and her uncle rebuked an evil spirit from her, suggesting that children and family tragedies could help soften a woman but also that strong-willed women were perhaps not entirely to blame for their tenaciousness.[77]

Through the medium of fiction, Gates communicated the need for women to act independently and respect polygamy even if it was abused in practice, to recognize religion as a noble inheritance, and not to base all their aspirations on marriage. She also combined messages about polygamy with other LDS principles. In the deathbed scene, Clara's unworthy husband could not understand her attempts to communicate, while the professor, the would-be polygamist whom Clara had refused, understood her perfectly. "Eternity, love, and mother," she said. "These were her parting messages to him; and he knew that sometime in the great Beyond he should meet and have joy with the soul who had so repented her rash conduct."[78] In the next life, Clara and the professor would be together and raise a family. Because of repentance, the mistakes Clara made on earth would not impede her eternal growth and happiness—a growth and happiness predicated on her embrace of plural marriage.[79]

From 1889 to 1896, Mormon women writers created images of independent womanhood, defended polygamy, and explored religious doctrines in the *YWJ*. As Utah moved toward and gained statehood, the Church tried to make itself more acceptable to the rest of the nation, and fiction in the *YWJ* after 1896 reflected the main-streaming of LDS culture.

The "New Woman in Fiction"

In January 1896, Utah became a state. Once they became politically connected to the United States, Utahns became increasingly connected to the country in cultural ways as well. Mormons struggled to put their aberrant past behind them. Isolationism had failed, and emphasizing the differences between themselves and the rest of the nation had seemed to hurt the LDS cause. Now they argued that polygamy was a "past issue"—once a major theme in *YWJ* stories, it would rarely be broached after Utah became a state.[80] In fact, the journal's fiction would become less about Mormon characters at all and more about ordinary Christian people striving for happiness.[81] Mormon women writers did, however, continue to voice their thoughts on women's equality and autonomy. After 1896, women's issues became the main focus of *YWJ* fiction.

Some have argued that after polygamy was rescinded and Utah was admitted as a suffrage state, women lost their incentive to work for further rights and moved away from a "visible and aggressive political activism" toward an emphasis on a woman's domestic role.[82] It is true that Mormons strove to "transform and improve their relations with the larger American society," but LDS women nevertheless continued to advance feminist ideas. The woman's movement had been mainstream in Utah and was becoming mainstream in the rest of the country. As historians have argued, the national woman's movement lost its cohesiveness after it won suffrage. This did not mean that women were less active. With the ratification of the Nineteenth Amendment, women who were once united in pursuit of a single cause separated into diverse, sometimes competing organizations and causes.[83] Mormons followed a similar pattern, but their shift came earlier when they secured the right to vote in 1896.

Evidence of women's work on behalf of their sex in the years after statehood is not difficult to find in the *YWJ*, as it continued to report on progress toward suffrage in other states, giving detailed accounts of national women's rights meetings, publishing letters from and information about women like Susan B. Anthony, and featuring articles that promoted equal pay and educational opportunities. It featured articles, poems, and stories that encouraged young women to take advantage of equality.[84] A 1902 article, "Some Things Our Girls Should Know," asserted that a woman "who lives by the light of the Gospel of Christ, sees herself, as she is, the equal … of her father, her husband and her son."[85] Other articles celebrated "the wide-awake girl" who sought "opportunities for intellectual growth ... found on every hand."[86] And the *YWJ* published information about "Girls in Our Church Colleges," noting that "young men and young women ... work shoulder to shoulder" in the same classes and that the female student "kept pace with her brother in the more intellectual studies."[87] In 1899, Susa Young Gates encouraged readers to listen to "the message of woman to woman" and to "heed" the call of women who "dare" to bring forth "sweet liberty and independence."[88] LDS women wanted their younger counterparts to recognize their "divine inheritance of perfect equality with man"—something that went beyond political rights.[89] They also promoted feminism in fiction, a 1900 article in the *YWJ* acknowledging the appearance of a "New Woman" in fiction and its author asserting that "we cannot pass her lightly for she was destined to change the ideas of man towards woman and give more strength and confidence in herself."[90]

Perhaps because Mormon fiction generally supported marriage and domesticity, scholars have missed the ways that it encouraged girls to understand their possibilities, gain confidence in themselves, and question their concepts of male-female relations. Even stories that ended "happily-ever-after" with husband and child could, and did, challenge traditional gender ideas and present other options. A close look reveals a connection between women's fiction and support for women's rights during a time of alleged "doldrums" for both LDS women and women nationally.[91]

Between 1896 and 1910, LDS women encouraged participation in a range of endeavors. An 1898 editorial suggested that "everywhere women are awakening from the long sleep of tradition and are determined to work ... with intelligence and apply mental progression to the solving of the old worn monotony of a woman's sphere."[92] Women had secured laws so that in Utah a woman could "engage in business in her own name"; keep her earnings and savings as a "separate estate without any express gift or contract of the husband"; "loan and invest them in her own name"; and "make contracts, sue and be sued in her own name."[93] They could legally enter any profession or occupation except mining, and all of Utah's institutions of higher learning admitted both sexes. Women could vote and hold office.[94] Indeed, in

Utah's first state elections, voters elected women to the state senate, house, and a number of city and county positions—including Ellen Jakeman as treasurer of Utah County.[95] The *YWJ* fiction encouraged girls to take advantage of the rights that had been won. It taught them to view themselves as capable and responsible, not to limit their activities to domestic endeavors.

Lillian Stewart Horsley's 1898 story, "The Duewell Household," featured a character named Jerome, who did not want his wife, Dorothy, to worry about his business failures so he kept them from her. Dorothy exhibited "the greater courage of the two" and found his lack of confidence disappointing. As they discussed plans for the future, Jerome admired the "sound logic of her reasoning" and proclaimed, "I had no idea you were such a wise little business woman." Even after this episode, however, Jerome had trouble learning that "they were one, and that he was not always that one."[96] As he watched Dorothy wisely stretch their meager resources to make their own life comfortable, even helping less fortunate neighbors, Jerome got the message and consulted her with a perplexing business question which she quickly resolved.

In Josephine Spencer's 1903 serial, "Love that Avails," the death of Ruth's parents left her responsible for her younger siblings.[97] As "a brave little woman, intelligent, refined and strong," a woman who refused to be defined as a "plaything and object of pity," Ruth let go of "every prop to which she had held with feminine clinging" and managed the family's affairs with skill and determination.[98] After turning down less respectful suitors, she eventually married a man who treated her as an equal. He was the ideal mate—one who encouraged her and opened "new vistas," including "new political economies," to her "mental vision."[99]

These writers wanted women to take advantage of the "new doors of thought, of progress, and of development for women everywhere."[100] They wished "every woman to wake up from the dull routine of unthinking labor … and to think … wisely and to a purpose."[101] When Luella, in Mary Kelly's 1901 serial, "Luella's Repentance," lost her job as a bookkeeper, she found the "enforced idleness … torture."[102] Josephine Spencer's 1904 serial, "By Natural Selection," featured a "defiant and independent" female protagonist whose beau took "keen pride" in her academic "proficiencies"; "the little triumphs of her superior [school] status had been dear to him as to her."[103] A 1902 story, "The Professor," featured an "exceedingly independent" young woman who excelled in a higher mathematics class and was, if anything, "a little too good," in her male instructor's mind.[104] An 1899 article praised English novelist George Eliot, "who dared defy conventionality and do what she thought right." Emily Calhoun Clowes's 1907 serialized plot, "The Boarding House Lady," likewise celebrated a woman as "free as the winter-wind of any form of conventionality."[105] Articles in the *YWJ* honored Susan B. Anthony and other activists as "heroines" and "Eves" who "pioneered the way" so those of the "second generation ... might be able to come into our divine inheritance of perfect equality with man."[106] The *YWJ* featured fictional local characters who took advantage of the new possibilities others had created for them and who rejected female subordination and incapacity.

An 1899 story by Christine D. Young, conspicuously entitled "Inner Resources," set a scene with "the conditions of happiness": shelves of books, musical instruments, orchards, and fields. But the "three girls that were the favored possessor of all this were evidently not happy," Young wrote. The young women complained of boredom and talked disparagingly about a party their friend Carrie recently hosted—a "confidential evening" that involved "talking about our plans, and dreams, and such nonsense. ... Of course chocolate ... was included" but "never a boy; not the faintest shadow of one." Just as the listless girls declared "there is simply nothing interesting around this old place, it is intolerable," the girls' moods were transformed by the appearance of two young gentlemen.[107]

Young contrasted this scene with a look at Carrie, who was home by herself for the afternoon. Her day was not spent in idle complaint. She walked around the budding trees and made a sketch, then settled down to read a book by one of "those authors that spoke to her deeper self ... and made her feel better and stronger and nearer to the fountain of her soul."[108] Carrie was playing the piano and singing when her mother returned. She did not need men; she had her own interests and dreams.

Josephine Spencer's 1909 story, "The Worth Whiles," made the same point. At first enchanted with parties, theaters, and boys, Ellice soon joined a nursing class and found the work exhilarating. It forced her to "stand on her own resources."[109] Contributors to the *YWJ* wanted young LDS women to realize they had abilities and opportunities for fulfillment that had nothing to do with men. Indeed, some of the fiction left out male characters altogether. Another of Spencer's stories, for example, centered on a poor girl who lived with two older women. The girl grew chrysanthemums, discovered she was a born artist, and made a career of her talent for arranging flowers.[110]

The stories in the *YWJ* suggested that a woman should determine her own direction in life even when it conflicted with the desires of her father, boyfriend, or husband. In her 1907 story, "Requital," Kate Thomas presented Hannah Davis, an unmarried woman who rescued a baby and, because the child's mother died, wanted to care for it. Her ornery father would not hear of it. Who would care for *him?* he wanted to know. Hannah, long "too tame," had her "say out for once" and reproached her father for his ungrateful selfishness. By the time Hannah finished her lecture, her father was "whimpering."[111] Defying him, she became a *single* mother.

Many stories featured similarly spirited characters who rebelled against the men in their lives or took alternative paths to traditional roles. A girl named Inid, in Josephine Spencer's 1899 short serial called "Cross Lines," was sarcastic and strong-willed.[112] In another story, a "kittenish" looking woman in Annie Pike's 1903 "A College Priscilla" is said to have "outwitted" some fraternity boys. Kate Thomas described the "bantering relationship" of a young couple in "The Reconciliation of Dick and Dorothy," published that same year. In Pike's 1904 "David Proposes," we are introduced to a feisty "advancement"-minded young woman, while Lella Marler Hoggan's "The Unwritten Law" tells of a woman who is determined "to live up to the dignity of her womanhood" and "see and know the world" better through a career in art.[113]

Like "Requital," however, these stories often presented an ambiguous message. Most of them ended with engagement scenes. In "Reconciliation," Thomas's main character, Dorothy, refused to take any suitor seriously. When Dick vowed to make Dorothy love him, she "indifferently" replied: "I value your friendship, but I cannot let you rule me."

Dick indeed won her love, but Dorothy continued to resist him. When "she heard the tone of mastery in his voice; she saw the mad exultation in his eyes. He had trapped her! ... His was the victory; hers the humiliation! A great wave of uncontrollable fury swept over her. She lifted her hand and struck him on his smiling mouth!" After this episode, Dorothy moved to California but soon reunited with Dick and resumed her banter with him. She wanted to apologize but was "determined that he should relent." She tried to make herself cry—"Woman's best weapon for all time was tears"—but only started laughing when she realized "the ridiculousness of it." Instead, Dick softened. He loved her but worried that unless he "broke" her, Dorothy's "will" would overpower her affections for him. He made her promise to marry him, insisting that she was "not capable of governing" herself.[114]

In Hoggan's "The Unwritten Law," Alice insists on "change." A "free, independent life" takes her to New York and brings her recognition as an artist. She has an impending marriage to a non-Mormon who will further her career and not tie her down with a home and family. Hoggan makes clear, however, that Alice has been "hypnotized" by the world's brightness, that her "desire to achieve fame and financial success" has caused her to lose "her peace of mind" and "true ideal of womanhood." The story ends with Alice becoming what Hoggan calls a "masterful woman" who returns to "her inmost soul" and "the quiet mountain valley of her home land," including a faithful man who served a mission while Alice had flitted about New York exploring her other options.[115]

The narrator in Annie Pike's "David Proposes" recounts how she came to be engaged. She wants to be taken seriously in her involvement in women's clubs and the freedoms she is accustomed to and at first refuses his proposal. After all, she might like to be a "public lecturer on women's questions" and believes that "a woman ought to have perfect freedom to work out her life as she sees fit." She thinks that if they just remain friends, they will have time for their respective careers. But Pike's story articulates ideas about independence in a mocking tone, which makes the "feminist" narrator out to be rather foolish; she talks about women's rights she doesn't really understand and is unable to decide on a particular career with so many choices available. She then accepts David's proposal after realizing how jealous she would be if he married someone else.[116]

Edyth Ellerbeck's 1903 story, "The Roses of Destiny," features the newly elected president of a woman's club, Kate, who is absorbed in speech writing and other club duties.[117] The male narrator is Kate's boyfriend who feels neglected and declares that he "disliked speech-making women—preferred to see them doing embroidery." Kate's eyes flash at this, and she replies, "If that is what you choose a wife for, I fear you have made a mistake in honoring me." The narrator pretends indifference but later, hopelessly in love, comes crawling back. Kate forgives him and promises she will learn how to embroider. He begs her not to (he hates embroidery) and insists that she "keep on making speeches—but make most of them to me!"[118]

Each of these stories featured strong-willed, independent women who challenged traditional female roles. They all ended with their female characters' surrender to males and marriage. Their capitulations, however, were not unequivocal. In two of these examples the female author spoke through a male narrator, and that narrator was given a number of traditionally female characteristics. Kate's boyfriend became strained under pressure and felt himself "flushing like a girl," and Dick was more emotional than Dorothy, who proved utterly incapable of falling back on traditional female escape routes like crying.[119] In addition, each of these stories portrayed men as being more committed to marriage ideals than women and often described them as the victims of love. In Thomas's and Pike's stories, the female characters, even to the very end, had a hard time taking the idea of romance and marriage seriously, and Hoggan's main character actually surrenders to her "true" self rather than to a man's wishes, and only after exploring other aspects of her nature and attaining success as an artist.

As these *YWJ* stories suggest, women writers confronted a deeper struggle than the one between the sexes. They also struggled with competing visions of themselves. The women's movement challenged traditional relationships between men and women, broadened "the range of choice offered to a girl," and gave her an "intense longing for the same freedom of action that her brothers have."[120] This longing was what one 1897 article described as "the distinguishing characteristic of the new woman."[121] It was a source of conflict as LDS women struggled to reconcile their longings for freedom with a national culture that both exalted motherhood and approved of women's participation in the public realm and with a religion whose first prophet supposedly ushered in the woman's movement but at the same time stressed families and sanctified women's traditional roles.

When Utah became a state, LDS leaders adopted the country's Victorian model of motherhood and began to emphasize a woman's place in the home.[122] Mormons had always honored motherhood, but before the LDS Church began assimilating into mainstream America, they had also discussed a woman's roles outside the domestic sphere. As Mormons moved into the twentieth century, women found that their Church was less willing to promote options beyond the home. As other scholars have noted, their stories conceded that a mother was the "divinest thing known on earth."[123] These women articulated the difficulties they and other Mormon women faced in denying themselves opportunities to pursue less traditional roles—roles they had fought for and celebrated. They wanted to fulfill the Church's ideal but could not deny that they "hungered for more."[124] Fiction writers showed their young counterparts the range of women's possibilities but also let them know those possibilities could be a source of conflict for women who recognized their individual potential and belonged to a religious community that idealized domestic motherhood.

Like many of the stories described above, *YWJ* editorials generally defined the longing women experienced as worldly ambition and warned young women about the dangers of seeking fame over home. A 1908 article explained:

> The idea now among the young people, it seems to me, is to draw away from home. The thought of home-making and devotion to home seems to be farther from their minds than ever before. ... I do not want to discourage any improvement along any line, but it should not be to the disadvantage of the home. The home must be the center and foundation of all.[125]

Dismissing "longings" as material or social aspiration, and setting young women's often unarticulated desires in direct opposition to home life, made clear the choices committed young women needed to make. But Mormon girls often confronted more complex messages than they had been told to expect, and their choices did not always fit neatly into simplistic and mutually exclusive categories. They were encouraged to be self-reliant and develop their talents; told to "get all the education possible and all the culture"; warned that they needed to cultivate "other interests, other sympathies to round out [their] character," and counseled to "grasp the idea of their possibilities." At the same time, they were advised that "there can be no higher ambition for a girl than to do well her part in the home."[126] Articles about Church schools, for instance, celebrated the equal academic opportunities LDS female students enjoyed, then added that "interwoven with this great co-educational chain, there exists a smaller one, designed for the girl's guidance in her own special sphere and office—that of the home and of motherhood."[127] In the *YWJ*, stories like "The Professor" upheld women's rights and excellence in academic pursuits, but the professor resolved to give his accomplished female pupil an A only after she skipped an examination to help a lost child.[128] At the same time, the *YWJ* taught that "there is no mental height to which a woman may not climb" and insisted on a woman's right to the franchise, "to demand an equal standard of life and morality." Women had "the right of choice," meaning the freedom to act without a man's permission. Still, there was no greater mission than motherhood. In "the beautiful future … woman will choose to be a woman and womanly"; "knowing the heights and the depths of a woman's possibilities, she will choose to be a fond wife, a loving mother, and a true woman."[129]

Such directives were likely to cause what social scientists would later identify as "role strain"—a tension "felt by educated women, reared to be wives and mothers but educated to be independent thinkers."[130] In *YWJ* fiction the tension between the ideal of home and family and the desire to leave traditional roles behind was acute. The stories upheld the model of wife and motherhood but also illustrated women's alternatives and acknowledged the difficulties LDS women faced in choosing conventional paths. Even fiction belittling the "new woman" presented girls with different ways of seeing themselves and the personal struggles involved with following the Church's prescription for "true" women. The frequency with which writers explored the contradictions between expanding opportunities on the one hand and traditional roles on the other hand indicates how much the younger generation was, or seemed to be, torn by the conflicting messages and range of options before them.

In Minnie Moore Brown's 1901 story, "Her Life-Work," the main character, Madge, asked a question: "Mamma, what can I do to be useful in this world—really and truly useful, I mean?" Her mother told her she could set the table, but then seriously replied: "Don't you know that every day at home you are doing more good things for us than we can count?" This failed to satisfy Madge. As she grew up, she kept asking the same question. She taught a kindergarten class but still "could not suppress a growing want at her heart—a feeling of emptiness and vague longing which grew every hour." Then came Allen Stuart who won her heart. They married. "Very happy now," Madge "almost forgot the little aching void," but soon enough the "old ache" returned and she wondered what was wrong with her. Her mother said to "wait awhile and maybe that want will be completely filled." Sure enough, the last scene of the story showed Madge with baby in arms, exclaiming: "I have found it at last. … What I have longed for all the time was the blessedness of motherhood."[131]

In Josephine Spencer's 1908 story, "The 'New' Woman," Janet lived according to the popular reform motto, "the greatest good to the greatest number." "President of a half dozen prominent clubs now, and past president of as many more … no woman in town had had the number of public honors accorded her." Her current project was an orphanage. She and her husband did not have children of their own because this would keep them from fulfilling her Progressive-era mantra. Then a tiny orphan "pining away for mother love" changed her outlook. As Janet held the "pitiful" infant, she felt "all the mother feeling, long dormant, starved, suppressed, surging in her heart." When she brought the baby home, her husband was overjoyed. He had evidently experienced something of the "mother feeling" already. His wife found herself turned into a "new woman … the old-fashioned kind," as Spencer put it.[132]

Kate Thomas wrote of longings in her 1901 story, "The Gobbles and Others, Principally Others." In her story, a woman named Minnie opted to cancel her wedding and pursue other options. When her fiancé, Brig, protested, she complained that men "don't understand." She exclaimed:

> I hate this place! I can't breathe here! I'm stagnating. … I used to think I'd run away, but I was too much of a coward. Then you came. It all changed. … But it didn't last. … The old longings came back. I tried to kill them, indeed I did. But they won't be still … I want light and laughter and music. I want my turn at the bright things. It has always been peg away, peg away, peg away. Oh … you don't know how hard it is to be a girl! … We want freedom. … It is awful to be tied down and to long and long and long.

Brig tried to console her. He told her of his dreams for their life together, but Minnie replied that "it sounds very lovely. But it wouldn't be that way." She was not to be dissuaded. Brig asked her to be "sensible"—to not "let this mad freak spoil our lives"—and Minnie said if she married him, she would end up hating him, so Brig finally let go. But by the end of the story, Minnie was back—nothing else seemed to satisfy her.

In their own way, these stories upheld traditional women's roles. Brown and Spencer glorified motherhood, while Thomas showed that "there's nothing in all the world like love." These writers also insisted, as Madge explained to her mother, that women "must still have something more"; Mormon women writers expressed the tension women felt in a culture that encouraged independent womanhood and sexual equality at the same time it idealized traditional dependent roles.[133]

"In Larger Perspective"[134]

Fiction writers for the *YWJ* presented characters who grew up longing to make a difference in the world, who were ambitious and aware of their possibilities. But eventually the characters in the stories relinquished their independent lives—the fame and success they found—for marriage and motherhood. It is just that they, and the writers who created them, did not silently acquiesce to traditional roles.[135] LDS women fiction writers voiced an "undefined longing for something better" that they and other women tried to reconcile with a religion that increasingly allowed only one true option for women.[136] Susa Young Gates once described herself as "one of the most dissatisfied members of my sex."[137] It seems fitting that the journal she created would become an outlet for Mormon women to proclaim: "How hard it is to be a girl! … We want freedom."[138]

Notes

1. *Woman's Exponent,* Sept. 1, 1889, 55. On Susa Young Gates, see Estelle Neff Caldwell, "Susa Young Gates," in *The History of the Young Ladies' Mutual Improvement Association of the Church of Jesus Christ of Latter-Day Saints from November 1869 to June 1910,* Susa Young Gates, ed. (Salt Lake City: General Board of the YLMIA, 1911): 121-26; Paul Cracroft, "Susa Young Gates: Her Life and Literary Work," M.A. thesis, University of Utah, 1951; Kenneth W. Godfrey, Audrey M. Godfrey, and Jill Mulvey Derr, *Women's Voices: An Untold History of the Latter-day Saints, 1830-1900* (Salt Lake City: Deseret Book Company, 1982): 325-37; Carolyn W. D. Person, "Susa Young Gates," in *Mormon Sisters: Women in Early Utah,* Claudia L. Bushman, ed. (Cambridge, MA: Emmeline Press, 1976): 199-223. In its initial years, the *YWJ* reached from 1,500-2,000 young women annually, but it had nearly 15,000 subscribers by 1910 (Gates, *History of YLMIA,* 112). In addition, those who had subscriptions shared their copies with others. Early issues had articles for young mothers, which of course future mothers also read.

2. See Carol Cornwall Madsen, "'Remember the Women of Zion:' A Study of the Editorial Content of the *Woman's Exponent,* A Mormon Woman's Journal," MA thesis, University of Utah, 1977; Sherilyn Cox Bennion, "The *Woman's Exponent:* Forty-two Years of Speaking for Woman," *Utah Historical Quarterly* 44 (Summer 1976): 222-39; Carol Lynn Pearson, *The Flight and the Nest* (Salt Lake City: Bookcraft, 1975).

3. Scholars have used both journals to illustrate Mormon feminism. See Carol Cornwall Madsen, "Emmeline B. Wells: Am I Not a Woman and a Sister," *BYU Studies* 22 (Spring 1982): 161-78.

4. *Young Woman's Journal,* Apr. 1890, 235.

5. George Q. Cannon, "Editorial Thoughts," *Juvenile Instructor,* Oct. 15, 1884, 312. The assault on fiction was part of a larger evangelical renunciation of the genre in both the United States and Britain. On this broad anti-fiction movement, see, e.g., Richard Altick, *The English Common Reader: A Social History of the Mass Reading Public, 1800-1900* (Chicago: University of Chicago

Press, 1957); and Mark Knight and Thomas Woodman, eds., *Biblical Religion and the Novel, 1700-2000* (Burlington, VT: Ashgate Publishing, 2006). Both the Godbeite and Christian Science movements advocated literary endeavors in Utah. The Godbeites, a group of apostate Mormons, started a literary magazine, and the Christian Scientists opened reading rooms in Utah. On the Godbeites, see Grant H. Palmer, "The Godbeite Movement: A Dissent Against Temporal Control," M.A. thesis, Brigham Young University, 1968; Ronald Walker, "The Commencement of the Godbeite Protest: Another View," *Utah Historical Quarterly* 42 (Summer 1974): 217-31; Ronald Walker, "The Godbeite Protest in the Making of Modern Utah," Ph.D. diss., University of Utah, 1977; Ronald Walker, *Wayward Saints: The Godbeites and Brigham Young* (Urbana and Chicago: University of Illinois Press, 1998).

6. Cannon, "Editorial Thoughts," 312.

7. Nephi Anderson, "A Plea for Fiction," *Improvement Era,* Jan. 1893, 186-88; B. H. Roberts, "Legitimate Fiction," *Contributor,* Feb. 1889, 135-36.

8. On Mormon economic self-reliance, see Leonard J. Arrington, *Great Basin Kingdom: An Economic History of the Latter-day Saints, 1830-1900* (Lincoln and London: University of Nebraska Press, 1958).

9. Women published fiction in all three Mormon youth periodicals, while independently publishing their own novels and short stories.

10. Susa Young Gates, *The Life Story of Brigham Young* (London: Jarrolds Publishers, 1930): 206.

11. See Matthew Durrant and Neal E. Lambert, "From Foe to Friend: The Mormon Embrace of Fiction," *Utah Historical Quarterly* 19 (Fall 1982): 325-39; Edward A. Geary, "Women Regionalists of Mormon Country," *Kate Chopin Newsletter,* fall 1976, 20-28.

12. See Barbara Bardes and Susan Gossett, *Declarations of Independence: Women and Political Power in Nineteenth-century American Fiction* (New Brunswick, NJ: Rutgers University Press, 1990), 10, 4; Mary Kelly, "Sentimentalists: Promise and Betrayal in the Home," *Fiction by American Women,* Winifred Farrant Bevilacqua, ed. (Port Washington, NY: Associated Faculty Press, 1983), 11-19; Joyce W. Warren, ed., *The (Other) American Traditions: Nineteenth-century Women Writers* (New Brunswick, NJ: Rutgers University Press, 1993); Nina Baym, *Feminism and American Literary History* (New Brunswick, NJ: Rutgers University Press, 1992); Nina Baym, *Novel, Readers and Reviewers: Responses to Fiction in Antebellum America* (Ithaca: Cornell University Press, 1984), 172.

13. See Susan Harris, "'But is it any good?' Evaluating Nineteenth-century American Women's Fiction," in *The (Other) American Traditions,* 265-71; Kelly, "Sentimentalists."

14. Before Congress instituted a territorial government in Utah, women held the franchise in civic matters between 1847 and 1852. They could also

vote on ecclesiastical matters under the Mormon doctrine of common consent, introduced by Joseph Smith three months after the Church's formation.

15. There is an extensive literature on Mormon women and the suffrage movement. In addition to works previously cited, see Thomas G. Alexander, "An Experiment in Progressive Legislation: The Granting of Woman Suffrage in Utah in 1870," *Utah Historical Quarterly* 38 (1970): 20-30; Lisa Bryner Bohman, "A Fresh Perspective: The Woman Suffrage Associations of Beaver and Farmington, Utah," *Utah Historical Quarterly* 59 (Winter 1991): 4-21; Jill C. Mulvay, "Eliza R. Snow and the Woman Question," *BYU Studies* 16 (Winter 1976): 250-64; Leon C. Thurgood, "An Analysis of the Rhetoric Used by Mormon Women to Argue Equal Suffrage in Utah, 1870-1896," M.A. thesis, University of Utah, 1973; Lola Van Wagenen, "In Their Own Behalf: The Politicization of Mormon Women and the 1870 Franchise," *Dialogue: A Journal of Mormon Thought* 24 (Winter 1991): 31-43; Jean Bickmore White, "Woman's Place Is in the Constitution: The Struggle for Equal Rights in Utah in 1895," *Utah Historical Quarterly* 42 (Fall 1974): 344-69.

16. This essay draws on a vast scholarship about the Mormon brand of feminism that blended Progressive ideas about women and allegiance to patriarchal religion. In addition to works previously cited, see Davis Bitton, "Polygamy Defended: One Side of a Nineteenth-Century Polemic," in *The Ritualization of Mormon History and Other Essays,* Davis Bitton, ed. (Urbana: University of Illinois Press, 1994); Judith Rasmussen Dushku, "Feminists," in *Mormon Sisters,* 194-95; Lawrence Foster, "From Frontier Activism to Neo-Victorian Domesticity: Mormon Women in the Nineteenth and Twentieth Centuries," *Journal of Mormon History* 6 (1979): 3-21; Joan Smyth Iversen, "A Debate on the American Home: The Antipolygamy Controversy, 1880-1890," *Journal of the History of Sexuality* 1 (April 1991): 585-602; Joan Iversen, "The Mormon-Suffrage Relationship: Personal and Political Quandaries," *Frontiers: A Journal of Women Studies* 11 (1990): 8-16; Joan Iversen, "Feminist Implications of Mormon Polygamy," *Feminist Studies* 10 (Fall 1984): 505-22; Anne Firor Scott, "Mormon Women, Other Women: Paradoxes and Challenges," *Journal of Mormon History* 13 (1986-1987): 3-19; Lola Van Wagenen, "Sister Wives and Suffragists: Polygamy and the Politics of Woman Suffrage, 1870-1896," M.A. thesis, New York University, 1991.

17. "Eve's Curse: Is it Never to Be Removed?" *Woman's Exponent,* July 1, 1875, 22. See Maureen Ursenbach Beecher and Lavina Fielding Anderson, eds., *Sisters in Spirit: Mormon Women in Historical and Cultural Perspective* (Urbana and Chicago: University of Illinois Press, 1987); Maxine Hanks, ed., *Women and Authority: Re-emerging Mormon Feminism* (Salt Lake City: Signature Books, 1992); Madsen, "Emmeline B. Wells," 171-73.

18. See Maureen Ursenbach Beecher, "The Leading Sisters: A Female Hierarchy in Nineteenth-Century Mormon Society," *Journal of Mormon History* 9 (1982): 25-39; Susa Young Gates, "The Open Door for Women," *YWJ,* Mar. 1905, 119; Louisa Greene Richards, *Woman's Exponent,* Jan. 1900 [1901], 69.

Most statements connecting the Relief Society and the women's movement were made after 1870, perhaps because only after this date were LDS women required to articulate their feminist views to non-Mormons.

19. Spiritual gifts later became the province of male priesthood holders. See Linda King Newell, "Gifts of the Spirit: Women's Share," in *Sisters in Spirit,* 111-50; Linda King Newell, "A Gift Given a Gift Taken: Washing, Anointing and Blessing the Sick among Mormon Women," *Sunstone,* Sept.-Oct. 1981, 16-25.

20. Eliza R. Snow, *Woman's Exponent,* Sept. 15, 1884, 61.

21. The Mormon church was (and is) headed by a prophet and twelve apostles, all male.

22. Many of the works previously cited in this essay explore Mormon women's loss of autonomy in their personal lives and Church structure during the twentieth century. There seems to be a connection between the Progressive-era drive to build an efficient and bureaucratic state and the major restructuring of the Mormon Church, which is what took away much of this female autonomy. See also Claudia L. Bushman, "Mystics and Healers," in *Mormon Sisters,* 1-23; Carol Cornwall Madsen, "Mormon Women and the Temple: Toward a New Understanding," in *Sisters in Spirit,* 80-110.

23. Works previously cited in this section document some of the personal and public interaction between Mormon women and women's rights advocates nationally.

24. See Carroll Smith-Rosenberg, "The Female World of Love and Ritual: Relations between Women in Nineteenth-Century America," *Signs: Journal of Women in Culture and Society* 1 (1975): 1-29; Maureen Ursenbach Beecher, "Sisters, Sister Wives, Sisters in the Faith: Support Systems among Nineteenth-Century Mormon Women," manuscript in the LDS Church Archives; Stephanie Smith Goodson, "Plural Wives," in *Mormon Sisters,* 89-111.

25. See Joan Iverson, "Feminist Implications of Mormon Polygamy," 505-22; Judith Rasmussen Dushku, "Feminists,"194-95.

26. See Bitton, "Polygamy Defended," 34-53; Nancy Tate Dredge, "Victims of the Conflict," in *Mormon Sisters,* 133-55; David J. Whittaker, "Early Mormon Polygamy Defenses in Early Mormon Pamphleteering," Ph.D. diss., Brigham Young University, 1982, 321-66.

27. While she advocated women's suffrage and feminist ideas before her editorship, Gates became one of Utah's foremost activists in the 1890s, speaking at national and international women's conferences, serving as press secretary for the National Woman Suffrage Association, and keeping a personal correspondence with Susan B. Anthony, Charlotte Perkins Gilman, and Anna Howard Shaw.

28. This figure does not include an average of two authors each year whose initials or pseudonym are unidentifiable. Eight women in 1906-1907 contrib-

uted two or more stories each (serialized installments counting as one story), as did three women in 1908. Five women had fiction in the magazine all three years and four women contributed twice, with an average of seven additional contributors each year. In earlier years the fiction is not listed separately in the contents and writers were less likely to sign their work, making it harder to categorize them. For 1899 and 1901, ten different fiction writers can be identified, and the figure for 1903 is sixteen.

29. Fiction during these years usually took the form of long-running serials or short sketches. The short pieces are sometimes hard to classify as fiction and I have not used them to represent the period even though they contain the same three themes.

30. Jakeman was a member of the Woman's Press Club, president of the Sanpete Country Suffrage Association, and a plural wife.

31. Ellen Jakeman, "The Western Boom," *YWJ*, Nov. 1890, 55.

32. Ibid.

33. Jakeman, "Western Boom," Mar. 1891, 252.

34. "Our Girls," *YWJ*, July 1891, 477. As this quote suggests, a similar reassessment of spinsterhood took place in American culture generally, partly as a result of the Civil War.

35. Census figures show that in 1890 and 1900, over 50 per cent of Utah's population was male. Statistics do not reveal, however, the proportion of "worthy" men to women, nor can they dismiss perceived threats. See Robert P. Porter and Carroll David Wright, *Compendium of the Eleventh Census* (Washington, D.C.: Government Printing Office, 1892-97), lxxviii; "Population General Report and Analysis," *Thirteenth Census of the United States* (Washington, D.C.: Government Printing Office, 1914), 1:270.

36. Jakeman, "Western Boom," Nov. 1890, 56.

37. Ibid., Dec. 1890, 106-7.

38. Ibid.

39. Ibid., Jan. 1891, 154.

40. Ibid., 155.

41. Ibid., 159.

42. Ibid., Mar. 1891, 255.

43. Ibid.

44. *YWJ*, Mar. 1890, 175.

45. Santiago [James H. Martineau], "Woman's Power," *YWJ*, Aug. 1890, 406.

46. "The National Women's Council," *YWJ*, Apr. 1891, 317.

47. Emily S. Richards, "Woman's Suffrage in Utah," an address delivered

before the National Woman's Suffrage Convention, Washington, D.C., Jan. 27, 1896, in *Collected Discourses*, comp. and ed. Brian H. Stuy, 5 vols. (Salt Lake City: BHS Publishing, 1987-1992), 4:419.

48. Jakeman, "Western Boom," Jan. 1891, 154.

49. Ibid., June 1891, 405.

50. There were exceptions, including Emma Smith, Joseph Smith's first wife, who "saw the new system as perpetuating rather than eliminating a double standard of moral conduct for men and women" (Jill Mulvay Derr, "'Strength in Our Union:' The Making of Mormon Sisterhood" in *Sisters in Spirit*, 161.

51. Delia Fish, "Words of Encouragement," *YWJ*, Apr. 1890, 227.

52. Kimball Young, *Isn't One Wife Enough?* (Westport, CT: Greenwood Press, 1970), 439.

53. Fish, "Words of Encouragement," 227.

54. Missionary work carried a degree of honor and prestige. Men who had served as missionaries were considered worthy of a woman's attentions and the respect of the community. It was a source of status that initially women only had access to through marriage or by accompanying a spouse on a mission. See Hanks, "Sister Missionaries and Authority," in *Women and Authority*, 315-34.

55. Ibid., 318.

56. Susa Young Gates, *History of the Young Ladies' Mutual Improvement Association* (Salt Lake City: Deseret News, 1911), 115.

57. One volume of the *YWJ* was sent gratis to Mormon missionaries, ca. 1900 (ibid, 114).

58. Qtd. in Derr, "Strength in Our Union," 174.

59. Jakeman, "Western Boom," July 1891, 451; June 1891, 405. Mormons who married in the temple made covenants to their spouse and to God.

60. Richards was the first editor of the *Woman's Exponent*, a member of the Woman's Press Club, and a plural wife.

61. Lulu Greene Richards, "Lights and Shades," *YWJ*, Oct. 1890, 13; Nov. 1890, 49.

62. Ibid., Dec. 1890, 113.

63. Ibid., Jan. 1891, 172, 174.

64. Ibid., Feb. 1891, 210.

65. Ibid., Sept. 1891, 539. Jill Mulvay Derr explains that plural marriage ceremonies "often included the first wife in a significant way" ("Strength in Our Union," 168).

66. Richards, "Lights and Shades," Dec. 1890, 116.

67. Mormons believed they could receive personal revelation from God and that children who died before reaching eight years of age would not be punished for their sins and would receive the highest degree of salvation.

68. Scholars have increasingly explored nineteenth-century ideas about childhood death, including its relationship to "family reconstitution" in the afterlife. See, e.g., Craig Thompson Friend, "Little Eva's Last Breath: Childhood Death and Parental Mourning in 'Our Family, White and Black,'" in *Family Values in the Old South,* Craig Thompson Friend and Anya Jabour, eds. (Tallahassee: University Press of Florida, 2009).

69. Homespun [Susa Young Gates], "Seven Times," *YWJ*, Dec. 1893, 118.

70. Ibid., 119. Jill Mulvay Derr asserts that "the Mormon practice of plural marriage ideologically sanctified" social relationships between women ("Strength in Our Union," 168).

71. Gates, "Seven Times," Jan. 1894, 185, 465.

72. Caldwell, "Susa Young Gates," 38.

73. Gates, "Seven Times," Jan. 1894, 184.

74. Ibid., Mar. 1894, 338.

75. Ibid., Feb. 1894, 242; Mar. 1894, 338. Gates, as was common, used the biblical image of Esau trading his birthright to his younger brother Jacob to represent the idea of marrying outside the Church.

76. Ibid., May 1894, 369.

77. Scholars such as Elizabeth Reis have noted that women have sometimes been able to act outside the confines of appropriate gendered behavior based on supernatural influences (Reis, *Damned Women: Sinners and Witches in Puritan New England* [Ithaca: Cornell University Press, 1997]).

78. Gates, "Seven Times," July 1894, 468.

79. This scene explored Mormon beliefs about the resurrection and eternal progression. Given Gates's first experience with marriage, this scene seems especially significant.

80. Out of seventy published stories (counting serialized episodes as one story) between 1898 and 1910, only one discussed polygamy. Almost all of the stories from the earlier period defended it.

81. "The Recent Triennial in Washington," *YWJ,* May, 1899, 207. Of seventy stories, only five (none of them serialized) were fundamentally Mormon. This does not mean, however, that authors did not talk about Utah, some aspect of Mormonism, or "the elect," although some did not. Susa Young Gates continued to write distinctly LDS stories.

82. See Foster, "Frontier Activism," 3-21; qtd. from Van Wagenen, "In Their Own Behalf," 32.

83. See Nancy F. Cott, *The Grounding of Modern Feminism* (New Haven: Yale University Press, 1987).

84. After their 1896 victory, Utah women considered themselves the vanguard of women's rights and took an authoritarian position on the subject.

85. "Some Things Our Girls Should Know," *YWJ*, Mar. 1902, 286-87.

86. "In the Realm of Girlhood: Lesson 1," *YWJ*, Sept. 1905, 447.

87. "Girls in Our Church Colleges," *YWJ*, Oct. 1900, 443-44.

88. Susa Young Gates, "With the Editor," *YWJ*, May 1899, 240.

89. Ibid.

90. Annie Pike, "The Influence of Fiction on Education," *YWJ*, Nov. 1900, 492.

91. See Eleanor Flexner, *Century of Struggle: The Woman's Rights Movement in the United States* (Cambridge, MA: Belknap of Harvard University Press, 1959); Foster, "Frontier Activism," 3-21. The fiction in the *YWJ* supports Maureen Ursenbach Beecher's contention that Mormon women "interpreted the doctrines and set the behavioral standards for their sisters ... discovered worthy causes and organized effective social programs ... made alliances and identified enemies" (Beecher, "Leading Sisters," 27).

92. "With the Editor," *YWJ*, Apr. 1898, 190.

93. Elizabeth Cady Stanton, Susan B. Anthony, Matilda Joslyn Gage, and Ida Husted Harper, eds., *The History of Woman Suffrage*, 6 vols. (New York: Fowler & Wells, 1881-1922), 4:951.

94. Ibid., 956.

95. Ibid., 953.

96. Lillian Stewert Horsely, "The Duewell Household," *YWJ*, Jan. 1898, 21-23.

97. On Josephine Spencer, see Kylie Neilson Turley, "The Life and Literature of Josephine Spencer," M.A. thesis, Brigham Young University, 1995; Rebecca de Schweinitz, "Josephine Spencer, Mormon Writer, Woman Writer," unpublished ms.

98. Josephine Spencer, "Love That Avails," *YWJ*, Mar. 1903, 119-20; Apr. 1903, 166.

99. Ibid, 170.

100. "With the Editor," *YWJ*, July 1898, 334.

101. Ibid., 335.

102. Mary F. Kelly, "Luella's Repentance," *YWJ*, Mar. 1901, 118.

103. Josephine Spencer, "By Natural Selection," *YWJ*, Oct. 1904, 447; Sept. 1904, 406.

104. Bethany, "The Professor," *YWJ*, Apr. 1902, 147.

105. Alice Louise Reynolds, "George Eliot's Religious Life," *YWJ*, Mar. 1899, 108; Emily Calhoun Clowes, "The Boarding House Lady," *YWJ*, June 1907, 254.

106. "With the Editor," *YWJ*, May 1890, 239.

107. Christine D. Young, "Inner Resources," *YWJ*, June 1899, 251-52.

108. Ibid., 253.

109. Josephine Spencer, "The Worth Whiles," *YWJ*, Apr. 1909, 168.

110. Josephine Spencer, "A Corner in Chrysanthemums," *YWJ*, Apr. 1902, 159.

111. Kate Thomas, "Requital," *YWJ*, Dec. 1907, 533, 536. On Thomas, see the Kate Thomas Collection, Utah State Historical Society, Salt Lake City. Some scholars have suggested that Thomas was lesbian. See, e.g., D. Michael Quinn, *Same Sex Dynamics among Nineteenth-Century Americans: A Mormon Example* (Chicago: University of Illinois Press, 1996).

112. Josephine Spencer, "Cross Lines," *YWJ*, Aug. 1899, 348-54; Sept. 1899, 395-99.

113. Annie Pike, "A College Priscilla," *YWJ*, Mar. 1903, 112-14; Kate Thomas, "The Reconciliation of Dick and Dorothy," *YWJ*, Dec. 1903, 548-53; Annie Pike, "David Proposes," *YWJ*, Feb. 1904, 74-77; Lella Marler Hoggan, "The Unwritten Law," *YWJ*, Jan. 1907, 17. Pike [later Greenwood] graduated from Brigham Young Academy and went on to publish in *The Nation* and *Atlantic Monthly*, as well as an autobiography.

114. Thomas, "Reconciliation," 549-53.

115. Hoggan, "The Unwritten Law," 16-19.

116. Pike, "David Proposes," 74-77.

117. Ellerbeck was the first wife of polygamist Charles Read and a member of the Utah State Legislature.

118. Edyth Ellerbeck, "The Roses of Destiny," *YWJ*, Nov. 1903, 498, 501.

119. Ibid.

120. "Ethical Studies: Fame vs. Home," *YWJ*, Sept. 1908, 544; Clara Nuttal, *YWJ*, Feb. 1897, 280.

121. Nuttal, *YWJ*, Feb. 1897, 281.

122. See Derr, "Strength in Our Union"; Linda P. Wilcox, "The Mormon Concept of a Mother in Heaven," in *Sisters in Spirit*, 64-77.

123. Christine D. Young. "In Larger Perspective," *YWJ*, Dec. 1899, 563-67; Nov. 1899, 507-13.

124. Ibid.

125. Augusta W. Grant, "The Ideal Home," *YWJ*, Aug. 1908, 380.

126. Ibid., 381.

127. "Girls in Our Church Colleges," 443.

128. Bethany, "Professor," 147-49.

129. "Some Things Our Girls Should Know: Woman," *YWJ*, July 1902, 287-88.

130. Rosalind Rosenberg, *Beyond Separate Spheres: Intellectual Roots of Modern Feminism* (Yale University Press: New Haven and London, 1982), 144.

131. Minnie Moore Brown, "Her Life Work," *YWJ*, Oct. 1901, 459, 461-62. Perhaps significantly the story ends with this scene, leaving no time for the longings to return as they had before.

132. Josephine Spencer, "The 'New' Woman," *YWJ*, Nov. 1908, 559, 602, 604.

133. Kate Thomas, "The Gobbles and Others, Principally Others," *YWJ*, Nov. 1901, 499-501; Brown, "Her Life Work," 459.

134. This was the title of a previously cited story by Christine Young.

135. Hoggan, "Unwritten Law," 16-19.

136. Young, "Larger Perspective," 511. In an era that saw the decline of women's autonomy and authority within the Mormon Church, fiction remained one of the only ways to express discontent. The *YWJ* was part of an "informal undercurrent" that "interrupted the formal [male power] system," as discussed by Beecher in "Leading Sisters." See also Jill Mulvay Derr and Brooklyn Derr, "Outside the Mormon Hierarchy: Alternative Aspects of Institutional Power," *Dialogue: A Journal of Mormon Thought* 15 (Winter 1982): 21-43.

137. Qtd. in the Register of the Susa Young Gates Collection, Utah State Historical Society, Salt Lake City, 2.

138. Thomas, "Gobbles and Others," 500.

Edward W. Tullidge and *The Women of Mormondom*

Claudia L. Bushman

In this paper, I sing the virtues of Edward W. Tullidge, English convert to the Church of Jesus Christ of Latter-day Saints, cultural enthusiast, and serious journalist and author. Tullidge, who was mercurial, changeable, and emotionally and perhaps mentally unstable, wrote despite his difficulties, turning out five long books, editing several periodicals, and contributing significant essays to others. Diligent and optimistic, he was a victim of his broad aspirations, falling short of what he might have done. Able, hard-working, and articulate, he was also a heavy drinker, given to emotional outbursts. Much of his work has been dismissed or ignored, valued primarily for the large chunks of undigested biographical material he included. I want to take him seriously.

Tullidge wore his heart on his sleeve, serving his current grand ideal, whatever it was. He had troubled relationships with the LDS Church, the RLDS Church, and the Godbeite movement. He yearned to be a devoted follower and to promote the virtues of an institution but could not stick; disillusioned, he moved on to more promising venues. He wanted the Church of Jesus Christ of Latter-day Saints to be part of something grand, to shine in a universal context. Historians label him a "rebel historian." Ronald Walker explains Tullidge as one who wanted Mormonism to be a "distinctive form of American culture."[1]

Tullidge was born in England in 1829 into a cultured, middle-class, Methodist family, then apprenticed to his cousin as a coach builder and painter. At the age of seventeen, he joined the Latter-day Saints. In 1848, at age twenty, he began twelve years of missionary activity in Great Britain without "purse or scrip," making money by mending shoes.[2] He wrote for the *Millennial Star,* published in Liverpool, where he exhibited considerable literary promise as well as mystical enthusiasm. He dramatically offered his services to Brigham Young to assist in developing culture and in writing an epic history for the Church. He foresaw a Mormon *Iliad* or *Paradise Lost,* with Young as the central hero. Tullidge envisioned "a truly national or Mormon literature, national education of every kind, national music, painting, and every branch of art." He wanted the church to rank in the "first class of civilized society" and for Zion to move toward greatness,[3] a vision which many of us in the humanities and social sciences like to promote today. He wrote to Brigham Young, "I shall never rest until I am in your hands, nor be satisfied until I am engaged in your service."[4] Young, more inclined toward action than talk, gave him limited encouragement.

Tullidge and Elias L. T. Harrison began the first of several periodicals in 1864. Tullidge wrote descriptive pieces on Mormon topics for Eastern periodicals, the *New York Galaxy* and the *American Phrenologist,* which were considered impartial and sophisticated. He was the first writer to bridge the gap between inside and outside views of the Church, a synthesis to which many LDS authors still aspire. Tullidge hoped his articles would inform the world, but Brigham Young told him not to expect too much, just to do his best and leave the result with the Lord.[5] Tullidge then wrote editorials for a new publication, favoring spiritual life and power, international brotherhood, and a call for Mormonism to grow and to assist in civilizing the world.

His friends Elias Harrison and William Godbe, disillusioned with the autocratic Brigham Young, moved toward Mormon reform and then into spiritualism. They were excommunicated for apostasy. Tullidge resigned his own membership in their support. He wrote a number of plays before reconciling with the LDS Church and writing a life of Brigham Young. He also wrote *The Women of Mormondom,*[6] this paper's subject, and *Life of Joseph the Prophet* before allying with the RLDS

Church, which bought an interest in the latter work. He served a mission for the RLDS Church, preaching against "polygamic theocracy" in Utah, but he soon left that group. He later wrote a *History of Salt Lake City and Its Founders,* which includes extensive historical and biographical material.[7] Although he projected a multi-volume series, it was never completed.[8]

Edward Tullidge married three times. His first two polygamous, childless marriages ended in divorce. His third marriage produced ten children. He died at 65 in 1894.

Quixotic, mercurial, self-destructive, Tullidge often discarded positions he had once profoundly claimed. He remained true to some Mormon ideals even as he warred with the Church. In a characteristically dramatic statement, he noted how hard he was working, "fighting with my characters and themes through the battles" to draw meaning from "their eventful trying lives." He threw himself "into brain fever or delirium for three weeks," barely escaping with his life. "I have, however, my will and nerve again and can execute my work as well as ever. In one thing at least I am a Mormon—I am hard to kill."[9] He was a cultural Mormon who preferred the pristine religion of Joseph Smith to the evolving frontier autocracy of Brigham Young.[10]

Now I would like to consider Tullidge's *Women of Mormondom,* a large book with 550 pages of text, a chronology from before Eve to the 1870s, with an international scope. What have historians said of this book? William Frank Lye, who taught at Ricks College and wrote an article on Tullidge in 1960, said little except that the book showers praise on Eliza R. Snow, a kindred poetic spirit.[11]

Ronald Walker, who wrote extensively of Tullidge and his Godbeite friends in *Wayward Saints,* dismisses *Women of Mormondom* as disjointed autobiographies of "prominent Mormon women tied loosely together by his epic prose." He notes that Tullidge wrote the book to kill Fanny Stenhouse's negative view of Mormon polygamy in *Tell It All,*[12] "not because she wars against her polygamic life with [her husband Thomas B. H.] Stenhouse, which is natural," Tullidge wrote, "nor against Brigham Young, which is also very natural with us Apostates, but because she has blasphemed against her sisters and the religious system that I have worshiped."[13] Tullidge, then, will favor the sisters and the system. Tullidge, Walker says, adorned the women with a "peculiar prose" and found them "collectively without a flaw." Walker notes that the book's exaggerated language, awkward syntax, and repeated exclamations fail to sustain a narrative, epic history.[14]

Davis Bitton and Leonard Arrington note that the book's defensive nature makes it panegyric, overwritten, and of patchwork organization. They find its greatest contributions are in its original histories. They do say, however, that Tullidge stood alone as a Mormon feminist historian before the revitalization of the women's movement in the 1970s.[15]

Such have been the dismissive evaluations of this man and his large book. One might wonder what the hard-lined Sister Snow thought of the boozy, changeable, apostate enthusiast. In fact, her attitudes toward him were also changeable.

Snow was involved in the *Women of Mormondom* from the beginning. She put her considerable prestige behind the book and was engaged in gathering funds for publication on subscription. The *Woman's Exponent* reports a meeting of the Senior and Junior Retrenchment societies where Miss Snow "laid the subject of the Woman's Book" before the group and "solicited [the sisters' aid] in behalf of the publishing of it." She also requested that "any special items in their lives, or spiritual manifestations which had been given them which they considered strong testimonies upon the principles of the gospel," be recorded and given to her or Mr. Tullidge.[16] The *Woman's Exponent* frequently spoke in favor of Tullidge as "one of the most gifted literary men of America." Tullidge returned the compliment. "There is a providence in the very attitude of Mormon women," he wrote in the *Exponent*. "The prophesy is distinctly pronounced in the whole history of their lives, that they shall be apostolic to the age."[17]

A letter from Snow to an unnamed correspondent documents her editorial and financial efforts on behalf of the book. "I wish you would get up some interesting items immediately," she writes. She is looking for "the testimonies of the sisters how they have lived polygamy—whether their hearts have been broken by it—whether they were forced into it &c." She notes that the author will "dress it up in his own style." She urges haste in sending the material, "(which will be good for your grand children to read) do not wait a day."[18] Tullidge himself noted that Utah women would be of interest to the general public and asked the Relief Society to choose which women should be engraved to illustrate the volume.[19] Clearly, Snow, Tullidge, and the Relief Society were collaborating closely, hoping to reap propagandistic and pecuniary benefits.

Yet in 1878, three years after soliciting her sisters, and a year after publication of the volume, Snow was carefully distancing herself from Tullidge. He had acknowledged her help in revising his Joseph Smith biography, assistance which she denied having offered. Where he had presented the manuscript for her perusal and she had suggested a few alterations to the biographical narrative, she loftily refused to be seen as a formal reviewer or critic. Neither she nor Joseph F. Smith cared to assist Tullidge in throwing "an air of Church authority around his work."[20]

The Women of Mormondom is shrouded in changing opinions, even as the author was perennially changing his own views. Yet it is still in print and is worthy, I decided, of another look. It provides real plums of quoted personal accounts which are undigested and under-synthesized, held together by a heroic dough. No need to recount the gems among the autobiographical plums. We all know the value of preserving accounts which the women might not have otherwise written and that might well have been lost. Instead, picking through the epic prose, the overwritten panegyric, the wild enthusiasm, the overwrought style, I sought for some sense of Tullidge's overall plan and explication, his ideas for illuminating the early sisters and their time. I wanted to see beyond his eccentricity as he speaks from his world to ours. I wanted to find what the book holds, apart from Tullidge's dramatically vacillating reputation.

Let us discuss three of Tullidge's general strategies. First, as I mentioned before, he wrote for audiences inside and outside the Church, on both sides of the abyss. He was not appreciated for that, being too sympathetic for the outsiders and too cool for the insiders. This is the problematic stance facing any Mormon writer. In 1875 when Tullidge was in New York City engaged in publishing his *Life of Brigham Young*,[21] he was described in the newspapers as "a man of talent and ability" who was "under the spiritual control of Joseph Smith."[22] He was too close to Mormonism to be considered reliable.

Yet the *Millennial Star* took him to task for his outsider ways. The *Star* dismissed his accounts of the lives of Brigham Young and Joseph Smith and *The Women of Mormondom* as lacking in authority. The *Star* proclaimed that all books dealing with doctrine, ordinances, and history should be issued under official Church authority. In the book on Young, Tullidge had written in the preface, "I have been, for many years, an apostate, and cannot be justly charged with a spirit of Mormon propagandism."[23] He assured President John Taylor, who called him on the statement, that he was not really an apostate, that the statement had been removed from the latest edition, and that he supposed it had only been included "with the expectation that it would make the book sell better in the East." President Taylor summed up, "Then, when in the East, you are an apostate, because it is expected your book will sell better, and here you are a Saint, because to be a Saint pays better."[24] Tullidge repudiated the remark, but the exchange frames an important issue for writers who are Mormons and tell the Mormon story. Writing for both audiences is a daunting effort, one for which we may well be dismissed by those on both sides of the gulf. However, I think we should all aspire to this position. Mormons must move beyond writing for ourselves to writing for a wider audience, as Tullidge attempted to do.

Second, Tullidge places Mormons in history and sees their saga within a long line of human activities. Mormons are often seen as an aberration, not part of the American story, or the grand human sweep, or anything significant. He puts the Church and individuals within it on a continuum. Church members are "the sons and daughters of the Pilgrim sires and mothers who founded this nation; sons and daughters of the patriots who fought the battles of independence and won for these United States a transcendent destiny." The pioneers descend from seventeenth-century Europeans who themselves had been pioneering for 250 years. The Huntington girls, Zina and Presendia, he delightedly tells us, are the grand-nieces of Samuel Huntington, signer of the Declaration of Independence, governor of Connecticut, and president of the Continental Congress. Lorenzo Snow's wife Harriet was born of *Mayflower* descendants. All this is tedious and repetitious, except for Tullidge's aim in making the Mormon story the pioneering story, a tale of repeated exile. Mormons are the worthy descendants of Pilgrim fathers and mothers.[25] He ennobles Mormon women as the natural successors to their honored American predecessors.

Third, Tullidge places the Latter-day Saints in literature, in a sense, through the genre of the romance. He notes that "the divine romance of the sisterhood best opens at Kirtland." He later says, "Presently we shall see that the romance of Mormonism has centred [sic] around the sisters abroad as well as at home."[26] This interesting phrase, "the romance of Mormonism," reframes the story, usually told as devotion, bravery, and sacrifice. A romance, according to the *American College Dictionary,* is "a tale depicting heroic or marvelous achievements, colorful events or scenes, chivalrous devotion, unusual, even supernatural, experiences or other matters of a kind to appeal to the imagination."[27] Tullidge writes this stylized story with its allegories of good and evil as a heroic, colorful, supernatural account. He shows interaction between humans and immortals, adventures with heroes and demons, elevating women to the status of magical creatures. Women are attuned and mystical, more sensitive and effective than the men and are the first to see the possibilities of great spiritual work in their age. This romantic view casts a bright light on women. Summing up these preliminary strategies, we see that Tullidge writes for a wide audience, puts Mormonism into history, and tells it literarily.

This female story, paralleling and intersecting the traditional male authoritarian story, makes the women's world and sisterhood, with the family consisting of mother and children, at the center rather than periphery of Mormon society. His purpose is to counter Fannie Stenhouse's blasphemy against her sisters, but he takes her on obliquely rather than directly.

Tullidge continually asserts the mystical aspects of the female adherents to the faith, who are more spiritually attuned than the men, according to *Women of Mormondom.* This familiar idea, given lip service today, did not originate with Tullidge; but let us consider his analysis. He sets up the mystical, spiritual world of Mormon women by noting that many people in Smith's time received the administration of angels. "Thousands both in America and Great Britain" recorded visions and intuitions, he explains. They had manifestations in which they foresaw elders bringing them the gospel. Mary Ann Whitney heard the voice of an angel from a cloud (45). Tullidge establishes the signs that follow the believers, such as reading a revelation from a medium's hands where "letters of light and letters of gold" appear on the medium's hands (56-57).

Not content to make women equal receivers of spiritual gifts, Tullidge makes them superior. The best receivers, he tells us, are among the sisters. "In modern spiritual parlance," they were more "inspirational." The sisters have always been the "best mediums." Tullidge further notes that the "gift of tongues" has been markedly the woman's gift (55-57, 475).

Tullidge's style was to make grand generalizations and illustrate them with homely examples. He says of the Kirtland temple that the apostles and elders laid the stone foundations, built up the arches, and put on the capstone. "But it was woman that did the 'inner work of the temple.'" What is this inner work? The women sewed the veils of the temple. He moves to "Joseph's instinctive appreciation of woman and her mission. Her place was *inside* the temple, and he was about to put her there" (76). When he generalizes, he does so in extravagant style:

> Once again woman had become an oracle of a new dispensation and a new civilization. She can only properly be this when a temple economy comes round in the unfolding of the ages. She can only be a legitimate oracle *in* the temple.
>
> When she dares to play the oracle, without her divine mission and anointing, she is accounted in society as a witch, a fortune-teller, a medium, who divines for hire and sells the gift of the invisibles for money.
>
> But in the temple woman is a sacred and sublime oracle. She is prophetess and a high priestess. Inside the temple she cannot but be as near the invisibles as man—nearer indeed, from her finer nature, inside the mystic veil, the emblems of which she has worked upon with her own hands.[28]

The temple interprets and protects woman. Her strong powers, which would be ridiculed in the greater world, are suited for the sanctuary. There she is not only at home, but she is also superior. Her great gifts not only predispose her for finer work, they make her unsuited for ordinary life. In a temple, she "is the medium of Jehovah" (78).

Through Eliza R. Snow, Tullidge tells of fast-and-testimony meetings in the Kirtland temple the first Thursday of each month. Spiritual gifts poured out of the women, especially the healing touch and tongues. On fast days, according to Snow, the veils which intersected at right angles divided the house into four parts. Each section had a leader to be watchful "lest a spirit of enthusiasm should creep in." At 4 p.m., the veils were drawn up and the congregations joined together, after which people could "speak or sing in tongues, prophesy, pray, interpret tongues, exhort or preach" for an hour as they wished (100-01). The united faith brought the saints into closer fellowship, but Snow noted the presence and the dangers of two powers, good and evil, and that when using the good power people were more open to its opposite.

Because of these two powers, the manifestations became known as "fire that could burn as well as bless." Fearing a confrontation between the two great forces, the Saints began to shy away from visions, angels, prophecy, and "speaking in tongues." Consequently, the sisters, who ever are the "best mediums" of spiritual gifts in the Church, were shorn of their glory (58). The danger of the opposing forces explains the loss of, or at least the hiding of, female spiritual power.

If the spiritual gifts sound foreign and distant, Tullidge's argument that Mormon women were Hebraic is equally difficult. But all things work together for Tullidge. Kirtland, he says, "is the place where this Israelitish drama of our times commenced its first distinguishing scenes,—the place where the first Mormon temple was built." The restoration was of the Old Testament gospel, much more than the New, is what Tullidge detects. Woman had been central and valued in old days, he suggests, and after she had fallen in the eyes of other religions, Joseph Smith restored her place. Woman, according to Tullidge, "was among the morning stars, when they sang together for joy, at the laying of the foundations of the earth." "The Mormon prophet rectified the divine drama," he goes on to say. "Man is nowhere where woman is not. Mormonism has restored woman to her pinnacle" (26, 177).

Eliza R. Snow was "deeply interested in the study of the ancient prophets," he notes, calling her "a prophetess in her very nature" (63):

> Her gifts are of race quality rather than of mere religious training or growth. They have come down to her from the ages. From her personal race indications, as well as from the whole tenor and mission of her life, she would readily be pronounced to be of Hebrew origin. One might very well fancy her to be a descendant of David himself; indeed the Prophet Joseph, in blessing her, pronounced her to be a daughter of Judah's royal house.[29]

This extravagant praise for the New England spinster, converted from Alexander Campbell's Disciples of Christ, sounds odd indeed. What is Tullidge getting at?

He equates Sidney Rigdon with a "voice crying in the wilderness, prepare ye the way of the Lord!" He says that Joseph is the sign of "Messiah's coming," that he came in "the spirit and power of Elijah" to "restore the covenant to Israel" (36). Tullidge rewrites Mormon history in the style of the Old Testament. He makes Mormonism part of a long religious story, a retelling of the Hebraic story of God working with his people.

He envisions a "Latter-day Israel." "The women," he says, did their full half in founding Mormondom. They comprehended, "as much as did their prototypes who came up out of Egypt, the significance of the name of Israel." "Out of Egypt the seed of promise, [came] to become a peculiar people, a holy nation, with a distinctive God and a distinctive destiny." "A Mormon *Iliad* in every view; and the sisters understanding it fully. Indeed perhaps they have best understood it." "Mormondom is no Christian sect, but an Israelitish nationality," he intones. "All America is the world's New Jerusalem!" (68, 71, 75). Mormon Israel acts out the Hebrew drama: Abraham leaves his father's house, heading to a promised land where he will found a great nation. In thee, Abraham is told, shall all families of the earth be blessed.

Tullidge's direction thus becomes clear. He sees Mormons, the spiritual sons and daughters of Abraham and Sarah, gathering to fulfill the familial promise. "A host of the daughters of New England—earnest and purest of women—many of them unmarried, and most of them in the bloom of womanhood—gathered to the virgin West to become the mothers of a nation" (73). They would then begin patriarchal marriage. So in the end, the book justifies polygamy. Why was I surprised, I wonder? I should have seen it coming.

Tullidge concedes that a woman's lot is difficult. "Comprehend this Hebraic religion of the sisters, and it can thus be comprehended somewhat how they have borne the cross of polygamy, with more than the courage of martyrs at the stake" (185). Yet plural marriage nonetheless exalts women in Israel, he says. After Bathsheba married George Albert Smith in 1841, they visited his family for a feast. John Smith, the groom's father, drank a toast to the newlyweds, "pronouncing the blessings of Abraham, Isaac and Jacob upon [them]." "I did not understand the import of this blessing as well then as I do now," the bride noted (155).

Tullidge comments that Anglo Saxons, the last race anyone would expect to embrace plural marriage, had reestablished it. "Hence, they have lifted it to a plane that, perhaps, no other race could have done—above mere sexual considerations, and, in its theories, altogether incompatible with the serfdom of women." He quotes Eliza R. Snow's curious defense of the practice at the mass meeting of 1870. She abjures the idea that Mormon women are slaves. The women of the Church have "performed and suffered what could never have been borne and accomplished by slaves" (379, 391).

Tullidge asserts that Israelitish Mormondom fully understands "the Abrahamic subject," while gentile Christendom never has. He sees Mormons closer to the ancient patriarchs than to Nephi and Mormon, whose civilization is now extinct. He notes that Snow, "a prophetess and high priestess of Hebraic Mormondom," traveled to Jerusalem and stood on the Mount of Olives, raising her "inspired voice to swell the divine command for Israel to gather" (480-81).

The idea then, that Mormonism is Hebraic, a restoration of the culture of the Hebrew Bible, has according to Tullidge confirmed the necessity of accepting plural marriage, a practice not very successful originally. This model caused women to accept, even welcome, sacrifice they could never have been forced to bear and the promise of numerous offspring and familial blessings.

A final idea is Tullidge's creation of a female theology. He names a "holy female trinity" of Eve, Sarah, and Zion—mothers in Israel at different times in history. Motherhood is the Mormon woman's everlasting theme. Eve is the Mother of a world, Sarah the mother of the covenant, and Zion a group name for polygamous wives who are the mothers of celestial sons and daughters. Eve is the first. God commanded Eve to be fruitful: "Thus opened creation, and the womb of everlasting motherhood throbbed with divine ecstacy." Tullidge credits Eve for breaking one commandment to fulfill another. The Mormon daughters of Eve must break the rules to "magnify the divine office of motherhood" (197-200). A Mormon woman is like Eve in the Creation and Fall and like Sarah in the covenant.

Sarah, the Old Testament wife of Abraham, incarnates the "very soul of patriarchal marriage," who gave her husband another wife in order to fulfill his covenant with the Lord. Tullidge emphasizes the extent of Sarah's sacrifice and the pain of both Sarah and Hagar. Yet Tullidge also reminds us that races and empires came of them. "From the courts above[,] the Mormon woman shall look down upon an endless posterity" (532, 535-36).

Zion personifies the woman of Tullidge's time. In his most mystical and opaque language, he expatiates on scriptures, concluding that each Mormon woman can be Zion if she is obedient. Then "Creation begins again! Zion—the New Jerusalem—is the Lamb's bride. She is the coming Eve" (546-47). As he places the Mormon story in history, so he also places the polygamous woman into the continuum of biblical history. He justifies Mormondom's strange marital practices by showing the progression from Eve and Sarah.

What then can we say about this mostly forgotten book? Tullidge, writing to make some money and defend the early Church, casts a bright light on the women of the 1870s. He sees them as potent, powerful creatures, willing to suffer for their beliefs. His defensive aim raises polygamy, this most criticized practice, to the central Church tenet. As a response to Stenhouse, his polygamy theme is transcendent. Yet men are left out entirely; this is a woman's choice. "The women of Mormondom, and the marriage question! Two of the greatest sensations of the age united!" "Marriage is the great question of the age. It is the woman's special subject," he noted in 1877 (496). How can Christendom hold the Bible divine and infallible, he asks, yet not follow it? "The Mormons and the Bible," he asserts, "stand or fall together" (497).

Because of the close collaboration with Eliza Snow, there can be no question that the spin Tullidge gave the topic is exactly the story the LDS women wanted told. Snow, who worked extensively on the manuscript, did see herself as an Hebraic high priestess. The Relief Society women told their stories to illustrate their devotion to the principles they lived. If Tullidge edited their work, as he was bound to do, he did not change their meanings. He was writing to please the sisters.

He promised them rewards: They would be redeemed from Eve's curse, he said. They would no longer bring forth their children in sorrow, nor would their husbands rule over them. "Woman will be redeemed from that curse, as sure as the coming of to-morrow's sun. No more, after this generation, shall civilized man rule over his mate, but 'they twain shall be one;' and the sisters are looking for that millennial day" (506).

Reading this book brings back whiffs of the nineteenth century, the flavors of a Mormon woman's lot: her oppression, her sacrifice, her obedience, her glorification. Better than any of his contemporaries, Tullidge brings Mormon women to life, puts them into history, and connects them to a past. He recreates the mystical and magical world of Utah's early female Zion, a world we frequently prefer to forget. Revisiting it does not mean that we have to relive it. For all his eccentricities and vacillations, Tullidge was a man of vision who still has something to say to us.

Notes

1. William Frank Lye, "Edward Wheelock Tullidge, the Mormons' Rebel Historian," *Utah Historical Quarterly* 28 (Jan. 1960): 56-75. Ronald W. Walker, "Edward Tullidge: Historian of the Mormon Commonwealth," *Journal of Mormon History* 3 (1976): 55.

2. Davis Bitton and Leonard J, Arrington, "Edward W. Tullidge: Celebrant of Mormon Nationalism," in *Mormons and Their Historians* (Salt Lake City:

University of Utah Press, 1988), 29-31. However, in "Edward Tullidge," Walker credits him with sixteen years of missionary activity rather than twelve.

3. Bitton and Arrington, *Mormons and Their Historians,* 31-32.

4. Walker, "Edward Tullidge," 58.

5. Bitton and Arrington, *Mormons and Their Historians,* 32-34.

6. Edward W. Tullidge, *The Women of Mormondom* (New York: Tullidge and Crandall, 1877).

7. Edward W. Tullidge, *History of Salt Lake City and Its Founders* (Salt Lake City: Star Printing Company, 1886).

8. Bitton and Arrington, *Mormons and Their Historians,* 34-40.

9. Edward W. Tullidge to B[athsheba] W[alker] S[mith], Jan. 18, 1875, Tullidge Name File, Historian's Office, LDS Church Archives, Salt Lake City.

10. Lye, "Edward Wheelock Tullidge," 72.

11. Ibid., 66.

12. Mrs. T. B. H. Stenhouse, *Tell It All: The Story of a Life's Experience in Mormonism: An Autobiography* (Hartford, CT: A. D. Worthington, 1874).

13. Walker, "Edward Tullidge," 65-66; Ronald Walker, *Wayward Saints: The Godbeites and Brigham Young* (Urbana: University of Illinois Press, 1998), 309-10.

14. Walker, "Edward Tullidge," 69.

15. Bitton and Arrington, *Mormons and Their Historians,* 37.

16. *Woman's Exponent,* Nov. 11, 1876.

17. Ibid., Jan. 1, 1878, 119; Aug. 15, 1877, 45.

18. E. R. Snow letter, n.d., Peterson family Papers, ca. 1844-1957, MS 2175, 37290, ARCH-88, LDS Church Archives, Salt Lake City, 2-3.

19. Tullidge to Smith, Jan. 18, 1875.

20. Eliza R. Snow letter, Oct. 7, 1878, published in the *Millennial Star,* Nov. 18, 1878.

21. Edward W. Tullidge, *Life of Brigham Young: or, Utah and Her Founders* (New York: 1876).

22. *Woman's Exponent,* Aug. 15, 1875), 45.

23. Tullidge, *Life of Brigham Young,* preface.

24. *Millennial Star,* Nov. 18, 1878.

25. Tullidge, *Women of Mormondom,* 27, 201-34, 438.

26. Ibid., 26, 215.

27. *The American College Dictionary,* 10th ed., 1956, s.v. "romance."

28. Tullidge, *Women of Mormondom,* 76-77.

29. Ibid., 31-32.

About the Contributors

Gary James Bergera is managing director in Salt Lake City of the Smith-Pettit Foundation, which sponsors historical research; former managing editor of *Dialogue: A Journal of Mormon Thought*; and former senior editor of Signature Books. He has authored or edited eight volumes, including *The Autobiography of B. H. Roberts* and *On Desert Trails with Everett Ruess*. He received a Best Article Award from the Mormon History Association for "The Orson Pratt-Brigham Young Controversies: Conflict within the Quorums." He currently serves as an MHA board member. His article, "Buckeye's Laments: Two Early Insider Exposés of Mormon Polygamy," appeared in the *Journal of the Illinois State Historical Society* in winter 2003.

Matthew Bowman received his Ph.D. from Georgetown University in 2011 when he was a Charlotte A. Newcombe Dissertation Fellow. He has received the Mormon History Association Award for Best Graduate Paper three years in a row, 2008-2010. He has published in *Fides et Historia*, the *Journal of the Early Republic*, *Religion and American Culture: A Journal of Interpretation*, and *Novo Religio*, as well as in two anthologies, *American Religious Responses to Kristallnacht* and *Between Pulpit and Pew: Mormon Encounters with the Paranormal*. "A Mormon Bigfoot: David Patten's Cain and the Conception of Evil in LDS Folklore" appeared in the *Journal of Mormon History* in fall 2007.

Martha Bradley-Evans is Associate Vice President for Academic Affairs and Dean of Undergraduate Studies at the University of Utah. She has been an Assistant Professor of History at Brigham Young University, Associate Professor of Architectural History at the University of Utah, and until recently Dean of the Honors College at the University of Utah. She is a past editor of *Dialogue: A Journal of Mormon Thought*. Of her six books, *Four Zinas: A Story of Mothers and Daughters on the Mormon Frontier* received the highest awards from both the Utah Historical Society and Mormon History Association. She is a member of the Utah State Board of History and a Utah Heritage Foundation board member. "Building Community: The Fundamentalist Mormon Concept of Space" appeared in *Communal Societies* in 2001 (vol. 21).

Newell G. Bringhurst is a retired Professor of History and Political Science, College of the Sequoias, and past president of both the Mormon History Association and John Whitmer Historical Association. He has written or edited nine books, including *Fawn McKay Brodie: A Biographer's Life*, which won the Mormon History Association Best Biography Award, and *The Mormon Quest for the Presidency*, which received a John Whitmer Historical Society Best Book Award. "The Private versus Public David O. McKay: Profile of a Complex Personality" appeared in the fall 1998 issue of *Dialogue: A Journal of Mormon Thought*.

Samuel M. Brown is Assistant Professor of Pulmonary and Critical Care Medicine and Division Associate in Medical Ethics and Humanities at the University of Utah School of Medicine. He has published in *Church History: Studies in Christianity and Culture*, the *Journal of the Early Republic*, and various Mormon studies journals. He is the translator of *Son of Man*, a work by Russian theologian Aleksandr Men, and author of the forthcoming book, *In Heaven as It Is on Earth: Joseph Smith and the Early Mormon Conquest of Death*. "The Translator and the Ghostwriter: Joseph Smith and William W. Phelps" (Mormon History Association Best Article Award) appeared in the *Journal of Mormon History* in winter 2008.

Claudia L. Bushman is an adjunct professor in the Mormon Studies Program at Claremont Graduate University, formerly Professor of American Studies at Columbia University and director of the Delaware Heritage Commission. She is a co-founder of the LDS-oriented magazine *Exponent II* and author of eleven books, including *In Old Virginia: Slavery, Farming, and Society in the Journal of John Walker*. The Mormon History Association has honored her with its highest prize, the Leonard

J. Arrington Award for "distinguished and meritorious service to Mormon history." "Edward W. Tullidge and *The Women of Mormondom*" appeared in *Dialogue: A Journal of Mormon Thought* in winter 2000.

Brian Q. Cannon is Professor of History and director of the Charles Redd Center for Western Studies at Brigham Young University. He is the author of *Remaking the Agrarian Dream: New Deal Rural Resettlement in the Mountain West* and *Reopening the Frontier: Homesteading in the Modern West,* editor of *Utah in the Twentieth Century,* and a contributor to several anthologies and encyclopedias. He has served as associate editor of *Agricultural History* and *BYU Studies*. He has won awards from the Agricultural History Society, Mormon History Association, and Western History Association. "Scandalous Films: The Campaign to Suppress Anti-Mormon Motion Pictures, 1911-1912" appeared in the *Journal of Mormon History* in fall 2003.

Douglas J. Davies is Professor in the Study of Religion and director of the Centre for Death and Life Studies at Durham University, England. He holds the higher D.Litt. degree from Oxford University and Honorary Doctor of Theology degree from Uppsala University. The author of twenty books, including *Joseph Smith, Jesus, and Satanic Opposition: Atonement, Evil, and the Mormon Vision* (2010), he also edited the *Encyclopedia of Cremation*. He has chaired the Religion Group of the British Sociological Association and is currently president of the British Association for the Study of Religion. He was elected to the Academy of Social Sciences in the U.K. in 2009. His article "Mormon Studies in a European Setting" appeared as his guest editor's preface to *Dialogue: A Journal of Mormon Thought* in fall/winter 2001.

Kathleen Flake is Associate Professor of American Religious History at Vanderbilt Divinity School. She is the author of *The Politics of American Religious Identity: The Seating of Senator Reed Smoot, Mormon Apostle,* which received a Mormon History Association Best Book Award. She is a contributor to two anthologies and author of several topical essays in three encyclopedias. She has published in *Biography: An Interdisciplinary Quarterly, Church History, Dialogue: A Journal of Mormon Thought, Journal of Religion, Journal of Ritual Studies, New Mexico Historical Review,* and *Religion and American Culture.* "Re-placing Memory: Latter-day Saint Use of Historical Monuments and Narrative in the

Early Twentieth Century" appeared in *Religion and American Culture* in winter 2003.

Lawrence Foster is Professor of American History at Georgia Tech in Atlanta. He has published widely in American social and religious history and served as president of the Communal Studies Association and the Mormon History Association, although he is not himself a Mormon. The first of his three books, *Religion and Sexuality* (Best Book Award, Mormon History Association), presents a comparative analysis of the celibate Shakers, "free love" Oneida Community, and polygamous Mormons in nineteenth-century America. "Sex and Prophetic Power: A Comparison of John Humphrey Noyes, Founder of the Oneida Community, with Joseph Smith Jr., the Mormon Prophet" appeared in *Dialogue: A Journal of Mormon Thought* in winter 1998.

Reinhold R. Hill is Dean of the College of Arts and Sciences at Governors State University in University Park, Illinois, south of Chicago, and until recently Associate Professor of Languages and Literature and Acting Dean of Arts and Sciences at Ferris State University in Michigan. He is active in the American Folklore Society and Modern Language Association. In 2004 he was a Fulbright Senior Lecturer at the University of Debrecen in Hungary. "God's Chosen People: Mormon Representations of the Jewish Other in Holocaust Literature" appeared in *Clio: A Journal of Literature, History, and the Philosophy of History* in January 2002.

Jacob W. Olmstead is a Ph.D. candidate at Texas Christian University in Fort Worth, Texas. He has published in *BYU Studies*, *Journal of Mormon History*, *Mormon Historical Studies* ("From Pentecost to Administration: A Reappraisal of the History of the Hosanna Shout"), and *Utah Historical Quarterly*. He is also a contributor to the *Encyclopedia of the Early Republic & Antebellum America* and to *Mormonism: A Historical Encyclopedia*. He has presented papers at the Mormon History Association meetings. "Scandalous Films: The Campaign to Suppress Anti-Mormon Motion Pictures, 1911-1912" appeared in the *Journal of Mormon History* in fall 2003.

Rebecca de Schweinitz is Assistant Professor of History at Brigham Young University and an executive committee member of the Society for the History of Children and Youth. She received her Ph.D. from the University of Virginia in 2004 (runner-up for the Southern Historical Association dissertation award). She is the author of *If We Could Change the World: Young People and America's Long Struggle for Racial Equality* and articles in professional journals. "Preaching the Gospel of Church and Sex: Mormon Women's Fiction in the *Young Woman's Journal*, 1889-1910" appeared in *Dialogue: A Journal of Mormon Thought* in winter 2000.

Jonathan A. Stapley is chief technology officer for DFI Corp., a biotechnical company that industrializes natural sweeteners. In his discipline, he has published in *Carbohydrate Research, Cereal Chemistry,* and elsewhere. In Mormon studies he has published in *Brigham Young University Studies* and the *Journal of Mormon History.* He is a regular contributor to the popular *By Common Consent* blog. "The Forms and the Power: The Development of Mormon Ritual Healing to 1847" appeared in the *Journal of Mormon History* in July 2009.

Brian H. Stuy is the owner of Research-China, an organization that provides parents with background information about their adopted children and works for ethical reform in Chinese adoptions. In LDS circles he is best known for his *Collected Discourses*, a five-volume sequel to the *Journal of Discourses* that makes available sermons delivered between 1886 and 1898. Many of these so-called lost sermons were written during the time that Church leaders were in hiding because of polygamy. Stuy has published other research in *Adoption Today, Dialogue: A Journal of Mormon Thought, Journal of Mormon History*, and *Sunstone* magazine. "Wilford Woodruff's Vision of the Signers of the Declaration of Independence" appeared in the *Journal of Mormon History* in spring 2000.

Stephen C. Taysom is Assistant Professor of Religious Studies at Cleveland State University and author of the new book, *Shakers, Mormons, and Religious Worlds: Conflicting Visions, Contested Boundaries.* He has contributed to the *Encyclopedia of Religious Revivals in America, Mormonism: A Historical Encyclopedia,* and *Telling the Story of Mormon History,* and he has published articles in *Dialogue: A Journal of Mormon Thought,* the *Journal of Mormon History, Mormon Historical Studies, Western Historical Quarterly,* and online at *Patheos.* "A Uniform and

Common Recollection: Joseph Smith's Legacy, Polygamy, and Public Memory, 1852-2002" appeared in *Dialogue* in fall 2002.

Kristine Wright has an M.A. in history from the University of Western Ontario. She has published articles in the *Journal of Mormon History* and online as a permanent blogger at *By Common Consent* and *Juvenile Instructor.* She has presented papers at the Mormon History Association meetings. "The Forms and the Power: The Development of Mormon Ritual Healing to 1847" appeared in the *Journal of Mormon History* in July 2009.